Introduction to Social Psychology
A European Perspective

Second Edition

Edited by

Miles Hewstone
Wolfgang Stroebe
Geoffrey M. Stephenson

Copyright © Blackwell Publishers Ltd, 1996

First published 1988
Reprinted 1989 (twice), 1990, 1992, 1993, 1994, 1995
Second edition published 1996
Reprinted 1996

Blackwell Publishers Ltd
108 Cowley Road
Oxford OX4 1JF, UK

Blackwell Publishers Inc.
238 Main Street
Cambridge, Massachusetts 02142, USA

British Library Cataloguing in Publication Data
A CIP catalogue record for this book is available from the British Library

Library of Congress Cataloging in Publication Data
Introduction to social psychology: a European perspective / [edited by Miles
Hewstone, Wolfgang Stroebe, Geoffrey M. Stephenson]. — 2nd ed.
p.   cm.
Includes bibliographical references and index.
ISBN 0-631-18585-2 (pbk : alk. paper)
1. Social psychology. 2. Social psychology—Europe.
I. Hewstone, Miles. II. Stroebe, Wolfgang. III. Stephenson, G. M. (Geoffrey
Michael)
HM251.I55   1996   95-30987
302—dc20   CIP

Commissioning Editor: Alison Mudditt
Editorial Coordinator: Alison Dunnett
Production Controller: Lisa Eaton
Picture Researcher: Thelma Gilbert

Typeset in 11 on 13pt Garamond
by Photoprint, Torquay
Printed in Great Britain by The Alden Press, Oxford

This book is printed on acid-free paper

Brief Contents

Contents

Part II Construction of the Social World 107

Part III Emotion, Communication and Relationships   277

16   Social Influence in Small Groups   487
EDDY VAN AVERMAET

Contributors

John Archer is at the University of Central Lancashire.
Hans W. Bierhoff is at the University of Bochum.
Rupert Brown is at the University of Kent.
Bram Buunk is at the University of Groningen.
Benoit Dardenne is at the Catholic University of Louvain.
Kevin Durkin is a the University of Western Australia.
Klaus Fiedler is at the University of Heidelberg.
Frank Fincham is at the University of Wales, Cardiff.
Dieter Frey is at the University of Munich.
Howard Giles is at the University of California, Santa Barbara.
Carl F. Graumann is at the University of Heidelberg.
Miles Hewstone is at the University of Wales, Cardiff.
Klaus Jonas at the University of Tübingen.
Jacques-Philippe Leyens is at the Catholic University of Louvain.
Anthony S R Manstead is at the University of Amsterdam.
Amélie Mummendey is at the University of Münster.
Klaus Scherer is at the University of Geneva.
Gün R Semin is at the Free University of Amsterdam.
Dagmar Stahlberg is at the University of Mannheim.
Geoffrey M Stephenson is at the University of Kent.
Wolfgang Stroebe is at the University of Utrecht.
John M Wiemann is at the University of California, Santa Barbara.
Eddy van Avermaet is at the University of Leuven.
Ad van Knippenberg is at the University of Nijmegen.
Henk Wilke is at the University of Leiden.

Preface to First Edition

The idea for this book grew out of many conversations the editors had with colleagues from all over Europe at various meetings of the European Association of Experimental Social Psychology. Members of the European Association teach social psychology in more than a dozen different countries and often use American textbooks. They typically report that texts which have been highly rated in the United States are not well received by European students. Since these students have to take more psychology courses than are required of American undergraduates they find American texts too basic. They also complain that most American textbooks do not adequately cover work done by European social psychologists and published in European journals. Thus, there seemed to be a need for a social psychology text that would be somewhat more advanced than American undergraduate textbooks and that would present the best of both American and European research in social psychology. Our 'European perspective' refers to the geographical location of our contributors, the literature they cite, and to a lesser extent to their conception of social psychology. There are undoubtedly more similarities than differences between European and North American social psychology, but the present volume is nonetheless distinctive in the attention it gives to such topics as minority influence and intergroup relations, areas in which Europeans have made their most significant contributions.

When we discussed this issue with our American colleagues, we were surprised to learn that many of them shared these views about the limitations of American social psychology texts. They argued that in the United States, there was also a need for a more advanced text that could be assigned in honours courses or in the initial stages of graduate training. Some even believed that such a text could be used in regular undergraduate social psychology classes.

While this idea may seem ambitious, it should be remembered that once upon a time there were textbooks of social psychology that were at the forefront of the field. These books were read not only by students but also by researchers and they were widely quoted in the research literature. Thus, the first generation of textbooks by Asch and Newcomb, and the second generation by Jones and Gerard, Brown, and Secord and Backman offered more than mere reviews. These books helped to shape the field by contributing new theoretical ideas, as well as their unique conceptions of social psychology. They tried to excite the reader with ideas rather than cartoons.

When we decided to produce a textbook in the tradition of those great books, and one that would also offer a representative survey of the field, we soon realized that this had to be an edited volume rather than a book written by the four editors. By making it an edited book, we could for each chapter commission a European social psychologist who was an expert in a given area and could thus be expected to give a 'state of the art' presentation of both European and American work. The danger of uneven writing styles and lack of integration could be avoided by giving explicit and extensive instructions to our authors.

After many discussions about who would be the ideal choice for each of the chapters, we had the gratifying experience of finding that our invitations to collaborate on this text were met with great enthusiasm and that all of our authors tried very hard to incorporate the suggestions made by the editors. We would like to use this opportunity to thank them for the patience with which they worked through several revisions of their initial drafts and for their willingness to accept editorial comments. We hope that they and the readers of this book – whether undergraduates, graduate students or teachers – will enjoy and benefit from the final version. We believe that it conveys a critical knowledge of and enthusiasm for social psychology, whatever its geographical provenance.

Miles Hewstone
Wolfgang Stroebe
Jean-Paul Codol
Geoffrey M. Stephenson

Preface to Second Edition

This is the second, completely revised and updated, edition of what has become a very successful and widely-adopted textbook. It consists of 18 chapters which cover the core of social psychology, each doing so in an accessible and engaging style, while focusing the student's attention on both the ideas (theories) that have had an impact on the field and the studies that have been carried out. As judged by sales and adoptions – both in the UK and on the European continent – the first edition did meet the perceived needs of a European audience of students and instructors, both in terms of **level** and **coverage**.

In terms of level, European undergraduate students typically specialize much earlier in (social) psychology than do their North American counterparts, often taking psychology as a single-honours degree course, sometimes as part of a joint-honours degree, and sometimes as a subsidiary subject. They therefore require a more detailed, advanced textbook than the typical American text which is too basic. Our students need *pages*, not lines, devoted to core areas of social psychology. In terms of coverage, we believe that students in Europe want to learn about the research conducted both in Europe and elsewhere, and that their understanding and appreciation of the field will be enhanced by examples and illustrations that have been chosen with them (not American undergraduates) in mind.

Although our first edition was successful (it has been translated into German, Hungarian, Italian, Spanish and even Japanese), we appreciate that the field of social psychology is growing at an impressive rate, and changing in the light of new theories, new findings, and new applications. We therefore decided to embark on a new edition, which includes the core of the old one, but also makes a number of significant changes in content, contributors, and style. In terms of content, we have included four completely new chapters, written by new authors. These reflect areas of growing interest (chapter 2: 'Evolutionary social psychology'), burgeoning parts of the field where we felt a second, more detailed chapter was required (chapter 6: 'Processing social information for judgements and decisions'), neglected topics (chapter 10: 'Emotion'), and popular topics where we wanted to publish a different perspective (chapter 12: 'Affiliation, attraction and close relationships').

We have also made stylistic changes, which we hope will make the book even more useful to students. The lay-out has been improved, there are more graphical illustrations to accompany the text on key studies, and there are more, but carefully-chosen, photographs whose aim is not merely to illustrate points but to make the reader think more deeply about the issues at hand (e.g., how do advertisements try to change our attitudes, when do we act on our stereotypes, and what are the consequences of social influence?). We have also added to the material presented at the end of each chapter. This now includes 'Further reading' to direct students' more detailed study; 'Discussion points', to check on their understanding of the text; 'Glossary terms', which highlight the main concepts around which each chapter can be organized; and 'Key studies', which direct students' attention to original research which we think is particularly instructive. The full text of these original papers is reprinted in the *Blackwell Reader in Social Psychology* which is published alongside this edition, where the studies are also critically discussed. Further help for instructors who adopt the book is available in the form of an Instructor's Manual, which can be obtained from the publishers.

Miles Hewstone, Cardiff
Wolfgang Stroebe, Utrecht
Geoffrey M. Stephenson, Canterbury

To:
Rebecca *and* William Hewstone
Katherine Stroebe
and
David Stephenson

Acknowledgements

The authors and publishers wish to thank the following who have kindly given permission for the use of copyright material:

Academic Press, Inc. for figure 8.7, Ajzen, Theory of planned behaviour, *Organizational Behaviour and Human Decision Processes*, 50, pp. 179–211. Figure 14.4, adapted from Zillman, Johnson and Day, Attribution of apparent arousal and proficiency of recovery from sympathetic activation affecting excitation transfer to aggressive behaviour, *Journal of Experimental Social Psychology*, 10, pp. 503–15. Copyright © 1991, 1974, Reprinted with permission of Academic Press, Inc.

American Psychological Association for figure 5.3, tree diagram depicting the clustering of trait attributes for the categories of extravert (left) and introvert (right), and figure 5.2, Associations between basic categories and upper-level categories from Andersen and Klatzky, Traits and social stereotypes: levels of categorization in person perception, *Journal of Personality and Social Psychology*, 39, pp. 1037–49. Figure 7.2 Miller, Culture and the development of everyday social explanation, *Journal of Personality and Social Psychology*, 46, pp. 961–78. Figure 7.3, Storms, Video tape and the attribution process: reserving actors' and observers' points of view, *Journal of Personality and Social Psychology*, 27, pp. 165–75. Figure 7.4, Passer, Kelley and Michela, Multidimensional scaling of the causes for negative interpersonal behaviour, *Journal of Personality and Social Psychology*, 36, pp. 951–62. Figure 8.5, Miller and Tessar, Effects of affective and cognitive focus on the attitude–behaviour relation, *Journal of Personality and Social Psychology*, 51, pp. 259–69. Figure 14.5, Tedeschi and Felson, A schematic of Berkowitz's cognitive neoassociationist approach and figure 14.7, The components of coercive actions, both from *Aggression and Coercive Actions: A Social Interventionist Perspective*. Copyright © 1987, 1987, 1980, 1984, 1973, 1978, 1994, 1994. Reprinted with the permission of the American Psychological Association.

A. Doyle for figure 3.2, Developmental patterns in the flexibility of children's ethnic attitudes. *Journal of Cross Cultural Psychology*, 19, pp. 3–18. Copyright © 1988. Reproduced with permission of the author.

P. Ekman for figure 10.2, Chevalier–Skolnikoff, J. Continuity of facial expression from chimpanzees to humans, *Darwin and Facial Expression*. Academic Press. Copyright © 1973.

P. Light for figure 3.1, Percentages of children succeeding on a complex computer test for each condition on each session, *European Journal of Psychology of Education*, 9, pp. 93–109. Copyright © 1994. Reproduced with permission of the author.

HMSO for figure 18.7, Known offenders as a percentage of the population by age and sex. Source: *Social Trends*, no. 24, 1994. Central Statistical Office. Crown Copyright 1994. Reproduced by the permission of the Controller of HMSO and the Central Statistical Office.

Holt, Rinehart and Winston for figure 8.1, adapted from *The Psychology of Attitudes* by Alice H. Eagly and Shelly Chaiken, p. 10. Copyright © 1993 by Harcourt, Brace & Company, reprinted by permission of Harcourt Brace & Company.

Plenum Press for figure 14.1, The weapons effect, p. 165; figure 14.2, The effects of noise and induced anger on the intensity of electric shocks delivered, p. 176; figure 14.3, curvilinear relation between negative affect and aggression, p. 146 – all from Baron, *Human Aggression*. Copyright © 1977. Reprinted with the permission of Plenum Press.

Sage Publications for figure 5.1, Leyens, Yzerbyt and Schadron, Stereotypes and social cognition; figure 8.3 adapted from Frey and Rosch, Information seeking after decisions: the role of novelty of information and decision reversibility, *Personality and Social Psychology Bulletin*, 10, pp 91–8. Figure 8.4 Shavitt and Fazio, Effects of attribute salience on the consistency between attitudes and behaviour predictions, *Personality and Social Psychology Bulletin*, 17, pp. 501–15. Copyright © 1994, 1984, 1991. Reprinted by permission of Sage Publications, Inc.

John Wiley & Sons Ltd for figure 14.6, Mummendey, Löschper and Linneweber, Perpective-specific divergence of initiator and re-actor in evaluating an aggressive action, *European Journal of Social Psychology*, 14, pp. 297–311. Copyright © 1984. Reprinted with permission of John Wiley & Sons Ltd.

Plates 21. Identical twins – Sally and Richard Greenhill; 2.2(a) Liz Taylor and husband – Rex Features; 2.2(b) Bill Wyman and wife – Press Association.

Plates 3.1 Secure base – provided by author; 3.2 Familiar routines – provided by author; 3.3, Conservation and social interaction: sharing fruit juice . . ., from *The Social Development of the Intellect*. Pergamon Press; 3.4 Babies Ad – Commission for Racial Equality.

Plate 4.1 Stills from 1965 film *Obedience* © Stanley Milgram as reproduced in *Obedience to Authority* by Stanley Milgram courtesy of Tavistock Publications.

Plates 5.1 Beer-drinking Belgian – Justin Leighton/Network Photographers; 5.2 Skinhead – Mike Goldwater/Impact Photos.

Plates 6.1 Wheelchair marathon competitor – Colorsport; 6.2 Earthquake newspaper – Evening Standard/John Frost Newspaper Service.

Plates 7.1 Cameroon football – Colorsport; 7.2 Tutorial – Format Photographers; 7.3 Examination hall – Martin Mayer/Network Photographers.

Plate 8.1 Anti-smoking Ad – Advertising Agency.

Plates 9.1 Anti-smoking Ad – Advertising Agency; 9.2 Seat-belt Ad – Advertising Agency.

Plate 10.1 Facial configuration used in the facial feedback experiment, adapted from *Journal of Personality and Social Psychology*, 54, pp. 768–77. Copyright © 1988.

Plates 11.1 Doctor–patient consultation – Format Photographers; 11.2 Interview – Format Photographers; 11.3 Elderly care – Martin Mayer/Network Photographers.

Plates 21.1 Love – Brian Shuel/Collections; 12.2 Women talking – Brian Shuel/Collections; 12.3 Attractive stereotype – Sandra Lousada/Collections.

Plates 13.1 Live Aid concert – Hulton Deutsch; 13.2 Oklahoma bomb – Associated Press.

Plates 14.1 Boxing and Rugby – Colorsport; 14.2 Sylvester Stallone – Kobal Collection; 14.3 Crowding on Underground – Geoff Howard/Collections; Crowding at disco – Geoff Howard/Collections.

Plates 15.1 Group mountaineering – Jess Stock/Stockshot; 15.2 Cabinet meeting – Press Association.

Plates 16.1 Swiss Sect chalets – Associated Press; 16.2 Henry Fonda – Kobal Collection; 16.3 Challenger – NASA/Science Photo Library; 16.4 Nuremberg war trials – Hulton Deutsch.

Plates 17.1 and 17.2 382 Introduction to Social Psychology (1st edition).

Plates 18.1 Guildford Four – Press Association; 18.2 Old and new football ground – Colorsport; 18.3 High rise and low rise developments – Format Photographers.

Every effort has been made to trace all the copyright holders but if any have been inadvertently overlooked the publishers will be pleased to make the necessary arrangement at the first opportunity.

PART I

Introduction

Contents

1 Introduction to a History of Social Psychology

Carl F. Graumann

Contents

Introduction: Why Study our History?

Individuals as well as groups, from families through institutions to nations, have their history. So do science and scientific disciplines. Getting to know any of these is a matter of trying to find out not only who and what they are at present, but what they have been and have done. In general, with social groups and systems we would not fully understand what their members are doing now unless we had some knowledge about what they (or their predecessors) had previously planned for the group to achieve. Social action as goal-directed behaviour can only be accounted for if we know who set the goal, when, and for which purpose. Since social inquiry, including social-psychological research, is a special case of social action, namely a collective enterprise, we should have some knowledge of disciplinary history if we want to understand why social psychologists are doing what they do and how they do it.

What we call 'history' is not something given that can be recorded and studied like other facts, physical or social. History has to be constructed. The data, figures, persons and events may be given. But which of these are to be considered and how they are weighted and related is a matter of construction and of purpose (see Graumann, 1983, 1987). Although we speak of historiography, i.e., the writing of history, it is important to realize that this writing is construction rather than recording.

One major concern and a plausible reason to construct a discipline's history can be the discipline's *identity*. What, for example, is the identity of social psychology? Is there a definition? There is no agreement, since neither the subject matter nor the methods nor the theories and models that are being traded will yield reliable and valid criteria for definition. We share the topics with neighbouring social, behavioural and biological disciplines. We tend to borrow the models from others, and most of our methods belong to the common arsenal of the social and behavioural sciences. Hence the traditional criteria of theory, method and research do not clearly distinguish social psychology from other fields. Distinction, however, is an important aspect of identity. Furthermore, it is a fact that different social psychologies exist side by side. At least for the two major variants, namely psychological social psychology (PSP) and sociological social psychology (SSP), it has been shown that they exist without much mutual notice (Wilson and Schafer, 1978). The explanation for this schism is as simple as it is problematic. The members of the two groups, as a rule, take different curricula; study, teach and work at different departments; read and write for different textbooks and journals; have different careers; and may adhere to different views of science. While psychologists focus on the mental (e.g. cognitive) structures and processes of individuals, sociological social psychologists tend to emphasize the functions of individuals in the context of social structures. Since this 'division of labour' has been going on for several generations of social psychologists we now find that members of PSP and of SSP have different histories, with different 'pioneers' and 'heroes': Lewin, Festinger, Schachter, Asch, Campbell and F. H. Allport for PSP; Mead, Goffman, French, Homans and Bales for SSP (Wilson and Schafer, 1978). It is the different histories that provide and maintain different identities. Hence, while it is the rule that textbooks on social psychology are written from either a psychological or a sociological viewpoint, a comprehensive historiography must account for all major variants of social psychology and their interrelationships.

In the establishment and maintenance of social identity, the psychologist recognizes a well-known feature of group formation; and in the display of identity, a technique familiar from the study of intergroup relations (see chapter 17). Hence, it is not surprising that historiography can be conceived as a 'social psychology of the past' (Watson, 1979).

There is one other, closely related function of history construction that has an equally social-psychological character: the *justificatory function*. Agassi (1963), Butterfield (1963) and others have argued that by historiographically relating ourselves and our own present research with 'classical' achievements, with reputed theories of the past or generally with 'great men', we justify our own work and possibly raise our scientific status. Connecting the present with a well-selected past establishes a kind of pedigree whose continuity from the oeuvre of a 'classical' ancestor (founding father or the like) to our present research work is interpreted as a mainstream line of progress, of accumulating knowledge (Graumann, 1987).

However, in order to be useful a history of a discipline must allow for the discontinuities, drawbacks, failures and dead ends as well as for continuity, success and progress. It must not pretend unity if there is pluralism as in social psychology. Finally, as with any phenomenon that we may study, we need information about the larger context. For disciplinary history the context is not only the system of sciences, but the social, political and economic system within which an individual discipline develops. That is why the sociology of science has become an essential part of disciplinary historiography (Danziger, 1990; Harvey, 1965; Lepenies, 1977; Woodward, 1980).

The following brief introduction to a history of social psychology cannot meet all these methodological demands. But whoever studies the history of science should have some knowledge of the principles of history construction. This should aid critical reading and the reconsideration of what, after all, is the use of studying the history of social psychology.

The Prehistory of Social-Psychological Thought

Social psychologists usually let their history begin in 1908 (or in the 1890s), while prehistory may extend as far back as Plato (427–347 BC) and Aristotle

(384–322 BC) or even the pre-Socratics (seventh to fifth century BC), depending on which philosophy of society and of science a historiographer of social psychology relies upon and on how broadly an author conceives of social psychology. The decision as to how far to extend the past or the history of social psychology and whom to include is a function of a writer's present conception of the social and the psychological.

Since there was no social psychology in either form or content before the end of the nineteenth century, our interest in its long prehistory is an interest in the history of social thought or social philosophy. Some of its central issues are:

1   Whether persons are conceived of as individuals, each of whom is unique, or as essentially like others;
2   Whether the individual person is seen as a function of the society or, inversely, society is seen as a product and function of the individuals composing it;
3   Whether the relationship between individual and society is at all a meaningful question or is an expression of a hidden ideology;
4   Whether the 'nature' of human beings is basically egoistic and needs techniques and processes of education, moralization or socialization to enable people to live together in groups, communes and states, or whether human beings are social by 'nature' and it is good or bad influences that make them social or antisocial;
5   Whether men and women are free and responsible agents or are determined by natural and social forces.

These and other anthropological questions have been asked and answered in a variety of ways by philosophers over the centuries. The different solutions offered are still controversial topics in contemporary thought and, inevitably, they become explicit or implicit assumptions of social-psychological theorizing. The primacy of the individual over the social, of mind over matter, of nature over nurture, of rationality over irrational forces, or the inverse positions – there is hardly a large-scale psychological theory that does not answer such questions in its own way. And it is here that the historical foundation of modern social thought is evident and acknowledged.

The acknowledgement may, for example, be seen in the fact that two major strands of social thought have come to be called Platonic and Aristotelian, respectively. Plato had emphasized the primacy of the state over the individual, who, in order to become truly social, had to be educated under the responsibility of authorities. For Aristotle, the human being is social by nature, and nature can be trusted to enable individuals to live together and to enter personal relationships from which families, tribes and ultimately the state will naturally develop. This difference in emphasis between Plato and Aristotle should not be exaggerated; however, they heralded two traditions of social thought which, in modern times, have been distinguished as the **socio-centred approach** and the **individuo-centred approach**. The former emphasizes the determining function of social structures (systems, institutions, groups) for individual experience and behaviour; by contrast, in the latter it is individual processes and functions from which the functions of the social systems are said to be explainable.

SOCIO-CENTRED APPROACH
INDIVIDUO-CENTRED APPROACH

In the history of social thought the conception of the primacy of the social has taken many forms. For Hegel (1770–1831), the German idealistic philosopher, the state is not only the ultimate form of society but the incarnation of the (objective) social mind of which individual minds are active participants. Later social-psychological ideas of a (supra-individual) **group mind** have been derived from Hegel's conception. For contemporaries who consider social psychology too exclusively individuo-centred, the philosophy of a social mind is a significant model (see Markova, 1982, 1983). Hence, a theory of society may be considered the framework within which social-psychological theorizing should originate, as is explicitly stated in the social psychology of G. H. Mead (1934) and in (the mainly SSP tradition of) symbolic interactionism (Manis and Meltzer, 1980).

GROUP MIND

While in the long prehistory of social psychology we may find other important theories of the primacy of the social and of society over the individual, we should now turn to a few examples of the opposite stance: the philosophical antecedents of an individuo-centred social science. Since, broadly speaking, psychology, and with it social psychology (PSP), is the study of individual experience and behaviour, we should expect major impacts of the varieties of **individualism** on psychology. Unfortunately, the term 'individualism' has too many different meanings to be useful without conceptual clarification (Lukes, 1973a). One such clarification, crucial for the psychologist, is the notion of the 'abstract individual', according to which the basic human psychological features (be they called instincts, needs, desires or wants) 'are assumed as given, independently of a social context' (1973a, p. 73). Since they are invariant, the group, the whole of society, is a mere union or product of such individual 'faculties'. PSP has from its beginning been defined as the scientific study of the individual in the social context. In its focus on the individual, PSP is very close, if not part of, general experimental psychology. A large portion of this individualism came historically under the names of hedonism and utilitarianism. The basic tenet of **hedonism** is the *pleasure principle*, according to which we act in order to secure and maintain pleasure and to avoid and reduce pain.

INDIVIDUALISM

HEDONISM

Since Jeremy Bentham (1748–1832), who theoretically transformed the pleasure principle into a principle of utility, **utilitarianism** – the doctrine that advocates the pursuit of the greatest happiness of the greatest number – has entered social thought to stay there. Over many variations of the doctrine and various combinations of individualism, utilitarianism and liberalism, there is one line of tradition leading directly into the foundation of psychology. For most modern theories of conditioning and of motivation, many of which are traded as

UTILITARIANISM

social-psychological theories, the underlying ideas of individual satisfaction (e.g., reinforcement, reward, profit; reduction of tension, of dissonance, of uncertainty) are variations of the pleasure or utility principle.

There were two other intellectual developments in the nineteenth century that contributed significantly to modern social psychology: sociology and evolutionary theory. As a term and a programme, **sociology** was created by Auguste Comte (1798–1857), who has also been praised and condemned as the father of **positivism**. For Comte (1853) positivism was a system of philosophy that implied a model of evolutionary progress of human knowledge from a theological through a metaphysical to a 'positive' stage of scientific knowledge, in which phenomena are taken to be real and certain, and knowledge is the description of such phenomena and their spatial and temporal order in terms of constancies and variations. Sociology was meant to be the culminating science, which would compare cultures as to their different stages of social evolution. Conventionally, however, Emile Durkheim (1858–1917) is credited with initiating a continuous tradition of sociology. He held that social facts are independent of and exterior to individual consciousness. Hence the 'collective representations' of a given society have an existence of their own. Although they may have emerged from the association and interaction of individuals their properties are different and independent from those of individual representations (Durkheim, 1898). While the relative autonomy of the social from the individual made Durkheim ask for a 'collective psychology' independent of individual psychology, most of the early conceptions of a social psychology around the turn of the century were fashioned after the model of a psychology of the individual. Only very much later did the French social psychologist Moscovici (1981) take up and revise Durkheim's theory of collective representations (see chapter 5 and Farr and Moscovici, 1984).

Finally, towards the end of the long prehistory there is the impact of the *theory of evolution*, one of the most powerful, popular, yet controversial intellectual innovations of the nineteenth century. Psychology has been much influenced by its major protagonist, Charles Darwin (1809–82), as well as by his followers. Darwin's antedated contribution to a social psychology is mainly to be found in *The Descent of Man* (1871) and its sibling volume on *The Expression of the Emotions in Man and Animals* (1872, 1896). Man is a social animal that has developed the capacity to adapt physically, socially and mentally to a changing environment, part of which is social, as for example the tribe or group. Hence, the expression of emotions has its social function in inter- and intra-species communication (see chapter 10). The British philosopher and (early) sociologist Herbert Spencer (1820–1903) generalized and popularized evolutionary theory, mainly in the social domain. But since he combined evolutionary theory with the doctrine of individualism and a *laissez-faire* attitude (let evolution take its course), historians of social psychology like Karpf (1932) and Hearnshaw (1964) have argued that Spencer did little to foster a social psychology. Even Darwin's own share in the

SOCIOLOGY

POSITIVISM

establishment of social psychology went unnoticed for a long time (cf. Farr, 1980) while his direct ancestry has been claimed both by human ethologists accounting for social behaviour (Hinde, 1974) and by sociobiologists (Wilson, 1975) (see chapter 2, this volume).

Transitions to Modern Social Psychology

So far, when we have spoken of social psychology's prehistory it has been to underline that the positions, briefly discussed, were not social psychologies in the modern sense of the word. But we saw that some of the doctrines that we referred to have led to present theorizing. When in this section we do not yet speak of modern social psychology, but only of a transient stage, the reason for this distinction must be seen in the fact that the research fields to be discussed had been given up or left to other social sciences before the institutionalization of social psychology was brought about.

We shall consider two major European approaches towards social psychology:

1 The *Völkerpsychologie* of Moritz Lazarus (1824–1903), Hermann Steinthal (1823–99) and Wilhelm Wundt (1832–1920);
2 The crowd psychology of late-nineteenth-century Italian and French writers such as Tarde (1843–1904) and Le Bon (1841–1931).

Both are examples of discontinuity since they had been given up before the modern (American) type of social psychology came into being. Both are conceptions of a social psychology that is socio-centred rather than individuo-centred, observational-interpretive rather than experimental. And both are nowadays reconsidered by those who try to broaden social psychology towards a (comparative) socio-cultural discipline, which includes the study of language, morality, customs, material culture, collective trends, and social change.

Völkerpsychologie

There is no hope of adequately translating this term into English (see Danziger, 1983). Literally, it is a psychology of peoples; in fact, it is a comparative and historical, social and cultural psychology which, in a European textbook, can be left as the German Völkerpsychologie. Instead of a series of definitions, an outline will be given of its basic rationale.

VÖLKER-PSYCHOLOGIE

Since, in agreement with Karpf (1932), we may rightly speak of the 'European background' of social psychology, it is inevitable that we should consider national traditions of social thought, as for example in Germany, France and England.

Völkerpsychologie, then, is the manifestation and prototype of German social-psychological thought, prepared in the eighteenth, elaborated in the nineteenth and brought to an end in the twentieth century. Reference to Germany emphasizes a particular national, i.e. political, social and cultural, development as the changing context of social and individual mind. In this tradition the key assumption was that the primary form of human association is the cultural community (*Gemeinschaft*), the *Volk*, in which the formation and education (*Bildung*) of the individual personality takes place. For philosophers and scholars like Herder, Hegel and Wilhelm von Humboldt, language was the medium in which the community shapes its individual members; these, in turn, actively contribute to their language, which is to be understood as a social product (Markova, 1983). While today the abstract 'society' is considered to be the social context of experience, action and interaction, in the eighteenth and nineteenth centuries for German scholars it was the national and cultural community of the *Volk*, whose mind or spirit (*Volksgeist*) was taken to be the unifying mental principle or idea.

Both *Volk* and *Volksgeist* became topics of the new discipline when it was institutionalized by and in a professional journal, the *Zeitschrift für Völkerpsychologie und Sprachwissenschaft*, in 1860 by M. Lazarus and H. Steinthal. From the beginning there was no doubt that the new discipline was closely connected with and also meant to contribute to the political efforts towards a German nation-state (Eckardt, 1971). Many enduring questions in social psychology were raised, but because the framework was national rather than social the questions were different from those of French crowd psychology (see below).

Wilhelm Wundt took up Völkerpsychologie as the equivalent and complement to experimental individual psychology as early as 1863, and with modifications, revocations and confirmations held on to this field until the year of his death in 1920 (Wundt, 1900–20, 1921). Although he was a major critic of Lazarus's and Steinthal's conception, it is possible to outline some common problems that were (or should have been) carried over to modern social psychology. The central question is obviously the nature of the individual–community relationship, which implies a host of theoretical, conceptual and methodological issues. However, there were no doubts about the intrinsically social nature of the individual; a purely individual experimental psychology is half a psychology.

An equally secular question is whether social psychology, in order to be truly social, should be a historical discipline, as has been postulated again by Gergen (1973, 1985). At least, Völkerpsychologie was a comparative historical study of the objective products of social (or collective) interaction, such as language, myth and custom; it was a cultural social psychology, in which the study of language had a central place. Except for the most elementary processes, no human experience or activity can (and should) be separated from its socio-cultural context, disregarding the evolutionary history of thought in language. Another feature of Völkerpsychologie that we hardly find in modern social psychology is the interest in the relationship between individuals as they act and interact and the products of their (inter)action – products that, in turn, affect and enrich the individual members' minds. They 'give rise in the individuals to novel accomplishments specific to community life' (Wundt, 1921, vol. I, pp. 20–1).

Today it is easy to find fault with Völkerpsychologie for its deficiency in empirical methodology and research. But if we try an imaginary inversion of perspective and look at the field of present-day social psychology from Wundt's viewpoint, we may also recognize the degree to which the cultural scope of the field has shrunk while it has methodologically improved (see Jaspars, 1983, 1986). In retrospect one gets the impression that perhaps not the whole idea but many of the major topics of Völkerpsychologie were handed over to neighbouring disciplines, mainly to anthropology and sociology, only to be rediscovered quite recently by European social psychologists. Jaspars (1986, p. 12) even presumed 'a return to the earliest scientific attempt to study social behaviour as advocated by Lazarus and Steinthal'.

Crowd psychology

The intellectual and scientific background of **crowd psychology** is complex. There are, on the one hand, the many techniques and conceptions of **suggestion**, such as the tradition (art, technique, doctrine and cult) of hypnotism, i.e. the induction of a sleep-like condition that subjects its target person, with certain limitations, to the suggestions of the hypnotist. Anton Mesmer (1734–1815), who could put people into a trance, had claimed to control a universal animal force ('magnetism') that would strengthen and enhance life and health. Hypnotic suggestion, as it was called later, was meant to lower a patient's level of consciousness, thus rendering her or his mind more 'primitive'. This technique figured as diagnostic and therapy respectively in the famous controversy between the rivalling French medical schools of Nancy and of the Salpétrière in Paris. But it also became one of the most important models of social influence and was appropriated by early crowd psychologists to account for the alleged irrationality, emotionality and 'primitivism' of crowds (see Barrows, 1981; Paicheler, 1985).

[margin: CROWD PSYCHOLOGY / SUGGESTION]

The other medical model, even more 'pathological' in origin and kind, was taken from epidemiology. In parallel with bacteriological contagion, which had recently become a scientific fact through the research of 'microbe hunters' like Louis Pasteur (1822–95) and Robert Koch (1843–1910), **mental contagion** was considered to be possible and to account for the spread of affect and 'anomie' in mob-like or otherwise agitated crowds.[1] Mental contagion, a key term in LeBon's influential crowd psychology (Le Bon, 1895), although he did not coin it himself (see Nye, 1975), was later interpreted in terms of 'circular reaction' (Allport, 1924) and 'interstimulation' (Blumer, 1946). It thus theoretically lost its

[margin: MENTAL CONTAGION]

'infectious disease' character (Milgram and Toch, 1969). The 'medical' distortions of the image of the crowd in nineteenth-century thought have been excellently documented by Barrows (1981; see also chapter 17).

The second scientific root of crowd psychology was criminology. What was a subconscious and affective state of mind from a medical viewpoint, in the juridical perspective was the *diminished responsibility* of the individual submerged in the crowd or even of the 'delinquent crowd' (Sighele, 1891; Tarde, 1895). The basic assumption of this medico-legal approach is again that in the crowd the individual becomes more primitive, more infantile than when alone, and hence less intelligent, less guided by reason and therefore less responsible. While all these ideas had been pronounced in a series of Italian and French publications before 1895, LeBon popularized them in his best seller without giving credit to the original authors. And it was LeBon to whom later students of crowd mind and behaviour referred as the master of crowd psychology (e.g. Freud, 1953; critically Nye, 1975; Moscovici, 1981).

If we take both sources, the medical and the criminological, together, this 'Latin' conception of the crowd is one of non-normalcy, associated with either disease or crime, at best allowing for mitigating circumstances. In order to understand why collective behaviour and its mental correlates were regarded as anomalous or 'anomic', it is necessary to look at the social and political context in which such conceptions developed; this is evident from the texts on the psychology of the crowd. The succession of revolutions (1789, 1830, 1848, 1871 in France); the radical economic and social changes due to rapid industrialization and urbanization; the rise and 'revolt of the masses'; the growing strength of the labour unions and of socialism, with strikes and May demonstrations; the corruption and scandals; the military defeat of France by Prussia in 1871, and the revolutionary Paris Commune and its bloody suppression in the same year; all this taken together became a threat to the established political, social and moral order and mainly to the bourgeoisie. As Barrows (1981) has convincingly argued, there was a general feeling of *décadence* and decline to be accounted for. The masses were 'discovered' (Moscovici, 1981) and feared as the causes of the general malaise, and science was required to analyse in detail the causal relationship between mass phenomena and the social evils. A criminological as well as a psychiatric or epidemiological 'explanation' suited the prevailing *Zeitgeist*. In spite of the controversial notions of the 'mental unit of the crowd' (LeBon, 1895) and of an entity-like 'crowd mind', which both carried well into the twentieth century (e.g., McDougall, 1920), it is important to see that a major concern of the Latin crowd psychology was the fate of the 'normal' individual who became somehow 'abnormal' under the social condition of the crowd. Whereas LeBon treated of mobs and juries, of mass demonstrations and parliaments, of criminal as well as religious aggregations, all under the category of 'crowds', today we give crowds, social movements, audiences and institutions different treatments. One important distinction, however, had already been made by Tarde (1901) and Park

(1972), namely that between the crowd and the public. While the former implies physical contact and spatial limitation, the latter, mainly owing to the modern media of communication (although only in the form of the press at that time), transcends spatial contiguity and spreads as 'public opinion'.

Like Völkerpsychologie, crowd psychology did not develop within the context of academic psychology after McDougall (1920) had once more invoked the 'group mind'. But, unlike the former, some of the major topics of crowd psychology were incorporated into the new social psychology after they had been individualized, and thereby became accessible for experimental analysis. Under the topic of social influence we recognize this continuity of what once was understood as the effects of suggestion, contagion and imitation (see Moscovici, 1985; Paicheler, 1985). But only recently the key problems of crowd mind and behaviour were given a fresh look and reinterpretation by Moscovici and others (Moscovici, 1981; see Graumann and Moscovici, 1986).

Modern Social Psychology

Social psychology as we know it today may be dated from around the turn of the century. American textbook authors prefer to fix the dates for its beginning at 1898 for the first experiment in social psychology and at 1908 for its first two textbooks. As a matter of fact, both 'firsts' have been shown to be wrong; but it does not make sense to replace them by other 'firsts'. In the late nineteenth century there was not only Völkerpsychologie and crowd psychology. There was also the term 'social psychology', applied to existing studies dealing with the individual in society, or a 'psychology of society' (Lindner, 1871; see Lück, 1987). Yet from the very first programmes of a social psychology we find two different emphases, which, in a nutshell, are: (1) as social *psychology* the new discipline should deal with the individual and with intra-individual processes, as does all psychology (e.g. McDougall, 1908; Simmel, 1908); (2) as *social* psychology it should focus on the role of the social (structural) context for individual processes (e.g. Lindner, 1871; Durkheim, see Lukes, 1973b; Ross, 1908). Although the much-cited books of 1908 were not the first textbooks in social psychology, they may well represent the two different emphases. McDougall's *Introduction to Social Psychology* was a (theoretical) book on 'the native propensities and capacities of the individual human mind' (1908, p. 18), i.e. an individualistic approach to social psychology by means of an instinct theory; in modern terms, a theory of motivation (see Farr, 1986). Ross, the sociologist, dealt in *Social Psychology* with the 'planes and currents that come into existence among men in consequence of their association' (1908, p. 1). His topic was the uniformities resulting from social influence due to interaction, partly in the tradition of crowd psychology, mainly a 'heartfelt homage to the genius of Gabriel Tarde' (p. viii). In his reflection on the history of social psychology, Pepitone (1981, p. 974) is right when he states that 'collective social psychology of the sort presented by Ross remained for the most part in sociology', whereas for psychology 'the individual was the only reality' and, hence, for a social psychology developing from it.

Social psychology in America

We have seen that social-psychological individualism had its roots in certain social philosophies. But with the establishment of a (psychological) discipline of social psychology this individualism acquired a methodological note. It may be that the 'emergence of social psychology as a distinctive field of empirical research . . . can be viewed . . . as a generational revolt against the armchair methods of social philosophy' (Cartwright, 1979, p. 83). But it definitely happened that, in the view and work of one of the first modern American social psychologists, F. H. Allport (1924), the individualist conception coincided and coalesced with a methodological orientation, the experimental–behavioural approach. For Allport, the first social psychologist in the behaviourist tradition, social psychology became 'the science which studies the behavior of the individual in so far as his behavior stimulates other individuals, or is itself a reaction to this behavior' (1924, p. 12). Yet while the 'behaviour viewpoint' was only a way of conceiving facts, it is the experimental method that yields them (p. vi). The combination of individualistic approach, 'behaviour viewpoint', and experimental method was meant to make social psychology a scientifically respectable discipline; this effort, according to Cartwright (1979, p. 84), took social psychology the first three or four decades of its existence.

While the greater part of this process took place in America and may historically be traced back to the model of F. H. Allport's early experiments on social facilitation (see chapter 15), one should note that Allport (1924) himself leaned heavily on the experimental work of several of Wundt's students (see Graumann, 1986). In this connection, Pepitone (1981, p. 975) speaks of 'the German roots of the experimental tradition in social psychology'. 'European roots' would have been even more precise, since there was not only the overly (and erroneously) cited example of Triplett, who in 1898 reported an experiment on the impact of co-acting others on an individual's working speed and quality (later to become known as 'social facilitation'). As Haines and Vaughan (1979) have shown, there were other experiments before 1898 deserving to be called social-psychological, mainly in the context of Binet's and Henri's studies of *suggestibility* (e.g., Binet and Henri, 1894), a topic that had been taken over from the hypnosis tradition discussed earlier.[2] Even earlier, in the 1880s, Ringelmann conducted investigations of group productivity (see chapter 15 and Kravitz and Martin, 1986). Historically, however, it is less interesting to find the truly first experiment (an arbitrary decision) than to observe that social psychologists are still trying to identify their history with the experimental rather than with any other methodology: a telling example of the identificatory function of historiography (see above).

In spite of the European roots of experimentalism, it happened mainly in the social and scientific climate of the United States after the First World War that social psychology more than elsewhere became a 'science of the individual' (Allport, 1924, p. 4). The effect of this limitation was that social psychology became largely removed from the study of social issues (Katz, 1978, p. 780). It has, at least in its research practice, isolated its subjects from their social context; until in economic and political crises, such as the Great Depression and the Second World War, 'the urgency of social problems overwhelmed the purists in their laboratories' (1978, p. 781), as we shall see below.

The major achievement in the 1930s and 1940s was the study and, mainly, the measurement of attitudes (see chapter 8), a preoccupation which was followed in the 1950s, and 1960s by a focus on conceptions of attitude change (see chapter 9). For the historian the many techniques of attitude measurement that have been developed since the mid-1920s are less interesting than the growing certainty, reconfirmed by each new technique, that 'attitudes can be measured' (Thurstone, 1928) and by their measurability, together with a growing sophistication of the experimental method, can enhance the scientific status of social psychology. Today the preference for experimental over field designs and for measurement over observation has been institutionalized in curricula and in criteria for the publication of research papers. In addition, fund-raising and grants depend to no small degree on the level of methodological sophistication. But also, what has been called the 'crisis' of social psychology in the 1970s, in which the social meaningfulness and relevance of its major research work was questioned from many angles, was largely attributed to the sovereignty of methods over problems (see Buss, 1979; Israel and Tajfel, 1972).

Historically, there have been deviations from this methodological mainstream whenever pressing social and political problems demanded the co-operation and commitment of social psychologists. This was the case when, during the 1930s, the Society for the Psychological Study of Social Issues was founded. It happened again in the 1940s, when, under the pressure of Nazi and Fascist domination and terror, social psychologists in the free countries not only tried to help win the war, but planned for a better world of democratic societies. One of them was Kurt Lewin (1890–1947), a Jewish refugee from Berlin, a member of the Gestalt group that was to influence social psychology in various direct and indirect ways.

Lewin, fully aware of what had happened in Germany and then in Europe, had become a social psychologist when he applied his *field theory* to groups (Lewin, 1948, 1951). Less a theory than a general methodology, this approach focused on the principle of interdependence, emphasizing the primacy of the whole (situation or field) over the parts, and made use of constructive rather than classificatory methods. This broad methodology permitted Lewin and his students to do experiments with groups (as prototypes of 'fields of forces'), but also to work with groups in everyday community life in order to change their conduct, morale, prejudice, style of leadership etc. – an approach that became known as *action research*. The list of his associates and students from his years at the University of Iowa's Child Welfare Research Station (1935–44) to those of his own foundation, the Research Center for Group Dynamics (then at MIT, now in Ann Arbor), is probably the most impressive and influential ever associated with one individual scholar after Wundt (see Festinger, 1980; Marrow, 1968).

Although Lewin died in 1947 it was largely Lewinians, such as Cartwright, Deutsch, Festinger, French, Kelley, Schachter and Thibaut, who shaped social psychology in America after the Second World War and, consequently, in Europe. Marx and Hillix (1979, p. 322) even conclude 'that it is hardly hyperbole to describe American social psychology as a Lewinian development'. If one adds those Americans who came to be influenced by the other emigrants, it is no exaggeration to summarize as did Cartwright (1979, p. 85): 'One can hardly imagine what the field would be like today if such people as Lewin, Heider, Köhler, Wertheimer, Katona, Lazarsfeld, and the Brunswiks had not come to the United States when they did.' It is important to remember this forced transfer of men and ideas from Europe to America if in American texts one occasionally reads that social psychology has become 'primarily an American product' (p. 85) or 'largely a North American phenomenon' (Jones, 1985, p. 47). The truth in such statements is that after the arrival of the emigrants many ideas had to be and indeed were transformed in a process of adaptation to the new social and scientific context (see Ash, 1985; Graumann, 1976). It is equally true that Hitler had emptied most of central Europe of whoever and whatever there was in social psychology. Into this vacuum poured 'American psychology' in the years after 1945; it was not the emigrants returning.

What actually happened in the decades after the Second World War in America and secondarily in Europe was, besides the ongoing methodological refinement, two theoretical changes: *from the behavioural to the cognitive viewpoint* and *from broader to more narrow theory ranges*. Both developments are not restricted to social psychology but apply to psychology in general. While the behavioural approach may be broadly characterized as a mainly American development (which owes key concepts to Pavlovian psychology), it has often been stated that the change or shift to a cognitive approach was brought about, or at least facilitated, by the appearance of Gestalt psychology in America. It is a historical fact that the first survey on cognitive theory, in a *Handbook of Social Psychology* (Scheerer, 1954), was, in effect, on Gestalt psychology. The situation had changed drastically when, fourteen years later, Zajonc (1968b, p. 391) succeeded Scheerer in the *Handbook*, noting 'with amazement how little in common we have with the previous generation of social psychologists'. Cognitive processes were now understood mainly as the 'underlying dynamics of social behavior' (p. 391). Since then, the situation has changed again: cognition has now come to mean the processing of information (Markus and Zajonc 1985).[3] Today it is less the (observable) social behaviour that is of interest than its cognitive representation, preceding (e.g. planning), accompanying (e.g. monitoring) and following (e.g. remembering) the behaviour (see chapters 5, 6, 7).

Together with the gradual transformation of the usage of social cognition we witness a proliferation and diminution of social-psychological theories. For the historian of psychology a pattern seems to recur. Just as, in the heyday of behaviourism, the kinds of learning proliferated, it is now the concept of cognition that seems to spawn the many mini-theories which, simultaneously, tend to spread over the whole field of social psychology.

One other social change has been noted in the development of American social psychology in the last 25 years, namely the change from a relatively low status and a marginal position within psychology to a more respected and central position. For Berscheid (1992, p. 531) it is even apparent 'that social psychology has emerged as a central pivot for much of contemporary psychology', an assessment which, if at all, may be true for the many new fields of applied social psychology: community, environment, health, law, organization (see chapter 18).

Social psychology in Europe

The situation of social psychology in postwar Europe can hardly be understood without the dialectics of the transatlantic interchange. There is, on the one hand, the American 'naturalization'. For psychology as a whole, Koch (1985, p. 25) made a convincing case that whatever the European contribution may have been historically – British post-Darwinian comparative psychology, Russia's Pavlovian conceptions, the Gestalt emigration, the discovery of Piaget, 'even' phenomenology and, of course, the neo-positivists' philosophy of the Vienna circle – it was all eagerly received, digested and transformed into something American, partly blended with the indigenous behaviourism and thoroughly individualistic. The vigour with which this was done had been made possible by an early and massive institutionalization. Koch, as others before him, is convinced that a cultural atmosphere favouring pragmatism and experimentalism in all walks of life facilitated the rise of psychology as a new science 'that seemed to promise prediction and control of human affairs' (Koch, 1985, p. 22). 'Naturalized' and institutionally strengthened psychology in the United States soon outnumbered and outweighed efforts in other countries. Psychology became an export commodity wherever there was demand, and demand was greatest in postwar Europe although in nationally different degrees and for different reasons. What was later critically called the 'Americanization' of European (e.g. German) psychology (see Cartwright, 1979, p. 85) was originally the much-needed and gratefully received reconstruction and internationalization of social science with American aid. Only to the degree that ideas, problems and their solutions were received and communicated in an uncritical attitude, may the term 'Americanization' have been justified.

What was the situation of social psychology in Europe before the war? Without proper institutionalization there were only individual scholars with some interest in social psychology. For example, in England there was Bartlett, whose major work on *remembering* (1932) has only recently gained interest among cognitive social psychologists. In Switzerland there was Piaget, who in his many volumes on child development also contributed to our present conception of socialization (see chapter 3), mainly by his focus on moral development (Piaget, 1932a). In Germany there was Moede, whose early experimental group psychology (Moede, 1920) had already impressed Floyd Allport (1924), and there was Hellpach, the founder of the (short-lived) first Institute for Social Psychology in 1921 and the author of the first systematic German textbook of social psychology (Hellpach, 1933). Yet none of these or other European scholars was founder or mediator of a social-psychological tradition; nor did they form a scientific community of social psychologists. After 1933 Hitler contributed to their separation.

Such was the situation in Europe after 1945. Although there were individuals and teams doing social-psychological research and teaching at various European universities, they were 'unaware of each other's existence, . . . the line of communication ran mainly between each centre and the United States', as the first editorial of the *European Journal of Social Psychology* stated in 1971. It was a first American initiative in the 1950s that, starting from Oslo, brought sociologists and social psychologists from seven European nations together for the purpose of an interdisciplinary cross-cultural study on threat and rejection (Schachter et al., 1954). But it took another effort, again initiated by American psychologists, to lay the foundation for a permanent grouping of European social psychologists.

When, in 1966, the European Association of Experimental Social Psychology (EAESP) was founded, it soon became the nucleus of a scientific community of social psychologists in Europe. From a small group in the mid-1960s it has grown into a large community comprising the vast majority of European social psychologists. Since its foundation during the 'cold war' it has been one of the Association's goals to include social psychologists from Eastern Europe in the growing network of communication.[4] As a special instrument, so-called East–West Conferences were held regularly, mostly in socialist and neutral countries, until in 1992 *every* EAESP member was free to participate.

The initial dependence on North American social psychology was gratefully acknowledged. But the lack of mutuality in the transatlantic exchange of ideas was also regretted, mainly by those founders of a European association who had hoped for a social psychology of a characteristically European vintage. Among the first to articulate this uneasiness and to search for the identity of social psychology in Europe were Tajfel and Moscovici who, each in his own way, pleaded for a more social social psychology than the one established and developed in America. Critics of the latter have repeatedly maintained that it is wedded to the 'cultural ethos' of 'self-contained individualism' (Sampson, 1977, p. 769). In contrast, Tajfel and his students have emphasized the *social dimension* of individual and group behaviour, i.e. the degree to which our experience and behaviour is embedded in and shaped by the properties of the culture and society we live in (Tajfel, 1981; 1984). Society, however, 'has its own structure which is not definable in terms of the characteristics of individuals' (Moscovici, 1972, p. 54). Therefore, 'social psychology can and must include in its theoretical and research preoccupations a direct concern with the relationship between human psychological functioning and the large-scale social processes and events which shape this functioning and are shaped by it' (Tajfel, 1981, p. 7).

It may be the diversity of social and cultural backgrounds characteristic of Europe that suggests this greater concern for the social (i.e. cultural) context of both social behaviour and its psychological investigation. The concern for social context is evident, for example, from Tajfel's own studies of stereotypes, prejudice and intergroup behaviour, and from Moscovici's work on social influence, minorities and social representations (see also Israel and Tajfel, 1972; Jaspars, 1986). However, it also belongs to the picture of diversity that many centres of social-psychological research in Europe have not been affected by the European quest for identity, are still 'following at a distance and with due delays the successive ebbs and flows of the mainstream of American social psychology' (Tajfel, 1981, p. 6), and are not noticeably different, in their theorizing and research, from any centre in North America. But whether there is an overall change in orientation in Europe's social psychology or whether this is restricted to some of its prominent protagonists, as Jaspars (1986, p. 12) wonders, the least one can say about the 'Europeanization' of social psychology is that it has succeeded in generating a more frequent and lively interaction among psychologists. The most important forum is the EAESP and the meetings, the journal and the monographs sponsored by it. Other positive symptoms are: the first European textbooks of social psychology, with contributors from several European countries and from North America (Moscovici, 1973, 1984; Tajfel and Fraser, 1978; and the first edition of this volume); and the recent annual series *European Review of Social Psychology*, a European counterpart to the successful North American *Advances in Experimental Social Psychology*.

Summary and Conclusions

A history of social psychology prepared for a European textbook is obviously written from a European perspective. Summing up, this means that if we emphasize the European background of contemporary social psychology we, at the same time, have to acknowledge that, in its modern form, social psychology is 'largely a North American phenomenon' (Jones, 1985), and that this is internationally so. The European background is not only to be found in the first-mentioned philosophical problems that have later been taken up by social-psychological science. It is also the 'German roots of the experimental tradition' (Pepitone, 1981) and, last but not least, the impact of such European emigrants as Katona, Lazarsfeld, Heider, Köhler, Wertheimer and, above all, Lewin who, mainly through their influential American disciples, helped shape modern social psychology.

Social psychology as it is presented in this textbook is not (and should not be) basically different from what it is in North America. Nevertheless it is possible to make distinctions. On the basis of an informal mail survey and a personal comparison of textbooks, Scherer (1992, 1993a) got the impression of 'an ever-widening gap between developments in European and North American social psychology' (1992, p. 184). His sample of approximately 80 social psychologists, members of the EAESP and of its North American counterpart, the Society for Experimental Social Psychology (SESP), seem to agree that American social psychology is more individualistic, ahistorical, ethnocentric and laboratory-oriented than is the case in Europe (1993a, p. 549). As to research topics there seems to be agreement that Europeans have a preference for 'intergroup relations, social identity, and social influence in terms of group factors' (1992, p. 184) while the individual's social cognitions, conceptualized as information processing and storage, are a preferential research topic and a 'major key development' in America (p. 188). The rationale of these assessments and their interpretation by Scherer is that in North America and Europe we have had differing key developments due to different orientations: there 'the individual and its functioning', here 'the social and cultural determinants of cognition and behaviour' (1993a, p. 520). If this accentuation is substantiated by more representative data, Jos Jaspars' predictive argument for the 'coming of age of social psychology in Europe' may be confirmed: 'We are moving . . . in the direction of studying more and more social behaviour in relation to a wider social context and appear to relate the results of our studies in a theoretically meaningful way to real social issues' (Jaspars, 1980, p. 427). (For further assessments of status and trends in social psychology see Leary, 1987; and Manstead, 1990.)

It may still be an open question whether this 'coming of age' will be brought about by 'bringing society into the laboratory' (Jaspars, 1980, p. 426) or by venturing into the field of social forces outside the laboratory. Yet since social psychology, as we have tried to show, started off with a much wider scope and agenda but 'narrowed down its task to gain scientific acceptance by employing experimental methods' (Jaspars, 1986, p. 13), it may now gain acceptance as a *social* science by addressing real social issues.

Notes

1 'Anomie' is Durkheim's term for a state in which dominant social norms are questioned, ignored or repudiated.

2 Haines and Vaughan (1979, p. 332) even wonder 'whether this experiment in any way inspired Solomon Asch's famous studies of conformity' (see chapter 16).

3 For the change of meaning of (social) cognition see Graumann (1987b).

4 Among them Hiebsch and Vorwerg (1980) had presented an explicitly Marxist social psychology.

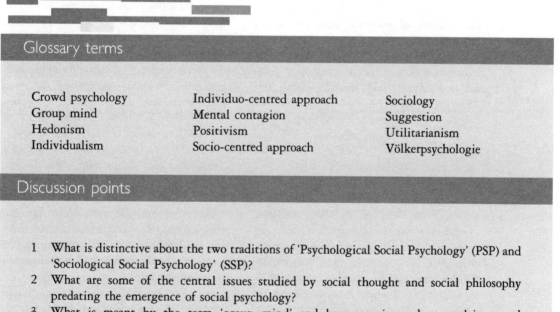

Glossary terms

Crowd psychology
Group mind
Hedonism
Individualism

Individuo-centred approach
Mental contagion
Positivism
Socio-centred approach

Sociology
Suggestion
Utilitarianism
Völkerpsychologie

Discussion points

1 What is distinctive about the two traditions of 'Psychological Social Psychology' (PSP) and 'Sociological Social Psychology' (SSP)?

2 What are some of the central issues studied by social thought and social philosophy predating the emergence of social psychology?

3 What is meant by the term 'group mind' and how was it used to explain crowd behaviour?

4 Discuss the main characteristics of 'Völkerpsychologie'?

5 What are the main similarities and differences between American and European approaches to social psychology?

6 When did social psychology first emerge as a recognizable discipline and what have been the most significant changes since that time?

Suggestions for further reading

There is no history of social psychology in print that is comprehensive, up to date and critically written. The following are second choices.

Allport, G. W. (1968) The historical background of modern social psychology. In G. Lindzey and E. Aronson (eds), *Handbook of Social Psychology* (vol. 1), 2nd edn. Reading, MA: Addison-Wesley, 1–80. This chapter appeared in the first edition of the *Handbook* in 1954 and still, though abridged, in the third edition of 1985. In spite of errors and other shortcomings it is the most frequently cited source for the history of social psychology. It sketches the European background of modern American social psychology.

Berscheid, E. (1992) A glance back at a quarter century of social psychology. *Journal of Personality and Social Psychology*, 63, 525–33. A selective and personal retrospective on the growth of social psychology in the United States between 1965 and 1990 by one of the leading women in social-psychological research.

Festinger, L. (ed.) (1980) *Retrospections on Social Psychology*. New York: Oxford University Press. Written by three academic generations of the Research Center for Group Dynamics, founded by Kurt Lewin, this is a very personal and historically limited but highly readable retrospective by some of the leading American figures of modern social psychology.

Jones, E. E. (1985) Major developments in social psychology during the past four decades. In G. Lindzey and E. Aronson (eds), *Handbook of Social Psychology* (vol. 1), 3rd edn. New York: Random House, 47–107. As a necessary addendum to the Allport chapter given above, the article surveys the recent development of social psychology in North America. References to research in Europe are arbitrary and rare.

Karpf, F. B. (1932) *American Social Psychology: its origins, development, and European background*. New York: Macmillan. The most comprehensive and erudite history of the European past of modern social psychology. Recommended to readers with a historical interest. An updating for the period till 1951 was published in 1952 as: American social psychology – 1951. *American Journal of Sociology*, 2, 187–93.

Patnoe, S. (1988) *A Narrative History of Experimental Social Psychology – The Lewin Tradition*. New York: Springer Verlag. Two generations of American students and students of students of Kurt Lewin's, altogether 20 social psychologists, were interviewed and report on their training within the 'Lewinian tradition' and on their contributions to social psychology.

Sahakian, W. S. (1982) *History and Systems of Social Psychology*, 2nd edn. Washington: Hemisphere. The only comprehensive history of social psychology in print that reviews not only the mainstream but also the psychoanalytical approach, social ethology and sociobiology. Its historiographical value is greatly diminished by errors and over-simplifications.

Scherer, K. R. (1992) Social psychology evolving. A progress report. In M. Dierkes and B. Bievert (eds), *European Social Science in Transition. Assessment and Outlook*. Frankfurt: Campus, 178–243. A report on recent key developments in American and European social psychology, based on an informal mail survey among approximately 80 members of EAESP and SESP.

Key study

Cartwright, D. (1979). Contemporary social psychology in historical perspective. *Social Psychology Quarterly*, 42, 82—93.

2 Evolutionary Social Psychology

John Archer

Contents

Introduction

There is a hidden ideological assumption about human beings that runs throughout most undergraduate social science courses. It entails two aspects. The first is that there is no such thing as human nature, or if there is, it has so little effect on people's social lives that it can be ignored. The second is that explanations of social behaviour can be derived from considering only societal roles and culture: within social psychology the origins of people's social dispositions and behaviour are usually viewed in terms of social roles and socialization (see chapter 3).

These assumptions are often referred to as the Standard Social Science Model (SSSM) by the growing numbers of researchers who have challenged them from the standpoint of modern Darwinian theory. This began with the writings of evolutionary biologists in the 1960s, and became known as **sociobiology** following the book of this name written by E. O. Wilson (1975), in which he set out to explain all animal and human social behaviour in terms of evolutionary and other biological principles. Since then, many of these principles have been used to study topics covered by the social sciences. A distinctive tradition has grown up within psychology which is now called **evolutionary psychology** (Buss, 1995). It differs in emphasis from the earlier sociobiology, which concentrated on the evolutionary origins of behaviour and tended to imply rigid genetic control. Instead, evolutionary principles are used to link the original function of behaviour to current psychological mechanisms, and flexibility of responding is a central part of such mechanisms.

SOCIOBIOLOGY

EVOLUTIONARY
PSYCHOLOGY

Evolutionary principles have been used to explain such well-known aspects of human behaviour as why it is that young males with few prospects are those most likely to kill and to be killed and why people are most likely to give their time and money to their relatives and to those who help them in return. They have also been used to derive novel and specific predictions, for example that relatives are more likely to comment that a baby resembles its father than its mother (Daly and Wilson, 1982) and that in parts of the world where parasites are prevalent, people place greater value on physical attractiveness when choosing a mate (Gangestad and Buss, 1993).

Before describing the theories which have been used to generate such predictions and the studies which have investigated them, it is necessary to outline the background to the evolutionary approach. It is not simply another area of theory and research within social psychology. Rather, it involves the transfer of principles from evolutionary biology – a quite separate academic discipline – to the subject matter of social psychology. It provides a different way of looking at the same material. Social psychologists have been concerned with processes and theories derived one at a time from specific phenomena, for example attribution, social identity, and cognitive dissonance (Buss, 1995).

Evolutionary psychologists begin with the principle of natural selection, which enables them to construct a theory of human nature, i.e. an overall view of how we should expect human beings to behave. From this, more specific theories and hypotheses are derived and tested, to investigate the sorts of issues outlined above.

Natural Selection and Behaviour

Since natural selection forms the basis of evolutionary psychology, we begin with a brief description of what it entails. Although Darwin and Wallace (1858) were not the first people to propose that common descent links humans with other creatures, and that a process of gradual change over many years (**evolution**) led to the diversity of life, their great achievement was to show *how* this process occurred. In Darwin's *Origin of Species* (1859) an analogy with the selective breeding of domesticated animals and plants formed the basis of the principle of **natural selection**. The human breeder selects certain heritable individual variations to be more strongly represented in the next generation. In the natural world, selection occurs because certain varieties are better able to survive and reproduce themselves in that particular environment than others are. Those that produce more viable offspring than others in the face of the forces of nature, such as a hostile climate, food shortage, and predation, are said to have greater **fitness** than their rivals. What enables them to do so is the possession of particular inherited physical and behavioural features which are well designed for life in that environment. Such animals are said to possess **adaptations** for their environment. For example, fish possess streamlined bodies and gills, which fit them well for life in water, but not on land; more specifically, a woodpecker's beak enables it to dig holes in live wood, and therefore to exploit this very specialized environment for feeding and nesting.

Darwin gradually came to realize that he had found many examples of such specific adaptations during his voyage on the Beagle (Desmond and Moore, 1991). The most famous of these concerned the finches of the Galapagos Islands, whose beaks had come to differ from the basic seed-eating type according to the feeding required in their particular environments. Thus, some ate insects on trees, and had become like warblers and woodpeckers, whereas others had become specialized for eating the seeds of different plants, including cacti (McFarland, 1993).

Darwin was mainly concerned with how physical structures had evolved. Modern Darwinians have been more interested in the evolution of behaviour (Cronin, 1991). Nevertheless, the same general principle of adaptation applies to any behaviour which has a heritable basis. Thus the tendency of most mammals and birds to form close emotional attachments with their young is an adaptation found in all animals which produce small numbers of vulnerable young and

(Margin terms:) EVOLUTION   NATURAL SELECTION   FITNESS   ADAPTATIONS

which live in dangerous environments. Without it, offspring survival (i.e., fitness) would be near to zero, and such animals would die out. A more specific behavioural adaptation is the tendency of a herring gull chick to peck at the red spot on its parent's beak (Tinbergen, 1951): this is only adaptive because in this particular social environment it elicits feeding by the parent. Again, chicks without this tendency would obtain little food and hence their fitness would be drastically reduced.

These examples illustrate a way of viewing the function of animal behaviour in terms of its past contribution to survival and reproduction. A very similar approach to human behaviour has been adopted by evolutionary social psychologists. For example, instead of regarding proneness to violence among young men in terms of social learning or frustration (Berkowitz, 1993; see chapter 14), it is understood as the result of its past contribution to obtaining resources and status, and access to women (Daly and Wilson, 1988).

When modern Darwinians first began to apply the principle of natural selection to the understanding of social behaviour, a number of issues were raised which were not apparent when considering the evolution of bodily structures. Foremost amongst these was how such an apparently 'selfish' process as natural selection, whereby some individuals leave more offspring than others, could have led to animals (and people) co-operating and helping one another. As we shall see in the next section, it can. More importantly, evolutionary theory identifies the conditions under which such helping behaviour would be expected.

Helping Others: the Problem of Altruistic Behaviour

Evolutionary biologists use the term **altruistic behaviour** to refer to behaviour which helps another individual's fitness despite a cost (in terms of fitness) to the donor. Apparently altruistic acts occur throughout the animal kingdom (Harcourt, 1991): examples are listed in table 2.1.

ALTRUISTIC BEHAVIOUR

We can add to these the many circumstances under which humans will help others: people may give money to a stranger begging or collecting money in the street, may help someone who has collapsed in a public place, and of course they are always doing large and small favours for relatives, friends and associates.

Table 2.1 Some examples of altruistic behaviour in animals

1	A male olive baboon helps another male defeat a rival despite the risk of injury.
2	Soldier castes defend a termite colony with their lives.
3	Mexican jays show co-operative breeding, feeding the young of others.
4	Many birds will mimic a broken wing to distract a predator from the nest.
5	Wild dogs hunt co-operatively, and share food with non-hunters.

Source: McFarland, 1993; Wilson, 1975.

HELPING
BEHAVIOUR

PROSOCIAL
BEHAVIOUR

Social psychologists have studied the conditions under which people show altruistic behaviour (also referred to as **helping behaviour**). In that context it is defined in terms not of fitness but of the willingness to benefit another person where there is the choice to do otherwise (see chapter 13 on **prosocial** behaviour). Research on this topic has considered the impact of variables such as personality, social norms, and the rewards and costs of performing particular acts.

At first sight there is a difficulty in reconciling such behaviour with the process of natural selection, which we have so far characterized as involving adaptations which are for the good of the individual. This way of portraying natural selection can be found in most of Darwin's writings (Cronin, 1991). But there was also another view, which gradually took hold of the thinking of a later generation of biologists, lasting until the late 1960s: they regarded adaptations as being primarily for the good of the group or species. On this view, explaining altruistic behaviour poses no problems, since feeding others or attracting attention to oneself by an alarm call would contribute to the greater good, despite any individual disadvantage.

ETHOLOGIST

One often-cited example of this way of thinking occurs in the book on animal and human aggression by the **ethologist**, Konrad Lorenz (1966). He attributed the apparent restraint that many animals show when fighting others of their own species to natural selection acting for the good of the species. Lorenz was not alone in espousing this view of natural selection, which flourished because hardly anyone stopped to ask precisely how it could work.

Acting for the good of the group or species may seem plausible at first sight, and indeed we can see the overall benefits of doing so in human affairs. But consider what would happen in a population of animals obeying the 'greater-good' convention if an individual who did not obey it came along. Suppose this individual's 'selfish' behaviour took the form of killing a rival and taking his/her resources, rather than merely threatening as others did. In the next generation such selfish individuals would be represented in greater numbers. Over succeeding generations this process would continue until we could imagine the entire population consisting of 'selfish' individuals rather than those following the greater-good convention.

When considered in this light, the evolution of altruism in the animal kingdom immediately poses a problem for the classical view of natural selection between individuals. But this problem was not realized for a long time, owing to the pervasiveness of the 'greater good' way of thinking.

The new form of Darwinism which arose in the 1960s differed from that found in Darwin's own writings not only because it concentrated on behaviour, but also because it concerned the basic units of heredity, the genes, rather than the species or individual (Cronin, 1991). The first enabled it to recognize the widespread occurrence of altruistic behaviour, and the second, to offer an explanation for it.

The central insight of modern Darwinism is that the reproductive process is about the transfer of genes to the next generation. It is therefore these genes (or packages of them, known as gene complexes) that are the true units of selection. Therefore genes that exert effects on structures and behaviour which aid adaptation will occur more and more frequently in future generations. Such a view again implies that there can be no mechanism for perpetuating a gene which causes behaviour that helps alternative genes to increase at the first one's expense. That is why Richard Dawkin (1976) called his book *The Selfish Gene*. However, there is a way in which genes helping other *individuals* could evolve.

Inclusive fitness

Genes are the units of evolutionary descent. They are the genetic instructions that act to produce others like us. The most obvious way in which they can do so is to produce an individual who is able to have many offspring. However, in the case of sexual reproduction, one parent's genes become 'diluted' with those from the other, so that each offspring only contains (on average) 50 per cent of each parent's genes. Brothers and sisters also share 50 per cent of the same genes. Thus, if it is a matter of life or death, saving a younger sibling with his/her whole reproductive life ahead will be equivalent to saving one of your own children of the same age. Saving your cousin's life will bring you less benefit in terms of passing on your genes since he/she has one-eighth of your own genes. In addition to these calculations we have to consider whether helping the relative is to occur instead of rearing one's own offspring or in addition to it (Grafen, 1982). In the first case, there may be no increase in overall fitness; there might even be a decrease (if, for example, an individual helped one cousin at the expense of its own offspring). In the second case, there would be a definite increase in overall fitness by helping the relative.

This wider concept of fitness, when helping relatives is balanced against reproduction, is called **inclusive fitness**. It was first widely understood following the paper by Hamilton (1964) in which he showed how it could be used to explain altruistic or helping behaviour in animals. It is now *the* major explanatory principle for this type of behaviour. The main exception is when helping is reciprocated at a later time (see section on *reciprocal altruism*). Of the examples listed in table 2.1, self-sacrifice in insects is entirely due to these sterile individuals (soldiers or workers) being more closely related to the reproducing queen's offspring than they would have been to their own (Dawkins, 1976, pp. 134–91). They are therefore aiding individuals who are more closely related to them than their own offspring would have been. Kinship underlies all sorts of alliances between social animals, for example the co-operative hunting of wild dogs. It is of course also responsible for the broken-wing displays used by bird parents to distract predators from the nest, but helping offspring is so much taken for granted that it is seldom viewed as a special case of a more general principle.

INCLUSIVE
FITNESS

When applied to humans, inclusive fitness can explain why kinship ties are important in all human societies (Crook, 1980), and why people give aid and resources to their close kin (see chapter 12). The emphasis on the use of strangers for laboratory experiments in social psychology (see chapter 4) has by-passed issues connected with kinship, and the present book contains only brief references to kin. Nevertheless, some evolutionary psychologists have viewed human behaviour in terms of inclusive fitness. Here we consider three examples, beginning with a recent application of Hamilton's principles to people's decisions to help others.

Burnstein, Crandall and Kitayama (1994) used social-psychological rating scale methods to test whether people would follow predictions from inclusive fitness when making hypothetical decisions concerning whom to help, either under life or death conditions or when only a small favour was involved. In each case the respondents were asked to choose between a series of three hypothetical target individuals differing in kinship, and in other characteristics such as sex, age, health and wealth. Over five studies, the choice of whom to help followed kinship in the way predicted from inclusive fitness, especially in response to the

Plate 2.1 Are genetically identical humans – monozygotic twins – more likely to be altruistic to one another? The available evidence, anecdotal and from research, indicates that twins feel a special affinity to each other, which can be explained in terms of 'kin selection'

life or death scenarios. People also used other criteria which were likely to reflect greater inclusive fitness, for example preferring younger and healthier individuals under life or death conditions.

Daly and Wilson (1988) examined cases of co-operative homicide in terms of kinship. Reasoning that killing someone is an extreme outcome of competition, and that collaborating to kill someone is a high-risk co-operative venture, they predicted from the principle of inclusive fitness that co-offenders would be much more closely related to one another than either would be to the victim. Using historical, criminological and ethnographic records, essentially they found this to be the case. Across a range of societies, the co-offenders were more closely related than were victims to offenders. For example, in thirteenth-century England, where two-thirds of homicides were collaborative, co-offenders were six times more likely to be related than were offender and victim. The main exception occurred when brothers were rivals for a substantial inheritance.

The principle of inclusive fitness can also be applied to the risk of child abuse from step-parents. The relevant prediction is one we encountered in passing in relation to the evolution of self-interested behaviour, that parental behaviour is costly, and therefore selection will strongly favour those individuals who selectively apply it only to their own offspring (Daly and Wilson, 1988, p. 83). Overall we should expect substitute parents to care less for their children than natural parents do, and for those who had least choice in adopting the parental role (step-parents) to care least of all. Statistics for rates of child abuse should reflect this lack of care. When Daly and Wilson first made this prediction, it was difficult to find statistics broken down by natural and step-parents. When broken down in this way, they did indeed support the prediction. Data from both the United States and Canada indicate a much higher incidence of abuse in homes containing a step-parent (nearly always a stepfather) and a natural parent than in those containing two natural parents (Daly and Wilson, 1985, 1988). The increased risk is such that abuse is about 100 times more likely to kill an American child in a home containing a step-parent. We should note that Daly and Wilson's comparison ruled out several possible confounding variables such as poverty, age, and size of the family

Inclusive fitness and xenophobia

Most modern treatments of inclusive fitness follow Hamilton in emphasizing the importance of distinguishing different degrees of relatedness for selecting the appropriate level of helping. However, in an earlier discussion of the idea behind inclusive fitness, Haldane (1955) referred to the case where animals live in small populations of related individuals, and mentioned that this probably applied to humans throughout history and prehistory. In such a population, he argued, natural selection would favour the spread of genes controlling certain types of altruistic behaviour. The form he identified was saving another individual at a small risk to oneself, for example saving a child from drowning where there would be a one in ten chance that you yourself would drown. In populations of closely related individuals (say cousin level and closer) all such altruistic acts would be generally advantageous (since you would be related by an eighth to a cousin yet be risking your life only one in ten times).

The logic of Haldane's argument is that for such isolated but interrelated groups it would pay to help any individual in the group irrespective of calculations of kin. A later discussion by Hamilton (1975) showed that this is most likely to occur where the contrast between close kin and neighbours is blurred, but there is a sharp drop in relatedness at the edge of the group. Haldane implied that once humans had evolved under such conditions, people would act altruistically towards someone in trouble even under modern urban conditions where the recipient was unlikely to be a close relative. Here he was making a point which is relevant to all evolutionary explanations, that they concern dispositions which evolved in the human ancestral environments, and which may or may not enhance fitness today, but are still with us.

If a general altruistic tendency did evolve in small groups, there would have to have been a way of discriminating between those to whom it was offered and those from whom it was withheld. To do so on the basis of group membership would fit the evolutionary analysis that non-membership originally coincided with a sharp drop in relatedness. Hostility to strangers by group members, or even to those within a group that are different in some way, is a widespread occurrence among animals who live in groups of close kin (Wilson, 1975).

Throughout human history most groups have shown *xenophobia* (hatred and dislike of strangers). Today's tribespeople in western New Guinea take it for granted that strangers will be killed if they stray into another group's territory (Diamond, 1991). In the so-called civilized world, there are numerous examples of bloody conflicts based on tribal loyalties. Daly and Wilson (1988) commented that, throughout human history, the criminal justice system applied only to those regarded as part of that particular society. Others have, throughout history and to this day, been persecuted, driven from their homes, tortured and killed – just because they belonged to a different group. The nature of such human killing is often on a large scale, well-planned and intentional. Although it does have small-scale parallels in the animal world, for example among our closest living relatives, the chimpanzees, its scale, efficiency and planning is unprecedented (Diamond, 1991).

The psychological mechanisms underlying this problematic human tendency are strong identification with one's own group, and negative stereotyping of those from other groups (see chapter 17). There are very varied criteria for deciding whom to kill and whom to help: people may be divided into 'us' and 'them' on the grounds of appearance, religion, customs, location, language or sexuality. This use of a wide variety of different distinguishing marks corresponds with social-psychological findings showing that people very readily develop a group identity on the basis of minimal identifying cues (see chapter 17). It seems that people will latch on to almost any cue to distinguish in-group and out-group members. Haldane's analysis suggests a likely evolutionary reason for this.

Reciprocal altruism

Although Haldane's early version of inclusive fitness may explain the tendency of humans to help those identified as 'one of us', modern sociobiology has generally by-passed it in favour of an emphasis on different degrees of altruism according to different degrees of kinship. There is also a further evolutionary explanation for altruism that does not depend on inclusive fitness. It concerns helping unrelated individuals, and therefore has attracted more attention from social psychologists whose research on altruism has involved strangers.

Reciprocal altruism (Trivers, 1971) can be described as 'I'll scratch your back and you scratch mine'. However, as with all evolutionary models, we are not concerned with intentions. We are asking under what conditions helping behaviour could have arisen by natural selection among individuals who do not share genes by common ancestry. Trivers' answer identified a fairly restricted set of conditions under which helping would confer fitness benefits: the benefit results from the recipient returning the favour later, and this must (obviously) entail the ability to recognize other individuals, in order to discriminate who is 'owed' a favour. Trivers also concluded that helping would evolve so as to occur selectively where the costs of helping were relatively low and the benefits relatively high, and where there was a way of identifying and excluding those individuals who received help but did not return it. The second of these points is particularly important, since it has been shown that reciprocal altruism would not be maintained unless most cheats were excluded. Indeed, some basic aspects of human reasoning in social situations entail a 'search for cheats' strategy (Cosmides, 1989).

The conditions set out above fit many examples of helping in intelligent social primates such as baboons, chimpanzees and of course humans. The principle of reciprocal altruism applies to the first example shown in table 2.1, a male olive baboon helping another male to defeat a rival.

We should again remember that for most of evolutionary history humans lived in relatively small bands. These conditions correspond more closely to those Trivers identified than is the case where people are called upon to help strangers, the situation most researched by social psychologists. Nevertheless, it is still possible to examine this research in terms of the conditions Trivers identified as enabling altruism to confer fitness benefits. Since the principle of reciprocity (i.e. knowing the person and having oneself received help, or seeing the prospect of receiving future help) is of primary importance (Thompson, 1980), it is predicted that people will generally be less helpful to strangers. Therefore, bystander intervention should be less common among larger anonymous communities than

RECIPROCAL
ALTRUSIM

among smaller integrated ones, as indeed it is. Between strangers, helping is more likely when it exacts a low cost from the donor, and confers a higher benefit on the recipient (chapter 13), again as Trivers predicted. For example, most of the reasons people offer for not helping someone after an accident involve costs to themselves. In practice, it is likely that help given to strangers also depends on considerations of shared group identity, to which Haldane's principles are more relevant.

Co-operation and Competition

The principles of inclusive fitness and reciprocal altruism, which indicate how helping behaviour could have arisen from the 'selfish' process of natural selection, are obviously of central importance to the understanding of the evolution of behaviour: without them, any further application of Darwinian theory to human (or for that matter animal) behaviour would be fruitless. Beyond the question of altruism lie a number of evolutionary principles and models which use the principle of natural selection as a starting point for working out in precise terms when individuals' fitness interests will coincide (when they are likely to co-operate) and when they will diverge (when they are likely to compete). The principles of *competition* and *co-operation* are central to the understanding of all forms of social interactions.

When considering natural selection, it is obvious that the process itself contains the seeds of competition. Because there are limits on resources important for survival and reproduction, genes from those individuals that are best able to obtain these will be perpetuated in future generations. As regards co-operation, we have already shown that kin have fitness interests in common (because of shared genes), and that this explains the evolution of helping behaviour. In other cases, animals co-operate because together they can achieve something they could not achieve alone, i.e., they do so for mutual benefit. Incidentally, reciprocal altruism is merely a case of mutual benefit separated in time, and therefore requiring ways of guarding against failure to reciprocate.

Parenting offers examples of two individuals co-operating for mutual benefit. Parents are unrelated, so that they will have no evolutionary reason for co-operating if either one can leave the other to bring up the offspring. In many species, two parents are needed to rear the young successfully: if either deserts, offspring survival may drop to zero. Both parents are equally related to the offspring and so will have the same fitness interests at stake. This sort of reasoning (Lazarus, 1990; Maynard Smith, 1977; Trivers, 1972) underlies the evolution of bi-parental care, which is characteristic of many species of birds, some primates (such as the gibbon), and the human species, but not of our nearest relatives, the chimpanzees.

Animals may show elements of both co-operation and competition in the same situation, as indeed people do. Parents may need one another to rear their offspring, but if either sex has the opportunity to increase fitness by an undetected mating with another partner, it will do so. This is true even for birds that were once thought to remain faithful (Mock and Fujioka, 1990). Infidelity among humans is of course more widely known, but its prevalence is probably higher than is generally believed, accounting for between 10 and 30 per cent of offspring born to stable couples (Bellis and Baker, 1990, Diamond, 1991). Thus co-operation with a long-term sexual partner to share parenting may occur alongside infidelity, in which case the fitness interests of the two partners will not coincide.

This example forms part of an extensive application of evolutionary principles to the analysis of sex differences in behaviour, which has in turn stimulated a considerable amount of research on humans. It goes beyond the immediate role of the two sexes in reproduction, to consider topics such as mate choice, violence and jealousy. The next section outlines the theory behind this research, and we then consider some of the research itself.

Sexual Selection and Parental Investment

Darwin (1871) realized that selection of, and different access to, sexual partners was a form of natural selection (which he called *sexual selection*), and that it had led to the evolution of most of the characteristic differences between the sexes found in the animal kingdom: for example, he saw the larger size of males, and their specialization for fighting, as a consequence of competing directly or indirectly for females. Females choose males with particular characteristics, leading to elaborate visual displays among the males of species such as the peacock.

It was not until 1972 that Trivers explained why sexual selection generally took the form of male competition and female choice. His great insight was to realize that these were not simply a consequence of the animal's sex, but of the imbalance in the parental contribution usually associated with the two sexes. Trivers used the term *parental investment* to refer to the time and effort spent in producing food for the egg cells, and all the feeding, incubating and protecting of the developing offspring that successful parenting entails. This is usually much greater in the female than in the male: it will therefore cost the female much more in time and effort to start again if her reproductive contribution is squandered, for example if she pairs with a male of poor fitness. The male, on the other hand, only has to produce more sperm in order to start again, and this is an inexpensive process.

Trivers saw that this imbalance would lead to different routes to fitness (or *reproductive strategies*) in the two sexes. Since females have more to lose by starting again, they will be selective in choosing a mate, preferring those with signs of a high level of fitness. Males could (in theory) fertilize many eggs, and therefore leave many offspring. In practice, this is limited by competition between males, and by female choice, leading to some males leaving many offspring and others leaving none. The resulting wider variation in male than female reproductive success applies to most species, including humans (Bateman, 1948; Trivers, 1972). Daly and Wilson (1988) cited an extreme example of competition – Emperor Moulay Ismail of Morocco (1672–1727), who was reputed to have fathered over a thousand children (Russell, 1987): his genes would be highly represented in the next generation whereas those of one of the eunuchs who guarded his harem would not be represented at all. We can contrast this with the most recorded children born to one woman, which is 69, from a Russian woman prone to multiple births (Russell, 1987). In the rest of the animal kingdom, it is not usually possible for one male to obtain such a mass of resources and reproductive output, but it is still the case that those males who compete more successfully with others will leave proportionately more descendants, and that the maximum number a female can produce is lower than that for a male.

Where both parents are necessary for the young's survival, male parental investment approaches that of the female, and intermale competition is reduced. As indicated in the previous section, males will still tend to revert to the basic male strategy if the opportunity arises (Trivers, 1972). In a minority of bird species, the male provides the higher parental investment, in the form of incubating the eggs (Jenni, 1974). This is associated with a mating system called POLYANDRY **polyandry**, where one female mates with several males. Typically there is a reversal of the usual sex differences in size and behaviour, thus supporting the link between the usual sex differences and parental investment.

Where fertilization is within the female's body and both sexes rear the offspring, there are no reliable cues as to paternity. Consequently, the male partner then runs the risk of bringing up another male's offspring, known as *cuckoldry*. Of course, this is not a possibility for the female, whose offspring will always be her own. There are signs of strong selection pressure for males to behave in ways which counter the possibility of cuckoldry: for example, they often guard females around the time of copulation (Berrill and Arsenault, 1982; Parker, 1974), and commonly kill a female's existing offspring before mating with her (e.g., Bertram, 1975; Hrdy, 1979).

Human Reproductive Behaviour

The principles outlined in the previous section (summarized in table 2.2) have been applied to several aspects of human behaviour, some examples of which are listed in table 2.3.

Let us first consider reproductive behaviour. Unlike our nearest relative, the chimpanzees, relationships between partners are long-term, and there is bi-parental care. In most industrialized societies this takes the form of *monogamous*

Table 2.2 An outline of Trivers' Parental Investment theory of sexual selection

1	Where there is no further parental investment, the imbalance in gamete production leads to male competition and female choice.
2	Where there is further parental investment, there is competition among the sex investing the lesser amount (usually the male), for access to the other, and choosiness by the one investing more (usually the female).
3	Where both parents are needed to rear the offspring, the sexes are similar.
4	Male competition is associated with a greater variation in reproductive success.
5	Where paternity is uncertain, there are counter-strategies such as mate guarding.

marriage (i.e., involving stable pairs of a male and a female). However, there is a size difference between men and women which suggests that, during evolutionary history, there was a degree of male competition, indicating a tendency towards **polygyny**. In a wide variety of cultures, men are allowed more than one wife (Ford and Beach, 1951). Where powerful men, such as autocratic rulers, are able to control or attract women, extreme polygyny occurs (Betzig, 1992). Where women choose famous men for short-term liaisons (as in the case of modern film and rock stars), a more promiscuous mating arrangement can occur. In one particular society where economic conditions are poor, *polyandry* is found, several brothers sharing one wife (Crook, 1980). There is therefore considerable variation in the mating arrangements of the human species.

POLYGYNY

A common explanation for this variation is that men will, if possible, seek sexual variety, but if this is prevented by female choice, they will – reluctantly – form monogamous (and in rare cases polyandrous) relationships. Females will show a more consistent tendency towards monogamy, except where there are great differences in fitness and resources between the available males – in which case they would tend towards polygyny (Ridley, 1994).

Symons (1979) argued that the preferred male strategy (many sexual partners) will be found where other men are the sexual partners, that is where men are not subject to female choice, or how women want them to behave. Likewise, the preferred female strategy (involving more stable relationships) will occur where other women are the sexual partners. Men from the pre-AIDS gay communities

Table 2.3 Some applications of Trivers' Parental Investment theory to human behaviour

1	Sex differences in preferred numbers of partners.
2	Risk-taking by young males.
3	Within-sex violence and homicide.
4	The need for reassurance over paternity.
5	Sexual jealousy and marital violence.
6	Mate selection criteria.

of the US did show vast numbers of sexual partners, whereas the sexual liaisons of lesbians were rather similar to those of heterosexual couples, and if anything more stable. This evidence supports the view that it is usually female choice which limits men's sexual activities.

Studies of what men and women say they would *like* to do provide another way of investigating differences in preferred numbers of partners. Symons and Ellis (1989) asked American undergraduates a number of questions, including whether they would have intercourse with an anonymous member of the opposite sex who was as attractive as their current partner, if there were no risks attached and no chance of forming a relationship. Men were four times more likely than women to answer that they certainly would, and women two and a half times more likely to say that they certainly would not. Buss and Schmitt (1993) found that, compared with females, male undergraduates desired more sexual partners over the long and short term, wanted intercourse after knowing a partner for a shorter time, and imposed less stringent standards in choosing a partner.

An alternative to the view that men are compromising in heterosexual relationships is that they can show *either* the tendency to behave polygynously (when this has a low cost) *or* the tendency to form longer-term relationships. Such a strategy, which is responsive to environmental cues associated with fitness, is called a conditional reproductive strategy. Buss and Schmitt (1993) found some

Plates 2.2 (a) and (b) From a sociobiological perspective, why might people react differently to 'younger man'/'older woman' and 'older man'/'younger woman' couples?

evidence for this view. Young American men used different criteria for selecting short-term and long-term partners, rating promiscuity as mildly desirable in the first case and highly undesirable in the second.

Trivers' theory has also led to predictions about the sorts of criteria the two sexes will look for when choosing a mate. Men should place more value on youth and physical attractiveness, which are both linked with health and reproductive potential (Buss, 1989; Singh, 1993). Since men's contribution to reproduction is less tied to age and indeed to physical attributes, these features should be lower priorities for women. Instead, female choice should be based on the male's status and on the resources he is likely to provide. Studies of human mate preferences have indeed found that women highly value indications of status and wealth, whereas men value physical attractiveness and youth (Buss, 1989, 1992; Ellis, 1992; Feingold, 1992b; Thiessen and Ross, 1990). In fact, according to cross-cultural research, regardless of country or class, men seek younger, physically attractive women, while women want partners who are mature and affluent (see Buss, 1995).

Trivers' analysis also predicted that females should choose males on the basis of genetic fitness, and this is likely to prove especially important in cases of short-term liaisons, for example with a high-status man. There has been some discussion as to the cues that females might use to distinguish males with good genes. One theory is that they are responsive to features signifying resistance to infectious agents such as parasites (Hamilton and Zuk, 1982). Gangestad and Buss (1993) found support for this among humans, in that physical attractiveness was valued more in areas of the world where there was a greater prevalence of pathogens.

Within-sex Competition and Homicide

Males generally show not only a wider variation in reproductive success than females, but also a shorter average life expectancy. This is attributed to the direct and indirect results of male competition. Trivers (1972) proposed that the greater the potential fitness benefits, the more males would risk their lives in competing with other males to obtain them. Computer simulations (Daly and Wilson, 1988) bear out his analysis.

Young men are known the world over to indulge in risky behaviour associated with gaining esteem and status from their peers and elders (Gilmore, 1990). Applied research on driver behaviour indicates that faster and more risky driving styles are associated with being young and male, and this has important practical implications in view of findings that it is rule-violations rather than errors that are associated with higher crash rates (Elander, West and French, 1993). Similarly, the curve for criminal convictions for serious crimes shows a pronounced peak for young males but not females (see chapter 18). Daly and

Wilson (1988) showed that same-sex killings also occur predominantly among young males in all societies that have been studied, and are particularly prevalent among those with little to lose. The disputes are usually about status within a masculine subculture or directly over women.

We can add to this evidence many more studies showing that most acts of physical aggression are more prevalent among males than females and especially among males of young ages (Archer, 1994). Verbal aggression is also more frequent among males, but the size of the difference is less in this case (e.g, Buss and Perry, 1992). Low-cost aggression such as indirect forms are more prevalent among females (Bjorkqvist, Osterman and Lagerspetz, 1994).

Cuckoldry and Jealousy

The term cuckoldry has long been used by humans to refer to the case of a man bringing up another's child. The need to reassure the supposed father of his paternity was demonstrated by Daly and Wilson (1982), who found that relatives' comments about which parent a new baby resembled were biased in favour of the father, in two samples of North Americans. Regalski and Gaulin (1993) replicated these results for a Mexican sample. Folklore and codified laws have consistently viewed a wife's adultery – which is likely to lead to cuckoldry – in terms of a violation of her husband's property rights. Indeed it is only modern Western societies that have anything approaching a single standard for adultery by men and women (Daly and Wilson, 1988).

Of course, it has long been recognized that adultery – or even the perceived threat of it – is dangerous in terms of the emotion that is aroused. Men who kill their wives generally act out of proprietary motives, either through sexual jealousy or in response to their actual or perceived intention to leave, whereas women who kill their husbands generally do so after a repeated pattern of severe abuse (Wilson and Daly, 1992). Men's motives for assaulting their wives similarly indicate proprietary feelings (Dobash and Dobash, 1977/8), a situation which parallels mate guarding in other animals.

Trivers predicted that male jealousy will be concerned with restricting sexual access to the partner, owing to the need to ensure paternity, whereas female jealousy will be concerned with the transfer of resources provided by the male (i.e. potential parental investment) to a rival. Buss et al. (1992; see Buss, 1995) asked undergraduates to imagine different sorts of infidelity by their partners, and to rate which one distressed them most. In various studies, male and female students were asked to imagine their partner either having sex with, forming an emotional attachment to, or falling in love with, another person. The results were as predicted. As measured by questionnaires, blood pressure and skin-conductivity tests, men rated the sexual scenario, and women the love scenario, as more distressing (see figure 2.1).

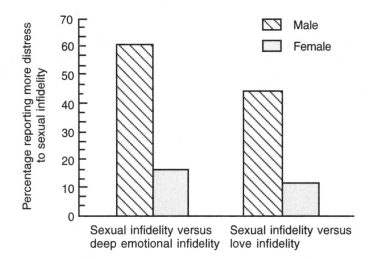

Figure 2.1 The percentage of respondents reporting more distress at cues indicating that their partner had shown sexual infidelity than at cues indicating emotional attachment or love infidelity (from Buss et al., 1992; reproduced with permission of Cambridge University Press and the author)

The Evolution of Flexibility

In the previous sections we have considered human sex differences in terms of principles derived from sexual selection theory. These have enabled predictions to be made (and tested) about the dispositions of men and women. It is important to emphasize that we are dealing with dispositions, and not fixed responses under rigid genetic control. It is now apparent that whenever aspects of the environment which are crucial to survival are likely to be uncertain or variable from time to time, widespread flexibility of responding evolves, so that behaviour can be flexible and varied according to the circumstances. This is the view of human nature that is found in modern evolutionary psychology.

One important source of uncertainty in an animal's environment is the behaviour of other animals: for most forms of social behaviour, whether it is adaptive will depend on how other animals respond to that behaviour. A significant breakthrough in analysing the implications of this was the application of *game theory* to animal fighting by Maynard Smith (1972, 1974). Particular types of social behaviour are viewed as strategies, with costs and benefits attached to their interaction with other strategies in the population. The aim of this form of game-theory modelling is to determine the **evolutionarily stable strategy** or **ESS**: this is the point where the strategy cannot be replaced by any other, given the current conditions of the population. Precisely what the ESS is in each case

EVOLUTIONARILY STABLE STRATEGY

ESS

depends on the types of strategy available, their frequencies, and the costs and benefits involved (see Archer, 1988).

Game theory has highlighted a number of general principles about animal fighting (Archer and Huntingford, 1994): for example, animals make assessments of the likely costs of fighting an opponent prior to a contest, and continue to do so throughout the fight, which typically involves a sequence of progressively more damaging actions. This will apply particularly when animals are capable of damaging one another, for example through dangerous natural weapons. Fights will also vary in severity according to what is at stake.

Summary and Conclusions

Evolutionary psychology is an attempt to make sense of human social behaviour – with all its flexibility and complexity – within the framework of a set of rules derived from natural selection. Ideally this should enable us to achieve something missing from conventional social psychology – a coherent view of human nature. Evolutionary psychologists argue that natural selection produces people who both behave within certain very general principles and can show the sort of flexibility according to circumstances that was outlined in the previous section.

As far as the general principles are concerned, we would not expect people to provide aid and to help others on an indiscriminate basis; we would not expect them to abandon their own children and look after those of strangers; we should not expect men and women to approach sexual relations in the same way, or to look for the same features when choosing a mate; we should not expect cautious behaviour to be the norm among young men. These activities are all within the realms of possibility for human beings (for they do not require wings or X-ray eyes or superhuman intelligence). Indeed we may be able to think of instances in which people do behave in these ways. The important point is that most humans in most societies do not behave like this, and the theory of natural selection indicates exactly why they do not. In this sense it provides an overall view of what we would expect human nature to be like.

As indicated in the Introduction, social psychology has derived concepts one at a time from research on how people actually behave. An alternative starting point is adopted by evolutionary psychologists. They use the principle of natural selection to deduce the types of general attributes and motives we would expect human beings to possess, and the circumstances under which these should vary in particular ways. They then set out to test specific hypotheses derived from this view. This not only provides a more consistent view of human nature but it also leads to predictions which can be contrasted with non-evolutionary ones. To take two examples: the most basic motivations of humans should be linked to their reproductive fitness rather than to their own survival as individuals; secondly, conflicts between parents and offspring should involve resources rather than (as in Freudian theory) sexual jealousies.

The evolutionary approach can also help to broaden the sources of data used in social-psychological investigations. Laboratory-based research involving under-graduate participants (see chapter 4) can be used to test hypotheses from conventional social psychology or from evolutionary theory: Buss has carried out a number of studies of this sort concerning mate choice. There is always the suspicion, however, that we may be dealing with a specialized group of individuals bounded by their place in history, geography and culture. To avoid this possibility, Buss supplemented his laboratory work with cross-cultural studies (Buss, 1989; Gangestad and Buss, 1993) and Daly and Wilson tested evolutionary-based theories about human violence wholly from archival data derived from historical, anthropological and criminological sources. Their use of these data bases provides an interesting parallel with researchers of very different theoretical inclinations, such as Gergen (1973), who have criticized the narrowness of the existing data-source in social psychology because it lacks historical and cultural dimensions. By coming to social psychology from a different vantage-point, evolutionary psychology can enrich both our theoretical understanding of it and the sources of evidence on which this understanding is based.

Glossary terms

Altruistic behaviour	Evolutionarily stable strategy	Polyandry
Adaptation	(ESS)	Polygyny
Ethologist	Fitness	Prosocial behaviour
Evolution	Helping behaviour	Reciprocal altruism
Evolutionary psychology	Inclusive fitness	Sociobiology
	Natural selection	

44 *John Archer*

Discussion points

1 How does the evolutionary approach to altruism differ from that found in conventional social psychology? (See also chapter 13.)
2 In what ways would human aggression be viewed differently by an evolutionary psychologist and a more typical social psychologist? (See also chapter 14.)
3 What implications for human nature can be derived from the theory of natural selection?
4 Do men and women look for the same characteristics in the opposite sex?
5 If you came across intelligent creatures from another planet, who had evolved by natural selection, how would you expect them to behave?
6 What might evolutionary theory predict about the sexuality of men and women?
7 Why is kinship a prominent feature in evolutionary psychology but not in conventional social psychology?
8 Can evolutionary theory and social identity theory be combined to help us understand xenophobia and racism? (See also chapter 17.)

Suggestions for further reading

Buss, D. M. (1995) *The Evolution of Desire*. New York: Basic Books. A fascinating book that emphasizes the importance of understanding human nature through our evolutionary past.

Daly, M. and Wilson, M. (1988) *Homicide*. New York: Aldine de Gruyter. This book describes the systematic application of selectionist thinking to research on homicide, using criminological, anthropological and historical sources.

Dawkins, R. (1976) *The Selfish Gene*. Oxford and New York: Oxford University Press. This classic book explains the basic principles of the then new evolutionary approach to behaviour. It is a popular science book in which the ideas are not watered down but clarified in a way that pulls the reader into the logic of the arguments.

Dawkins, R. (1986) *The Blind Watchmaker*. London: Longman. The logic of natural selection and the objections to alternative accounts of our origins are explained in a way that surpasses even *The Selfish Gene* as exemplary popular science writing.

Diamond, J. (1991) *The Rise and Fall of the Third Chimpanzee*. London: Radius Books. This is another, yet rather different, impressive piece of popular science writing, and is probably more accessible than are Dawkins's books. Diamond views all aspects of human behaviour, good and bad, from the vantage point of evolution.

McFarland, D. J. (1993) *Animal Behaviour*, 2nd edn. London: Pitman. Chapters 5–9 inclusive contain excellent coverage of the evolutionary principles which have been applied to animal behaviour, with some reference to their extension to human behaviour.

Symons, D. (1979) *The Evolution of Human Sexuality*. New York: Oxford University Press. The application of sexual selection to human behaviour. A well-written book full of ideas and illustrations from many sources. Despite the enormous growth of research in this area, the book has dated little.

Key study

Buss, D. M., Larsen, R. J., Westen, D. and Semmelroth, J. (1992). Sex differences in jealousy: evolution, physiology and psychology. *Psychological Science*, 3, 251—5.

3 Developmental Social Psychology

Kevin Durkin

Contents

Introduction

How do we get into the social world in the first place? As a student of social psychology, you will be giving a lot of thought to processes of interpersonal and intergroup behaviour, to the ways in which cognitive activity mediates and reflects social actions, to social influences, to attitude formation and change, and to the contexts in which people behave aggressively – or generously, or competitively, or co-operatively, or seductively. Flicking through the pages ahead, you can gauge already that the agenda is lengthy and fascinating. But to each topic, there is a preface, and the preface is headed: how does it all begin?

Responding to other people, discerning their properties, evaluating their merits and negotiating understandings with them are not phenomena unique to the adult world. They do not commence with the age of majority, and it is unlikely that their developmental histories are irrelevant to their mature functioning. We develop as social beings over a long time, and development ceases only with death. We happen not only to *be*, but also to *live among*, developing social beings. A social psychology without a developmental component would have to proceed in defiance of one of the principal axioms of scientific enquiry: first *describe* the phenomena under investigation. By and large, social psychologists do come perilously close to overlooking *development*. They rarely describe the developmental aspects of their concerns, and rarely entertain a developmental dimension to their explanations. At the same time, developmentalists often disregard the *social* contexts of human development. They focus instead on the individual child, and strive to uncover her or his capacities, deficiencies and changes as though these were quite independent of her or his interactions with others.

There is an alternative to non-developmental social psychology and to asocial developmentalism. This chapter provides an introduction to the new and growing field of developmental social psychology. Developmental social psychology draws upon both of the sub-disciplines incorporated in its title, and aims to investigate the developmental courses and the social contexts of human social behaviour (Durkin, 1995). In this introduction, four main themes will be addressed. First, responding to our initial question of how a person gets into social life in the first place, we consider the nature of **socialization**. Socialization   SOCIALIZATION
is so familiar a colloquial term that what it entails is often taken for granted, as a process of 'moulding' or 'conditioning'; we will see that it is much more complex – indeed, much more social. Secondly, we consider the development of *relationships*, and development within relationships. It turns out that social life begins in social life, and social development proceeds in social contexts. If this sounds obvious, you are already on your way to becoming a developmental social psychologist, but you may be surprised later to find that not all social and developmental psychologists share your perspective. Thirdly, we consider the development of language, the pre-eminent medium of human *communication*. Although often treated as an individual achievement, we will see that language

acquisition is inseparable from social context. Finally, we examine aspects of the development of *social knowledge*. Human social functioning requires the ability to represent and interpret the social world; we will see that developmental social psychologists' investigations of these capacities highlight the mutual relevance of the study of change and the study of social context.

The Nature of Socialization

Socialization is the process whereby people acquire the rules of behaviour and the systems of beliefs and attitudes that equip a person to function effectively as a member of society. In some areas of psychology and the neighbouring social sciences, socialization has often been taken to refer to processes by which an individual is shaped or restrained so as to fit into the society to which he or she belongs. It is seen as something which is 'done to' a malleable target or a potential menace to ensure that he or she behaves acceptably. Research in developmental social psychology has called this notion seriously into question.

Discussing some of the conceptual issues, Schaffer (1984a) points out that traditional models represent socialization as a largely *unidirectional* process with the impetus for change and regulation coming from outside the individual being socialized. Early American behaviourism provides the most influential example of this perspective (e.g., Watson, 1928). On the other hand, there are theories of socialization which see the child as arriving in society with a range of instincts and desires which she or he is disposed to vent or gratify with little concern initially for the feelings and desires of others. For example, Freud (1953) stressed that young children are impulsive, with easily aroused emotions and little ability to restrain or delay gratification, and he regarded socialization as the process whereby society (primarily represented by the parents) repressed and disciplined the reluctant child into publicly accepted conventions.

Both of these theories have intuitive appeal. At the beginning of life, children do not seem fully informed on the values of the surrounding culture, and it falls to others to advise them. We know that people growing up in different communities around the world acquire markedly different sets of values and ways of behaving (Shweder, 1991; Triandis, 1994). Surely people *are* malleable, perhaps infinitely so? On the other hand, if you have ever tried to control a two-year-old within range of chocolate mousse and a banana milk shake, you will agree that junior members of the species do appear to have a will of their own, and can resist violently if necessary any cultural practices that stand in the way of immediate consumption. We can beat them down in the end, but perhaps humans *are* initially impulsive, hedonistic and in need of restraint? Our intuitions, like our scientific leaders, have just led us to two diametrically opposed conceptions of socialization. There are more, but you get the point: explaining everyday processes such as socialization proves much more contentious than we might have at first thought.

As indicated above, in developing and testing our theories, much depends on what we choose to observe. However, during the 1970s our observational facilities improved somewhat with the advent of videorecording. This technology enabled researchers to look more closely at the very beginnings of socialization – the early interactions between infants and their caregivers. In the course of this work, a new perspective on socialization gained ground, a perspective which Schaffer (1984a) calls the *mutuality model*. In contrast to both of the unidirectional theories sketched above, the mutuality model represents the child as an active participant in her or his own social development and it stresses the interdependence of parent and child in much of their social transactions. It does not, of course, maintain that there is no conflict in parent–child relations (a claim which most parents would see as contrary to daily reality, and which researchers have demonstrated to be contrary to readily obtained evidence; cf. Rijt-Plooj and Plooj, 1993). Nor does it suppose that there is no influence of adult upon child. But it does stress that the diverse processes that are entailed in social development are from the outset negotiated through mutual exploration and stimulation. Let us examine the beginnings of these processes.

Children as social beings from birth

Recent advances in infancy research have dispelled the early behaviourists' notion that children are blank slates at birth. There is abundant evidence that neonates bring reflexes, capacities and predispositions into the world, and that they explore and initiate as well as respond to people and things around them (Bremner, 1994). Studies of infants using measures of attentional preference and discrimination have found that from very early in life they are particularly interested in the kinds of sensory experiences that other human beings provide. For example, they prefer parents who move and talk, rather than parents who (at the experimenter's request) sit still and show no acknowledgement of their presence (Gusella, Muir and Tronick, 1988; Legerstee, 1991). They prefer human voices to other sounds (Fernald, 1989). Among visual stimuli, they prefer faces to other symmetrical shapes (Johnson and Morton, 1991). In sum, the infant's perceptual capacities ensure that it attends to other people. And other people, for their part, are usually very interested in the behaviour of infants – especially their own. This fortunate coincidence results in social activities which often involve synchrony and co-operation with parental behaviour rather than opposition and reluctance (Papousek and Papousek, 1989; Schaffer, 1984b, 1989).

Research into parent–child interaction has exploited microanalytic techniques to examine moment-by-moment the expressive and communicative behaviours of both parent and infant (Kaye, 1982; Schaffer *et al.*, 1977; Stern, 1985). Starting among the most elementary of observations, it is obvious that caregivers set the scene for interactions by maximizing the physical opportunities for mutual interest: they hold the baby so that they are face-to-face. This simple manipulation takes advantage of both parties' interests. The baby finds a face and voice presented conveniently for attention and familiarization, and the caregiver has extensive scope to search this highly attractive new person for any and all signs of inquisitiveness, enjoyment or distress. More interestingly, a distribution of power is achieved. While the adult has greater scope for mobility and manipulation, the baby has influential resources, too: he or she can affect the intensity and pace of an interaction by withdrawing or averting gaze (Stern, 1985; Trevarthen, 1982).

In fact, when the flow of the interactions is studied, patterns are found which indicate reciprocal effects rather than unidirectionality. Kaye (1982), for example, analysed the stop–start organization of breastfeeding, wherein mothers period-ically 'jiggle' the baby to encourage him or her to resume sucking. During the first few weeks, mother–infant dyads evolve a rhythm to their burst–pause engagements, almost as though they were practising one of the distinctive features of human conversational interaction, namely turn-taking. Elsewhere in everyday interactions, parent and infant adjust in response to each other's movements, rather like dancers co-ordinating their steps (Stern, 1985). By at least the end of the first year, vocal interchanges between mothers and infants reveal turn-taking (switches from one 'speaker' to the other) that are virtually as smooth as adult–adult conversations (Rutter and Durkin, 1987; Schaffer, Collis and Parsons, 1977).

Early interactions, then, exhibit a good deal of mutuality. From the start, the infant is actively involved in her or his own social development. There is controversy among researchers concerning the relative contributions of caregiver and child to the kinds of processes summarized here, but broad agreement that progress is only possible because of some level of *joint* activity. This does not end the story of socialization, but it does cast its beginnings in a new light. The infant is neither an infinitely malleable lump of clay nor a wilful beast in need of restraint. Instead, she or he is a social participant, less skilled and less informed than others, to be sure, but oriented by predispositions and circumstances to engage *with* others in the collective construction of a social world.

Socialization and social psychology

The findings just summarized seem interesting enough in their own terms, but why should they bear on the concerns of the social psychologist (who, after all, deals with people who have already been socialized)? In fact, socialization was once regarded as the central theme of social psychology (Sherif, 1948) and there are at least two reasons why its relevance needs to be reasserted. First, there is the 'preface' reason: this is where it all begins. From the social processes described above develop patterns of interaction that are fundamental to all of our face-to-face interactions throughout life. Part of the scientific task is to investigate changes and continuities in these competencies. Secondly, there is a conceptual reason, relating to one of the central concerns of social psychology – the study of social influence (see chapter 16). Social influences upon adults are sometimes conceived of in unidirectional terms, as if other people or 'society' compel the individual to behave in a particular manner or to subscribe to a particular belief. Yet, as we have seen, if we examine supposedly the most influenceable of human subjects, young children, we find that unidirectionality is not the norm. Social influence involves complex processes of interpersonal and cultural negotiations and these negotiations are prevalent from childhood onwards (Emler and Dickinson, 1993).

It might be conceded that socialization is not just a one-way street, but it remains the case that people develop in different ways in different contexts. We need still to account for the ways in which the dynamic negotiations of socialization can result in particular patterns of social behaviour and shared systems of belief. These questions recur in relation to each of the three other major themes of developmental social psychology that will be addressed here, namely the development of relationships, the development of language and the development of social knowledge.

The Development of Relationships

At the very core of becoming a social being is involvement in relationships with others. As we have already seen, in all but the most severely deprived circumstances, the initiation of relationships is virtually inevitable because of both the infant's inherent orientation towards some of the features of other people and other people's strong interest in the infant. One of the key themes to emerge from studies of young children's social development concerns the implications of the first relationships (with caregivers) for subsequent relationships (with peers and other people). Numerous studies have demonstrated that what happens at home is associated with what happens at the preschool and school (Olweus, 1993; Promnitz, 1992; Turner, 1993). Relationships have implications for other relationships (Duck, 1992; Erwin, 1993). In order to explore the possible relevance of the study of early relationships for social psychology we need to focus on a particular topic that has been very influential in the field of social development – the study of **attachment**.   ATTACHMENT

Attachment

An attachment is a specific, enduring affectional tie formed between one person and another (Ainsworth, Blehar, Waters and Wall, 1978). The formation of an attachment is reflected in a repertoire of attachment behaviours, which serve essentially to maintain proximity to the attachment figure. Examples of attachment behaviours include preferential attention, touching, clinging, calling for, and crying in the absence of the specific individual or smiling in her or his presence. Such behaviours are commonly observed in infants from the second half of the first year (Schaffer, 1990). It should be noted in passing that these phenomena are by no means peculiar to infants, and attachments (as well as most of the above attachment behaviours) occur among individuals throughout life; we will return to this point. For the moment, though, let us concentrate on children's attachments, the focus of the majority of the relevant research.

An attachment between a child and his or her caregiver is so commonplace that on first sight it seems banal – a 'natural' dependency. However, it raises a number of puzzles and seems to have so many implications for the child's subsequent development that it has attracted a great deal of research attention. Consider first of all *why* a child might become attached. Obviously, caregivers have some very endearing features: they keep showing up in times of need (especially if you cry out) and they provide invaluable services, such as cuddling, cleaning and, finest of all, feeding. In short, at the start of life caregivers are your best bet for meeting your primary needs. It follows that you should develop positive feelings towards them.

This line of reasoning underpins an influential early theory of Dollard and Miller (1950): the *secondary drive hypothesis*. This theory holds that caregivers, especially mothers, become associated with meeting the primary drives (feeding, bodily comfort). The basic idea is that because she meets the primary needs and thus provides several thousand positive reinforcements a year, proximity to the mother itself becomes a need (a secondary drive). However, there are problems for this initially very plausible explanation. One is that children often form attachments to persons who do not undertake the principal caregiving tasks, and hence are not directly associated with the gratification of primary needs. For example, in traditional households where the mother attends to the baby's physical needs, infants often become attached not only to the mother but also to the father, to older siblings or to other members of the extended family (Schaffer and Emerson, 1964). In some contexts, children become attached to parents who neglect or abuse them (Bowlby, 1969; Schaffer, 1971).

Although there is a variety of other theoretical positions on the origins of infant–parent attachment, by far the most influential has been that developed by the British psychiatrist John Bowlby (1969, 1988) and extended by the American social developmentalist Mary Ainsworth (Ainsworth et al., 1978). Drawing heavily on ethological theory and research (see chapter 2), Bowlby interpreted attachment as an adaptive system of behaviour that has evolved to maximize the infant's survival prospects. Attachment behaviours, as we have seen, serve to maximize proximity to a potential caregiver and to elicit responses from her or him. They increase the likelihood that a vulnerable or distressed infant can obtain help, and they help ensure that the infant develops a **secure base** – a reliable, specific individual whose attention and affection can be depended upon as one begins to explore the wider environment. This theory does not maintain that learning experiences with actual caregivers are irrelevant to the

SECURE BASE

development and consequences of attachment, but it does hold that the capacities and organization of behaviours that promote attachment are built in by nature rather than emerging as a result of reinforcement contingencies. Importantly, for Bowlby the secure base of a stable attachment is crucial to a child's well-being and developmental prospects.

Types of attachment

Studies of infants and parents in quite diverse social systems around the world confirm that attachment is a normative development, occurring in almost all children within roughly the same age span (cf. van IJzendoorn, 1990). However, researchers soon noticed that there were individual differences in the nature of infant–caregiver relationships and in children's responses to separation from and reappearance of the caregiver. Ainsworth et al. (1978) devised a carefully controlled laboratory procedure within which children's reactions to these kinds of events could be observed systematically. They identified three main types of attachment relationship. These are *Type A*, *Anxious/avoidant* (these babies show relatively little distress on the removal of the mother, and appear disinterested in interaction with her during the reunion stages of the procedure); *Type B*, *Securely attached* (who seek actively to maintain proximity and interaction with the mother; they wander and explore confidently when she is present and may show distress on her departure; they greet her return enthusiastically); and *Type C*,

Plate 3.1 A secure base

Anxious/ambivalent (who manifest distress on the removal of the mother, yet resist contact and sometimes appear angry during the reunion episodes). In most samples, approximately 70 per cent of infants display Type B relationships; about 20 per cent fall into Type A, and 10 per cent into Type C (Ainsworth et al., 1978).

Researchers have attempted to discover the correlates of attachment type. The most common finding is evidence of a social and developmental advantage to Type B, securely attached, children. Among other things, children identified during their second year as having Type B attachments have been found during their preschool and kindergarten years to score higher on measures of interpersonal competence, cognitive development, toy play, exploratory skills and eagerness to learn (Lutkenhaus, Grossman and Grossman, 1985; Suess, Grossmann and Sroufe, 1992; Youngblade and Belsky, 1992). These kinds of findings are consistent with the attachment theorist's premise that the provision of a secure base is fundamental to subsequent development. Overall, attachment research amplifies our earlier conclusion: relationships have implications for other relationships.

Relationships, social development and social psychology

The study of relationships has long held a prominent place in the work of social psychologists (see chapter 12; Fletcher and Fincham, 1991) and is one of the most promising areas for fruitful collaborations between social and developmental psychologists (Hartup, 1991). Even so, surely the study of attachment in particular is a concern for the developmentalist rather than the social psychologist? It appears to be something to do with children and whether they grow up feeling good around people. But there are several reasons why the topic merits more careful attention from social psychologists.

First, attachment is bi-directional. It is important not only for the child but also for the caregiver(s). Consider the implications of attachment for the mother. One of the most controversial themes of attachment research has been the question of whether the relationship between the child and his or her natural mother is crucial to the child's healthy development. If it is, and the child needs not just any secure base but the maternal one, then it may follow that mothers should be encouraged to organize their lives so that they are predominant in the preschool child's early experiences. Perhaps it would be best, for example, if mothers did not go out to work but stayed at home with their toddlers? Some early attachment theorists were adamant that this was the case (although their views were moderated subsequently; see Bowlby, 1988). While these issues remain the focus of vigorous debate and research in the developmental arena (see Birns and Hay, 1988; Schaffer, 1990), it should be obvious that they are also very pertinent to social-psychological investigation of adult gender roles and relationships. In fact, many young women and men, on the verge of career entry (leaving university), believe that nature has designed women for maternal attachment rather than professional involvement, and this belief frames their career plans (Wetherell, Stiven and Potter, 1987). Individuals' developmental contexts and expectations influence their social contexts, and vice versa.

A second reason why attachment might be important to the social psychologist returns us to an earlier point, which was that we form attachments throughout life and they are very important to us (Levitt, 1991). It has been proposed by attachment theorists that early attachments furnish working models of social relationships, and thus influence how a person approaches new relationships (Bowlby, 1988; Bretherton, 1992). Suppose that a person with a developmental history of a particular attachment type were as an adult to form a new relationship, with a lover or spouse. What expectations would he or she bring to the relationship, how would he or she relate to the new partner, and what is the prognosis for the future of the involvement? Interesting studies by Shaver and colleagues indicate that adults' romantic orientations can be categorized in three major patterns that are very similar to Ainsworth's typology of infant–caregiver relationships (Hazan and Shaver, 1987; Shaver, Hazan and Bradshaw, 1988). Adults, too, exhibit the characteristics of secure, anxious/ ambivalent and avoidant attachments. And, just like infants, securely attached lovers seem to have an advantage. They find close personal relationships comfortable and rewarding. They feel they can rely upon their partner but allow him or her space as an independent person. Anxious/ambivalent adults are more uncertain about their relationships, they worry that their partner may not love them enough and may leave, they demand assurances yet are inconsistent in their own displays of affection. Avoidant lovers find close relationships uncomfortable and are reluctant to commit themselves fully to their partner (see Feeney, Noller and Patty, 1993).

There is a third reason why attachment is an important topic for social psychologists. Attachment may be relevant not only to interpersonal relations, but also to the study of individuals' orientation to society more generally. For example, Feshbach (1991) found evidence of an association between the quality of early attachments to fathers and adults' degree of patriotism (attachment to the fatherland): securely attached individuals may grow up to love their country while the insecurely attached may be more preoccupied with themes of national dominance. Kirkpatrick and Shaver (1992) found that persons with different attachment styles revealed different types of religious commitment – once again, the secure seemed to have a better relationship with their God. Attachment style appears also to be associated with differences in how individuals respond to societal events, including crises. A topical illustration is provided by Mikulincer, Florian and Weller (1993), who investigated the reactions of young Israeli adults to the Iraqi Scud missile attacks during the Gulf War. While secure types coped with the trauma by seeking support from others, ambivalent people become more emotionally volatile, and avoidant people tried to distance themselves psychologically from the events. In general, insecure people suffered greater psychological distress – lacking a secure base, they found it more difficult to deal with perilous events.

This area of research reminds us that human beings are emotional and socially entangled creatures. Our lives are influenced profoundly by relations to others, feelings, attractions, fears of losses, dependencies and obligations (see chapters 10 to 12). Social psychologists acknowledge these points – though they have not always been prominent in the wake of the cognitive revolution – but it becomes clear that their origins and import can only be understood fully with a developmental perspective.

The Development of Language

We could say the same about language. Much of the excitement of psycholinguistics since the 1960s has been associated with debates about the origins of language and about its import for our understanding of human nature. Following the early work of the American linguist Noam Chomsky (1959, 1965), controversy has raged over the proposition that the grammatical complexities of natural languages are such that only a species endowed with highly specific knowledge could master a language within the space of a few years (see Pinker, 1994, for an overview of the evolutionary arguments). Chomsky maintained that innate knowledge made possible the normal preschooler's rapid progress with the formidable structures of syntax in the face of the impoverished, fragmentary models provided in everyday speech. If this hypothesis is correct, then it certainly hammers a very long nail into the conceptual coffins of those who hold that human knowledge is given by experience, and that children are infinitely malleable. From this theoretical perspective, 'where it all begins' is set back very early indeed, in the child's genetic endowment.

Language raises important issues for psychology as a whole. To a large extent these issues are pursued by researchers outside of social psychology, such as psycholinguists (interested in comprehension and production processes, and in the mental representation of linguistic knowledge) and developmental psycholinguists (who study the emergence of these phenomena in infants and children). However, if we follow the paths of those who have tried to explain the acquisition of language, we soon find that they lead directly to factors which call for the attention of developmental social psychologists.

Social factors in the acquisition of language

Chomsky's provocative ideas set off an explosion of research into the early stages of language acquisition. Many saw support for the innateness hypothesis in the intricacies and rapidity of normal development; this remains the dominant theoretical standpoint among linguists (Goodluck, 1991). Others were equally impressed by the child's early achievements but saw connections between language acquisition and other developments, especially cognitive development (Brown, 1973; Cromer, 1991; Sinclair-de-Zwart, 1967). The outcome was that, for a while, much attention was focused on that classic problem area of psychology, the language–thought relationship (see, for example, Piatelli-Palmarini, 1980).

Social aspects of language development were not widely studied during this era, largely because the idea that interpersonal or environmental factors may be relevant seemed to have been undermined by some of the early discoveries of developmental psycholinguists. For example, children develop forms according to rules rather than simply copying adult models (as when they produce over-regularizations such as 'runned', 'mouses', 'mans', which are not imitations of adult utterances, but do appear to have a systematic basis); children are often impervious to the attempts of caregivers to correct their linguistic 'mistakes' (McNeill, 1970). Tests of the correlation between the order of emergence of particular grammatical elements and their frequencies in parental speech revealed no relationship (Brown, 1973).

However, Brown's (1973) detailed longitudinal study of the language of three American preschoolers showed that one of the most fruitful means of investigating language development is to study it as it occurs spontaneously in its natural contexts. Many other researchers followed suit, and it soon became clear that what the child is producing *is* related to its social experiences: to what other people are saying and doing, to the ways in which they phrase their speech to the learner, to the opportunities and feedback they provide. Reflecting increasing sensitivity to these matters, during the 1980s a new wave of child language research began to dissect the social contexts of language development (Golinkoff, 1983; Robinson, 1984; Snow, 1986). Among other issues, this led researchers to investigate the implications of reciprocity in early caregiver–child relations for language learning, the kinds of support that adults may give to the acquisition process, and the nature of the linguistic input that is made available. It is helpful to consider examples of each in turn.

Reciprocity

When we considered findings supporting the mutuality model of socialization above, we noted that caregivers and infants show accommodations to each others' behaviour from the outset, and that they strive to achieve communication through the repertoire of perceptual and motor skills they have available. Well before the appearance of the first words, caregiver and child are communicating and sharing reactions to the world and to each other. We saw that one feature of early interactions is the ability to take turns quite smoothly, just as in a conversation. The baby is not yet using recognizable words but the parent often frames a dialogue *as though* the infant were responding conversationally. The possibility arises that these simple exchanges – repeated countless times in the course of everyday caregiving – serve as a precursor to the essential skills of conversational behaviour.

Support for language

Turn taker or not, the infant still needs some words to make headway in a conversation. In this respect, other researchers have shown that parents work hard to develop and then exploit a meaningful shared context for language experiences (Bruner, 1983; D'Odorico and Franco, 1985; Messer, 1983). They monitor the child's attention and orient their talk to his or her interests and actions. Bruner has argued that the repetitive routines and games of parent–infant exchanges provide ideal settings or *formats* for the teaching of labelling (Bruner, 1978, 1983). For example, everyday activities like picturebook reading involve the 'That's an X' format, where useful new information such as the names for things is inserted into a familiar structure ('That's a lion,' 'That's a gorilla,' 'That's an elephant'). Once the format is well practised, the routine part of it ('That's a') may signal that an attention-worthy word is forthcoming, giving the child optimal conditions within which to attend to the novel label. There is certainly much evidence that new words can be introduced or stressed in relation to objects and activities which are the current focus of shared attention (Akhtar, Dunham and Dunham, 1991), and that infants begin to co-ordinate their vocalizations with their responses to specific demands of routine play (Rome-Flanders and Richard, 1992).

Linguistic input

Another feature of the social context of language acquisition is the nature of the speech addressed to children. Chomsky had asserted that the models available to normal language learners provided inconsistent and unreliable examples of the grammatical structures to be learned. Part of his reasoning was that in everyday speech we make speech errors, leave sentences incomplete, change our minds in mid-utterance, and so on: this presents the learner with a very untidy basis from which to launch into an already immense task of working out what are the rules for putting words in order.

Critics pointed out that Chomsky was overlooking an important body of evidence. If you listen to an adult speaking to a young language user, it soon becomes apparent that adults modify their language to children. If you have ever heard or participated in such a conversation, other features will be familiar to you: the mother raises her pitch, speaks slowly, and emphasizes key words. These are all typical features of what is known as *parentese* (sometimes called child-addressed-speech), and they seem to be invoked almost automatically when we talk to infants and toddlers (Garton, 1992; Snow, 1986). The possibility arises that through these modifications parents simplify the input and thus facilitate

Plate 3.2 Everday routines may promote vocabulary acquisition

the learner's task. If you were learning a language, would you prefer a teacher who spoke clearly and slowly, or one who rattled away at native-speaker speed?

So, it seems that children get practice at the framework of conversations for quite a while before they begin them, that patient caregivers often strive to make the basics of vocabulary accessible, and that almost anyone speaking to a young language user tends to slow down, to shorten and repeat utterances. It is tempting to conclude that adults do teach language after all, and there are some strong arguments to that effect in the literature (e.g., Moerk, 1992). But there are some serious problems for this hypothesis, too.

Problems for the social-basis hypothesis

One of the problems is that if parents and children achieve such smooth interactions and readily shared understandings, then the question arises: why would the child need to bother learning language anyway (Brown, 1973)? Another is that the relationship between the patterns of early interaction and language acquisition is not clear. We pointed above to a broad analogy between the toing and froing of parent–child interaction and the turn-taking of fully fledged conversation – but broad analogy may be as far as it goes. Some other species are just as capable of alternating vocalizations (such as birds in song) but their young do not learn language (Collis, 1985). Although taking turns is a useful precursor to conversing, it does not in itself provide the *content* of a conversation, including the vocabulary, the grammatical knowledge and the coherence of organized discourse (Collis, 1985; Durkin, 1987).

The evidence that parental support for language acquisition can facilitate (accelerate) some aspects of vocabulary and grammatical knowledge is somewhat stronger (Baker and Nelson, 1984; Whitehurst, Falco, Lonigan et al., 1988). However, this is not evidence that such contexts are *essential* (Nelson, Bonivillian, Denninger et al., 1984). Children in quite diverse contexts acquire a language on roughly the same developmental schedule, even if they grow up in cultures where their parents are much less likely to engage in the kinds of reciprocal interchanges with infants that are typical of middle-class Westerners (cf. Schieffelin, 1990).

The simplicity of parental speech proved to be something of an illusion, too. Some critics have pointed out that although the utterances of parentese tend on average to be shorter, that is because many of them are single words or interjections, and many of the sentences are imperatives or questions: it could be argued that this fails to provide all of the information about the target language that the child will need (Gleitman and Wanner, 1982; Wexler, 1982). Others point to ungrammatical and contradictory information in parentese (Chafetz et al., 1992; Durkin, 1987). It has also been shown that speech modifications when addressing pets bear similarities to the features of parentese (Hirsh-Pasek and Treiman, 1982) – but if our animal companions have profited linguistically from these experiences, they have not yet said so.

These points do not refute the relevance of a social perspective on language acquisition. No child has yet been discovered who learned language without interacting with other language users (though several have been found who failed to learn language in the face of extreme social deprivation; cf. Curtiss, 1989). They do, however, remind us of the limitations of supposedly social theories which see the learning process as one-way, from adult to child, from teacher to learner. Social perspectives which assume bi-directionality may ultimately prove more successful in accounting for the (still mysterious) processes whereby children acquire language.

The pervasiveness of language

We have considered here only the beginnings. Acquiring a language is an impressive enough feat – but you also have to use and respond to it. There are many other ways in which language permeates, facilitates and affects the nature of our social worlds. The development of conversational skills continues well beyond the turn-taking of early childhood, requiring increasing linguistic sophistication, the ability to maintain topics, repair breakdowns, and achieve awareness of others' perspectives (Mannle, Barton and Tomasello, 1992; McTear,

1985; Robinson and Whittaker, 1986). Language is the principal medium through which children receive guidance about social rules: about 25 per cent of maternal speech to preschoolers is concerned with regulating social behaviour by means of instructions, questions, authority assertions, and statements about possession rights and roles (Halle and Shatz, 1994). Children have to master the politeness conventions concerning when and with whom we might use direct speech ('Gimme that cookie!') versus indirect speech ('I feel hungry') (see Baroni and Axia, 1989). Language is also important as a social marker (Giles and Powesland, 1975); children have to learn that one's language informs others about the group(s) to which one belongs and serves to identify others' group memberships in the same way. Socially shared beliefs and prejudices about the relative merits of different variants of language abound in our educational systems, and these can have profound consequences for teachers' expectations for the performance of individual pupils (Edwards, 1989). Above all, language serves to label, and hence to share, our understandings of the social and physical world.

Language and social psychology

Clearly, these issues raise vital matters for developmentalists, but do they bear on the work of social psychologists? We encounter the 'preface' point again: all of the aspects of language we have touched upon here are relevant to adult communicative processes. Language is crucial to our involvements with others throughout life. It is integral to interpersonal relations, to the sharing of cultural understandings, to the expression and regulation of social status, and to the recording and transmission of societies' achievements, beliefs and aspirations (Fraser and Scherer, 1984; Giles and Robinson, 1990; Semin and Fiedler, 1992; see also chapter 11). These are inextricably developmental and social processes.

The Development of Social Knowledge

As we have seen, if you are going to participate in the social world, you need to be able to orient to others, to form relationships with selected individuals, to learn the local system of communication – but there is more. You need also to find ways of sharing ideas with other people, of learning from what they know, of developing solutions jointly; you need to understand what people are, how they function psychologically and how they organize social relations. These are among the principal tasks of the development of social cognition. In this section, we consider research into these topics under two main headings: social interaction and understanding, and understanding the social world.

Social interaction and understanding

It will have seemed obvious to you earlier that social development entailed social experience. Oddly enough, this has not always been obvious or especially interesting to developmental psychologists. Developmentalists have overlooked the social contexts of childhood in much of their work through the twentieth century because they have been concerned primarily with how the child could come to understand the logical and physical properties of the world (Light, 1986). This focus is due in part to the influence of the great Swiss psychologist Jean Piaget (1896–1980), whose imaginative and pioneering studies of the development of reasoning in childhood have guided and inspired countless investigations by his followers and critics into how children construct their theories of knowledge. Piaget himself acknowledged the relevance of social psychology to the kinds of problems he addressed (e.g. 1973), and he maintained that interactions with peers were a crucial factor in the development of reasoning about social topics (such as moral understanding; Piaget, 1932a). However, in practice much of his work and that of other Piagetians focused on the cognitive achievements of the 'individual' child, who was represented in the theory as a kind of mini-scientist evolving, testing and revising his or her understanding through logically progressive stages of reasoning.

As a reminder, let us review briefly Piaget's standard conservation experiments. In the best-known version, the child is presented with two identical amounts of liquid in identical beakers. Once the child has confirmed that they are the same amount, the contents of one of the original beakers is transferred to a third beaker of a different shape: say, taller and thinner. Then, the child is asked whether the new beaker contains the same amount of liquid as the remaining original beaker. Intriguingly, children aged below about six years usually declare that the contents of the new beaker are different – either more or less than the original. Often, they add explanations like "cos it's taller' or 'that one's thinner'. In other words, children seem to fail to conserve mentally the volume of the transferred liquid, and instead are seduced by the perceptual transformation that makes it look greater or less than the original. A child who gives this sort of response is usually termed a 'non-conserver'.

If you run this experiment with a five-year-old you will get a sense of the alluring questions that Piaget's simple but ingenious techniques provoke. His studies of problems such as conservation and many other aspects of children's reasoning set the scene for what turned out to be decades of research into cognitive development. The questions of whether or not Piaget's explanation is correct, and the extent to which methodological procedures in tasks such as the conservation test might distort our impressions of children's underlying abilities, have occasioned much dispute among developmentalists. In the course of this work, the child's involvement with other people was not always a foremost consideration, and the central question was usually: 'How does the mini-scientist tackle this or that logical or mathematical problem?' Recent developments in European developmental social psychology have cast these issues in a new, more social, perspective. A group of Genevan psychologists and their collaborators have revived interest in Piaget's (1932) early argument that cognitive disagreement among peers promoted cognitive development (Doise and Mugny, 1984; Doise and Palmonari, 1984; Perret-Clermont, 1980).

Peer interaction and cognitive development

The starting point of this work was a study in 1975 by Doise, Mugny and Perret-Clermont. Using a conservation-of-liquid task, these researchers reported the interesting finding that six- to seven-year-olds working together (in twos or threes) performed at a higher level than they had done individually in pre-tests. Furthermore, initially non-conserving children who worked with peers who could conserve subsequently performed at a higher level on post-tests than children who did not participate in the collaborative sessions.

It might be argued that, noteworthy as such an outcome is, the children have merely learned to imitate the behaviour of more competent peers, and have not actually advanced their understanding of the cognitive problem posed to them. However, the children were able to provide explanations of their judgements at a higher level than at the outset, making reference now to matters such as reversibility, compensations for changes in height or width and so on – responses which suggest that definite insights had been gained.

Plate 3.3 Conservation and social interaction: Sharing fruit juice can promote attention and insight (Doise and Mugny, 1984)

Even so, in this study at least one of the participants knew the 'correct' answer, and could pass the explanation on to her or his peers. Still more interesting are other experiments which show that non-conserving children can profit from social interaction with other non-conservers (see, for example, Mugny, Levy and Doise, 1978; Rijsman et al., 1980). It seems that generating contradictory perspectives – even if each perspective is erroneous – may promote awareness that more than one dimension (e.g. height and width) needs to be taken into account in judging the transformation. Other research using similar experimental paradigms has shown that gains acquired through social interaction can be obtained elsewhere, such as in other Piagetian tasks (Perret-Clermont, 1980), and through tasks using different material and formats from those used at pre-test (Valiant, Glachan and Emler, 1982). Improved performance as a result of social interaction on more advanced cognitive tasks has also been demonstrated with older children and adolescents (Aboud, 1989; Doise and Hanselmann, 1990; Howe, Tolmie and Rodgers, 1992; Light, Littleton, Messer and Joiner, 1994). For example, Light et al. (1994) found that eleven-year-olds, given a complex computer task over a series of sessions, fared better if working in pairs; importantly, the relative advantage to children who had worked jointly (in Sessions 1 and 2, in figure 3.1) was sustained even when they were tested again individually (Session 3).

This work in turn has led to differences of opinion among psychologists as to what is entailed in the social interactive processes (Carugati and Gilly, 1993). Doise and Mugny (1984) emphasize **socio-cognitive conflict**, but others stress the *intra*psychological processes that may be engaged by the tasks (Emler and Valiant, 1982; Gilly, 1989; Howe et al., 1990), the importance of confirming the correct answer (Bijstra et al., 1991), and the role of imitation (Winnykamen,

SOCIO-
COGNITIVE
CONFLICT

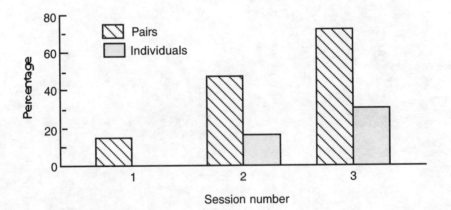

Figure 3.1 Percentages of children succeeding on a complex computer task for each condition on each session, note that on Session 3 all children are working individually so that here 'pairs' denotes those who *previously* worked in pairs. (Light et al., 1994)

1990). Many researchers have found inspiration in another social theory, that of the Soviet psychologist Vygotsky (1962, 1978), which emphasizes the role of more advanced tutors (parents, teachers, more competent peers) in guiding children's learning. From a Vygotskyan perspective, the child is seen as an active apprentice (Rogoff, 1990; Wertsch and Tulviste, 1992) rather than as a scientist engaged in dispute with her or his peers. Although debate continues, these scientific perspectives may not be mutually exclusive, and it is likely that the ways in which social processes contribute to cognitive development will turn out to be varied. Certainly, one major contribution of these lines of research has been that they have affected the character of cognitive developmental research by bringing social processes to the fore. In this respect, they illustrate one of the principal ways in which developmental psychology has begun to profit from a closer relationship with social psychology. Let us turn now to another.

Understanding the social world

The work we have just considered highlights the social *contexts* within which cognitive development proceeds. We turn now to the social *content*. Note first that the actual tasks used in the kinds of studies described above tend to be those traditionally of interest to developmental and educational psychologists. Subjects may work together but they are focused on the conservation of liquid, or some abstract problem concerned with logical and spatio-temporal variables. In everyday life children have to learn a great deal, too, about the social world itself: the differences among people, the reasons for people's behaviour, the nature of society. In this sense, we are concerned with the social content of cognition (see chapter 5), asking, how do children come to understand how people function and the ways in which society is structured?

Understanding people

Knowledge of the personal attributes and mental processes of others is a prerequisite to many tasks in social reasoning and is essential to social relations. The child needs to grasp that other people have unique characteristics, which help us to distinguish among them, and to appreciate that they are thinking, knowing and feeling entities, which helps us to interact with them. These are vital but elusive matters. After all, from the preschool on, it is adaptive to know who is who and what different individuals are likely to do for – or to – you. The task is made more difficult by the fact that we can never observe directly other people's mental activities or even their emotions. At most, we witness external correlates or outcomes and from these we make inferences about what underlies a person's behaviour. How, then, do children piece together this complex information? It appears that both *intra*psychological, developmental changes in cognitive abilities and *inter*psychological, social experiences are entailed, though exactly how these interrelate remains a pressing research question.

The child's cognitive processing is studied in research which requires explanation or decisions about social phenomena. For example, one important line of enquiry has attempted to uncover developmental changes in knowledge about personal attributes. Livesley and Bromley (1973) and Peevers and Secord (1973) elicited children's descriptions of others (their friends, or people they knew) and investigated age-related changes in the kinds of characteristics that were focused upon. Drawing on Piagetian theory, they expected and found that younger children refer most often to peripheral or external phenomena (the person's physical appearance, dress, possessions, kinship status and so on), while from around age seven or eight years there was a notable increase in the amount and sophistication of reference to internal psychological properties (such as traits, needs, motives and attitudes). Subsequent research has confirmed that person *descriptions* do become more focused on internal, psychological properties with age (Newman, 1991; Yuill, 1992). During middle childhood, understanding of these and other essential social matters is refined, and concepts of friends, of friendship, and of the mutual responsibilities and obligations among peers develop (Erwin, 1993; Selman, 1980; Youniss, 1989).

These kinds of findings raise many questions about the nature of changes in children's thinking and about the ways in which young children conceive of other people. Note that description tasks depend on production of relatively uncommon vocabulary. In tasks using different methodologies, it has been demonstrated that by at least five years children can use information about a person's psychological attributes to predict how he or she will behave in another situation (Bennett, 1985–86; Berndt and Heller, 1985; Yuill, 1993). Even earlier, children are developing a 'theory of mind' – an understanding that they and other people have mental processes, such as thought, perception and memory (Frye and Moore, 1991; Leekam, 1993; Pratt, 1993).

Although there is much still to be investigated, it appears that children achieve some insights into the complexities of human psychological phenomena surprisingly early. The next, closely related, issue is: how do they find out? It seems that learning about the psychological world depends crucially upon involvement in social contexts. Stimuli to discovery may occur in each direction: inner to outer, and vice versa. For example, in studies of the development of emotional understanding, Harris (1989) argues that the beginnings of the process are to be detected in an 'imaginative leap' that the young child makes from his or her own feelings to the eventual grasp of the possibility that other people may have similar sensations. But it is also the case that other people may alert us to possible and situationally appropriate emotions by their verbal accounts and by their interventions in our experiences (Dunn, 1988).

An interesting example is provided in a study by Semin and Papadopoulou (1990). These investigators asked mothers to estimate their own and their child's embarrassment in the course of everyday mishaps (such as dropping a bottle in a supermarket, spilling soup in a restaurant). The older the child, the greater the degree of embarrassment the mother expected him or her to feel. But the less embarrassment the child felt, the more the mother anticipated for herself. It appears that the parent perceives herself and her child as a unit, and feels a responsibility for the unit to meet public requirements. Although it is recognized that the younger child cannot undertake his or her full share of the relevant emotion, over time he or she is gradually encouraged to do so. In such ways, it may be that we learn much about feelings through involvement with those who already have them.

What becomes clear, then, is that the social content of cognition is inseparable from the social context, since this body of knowledge can only be obtained in social environments. Family and peer relationships provide the natural starting point for discoveries about other people's characteristics, including their beliefs, intentions and emotions (Dunn, 1988, 1993).

Understanding society

As if people themselves were not complicated enough, they also form into social structures and organize transactions through socially shared mechanisms. Some of these impinge directly on the young child's life (the family, school, shops, the community) and others are more remote, though still salient because of their frequency in everyday discourse (e.g., the government, the economic system, the country, foreign nations). Coming to understand the nature and functions of these various societal arrangements is another important dimension of the development of social cognition.

Some of the most fruitful investigations have drawn upon Piagetian or neo-Piagetian stage-sequence theory (Berti and Bombi, 1988; Cram and Ng, 1994; Furth, 1980). Furth (1980) proposed that understanding of both local and remote aspects of the societal structure advances in stages, and that these stages take several years. For example, he found that a local institution such as the shop is understood in quite simple, undifferentiated terms by most five-year-olds, who see shopping as facilitated by adults' apparently unlimited access to money, and by the generosity of the shopkeeper who provides even more money (change) to finance future consumption. Over the next few years, theories of how shops operate are enriched as children come to understand the rituals of payment, but even so the notion of profit margins is rarely grasped and the destination of funds in the till is uncertain: seven- to eight-year-olds often suppose it is given to poor or blind people, or collected (in England at least) by the Queen. By age ten to eleven years understanding is fuller, though there is still little or no awareness of considerations such as the expenses of running the shop. Berti and Bombi (1988), interviewing Italian children about their understanding of the ownership of the local bus, found broadly similar patterns.

These kinds of findings fit well with Piagetian theory, and these investigators maintain that understanding of society is closely related to cognitive development in general. However, it must be stressed that the converse holds equally:

cognitive development needs to be investigated in relation to social experience. Although children may have often fantastic notions about the nature of societal phenomena, it is important to bear in mind that their experiences of these processes are very limited and vary with culture (see Jahoda, 1983, 1984).

Turning to one of the most prominent extra-familial social institutions in children's lives – the school – we find further evidence that social experiences are associated with variations in social reasoning. For example, Emler, Ohana and Moscovici (1987) found that seven- to 11-year-olds' understanding of the role of the teacher showed some similarities to the patterns of development uncovered in neo-Piagetian studies: by late childhood, subjects had a better grasp of the hierarchy of authority relations within the school and they understood the need for rules. However, Emler et al. drew their subjects from two different countries, Scotland and France, and there were differences in how the children from each society saw things. The Scottish subjects tended to regard teachers as obligated to enforce the school rules irrespective of their own personal feelings about whether the rules were fair. The French children were more inclined to the view that the teacher should always do what was fair, irrespective of what the rules dictated. Perhaps this tells us something about variations in national ideologies (readers prone to stereotyping might surmise that the French are romantic revolutionaries, and the Scots dour rule followers) or perhaps it tells us something about the regimes in the particular schools from which the researchers drew their subjects. The important point is that the young subjects seemed to share the outlooks of their respective communities: aspects of social cognition may vary with social context.

A final example of the interweaving of developmental changes in social understanding and the impact of social experiences is presented by research concerned with national and ethnic categorization. Again, these are abstract and in some respects rather remote social concepts. Even so, there is evidence that some perception of their importance is attained relatively early in life. Although children below around age seven tend to have rather confused notions of nationality (Jahoda, 1963; Piaget and Weil, 1951), they have already developed affective orientations, such that they like some nationalities (especially their own) more than others (Tajfel, 1981; Tajfel and Jahoda, 1966). A recent illustration is provided by Barrett and Short (1992), who investigated five- to ten-year-old English children's knowledge of and attitudes towards people from other European countries. The younger children's factual knowledge was slight, but their preferences were clear: French and Spanish people were liked most, followed by Italians, and Germans were liked least.

For Tajfel, the importance of these kinds of findings is that they provide 'evidence of the very high sensitivity of young children to the more primitive aspects of the value systems of their societies' (1981, p. 206). However, there appears to be more to the development of national and ethnic prejudices than the direct absorption of adult prejudices (Aboud, 1988). In a review of several

Plate 3.4 This advertisement, part of an anti-racism campaign run by the Commission for Racial Equality, raises the question: 'when does prejudice develop?'

decades' research into children's prejudices, Aboud shows that children's views are not invariably direct replicas of those of their parents or other salient community sources. In fact, at around ages four or five, children's ethnic biases are often *stronger* than those of adults. Aboud argues that this is a function of an early social-cognitive reliance on perceptual features (such as colour of skin, clothing, language) that provide an easy basis for comparing self with others. Once a distinction is made, then it tends to be accompanied with a strong affective orientation – typically, wariness or even dislike of the outgroup. With further social-cognitive development, children build up a greater amount of factual knowledge about other social categories and increasing awareness that intergroup relations are reciprocal (i.e., that if you are a foreigner to me, then perhaps I am a foreigner to you). This may mitigate the simplistic concepts and starker prejudices of the younger child (see Doyle, Beaudet and Aboud, 1988, illustrated in figure 3.2; Tajfel et al., 1970).

In sum, part of the developing person's task is to discover what the social world is like: what are the properties of people, how are things organized, what are the rules, and so on. But these are not just interesting intellectual puzzles for the mini-social psychologist to work on in preparation for adulthood. From the outset, the child is learning through participation, and participation affects the content and processes of learning. Part of the challenge of developmental social

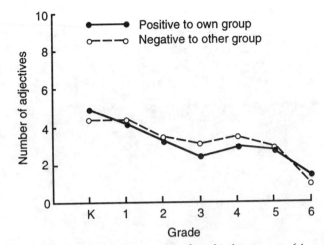

Figure 3.2 Children's views of own and other group from kindergarten to 6th grade (Doyle et al. 1988)

psychology is to account for the dynamic tensions arising from the intersection of developmental changes in capacities and the social contexts in which development comes about.

Social knowledge and social psychology

Why should all this matter to the social psychologist? Once again, is it not reasonable to assume that adults have already dealt with these matters, and by the time they get to the laboratory are fully functioning in mature state? As above, part of the answer rests on the preface argument: a comprehensive account of human social reasoning entails an understanding of its origins and development. In fact, recent work in developmental social psychology has shown that all of the central processes of interest to investigators of adult social cognition, to be discussed in more detail in chapters 5 to 7, have complex developmental histories (Durkin, 1995). It is also the case that biases in social reasoning may reflect strategies that proved useful at earlier stages of development. For example, it was an early observation of Piaget's (1928) – that the first thing to interest a child about a country was its name – which provided a starting point to Tajfel's later studies of the influence of group membership and group identity upon social judgements (see chapter 17).

Summary and Conclusions

We have considered just some of the issues that arise when social psychologists engage in interaction with their developmental colleagues and ask: how does it all begin? There are many more topics that could be pursued in like fashion – as many as there are in the remainder of this book – but some important conclusions can be established on the basis of the work we have reviewed here.

First, it is clear that from infancy through to adulthood, the young person is immersed in a social world in which the content and the processes of development depend critically upon interactions with other people. In discussing the concept of socialization, we saw that these processes amount to much more than an 'injection' of information or instructions from adults. From the beginnings, social participation and social discovery involve mutual responsiveness, toing and froing, and negotiations rather than repression. Secondly, social participation leads swiftly beyond the delights of perceptual stimulation and need gratification to the emergence of selective, emotionally significant relationships. This remains an essential fact of human social organization throughout our lives, and we considered some evidence which suggests the relevance of developmental models of relationships (especially, attachments) for the study of adult relations, both to other people and to society more generally. Thirdly, social participation normally requires mastery of one of the species's most distinctive skills, language. We saw that although language acquisition was for some time regarded as a mystery for linguists and cognitive developmentalists to explain, research into language in its natural contexts soon brought home that it is a fundamentally social activity. This does not ease the task of explaining how we do it, but it does cast the enquiry in a more appropriate light – and, in the process, it illuminates new directions for social psychology. Fourthly, social participation offers prospects of learning with and from others, as well as the challenges of discovering how others function and what kind of a world they have set up for us. The once highly individualistic theories of cognitive development are being broadened by exposure to more social perspectives. The study of the contents of social knowledge is being informed by the analysis of their origins and developmental changes.

In each case, we have seen that there are good grounds for drawing together both social and developmental perspectives on these various problems. Often, researchers in the respective sub-disciplines have not been energetic in seeking each other's views, but we have noted several exceptions where important new research directions have emerged as a result of the work of those who are willing to cross boundaries. But the developmental story does not end there. The next question is: how does it all continue? Humans continue to develop throughout adulthood, though the scale of the developments is sometimes less apparent to us because we are right in the midst of them. Perhaps, as you continue through this book and other readings in social psychology, you might ask yourself the preface questions from time to time: how do people come to do that? How do their developmental experiences affect their current behaviours? And then, ask the continuation questions: might people do that differently at different points in their lives, or in response to age differences in the people they are interacting with? The answers to the continuation questions, invariably, will be 'yes, of course'. This answer will remind you that a social psychology without a developmental aspect defies a principal axiom of scientific enquiry.

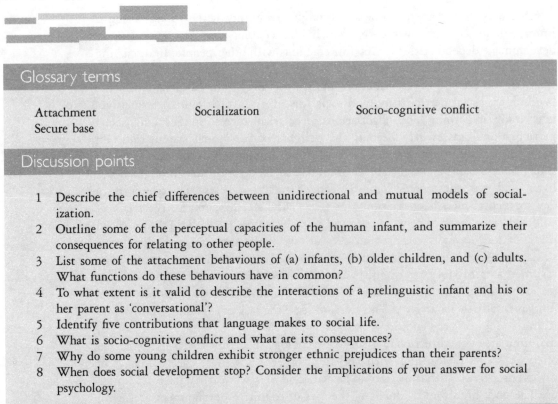

Glossary terms

Attachment   Socialization   Socio-cognitive conflict
Secure base

Discussion points

1 Describe the chief differences between unidirectional and mutual models of social-ization.
2 Outline some of the perceptual capacities of the human infant, and summarize their consequences for relating to other people.
3 List some of the attachment behaviours of (a) infants, (b) older children, and (c) adults. What functions do these behaviours have in common?
4 To what extent is it valid to describe the interactions of a prelinguistic infant and his or her parent as 'conversational'?
5 Identify five contributions that language makes to social life.
6 What is socio-cognitive conflict and what are its consequences?
7 Why do some young children exhibit stronger ethnic prejudices than their parents?
8 When does social development stop? Consider the implications of your answer for social psychology.

Suggestions for further reading

Aboud, F. (1988) *Children and Prejudice*. Oxford: Blackwell. A review of research into ethnic prejudice in children and a new social-cognitive model of developmental changes.

Bennett, M. (ed.) (1993) *The Child as Psychologist. An introduction to the development of social cognition*. New York: Harvester-Wheatsheaf. A valuable set of essays on recent work in developmental social cognition.

Bretherton, I. (1992) The origins of attachment theory: John Bowlby and Mary Ainsworth. *Developmental Psychology*, 28, 759–75. Discusses the history of attachment theory, and provides a succinct review of current issues.

Doise, W. and Mugny, G. (1984) *The Social Development of the Intellect*. Oxford: Pergamon. A seminal work on socio-cognitive conflict and the social influences on intellectual operations in childhood.

Dunn, J. (1988) *The Beginnings of Social Understanding*. Oxford: Blackwell. An examination of the earliest stages of social knowledge and reasoning in the social contexts of the family.

Durkin, K. (1995) *Developmental Social Psychology: From Infancy to Old Age*. Oxford: Blackwell. A fuller account of the issues introduced in this chapter and of other key topics in developmental social psychology.

Erwin, P. (1993) *Friendship and Peer Relations in Children*. Chichester: Wiley. A comprehensive discussion of research into children's peer relations, including problems and interventions.

Key study

Tajfel, H., Nemeth, C., Jahoda, G., Campbell, J. D. and Johnson, N. B. (1970). The development of children's preference for their own country: a cross-national study. *International Journal of Psychology*, 6, 245–53.

4 Methodology in Social Psychology: Putting Ideas to the Test

Antony S. R. Manstead and Gün R. Semin

Contents

Introduction

Selection of research strategies
   Survey research
   Experiments and quasi-experiments
   Key features of the social-psychological experiment
   Experimental designs
   Threats to validity in experimental research

Data collection techniques
   Observational measures
   Self-report measures
   Choosing a measure

Problems with experimentation

Summary and conclusions

Introduction

Procedures for gathering information in any discipline are known as *methods*. Methods provide a means of translating a researcher's ideas into actions. The researcher's ideas will generally revolve around one or more questions about a phenomenon. An example of such a question in social psychology would be: 'How can a group of capable people make a decision that is stupid and could have been shown to be so at the time the decision was taken?' (cf. Janis, 1972; and chapter 17 of this book). A researcher interested in this question might have a hunch or a theory to explain this phenomenon. For example, it might be thought that the poor decision arises from the fact that the group has a powerful leader who expresses a preference early in the decision-making process and thereby stifles systematic evaluation of superior options. Assessing the correctness of this hunch would necessitate the collection of information about styles of leadership in groups making poor decisions. Methods are the procedures the researcher would follow in gathering that information, and *methodology* is a term used to refer to all aspects of the implementation of methods.

Although this chapter is concerned above all with the methods used by social psychologists to test the validity of their ideas, it is worth giving some consideration to the issue of where these ideas originate. In the typical case, the researcher begins with a **theory** about the phenomenon under investigation. THEORY Where does such a theory come from? One obvious source is observation of real-world events. For example, Janis's (1972) theory concerning the poor quality of decision-making that is sometimes apparent in groups, even when the groups consist of competent and experienced persons, was stimulated by reading accounts of how the United States government took the decision to invade Cuba in 1961, a decision that has been called 'the perfect failure'. Here is the starting point for Janis's theory of defective decision-making by groups: a puzzling real-world phenomenon, namely the ability of a highly qualified group of individuals to arrive at a remarkably poor decision. Having previously conducted a good deal of research on group dynamics, Janis was acquainted with the way in which strong normative pressures can build up in groups, encouraging their members to maintain friendly relations with each other at the expense of critical thinking. The undermining of critical and independent thinking in social groups that results from strong pressures towards uniformity is what Janis called 'group-think'. Thus a second important element of theory-building in social psychology is existing theory. The fact that Janis was already conversant with research on group processes and social influence in groups provided him with a conceptual armoury that he could use to explain defective decision-making by groups.

Another version of this process of theory building begins not with a puzzling real-world phenomenon but with a puzzling set of apparently conflicting findings from previous research. A well-known example in social psychology is Zajonc's (1965) attempt to reconcile conflicting findings in previous studies of the effects on individual task performance of being observed by others (see chapter 16). Zajonc observed that some researchers had found that being observed by others had beneficial effects on task performance, whereas other researchers had found that being observed by others resulted in poorer performance. To explain these conflicting findings, Zajonc drew on principles derived from learning theory. Once again, then, the theorist began with a phenomenon that required an explanation, and drew on existing theoretical concepts and processes to make sense of that phenomenon.

In what sense does a theory 'explain' a phenomenon such as the defective decision-making of high-calibre groups, or the conflicting effects of being observed on task performance? Social-psychological theories usually consist of a set of concepts and a set of statements concerning the relationships among these concepts. For example, Janis's (1972) theory consists of one group of concepts representing the antecedent conditions of groupthink, another set representing the symptoms of groupthink, and a third set representing the process linking antecedent conditions with symptoms. An example of an antecedent condition is a 'cohesive group', that is a group whose members are psychologically dependent on the group. Because they are dependent on their group membership, reasoned Janis, they will be more likely to conform to what they believe to be the consensus position in the group. An example of a symptom of groupthink is the presence in the group of 'mind guards', the term Janis used to describe group members who take it upon themselves to protect the group from information that would question the correctness or morality of the emerging decision. The mediating process specified by Janis is 'concurrence-seeking tendency', a powerful preference for agreement with fellow group members. Thus antecedent conditions are linked to symptoms via a mediating process.

CONSTRUCT

Three important concepts need to be introduced at this point. **Construct** is the term used to refer to abstract concepts in a theory. For example, in Janis's theory concepts such as group cohesiveness and concurrence-seeking tendency are theoretical *constructs*. **Variable** is a term used to refer to a measurable representation of a construct. To represent the construct of group cohesiveness, for example, we might measure one or more of the following variables: how long the group has been in existence; the extent to which group members nominate each other as personal friends; how much group members say they value their membership of the group; and how much conflict and dissent is expressed within the group. Here we can see that the construct of cohesiveness has several possible ways of being represented as a variable. In their research, social psychologists work with variables, rather than constructs, because variables can be measured.

VARIABLE

How can a theory be used to guide research? Having proposed a theory, one normally derives predictions from it. In the case of Janis's theory, one prediction that can be logically derived from the theory is that groups that are characterized by greater cohesiveness should be more prone to making poor quality decisions than groups that are lower in cohesiveness. Armed with such a prediction (or **hypothesis**), the researcher will then set about trying to accumulate evidence to support the prediction. To the extent that the evidence is consistent with the prediction, confidence in the theory from which the prediction was derived is enhanced. Correspondingly, if the evidence is inconsistent with the prediction, confidence in the underlying theory is weakened. Methods are the means by which researchers put their ideas to the test.

HYPOTHESIS

It is useful at this point to distinguish between three broad types of research: descriptive, correlational and experimental. *Descriptive research* is intended to provide the researcher with an accurate description of the phenomenon in question ('Does *A* occur?'). For example, a researcher may want to know (as did Milgram, 1963) whether the average adult would obey orders from an authority figure to administer painful and potentially lethal electric shocks to a fellow human. The researcher would begin by observing and recording the proportion of adults that obeys an authority's orders. This simply describes the phenomenon. Social-psychological research rarely stops at this point. The researcher typically wants to know *why* people behave as they do. If one finds, as did Milgram, that 65 per cent of a sample of adults are fully obedient to orders to administer shocks, an obvious question is 'Why?'

Correlational research takes us part of the way to answering this question. The goal here is to describe the extent to which variations in some behaviour, such as obedience, are related systematically to variations in some other factor ('Is *A* related to *B*?'). For example, do those who obey orders tend to be particular *types* of persons (men rather than women, introverts rather than extroverts, and so on)? In posing such questions, the researcher is looking for relationships, or *correlations*, between the measured variables. Discovering such a relationship is a helpful first step in establishing why a phenomenon occurs, but causal conclusions cannot be unambiguously drawn on the basis of correlational information. To understand why this is so, take the case of a correlational finding from Milgram's (1965) study of obedience. It was found that persons who were more obedient tended also to report experiencing more tension during their participation in the study. How should we interpret this correlation? Is the tension a sign of fear of the consequences of disobedience, which would suggest that obedience is 'caused' by individuals' fears about what might happen to them if they were disobedient? Alternatively, might the tension simply reflect concern about the possible harm befalling the 'victim'? In the first case the relationship between obedience (*A*) and tension (*B*) is explained as '*B* leads to *A*'; in the second case, the same relationship is interpreted as '*A* leads to *B*'. Yet another possibility is that the relationship between *A* and *B* is caused by some third variable, *C*. In the Milgram case, for example, one possibility is that both the obedience and the tension are caused by aggressiveness, and that the relationship between obedience and tension is therefore not a causal one at all. In the absence of further information, any of these interpretations is plausible. This is why it is usually impossible to infer causality from correlational research.

Experimental research is explicitly designed to yield causal information. The goal

EXPERIMENT

of an **experiment** is to see what happens to a phenomenon, such as obedience, when the researcher deliberately modifies some feature of the environment in which the phenomenon occurs ('If I change variable B, will there be resulting changes in variable A?'). By controlling the variation in B, the researcher can arrive at stronger conclusions about causality if it is found that A and B are related. Instead of simply knowing that more of variable A is associated with more of variable B, the experimental researcher discovers whether A increases when B is increased, decreases when B is reduced, remains stable when B is left unchanged, and so on. Such a pattern of results would suggest that the manipulated variations in B *cause* the observed variations in A. We will have a lot more to say about experimental research below.

The descriptive, correlational and experimental research types are very general kinds of research method, and are by no means specific to psychology or social psychology. Which of these approaches is adopted by a researcher in conducting a particular investigation depends to a large extent on the type of question he or she is trying to answer. Although the typical case in social-psychological research is one in which the researcher's goal is to test a specific prediction, there are also cases where the researcher's goal is more exploratory and descriptive. If the research goal is to *describe* some phenomenon (for example, to establish whether it exists, the conditions under which it is found, and so on), this implies a different type of method from the one suggested by the research goal of *hypothesis testing*. Note that descriptive research can often be a prelude to hypothesis-testing research. For example, if in the course of descriptive research an investigator notices that a phenomenon often occurs under a particular set of conditions, this observation can form the basis of a theory concerning the relationship between the conditions and the phenomenon, and thereby lead to specific predictions and thus to hypothesis-testing research. The ultimate goal of most social psychological research is *explanation*, and the steps by which explanations are arrived at are (1) the formulation of theoretical statements about the relationships between constructs, and (2) the conduct of empirical research in which evidence concerning these relationships is gathered. This type of research endeavour is typical of what is often called 'psychological social psychology' (see chapter 1).

Our general goal in the present chapter is to present an overview of research methods as practised by social psychologists whose ultimate goal is the explanation of social phenomena by observing relationships between constructs, by proposing theories to account for such relationships, by deriving predictions from these theories, and by collecting evidence to test such predictions. These are the research methods most often employed in social-psychological research. Our principal aim here is to enable the reader to evaluate social-psychological research, as it is presented in subsequent chapters of this book; a secondary aim is to provide some preliminary guidance for the conduct of this type of research.

To facilitate the process of describing and discussing research methods, we will consider separately two facets of research methodology. First, we will describe various *research strategies*; by research strategy we mean the broad orientation one adopts in addressing a question. Then we shall describe some of the most popular *data collection techniques*; these are the specific procedures the researcher follows in gathering information. The selection of a particular technique will be determined partly by the researcher's objectives and partly by the available resources.

Selection of Research Strategies

The strategies available for social-psychological research differ in terms of several attributes. Three that we highlight here are: the *representativeness* of the data that are collected, the *realism* of the setting in which data are collected, and the degree of *control* over the setting in which the data are collected. In this section we provide an overview of what we regard as the major research strategies available to social psychologists and briefly describe the distinctive attributes of each strategy.

Survey research

One strategy for gathering information is to survey public opinion and/or behaviour, either by interview or by questionnaire. This type of research strategy is known as a **sample survey**, and is well known in everyday life in the form of opinion polls (Schuman and Kalton, 1985). This strategy does not directly address questions of causality; rather, the objective is to describe the characteristics of one or more groups of people. Such descriptions can range from the simple (e.g., describing the percentage of persons eligible to vote in a particular constituency who say that they intend to vote for a particular political candidate) to the more complex (e.g., describing the personal and social characteristics associated with illegal use of drugs among school-age children and teenagers). Note that the first type of description is 'pure' description, while the second describes relationships between variables – such as those between drug use, on the one hand, and age, sex, socioeconomic status, educational achievement, on the other, and thereby constitutes correlational research.

The survey researcher's primary concern is with the extent to which the respondents are representative of a population (such as all adults living in a particular community, region or country). How does the survey researcher tackle the issue of representativeness? One solution to this issue would be to interview or collect completed questionnaires from the entire population in question (as is done in a census). Here the issue of representativeness is circumvented by

SAMPLE SURVEY

collecting data from all members of the population: if you are really able to describe the entire population, there can be little doubt that the findings are 'representative' of that population. In most cases, however, interviewing or administering questionnaires to all members of a population is simply not practicable. Then the survey researcher is confronted with the business of choosing which members of that population should receive questionnaires or be interviewed. The process of selecting a subset of members of a population with a view to describing the population from which they are taken is known as **sampling**.

Two main types of sampling are used in survey research: probabilistic and non-probabilistic. The most basic form of probabilistic sampling is the **simple random sample**. A simple random sample is one which satisfies two conditions: first, each member of the population has an equal chance of being selected; second, the selection of every possible combination of the desired number of members is equally likely. To explain the second condition, imagine that the population size is 10 (consisting of persons labelled A to J) and the sample size is 2. There are 45 possible combinations of 2 members of the population (A + B, A + C, A + D, and so on, to I + J). In simple random sampling each of these 45 possible combinations of 2 members has to be equally likely. In practice this kind of sampling is achieved by allocating numbers to each member of the population, and then using computer-generated random numbers to select a sample of the required size. Thus the first randomly-generated number defines the first member of the population to be sampled, and so on, until the sample is full. Even if you do not have access to a computer program that generates random numbers, most statistics textbooks contain tables of random numbers that can be used for this purpose.

Because it is expensive and time-consuming to do probability sampling, non-probability sampling is more commonly used for research purposes. The most typical form of non-probability sample is the **quota sample**. In a quota sample, the objective is to select a sample that reflects the basic attributes of the population. These attributes might be age and sex. Thus if you know the age and sex composition of the population concerned, you ensure that the age and sex composition of the sample faithfully reflects that of the population. The term 'quota' refers to the number of persons of a given type (e.g., females between the ages of 55 and 60) who have to be interviewed. The major advantage of quota sampling is that the interviewer can approach potential respondents until all quotas are filled, without needing to recruit a specifically identified respondent. In simple random sampling, by contrast, the members of the population who are thrown up by the random number selection process are the ones who have to be interviewed, but some of these persons may be difficult to contact or unco-operative, requiring several repeat calls and visits. Although quota sampling saves time and money for the researcher, there is a necessary loss of accuracy involved, as compared with probability sampling. Detailed discussion of the advantages and disadvantages of the two methods are beyond the scope of this chapter, and readers are referred to Schuman and Kalton (1985) for a more specialist treatment.

Experiments and quasi-experiments

The survey researcher is not concerned about the physical and social setting in which the data are collected (e.g., the respondent's home, a shopping mall, or a street corner) and assumes this to be irrelevant. The setting in which data are collected is much more of a concern for other researchers, typically because they want to examine the relationship between certain features of the setting, ranging from social features (such as whether it is a public or private one) to physical features (for example, how rainy it is or how hot it is) and certain aspects of an individual's or group's behaviour (such as how conformist their expressed attitudes are, how positive their social judgements are, or how aggressive their behaviour is). This type of research is much more geared towards causal explanation than is survey research.

To address the issue of causality, social psychologists typically use some variation on the general theme of the experimental method. However, this is a theme with many variations. Two of the most common of these variations are the **quasi-experiment** and the **true randomized experiment**. They differ with respect to two of the attributes of research strategies that we listed earlier, namely the realism of the setting in which the data are collected, and the degree of control that the researcher has over that setting. In the typical case the quasi-experiment is one conducted in a natural, everyday life setting, over which the researcher has less than complete control. The lack of control over the setting arises from the very fact that it is an everyday life setting. Here the realism of the setting is relatively high, the control relatively low. The true randomized experiment, by contrast, is one in which the researcher has complete control over key features of the setting; however, this degree of control often involves a loss of realism.

QUASI-EXPERIMENT

TRUE RANDOMIZED EXPERIMENT

To grasp the essential difference between a quasi-experiment and a true experiment we need to define what we mean by the term 'experiment'. Experiments are studies in which the researcher examines the effects of one class of variables (independent variables) on another class of variables (dependent variables). In a true randomized experiment the researcher has control over the independent variable and also over who is exposed to this variable. Most importantly, the researcher is able to allocate research participants *randomly* to different conditions of the experiment. True experiments are often conducted in laboratory settings, where the researcher is able to control many features of the setting. In a quasi-experiment the researcher cannot control who is exposed to the independent variable. In a typical quasi-experiment pre-existing groups of people are either exposed or not exposed to the independent variable. Quasi-experiments are often conducted in natural, or 'field' contexts, where the researcher has less control over the setting. Examples of each method may help to bring out the points of difference.

As will be clear from chapter 14, an issue much studied by social psychologists interested in aggression is whether exposure to violent film and television material has an impact on the subsequent behaviour of the viewer. This is an issue that can be studied using true randomized experiments or quasi-experiments. An example of a true experiment on this issue is the study reported by Liebert and Baron (1972). Male and female children in each of two age groups were randomly allocated to one of two experimental conditions, one in which they viewed an excerpt from a violent television programme and another in which they viewed an exciting athletics race. Later both groups of children were ostensibly given the opportunity to hurt another child. Those who had seen the violent material were more likely to use this opportunity than were those who had seen the non-violent material. Because children had been allocated to the violent and non-violent conditions randomly, the observed difference can be attributed with confidence to the difference in type of material seen, rather than to any difference in the type of children who saw the material.

An example of a quasi-experimental study of the same issue is the study reported by Black and Bevan (1992). They asked people to complete a short questionnaire as a measure of tendency to engage in aggressive behaviour under one of four conditions: while waiting in line outside a cinema to see a violent movie; while waiting in line to see a non-violent movie; having just seen a violent movie; and having just seen a non-violent movie. The researchers found that: (1) those waiting to see the violent film had higher aggression scores than those waiting to see the non-violent film; (2) those who had just seen the violent film scored higher than those waiting to see the violent film; (3) there was no difference in aggression scores between those who had just seen a non-violent movie and those waiting to see a non-violent movie. While this pattern of findings is consistent with the conclusion that viewing a violent movie increases the tendency to aggress, the fact that subjects were not allocated at random to the different conditions of the study means that other explanations cannot be ruled out. For example, it may be that violent movies only increase aggressive tendencies among those who are attracted to view such movies in the first place.

Reflection on the strengths and weaknesses of real experiments and quasi-experiments suggests that they each have an important part to play in social-psychological research. The prime quality of the real experiment is the confidence with which causal inferences can be drawn concerning the observed relationships between independent and dependent variables. Its major drawback is the artificial nature of the setting in which data are gathered, which raises questions about the degree to which the observed cause–effect relationships are ones that occur outside the context of the experimental laboratory. A prime quality of the quasi-experiment is that it can be conducted under relatively natural conditions. As far as drawing causal conclusions is concerned, the quasi-experiment is inferior to the real experiment, which means that the real experiment has to be the preferred method if one is interested in testing predictions about cause–effect relationships. One way to combine the best of both approaches is to conduct both true experiments and quasi-experiments to test a given prediction. To the extent that the findings are consistent across methods, confidence in the validity of the underlying theory will be enhanced.

The fact that quasi-experiments can be conducted under natural conditions is not the only reason for using this strategy. Often the only way in which to conduct an experimental study of a social phenomenon is via a quasi-experiment. Ethical and practical considerations frequently make it impossible to allocate people randomly to different experimental conditions. If, like Stroebe, Stroebe and Domittner (1988), you wish to study the effects of bereavement, for example, you obviously cannot randomly allocate research participants to a 'bereaved' and 'non-bereaved' condition. The same problem applies in many other fields of research. All social interventions, such as new teaching methods in schools, new ways of treating those who are suffering from physical or psychological disorders, new public information campaigns, and new management techniques, share the characteristic that people are not randomly assigned to participate or not to participate in these programmes. Either they themselves choose to participate in such a programme (for example, by volunteering for a new method of psychological treatment) or someone else chooses for them but does so on a non-random basis (such as when the board of directors of a corporation decides to introduce a new management system in one factory but not in another). The effects of such interventions can only be studied quasi-experimentally. Thus the choice of research strategy is often a compromise between what is optimal and what is practicable. Fortunately, the sophistication of some quasi-experimental designs is such that it is possible to draw conclusions about causality (Judd and Kenny, 1981).

Key features of the social-psychological experiment

As noted earlier, experimentation has been the dominant research method in social psychology, mainly because it is without equal as a method for testing theories that predict causal relationships between variables. Standard guides to research in social psychology (e.g. Aronson, Ellsworth, Carlsmith and Gonzales, 1976; Aronson, Brewer and Carlsmith, 1985) tend to treat experimentation as the preferred research method. In fact there are grounds for questioning the extent to which experimental studies provide unambiguous evidence about causation, as we shall see later. However, first we will describe the principal features of the experimental approach to social-psychological research. To assist this process of description, we will use one experiment as an illustrative example.

The work in question is the well-known study of obedience conducted by Milgram (1965), already referred to at the beginning of this chapter (also see chapter16 for a fuller discussion of this study).

EXPERIMENTAL
SCENARIO

The **experimental scenario** is the context in which the study is presented. In a field experiment the scenario would ideally be one that occurs naturally, without contrivance on the experimenter's part. In laboratory settings, however, it is important to devise a scenario for which there is a convincing and well-integrated rationale, because the situation should strike participants as realistic and involving, and the experimental manipulations and the measurement process should not 'leap out' at the subject. There is a sense in which the typical laboratory experiment is like staging a play, with the exception that the subject's lines are unscripted. In the case of Milgram's study, the scenario presented to subjects was that of an investigation of the effects of punishment on learning. The subject was allocated, apparently at random, the role of 'teacher', while an accomplice of the experimenter, posing as another subject, took the role of 'learner'. (It is worth noting in passing that an accomplice of the experimenter who performs a prescribed role in an experiment is generally referred to as a

CONFEDERATE

confederate, or stooge.) The learner's ostensible task was to memorize a list of word pairs. The teacher's task was to read out the first word of each pair, to see whether the learner could correctly remember the second word, and to administer a graded series of punishments, in the form of electric shocks of increasing severity, if the learner failed to recall the correct word (which he had been instructed to do from time to time). The experimental scenario was set up with a view to convincing the subject that the shocks were genuine (which they were not), and that the learner was indeed a fellow-subject who was actually receiving the shocks. Thus what was actually a study of the extent to which subjects would obey the experimenter's instruction to deliver steadily increasing electric shocks was presented as a study of the effects of punishment on learning.

INDEPENDENT
VARIABLE

The **independent variable** is the variable that is deliberately manipulated by the experimenter. All other aspects of the experimental scenario are held constant, and the independent variable is changed in some respect with a view to assessing the consequences of this manipulation. Each change in the independent variable produces a new 'condition' of the experiment: one change yields two conditions, two changes yield three conditions, and so on. For example, in Milgram's study a key independent variable was the proximity of the 'learner' to the 'teacher'. In one condition, learner and teacher were in separate rooms, and the teacher could not hear or see the learner's reactions to the shocks; in a second condition, the teacher could hear the learner, but still could not see him; in the third condition, the teacher could both see and hear the learner's reactions; in the fourth condition, the teacher had to hold the learner's hand down on a metal plate in order for the shock to be delivered (the Touch-Proximity Condition, see plate 4.1). All other aspects of the experimental setting were held constant, so that variations in the teacher-subjects' behaviour in these four different conditions should have been attributable only to the change in proximity between teacher and learner. The adequacy of an experiment often hinges on the effectiveness of manipulations of the independent variable. By *effectiveness* we mean (1) the extent to which changes in the independent variable capture the essential qualities of the construct that is theoretically expected to have a causal influence on behaviour; and (2) the size of the changes that are introduced. For example, in Milgram's study, we should consider how well the four proximity conditions capture the construct of proximity. What is being manipulated, quite clearly, is *physical* proximity (rather than, say, psychological proximity); as long as this is what the experimenter intends to manipulate, all well and good. We should also consider whether the changes between the four conditions are sufficiently large to have an effect. In this particular case, it is difficult to see how the proximity variable could have been manipulated more powerfully, but an investigator who adopts weaker manipulations runs the risk of failing to find the predicted effects simply because the variations across levels of the independent variable are too subtle to have any impact. It has become standard practice in social-psychological experiments to include among the measured variables one or

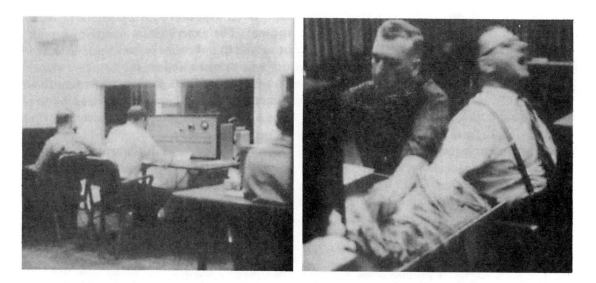

Plate 4.1 General arrangement for Touch-Proximity Condition and obedient subject in Touch-Proximity Condition in Milgram's (1963) study. (Stills from 1965 film *Obedience* © Stanley Milgram as reproduced in *Obedience to Authority* by Stanley Milgram courtesy of Tavistock Publications)

more measures of the effectiveness of the manipulation, and these measures are known as manipulation checks. We will have more to say about these later.

As we have already seen, a key feature of the true experiment is that subjects should be randomly allocated to different experimental conditions. Failure to adhere to this stipulation interferes with one's ability to draw causal inferences from the results. For example, in the four conditions of Milgram's study described above, it was found that the number of shocks teacher-subjects were prepared to administer steadily declined as the proximity between teacher and learner increased. This appears to show that obedience to the experimenter's instructions diminished as the learner's suffering became more salient to the teacher. Such an inference could *not* be drawn if there were grounds for thinking that the type of subject recruited for the four conditions differed in some systematic way.

Assessing the impact of an independent variable requires the experimenter to measure some feature of the subject's behaviour or internal state. This measured

DEPENDENT VARIABLE

variable is known as the **dependent variable**, so called because systematic changes in this measured variable should depend upon the impact of the independent variable. In the Milgram study, the dependent variable was the number of shocks in a 30-step sequence that the teacher was prepared to deliver by throwing switches corresponding to each shock level. A key question to ask of any dependent variable is the extent to which it is a good measure of the underlying theoretical construct. For example, is the willingness to deliver what appear to be increasingly strong shocks to another person a good measure of 'destructive obedience'? In addition to this question of the 'fit' between a theoretical construct and the measured or dependent variable, the most important issue involved in designing dependent variables is what type of measure to use. This is a matter that will be discussed in more detail below.

As well as measuring the main dependent variables, the experimenter usually tries to collect other kinds of measures. One of the most important of these supplementary measures is the **manipulation check**, referred to earlier as an

MANIPULATION CHECK

assessment of the effectiveness of the independent variable. A typical manipulation check is designed to measure subjects' perceptions of those features of the experimental scenario that are relevant to the manipulation in question. For example, Isen, Daubman and Nowicki (1987) conducted four experimental studies of the impact of positive affect on creative problem solving, to test the prediction that positive affect promotes creativity. In their second experiment they manipulated affect in two different ways (by showing comedy films or giving subjects a candy bar) and measured subjects' performance on a test of creativity. In addition, they checked the manipulation of subjects' affective state by asking them to rate their affective state, after the manipulation but before the creativity test. They found that the film manipulation did have a significant impact on subjects' reported affective state, whereas the candy bar gift did not. Interestingly, creative problem solving was enhanced in the comedy film condition (relative to negative and neutral film conditions) but was no better in the candy bar condition than in a no-gift condition. Thus the negative results for the gift condition may have been attributable to the ineffectiveness of the manipulation. A major function of the manipulation check, then, is to aid in interpretation of the findings, especially in the case where the independent variable does not have the predicted effect on the dependent variable.

Debriefing takes place at the end of the experimental session and refers to the process of informing the subject as fully as possible about the nature and purpose of the experiment, and the role their particular participation played in the study as a whole. Although debriefing research participants is good practice in any form of research using human subjects, it is particularly important wherever the subject has been deceived about the purpose of the experiment and/or about some aspects of the experimental procedure. In Milgram's study, for example, care was taken to assure subjects that the 'shocks' they had administered were in fact bogus, and that the learner had not been harmed in any way. Ideally, the debriefing process should leave subjects understanding the purpose of the research, satisfied with their role in the experiment, and with as much self-respect as they had before participating in the study. DEBRIEFING

Experimental designs

We have already seen that it is important (1) that experimenters keep all theoretically irrelevant features of the experimental setting constant across conditions, manipulating just the key independent variable, and (2) that subjects are allocated randomly to the different conditions of an experiment. Failure to achieve these goals hinders the researcher's ability to draw the inference that observed differences in the dependent variable across conditions result from changes in the independent variable. We shall now examine more closely the question of designing experiments in such a way that alternative inferences are ruled out as far as possible.

Consider first a design for a study that may *appear* to be an experiment but cannot truly be described as an experimental design. This is the so-called **one-shot case study**. Following Cook and Campbell (1979), we shall use the symbol X to stand for a manipulation (i.e. of the independent variable) and the symbol O to stand for observation (i.e. the dependent variable). In these terms the one-shot design looks like this: ONE-SHOT CASE STUDY

$$X \qquad O$$
$$\longrightarrow$$
$$time$$

To take a concrete example, imagine that an educational researcher wanted to know the effect of a new teaching method on learning. The researcher takes a class of students, introduces the new method (X), and measures the students' comprehension of the taught material (O). What conclusions can be drawn from such a design? Strictly speaking, the answer is none; the point is that there is nothing with which O can be compared, so the researcher cannot infer whether the observed comprehension is good, poor or indifferent.

A simple extension of the one-shot design provides the minimum requirements for a true experimental design, and is known as the **post-test only control group design**. Let R stand for random assignment of subjects to conditions, and X and O stand for manipulation and observation, as before. This design looks like this:

POST-TEST
ONLY CONTROL
GROUP DESIGN

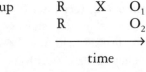

Experimental group   R   X O_1
Control group   R O_2
$\longrightarrow$
time

EXPERIMENTAL
GROUP

CONTROL
GROUP

Compared with the one-shot design, there are two important modifications. First, there are two conditions. In one the subjects are exposed to the manipulation (this is usually referred to as the experimental condition, and subjects in this condition are known as the **experimental group**), and possible effects of the manipulation are measured. In the other no manipulation is introduced (this is usually referred to as the control condition, and subjects in this condition are known as the **control group**), but these subjects are also observed on the same dependent variable and at the same time-point as the experimental group. Now the observation made in the experimental condition (O_1) *can* be compared with something, namely the observation made in the control condition (O_2). In the example we have been using, the researcher might compare one group of students who have been exposed to the new teaching method with another group who have continued to receive the normal method, with respect to their comprehension of the taught material. The second important modification is that, in this design, subjects are randomly allocated to the two conditions, ruling out the possibility that differences between O_1 and O_2 are due to differences between the two groups of subjects that were present before X was implemented. It follows that if O_1 and O_2 differ markedly it is reasonable to infer that this difference is caused by X.

Although the post-test only control group design is one of the more commonly used experimental designs in social psychology, there are several other more sophisticated and complex designs, each representing a more complete attempt to rule out the possibility that observed differences between conditions result from something other than the manipulation of the independent variable (see Cook and Campbell, 1979, for a full discussion). The prime object of experimental design, then, is to enhance the validity of the researcher's inference that differences in the dependent variable result from changes in the independent variable.

A very common design in social-psychological experiments is the **factorial** FACTORIAL EXPERIMENT **experiment**, in which two or more independent variables are manipulated within the same design. The most simple case can be represented diagrammatically as follows, where R stands for random assignment of subjects to conditions, X stands for one variable with 2 levels (X_1 and X_2) and Y stands for another variable with 2 levels (Y_1 and Y_2):

$$
\begin{array}{lll}
R & X_1Y_1 & O_1 \\
R & X_1Y_2 & O_2 \\
R & X_2Y_1 & O_3 \\
R & X_2Y_2 & O_4 \\
\end{array}
$$

$$\longrightarrow$$
$$\text{time}$$

The essential feature of a factorial design is that it contains all possible combinations of the independent variables. In the design shown above, each independent variable has two levels, resulting in four conditions (2×2). Adding one level to each variable would result in nine conditions (3×3), whereas adding another two-level variable would result in eight conditions ($2 \times 2 \times 2$). The main benefit of a factorial design is that it allows the researcher to examine the separate and combined effects of two or more independent variables. The separate effects of each independent variable are known as **main effects**. If the combined effects   MAIN EFFECTS
of two independent variables differ from the sum of their two main effects, the combination is known as an **interaction effect**.   INTERACTION EFFECT

To illustrate such an interaction, let us consider a hypothetical set of results from a study of attitude change in which two variables are manipulated: argument quality, i.e., whether a persuasive message that subjects are given to read consists of strong arguments or weak arguments; and involvement, i.e., whether subjects' involvement with the topic of the message is high or low. Such a design tests one of the basic predictions derived from Petty and Cacioppo's (1986b) elaboration-likelihood model of persuasion (see chapter 9). The prediction is that argument quality will have a stronger influence on attitudes when subjects are involved with the message topic than when they are not. Figure 4.1 shows hypothetical data from such a study. It can be seen (panel a) that argument quality does have a main effect on attitudes, such that strong messages are more persuasive than weak ones. Involvement has no main effect on attitudes (see panel b): attitudes do not vary as a function of level of involvement. However, when the combined effects of these two variables are examined (see panel c), it is clear that there is an interaction: the effect of argument quality is much greater when involvement is high than when it is low, just as the theory predicts. Because the predicted effect is an interaction, testing this prediction requires conducting a factorial experiment.

Threats to validity in experimental research

In the context of research, validity refers to the extent to which one is justified in drawing inferences from one's findings. Experimental research attempts to maximize each of three types of validity: internal validity, construct validity and external validity.

INTERNAL
VALIDITY

   Internal validity refers to the validity of the conclusion that an observed relationship between independent and dependent variables reflects a *causal* relationship, and is promoted by the use of a sound experimental design. We have already seen that the use of a control group greatly enhances internal validity, but even if one uses a control group there remain many potential threats to internal validity (Cook and Campbell, 1979). Among these is the possibility

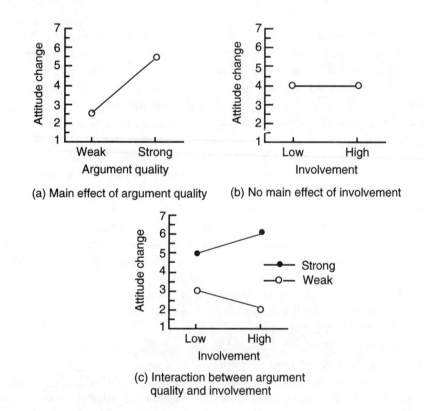

(a) Main effect of argument quality

(b) No main effect of involvement

(c) Interaction between argument
quality and involvement

Figure 4.1 Hypothetical data illustrating a main effect (panel a), an absence of a main effect (panel b), and an interaction effect (panel c)

that the groups being compared differ with respect to more than the independent variable of interest.

For example, assume for one moment that in the experiment described previously Milgram had used a different experimenter for each of the four conditions, such that experimenter 1 ran all subjects in one condition, experimenter 2 ran all subjects in the next condition, and so on. Although it might seem sensible to divide the work of running the conditions among different experimenters, to do so in this way poses a major threat to the *internal validity* of the experiment. This is because the four conditions would no longer differ *solely* in terms of the physical proximity of the 'victim'; they would also differ in that each would be conducted by a different experimenter. Thus the differing amounts of obedience observed in the four conditions *might* reflect the causal influence of the physical proximity independent variable, *or* the influence of the different experimenters (or, indeed, some combination of these two factors). The problem is that the physical proximity variable would be *confounded* with a second variable, namely experimenter identity. It is impossible to disentangle the effects of confounded variables (see **confounding**).

CONFOUNDING

Even when we are confident that the relationship between X and O is a causal one, in the sense that internal validity is high, we need to consider carefully the nature of the constructs involved in this relationship. **Construct validity** refers to the validity of the assumption that independent or dependent variables adequately capture the variables (or 'constructs') they are supposed to represent.

CONSTRUCT VALIDITY

With regard to the construct validity of independent variables, the issue is whether the independent variable really represents a manipulation of the intended theoretical construct. For example, in a well-known experiment Aronson and Mills (1959) found that subjects who underwent an embarrassing initiation in order to join what turned out to be a tedious sex discussion group subsequently reported greater liking for that group than did subjects who underwent a milder initiation. This was interpreted as evidence in support of a prediction derived from dissonance theory (see chapter 8). According to dissonance theory, the knowledge that one has suffered in order to attain a goal is inconsistent with the knowledge that the goal turns out to be worthless, thereby generating cognitive dissonance. To reduce this uncomfortable state of dissonance, it is argued, the individual re-evaluates the goal more positively. Gerard and Mathewson (1966) pointed out that Aronson and Mills' findings are open to alternative interpretations which accept that the initiation manipulation used by Aronson and Mills was responsible for the observed differences in liking for the discussion group, but assert that this effect resulted from something other than the differing amounts of dissonance supposedly experienced by the two groups of subjects. For example, it could be argued that the fact that the discussion was tedious was actually a relief to those subjects who had undergone the embarrassing initiation, who as a consequence found it more pleasant than did subjects who had undergone a milder initiation. To rule out this alternative explanation (and others like it) Gerard and Mathewson devised an experimental condition in which participation in the group discussion followed an aversive experience but was not contingent upon that experience. For the alternative explanation it should make no difference whether or not the discussion is dependent on the aversive experience, whereas for dissonance theory the contingent relationship between 'suffering' and the group discussion is crucial. Gerard and Mathewson showed that increased liking for the discussion group was only positively related to the severity of the prior experience when group membership was dependent upon that experience.

Even if the researcher has reason to feel satisfied with the construct validity of the independent variable, there remains the question of whether the dependent variables actually assess what they were intended to assess. As we shall see below, devising a measure to capture the essence of a social-psychological construct is by no means straightforward. There are three main types of threat to the construct validity of dependent variables in social-psychological experimentation: social desirability, demand characteristics and experimenter expectancy.

SOCIAL
DESIRABILITY

Social desirability is a term used to describe the fact that subjects are usually keen to be seen in a positive light, and may therefore be reluctant to provide honest reports of fears, anxieties, feelings of hostility or prejudice, or any other quality which they think would be regarded negatively. Equally, subjects may 'censor' some of their behaviours so as to avoid being evaluated negatively. To the extent that a researcher's measures are contaminated by social desirability effects, they will obviously be failing to assess the theoretical construct of interest. The most obvious means of reducing social desirability effects is to make the measurement process as unobtrusive as possible, on the premise that if subjects do not know what it is that is being measured, they will be unable to modify their behaviour.

DEMAND
CHARACTERISTICS

Demand characteristics are cues in the experimental setting which convey to the subject the nature of the experimenter's hypothesis. The point here is that individuals who know that they are being studied will often be curious about what the experimenter is looking at and what types of responses are expected. Subjects may then attempt to provide the expected responses in order to please the experimenter. When behaviour is enacted with the intention of fulfilling the experimenter's hypotheses, it is said to be a response to the demand characteristics of the experiment. Orne (1962, 1969) has conducted a great deal of research into demand characteristics, and has suggested various methods of pinpointing the role they play in any given experimental situation. For example, he advocates

POST-
EXPERIMENTAL
ENQUIRY

the use of in-depth **post-experimental enquiry** in the form of an interview, preferably conducted by someone other than the experimenter, the object of which is to elicit from the subject what he or she believed to be the aim of the experiment, and the extent to which this belief affected behaviour in the experiment. Clearly, researchers should do all they can to minimize the operation of demand characteristics, for example by using **unobtrusive measures**, or by telling subjects that the purpose of the experiment cannot be revealed until the end of the study and that in the meantime it is important that they do *not* attempt to guess the hypothesis. A **cover story** which leads subjects to believe that the purpose of the study is something other than the real purpose is a widely used means of lessening the impact of demand characteristics. However, an unconvincing cover story can create more problems than it solves, raising doubts in the mind of the subject that otherwise might not have arisen.

Experimenter expectancy refers to the experimenter's own hypothesis or expectations about the outcome of the research. This expectancy can unintentionally influence the experimenter's behaviour towards subjects in such a way as to enhance the likelihood that they will confirm his or her hypothesis. Rosenthal (1966) called this type of influence the **experimenter expectancy effect**. The processes mediating experimenter expectancy effects are complex, but non-verbal communication is centrally involved. The extent to which experimenter expectancy can influence a phenomenon may be assessed by using several experimenters and manipulating their expectations about the experimental outcome. An obvious strategy for reducing these effects is to keep experimenters 'blind' to the hypothesis under test, or at least blind to the condition to which a given subject has been allocated; other possibilities include minimizing the interaction between experimenter and subject, and automating the experiment as far as possible. The goal in each case is to reduce the opportunity for the experimenter to communicate his or her expectancies.

Even if the experimenter manages to circumvent all the above threats to internal and construct validity, an important question concerning validity remains: to what extent can the causal relationship between X and O be generalized beyond the particular circumstances of the experiment? **External validity** refers to the generalizability of an observed relationship beyond the specific circumstances in which it was observed by the researcher. One important feature of the experimental circumstances, of course, is the type of person who participates in the experiment. In many cases subjects volunteer their participation, and to establish external validity it is important to consider whether results obtained using volunteers can be generalized to other populations. There is a good deal of research on differences between volunteers and non-volunteers in psychological studies (see Rosenthal and Rosnow, 1975, for a review; and Cowles and Davis, 1987, for an example of a study). The general conclusion is that there *are* systematic personality differences between volunteers and non-volunteers. More importantly, in studies such as one reported by Horowitz (1969) it has been found that the effects of some manipulations used in attitude change research were actually *opposite* for volunteers and non-volunteers. Such findings are explained in terms of volunteers' supposedly greater sensitivity to, and willingness to comply with, demand characteristics. The external validity of studies based only on volunteers' behaviour is therefore open to question, and the solution to this problem is to use a 'captive' population, preferably in a field setting.

Data Collection Techniques

Whichever research strategy is adopted by an investigator, he or she will need to measure one or more variables. In correlational designs the researcher has to measure each of the variables that are expected to correlate. In experimental designs the researcher needs to measure the dependent variable. In either case, the investigator is confronted with the task of translating a theoretical construct (for example, aggression or attraction) into a measurable variable (for example, willingness to harm someone, or willingness to help someone). Two important issues arise in connection with this process. Any psychological measure should be both reliable and valid. **Reliability** here refers to the stability of the measure. If you measure an adult's height (assuming you are doing it carefully), the measurement will be highly stable from one day to the next, and will also be independent of who is doing the measuring. These are the hallmarks of a reliable measure: it is not dependent on the time of measurement or on the person taking the measurement. However, a measure can be highly reliable and yet be low in validity. To pursue the height measurement example, let us imagine that what you *really* want to measure is a person's weight. In the absence of a proper weighing scale you decide to measure height instead, because you do have a tape-measure. Of course, height and weight are correlated with each other, so height may be a better measure of weight than simple guesswork. But clearly height is not especially valid as a measure of weight. Thus **validity** in this context refers to the extent to which the measured variable really captures the underlying construct.

RELIABILITY

VALIDITY

The researcher's first goal should be to specify what it is that he or she wants to record in order to represent the construct in a meaningful way. Imagine that a researcher wishes to measure aggressive behaviour. Would willingness to deliver a painful shock to another person, expressed behaviourally, be a *valid* index of the construct of aggression as conceptualized by the investigator, or would it be better to adopt another index, such as the number of verbal insults directed at the person (cf. chapter 14)? Having decided what general form the measured variable should take, the next task of the researcher is to try to ensure that the measure is *reliable*. In social-psychological research the investigator typically chooses to measure a variable using either observational measures or self-report measures.

Observational measures

If the object of one's research is to collect information about social *behaviour*, an obvious means of doing so is by observation. Many behaviours that are of interest to social psychologists are detectable without the assistance of sophisticated equipment and are enacted in public settings, which makes them suitable for observation. Although observational methods vary in kind, as we shall see, from the relatively informal and unstructured to the highly formal and structured, the object in each case is the same: to abstract from the complex flux of social behaviour those actions that are of potential significance to the research question, and to record each instance of such actions over some period (Weick, 1985).

Sometimes the nature of the research setting or topic dictates that observation is conducted in a relatively informal and unstructured manner, with the researcher posing as a member of the group being observed. A classic example of research employing this method is Festinger, Riecken and Schachter's (1956) study of the consequences of blatant disconfirmation of strongly held beliefs. The investigators identified a religious sect which predicted that the northern hemisphere would be destroyed by flood on a certain date. By joining that sect, members of the research team were able to observe what happened when the predicted events failed to materialize. Under such circumstances, observation clearly has to be covert and informal: if other sect members suspected that the researchers were not *bona fide* believers, the opportunity for observation would be removed. This type of observation is known as **participant observation**, for the obvious reason that the observer participates in the activities of the group that is being observed.

PARTICIPANT OBSERVATION

More formal methods of observation can be used when it is possible to record actions relevant to the research question without disrupting the occurrence of the behaviour. An example is Carey's (1978) series of studies investigating the hypothesis that when one pedestrian approaches another on the street, a rule of 'civil inattention' applies, whereby each looks at the other up to the point where they are approximately eight feet apart, after which their gaze is averted. This hypothesis was first advanced by Goffman (1963), on the basis of informal observation. Carey's purpose was to verify, using more formal methods, the existence of this rule, and to establish parameters such as the distance between pedestrians when gaze is first averted. He covertly photographed pairs of pedestrians as they approached and passed each other on a street, taking the photographs from upper storeys of buildings overlooking the street. The resulting still photographs were then coded for variables such as distance between the pair, whether their heads and eyelids were level or lowered, and whether gaze direction was towards or away from the approaching person.

The two examples cited above have in common the fact that the targets of the researchers' observations were unaware that they were being observed. Although such failure to inform persons of their involuntary participation in a research project may raise tricky ethical questions, it does overcome a problem peculiar to any research that uses humans as subjects, namely the tendency for the measurement process itself to have an impact on subjects' behaviour, a phenomenon known as **reactivity**. It is well established that the simple knowledge that one is being observed can influence behaviour enacted in front of observers. The best known instance of such an effect is a study of worker productivity conducted at the Hawthorne plant of the Western Electric Company (Roethlisberger and Dickson, 1939), where it was found that merely observing workers raised their motivation and thereby increased productivity. Instances of such influence have come to be known as **Hawthorne effects**. Awareness of this problem has led many researchers to develop unobtrusive methods of observing and measuring behaviour. An entertaining and very useful sourcebook of methods of unobtrusive measurement has been compiled by Webb et al. (1981).

The most formal type of observational method is one in which the researcher uses a category system for scoring social behaviour. A well-known example of such a system is Bales' (1950) *interaction process analysis (IPA)* (see chapter 15), developed to study interaction in small social groups. IPA consists of the 12 categories shown in figure 4.2. The observer's task in using this system is to concentrate on the verbal interaction taking place between members of a group, and to place individual statements or 'thought units' into one of the 12 categories, noting at the same time who made the statement and to whom it was directed. Such a system should be simple enough for codings to be made in real time, general enough to be applicable to most types of group, and yet specific enough to tap important facets of verbal interaction. The IPA system is a fairly successful one, judged by these criteria, but some of its limitations are apparent if one remembers that non-verbal behaviour (widely acknowledged to be an important feature of interaction – see chapter 11) is almost totally ignored.

Observational methods of data collection have two main advantages over the self-report methods we shall consider below: first, they can often be made unobtrusively; secondly, even where the subject knows that his or her behaviour is being observed, enacting the behaviour is typically quite engrossing, with the result that subjects have less opportunity to modify their behaviour than they would when completing a questionnaire. Nevertheless, there are some types of behaviour that are either impossible to observe directly (because they took place in the past) or difficult to observe directly (because they are normally enacted in private). Moreover, social psychologists are often interested in measuring *people's perceptions, cognitions or evaluations*, none of which can be directly assessed simply through observation. For these reasons, researchers often make use of self-report measures.

Self-report measures

The essential feature of data collection using self-report measures is that questions about the subject's beliefs, attitudes, behaviour or whatever are put directly to the subject. His or her responses constitute self-report data. Self-report measurement is usually quicker, cheaper and easier to use than observational

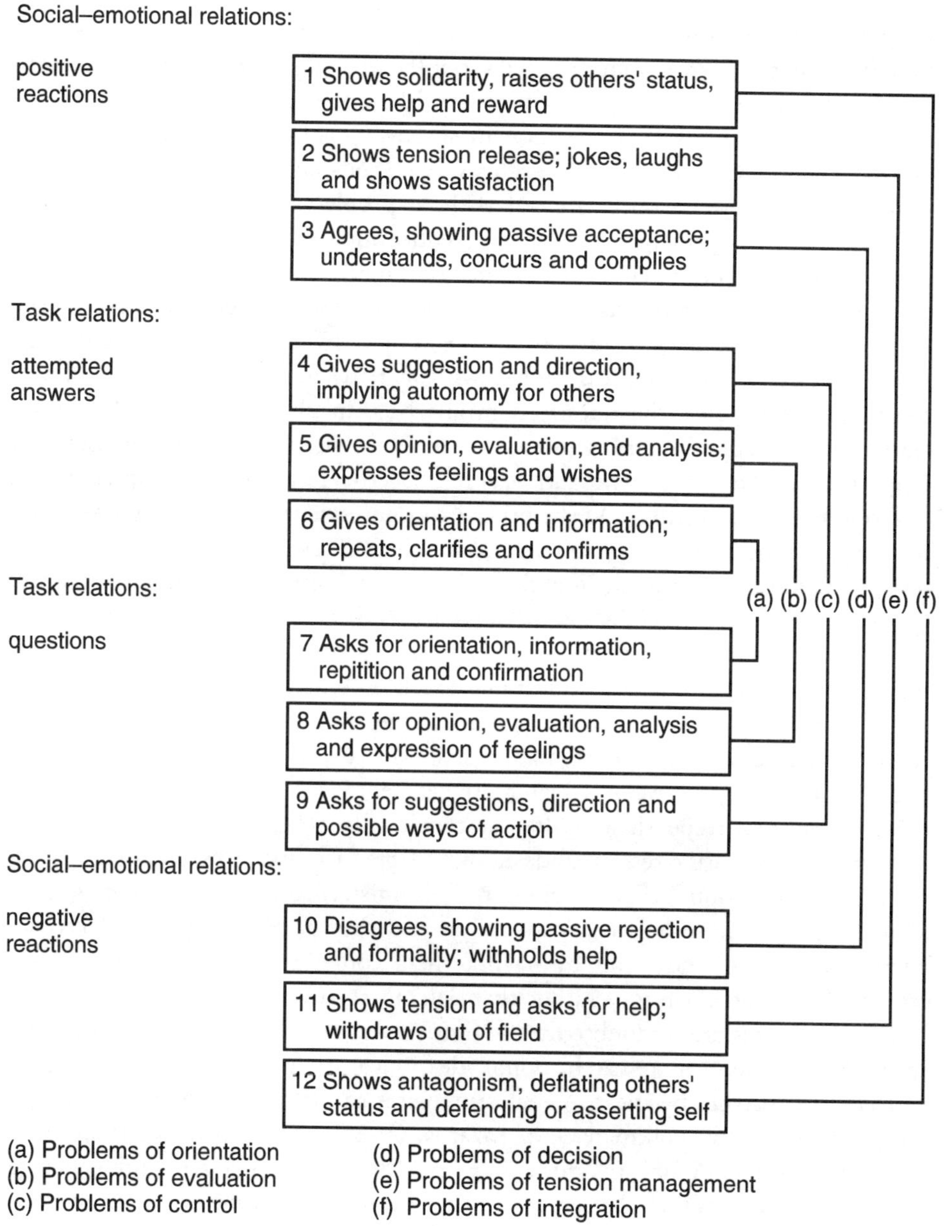

Social–emotional relations:

positive
reactions

| 1 Shows solidarity, raises others' status, gives help and reward |
| 2 Shows tension release; jokes, laughs and shows satisfaction |
| 3 Agrees, showing passive acceptance; understands, concurs and complies |

Task relations:

attempted
answers

| 4 Gives suggestion and direction, implying autonomy for others |
| 5 Gives opinion, evaluation, and analysis; expresses feelings and wishes |
| 6 Gives orientation and information; repeats, clarifies and confirms |

Task relations:

questions

(a) (b) (c) (d) (e) (f)

| 7 Asks for orientation, information, repitition and confirmation |
| 8 Asks for opinion, evaluation, analysis and expression of feelings |
| 9 Asks for suggestions, direction and possible ways of action |

Social–emotional relations:

negative
reactions

| 10 Disagrees, showing passive rejection and formality; withholds help |
| 11 Shows tension and asks for help; withdraws out of field |
| 12 Shows antagonism, deflating others' status and defending or asserting self |

(a) Problems of orientation
(b) Problems of evaluation
(c) Problems of control
(d) Problems of decision
(e) Problems of tension management
(f) Problems of integration

Figure 4.2 Categories of socio-emotional (directed at friendship and emotional needs) and task-related (directed at achieving concrete problem-solving) interactions in small groups (Bales, 1950b)

measurement. The researcher does not have to contrive a laboratory setting or find a natural setting in which to observe a behavioural response; furthermore, there is typically no need to train observers or to use recording equipment, for self-reports are usually recorded by the subject in the form of written responses. Finally, as noted above, some of the variables that are of most significance to social psychologists are not directly observable. For these various reasons, self-report measurement is very common in social-psychological research, and it is not unusual for studies to depend exclusively on self-report data. As we shall see, however, self-report measures are not without problems.

There are two principal methods of collecting self-report data: the questionnaire and the interview. In the *questionnaire* method, subjects are handed a set of questions, along with instructions on how to record their answers. In the *interview* method, questions are put to the subject by an interviewer, who then records the subject's responses. Interviewing is particularly useful when there is reason to believe that the questions might be difficult to understand without clarification. A tactful and sensitive interviewer should be able to establish rapport with the respondent and ensure that the latter fully comprehends a question before answering. On the other hand, interviewing is a costly procedure in terms of time and money, and a poorly trained interviewer can easily bias the respondent's answers by hinting at a desired or socially acceptable response. Questionnaires are especially useful for gathering data from large numbers of subjects with minimal expense, and the comparative anonymity of the process might be preferable when the questions touch on sensitive issues. On the other hand, many people who are given questionnaires fail to complete and/or return them. Response rates for questionnaires sent by mail to randomly selected names and addresses vary between 10 and 50 per cent. Because there is always the danger that non-respondents differ systematically from respondents in some respect, low response rates are undesirable. In practice, social psychologists often manage to get round this problem by administering their questionnaires to subjects who are in some sense 'captive', in that they have already volunteered to participate in the study, and by having them complete the questionnaire in a lecture theatre or laboratory rather than letting them take it home.

Questionnaires are undoubtedly the most widely used form of data collection in social-psychological research. Some idea of the richness and variety of data collected exclusively by means of questionnaires can be gained by considering a study reported by Folkman and Lazarus (1985). These investigators used questionnaire techniques to study how people appraised a stressful event (a university examination), what emotions they experienced as the event approached and passed, and how they coped with the stress induced by the event. It is difficult to envisage how Folkman and Lazarus could have conducted such a study without using questionnaires. It is certainly possible to measure some psycho-physiological indices of stress, such as heart rate, before, during and after exposure to a noxious stimulus such as an electric shock; but one cannot assume that the short-term stress induced by shock in a laboratory is comparable with the longer-term stress induced by 'natural' events such as examinations, ill health, divorce or bereavement. Furthermore, the individual's appraisals, emotions and coping strategies could not be assessed satisfactorily without the use of self-report measures.

Devising a good questionnaire or interview schedule is a harder task than one might imagine. As with any psychological measure, the goal is to produce questions that are reliable and valid. Reliability in this context means that the questions would evoke the same response from a given individual if he or she were tested more than once under similar circumstances. Validity means that the questions measure exactly what the researcher intends them to measure. Although there are many potential sources of unreliability in the construction of questionnaires, the most serious threat to question reliability is *ambiguity*: if a question is ambiguous, a given respondent might well interpret it differently on different occasions and therefore give different answers. The most serious threat to question validity is failure on the part of the investigator to have *specific objectives* for each question: the hazier the intent of the researcher in posing a particular question, the greater are the chances that it will fail to elicit information relevant to his or her objectives. Even if a question is unambiguous, however, and has been formulated with a clear goal in mind, there are other sources of unreliability and invalidity which cannot easily be controlled. A simple rule-of-thumb in questionnaire research is never to assume that answers to a single question will reliably or validly measure any construct. If the average of two (or preferably more) items is used to measure that construct, the various factors (such as question ambiguity, misunderstanding on the part of the subject, the context provided by the immediately preceding question) that decrease reliability and validity of responses to any single question should cancel each other out, and the resulting measure will be a purer reflection of the underlying construct.

Because it is difficult to envisage all the potential pitfalls in questionnaire construction, there is no substitute for pilot work in which prototypes of the final questionnaire are administered to groups of subjects, whose answers and comments provide a basis for revision. Constructing an entirely fresh questionnaire can therefore be a time-consuming and painstaking process. Fortunately, there are collections of previously developed and pre-tested questionnaires, such as the one edited by Robinson, Shaver and Wrightsman (1991). It is worth checking such a source before setting out to construct an original questionnaire. If no suitable questionnaire already exists, the researcher should consult a text on questionnaire design such as the one by Oppenheim (1992) before devising a fresh questionnaire. It is also advisable to familiarize oneself with recent research on the cognitive processes that underlie respondents' answers to survey questions (see Schwarz, 1990).

As we have seen, self-report measures have several advantages; what are the drawbacks? Chief among these is the fact that it is not possible to collect self-report data completely unobtrusively: subjects are always aware that they are under investigation, and may modify their responses as a result of this awareness. In particular, there is ample opportunity for the respondent's answers to be influenced by motivational factors, such as social desirability. There is no simple solution to this problem, although there are some steps that can be taken which together should reduce the scale of the problem. First, it is worth emphasizing to subjects whenever possible that their responses are anonymous. Secondly, it is worth stressing the point that there are no right or wrong answers. Thirdly, it is often possible to increase subjects' motivation to respond truthfully by treating them as research accomplices rather than as 'guinea-pigs'.

Choosing a measure

As we have seen, both types of measure considered here have certain advantages and disadvantages. Although there are no hard-and-fast rules for choosing one type of measure rather than the other, there are two points that should be borne in mind when judging the appropriateness of a dependent measure. First, the two types of measure – observational and self-report – can be used in conjunction with each other in many types of research. Secondly, the two types of measure differ in terms of the type of information they yield. Let us consider each of these points more closely.

Assume that you wish to study interpersonal attraction. Under laboratory or field conditions you introduce two people, previously unknown to each other, and ask them to get to know each other in the course of a 15-minute discussion. If you want to measure how much these two like each other at the end of the session, you could simply depend on self-report measures, such as responses to questions about how much each person liked the other, would be prepared to work with the other, and so on. You could also use observational measures: unobtrusively videorecording the interaction would permit you to measure various aspects of behaviour, both verbal (such as the extent to which the two persons discovered mutual interests or shared attitudes) and non-verbal (such as the amount of smiling or directly looking at the other person).

Consider the advantages of using both types of measure. First, the observational data provide one type of check on the validity of the self-report data, and vice versa. Just as questionnaire data can be distorted by the respondents' motivations, so too can observers' perceptions be distorted by the nature of the coding system they are using. If both kinds of data point to the same conclusion, this will enhance confidence in their validity. A second, potentially more important, advantage is that while self-reported attraction can be said to be an *outcome* of the interaction, observational measures provide an insight into the *processes* that might mediate that outcome. Researchers would typically be interested in finding out *why* people did or did not like each other; examining the behaviours that occurred during the interaction might shed some light on this.

In summary, using more than one type of measure is often helpful to the researcher. If observational and self-report measures of the same conceptual variable point to the same conclusion, this enhances confidence in that conclusion. Furthermore, self-report measures often assess the outcome of a process; by using observational measures as well, the researcher may gain insight into the process responsible for that outcome.

Problems with Experimentation

It is widely assumed that the experimental method provides the 'royal road' to causal inference (cf. Aronson, Brewer and Carlsmith, 1985). In fact causal inference from the results of experiments is more problematic than some commentators allow. One problem concerns what Gergen (1978) has called the *cultural embeddedness* of social events, by which he means that 'few stimulus events considered independently have the capacity to elicit predictable social behavior' (p. 509). It follows that, even in the most tightly controlled laboratory experimental demonstration that the manipulation of independent variable X has a causal impact on dependent variable O, the circumstances in which X was manipulated may play a key role in producing the observed effects on O. The inference that 'X causes O' may therefore only be true under particular circumstances.

A related problem, also articulated by Gergen, is that although the experimental method purportedly allows us to trace the causal sequence from antecedent conditions to the behaviour of interest, its capacity to do so depends on the assumption that external events are related in a one-to-one fashion with particular states or processes in the individual. Gergen argues: 'In dealing with human beings in a social setting it is virtually impossible to manipulate any variable in isolation of all the others. Even the most elemental variations in an independent variable have the capacity to elicit a host of intervening reactions' (1978, p. 515). The result is that what one experimenter believes to be a demonstration of the effect of X on O via the mediating process Z, another will prefer to explain in terms of an alternative mediating process. Social psychology abounds with such debates between rival accounts for findings (see Greenwald, 1975b; Ostrom, 1977; Tetlock and Levi, 1982; Tetlock and Manstead, 1985), and some have come to the view that experimentation is not a suitable way to settle such between-theory disputes.

Yet another inferential problem confronting the experimental researcher in social psychology also arises from the fact that social behaviour is culturally embedded. In every culture there are norms that define the boundaries of appropriate social behaviour in particular settings, with the result that most individuals behave quite similarly in such settings. Such behaviour is best regarded as the product of that culture's conventions or rules, rather than of intra-individual psychological processes. Experimental settings are not free from the operation of cultural norms; indeed, there are grounds for thinking that laboratory experiments may promote the occurrence of behaviours that are guided by norms (Semin and Manstead, 1979). Inferential difficulties can arise when behaviour in such settings is interpreted exclusively in terms of hypothetical internal processes. For example, it might be argued that cultural norms prescribe that one does not question the instructions of someone running a scientific experiment, and that when one is asked to deliver an increasingly strong series of shocks to another person, apparently in the interests of scientific research, one should do so. That people are willing to do so, even when the shocks are strong enough to produce fatal results, is by no means uninteresting; but whether it reveals something about the psychological processes mediating obedience to authority is another matter. In short, it is important to avoid the temptation to formulate causal laws in terms of psychological processes where there are grounds for thinking that the phenomena being 'explained' have their origins in cultural convention (cf. Brandstädter, 1990; Semin, 1986; Smedslund, 1985).

One final and related problem worth mentioning in this context is that although the ostensible goal of social-psychological experimentation is the accumulation of scientific knowledge, in the form of laws or principles of social behaviour that are valid across time, there is some reason to doubt whether experimentation (or, indeed, any other method) is capable of generating evidence that could be the basis of such laws. To understand why this is the case in social sciences but not in natural sciences, we need to take account of the fact that the relationship between the researcher and the object of the research is radically different in the two types of science. The testing of theories in the natural sciences is concerned with the analysis and explanation of the *object world*, a world that does not engage in the construction and interpretation of the meaning of its own activity. This contrasts with the objects of investigation in social sciences: being people, these 'objects' do of course attribute meaning and significance to their actions. Social psychology cannot therefore be neatly distinguished from what it studies; lay persons and social psychologists alike are concerned with understanding and interpreting their social environments. Lay persons are able to acquire social-psychological knowledge and use it to modify their actions in a way that atoms, elements and particles cannot. As Giddens (1982) puts it: 'The fact that the "findings" of the social sciences can be taken up by those to whose behaviour they refer is not a phenomenon that can, or should be marginalised, but it is integral to their very nature. . . . Human beings . . . are not merely inert objects of knowledge, but agents able to – and prone to – incorporate theory and research within their own action' (pp. 14–16).

One implication of this is that social-psychological theories should not be regarded as embodying 'laws' that will necessarily hold good across time: if learning about a social-psychological theory leads people to modify the very behaviour that the theory tries to explain, it is clear that the theory has only limited temporal validity. Gergen (1973, 1978) has been the leading advocate of this sobering view, although his arguments have been challenged by Schlenker (1974) and by Semin and Manstead (1983). It is also worth noting that some of the problems of accumulation of knowledge in social psychology can be addressed through the use of **meta-analysis**, a relatively recently developed technique for statistically integrating the results of independent studies of the same phenomenon in order to establish whether findings are reliable across a number of independent investigations (see Cooper, 1990; Hedges and Olkin, 1985).

META-
ANALYSIS

What are the implications of these problems for the status of experimentation in social-psychological research? It should be noted that even some of the severest critics of the experimental approach do not advocate the abandonment of experimentation. For example, Gergen acknowledges that experiments will continue to play an important role in the explication of the relationship between biological processes (such as physiological arousal) and social behaviour; that studies such as the Milgram experiment are useful for raising consciousness about the insidious nature of social influence; that experiments can increase the impact of theories by providing vivid demonstrations of conditions under which a theory does make successful predictions; and that experimentation can be useful to evaluate social reforms, such as the effectiveness of measures designed to conserve energy. Thus the debate about the utility of experimentation revolves around the types of inference that can reasonably be made on the basis of experimental evidence, with 'traditionalists' such as Aronson, Brewer and Carlsmith (1985) sticking to the view that experimentation provides a firm basis on which to build knowledge, and critics such as Gergen questioning this assumption.

Summary and Conclusions

Methods are procedures followed by researchers in gathering information that helps them to answer research questions. Methodology is the term used to refer to all aspects of the implementation of these methods. The type of method used by a given researcher will depend to a large extent on the kind of question he or she is addressing. We distinguished between three basic types of research – descriptive, correlational and experimental – and we noted that social-psychological research is typically experimental or quasi-experimental in nature, having the goal of explaining the phenomena under investigation.

In describing methods in more detail, we drew a distinction between research strategies and data-collection techniques. Three research strategies were described: survey research, quasi-experiments and true randomized experiments. Two key ways in which these strategies differ are in terms of (1) the degree to which one is able to generalize to a population, and (2) the degree to which one can draw inferences about causality.

Experimentation was singled out for more detailed discussion because of its prominence as a research strategy in social psychology during the last four decades. The main features of experimentation were identified as: the experimental scenario; the independent variable; the dependent variable; the manipulation check; and debriefing.

A true experimental design is one that enables the researcher to infer that changes in the independent variable produce changes in the dependent variable. Such a design must therefore incorporate more than one condition, allowing the researcher to compare observations made under different conditions. The minimal true experimental design is the post-test only control group design, in which subjects are randomly allocated to one of two conditions, only one of which involves being exposed to the manipulation. Several more complex designs are available, and of these the factorial design is very commonly used, mainly because of its ability to test predictions concerning interaction effects.

Drawing strong inferences from social-psychological research depends on three types of validity: internal, construct and external. We identified confounding as a threat to internal validity; social desirability effects, demand characteristics and experimenter effects as threats to construct validity; and volunteer/non-volunteer differences as a threat to external validity.

We identified two principal methods of collecting data in social-psychological research: observational measurement and self-report measurement. Observational measures have the advantage of being less susceptible to social desirability effects, and can be made completely unobtrusive. On the other hand, they cannot directly tap covert cognitive phenomena such as causal attributions (see chapters 5–7). Here the researcher must rely on self-report measures, although the advantages of using both types of measure in conjunction should not be overlooked.

Finally, we noted that some social psychologists have questioned the utility of conventional methods, and of laboratory experiments in particular. The cultural embeddedness of social behaviour, the fact that social behaviour is determined by multiple factors, the difficulty of discriminating between normative and psychological causation, and the ability of humans to modify their behaviour in the light of social-psychological theories, were identified as grounds for questioning the assumption that experimentation generates cumulative knowledge of the laws governing social behaviour.

Glossary terms

Confederate
Confounding
Construct
Construct validity
Control group
Cover story
Debriefing
Demand characteristics
Dependent variable
Experiment
Experimental group
Experimental scenario
Experimenter expectancy
   effects
External validity

Factorial experiment
Hawthorne effect
Hypothesis
Independent variable
Interaction effect
Internal validity
Main effect
Manipulation check
Meta-analysis
One-shot case-study
Participant observation
Post-experimental enquiry
Post-test only control group
   design

Quasi-experiment
Quota sample
Random allocation
Reactivity
Reliability
Sample survey
Sampling
Simple random sample
Social desirability
Theory
True randomized experiment
Unobtrusive measures
Validity
Variable

Discussion points

1   What are the differences between correlational and experimental research?
2   What are potential shortcomings of quasi-experiments?
3   What is an independent variable, and how can multiple independent variables be manipulated in one experiment?
4   In which ways is a factorial design superior to a post-test only control design?
5   What is construct validity and which factors constitute potential threats to it?
6   What types of observational measures are there and what are their shortcomings?
7   What are the types of issues that one should consider in choosing a dependent measure?
8   To what extent can the 'cultural embeddedness' of social behaviour limit its predictability?

Suggestions for further reading

Aronson, E., Ellsworth, P. C., Carlsmith, J. M., and Gonzales, M. H. (1990) *Methods of Research in Social Psychology*, 2nd edn. New York: McGraw-Hill. A comprehensive introduction to research methods in social psychology, with an emphasis on experimentation.

Cook, T. D. and Campbell, D. T. (1979) *Quasi-Experimentation: Design and Analysis Issues for Field Experimentation*. Chicago: Rand McNally. An authoritative account of how to minimize threats to validity by careful research design.

Gergen, K. J. (1978) Experimentation in social psychology: a reappraisal. *European Journal of Social Psychology*, **8**, 507–27. A thought-provoking analysis by one of the leading critics of the use of experimentation in social psychology.

Greenberg, J. and Folger, R. (1988) *Controversial Issues in Social Research Methods*. New York: Springer. This books does a good job of presenting the *debates* concerning key issues in research.

Greenwood, J. D. (1989) *Explanation and Experiment in Social Psychological Science: Realism and the Social Constitution of Action*. New York: Springer. An interesting, critical treatment of the philosophical background to research methods.

Jones, R. A. (1985) *Research Methods in the Social and Behavioral Sciences*. Sunderland, MA: Sinauer. This is an unusual book: it presents the whole gamut of methods used by social scientists in an intelligent, informative and entertaining way. Highly recommended.

Lindzey, G. and Aronson, E. (eds) (1985) *Handbook of Social Psychology* (vol. 1), 3rd edn. New York: Random House. The most recent edition of this essential handbook, containing contributions on laboratory experimentation (ch. 8), observational methods (ch. 11), survey methods (ch. 12) and attitude measurement (ch. 10).

Key study

Gergen, K. J. (19978). Experimentation in social psychology: a reappraisal. *European Journal of Social Psychology*, 8, 507–27.

PART II

Construction of the Social World

Contents

5 Basic Concepts and Approaches in Social Cognition

Jacques-Philippe Leyens and Benoit Dardenne

Contents

Introduction

The field of social cognition
Definition
What cognition is

Categorization and schemata
Categorization
Schemata

What is social in social cognition?
The content of social cognition
The social origin of cognition
Shared social cognitions

Five approaches to the person as a social cognizer
The consistent or rationalizing person
The naive scientist
The data-processing trainee
The cognitive miser
The motivated tactician or the social agent

Summary and conclusions

Introduction

Hannah, a 9-year-old girl, is videotaped in her neighbourhood and in her school playground. For half of the subjects who see Hannah, it is clear that she comes from a relatively impoverished family; Hannah's school is located in a poor urban neighbourhood which is quite run down and her school is equally dilapidated and unappealing. For the remaining half of the subjects, Hannah is from a middle-class family; her home and school are located in a residential area and her modern school building is situated near a well-maintained playground. After watching the video, subjects estimate Hannah's academic abilities in reading, maths, and liberal arts. Subjects do not differentiate between the rich Hannah and the poor Hannah; all subjects judge Hannah to be as academically capable as any typical 9-year-old child.

For another group of subjects, the first video of Hannah playing at school is followed by a second video. In this tape, Hannah, seen from behind, responds in an ambiguous fashion to an alleged intelligence test. This second video is designed in such a way that it does not provide any diagnostic information about Hannah's intelligence. However, this time, when subjects rate Hannah's academic abilities, the rich Hannah is judged to be better across all domains than the poor Hannah. One might even think that there were two different intelligence test videotapes, one for the rich and one for the poor Hannah: subjects not only perceive the intelligence test to be more difficult for the rich Hannah than for the poor Hannah, they even believe that the rich Hannah has passed on more items and performed in a more adaptive way than the poor Hannah!

This experiment, conducted by Darley and Gross (1983), illustrates how several important processes function in our perception of others. The subjects saw an attractive or a dilapidated school (first video), just as they 'saw' the success or failure in items on the test (second video), and they then took all these data into account. Subjects also entertain hypotheses, or theories, about the data available to them, in this case the information given to them on videotape. These hypotheses work in such a way that the ambiguous behaviour (second video) coming from a child of privileged background is interpreted as more adaptive. Finally, subjects have theories about their own judgements and they will refrain from risking a judgement that would be based solely on socioeconomic status (first video), whereas it obviously shapes their judgements if they can 'see' confirmation (second video). Throughout this chapter, we will consider several explanations for Darley and Gross's findings.

It seems likely that our conception of the social world rests essentially on three aspects: so-called objective facts or data, theories concerning these data, and theories about judgements. According to their theoretical preferences, researchers studying the judgement process will either promote one of these aspects as more important than the others, or they may study the conditions under which one aspect becomes more relevant. Until recently, most research attention was focused on the first two aspects (Leyens and Fiske, 1994), especially on understanding the theories about data.

Consider, for example, **implicit personality theories** (Leyens, 1991; Schneider, 1973). This concept addresses general beliefs about the frequency and variability of personality traits for individuals or groups, and also beliefs about the correlations between these traits. These general beliefs constitute theories about data since they can lead people to believe, for example, that bulging eyes are a sign of extroversion, while recessed eyes are a sign of introversion. Since social data are often ambiguous, theories about them need to be very flexible. Indeed, depending on the circumstances, people are able to think about another's personality in terms of associations (for example, intelligence is correlated with resourcefulness); in terms of dimensional relationships (for example, sociability is negatively correlated with timidity, but these two traits both fall along a dimension of extroversion/introversion); and in terms of clusters (for example, the 'intellectual' type is intelligent, efficient, competent and studious). These different strategies can often lead to different portraits of the same person. For example, the traits 'outgoing' and 'self-centred' do not easily go together, unless one considers a Hollywood star (Anderson and Sedikides, 1991; Sedikides and Anderson, 1994). Along these lines types of person, or clusters, often correspond to **stereotypes**, that is to say, there are shared beliefs about personality traits and behaviours of group members (Leyens, Yzerbyt and Schadron, 1994; Oakes, Haslam and Turner, 1994).

IMPLICIT
PERSONALITY
THEORIES

STEREOTYPES

The Field of Social Cognition

Definition

The preceding examples demonstrate that people do not just receive external information; they also process it and become the architects of their own social environment (Markus and Zajonc, 1985). Understanding how people arrive at their particular construction of the social world is the domain of social cognition (e.g., Arcuri, 1985; Beauvois, 1984; Devine, Hamilton and Ostrom, 1994; Fiske and Taylor, 1991).

Just what does 'social cognition' mean? The least one can say is that social cognition concerns not only people's perception of themselves and others but also the *'naive' theories* they entertain to justify those perceptions. Not only do people think about themselves and others, but they think about how they think. Very often, the study of these processes is influenced by theories and methods from cognitive psychology that centre on: (1) how information is processed; and (2) how the process influences the results, the judgement.

This chapter is limited to introducing the principal concepts of social cognition. We illustrate these concepts via different metaphors that researchers have maintained about human beings, metaphors that are themselves the naive theories of experts in the field of social cognition. The more specific aspects of information processing are the topic of the following chapter and will not be discussed here.

What cognition is

Everyone is continuously subjected to vast amounts of highly varied information: some of it comes from the senses, some from memory, some of it is inferred from prior knowledge. Cognition refers to the set of activities through which all this information is processed. It is convenient to describe the process as operating from a beginning to an end, through multiple steps intervening between stimulus and response. From this information-processing point of view, 'cognition is the activity of knowing: the acquisition, organization, and use of knowledge' (Neisser, 1976, p. 1). The tools which give rise to such knowledge are perception, memory, thought elaboration processes, language and so on. All these phenomena are tightly embedded; for instance, knowledge comes from memory and from inferences, and people are sometimes unable to discriminate between these sources. These phenomena are also interwoven, in that they continuously interact, preceding and following each other.

Cognition is an activity which bears on 'objects'. In its primary and broadest sense, an object is anything that is exterior to the organism and which affects the senses, regardless of its complexity. Both a light source and an artistic style are objects, just like a tool or a person. While such objects are very different from each other, the fundamental principles of cognition still apply to them.

So far we have explained what cognition is but we have said nothing about what the act of knowing is aimed at. Cognitive psychology must ultimately propose an acceptable answer to this question if it is to endure. In short, the study of cognition must explain what ordinary people do, or at least think, in their everyday lives.

Categorization and Schemata

Categorization

Studies on the psychology of perception have long shown that individuals record only part of the signals provided by their environment. The ability to process information is in fact very limited relative to the amount of information people are exposed to. To reduce the processing tasks that are too difficult, people devise all sorts of short-cut strategies. Information intake is thus subject to laws and processes that deform perception and that function, for instance, by selection, rigidity and simplification.

One such means of simplification is the categorization process. A **category** (or   CATEGORY
a **concept**) is the grouping of two or more distinguishable objects that are   CONCEPT
treated in a similar way. The categorization process promotes cognitive economy
(Rosch, 1975), enables the categorizer to 'go beyond the information given'
(Bruner, Goodnow, and Austin, 1956) and, when categories are combined, it
permits them to form complex concepts (Osherson and Smith, 1981). There is
nothing more basic to our perception, memory, thought, and action than
categorization. As stated by Smith and Medin (1981, p. 1), 'Without concepts,
mental life would be chaotic.'

During the last forty years, the nature of categories has been studied at great
length (see Komatsu, 1992, for an overview). The *classical view* of categories was
reviewed in Bruner et al.'s seminal book: *A Study of Thinking* (1956). According
to this early approach, membership of a category is determined by the necessary
and sufficient attributes of the object. All objects which fit the definition of a
category are equally 'good' members. Thus a square is defined by four straight
lines of equal length joined at right angles. It is not important whether the
square is small or large, green or blue, sitting on its side or at an angle.
According to this definition, the boundaries between categories are clear and
easily established: an object either belongs or does not belong to a given category.
Moreover, and this is essential, categories are arbitrary. Nothing in the world or
in the cognitive system predetermines them. Categories are thus based on culture
or on language (Whorf, 1956).

It soon became evident that there were important inadequacies when fitting
this approach to natural categories, such as birds or flowers (Medin, 1989; Rosch,
1978). Membership of natural categories is *probabilistic* rather than all-or-none,
and consequently there is a gradient of representativeness or typicality, from the
less typical member to the most typical one, or **prototype** – either a kind of   PROTOTYPE
average or an ideal (see Barsalou, 1985, 1991). That is, members of a category
share something in common; there is a 'family resemblance' such that some
features are present for some members but can be absent for other members,
which are nevertheless not thrown out of the category (for example, most but not
all Belgians love beer). So, the probability of categorizing an object as belonging
to one category or another depends on how similar it is to the category's
prototype. Since an object may share similarities with numerous prototypes, the
boundaries between categories are rather fuzzy. Figure 5.1 shows two categories:
birds and mammals. Assume that a sparrow is the prototype for the birds
category and that a cow is the prototype for the mammals category. See the
location of a (female!) bat in this figure: it flies like a bird but has milk-secreting
organs like a mammal.

The prototype view of concepts has been challenged by the *exemplar view*,
which argues that a concept is made of memory traces for specific *instances* (Estes,
1986; Hintzmann, 1986; Medin and Schaffer, 1978). For instance, when
encountering someone with a Portuguese name, you may decide this person is

Plate 5.1 This person shares at least one feature ('beer-drinking') with the prototypical 'Belgian'

Portuguese because she resembles the other Portuguese that you remember. The abstraction of a prototype is again central to the exemplar view, but now the abstraction takes place during the retrieval of the information and not during the encoding. The family resemblance and the exemplar views are difficult to

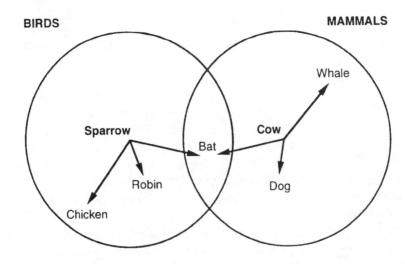

Figure 5.1 Representation of prototypes and category fuzziness (the prototype is shown in bold; length of the arrows represents the degree of deviation from prototypicality)

disentangle because both rely on a similarity principle (Malt, 1989; see also Medin, Goldstone and Gentner, 1993): if two objects are similar, they are both in the same category.

A few theorists have proposed that some concepts, particularly natural ones, may be composed of probabilistic features, like the prototype, and a *core*, which is a set of sufficient and necessary conditions (Smith, 1988, 1990; Smith and Medin, 1981). The category *grandmother*, for instance, has defining properties such as *female* and *parent of a parent*. However, *being old* is more visible and is certainly nearer to the prototype than *parent of a parent*, which is closer to the core of the category. The prototype can thus be seen as a 'blunt' tool with which to categorize, being less diagnostic than the core. In fact, it does not matter whether such a core exists in reality, because people treat the world as if such cores exist (Malt, 1990). This proposition leads us to view the core as the essential part of a category, coming from folk psychology or the naive theories people hold about the world (Murphy and Medin, 1985; Wattenmaker, Nakamura and Medin, 1988). Such naive theories do not need to be true; they can be wrong. Again, this is not very important as long as these theories give a meaningful structure to the world and as long as they are not too far from reality.

Natural categories (containing objects that are independent of people's existence, such as birds, flowers and stones) and artefactual categories (with objects dependent on people's activities, such as books, chairs and pianos) are only two pieces of the puzzle. People, unlike other objects, are most often classified according to social categories: occupation, sex, ethnicity, religion or nationality. Social categories have a core and a prototype. As Rothbart and Taylor (1992, p. 12) point out, the core of a social category, its underlying essence, leads us to 'infer deep essential qualities on the basis of surface appearance, a tendency to treat even independent categories as if they were mutually exclusive, and a tendency to imbue even arbitrary categorizations with deep meaning'. As for social prototypes, they correspond to stereotypes.

There are many reasons for grouping objects together, such as the fact that often the environment presents certain things together (for example, most birds sing), the fact that certain objects are used when performing the same function (a book, a pen, and an office do not objectively have many physical features in common), or the cause-and-effect relationship perceived between objects (Michotte, 1963). The notion of a 'common characteristic' should be considered here in a very broad sense. Any naive theory (reason) for which a mental system groups some objects together is a common characteristic of those objects. These naive theories give coherence to the category. According to this naive-theories point of view, categories are based less on a gradient of representativeness or on objective reality than on people's explanatory (e.g., biological) theory linking surface similarity (for example, skin colour) and underlying principles (such as personality traits) (for a review see Corneille and Leyens, 1994).

Schemata

We have so far explained what is represented in a category; we now turn to how it is represented. The study of category structure has principally investigated the cognitive representation of the prototype, although the core is presumably represented as the prototype is.

Consider the concept of *politics*. It can include a minister, a party, laws and votes. Moreover, Senate and Parliament can also be part of the representation. On the basis of personal or social experiences involving a given object, people tend to generalize in time and in space about that given object's characteristics and properties. Generalization, in turn, influences the subsequent information-filtering, integration, and organization processes concerning objects (see Alba and Hasher, 1983, for a review). The general form of this generalization and its outcome are usually called a 'schema' (Anderson, 1980).

SCHEMA

Cognitive schemata organize the representations that people make of a given aspect of the environment. This organization is hierarchic, having lower (*sparrow*), basic (*bird*) and upper (*animal*) levels. The most useful level, permitting inferences and thus anticipation, is the basic level. This level is rich in associations and relatively concrete (Cantor and Mischel, 1979). As an example, here is the summary of a research programme conducted by Andersen and Klatzky (1987). These authors gave to their subjects the words 'extraverted', 'introverted', 18 adjectives usually associated with being extraverted (e.g., boisterous, ambitious, domineering), and 12 adjectives usually associated with being introverted (e.g., inhibited, contemplative). Subjects were asked to sort the 32 words into piles. Figure 5.2 shows how the words clustered together, that is, how similar they were according to the subjects' sortings. The upper-level category 'extravert type' is divided into three basic categories: politician, clown, and bully. Each of these basic categories is further divided into lower-level categories: the ambitious persons, the diplomatic individuals, etc. The upper-level category 'introvert type' is divided into three basic categories (brain, guru, and neurotic), each one being further divided into lower-level categories (e.g., studious, brainy). To other subjects, Andersen and Klatzky presented the labels of the 8 upper and basic categories and asked them to rate how much 31 attributes commonly associated with one of these 8 categories applied to each of them. Figure 5.3 shows that basic categories are richer and more distinctive in associations than upper-level categories.

Schemata cannot be dissociated from the inference process. Unlike Andersen and Klatzky's subjects, people are not provided with a complete set of attributes in their everyday life. They may, however, reconstruct, or infer, much of it. First, any concept has a default value; in the absence of information to the contrary, the concept (or category) *clown* has the attribute 'entertaining' as a default. Secondly, several schemata may be linked to each other in a semantic network. The more closely linked two schemata are, the more likely it is that they will be activated at the same time, providing useful information (for example, the schema of a politician may easily activate the schema of a bully, much more easily than the schema of a brainy person). Thirdly, the relations between attributes are also the source of a wide set of inferences. For instance, the bully is socially offensive and thus can be obnoxious. Finally, a higher level (such as 'extrovert type') can be inferred from a lower level (such as 'comedian').

What is Social in Social Cognition?

We mentioned earlier that research on social cognition was and still is highly influenced by experimental cognitive psychology; if, however, cognition stems essentially from individual processes, then what is 'social' about social cognition aside from its object? Perhaps studies of social cognition are nothing more than particular applications of cognitive psychology? Social psychologists in general, and European psychologists in particular, wish to stress the original contributions of social psychology (Israel and Tajfel, 1972; Tajfel, 1984; Taylor and Brown, 1979). Does the current enthusiasm for studies in social cognition support or, on the contrary, undermine this peculiarity?

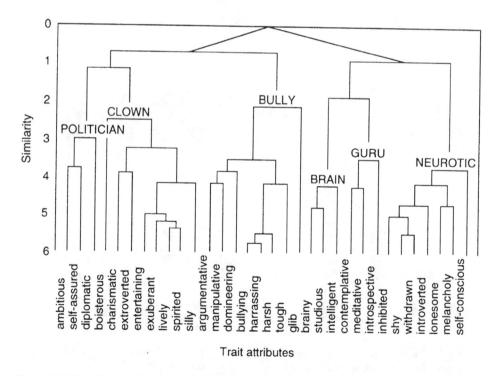

Figure 5.2 Tree diagram depicting the clustering of trait attributes for the categories extrovert (left) and introvert (right) (Andersen and Klatzky, 1987)

In this chapter, we defend the idea that cognition may be qualified as social in three ways. First, and most obviously, it has a social object since it deals with thinking about things which are social. Secondly, it has a social origin, being created or reinforced through social interaction. Thirdly, it is socially shared, being common to different members in a given society or group.

The content of social cognition

The ideas and concepts used in the study of social cognition have been applied to many social objects: the self (e.g., Codol, 1986; Linville and Carlston, 1994), others (e.g., Kenny, 1991), imaginary persons (e.g., Fiske and Neuberg, 1990), interpersonal relationships (e.g., Flament, 1982; Mackie, 1987), groups (e.g., Leyens, Yzerbyt and Schadron, 1994; Oakes, Haslam and Turner, 1994), and memory for social information (e.g., Smith and Zárate, 1992; Wyer and Srull, 1989). It is not possible to discuss thoroughly all of these aspects in one chapter. In Europe as elsewhere, research on stereotypes has increased recently, primarily

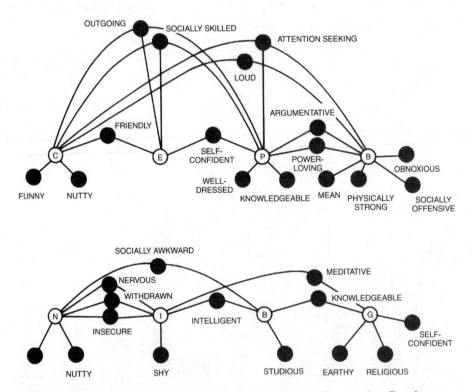

Figure 5.3 Associations between basic categories and upper-level categories. For the category 'extravert' (top): C = Comedian; E = Extrovert; P = Politician; B = Bully. For the category introvert (bottom): N = Neurotic; I = Introvert; B = Brain; G = Guru (Andersen and Klatzky, 1987)

owing to progress in social cognition. For this reason, our experimental illustrations will focus on this particular area of research.

In its present meaning, the word stereotype first appeared in the writing of a journalist, Walter Lippmann, in 1922. Not until 1933, however, did we see the first measures of the concept, by Katz and Braly. Several later studies assessed the contents of stereotypes, compared them, and evaluated their changes over time (see Stroebe and Insko, 1989). At that time there was no study of the *process* of stereotyping. In 1969, Tajfel published an important article giving the field a fresh direction. Tajfel proposed that stereotypes could be viewed as special cases of categorization, with an accentuation of similarities within groups and of differences between groups. Social cognition was an intellectual catalyst for taking a process approach to stereotypes.

The social origin of cognition

Stereotypes are usually defined as shared beliefs about personal attributes, usually personality traits but often also behaviours of a group of people. Such a definition implies that personality traits are important in order to distinguish an ingroup from outgroups. However, an increasing amount of research testifies that traits are not the universally preferred way of thinking about people (see Markus and Kitayama, 1991).

Cousins (1989), for instance, asked American and Japanese subjects to answer two versions of the 'Who am I?' test. For the usual, decontextualized, version ('Who am I?'), personality traits were four times more frequent in the American sample than in the Japanese one; social roles and situations, on the other hand, were three times more frequent among Japanese than among Americans. By contrast, and for a contextualized version ('Who am I at home, in school, etc.?'), Japanese subjects gave one and a half times more personality traits than Americans. According to Cousins, these results illustrate that Americans think of themselves as autonomous entities whereas Japanese consider themselves in terms of social contexts. At any rate, these differences support the idea that cognition has a social origin. If the social environment has such impact on the way people think of themselves, it certainly also has an enormous influence on other objects of cognition.

Shared social cognitions

People do not all share the same knowledge constructs nor do they all form precisely the same opinion about another person. Consider the last time you were talking with a friend about 'someone' who you think is outgoing, only to realize that your friend finds this person loud and obnoxious. This frequent experience highlights the fact that cognition does not depend essentially on the material or 'objective' characteristics of objects. Rather, cognition is the mental reconstruction of that which is real, based on an individual's past experience, needs, desires and intentions. Since there are no two individuals on earth who are strictly identical in every way, no two people will share strictly identical cognitions.

It is apparent, however, that a great deal of information, and hence meaning, is collectively shared by sets of individuals, groups or societies. This is a natural consequence of the social life we lead, which involves a plethora of communication and sources of influence. As many studies have shown, our perception is determined by the ecological context in which we exist. Our religious beliefs, political and social ideologies, ideas about right and wrong, and even scientific theories are for the most part defined by the social contexts in which they develop (Deconchy, 1984).

SOCIAL
REPRESENTATION

The issue of shared cognition has especially interested certain European authors who have conducted theoretical analyses and empirical studies on the notion of **social representation** (see Abric, 1994; Jodelet, 1984). This notion is a social-psychological adaptation by Moscovici (1961; revised in 1976) of a sociological concept (Durkheim, 1898). Moscovici has defined social representations as follows:

> By social representations we mean a set of concepts, statements and explanations originating in daily life in the course of inter-individual communications.They are the equivalent, in our society, of the myths and belief systems in traditional societies; they might even be said to be the contemporary version of common sense. (Moscovici, 1981, p. 181)

In contrast to an implicit personality theory and a schema, its objects are almost without limits, including 'ideas, thoughts, images, and knowledge which members of a collectivity share' (Augoustinos and Innes, 1990, p. 215). Few of us could define exactly what are nuclear physics, biochemistry, the sociology of science or ethology. However, this lack of precise knowledge does not prevent most of us from discussing these matters. Indeed, we have categorized some information about these sciences, and the resulting simplicity, shared by the community, allows us to communicate about them. These are precisely the two main functions of social representations: to help the individual to master and make sense of the world and to facilitate communication. Thus, in a sense, the study of social representations is the study of the transformation from knowledge to common sense (Moscovici and Hewstone, 1983). Put yet another way, the theory of social representations 'explains how the strange and the unfamiliar become, in time, the familiar' (Farr and Moscovici, 1984, ix; see also, Moscovici, 1982).

Supporters of this position claim that people use two main processes to realize these two functions of social representations: anchoring and objectifying. As stated by Jodelet (1984), people need to anchor new ideas into a pre-existing system. Yet this is not enough. The abstract must be made concrete, almost visual, by the process of objectifying. Moscovici and Hewstone (1983) suggested that this process can take two routes: personification and figuration.

As shown by Moscovici (1961; 1976), people have simple, and often incorrect, ideas about psychoanalysis but they still know the name 'Freud' – and that name is linked to psychological complexes. Likewise, few people know the details underlying the theory of relativity, but it is enough to remember the name 'Einstein'. This is personification in the sense that the theories or ideas are linked to a particular person's name, which represents them. When we think and speak of psychoanalysis, on the other hand, we often see a three-storey building. The first floor – the id – is untidy. The second – the ego – is where you receive people. In the third there is a mysterious person – the super-ego – somewhat like your father or teacher, who gives you orders and blames you because you have not yet put the first floor in order. This is an example of figuration, as is the visualization of the equation $E = mc^2$ when we think about relativity. Amazingly, even this trivial amount of knowledge is sufficient to maintain conversation at a party, which is good evidence that cognitions can be socially shared.

One cannot, though, conclude from the above explanation that social representations are above all else consensual (Doise, Clémence and Lorenzi-Cioldi, 1992). Groups, and likewise individuals, can differ as to the contents of social representations. Nevertheless, social representations constitute the principal organizing agents for the contents of individual thought.

The framework of social representations has stimulated research across different areas, in the laboratory and in the field, using sophisticated quantitative as well as more intuitive qualitative data analyses. Its fuzziness, however, has raised vigorous criticisms (e.g., Jahoda, 1988). Also, it does not do much to suggest hypotheses that can be tested (for exceptions, see, for example, Di Giacomo, 1980; Echebarria and Paez, 1989; Guimelli, 1993), and it certainly does not appear falsifiable.

Five Approaches to the Person as a Social Cognizer

Having explained social cognition, emphasizing the social nature of its origins and content, we now review the different perspectives for conceptualizing the lay person as a social thinker. For historical as well as illustrative reasons, we distinguish five different approaches: the rationalizing person, the naive scientist, the data-processing trainee, the cognitive miser, and the motivated tactician/ social agent.

The consistent or rationalizing person

A first approach refers to several proposals based upon the idea that inconsistency between cognitions raises an unpleasant psychological tension which must be reduced by a search for consistency (see also chapter 9). This psychological inconsistency has received several labels: cognitive imbalance (Heider, 1958), asymmetry (Newcomb, 1953), incongruence (Osgood and Tannenbaum, 1955) and dissonance (Festinger, 1957).

Let us briefly illustrate the most influential theory in this approach, namely cognitive dissonance theory. Cognitive dissonance exists between two cognitions if, considering the two alone, the inverse of one would follow from the other. For example, we smoke and we know that smoking promotes cancer. The most obvious way to eliminate dissonance would be to stop smoking. Unfortunately there are other ways of reducing the tension. Since there is no direct causal relationship between smoking and cancer, it may well be that only smokers with a certain kind of personality get cancer, and, of course, we do not have that personality; moreover, we know very old people who have smoked all their lives; also, we would prefer to die happy at the age of 90 rather than peevish and bored at the age of 100! As this example shows, the search for consistency very often involves rationalizing (Beauvois and Joule, in press).

The naive scientist

If one has to date the foundation of present-day social cognition, the year 1946 undoubtedly stands out; it is the publication date of Asch's studies on lay impressions of personality. Asch was a Gestaltist who proposed a threefold question. First, is it possible for people to form a consensual and coherent image of another person when starting off with disparate pieces of information about the person? Secondly, among the many possible pieces of information, do some pieces have a particular status such that they are capable of organizing perception? Thirdly, are impressions guided by information that was received earlier in the process?

To answer these questions, Asch gave the following instructions to his subjects: 'Here is a list of personality traits of an imaginary person called X. Take note of them. We shall ask you later who X is.' This was followed by a list of traits about X: 'intelligent, skilful, industrious, warm, determined, practical, cautious'. First, Asch asked his subjects to write a free description of X. This did not pose any difficulty for his subjects. Secondly, Asch presented a list of opposite-trait pairs to his subjects who then had to choose, from each pair, which trait best described X. The results are presented in table 5.1 and show a high consensus among subjects' responses. For the first question, then, Asch received a positive response: people are capable of creating a coherent and socially shared image of someone, starting only from miscellaneous bits of information.

To another group of subjects, Asch gave the same list of traits, except that he replaced the word 'warm' with either 'cold', or 'polite', or 'blunt'. The results of the questionnaire for the lists with 'warm'/'cold' are given in table 5.1 (first 2 columns). Like the free descriptions, these show that the 'cold X' is completely different from the 'warm X'. This result was not replicated when 'polite' was

Table 5.1 Trait inference as a function of the type of list presented to the subjects (in percentages)

		Type of list		
	Warm	*Cold*	*Intelligent*	*Envious*
1 Generous	91	8	24	10
2 Wise	65	25	18	17
3 Happy	90	34	32	5
4 Good-natured	94	17	18	0
5 Humorous	77	13	52	21
6 Sociable	91	38	56	27
7 Popular	84	28	35	14
8 Reliable	94	99	84	91
9 Important	88	99	85	90
10 Humane	86	31	36	21
11 Good-looking	77	69	74	35
12 Persistent	100	97	82	87
13 Serious	100	99	97	100
14 Restrained	77	89	64	9
15 Altruistic	69	18	6	5
16 Imaginative	51	19	26	14
17 Strong	98	95	94	73
18 Honest	98	94	80	79

Source: Asch, 1946.

contrasted with 'blunt': the descriptions and the traits did not differ. Thus, in answer to Asch's second question, certain traits are **central traits** because they are capable of tipping the scales of perception while others are not. CENTRAL TRAITS

To test the direction of perception, Asch gave the following description of X to half of another group of subjects: 'intelligent, industrious, impulsive, critical, stubborn, envious'. The remaining half of the subjects received the same list, except that the order of the list was reversed – so, starting with envious. The results of the questionnaire clearly show that the first list produced a much more favourable image of X than the second, reversed list (see table 5.1, last 2 columns). Asch's third hypothesis was therefore confirmed: perception is directed by the first elements of information available. This phenomenon is called a **primacy effect**. **Recency effects**, when the last pieces of information have the greatest influence, have since been investigated and found to be uncommon in impression formation. PRIMACY EFFECT RECENCY EFFECTS

In time, it was apparent that Asch's results had implications reaching well beyond his three questions. First, these results implied holistic information processing rather than elemental processing (Fiske and Taylor, 1991). On the basis of a few elements, people form a global portrait of another person which, in essence, corresponds to a category. In other words, people have at their disposal theories about data, hypotheses, or implicit personality theories, which determine how they process the data. Secondly, judgements are made on-line rather than based on memory (Hastie and Park, 1986). People form impressions as they receive information and do not wait until some magic moment to sit back and reflect upon all they have learned about another person.

The fact that people can be so quickly guided by categories, by their theories about data, does not, in turn, mean that they are insensitive to the data. Indeed, the third implication of Asch's research is that the data (i.e., the personality traits) are important in as much as they bring to bear information about the target. Such is the case with the primacy effect. People are very sensitive to early information because, in fact, they have no other information to guide them. Similarly, people are sensitive to central traits like 'warm' and 'cold'. Wishner (1960) later proposed that these central traits correlated highly with the traits on Asch's questionnaire. Rosenberg, Nelson and Vivekanathan (1968) have proposed, however, that central traits are central because they provide information about a new dimension previously unknown to the subjects. Recall that in Asch's experiment the early information on the list was relevant to the dimension of intelligence. When subjects encounter the traits 'warm' and 'cold' they have information about a new dimension: sociability. It is not surprising then that subjects' ratings varied greatly for traits related to sociability, but not for traits related to intelligence, which was not manipulated within the list.

The data-processing trainee

Asch's work and his interpretation created much debate. The most unremitting critic of his approach was Anderson (1981), who maintains that data take precedence over theories about data. Anderson emphasizes the personality traits he presents to his subjects, rather than the theories the subjects possess about those traits.

In Anderson's way of thinking, for example, the primacy effect (i.e., the strong effect of early traits on later processing) is due not to a continuous organization of the traits but to the lowering of the subjects' attention level. He believes the subjects invest all their interest in the initial adjectives presented to them, paying less and less attention as they read down the list. Owing to their unfavourable position in the list, the final traits cannot influence the subjects, unless the experimenter can somehow keep the subjects' attention throughout the task (Anderson and Hubert, 1963).

According to Anderson, the final answer is the result not of a general impression or an implicit theory of personality but of the 'algebraic linear integration of the weighted evaluations of ratings' attributed to the various traits.

Since you probably never considered the impression you have of someone as being the result of the 'algebraic linear integration of the weighted evaluations of ratings' of the information available to you, let us explain this concept a bit further. In each culture, personality traits can be rated positively or negatively. Anderson has determined the different ratings of personality traits in American culture. These data are very important to his perspective because the final evaluation of a person is a function of the ratings of each of the known traits of that person. What is important is how these ratings are integrated: by simple addition, by averaging, or by some other method.

We might imagine, for example, that the final impression we have of a person is a function of the sum of all the points attributed to the various characteristics of the person (**additive model**), or it is a function of the average of those points (**averaging model**). If we know that Diana is spontaneous (+ 3), funny (+ 3) and beautiful (+ 3), and that Margaret is attentive (+ 8) and ugly (− 1), then Diana would 'win' using the additive model (3 + 3 + 3 = 9, which is greater than 8 − 1 = 7). However, Margaret would 'win' using the averaging model (7/2 is greater than 9/3) (see table 5.2). The ratings are not the same in all contexts either. If it is a friend one is evaluating, then beauty is not very important and is weighted 1, but spontaneity, attentiveness and humour are weighted 10. In contrast, if it is a fashion model one wishes to hire, then beauty is weighted 10 and the other traits only 1.

ADDITIVE
MODEL

AVERAGING
MODEL

According to Anderson (in a version we deliberately simplify), the best model is one that accounts for the weighted averages. Table 5.2 provides the numerical details of our example. In the friendship situation, then, Margaret would win; her score of 39.5 is greater than Diana's score of 21. Diana, however, would have an advantage as a fashion model, where her score of 12 is greater than Margaret's score of − 1.

Table 5.2 Adding versus averaging in the integration of impressions

Attributes (A) (no. N)	No weight	Weighted: friendship	Weighted: fashion model
Diana			
Spontaneous	3	3 × 10	3 × 1
Funny	3	3 × 10	3 × 1
Beautiful	3	3 × 1	3 × 10
Sum A	9	63	36
Average A/N	3	21	12
Margaret			
Attentive	8	8 × 10	8 × 1
Ugly	−1	−1 × 1	−1 × 10
Sum A	7	79	−2
Average A/N	3.5	39.5	−1

The two approaches advocated by Asch and Anderson are quite different from one another. They reflect two distinct conceptions of human beings. Asch's conception corresponds to a naive-scientist metaphor, in which people process information more on the basis of their theories than on a detailed examination of the data. Anderson's conception, in contrast, is of a data-processor who approaches the facts objectively, examining the data without preconceptions.

Although expressed in unfalsifiable terms, these two antithetical approaches have nevertheless attracted advocates and generated debate for many years. In 1977, Ostrom unsuccessfully called for a cease-fire, arguing that it was an unproductive war. Devine and Ostrom (1988) argued once again for a change in perspective some years later. They proposed a redirection to different measures (judgements, reaction times, recall, recognition, etc.) that would be more sensitive to evaluating the *processes* at work at the time of impression formation. What is important is to see how people construct or represent their initial categories and what are the required characteristics for the data either to be considered with the categories or to supplant them (Leyens and Fiske, 1994). This was, in fact, the onset of social-cognition research.

The cognitive miser

For quite some time, psychologists tended to see social perception as some kind of problem-solving task. Much of their research revealed that people were quite deficient at this task, presumably because they were intellectually lazy (e.g., Nisbett and Ross, 1980). Often, social psychologists portrayed people as cognitive misers who relied mostly on 'heuristics', that is, quick and economical ways of reasoning that are normally efficient, but can also lead to serious mistakes (see chapter 6 for a taxonomy of heuristics).

Cognitive laziness also explains why people preferentially process information that stands out, that is salient. This phenomenon accounts for the fact that we are spontaneously more apt, for example, to notice – and to stereotype – the behaviour of a woman if she is surrounded by men or of a man among several women – the uniqueness is silhouetted against the background (Taylor and Fiske, 1978).

People are also reluctant to reconsider facts. A study conducted by Anderson, Lepper and Ross (1980, expt 2) is an excellent illustration of this type of bias. In their experiment, subjects received two case-studies, leading them to believe that success in the profession of fire-fighter was correlated with either caution or risk-taking. Some subjects were invited to write down their explanation for the correlation and were then told whether or not the cases were fictitious and that the direction of the correlation had been given arbitrarily. No explanation was asked of the remaining subjects, who were not debriefed concerning the fictitious character of the material. Finally, all subjects estimated to what extent they believed good fire-fighters were cautious or liked taking risks. Figure 5.4 shows the results. Subjects were clearly influenced by the correlation described in the case-studies. The debriefing was insufficient to erase this influence, especially among subjects who had explained the direction of the correlation.

To the same extent that people persevere in their beliefs, they also tend to rely on their expectations, their theories about data. Remember the subjects who evaluated Hannah after her ambiguous performance in an alleged intelligence test. Subjects who saw the rich Hannah performing the test thought that she was more advanced in school than the poor Hannah, and that her performance was better in spite of a more difficult test (Darley and Gross, 1983). These subjects confirmed their hypothesis about a link between socioeconomic status and intelligence via completely ambiguous information (see also Duncan, 1976; Sagar and Schofield, 1980).

People do not rely hazardously only on category-based knowledge. Amazingly, they sometimes also afford undue weight to non-diagnostic individuating information (a phenomenon called **dilution of stereotypes**). For example, in a series of studies conducted by Hilton and Fein (1989, expts 2 and 3), subjects were invited to evaluate the competitiveness of a typical business student; when they subsequently heard that this student used to rent Fellini movies at weekends, they rated his competitiveness as less important than before. In other

DILUTION OF
STEREOTYPES

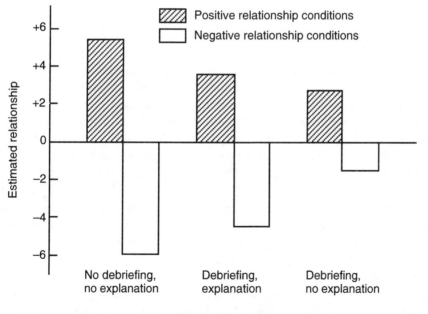

Figure 5.4 Estimation of success for fire-fighters depending on the degree of cautiousness (either cautious or risk-taking) (Anderson et al., 1980, expt 2)

words, subjects 'diluted' their stereotype about business students when they were provided with pseudo-relevant information – that is, information that is usually relevant but not for the task at hand (see also Nisbett, Zukier and Lemley, 1981; Locksley, Hepburn and Ortiz, 1982).

The motivated tactician or the social agent

The cognitive-miser metaphor presents a negative picture of people. Almost as soon as Fiske and Taylor (1991) coined the term 'cognitive miser' a new perspective was unfolding, placing motivation and emotions at the forefront of research questions. This new perspective has since been dubbed 'the motivated tactician' (Fiske and Taylor, 1991; see also Kruglanski, 1990). The motivated tactician is 'a fully engaged thinker who has multiple cognitive strategies available and chooses among them based on goals, motives, and needs' (Fiske and Taylor, 1991, p. 13).

This perspective suggests that people are as ridiculous as either their theories or experiments lead them to be, and as sophisticated as their theories or experiments permit them to be. People appear ridiculous from a normative point of view because they are biased, but these biases have the perverse effects of being efficient most of the time – this is the cognitive-miser perspective. When people are dependent on others or are otherwise motivated, and when they have plenty of time, they process the information available more carefully and select the strategies most suitable for their goals – this is the motivated-tactician perspective. Perceivers' cognitive resources, motivation, and goals are thus key aspects of the tactician perspective. We will illustrate each of these aspects.

Some theorists assert that stereotypes are used automatically when people are too busy or otherwise lack resources and control over their reactions (Devine, 1989). This is not necessarily the case (Gilbert and Hixon, 1991): people do not stereotype in an automatic manner, and the example of little Hannah at the beginning of this chapter demonstrates this fact. Nevertheless, when a stereotype is activated it becomes extremely influential and can save cognitive energy. In an experiment conducted by Macrae, Milne and Bodenhausen (1994, expt 3), subjects were required to switch off a randomly presented auditory signal while forming impressions of four targets. Subjects observed on a computer screen a target's name and ten personality traits. The target's name was accompanied, supra- or sub-liminally, by a label serving as a stereotype (such as artist, skinhead), or no label at all was provided. Half of the traits were stereotypical (for example, the skinhead was rebellious, dangerous, etc.), and the other half were neutral. During the impression–formation task, the computer periodically emitted a bleeping sound and the subjects were asked to turn off the sound. The results are straightforward. First, subjects recalled more traits when a label was present than when it was absent. Secondly, subjects with a supra-liminal label recalled more stereotypical traits than subjects who did not receive the label.

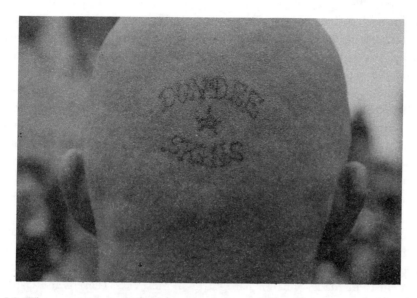

Plate 5.2 When your stereotype of 'skinheads' is activated, what traits come to mind? And could this process save cognitive energy?

Thirdly, subjects with no label reacted more slowly to the random signal than the other subjects. Thus, not only was the recall performance better in the (stereotypical) label conditions than in the no-label condition, but the presence of this label also economized energy that could be spent on the auditory task.

Often, motivation can supply cognitive resources. In a series of experiments, Kruglanski and Freund (1983) manipulated two motivational factors: subjects had limited or unlimited time to perform a task (need for closure, see Webster and Kruglanski, 1994) and they did or did not expect their performance to be evaluated (fear of invalidity). In one of the studies, students had to judge a dissertation written by an unknown peer of either prestigious or less prestigious ethnic origin. Those who were under pressure to give an answer but had no fear of evaluation were especially likely to take into account the ethnic origin of the writer and to downgrade the dissertation on this basis.

Fiske and Neuberg (1990) have proposed a model that accounts precisely for the integration of both stereotypic and **individuating information**. According to these authors, the first reaction people have to others is to categorize them and then to rely on their stereotypes. Assuming people are motivated and have adequate cognitive resources, they will try to make sense of individuating information that contradicts their initial categorizations. When possible, people will recategorize or subcategorize a person to make sense of contradictory information. For example, the departmental chairperson who is always available to students might be recategorized as an extrovert or a mentor. If recategorization

INDIVIDUATING
INFORMATION

is not possible, people proceed in 'piecemeal' fashion and arrive at an individualized judgement, attributing particular internal dispositions to the target (see also Brewer, 1988). According to this 'continuum model', the goals of the perceivers will have an impact upon motivation and attention to information. Suppose you expect to work with Edmund and the only information you have about Edmund is that he is highly skilled, or that he is inexperienced and unskilled. This information activates a stereotype. Later on, when you learn more about Edmund, you will pay differential attention to this individuating information as a function of its consistency with your expectations and of your dependence on Edmund. For instance, if you depend on Edmund's performance to win a prize, and if the individuating information is inconsistent with your expectations, you will pay particular attention to this information (Erber and Fiske, 1984, expt 1).

The motivated-tactician metaphor may give the impression that people are strategists who, provided that they are sufficiently motivated, always have choices between tactics. This perspective also implies that there is ultimately a correct judgement to be made, which is hardly true in most cases (Leyens and Dardenne, 1994). Given these two implicit assumptions, we prefer to regard people as social agents rather than as motivated tacticians. Being a social agent assumes that actions are performed in the service of interactions. Social perception is more in the domain of action than of the intellect. Expressing judgements about people goes beyond the integration of individuating (data) and category-based (theories about data) information in order to match objective reality as accurately as possible. Judgements need to be socially valid, and perceivers also have theories about judgements. For example, there is an implicit social rule that people

CATEGORIAL
INFORMATION

should not rely upon mere **categorial information**, nor on irrelevant individuating information in order to express a judgement about a specific person. In other words, people feel entitled to make judgements to the extent that they have received enough information about the target.

This rule applies to the example which opened this chapter. Darley and Gross (1983), who observed Hannah in her neighbourhood and her school, did not take a position on her intelligence because the only information they had about Hannah was her social class. Whereas Darley and Gross believed that people express a judgement only to the extent that they are able to confirm their initial hypotheses, Yzerbyt, Schadron, Leyens and Rocher (1994) found that this hypothesis confirmation was not necessary. They tested this idea by having subjects receive no information but deluding them that they had, in fact, received some. In one study, subjects thought they were part of a research programme on the influence of daily activities on social judgement processes. The experiment consisted of three parts. Subjects first received, via a taped interview, minimal category information about some person (the person was either a comedian or an archivist, that is to say, their profession activated the stereotypes of extroversion or introversion). Secondly, subjects were asked to 'shadow' a text during a dichotic listening task. In no way was the material related to introversion or extraversion. Upon completion of the vigilance task, presented as the formal equivalent of the pressure of daily activities, half of the subjects proceeded immediately to the third part of the experiment. The other persons were told that, unknown to them, they had been given information about the target during the dichotic task, in the non-listening ear. Finally, all subjects rated the target on a series of questionnaires. One questionnaire contained items related to introversion and extraversion and each of the items could be answered 'True', 'False', or 'Don't know'. Subjects with the illusion of having received individuating information gave answers congruent with the stereotype activated by the profession. Subjects in the no-information conditions refrained from judging and mostly gave 'Don't know' answers (see figure 5.5).

What this research indicates is that, besides data and theories about data, people also pay attention to their theories about judgements when answering the question: 'When is it OK to judge?' This approach has been called the 'social judgeability' theory because it focuses on the conditions under which people feel entitled to judge (Leyens, Yzerbyt and Schadron, 1992, 1994; Schadron and Yzerbyt, 1991; Yzerbyt and Schadron, 1994).

The social judgeability theory also accounts for the dilution of stereotypes. When the pseudo-relevant diagnostic information is given simultaneously with the categorial information (e.g. the business student who rents Fellini movies during the week-end), subjects do not dilute the stereotype but, on the contrary, they give stereotypical judgements. When the pseudo-relevant information is given after a stereotypical judgement based on category information, subjects

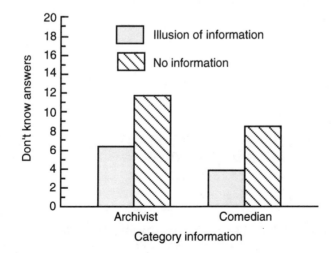

Figure 5.5 'Don't know' answers as a function of category membership and information status (after Yzerbyt et al., 1994)

depolarize their previous judgement, that is, they dilute the stereotype. In the first case, the structure of the information gives the pseudo-relevant information the status of illusory information; in the second case, the structure individualizes the previously stereotypical target.

Studies on social perception are too often conducted in a 'get to know' context rather than in a 'get along' context (Snyder, 1992; e.g., Dardenne and Leyens, 1995), or in an 'assessment set' rather than in an 'action set' (Hilton and Darley, 1991). With the exception of those people whose professions require the search for ultimate truths (psychologists, for example), social agents search for enough truth to manage their interactions, or to act in and better comprehend their environment. From this new perspective, it seems that people are 'good-enough perceivers' (Fiske, 1992, 1993; Funder, 1987; Swann, 1984).

Summary and Conclusions

In a very general way, cognition refers to all those activities through which a mental system organizes information into knowledge. More specifically, social cognition studies how people think about others and how they believe they think about others.

Throughout this chapter we have chronicled how, at different times in the history of social psychology, researchers have given priority to one of the facets of the social knowledge acquisition process: motivation, which induces error, the naive search to validate a construction of reality, systematic but deficient information processing, and a pragmatic view of social perception within interactions. Each of these preferences involves a different conception of the person faced with a social object.

Glossary terms

Additive model	Concept	Prototype
Averaging model	Dilution of stereotypes	Recency effect
Categorial information	Implicit personality theory	Schema
Category	Individuating information	Social representation
Central traits	Primacy effect	Stereotype

Discussion points

1   What are the main differences between a prototype and a schema?
2   Are there situations when you use a prototype view and other circumstances when you use an exemplar view of categorization?
3   What are the main differences between a schema and a social representation?
4   When are you usually confident in your judgements about other people? When do you think you should be less confident than you are?
5   When could stereotypes be useful?

Suggestions for further reading

Bar-Tal, D., Graumann, C. F., Kruglanski, A. W. and Stroebe, W. (eds) (1989) *Stereotyping and Prejudice: Changing Conceptions*. New York: Springer-Verlag. This edited volume is concerned with the possibility of formulating general epistemic models to account for the formation of all knowledge.

Devine, P. G., Hamilton, D. L. and Ostrom, T. M. (eds) (1994) *Social Cognition: Contributions to Classic Issues in Social Psychology*. New York: Springer-Verlag. Leading experts discuss how social cognition has affected social psychology as a whole. They cover issues such as impression formation, attribution, person perception, the self, attitudes, persuasion, conformity, stereotyping and intergroup relations.

Fiske, S. T. and Taylor, S. E. (1991) *Social Cognition* (2nd edn). New York: McGraw-Hill. In a single volume, this second edition is certainly the most complete and up-to-date compendium on contemporary social cognition. Chapters cover topics such as social schemata, person memory, and affect.

Leyens, J.-P., Yzerbyt, V. Y. and Schadron, G. (1994). *Stereotypes and Social Cognition*. London: Sage. This books integrates cognition and motivation and ties in the social rules that guide judgement processes, reviewing classic and current work in stereotyping, attribution and impression formation.

Martin, L. L. and Tesser, A. (eds) (1992) *The Construction of Social Judgments*. Hillsdale, NJ: Erlbaum. Each of the chapters presents current work showing that perceivers integrate different types of knowledge in different ways to create or construct their judgements.

Nisbett, R. E. and Ross, L. (1980) *Human Inference: Strategies and Shortcomings of Social Judgment*. Englewood-Cliffs, NJ: Prentice-Hall. This book is a landmark in the history of social cognition. With style and striking examples, the authors report where, how and why we make so many erroneous inferences in our social judgements.

Resnick, L. B., Levine, J. L. and Teasley, S. D. (eds) (1991) *Perspectives on Socially Shared Cognition*. Washington, DC: American Psychological Association. This book examines the reciprocal relations between cognition and social interaction, from the point of view of cognitive, social, and developmental psychology.

Uleman, J. S. and Bargh, J. A. (eds) (1989) *Unintended Thought: Limits of Awareness, Intention and Control*. New York: Guilford. This volume presents an impressive series of chapters dealing with the control of cognition and providing a balanced view of basic processes and of practical issues.

Key studies

Asch, S. E. (1946). Forming impressions of personality. *Journal of Abnormal and Social Psychology*, 41, 258–90.

Darley, J. M. and Gross, P. H. (1983). A hypothesis-confirming bias in labelling effects. *Journal of Personality and Social Psychology*, 44, 20–33.

6 Processing Social Information for Judgements and Decisions

Klaus Fiedler

Contents

Introduction: The Cognitive and the Social in Social Cognition

The modern discipline of social cognition as it now appears in journals and textbooks has become a broad and general perspective applicable to almost every topic in social psychology. The cognitive approach provides a theoretical framework for many heterogeneous issues, including some of the most fertile and popular endeavours of social psychology, namely, attitude change (see chapter 9), attribution research (see chapter 7), and stereotyping (see chapters 5 and 17). It is a melting pot for theoretical developments that share as a common denominator the basic assumption that in order to understand and explain social behaviour we need to take into account the hidden cognitive processes that mediate between external stimuli and overt behavioural responses. To exclude cognitive processes and representations from social-psychological research would result in a severely impoverished picture of human conduct. To quote from one of the most prominent European social psychologists, Henri Tajfel (1969):

> the greatest adaptive advantage of man is his capacity to modify his behavior as a function of the way in which he perceives and understands a situation (p. 81)

There is a good deal of humanistic optimism in Tajfel's statement. He intends to claim that cognitive mediation serves to loosen the restrictions imposed on human behaviour by the instincts or innate programmes emphasized by biologists (see chapter 2) or the unconscious forces stressed by psychoanalysts. Consider, for example, a forty-year-old personnel manager named Harry Olds, who is prejudiced against women and who treats female job applicants in a discriminatory fashion. To understand and predict his sexist behaviour, it may be more important to analyse Harry's cognitive structure and knowledge about women and gender roles, and the way he interprets intersexual encounters, rather than to look for real conflicts or unconscious motives – and Tajfel would have quickly added that the cognitive approach affords a useful key to influencing or changing prejudiced behaviour. In any case, the core assumption of the cognitive approach is the flexibility of cognitive mediation rather than any restriction to biological programmes. However, cognition is by no means confined to 'cold rationality'. Indeed, the proponents and promoters of the social-cognition approach have been interested in affect and emotion (see Isen, 1994), irrational behaviour (Kahneman, Slovic and Tversky, 1982), and intergroup affairs just as much as in purely intellectual processes of thinking, judging and recalling (see Wyer and Srull, 1989).

The emphasis on *cognitive* processes is but one side of the social-cognition coin; the other component of the term stresses the *social* nature of information processing. Just as a young child could hardly learn her first language from a radio receiver, or just as social interaction in peer groups is a necessary condition in Piaget's (1932b) theory of cognitive development (cf. chapter 3), the most important message guiding the present chapter is that (social) cognition is a genuinely social process. This message is at the heart of Bruner and Goodman's (1947) seminal work on social perception, as, for instance, in their demonstration that the over-estimation of the size of valuable objects (for example, coins as compared with cardboard discs of equal size) is more pronounced in working-class children than in middle-class children.

Some very recent studies continue to teach us this essential lesson. For instance, Cosmides (1989) argues that the persistent failure of even the most intelligent human subjects in logical reasoning tasks is due to the fact that reasoning experiments are often detached from the social context in which the reasoning ability has evolved, biologically. In a typical research paradigm modelled after Wason (1966), four cards are presented displaying the symbols 2, A, B, 1, and the participants are told that each card has a letter on one side and a number on the other. Their task is to select those cards that allow a logically sound test of a rule such as *If a vowel is on one side, an even number is on the other.* While the modal response to this reasoning task is to select the A and 2 cards (i.e., the cards matching the attributes mentioned in the rule), the logically correct solution would be to select A and 1. The symbol 1 is crucial because it implies that no vowel must be on the other side, but the 2 card is irrelevant because the rule does not exclude that an even number may also co-occur with consonants. Two decades of research on this particular task have conveyed a rather pessimistic picture of human reasoning ability. Even when the rule refers to familiar and meaningful content, the reasoning errors will sometimes persist. However, Cosmides has reported a series of very influential studies which demonstrate that people have no difficulty in solving logically equivalent problems if the rule constitutes a social contract that is reminiscent of social-exchange principles. Given a rule like: *If somebody is drunk, she is not allowed to drive a car,* social intelligence tells us that we have to look for both people who are drunk and those who drive a car, in order to detect 'cheats' who violate social contracts (Gigerenzer and Hug, 1991).

Another example of how social involvement may trigger logical thinking is evident from Schaller's (1992) recent work on statistical reasoning. If students are presented with statistical tables indicating that, say, female performance is inferior to male performance, they usually fail to consider the spurious character of such a correlation. That is, they fail to recognize that the seeming relationship between gender and performance might be due to some third variable (such as the fact that women have to work under less favourable conditions). However, statistical reasoning can be markedly improved when respondents are socially or emotionally involved, as when female or feminist participants are motivated to defend the gender group to which they belong.

Apart from the influence of affective involvement and personal relevance, however, there is another, equally important but less obvious, answer to the question of 'what is social about social cognition?' While the physical environment consists of stimulus attributes such as colour, size or pitch that are amenable to direct perception and for which we have developed sensory receptors, the social ecology extends to numerous attributes that cannot be perceived directly or assessed objectively. In fact, the attributes of most interest in social and applied psychology, such as *risk, intelligence, honesty, love, danger, gains* and *losses,* refer to distal or latent entities that have to be inferred or construed from more proximal cues and sometimes have no objective existence at all. Therefore, the variables of major interest, that is, the causes, goals or consequences of behaviour, are often ill-defined. For instance, the frequent use in Western cultures of personality traits or dispositional terms such as 'extroversion' or 'independence' does not rely on direct experience of the traits themselves, but on indirect experience of behavioural cues (talkativeness, voice quality, style of clothing and so on) that are used to construe the 'perception' of such traits. Thus, an apparent correlation between, say, extraversion and leadership may be due to the fact that both traits are construed or inferred from the same behavioural cues (cf. Shweder, 1975). In a similar vein, personnel manager Harry Olds's stereotypical belief that male workers are more rational and logical than female employees may be hard to falsify, simply because the 'perception' of masculinity is based on the same cues (e.g., reduced emotional expression, deep voice, dominant communication style) as the 'perception' of rationality. It is this conventional and constructive nature of the social world which creates the potential for illusions and stereotypes that are so resistant to change.

The Cognitive Stages of Social Information Processing

Let us now turn to empirical evidence and insights into human information processing in such a complex and fallible ecology. Borrowing a familiar scheme from cognitive psychology, we can decompose the sequence of cognitive processes into the stages depicted in figure 6.1. Although the successive process stages, from perceptual input to behavioural output, are highly interdependent and characterized by various feedback loops, the ordering has a sound logical basis in that later stages (e.g., categorization) take earlier stages (e.g., perception) for granted, whereas the reverse influence is not necessary, albeit possible. Thus, we cannot categorize a face as belonging to some ethnic group unless we have perceived the face, but we can perceive facial attributes independently of social categorization. Likewise, the organization of memory presupposes the categorical coding of the stimulus input; that is, memory for faces cannot be organized in terms of ethnic similarities unless the faces are categorized in the first place. In a similar vein, inferences presuppose an organized knowledge structure, recall or retrieval takes inferences and organized knowledge as an input, and the final decision stage is triggered by the products of retrieval.

However, the feedback loops between all adjacent stages in figure 6.1 remind us that prior stages are often influenced by backward or 'top-down' influences

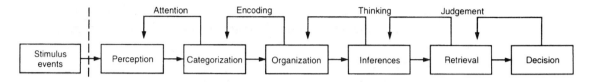

Figure 6.1 Conceptual framework of cognitive stages in information processing

from later stages. Thus, social perception may be guided by ethnic categories (Secord, 1959), just as the organization of memory can influence the logically preceding process of categorization, or the ultimate decision problem can restrict the retrieval of information from memory. Social-cognition research in the last two decades has generated many interesting findings that illuminate the nature of all these processing stages.

Perception

The initial stage of perception highlights the interplay of internal cognitive processes and external stimulus events in the environment. Traditionally, the social approach to perception has been influenced by the Gestalt psychology view that perceptual organization is guided by innate principles of organization such as similarity, good patterns, or cognitive consistency (Festinger, 1957; Heider, 1958). According to such principles, we tend to perceive causes which resemble the behaviours or events they produce (e.g., bad causes for bad events or extraordinary causes for abnormal behaviour; Heider, 1944; Michotte, 1963), or we group our observations in terms of spatial or temporal closeness. The holistic Gestalt approach is evident in Asch's (1946) seminal work on impression formation, as described in chapter 5.

In contrast to this early emphasis on 'top-down' influences from prior knowledge on novel stimuli, the environmentalist approach (Gibson, 1979; Zebrowitz McArthur and Baron, 1983) stresses the opposite view, that perception is often determined by external events. To the extent that organisms have sensory devices to perceive certain stimulus characteristics but not others, and that they are prepared biologically to give attention to specific information, the process of perception amounts to picking up the crucial signs or symptoms in the environment, with little room for interpretation or social inference.

At first glance, this ecological view seems to contradict the Gestalt view, or the above notion that social perception is often constructive and driven by stereotypical conventions rather than 'objective data'. However, the contradiction is more apparent than real, and the two positions are but two aspects of the same issue. Thus, consider the case of emotion perception. Even though different individuals in different cultures may use the same proximal cues to identify emotions (for example, the facial or vocal cues identified in chapter 10), the picking up of the proximal cues should not be equated with the perception of the emotion itself. A completely authentic angry expression produced in the context of a comedy may not be perceived as anger, indicating that the hard ecological data leave considerable latitude for contextual and subjective interpretation. The inferential nature of emotion perception is particularly evident from Wilson, Laser and Stone's (1982) findings regarding emotion perception in the self and others. Contrary to our intuitive conviction that we have private access to the internal processes within our body and soul, Wilson and colleagues have shown that to identify our own emotional states we largely rely on the same situational and expressive cues that we use to infer others' emotions. In other words, observers are often as accurate in identifying another person's emotion as that person herself or himself.

Categorization

Although the boundary between perception and categorization is fuzzy, the former stage is stimulus driven while the latter stage emphasizes the influence of prior knowledge. Once a stimulus is classified into some meaningful category, the perception is enriched with stimulus-independent knowledge about that category. This 'going beyond the information given' (Bruner, 1957) is evident, for instance, when sexist Harry's categorizing a person as female rather than male lends completely different meaning to that person's behaviour. For instance, the same careless behaviour (such as forgetting to ask for permission) may be interpreted as a sign of autonomy in male people but as a sign of negligence in females. Thus, we have to realize that perception comes to interact with the categories comprising the perceiver's knowledge of the world. The fate of a stimulus event depends on what category happens to be accessible in the perceiver's memory for interpreting and understanding the event, especially when the stimulus is ambiguous and open to different interpretations.

PRIMING
EFFECT
    This is evident in the so-called **priming effect** as demonstrated in a well-known experiment by Higgins, Rholes and Jones (1977). Participants had to form an impression of a target person who was described, in a written personality sketch, as a highly self-confident person who would engage in many risky and dangerous activities. While the topic of description was clearly defined and obviously related to courage and autonomy, the evaluative tone of the description was unclear, allowing for positive as well as negative interpretations. The same behaviour could be interpreted either as self-confident and persistent or as reckless and aloof.

    The priming treatment was hidden in a verbal-learning task that preceded the impression-information task, as part of a seemingly unrelated experiment.

Participants had to memorize (for 8–10 seconds) several words while naming the colours of slides. The words to be memorized differed in valence and in applicability to the behaviour descriptions, yielding four experimental conditions. In the *Positive–Applicable* condition, the words pertained to favourable traits that were clearly relevant to the description of the target (i.e., adventurous, self-confident, independent, persistent). In the *Negative–Applicable* condition, the trait terms were similarly relevant but negative in valence (reckless, conceited, aloof, stubborn). In two other conditions, the words used for priming were *Positive–Non-applicable* (obedient, neat, satirical, grateful) or *Negative–Non-applicable* (disrespectful, listless, clumsy, sly).

Priming of positive trait categories prior to reading the stimulus sketch resulted in more favourable impressions of the target person than priming of negative trait categories, and the effect was even more pronounced after an interval of 10 to 14 days. However, this priming influence was completely confined to the applicable condition, where the trait terms were clearly relevant to the specific contents of the behaviour description. Priming of non-applicable categories did not affect the impressions at all.

Theoretically, the influence of category priming can be explained within an associative-network model of human memory, in which concepts are represented as nodes and the distance between nodes indicates their dissimilarity (see figure 6.5 below). The more similar two concepts are in meaning, the smaller is the distance between their nodes in an associative network. In such a framework, 'priming' can be understood as a process of spreading activation from one node (the prime) to adjacent nodes in the network, and the strength of this effect should dissipate with increasing distance from the origin of activation. For instance, if the 'reckless' and 'aloof' nodes are primed (in a verbal-learning task), the activation should spread to other negatively valenced nodes related to adventurous behaviours. As a consequence, negative concepts should become more accessible and subsequent judgements should be biased accordingly.

It seems plausible that such a priming effect is most apparent in the applicable conditions, because the primed concepts (reckless, aloof) and the activated stimulus behaviours (skydiving, for example, or crossing the Atlantic in a sailing boat) pertain to closely related nodes and their joint activation should amplify the effect. However, the theory does not strictly exclude an effect of non-applicable primes, which only convey a positive or negative evaluation but are not descriptively relevant. Note that the prime words used by Higgins et al. are descriptively very homogeneous, revolving around the same behavioural topic. If, however, heterogeneous primes are used that are not confined to one descriptive topic but only share, as a common denominator, a positive or negative evaluation, then the priming effect should be broader and less specific. *Evaluative priming* of this kind should activate the diffuse feeling that the target person is unlikable (as opposed to likable). In any case, priming effects may be much less restrictive than suggested by Higgins et al. if only the primed category is broad enough, and this is exactly what research by Wyer and Gordon (1982) and others demonstrates.

Another possible restriction pertains to the timing of category priming. In the experiment by Higgins et al., above, the trait categories were activated *before* the presentation and encoding of the behaviour description. Several studies suggest that the encoding stage is especially sensitive to priming effects. For instance, Srull and Wyer (1980) manipulated the order in which the priming task, the presentation of stimulus information and the impression-judgement task were applied. They only obtained an effect when the priming treatment was administered before the target information, but no effect when categories were primed after stimulus encoding.

However, there is at least some evidence to suggest that, under certain conditions at least, an already formed impression may be changed by categories primed *afterwards*. One such demonstration comes from Snyder and Uranowitz (1978), who provided their participants with a written personality sketch about a female target person named Betty K. that resulted in a moderately favourable impression. Later on, the participants of one experimental condition received additional information about Betty's lesbian life-style. The activation of this category led to a substantial updating of judgements about Betty; not surprisingly, the resulting impression was less favourable and biased in a stereotypical fashion.

Although it is unclear whether the Snyder and Uranowitz findings reflect a reconstructive updating of memory contents or merely a memory-independent judgement bias (cf. Bellezza and Bower, 1981), a number of other studies have shown that post-encoding information can in principle have a retrograde influence on already existing memory representations (Belli, 1989; Tversky and Tuchin, 1989).

Interpreting stimulus observations in terms of primed categories does not require an intentional or conscious process, to be sure. For example, Bargh and Pietromonaco (1982) have reported a judgement bias towards semantic categories presented so quickly that conscious recognition was made impossible. On the contrary, too high a degree of consciousness may undermine or even reverse the effect of priming. Note that the priming treatment in the study by Higgins et al. described above (as well as in many other experiments) was disguised rather than blatantly obvious. However, if participants get the feeling that blatant priming procedures may influence the outcome of their impression formation, they may attribute their biased impression to the external influence attempt and correct their judgements in the opposite direction. Lombardi, Higgins and Bargh (1987) used the same priming and stimulus materials as in the study by Higgins et al. (1977) and showed that the judgement bias disappeared in those participants who recalled the concepts primed in the preceding verbal-learning tasks. Similarly, Strack, Schwarz, Bless, Kübler, and Wänke (1993) found that a priming effect can be eliminated and even reversed when judges are reminded of the priming episode. Thus, awareness is not a precondition but may actually interfere with the priming effect.

Organization

The most natural way of organizing social information in memory is by categories, and a most prominent type of category is the individual person. When complex social information refers, in mixed order, to different persons' behaviours with reference to different topics (such as group discussions, parties, etc.), people tend to organize their memories in a person-by-person fashion (Sedikides and Ostrom, 1988). The order in which the information is recalled reveals person clusters rather than topic clusters; that is, behaviours belonging to the same person are grouped together in memory.

However, person units are by no means the only way in which a categorical structure may help to organize memory in an economical fashion. When all information pertains to the same individual target person, memory for the target's behaviours can be organized around goals or traits. Imagine you get acquainted with somebody who tells you about her hobbies or interests. Altogether, she talks about 12 different interest categories (e.g., sports, finance) with four different items per category (e.g., tennis, handball, boxing, rowing; stock exchange, interest rates, share capital, foreign currencies) but in a random order. A highly efficient strategy for memorizing a remarkably high amount of information in such an overloaded task is to form a memory code at the categorical level. Rather than trying in vain to memorize all the 48 original items, the subject can rely on categorical information such as *she is interested in all kinds of sports* or *she is interested in some financial topics*. Reducing memory load from 48 specific to 12 more abstract units, subjects can then use their world knowledge to reconstruct the specific contents of the stimulus information. In several studies (e.g. Fiedler, 1986), people have been shown to use such higher-order memory codes in highly efficient and economical ways.

The organization of information in memory is greatly affected by the processing goal or task instructions. In a relevant study, Hamilton, Katz and Leirer (1980) presented subjects with behaviour descriptions. Subjects in one experimental condition were explicitly asked to memorize the stimulus behaviours, whereas another group of subjects was instructed to form an impression of the target person. Although there was no mention of a memory test in the impression-formation condition, the recall performance was higher than under memory instructions. This advantage of incidental over intentional learning reflects the impact of an impression-formation goal on the formation of a coherent memory representation which can then be used for efficient retrieval.

Plate 6.1 Is this picture inconsistent with your view of the category 'disabled people'? How likely are you to remember it?

This result can be related to another intriguing finding, namely, that inconsistent or unexpected information is often recalled better than information consistent with a categorical expectation (Hastie, 1980). Thus, surprising information may have a recall advantage, as when we learn that a priest has robbed an old lady or that an active sportsman is physically handicapped. As Srull (1981) has shown, an explicit impression-formation instruction serves to reinforce this advantage of inconsistent information. This is because the goal of forming an overall impression highlights the need to integrate and make sense of the inconsistent information and thereby forces the subject to invest extra cognitive effort in the processing of inconsistent information. The same assumption may also explain why the enhanced memory for inconsistent information disappears when stimulus behaviours refer to groups rather than to individuals (Stern, Marrs, Millar and Cole, 1984); obviously, the group as an organizing unit imposes much weaker consistency constraints on memory than person units do. Inconsistencies between different members of the same group are much more likely than within the same individual. In accordance with this explanation in terms of the deeper cognitive elaboration of inconsistent items, Bargh and Thein (1985) found that the inconsistency advantage may be eliminated when stimuli are presented at a rate fast enough to prevent extra processing.

Retrieval

Although many person-memory studies report a net advantage of inconsistent information, this is not to say that consistent information is easily forgotten. On the one hand, the recallability of inconsistent items gains from the extra processing of individual items, as noted above. On the other hand, however, consistent information may also be highly recallable because it can be derived from a meaningful knowledge structure. The relative superiority should therefore depend on whether the recall process is guided by superordinate structures or has to rely on retrieval of the specific raw events. A comprehensive review and statistical meta-analysis of all relevant studies on memory for *consistent versus inconsistent information* was conducted by Stangor and McMillan (1992). When memory performance is measured in terms of *recall*, expectancy-incongruent information is superior to expectancy-congruent information. When *recognition* measures are used, the same conclusion holds for accurate retrieval of information at the specific-item level. At the same time, however, there is a general response bias towards inferring information that is congruent with an expectation or superordinate category, regardless of whether these inferences are accurate or not. For instance, even though criminal behaviour by a monk may be likely to be recalled correctly, benevolent behaviour may be inferred on a recognition test, whether correctly or incorrectly.

To the extent that natural judgement or decision problems involve cueing and reconstruction, in addition to accurate recall of authentic stimulus items, expectancy-congruent inferences may override the superior recall of incongruent information. This is obviously the case when social stereotypes are maintained in spite of contradictory observations. For instance, our sexist personnel manager Harry Olds may be exposed to frequent observations of women performing well in their job and outperforming their male colleagues. These expectancy-inconsistent events should be particularly well remembered, and Harry's stereotype should soon be changed through selective memory. However, the principle discovered by Stangor and McMillan tells us that this will hardly be the case. Since Harry's memory is presumably organized by a network of sexist categories, he will use these categories as retrieval cues. That is, he will probably scan his memory for instances of female naïveté, unreliability, or hysterical reactions, and these retrieval cues as starting points may override the primary memory advantage of stereotype-inconsistent observations.

In the discussion of category priming above, we have already presupposed that category-congruent rather than incongruent recall is facilitated when a category prime is given as a cue. Now we recognize that this need not contradict the later claim that incongruent items may be especially well recalled. Both conclusions are valid if the distinction between category-driven and stimulus-driven retrieval is taken into account. When no category cue is available and the retrieval process depends on the strength of individual item traces, incongruent items profit from the extra processing they receive during encoding. However, congruent information is more likely to be recalled when superordinate categories or schemata are primed to guide the retrieval process. Cognitive psychologists often use the term *schema* to refer to stable categories that have become part of the permanent knowledge structure.

In general, retrieval is facilitated when the recall task reinstates the same task conditions that characterized the learning or encoding task. This is known as the principle of *encoding specificity* (Tulving and Thompson, 1973). Applying this same principle to person memory, it is particularly likely for Harry to reproduce his prejudiced knowledge about women in the same context in which that knowledge was acquired (for example, in sexist conversations among men or in the context of job interviews with female applicants). The same principle can account for mood-state dependent memory (Bower, 1981; Isen, 1994), that is, enhanced recall when the mood state at the time of retrieval matches the mood at the time of learning. Thus, an eye-witness who experienced extreme fear or arousal while watching a violent crime may be blocked from remembering it unless the same extreme arousal is reinstated.

Inferences

The distinction between inferences and retrieval is often arbitrary, resting mainly on the assumption that retrieved information is authentic (i.e., identical with what has been learned before), whereas inferred information is the product of creative invention. Proponents of a constructivist memory view would not even maintain this assumption, because recalled information is no longer a retrieved copy of the original information. Bearing the strong resemblance between the two concepts in mind, the notion of social inferences is intended here to highlight the creative nature of social cognition.

Most research on social inference is concerned with inferences from behaviour to dispositional traits (see also chapter 7 on attribution theory). An ingenious investigation by Reeder and Brewer (1979) elucidates the *schema* structures which determine such inferences. For example, in the domain of morality, inferences from negative behaviour (e.g., lying) to corresponding traits (dishonesty) are drawn more readily than are inferences from positive behaviour (telling the truth) to positive traits (honesty). In other words, more positive than negative behaviours are necessary to confirm a trait by repeated observation or induction. This pattern of inference data is predicted by the asymmetric schema depicted in the right panel of figure 6.2. In the domain of morality, the inference schema places stronger restrictions on positive than on negative traits: an honest person is expected to show positive or at least neutral behaviour, but hardly ever negative behaviour. By contrast, a dishonest person is not expected to lie or cheat all the time; rather, the trait of dishonesty is compatible with a broader range of negative, neutral and positive behaviour. As a consequence of this asymmetry,

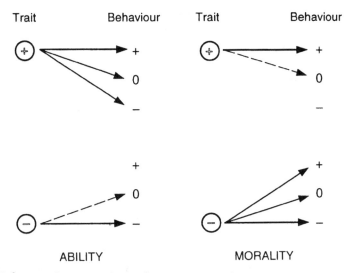

Figure 6.2 Inference schemata mediating behaviour-trait inferences in the domains of ability and morality (according to Reeder and Brewer, 1979). Negative behaviours are considered to be more diagnostic of a morality-related trait than are positive behaviours, but in the ability domain, positive behaviours are thought to be more diagnostic than negative behaviours

negative information is more diagnostic and receives more weight in social judgement than positive information (Skrowronski and Carlston, 1989), because negative behaviour is clearly indicative of negative traits whereas positive behaviour occurs with positive as well as negative traits.

Interestingly enough, however, the asymmetry is reversed in the ability domain (see left panel of figure 6.2), where positive behaviour is more diagnostic than negative behaviour. Thus, seeing an athlete jumping as high as 2.20 metres on a single occasion is sufficient evidence to infer his high ability even when he fails at 1.60 metres on other occasions.

Another type of inferential scheme is based on **analogies** to past experiences, ANALOGIES as illustrated in an intriguing study by Gilovich (1981) titled 'seeing the past in the present'. American students were presented with a brief sketch about a foreign-policy dilemma involving the aggressive invasion by one country into another, smaller country that ought to have been protected by the participants' own country. Two different historical analogies were raised in different experimental conditions: either Hitler's Blitzkrieg invasion in World War II or the Vietnam War in the sixties. This was accomplished by subtle primes such as the name of the lecture hall where the study took place (either Winston Churchill Hall or Dean Rusk Hall), allusions to the contemporary US president's home state (either New York for F. D. Roosevelt or Texas for L. B. Johnson, respectively), or whether the civilian people in the sketch were fleeing via boxcars on freight trains or via small boats sailing up the coast. In a control condition, neutral primes were used that did not raise any historical analogy. Although participants did not notice the subtle influence attempts, their judgements and recommended political actions were determined by the historical analogies, which suggested intervention in the World War II condition (because history says the Allies ought to have stopped Hitler's Blitzkrieg) but no intervention in the Vietnam War condition (because history tells the reverse story in this case).

Judgements and decisions

The ultimate products of cognitive processes are typically manifested in judgements and decisions. The judgemental nature of the cognitive output may be obvious and explicit, as in teachers' judgements of their pupils' performance, jurors' judgements of guilt or innocence, or diagnostic and prognostic judgements of medical experts. On other tasks, the judgement stage may be concealed by a different naming of the experimental task. After all, a memory test involves judgements of previous occurrences (Mandler, 1980), decisions are combinations of risk judgements and judgements of values and costs, and attitudes entail judgements of the relevance and convincingness of statements and arguments.

Because judgements constitute the visible result, it has seemed natural to conceive the cognitive process as a causal path leading from memory to judgements. For example, in Hovland, Janis and Kelley's (1953) early approach to attitude change, the persuasiveness of a message was understood as a function of memory for pro and contra arguments. The same one-sided assumption that memory triggers judgement, and not vice versa, has dominated the modern

JUDGEMENTAL
HEURISTICS

research programme on **judgemental heuristics** (Kahneman, Slovic and Tversky, 1982). The notion of a heuristic highlights the fact that cognitive information processing is rarely exhaustive and guided by logical norms but has to reach a compromise between rationality and economy. Thus, a heuristic is a cognitive device that enables the social individual to make quite economic judgements by rules-of-thumb that require little effort but yield quite valid results most of the time. However, the price of such economy is systematically biased judgements under certain conditions. An overview of the most important heuristics and fields of application is given in table 6.1.

AVAILABILITY

Judgements of frequency and probability can be obtained by the so-called **availability** heuristic (Tversky and Kahneman, 1973), even when valid statistical information is lacking. For instance, even if we did not count the number of rainy and sunny days in 1995, we can estimate the respective frequencies from the availability of relevant information in memory. If a brief memory scanning makes as many sunny as rainy days available, our numerical estimates will also tend to be equal. However, while this heuristic procedure is often quite accurate, the resulting judgements may be biased when the memory sample is biased. Thus, if we selectively recall more sunny than rainy experiences, the frequency estimates will be biased in the same direction. A more serious illustration is given by Combs and Slovic (1979), who demonstrate that judgements of lethal risks are biased towards the frequencies with which newspapers report on causes of death. Since the media are more likely to make available spectacular events like catastrophes or homicides rather than heart diseases or suicide, the frequency of the former events is overestimated relative to the latter.

Although the availability heuristic does not assume an exhaustive memory search, but only a small sample of recallable events, it was nevertheless conceived

Plate 6.2 What effect do media headlines have on your judgements of lethal risks?

Table 6.1 Overview of the most popular judgement heuristics

Heuristic	Field of Application	Illustration/Example
Availability	Judgements of frequency or probability	Recallability of risk episodes determines judgements of risk.
Representativeness	Judgements of likelihood that observations belong to a category	Birth order son–daughter–son–daughter more representative of random event than son–son–son–son.
Anchoring and adjustment	Quantitative estimates	Cost calculations biased towards starting value.
Simulation heuristic	Counterfactual reasoning	More regret experienced when missing train by 2 minutes than by 20 minutes because it is easier to mentally undo the former event.

in terms of a causal influence of recall on judgements. This assumption has even been generalized from statistical judgements of frequency and probability to other kinds of social judgements. For instance, juridical judgements of guilt and appropriate punishment have been found to be correlated with the availability in memory of facts and arguments that excuse or accuse the defendant (Reyes, Thompson and Bower, 1980) and such correlations were often interpreted in terms of a causal dependence of judgement on recall.

REPRESENTATIVE-NESS

The same assumption is implicit in other judgement heuristics. According to the **representativeness** heuristic (Kahneman and Tversky, 1972), a person described as interested in model aircraft, chess and computers may be more likely to be classified as a physicist than as a teacher, simply because the information is more representative of the former than of the latter profession. In fact, the baserate of teachers (i.e., their relative frequency in the population) is much higher than that of physicists so that this judgement is probably wrong. However, the heuristic is guided by semantic resemblance (between concepts such as physicist, aircraft, and computers) rather than by statistical baserates.

ANCHORING AND ADJUSTMENT

The **anchoring and adjustment** heuristic (Tversky and Kahneman, 1974) implies that quantitative judgements are often biased towards an initial anchor because a memory-based adjustment process is often incomplete. Imagine you are planning a two-week holiday in Florida and you want to calculate the costs in advance. You may start from a low anchor of $300 for the flight ticket and think about additional costs in an upward adjustment process. Alternatively, you may start from the high anchor of $2000 that your well-off friend spent on a similar trip, and subtract whatever expenditures could be saved. Since the memory search for costs to be added or saved is typically incomplete, the upward adjustment process will usually result in a lower estimate than the downward adjustment process. To give another example of anchoring, in lie detection the judged credibility of a communication depends on the order of two tasks, to detect lies and to understand the communicator's message. If comprehension comes before lie detection, the message appears more truthful than when the order is reversed and the lie detection task determines the anchor from which to begin (Zuckerman, Koestner, Colella and Alton, 1984).

While most research on social judgements has treated judgements as a dependent variable and memory as an independent variable, however, it is by now clear that a simple uni-causal model cannot account for the relationship between memory and judgement. More systematic accounts of the empirical evidence suggest that recall measures are often uncorrelated with judgemental tendencies (Hastie and Park, 1986). This is because many social judgements are already 'pre-formed' and stored in memory when a judgement is called for and do not have to be formed on the basis of memorized raw information. Thus, a woman who is asked to judge the jealousy of her husband need not scan her memory for relevant experience but already knows that he is notoriously jealous. Pre-formed judgements of this kind make up a considerable part of social memory. As Hastie and Park (1986) have shown, only **memory-based** judgements that cannot use pre-formed **'on-line' judgments** should bear a substantial correlation with recall of stimulus information. Of course, if you are to estimate the number of children in your street and you have never thought about this issue before, your judgement *has to rely* on available memories.

MEMORY-BASED JUDGMENTS

'ON-LINE' JUDGMENTS

Even for memory-based judgements, the best predictor need not be the amount of recallable information. A refined version of the availability heuristic proposed by Schwarz et al. (1991) states that judgements reflect the experienced **ease of retrieval** rather than the recall output itself. Thus, if participants are asked to think about either six or twelve episodes in which they have shown self-assertive behaviour, they come out with more recalled items in the latter than the former condition. However, subsequent self-ratings of assertiveness exhibit an opposite bias. As thinking about few examples is experienced as easier and less effortful than thinking about many examples, enhanced assertiveness can be inferred from the experienced ease of recalling examples. Other studies have shown that the effect disappears when the experienced ease of retrieval can be attributed to an external cause (such as the alleged facilitative effect of music). This reformulation of the availability heuristic comes quite close to the meaning of the **simulation heuristic**, which says that the ease with which possible events or outcomes can be imagined or mentally simulated is often crucial to judgements. Thus, in judging the risk of driving after drinking alcohol, memories of past accidents should be less relevant than one's ability to imagine or 'mentally simulate' being involved in an accident. Our reluctance to create such a mental scenario will typically lead to an under-estimation of the actual risk.

EASE OF RETRIEVAL

SIMULATION HEURISTIC

152 *Klaus Fiedler*

ASSIMILATION
CONTRAST

At the descriptive level, judgemental tendencies can be characterized as **assimilation** or **contrast** effects, depending on whether the judged position of a stimulus on an attribute dimension is biased towards or away from the position of a context stimulus. Thus, we may judge our present situation more pleasant when he have just remembered other pleasant experiences (assimilation), but it is also possible that our present situation will appear less pleasant (contrast) if compared with the standard of a most pleasant experience (Strack, Schwarz and Gschneidinger, 1985).

Whether assimilation or contrast is obtained depends on the way in which a context stimulus is represented, that is, if a context stimulus is either *included* in the same category as the focal stimulus to be judged or *excluded* as part of a comparison category (Schwartz and Bless, 1992). For instance, politicians of the Christian Democratic Union (CDU) in Germany may be judged either more favourably or unfavourably when the highly respected former President of Germany Richard von Weizsäcker is used as a context stimulus. If von Weizsäcker is introduced as a CDU member, the context cue is included in the stimulus category of CDU politicians, and judgements become more favourable (assimilation). However, if he is referred to as the independent head of the state, the context cue is excluded from the stimulus category and a contrast effect results in more unfavourable judgements of CDU politicians. In general, the likelihood of assimilation decreases as the distance between stimulus and context category increases (Herr, Sherman and Fazio, 1983; Sherif and Hovland, 1961).

Verification and Falsification of Social Hypotheses

In everyday life, the cognitive operations of encoding, retrieval and judgement (see figure 6.1 above) are not isolated, as in a well-controlled priming experiment, but embedded in goal-directed action or problem solving. A teacher has to evaluate her students' achievement, a personnel manager (like Harry Olds) has to select among job applicants, and we all have to structure the social world as we acquire conceptions of various social groups. Let us refer to these everyday problems as **social hypothesis testing**. The teacher's job requires the testing and updating of hypotheses about students, while the personnel manager is concerned with hypotheses about the applicants' abilities and aptitudes, as they relate to gender and other personality factors.

SOCIAL
HYPOTHESIS
TESTING

Stereotypes and illusory correlations

Hypotheses about social groups are usually referred to as social stereotypes. More precisely, stereotypes can be conceived of as subjectively expected correlations between attributes and group membership. Harry's sexist stereotype may assume a correlation between gender groups and formal thinking such as that girls are supposed to have lower logical abilities than boys. Such hypothetical or stereotypical correlations have been shown to affect information processing at virtually all process stages (Hamilton, 1981). Harry is inclined to *judge* women and girls more negatively in regard to logical ability because he more readily *retrieves* stereotype-confirming information from his memory. Moreover, he may *encode* confirming evidence more efficiently and integrate it into the global memory *organization*. The stereotype may even influence his *attention* and *perception* in such a way that Harry 'perceives' the same logical achievement to be higher in a boy than in a girl.

When a stereotypical expectation overrides the correlation which actually describes a series of stimulus observations, we refer to an **illusory correlation** to highlight the illusion inherent in stereotypical thinking. In a typical experiment, Hamilton and Rose (1980) presented their participants with a series of sentences about members of three vocational groups (accountants, doctors, salesmen), with each sentence describing a person by two trait terms. Stimulus traits varied in stereotypicality for the various professions (for example, accountant – perfectionist vs accountant – helpful). However, the series was constructed such that each occupational group was described by each trait adjective exactly twice. Nevertheless, subjects' frequency judgements were biased towards the stereotypes so that the co-occurrence of typical traits with the occupational groups was overestimated. Since it would have been impossible for them to remember the group associations of so many stimulus behaviours, subjects must often have resorted to guessing and relied on stereotypical knowledge when they tried to reconstruct what they had observed. This is completely in line with our earlier contention that social memory is biased towards expectancy-congruent material when guessing or response tendencies are allowed to influence the recall process, even though incongruent stimuli may have a primary encoding advantage (Stangor and McMillan, 1992).

ILLUSORY CORRELATIONS

In a similar experiment, Fiedler, Hemmeter and Hofmann (1984) demonstrated an illusory correlation between social categories and attitude statements such that students were erroneously reported to propose more liberal educational attitudes than were conservative clerks. Again, the biased frequency judgements were correlated with a corresponding recall bias, but the illusion was also shown to reflect the perception and comprehension of the attitude statements. That is, exactly the same attitude statements were interpreted as more liberal when they were proposed by a student than by a clerk.

These stereotypical biases in the perception, encoding and recall of relevant observations help to explain the persistence of many social stereotypes in spite of disconfirming evidence. Quite independent of any sentiments and affectively-charged prejudices, the expectancy-driven nature of human information processing provides a universal source of stereotyping. To keep within our example, even when girls exhibit formal thinking as often and obviously as boys, the formal qualities of girls may go unnoticed, or may be forgotten, as memory for the original observations declines and stereotypes continue to determine the reconstruction of memories. As a result of such a 'vicious circle', it may be difficult to change a stereotype even when disconfirming evidence is available. If anything, stereotype change is most likely when disconfirming evidence is unambiguous and clearly pertains to prototypical members of the stereotyped group (Hewstone, 1994; Rothbart and Lewis, 1988). That is, the girl who disconfirms the stereotype, showing superb formal thinking, should have clearly feminine education and appearance to be influential. Otherwise, a subtyping process may protect the stereotype from falsification (Johnston and Hewstone, 1992; Weber and Crocker, 1983). That is, the high-performing girl may be classified as belonging to a rather exceptional subtype of girls, who are more like boys.

Self-verification processes

The tendency of hypothetical expectations to become social reality is, however, not solely determined through biases in the hidden cognitive stages of perception, encoding, retrieval and judgement. Rather, the manner in which social hypotheses are tested in social interaction may help the hypothesis to come true. In an intriguing series of studies, Snyder and Swann (1978) asked their subjects to find out whether their interaction partner was an extrovert, or an introvert, depending on the experimental conditions. There was a strong tendency for the resulting impression to be biased in the same direction as the question; when the question referred to extroversion, a more extrovert impression of the partner emerged than in the other condition where the question referred to introversion. Closer analyses revealed that this was due to the subjects' one-sided information search in verbal interaction. In the extroversion condition, they asked their partners questions such as 'What would you do if you wanted to liven things up at a party?' or 'What kind of situation do you seek out if you want to meet new people?' By contrast, in the introvert condition, the typical interview questions were 'In what situations do you wish you could be more outgoing?' or 'What things do you dislike about loud parties?' Since the discussion partners had equally good reasons for providing confirming evidence for both sets of questions (because almost everybody sometimes engages in extrovert and sometimes in introvert action), the questions evoked confirmatory evidence for either personality traits. Furthermore, observers of the videotaped interaction were biased in the same direction in that they inferred a disposition from the respondents' extrovert or introvert answers, disregarding the one-sided questions that evoked those answers. Unfortunately, this intriguing demonstration of how 'belief creates reality' (Snyder, 1984) has been confusingly explained by an alleged confirmation bias, which is not justified logically. It is not really appropriate to interpret the interviewers' behaviour as a selective search for information which confirms the hypothesis. What brings about the confirmation of the extroversion question is not the selection of parties or friends as conversation topics; after all, the target persons could deny any sociability in these encounters. Rather, what creates the confirmatory evidence is human communicators' readiness to co-operate with most conversation topics (Grice, 1975) and to provide positive evidence for many topics. We are all at times extrovert and at other times introvert, and this explains the tendency of hypotheses to come true in social interaction.

Semin and Strack (1980) later clarified the distinction neglected by Snyder and Swann (1978). They manipulated the subject's actual hypothesis independently of the direction of the experimental question. Subjects were again asked to find out whether their interaction partner was extrovert or introvert, but, within both conditions, different subgroups of subjects were led to expect that the target person was probably an extrovert, or an introvert, or no expectation was induced. As it turned out, the biased information search was not determined by the expectation itself but by the direction of the question. Thus, if the question called for a test of the target's extraversion, the verbal interaction was biased towards typically extrovert topics even when the perceiver was led to expect an introvert.

Although a confirmation bias does not seem to be essential for the question content to become true, Snyder (1984) continued to emphasize the role of behavioural confirmation. Thus, the crucial factor is that the interaction partner must really provide confirming responses to the one-sided questions; otherwise no judgement bias would be expected. However, according to Snyder's theory, such confirming evidence need not be explicit but may be implicit. That is, interviewers may simply assume or imagine that the target would presumably confirm the question, or implicit confirmation may be 'conjectural'. For instance, Swann, Giuliano and Wegner (1982) used audiotaped interactions involving a female interviewer asking about either extravert or introvert topics to respondents who were instructed to respond spontaneously. Afterwards, the audiotaped conversations were presented to observers, who had to rate the respondent for extraversion versus introversion. Depending on the experimental condition, the tape included (a) only the interviewer's questions, (b) only the respondent's answers, (c) the questions plus the answers, or (d) nothing but minimal background information about the respondent. Relative to the latter control condition, the resulting impressions in all other conditions were clearly biased in the direction suggested by the interviewers' questions. It did not matter whether observers received the respondents' answers as behavioural evidence or only the question contents; the effect was substantial in all experimental conditions (see figure 6.3). According to Swann et al. (1982), observers take the question as implicit 'conjectural evidence' for the view of the respondent implied by the

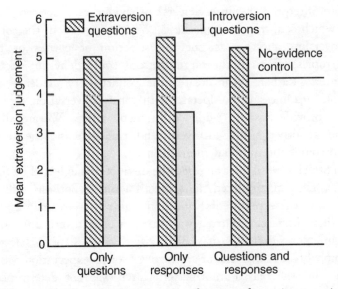

Figure 6.3 Mean attribution of extraversion as a function of question type (extraversion vs. introversion) and evidence type (only questions; only responses; questions plus responses; or no-evidence control) (after Swann et al., 1982)

experimenter: if she asks these questions she will presumably have background information that justifies such leading questions.

Other evidence suggests that the self-verification of hypotheses occurs not only in the absence of behavioural confirmation but even in spite of disconfirming evidence. For example, Wegner, Wenzlaff, Kerker and Beattie (1981) were concerned with the effects of incriminating innuendo in the mass media, such as the incriminating question 'Is Bob Talbert Linked With Mafia?' The audience's impression of the target was swayed in a negative direction, even when the innuendo entailed a denial ('Bob Talbert Not Linked With Mafia'). This finding is hardly compatible with the view that confirmatory evidence (either explicit or implicit) is necessary for innuendo effects. Instead, it may reflect a truly **constructive memory** process of the same type that has been demonstrated in research on eyewitness testimony (Loftus, 1979). Asking a witness if there was a stop sign when the car turned right and caused a major crash may cause the intrusion of a stop sign in the witness's memory representation. In a similar vein, the mental act of thinking about Bob Talbert linked with the Mafia may force the subject to construe Bob Talbert for a moment in the semantic context of Mafia and criminality, if only to deny the innuendo. However, this constructive experience may be sufficient to leave a trace in the memory, because, over time, social memory tends to confuse information stemming from different sources (Johnson and Raye, 1981), making it difficult, later on, to distinguish between original and constructed information.

CONSTRUCTIVE
MEMORY

Cognitive Adaptation in a Social Environment

In order to understand social cognition and behaviour, it is first of all important to describe the stimulus environment that impinges on the social individual. In the final section of this chapter, we shall illustrate the interplay of cognitive processes and environmental influences with reference to three intriguing issues. We first show that judgement biases may reflect the distributions of stimuli in the social world before any cognitive distortions or motivational forces come into play. Then we briefly address the impact of language as one of the most powerful aspects of the human environment. And finally, we shall consider the interplay of cognition and emotional states.

Distribution of stimulus information

What seems at first sight to be a serious cognitive bias may turn out to be adaptive behaviour, upon closer inspection. The following phenomenon of **probability matching** may illustrate this point. Imagine there are two routes between your work place and your home. The likelihood of being caught in a traffic jam is 75 per cent on route A and 25 per cent on route B. Obviously, the frustration and time costs can be minimized if you take route B every day. However, a typical strategy in such a situation is to match the probabilities and take routes A and B on 75 per cent and 25 per cent of the days, respectively. Although this strategy seems to reflect a lack of rational action, it has an important adaptive advantage. If we always select the optimal action and never try out the less optimal alternatives, we no longer learn about possible changes in the environment. After all, the traffic conditions might change, and probability matching is an adaptive compromise that makes frustration rather unlikely but 'sacrifices' some trials for the purpose of learning.

PROBABILITY MATCHING

Another demonstration of a cognitive illusion that originates in a skewed stimulus distribution is the illusory correlation phenomenon first shown by Hamilton and Gifford (1976). They constructed a series of desirable and undesirable behaviours by two groups, denoted A and B to avoid any associations which real groups. The series included 18 positive behaviours of group A, 8 negative A behaviours, 9 positive behaviours of a smaller group B, and 4 negative B behaviours. Thus, while the ratio of positive to negative behaviours was the same in both groups (18+/8− = 9+/4−) so that positivity was not correlated with group membership, the stimulus distribution was skewed: observations about group B were less frequent than those about group A, rendering B a minority and A a majority. Moreover, negative behaviours were less frequent than positive behaviours, which is also representative of the social world, because negative behaviour deviates from social norms (Skowronski and Carlston, 1989). Therefore, Hamilton and Gifford's stimulus series can be considered an experimental analogue of an actual social environment in which a majority and a minority do not differ in positivity. Nevertheless, a more negative impression was created of the minority B than of the majority A in this paradigm. This was evident in biased group-impression ratings, frequency estimates of the relative number of positive versus negative behaviours in both groups, and a tendency to associate many negative behaviours with the minority in a recall test.

This phenomenon has been replicated in numerous experiments (Mullen and Johnson, 1990) and can be considered a permanent source of minority derogation. Hamilton and colleagues originally explained the illusion in terms of the distinctiveness of the most infrequent event category. They assumed that negative behaviours of the minority were particularly salient and had a memory advantage over the more frequent event categories. However, more recent research by Fiedler (1991) and computer simulations by E. Smith (1991) have clearly shown that one need not assume a biased memory process to explain and predict this sort of anti-minority bias. Even when all stimulus events are given the same weight and are equally likely to be retained in memory, the prevalence of positive over negative behaviours is more likely to be detected in the majority than in the minority, simply because the 18+/8– ratio rests on a larger sample of observations than the 9+/4– ratio. Just as any reasonable learning theory predicts that rule learning will increase with the number of trials, the 26 (18 + 8) learning trials on the majority convey the prevailing positivity more efficiently than the 13 (9 + 4) minority trials. To the extent that information processing is sensitive to sample size, then, we begin to understand that cognitive processes may be pre-determined by the frequency distribution of stimuli in the environment.

Language and communication

Language is the medium within which social knowledge is acquired and communicated in books, mass media and face-to-face interaction. Therefore, a considerable part of social knowledge is built into the lexicon and the rules of language. The socially shared word meanings and communication rules provide an important external store of social knowledge, quite independent of the internal representations within individual persons' brains. At the lexical level, to begin with, the choice of the words we use to describe people and their behaviour has rich implications for cognitive inferences and implicit attributions. For instance, the notion of *implicit verb causality* (Brown and Fish, 1983; Fiedler and Semin, 1988) refers to the systematically different causal attributions suggested by *action verbs* (help, hurt, comply with) and *state verbs* (abhor, like, respect). Thus, the same behaviour might be described by the sentence 'The student complies with the teacher' (action verb) or 'The student respects the teacher' (state verb). However, the former sentence attributes the behaviour to the student's compliance, whereas the latter sentence suggests an attribution to the teacher's respectability. In general, the semantic meaning of action verbs implies subject causation, whereas the meaning of most state verbs implies object causation.

The adjectives we use to characterize the traits and dispositions of persons and groups differ markedly with respect to the variety of behaviours they refer to and the amount of behavioural evidence that is necessary to confirm or disconfirm a trait hypothesis (Rothbart and Park, 1986). An *honest* person is honest most of the time whereas the antonym *dishonest* is already justified by very few observations of dishonest behaviour. Likewise, *talkative* refers to a more narrow range of behaviour than *extravert*. Therefore, the latter term conveys a more global and broadly applicable attribution than the former, although both terms might be used to describe the very same behaviour in the same situation. It is no wonder, then, that the words used to describe people and behaviour can greatly affect the formation and change of social stereotypes. For instance, little evidence is necessary to verify that someone (or a group of people) is *dishonest*, but once the stereotype is established, it has broad implications, and many observations are required to falsify the stereotype and to verify that the person or group is in fact *honest*.

A systematic taxonomy of the verbs and adjectives that make up interpersonal language has been proposed by Semin and Fiedler (1988, 1991). At the most concrete level, *descriptive action verbs* refer to specific behaviours in specific situations, with little interpretation beyond the observable behaviour (e.g., to shake hands, to kiss, to turn away from). *Interpretive action verbs* (to help, to hurt, to hinder) also refer to singular action episodes but abstract from the physical and perceptual features by which the action is manifested. At the next level of abstractness, *state verbs* (to love, to respect, to dislike) refer to more enduring, affective or mental states that abstract from a single action episode. At the highest level, *adjectives* (honest, unreliable, brutal) are used to abstract from specific actions, situations, as well as object persons.

The choice of *linguistic categories* has important implications for the way in which social behaviour is interpreted and represented cognitively. As one moves up the abstractness scale from descriptive action verbs to adjectives, quite different attributions can be suggested for the same behaviour. For instance, Susy's verbal behaviour may be characterized as *speaking softly* and *hesitating before speaking* (descriptive and interpretive action verbs) or as *timid* and *not self-confident* (adjectives). The latter, more abstract style appears to reveal a lot about Susy's personality, suggests a stable attribution, and a lack of voluntary control (i.e., adjectives rarely allow for an imperative: 'Stop being timid!'). By contrast, the former, less abstract language style implies a much less stable attribution, a higher degree of context dependence (i.e., Susy may behave differently in another context), and a higher level of voluntary control. Moreover, specific terms entail much clearer references to the empirical world, rendering critical tests and falsification attempts more likely than in the case of abstract adjectives. Regarding the role of language for stereotyping, it should be added that abstract

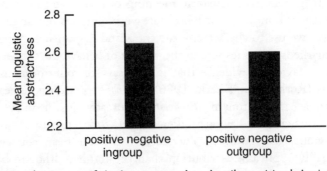

Figure 6.4 Mean abstractness of the language used to describe positive behaviours and negative behaviours of ingroup and outgroup members (after Maass et al., 1989)

language plays an important role in Harry Olds' sexist language about female performance.

Maass, Salvi, Arcuri and Semin (1989) have applied the above linguistic-category model to the study of intergroup behaviour in natural settings, with Palio teams as participants. Palio is a traditional horse-racing competition between North-Italian towns, with considerable between-group animosities. Maass et al. presented their subjects with cartoon-like scenes depicting desirable and undesirable behaviours by members of either their own or the opposing team. Respondents were free to select any of the above language levels to describe the behaviour in question. A *linguistic intergroup bias* was manifested in a systematic tendency to describe negative outgroup behaviour and positive ingroup behaviour in more abstract terms than positive outgroup and negative ingroup behaviour (see figure 6.4). The important social-psychological implication of this finding is that independently of any cognitive biases or affective conflicts within individual people, the language used to communicate social knowledge between people and in the media (Maass, Corvino, and Arcuri, 1994) will serve to reinforce and maintain an ingroup-serving bias. Rather than denying the occurrence of positive outgroup and negative ingroup behaviour, the linguistic intergroup bias operates in a more subtle and refined manner, raising stereotypically expected behaviour to a more abstract level.

Cognitive–affective regulation

Not only does the social environment serve to provide the cognitive system with informational input; rather, the interface between cognition and the environment is charged with emotional experience as the stimulus events are relevant to the individual's wishes and personal values. Countless studies in the last decade have addressed the interplay of affect and cognition, but we are only just beginning to understand this fundamental issue of behaviour regulation.

The term 'behaviour regulation' here alludes to the double function of cognitive processes which have to support emotional reactions on the one hand and prevent perpetuating reactions on the other. The former aspect has been widely noted as the principle of **mood congruency** (Bower, 1981; Isen, 1994). There is a basic selective tendency for people in a positive mood state to perceive, encode and retrieve positive material more efficiently than negative information, and a relative processing advantage for negative information in negative mood states. This principle can account for the pessimistic contents of depressive people's thoughts and memories as well as the ability of elated mood states to facilitate the recall of pleasant memories (Bower, 1981) and benevolent social judgements (Forgas and Bower, 1987). Such congruency effects can be understood in terms of an associative network: given that positive mood states are represented in the associative neighbourhood of other pleasant stimuli or events (see figure 6.5), the spreading activation that emanates from the positive-mood node should raise the activation level of other positive memory contents (pertaining to pleasant stimuli) but not enhance, or even block, the activation of affectively incongruent nodes (pertaining to unpleasant contents). As a consequence, a positive affective state leads to more positive and optimistic social judgements (Mayer and Salovey, 1988) and to decreasing judgements of risk and danger (Johnson and Tversky, 1983), presumably because associative memory facilitates mood-congruent pathways.

The congruency principle alone would lead to a perpetuating effect that might contribute to pathological developments. For instance, a depressive state may result in pessimistic memory contents and pessimistic social judgements, which may become manifested in antisocial behaviour. The social environment will react aversively to such antisocial behaviour, causing an even stronger depressive reaction which may in turn lead to further pessimistic cognitions, and so on. Analogous to such a vicious circle, Isen, Shalkner, Clark and Karp (1978) have proposed a positive loop to account for the altruistic influence of positive mood states. Good mood appears to trigger positive memory content and benevolent judgement and treatment of other people, who will, in turn, mirror the prosocial behaviour brought about by the positive mood state, thus reinforcing the positive emotional state, and so forth (see chapter 13).

Fortunately for the adaptation of the individual, the free and uncontrolled operation of these self-perpetuating circles is countered by several regulatory processes. First, there is good evidence for a meta-cognitive process working against, or correcting, too obvious or blatant mood influences. Thus, the congruent influence of good weather on judgements of well-being disappears when the respondent is reminded of the good weather immediately before making the judgement, as if the respondent were detecting and correcting the mood-dependent judgement bias. In a similar vein, a mood-congruent judgement bias may vanish if the respondent attributes her current mood to an experimental manipulation (Schwartz and Clore, 1988).

Secondly, the associative effect of mood congruency may be corrected by motivated processes of 'mood-repair', which create a basic asymmetry in the cognitive effects of positive versus negative affect. While there is no reason for people in elated mood states to change their positive thought contents, people in a depressed state will typically attempt to improve their situation by actively avoiding unpleasant thoughts or consciously seeking more pleasant thought contents. The net outcome is a generally much weaker congruency effect for negative than for positive moods (cf. Isen, 1994).

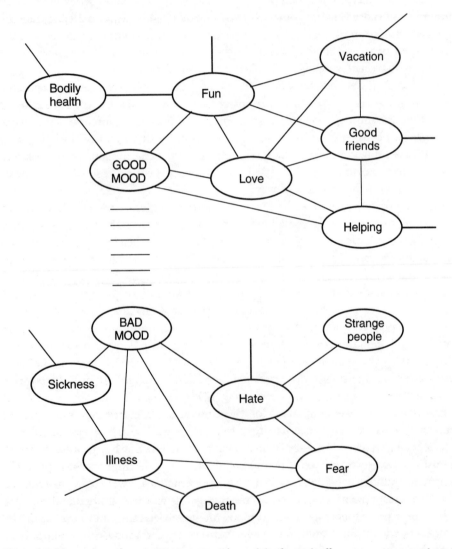

Figure 6.5 Illustration of an associative-network model of mood effects on memory and social judgements

A third process of mood-contingent regulation refers to the different cognitive styles triggered by emotional states and suggests some of the cognitive strategies that can be used to repair one's negative mood or to prevent one's elated mood from being perpetuated. There is converging evidence from many studies that negative emotional states elicit more systematic processing and cognitive discipline (Isen, Means, Patrick and Nowicki, 1982). In contrast, positive mood states elicit a more creative style (Isen, Daubman and Nowicki, 1987) that sometimes interferes with exhaustive or accurate processing. Particularly, people in a positive mood produce less common word associations (Isen, Johnson, Hertz and Robinson, 1985), seek less information before decisions (Isen et al., 1982), and sometimes make less accurate judgements (Sinclair and Mark, 1992). However, good mood may lead to better performance than bad mood on demanding tasks that call for creativity and productive thinking (Ellis and Ashbrook, 1988; Murray, Surjan, Hirt and Surjan, 1990).

A study by Bless, Bohner, Schwarz and Strack (1990) illustrates the different cognitive styles of people in good and bad moods with reference to the impact of persuasive communication. Subjects who had written a vivid and detailed report on a happy or sad life event, as a mood manipulation, were then exposed to a tape-recorded communication that argued for an increase in the fees to be paid by students. Sad subjects were influenced by this counter-attitudinal message only if the arguments were strong, but happy subjects were equally persuaded by strong and by weak arguments. An analysis of thoughts listed in response to the communication supported the interpretation that happy subjects simply engaged in less systematic elaboration of the message. In accordance with this account, the sad subjects' sensitivity to argument quality disappeared when a distractor task was included that prevented them from cognitive elaboration.

While the empirical evidence for mood-contingent cognition is strong and uncontestable, the theoretical explanation is less than clear. It is possible, of course, that the experience of positive affect occupies cognitive resources or capacity, or that happy subjects are generally inclined to avoid cognitive effort that might spoil their pleasant state. Research by Martin, Ward, Achee and Wyer (1993) suggests that mood effects on cognitive elaboration reflect adaptive strategies rather than absolute capacity constraints. Participants read a series of behaviours to form an impression of a target person. When told to stop reading 'when you feel you have enough information', happy subjects stopped sooner than sad subjects. However, when instructed to read behaviours 'until you no longer enjoy' the task, positive mood led subjects to engage in longer, seemingly more elaborated information processing. This experiment nicely illustrates the flexibility and adaptability of affective–cognitive regulation. The influence of mood states on cognitive processing depends on the meaning of the task. If the tasks calls for carefulness and scrutiny, performance may profit from negative mood states. If, however, the same task is framed in terms of enjoyment, it is more likely to be supported by positive affective states.

Summary and Conclusions

The social-cognition approach emphasizes the cognitive mediation of social behaviour, and, vice versa, the social impact on cognitive processes. Personal involvement, affective states, or environmental factors can have a considerable influence on logical thinking, stereotyping, social judgements and decisions.

In accordance with cognitive psychology, we have decomposed the scope of social cognition into sequential stages of information processing, such as perception, encoding, organization, inference making, retrieval, and judgement. At all stages, the individual's expectations or older knowledge structures come to interact with new input information. In many cases, the prior knowledge or stereotypical expectations are stronger than unexpected or inconsistent information. But we have also noted a primary memory advantage of inconsistent or unexpected information. The phenomenon of priming effects is due to the memory activation of semantic categories (such as negative traits) that may influence subsequent judgements, unless the priming is too weak or too blatant. However, the priming of certain categories does not always result in a congruent, assimilation effect on judgement (for example, negative priming causing negative judgements). If the primed category is not included in the same category as the judgement target but excluded as a standard of comparison, the outcome may be a contrast effect (more positive judgements after negative priming, for example).

The manner in which social hypotheses are tested in conversation and social interaction may help the hypotheses to come true. Asking someone questions about extravert behaviour may help to create the impression of an extrovert person; talking about criminal behaviour may leave the impression that the conversation partner is at least somewhat associated with criminality. These self-verification effects may be due to constructive memory processes elicited by the question contents, and to the tendency of interaction partners to exhibit the kind of behaviour suggested by the question contents.

Finally, we have to recognize that the outcome of cognitive processes is not solely determined by cognitive and motivational forces within the individual, but partly pre-determined by the environment impinging on the social individual. In this respect, we have addressed the differential impact of large and small stimulus classes (majorities vs minorities), the subtle implications of the language used to describe interpersonal behaviour, and the affective influences on cognitive processes that arise from the subject's coping with the social environment. All the issues covered in this chapter have obvious implications for judgements and decisions in important natural settings such as the court-room, marketing, politics, diagnostics, or intergroup encounters.

Glossary terms

Analogy
Anchoring and adjustment
Assimilation
Availability
Constructive memory
Contrast

Ease of retrieval
Illusory correlation
Judgemental heuristics
Memory-based
    judgements
Mood congruency

On-line judgements
Priming effect
Probability matching
Representativeness
Simulation heuristic
Social hypothesis testing

Discussion points

1   What are the genuinely social aspects that distinguish social cognition from cognitive psychology?
2   What could be done to correct unjustified social stereotypes at the various stages of cognitive processing that are depicted in figure 6.1?
3   Try to think about the irrationality versus adaptive value of judgemental heuristics under natural conditions.
4   What are the most intriguing examples of self-verification in social life? Under what conditions can hypothesis-testing be debiased?
5   How could language analysis be used to analyse political bias in newspapers?

Suggestions for further reading

Eagly, A. H. and Chaiken, S. (1993) *The Psychology of Attitudes*. New York: Harcourt Brace Jovanovich. This recently published volume is currently the most comprehensive reference for students of attitude and persuasion, and it will certainly continue to be so in the next decade.

Fiske, S. T. and Taylor, S. E. (1991) *Social Cognition*, 2nd edn. New York: McGraw-Hill. The Fiske–Taylor textbook is uncontestably the most frequently cited textbook that is specially devoted to the cognitive approach in social psychology.

Kahneman, D., Slovic, P. and Tversky, A. (1982) *Judgment under Uncertainty: Heuristics and Biases*. Hillsdale, NJ: Erlbaum. This edited volume contains reprints of the most important original articles on cognitive fallacies and biases.

Markus, H. and Zajonc, R. B. (1985) The cognitive perspective in social psychology. In G. Lindzey and E. Aronson (eds), *Handbook of Social Psychology*,3rd edn, vol. 1. New York: Random House, 137–230. This handbook article is less up-to-date than the volumes of the Wyer–Srull handbook, but it provides a more condensed alternative.

McArthur, L. (1990) *Social Perception*. Buckingham: Open University Press. If you are looking for a quick and easy introduction written by an informed author you might choose this paperback textbook.

Wyer, R. S. and Srull, T. K. (eds) (1994) *Handbook of Social Cognition* 2nd edn, 2 volumes. Hillsdale, NJ: Erlbaum. A comprehensive sourcebook covering even very recent developments in cognitive social psychology, written clearly and interestingly by distinguished scientists.

Key studies

Hamilton, D. L., Katz, L. B. and Leirer, V. O. (1980). Cognitive representation of personality impressions: Organizational processes in first impression formation. *Journal of Personality and Social Psychology*, 39, 1050–63.

Snyder, M. and Uranowitz, S. W. (1978). Reconstructing the past: Some cognitive consequences of person perception. *Journal of Personality and Social Psychology*, 36, 941–50.

7 Attribution Theory and Research: Basic Issues and Applications

Miles Hewstone and Frank Fincham

Contents

Introduction

Theories of causal attribution
The naive analysis of action
Correspondent inference theory
Covariation and configuration

Fundamental questions for attribution research
The nature of causal attribution
The instigation of causal attributions
Errors and biases in the attribution process
The process of causal attribution

Applications of attribution theory
Attributions and motivation
Attributions and clinical psychology
Close relationships

Summary and conclusions

Introduction

Imagine you have just found out that you failed the statistics exam you took last month. Why? The research we review in this chapter deals with how you answer such 'why?' questions. We look at the kind of information you use, and how you process it; for example, do you compare your own outcome with that of other students? We also look at the consequences that follow from your explanation. For example, if you ascribe your failure to a lack of ability you may experience a loss of self-esteem and not bother to study for the re-take. On the other hand, if you attribute the failure to lack of effort you can take a positive approach and work hard to make sure that you pass next time. You can see that the topic of **causal attribution**, how people attribute effects to causes, is an important one. Studying these issues has been one of the most active pursuits of social psychologists, and continues to be so: well over 300 journal articles on the topic of **attribution theory** were published in 1990 (see Smith, 1994).

    In this chapter we are concerned with people's causal attributions for social events, including their own and other people's behaviour. We will deal, first, with the three classic theories about the way people *attribute* behaviour to discrete causes. We will then consider some of the most interesting theoretical questions and research relating to four central issues: the nature of, biases in, and the instigation and process of causal attribution (see Hewstone, 1989, for a more detailed treatment of these questions). In the second half of the chapter we look at applications of attribution theory, focusing on three main topics: motivation, clinical psychology and close relationships.

CAUSAL ATTRIBUTION

ATTRIBUTION THEORY

Theories of Causal Attribution

The naive analysis of action

What do people do when they try to explain events in their social and physical world? Heider (1958) viewed the lay person as a *naive scientist*, linking observable behaviour to unobservable causes. We will highlight here what was perhaps Heider's major contribution to attribution theory – the division of potential sources of action into personal (or internal) and environmental (or external) types. According to Heider, the job of the perceiver is to decide whether a given action is due to something within the person who is performing it (such as ability, effort, intention), or to something outside the person (such as the difficulty of the task, or luck). Understanding which set of factors should be used to interpret the behaviour of another person will, according to Heider, make the perceiver's world more predictable, and give a sense of control. Heider's (1958) insights provided the blueprint for succeeding theories, which we will now consider (see Hewstone, 1989; Ross and Fletcher, 1985).

Correspondent inference theory

According to 'correspondent inference theory' (Jones and Davis, 1965; Jones and McGillis, 1976) the goal of the attribution process is to *infer* that observed behaviour and the intention that produced it *correspond* to some underlying stable quality in the person or actor. The central concept of the theory, the **correspondent inference**, refers to the perceiver's judgement that the actor's behaviour is caused by, or corresponds to, a particular trait (for example, someone's hostile behaviour is ascribed to the trait 'hostility'). There are two major stages in the process of inferring personal dispositions: the attribution of intention ('did he mean to do it?'), and the attribution of dispositions ('which personal characteristic(s) caused him to do it?').

CORRESPONDENT
INFERENCE

Attribution of intention

The perceiver's first problem is to decide which effects of an observed action, if any, were intended by the actor. According to Jones and Davis, to infer that any of the effects of an action were intended, the perceiver must believe that the actor *knew* the consequences of his action, and that he had the *ability* (e.g., the physical strength) to perform the action.

Attribution of dispositions

One key influence on dispositional attribution is the perceiver's beliefs about what other people would do in the same situation (*social desirability*). Correspondent inferences are stronger when the consequences of the chosen behaviour are socially *un*desirable. More generally, only behaviours that disconfirm expectations are truly informative about the actor. When people say what is expected of them in a particular situation, or while playing a particular role, then we learn little about them. This hypothesis was supported in Jones, Davis and Gergen's (1961) study in which subjects judged candidates being interviewed for the job of either a submariner or an astronaut. The behaviour of candidates who presented themselves as fitting the desired type (that is, they were 'other directed' for the submariner's job, 'inner directed' for the astronaut's job) was judged relatively uninformative about the individual's personal characteristics. In contrast, when the candidates answered questions in a manner inconsistent with the role expectations (expectancy-disconfirming or out-of-role behaviour), inferences about their personalities were stronger and made with more confidence.

Biases in the inference process

Jones and Davis anticipated later work by distinguishing two kinds of **attributional bias** – motivational and cognitive. Motivational biases were triggered by the personal involvement of the perceiver in another person's actions. For example, perceivers were more likely to make a correspondent inference when the actor's choice had positive or negative effects for them

ATTRIBUTIONAL
BIAS

('hedonic relevance'). The main cognitive bias identified was the over-estimation of personal factors and the under-estimation of situational factors. This bias came to be called the **fundamental attribution error** and is discussed in more detail below.

Critical issues relating to correspondent inference theory

Although experimental studies have yielded some support for the theory, it has three main limitations. (1) Although the theory argues that attribution of intention must precede a dispositional inference, some dispositions are defined in terms of unintentional behaviours (clumsiness, for example). Thus the theory is applicable only to 'actions', which have some element of choice. (2) Although behaviour that disconfirms expectancies is obviously informative, expectancy-confirming behaviour can also be so (such as behaviour that confirms stereotypes). (3) Most of the studies generated by the theory did not measure *causal* attributions. Inferring a disposition is not the same task as inferring a cause and, as we see below, each appears to reflect different underlying processes.

Current work

Current work on dispositional inference investigates the different components or stages involved in trait attribution. Three stages are suggested: (1) the trait implications of a behaviour are *identified*; (2) the identified trait is *attributed* to the actor; (3) a *situational correction* is made to adjust the trait attribution for external factors (see Gilbert, 1995, for a review). When a person's behaviour has clear trait implications, perceivers seem to make inferences automatically (that is, without effort, intention or awareness; e.g. Winter, Uleman and Cunniff, 1985). In contrast, situational correction is not an automatic component of the attribution process (e.g., Gilbert, Pelham and Krull, 1988).

Covariation and configuration

The next addition to attribution theory was Kelley's (1967, 1973) model. Kelley begins with the question of what information is used to arrive at a causal attribution. He outlines two different cases, which depend on the amount of information available to the perceiver. In the first case the perceiver has information from multiple sources, occasions and modalities, and can perceive the *covariation* of an observed effect and its possible causes. For example, if you have just failed a statistics examination, how do you explain this? If you know that you failed the same subject last year, that you passed all your other exams, and that several of your friends also failed statistics, you will be more likely to attribute this failure to the particular examination (for example, its nature or topic) than to yourself. In the second case, the perceiver is faced with a single observation and must take account of the *configuration* of factors that are plausible causes of the observed effect. For example, if you see a car knock down a pedestrian, you cannot normally ask about the number of previous accidents involving either driver or pedestrian. You have to take note of such factors as a wet road surface, whether the driver was drunk, and so on. We deal with both covariation and configuration in turn.

Attributions based on multiple observations: covariation

Where the perceiver has information from multiple sources, Kelley (1967, 1973) suggests that her purpose, like the scientist's, is to separate out which effects are to be attributed to which of several factors. He proposes that a **covariation**   COVARIATION
principle is used: an effect is attributed to a condition that is present when the   PRINCIPLE
effect is present, and absent when the effect is absent. Kelley based his model on a statistical technique, the analysis of variance (ANOVA), which examines changes in a dependent variable (the effect) by varying independent variables (the conditions).

We can demonstrate the ANOVA model by considering an example studied by McArthur (1972): 'John laughs at the comedian.' This outcome could be caused by something in the person (John), the circumstances (for example, the occasion on which the outcome occurred), the entity or stimulus (the comedian), or some combination of these factors. The independent variables constitute the three possible ways of examining variations in effects (see figure 7.1): (a) over

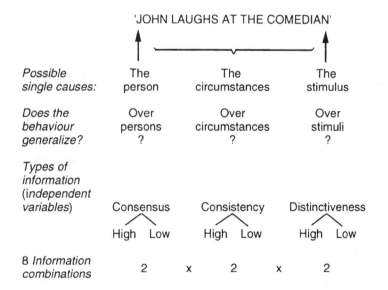

Figure 7.1 The analysis of variance model of covariation

Note: An explanation for a simple sentence of this type can be generated by identifying each possible single cause (person/circumstance/stimulus), asking whether the behaviour generalizes across persons, circumstances and stimuli, and thus specifying the level of information in each case (from Hewstone, 1989; after Kelley, 1967; McArthur, 1972).

persons (from which *consensus* information is derived); (b) over time/modalities (from which *consistency* is derived); and (c) over stimuli (from which *distinctiveness* is derived). The dependent variable is, of course, whether the effect occurs or not. The covariation principle suggests that the effect is seen as having been caused by the factor with which it covaries. Thus if only John laughs at the comedian (low consensus), he has done so in the past (high consistency), and he also laughs at all other comedians (low distinctiveness), then the effect is seen as caused by something in the person (John).

If we assume that each type of information could be given a high or a low value, then we could generate a total of eight different patterns of information. McArthur (1972) did this and produced results apparently consistent with the model, confirming that consensus, distinctiveness and consistency did indeed affect the attribution of causality in the way predicted by Kelley and in line with the covariation principle.

Critical issues relating to the covariation principle

Although initial studies seemed to support the model, it has since been criticized on three major grounds. (1) The covariation principle is limited as a basis for inferring causality. As statistics books remind us, correlation does not necessarily imply correlation (for example, we all know that sexual intercourse is the cause of pregnancy, but the two are not, in fact, highly correlated; see Einhorn and Hogarth, 1986). (2) In the type of experiment used to test the model (e.g. McArthur, 1972), subjects are provided with 'prepackaged' covariation information which, under normal circumstances, they might neither seek out, nor use (see Garland, Hardy and Stephenson, 1975). This limitation is made more serious by the fact that people are not very skilled at assessing covariation between events (Alloy and Tabachnik, 1984). (3) Although subjects' attributions may appear *as if* they used the covariation principle, their actual information processing may be completely different from that set out by Kelley. Just because people's attributions seem to fit the ANOVA framework, this does not mean that they are doing anything like that in their heads. Can you? Most of us find it hard enough with a calculator, or even a computer. We will return below to the interesting question of the cognitive processes involved in causal attribution.

Current work

Recent and current work on this theory has focused on exactly *how* perceivers make causal attributions, given consensus, consistency and distinctiveness information. Hewstone and Jaspars (1987) proposed a 'logical model' of the attribution process, which presented a method by which perceivers could analyse covariation (and identify necessary and sufficient conditions for the occurrence of an effect) but without computing a mental analysis of variance. Although this model does a better job of predicting perceivers' attributions, it is an extremely complex model of the lay person. An alternative, the 'abnormal conditions focus'

(ACF) model (Hilton and Slugoski, 1986), provides an elegant, but simple, analysis. According to this model, we select as a cause the necessary condition that is *abnormal* when compared with the background of the target event. The ACF model proposes that subjects treat consensus, distinctiveness and consistency information as 'contrast cases' that define the abnormal conditions facilitating the production of the event. The abnormal conditions are then treated as the causes of the event. Specifically, Hilton and Slugoski suggest that *low consensus* information ('hardly anyone else does it') identifies the target *person* as abnormal; *high distinctiveness* information ('the target person does it to hardly anything else') identifies the *stimulus* as abnormal; and *low consistency* information ('the target event has hardly ever happened before') identifies the present *circumstances* as abnormal. Kelley's model continues to be refined and extended, from alternative perspectives (see Cheng and Novick, 1990; Försterling, 1995).

Attributions based on a single observation: configuration

Another drawback of the covariation model is that it requires multiple observations, yielding consensus, consistency and distinctiveness information. Yet we often do not have that information when making attributions in everyday life. Kelley (1972) acknowledged that the ANOVA model was 'idealized' and that there are many occasions on which the perceiver lacks the information, time or motivation to examine multiple observations. In these cases of incomplete data, attributions are made using **causal schemata**. These schemata are ready-made beliefs, preconceptions and even theories, built up from experience, about how certain kinds of causes interact to produce a specific kind of effect. A perceiver can interpret information by comparing it, and integrating it, with a schema (see chapters 5 and 6).

CAUSAL SCHEMATA

One of the simplest causal schemata is the multiple sufficient cause (MSC) schema (Kelley, 1972). According to this schema, any of several causes (such as problems at home, poor school environment, or lack of effort) acting individually can produce the same effect (examination failure, for example). Kelley also put forward a number of attributional principles that accompany the causal schemata. The MSC schema is associated with the **discounting principle**: given that different causes can produce the same effect, the role of a given cause in producing the effect is *discounted* if other plausible causes are present. Thus a child whose parent died recently may have an examination failure attributed to this cause rather than to lack of effort. Kelley (1972) also proposed an **augmentation principle**: the role of a given cause is *augmented* (increased) if an effect occurs in the presence of an inhibitory cause. Thus a student who succeeds in an examination despite suffering from glandular fever should have her performance attributed more to effort and ability than would be that of a healthy student. The augmentation principle applies both to the MSC and to the more complex multiple necessary cause (MNC) schema (Kelley, 1972). According to the MNC schema, several causes must operate together to produce the effect.

DISCOUNTING PRINCIPLE

AUGMENTATION PRINCIPLE

Kelley hypothesized that this schema would be invoked to account for unusual or extreme effects (Cunningham and Kelley, 1975).

Kelley (1972) proposed that there are many other kinds of causal schema available to the lay person, and they are important for three main reasons: (1) they help the perceiver to make attributions when information is incomplete; (2) they are general conceptions about causes and effects which may apply across content areas; (3) they provide the perceiver with a 'causal shorthand' for carrying out complex inferences quickly and easily (Fiske and Taylor, 1991).

Critical issues relating to causal schemata

Despite the apparent advantages of causal schemata, there are still issues which require theoretical and empirical attention. According to Fiedler (1982), two issues are central. (1) The existence and functioning of causal schemata, while intuitively plausible, have not been successfully demonstrated. Fiedler criticizes some of the research for being artificial, and for having a built-in device for finding a causal schema in any kind of attribution by the subject. Thus different responses are seen as evidence of the use of different kinds of schemata. But how do we know that a schema was used at all? All we can say, at present, is that people act *as if* they use schemata. (2) Fiedler also criticized the abstract, content-free conception of the schema. A schema should represent organized knowledge based on cultural experience, and not just an abstract relation between cause and effect.

Covariation and configuration: an integration

In spite of the critical issues raised by our discussion, both covariation and configuration notions are central to attribution research. There has been extended discussion of whether attributions are 'data driven' (by covariation) or 'theory driven' (by configuration). In fact, there is an interaction between data and expectations, with preconceptions influencing not only how, but what, data are processed (Alloy and Tabachnik, 1984).

Theories of causal attribution: a summary

The three theories outlined above – those of Heider, Jones and Davis, and Kelley – are generally considered the building blocks for subsequent research. They converge on the following general themes: mediation between stimulus and response; active and constructive causal interpretation; and the perspective of the naive scientist or lay person. Most importantly, all share a concern with common-sense explanations and answers to the question 'why'? Based on the rich, descriptive work of Heider (1958), the theories of Jones and Davis (1965) and Kelley (1973) tried ambitiously to formalize the rules people might be using to make causal attributions. They answered many questions, and raised a great deal more, about the nature of common-sense explanations, and when and how they are made. We now consider these questions.

Fundamental Questions for Attribution Research

The initial enthusiasm for attribution research, stimulated by the testable theories reviewed above, was followed by deeper, more critical research and theorizing on fundamental issues: what exactly are causal attributions; how are they biased; when do they occur; and how do perceivers make them?

The nature of causal attribution

Internal versus external attributions

Since Heider's (1958) work, there has been a great emphasis on the distinction between internal and external attributions. Although this distinction is important, two major problems threaten its use and value (Miller, Smith and Uleman, 1981).

First, what is the relation between internal and external attributions? Heider proposed an inverse relation between personal and situational causality. The more the person is seen as causing the action, the less the environment will be perceived as causal (and vice versa). According to this view, measures of personal and situational attribution should be negatively correlated. However, several studies have reported positive or only slightly negative correlations between attributions to the person and attributions to the situation when rated on separate scales (e.g., Taylor and Koivumaki, 1976). It should also be noted that people are more likely to employ combinations of both internal and external attributions under certain conditions, such as when explaining extreme events (Kelley, 1973) or complex interpersonal events such as marital interaction (Fincham, 1985).

Secondly, can internal and external attributions be distinguished? A central problem is that statements which seem to imply external attributions can be rephrased as statements implying internal attributions (and vice versa; Ross, 1977). This problem is particularly evident where researchers have attempted to code attributions from a free-response format. Nisbett et al. (1973, study 2) asked subjects to write brief paragraphs describing why they had chosen their college degree subject. A statement such as 'I want to make a lot of money' was coded as internal, while 'Chemistry is a high-paying field' was coded as external. An obvious criticism of this method is that the two types of statements contain similar information and in fact imply one another. A number of researchers have also noted that the categories of internal and external causality are very broad, containing a heterogeneous collection of attributions (see Lalljee, 1981). Some researchers have reported that many of their subjects failed to understand the distinction, and/or did not find it meaningful (Taylor and Koivumaki, 1976).

This research raises serious questions about the validity of the distinction between internal and external attribution. An improved and multi-dimensional approach to the structure of perceived causality has been developed over some years by Weiner and colleagues (see Weiner, 1986), which we shall look at in the second half of the chapter.

Causal and other explanations in common sense

Although the vast majority of attribution research has dealt with *causal* attributions, common-sense explanations include a rich variety of other kinds of explanations. Two distinctions have received most attention.

Buss (1978), drawing on a long philosophical tradition, argued that *causes* and *reasons* are logically distinct categories for explaining different aspects of behaviour. He defined a cause as 'that which brings about a change' and a reason as 'that for which a change is brought about' (1978, p. 1311). Buss's article raised a number of interesting issues (see Locke and Pennington, 1982), yet it is fair to say that this distinction has had little impact on subsequent research.

The distinction between *excuses* and *justifications* has had greater impact, albeit in generating research on 'accounts' that extends well beyond attribution theory (see Harvey, Weber and Orbuch, 1990; McLaughlin, Cody and Read, 1992). Scott and Lyman (1968) distinguished between excuses (where one admits a bad or wrong act, but denies responsibility) and justifications (where one accepts responsibility, but denies the pejorative quality associated with it). Two published studies have shown that prison inmates' explanations for their violent behaviour were far more likely to be justifications than excuses (Felson and Ribner, 1981; Henderson and Hewstone, 1984). Henderson and Hewstone analysed these explanations using both attributional and accounting coding-schemes. This analysis showed the importance of distinguishing between the attribution of causality and that of responsibility. The offenders did sometimes accept their ultimate causal role (self-attribution) but they could excuse this behaviour (for example, claiming it was an accident) or justify it (for example, through the norm of self-defence).

The instigation of causal attributions

'Spontaneous' causal attribution

When do people make attributions? To answer this question, Weiner (1985) reviewed all the available evidence for what he called 'spontaneous' causal thinking. He deliberately excluded all studies that had measured attributions obtrusively, and concentrated on studies where normal (verbal) behaviour had been observed and coded. For example, Lau and Russell (1980) content-analysed attributions in the sports pages of newspapers and found, as one would predict, that unexpected outcomes elicited a greater number of attempts at explanation than did expected results. Similarly, Seligman and his colleagues have coded attributions from a variety of sources including diaries, election speeches, and psychotherapy sessions (see Peterson, Maier and Seligman, 1993). From his review Weiner concluded that there were two key factors in eliciting attributions: unexpected (vs. expected) events, and non-attainment (vs. attainment) of a goal. Before concluding that causal attributions are spontaneous, however, we recommend that you read the section on 'process' below.

Other instigating factors

Researchers have also identified a number of additional triggers of attributional activity, including loss of control (Liu and Steele, 1986), and negative mood states (Bohner, Bless, Schwarz and Strack, 1988). A quite different approach to the instigation of attributions involves looking at the conversational context in which attributions are made (see Hilton, 1990, 1991). For example, Turnbull and Slugoski (1988) demonstrated that speakers followed the kinds of rules discussed by Grice (1975) and only offered explanations that were informative from the listener's point of view. In other words, the same event might receive different explanations (or perhaps no explanation at all), depending on the conversational context.

Errors and biases in the attribution process

Classic models of the attribution process, as we saw earlier, tended to view the perceiver as a fairly rational person. Kelley's (1967) **ANOVA** model was actually given the status of a **normative model**, which indicated how perceivers *should*

NORMATIVE MODEL

Plate 7.1 Unexpected outcomes (Cameroon beating Argentina, 1:0, in the 1990 World Cup) are more likely to lead to attempted explanations than are expected results

make accurate causal attributions. In practice perceivers do not act like scientists in following such detailed and formal models. Rather, they make attributions quickly, using much less information and showing clear tendencies to offer certain sorts of explanation. We need, then, to consider more *descriptive* models of *how* perceivers actually make attributions.

A number of studies have concluded that, compared with scientists or statisticians, lay people are biased and make attribution 'errors'. Are we justified in referring to such tendencies as errors or biases? The term *error* should be reserved for deviations from a normative model (Fiske and Taylor, 1991) or departures from some accepted criterion of validity (Kruglanski and Ajzen, 1983). Such models or criteria are, however, rarely available for attribution research. For this reason the term *bias* should be used, although we still use the term *error* where the original, if inaccurate, label has stuck. A bias occurs if the social perceiver systematically distorts (e.g., over- or under-uses) some otherwise correct procedure (Fiske and Taylor, 1991). A rather different view has been put forward by Funder (1987), who argues that what have been termed 'errors' are largely a function of the laboratory context and might not result in 'mistakes' in the real world. From different perspectives, researchers have also shown that even well-established attributional biases can be reversed by re-framing problems or by subtle changes in the information presented (Cheng and Novick, 1992; Försterling, 1995). As we will see, such biases can help to provide a better descriptive analysis of causal attribution than do complex normative models, and we will look now at some of the best-known biases.

The fundamental attribution error

We referred earlier to the fundamental attribution error in discussing correspondent-inference theory. Many studies show that perceivers seem to attach too little weight to the situation and too much weight to the person (e.g. Jones and Harris, 1967; Ross, Amabile and Steinmetz, 1977). What causes this effect? Cognitive accounts emphasize the knowledge base of attributions and social information processing. One explanation is that the actor's behaviour is often more salient than the situation. A general salience explanation is supported by Rholes and Pryor's (1982) demonstration that increasing the ease with which situational constructs could be brought to mind increased the likelihood that situational factors would be considered in explaining a target's behaviour. Another cognitive explanation refers to differential rates of forgetting for situational and dispositional causes. Moore et al. (1979) and Peterson (1980) have reported that self-attributions made some time after the behaviour in question tended to emphasize dispositional causes more, and situational causes less, than attributions made immediately (but cf. Funder, 1982; Miller and Porter, 1980). Although there is evidence of shifts in attribution over time, these are not consistent enough to provide a complete explanation for the fundamental attribution error.

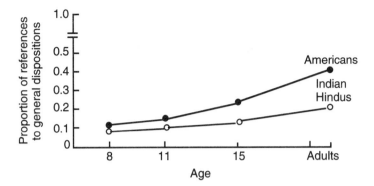

Figure 7.2 Cultural and developmental patterns of dispositional attribution (data from Miller, 1984, © 1984 by the American Psychological Association, adapted with the permission of the publisher and author)

An alternative explanation is cultural. Miller (1984) reported a developmental increase in reference to dispositional factors in an American sample, but an increase in reference to contextual factors in an Indian-Hindu sample (see figure 7.2). Studies have also shown that as children in a Western culture develop, they come to hold an increasingly dispositional view of the causes of behaviour (Higgins and Bryant, 1982).

Linguistic aspects of attribution may also help to explain the fundamental attribution error. A general dispositional theory may be culturally prescribed in our language, whereby certain inferences are systematically triggered by different types of verbs. Semin and Fiedler (1991) point out that the general bias towards explaining behaviour in terms of the internal dispositions of animated subjects (rather than external, environmental factors) corresponds to a pervasive tendency to use abstract language (see Fiedler, Semin and Bolten, 1989).

How fundamental is the fundamental attribution error (Harvey, Town and Yarkin, 1981)? Despite its name, there are circumstances under which people will over-attribute another person's behaviour to situational factors: most notably, when behaviour is inconsistent with prior expectations (Kulik, 1983), and when attention is focused on situational factors that could have produced a person's behaviour (e.g., Quattrone, 1982). In view of the fact that the bias is far from universal, and the criteria for accuracy are lacking, we should prefer a more modest label for this nonetheless important effect – the **correspondence bias** refers to the attribution of behaviour to dispositions, even in cases where we should not make such an attribution (Gilbert, 1995; Jones, 1990).

CORRESPONDENCE BIAS

Actor–observer differences

Jones and Nisbett (1972) proposed that actors tended to attribute their actions to the situation, whereas observers tended to attribute the same actions to stable personal dispositions. Watson (1982) has provided a comprehensive review of these **actor–observer differences**. He prefers the terms *self* and *other* rather than actor and observer, because in many studies there is not, in fact, one person acting while another observes. As Watson shows, there *is* an effect, but it is confined to self–other differences in situational attribution: self-attributions to situations are more commonly found than other-attributions to situations. For example, we attribute our own shyness in tutorials to the situation more than we do for other students.

Why does this self–other effect occur? There are three main explanations. One hypothesis is that self–other differences arise from the greater amount of *information* available to the actors or self-raters. We know more about our own past behaviour, and its variability across situations, than we know about the behaviour of others (e.g., Nisbett et al., 1973, study 2). There has been far more research on the, admittedly more interesting, hypothesis that *focus of attention* explains actor–observer differences. An ingenious experiment by Storms (1973) followed up the most fundamental difference between self and other: the fact that they have, quite literally, different 'points of view'. Storms set up a getting-acquainted conversation involving two strangers, A and B, each watched by one observer, and each filmed by one video camera (see figure 7.3). He hypothesized that it should be possible to change the way actors and observers interpret

Plate 7.2 If *you* feel shy in tutorials, you are more likely to attribute this to situational factors than you do for other students

behaviour by changing their visual orientations: actors who come to see themselves should make more dispositional attributions about their own behaviour; and observers who come to see another aspect of the actor's situation should become more situational in attributing the actor's behaviour. Storms compared three orientation conditions: *no video* (control); *same orientation* (video

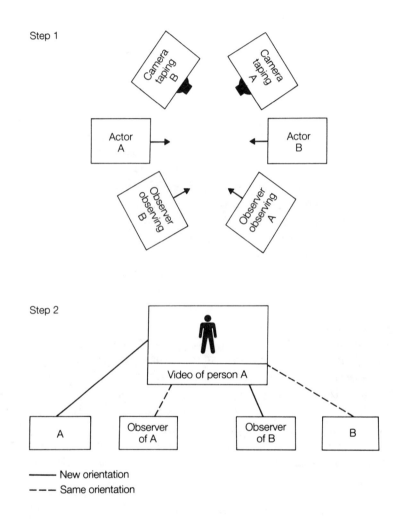

Figure 7.3 Testing the perceptual explanation for the actor–observer effect (Fiske and Taylor, 1991, based on Storms, 1973)

used simply to repeat the subject's original orientation); and *new orientation* (video used to reverse the orientation of actors and observers).

Storms found, as predicted, a reversal of actors' and observers' attributions when subjects were shown a new orientation: actors' attributions became *less* situational, and observers' became *more* situational. Unfortunately, Storms's findings have not always been replicated. It seems that the participant in the centre of the visual field (person A to the observer of A, person B to the observer of B) *is* rated as more causally important, but that this weighting does not always have a clear effect on dispositional and situational attributions (Taylor et al., 1979). Nevertheless Storms's findings underline the general point that methods exist for shifting the perspectives of actors and observers. **Salience** effects on the weighting of dispositional and situational attributions have also been found in other studies. For example, McArthur and Post (1977) had observers watch a conversation in which one conversant was made salient (by being illuminated with a bright light, for example), while the other was non-salient (dim light). Observers rated the salient conversant's behaviour as more dispositionally, and less situationally, caused.

SALIENCE

Linguistic factors have again been implicated in this bias. Semin and Fiedler (1989) found that actors and observers use different linguistic devices. Actor-attributors typically avoided statements about themselves in general and abstract terms which ascribed dispositional attributes to themselves in particular. In contrast, observer-attributors typically tended to describe actors in relatively more abstract terms that implied enduring, dispositional properties.

Buehler, Griffin and Ross (1995) have recently extended actor–observer differences to other kinds of judgement. They examined people's predictions of how long it would take them to complete various tasks and activities. They found evidence of an optimistic bias whereby people under-estimate their own completion times. But this optimistic bias disappears when observers make forecasts concerning the completion times of other people. Indeed, these observers' estimates show a pessimistic bias whereby observers over-estimate the time taken for completion by others. The same pattern emerged from a study on forecasts concerning the future course of romantic relationships. Actors were too optimistic and observers were too pessimistic. Thus differences in perspective are likely to have important and interesting effects on many different types of interpersonal relations.

Self-serving biases

Kingdon (1967) interviewed successful and unsuccessful American politicians about five months after elections and asked them to summarize the major factors (causes) that had led to their victories or defeats over the years. The politicians attributed their wins to internal factors – their hard work, personal service to constituents, matters of campaign strategy, building a reputation, and publicizing themselves. They attributed their losses to external factors – the party make-up of the district, the familiar name of their opponent, national and state trends, and lack of money. This is an example of a more general **self-serving bias**, whereby people are more likely to attribute their successes to internal dispositions, such as abilities, whereas they attribute failures to situational causes, such as the difficulty of the task. Taking credit for success and avoiding the blame for failure is something that most of us do at least some of the time. This bias is well established, but a controversy continues over whether it should be explained in cognitive (information-processing) or motivational (need-serving) terms. The debate has useful lessons for our attempts to explain any biases.

SELF-SERVING BIAS

Is it a *cognitive* bias? There are, in fact, two biases at issue here – a self-enhancing bias (taking credit for success) and a self-protecting bias (denying responsibility for failure). Miller and Ross (1975) claimed support only for the self-enhancing bias, and they argued that it could be explained by cognitive factors. For example, if people intend and expect to succeed, and if behaviour can be seen as due to their efforts (whereas failure occurs *despite* their efforts), then it may be perfectly reasonable to accept more responsibility for success than for failure.

Is it a *motivational* bias? Zuckerman's (1979) systematic summary of the literature concluded that the need to maintain self-esteem directly affected the attribution of task outcomes. But he argued that the strength of this effect depended on factors that included the extent to which self-esteem concerns were aroused in experimental subjects. He concluded that there are self-serving effects for both success and failure in most, but not all, experimental paradigms. Weary (1980) discussed self-serving attributions in the context of self-presentation. People may attribute outcomes in ways that avoid embarrassment and/or gain public approval, especially under public vs private conditions (e.g., Weary et al., 1982).

Researchers have tried to distinguish the cognitive and motivational accounts, but they have encountered a number of problems. It has been claimed that the cognitive explanations actually contain motivational aspects (Zuckerman, 1979), and that the cognitive research programme is so flexible that it can generate the predictions of virtually any motivational theory (Tetlock and Levi, 1982). In addition, motivational factors can have an effect on information processing. Thus it appears impossible to choose between the cognitive and the motivational perspectives (see Tetlock and Manstead, 1985).

Group-serving biases

There is now extensive evidence that attribution biases are influenced by group membership. For example, success and especially failure by members of the 'ingroup' and 'outgroup' may receive quite different explanations (see Hewstone, 1990). This bias acts to preserve and protect stereotypes of the ingroup ('we are intelligent') and of the outgroup ('they are stupid'). Islam and Hewstone (1993) investigated intergroup attributions by members of majority and minority groups. Group members attributed imagined positive and negative behaviours by outgroup and ingroup members, and then gave their affective reactions. The groups used were Hindus (the minority) and Muslims (the majority) in Bangladesh. The results showed robust intergroup attributional bias by members of the Muslim majority group; the Muslims both favoured their own group and derogated the Hindus. In contrast, Hindus' attributions showed only a very mild form of ingroup-favouritism. Islam and Hewstone also found that causal dimensions were predictive of negative and, especially, positive affects, but primarily for outcomes associated with ingroup actors. For example, for Muslims, feelings of happiness and pride were maximized when the cause of a positive outcome by a Muslim was perceived as internal and global.

Again, linguistic factors may provide at least part of the explanation for this bias. Maass, Salvi, Arcuri and Semin (1989) reported that the same visually-presented positive act was encoded at a higher level of abstraction (for example, by the use of certain types of verbs, or specific adjectives) when performed by an ingroup versus an outgroup member; and the same negative act was encoded at a lower level of abstraction when performed by an ingroup versus an outgroup member. Given that information encoded at an abstract level is relatively resistant to disconfirmation and implies high stability over time (Semin and Fiedler, 1991), this 'linguistic intergroup bias' could contribute to the persistence of stereotypic beliefs (see chapter 17).

The process of causal attribution

Having looked at some of the most prominent attribution biases, it does seem that causal attribution may often be a rapid process based on limited information processing. A major new influence on attribution research has been the rise of social cognition (see Smith, 1994; and chapter 6 of this volume). As social psychologists have become more interested in how much, and how, social information is processed they have used a variety of sophisticated cognitive measures, all of which are attempts to sidestep a major methodological problem – the fact that we can never tap directly what is going on in the heads of our research subjects (Taylor and Fiske, 1981). Borrowing from cognitive psychology, social psychologists have begun to use measures such as visual attention, information search, memory and, especially, response time.

Smith and Miller's (1983) study illustrates some of the benefits of response-time methodology (see also Macrae and Shepherd, 1991). Smith and Miller distinguished the different types of inference used in attribution research – for example, causal judgements, trait judgements about an actor, and judgements of the actor's intent – and measured how long subjects took to make each kind of inference. The rationale for using response-time measures is simple (Hamilton, 1988). If the question corresponds to a process that occurs spontaneously during the initial comprehension of behaviour, then the answer to the question will be readily available and subjects' response time will be short. In contrast, if the

Table 7.1 Response times to different questions in Smith and Miller's (1983) research

Question	Response time[a]	
	Study 1	Study 2
Gender	2.14	4.24
Intention	2.41	4.56
True trait	2.48	4.37
False trait	3.02	5.09
Person cause	3.42	5.68
Situation cause	3.80	6.05

[a]Response times are in seconds. In Study 1 responses indicate question-answering time, in Study 2 responses indicate time taken to read a sentence and answer a question about it. *Source*: Data drawn from Smith and Miller, 1983, © by the American Psychological Association, reprinted with the permission of the publisher and author.

question asks about something not inferred from the comprehension stage, then the subject must retrieve the relevant information and make the inference before responding to the question, leading to a longer response time.

Smith and Miller reported that judgements of intention and trait inferences did not take significantly more time than a 'control' question concerning the actor's gender (see table 7.1). This finding suggested that these judgements may also be made during comprehension, or at least that they could be easily inferred. The slowest responses were to person-cause and situation-cause questions. Smith and Miller concluded that the 'basic' attribution (probably made during the initial process of comprehension) was a judgement of intention or a trait attribution or both (see Winter et al., 1985), *not* a person- or situation-cause. The longer response time for person- and situation-cause questions could also be due to the fact that people are not used to thinking about and answering questions in these terms. From these data causal processing does not appear to be automatic. What occurs during the comprehension phase seems to be a simple trait inference, with no attempt to understand the causal basis of the behaviour.

This kind of process analysis offers methodological precision and theoretical sophistication. But process analysis also has limitations. First, measures such as response times are best used to rule out alternative models rather than to support a particular model. Secondly, by definition the attempt to measure cognitive processes interferes with normal thinking. Measures such as recall and response times may not be informative about normal, extra-laboratory information use. Thirdly, and consequently, there may be a trade-off between precision of measurement and generalizability of results. Thus we see mini-experiments with cognitive measures as a complement to studies of thinking and behaviour outside the laboratory, as we now see in considering applied research on attribution theory.

Applications of Attribution Theory

Why is it claimed that 'attribution theory is the most important development in social psychology' (Anderson, 1991, p. 12)? After all, studies on attribution *theories* (e.g. correspondent-inference theory, Kelley's ANOVA model) no longer dominate basic research as they did during their heyday in the 1970s and early 1980s. A complete answer to this question requires consideration of the application of attribution theory. It is no exaggeration to say that few applied problems have escaped analysis from the perspective of attribution theory. Some idea of the scope of application is indicated by the following very incomplete list of problems analysed from an attribution perspective: shyness, helping, mortality in old age, smoking, stigma, intergroup conflict, depression, sales performance, HIV infection, spouse and child abuse, pain management, physical illness, anxiety, international relations, sport, and consumer satisfaction (see Weiner, 1995). Extensive attribution literatures now exist in many applied areas.

A key element in understanding the importance accorded attribution theory therefore lies in the extent to which it lends itself to the analysis of applied problems. Weiner (1995) argues that attribution theory has been so amenable to practical use because many of the pioneers in this area were committed to both theory development and theory utilization and did basic research on issues that lend themselves to application. Before illustrating some applications of attribution theory, it is important to note that the relation between the attribution models described earlier and applied research is often not straightforward. There are three reasons for this circumstance. First, some attribution principles (such as the covariation principle) are so pervasive that they are no longer associated with a particular model (e.g. the ANOVA model) and they often remain implicit in analyses of applied problems.

Secondly, findings obtained in basic attribution research cannot simply be extrapolated to applied settings without further examination. For example, much basic attribution research examines attributions made for hypothetical others, but it has been found that attributions vary as a function of (a) expected interaction with the attribution target (Knight and Vallacher, 1981), (b) the nature of the attributor's relationship (acquaintance, friend, spouse) to the attribution target (Taylor and Koivumaki, 1976), and (c) the affect experienced towards the attribution target (Regan, Straus and Fazio, 1974).

Thirdly, applied work has generated ideas that are not found in the writings on attribution theory and has also led to slightly different perspectives on some existing attribution ideas. An example concerns individual differences in attributions; references to constructs such as attributional style (labelled 'explanatory style' by some researchers) are frequently found in applied writings despite their absence from the models described earlier in the chapter. Similarly, the analysis of responsibility attribution, which deals not with who or what caused an event but with accountability for the event, has been considerably expanded in applied work.

In the remainder of this section, we illustrate the application of attribution theory in three broad areas, motivation, clinical psychology, and close relationships.

Attributions and motivation

Recall that statistics exam that you have just failed. No doubt you will experience some general negative affect. But what specific affect will you feel? Who will be the target of that affect? And what implications, if any, will this experience have for your future behaviour? Weiner (1986, 1995) has developed an attributional theory of motivation that provides answers to such questions. According to Weiner, the specific answers will depend on what you perceive to be the cause of your exam failure.

Plate 7.3 Your attributions for exam failure are likely to affect motivation and affect

Let us say you were distracted by extra-curricular activities and you just did not study for this test. You would probably feel some guilt. If your tutor believed that your failure was due to lack of effort he or she would most probably experience anger and act in a punitive manner towards you. After all, you could have made an effort and cut back on these other activities. But what if you attributed your failure to lack of intellectual ability? In this case you would probably experience shame. If you viewed your ability as something that was unlikely to change, you would also experience hopelessness and expect to fail on future statistics exams. Perhaps you might even withdraw from studying psychology altogether. In this case, your teacher would most probably experience pity or sympathy and be inclined to act in a helpful manner. Contrast these responses with the response you would have if you thought you had failed because the marking was unfair or the test was inappropriately difficult. In these circumstances you would be most likely to experience anger towards the person who marked or who set the test and you would not draw any adverse conclusions about your performance on other psychology tests.

This example contains the essential features of Weiner's (1986) extensively researched theory of motivation. It can be summarized in the following way:

Event (exam failure) → outcome-dependent affect → causal attribution →
  psychological consequences (future expectancies, affect) → behaviour

Critical to this theory is the analysis of causal attribution. Weiner offers a *logical* analysis of the underlying dimensions of causes, arguing that it is these dimensions that determine the psychological consequences of attributions.

Following Heider, he initially focused on the locus of causality but soon found that achievement evaluation was influenced more by effort than by ability despite the fact that both are internal causes (Weiner and Kukla, 1970). This led him to postulate that effort and ability differ in causal stability, or lability over time, and to show that expectations relating to future performance are determined by causal stability rather than causal locus. This was an important advance and the resulting fourfold classification of causes (see table 7.2) dominated this research area in the 1970s.

Again, however, differential evaluation of causes within one of the cells led to further refinement of the topology; lack of effort was found to elicit more punishment than poor strategy as a cause of failure, even though both are internal, variable causes. Weiner (1979) therefore postulated a third causal dimension, which he labelled 'controllability'. Thus, effort and ability differ not only in stability but also in controllability and either dimension may be responsible for their differential evaluation. As it turns out, controllability is the mediator of reward and punishment (Weiner, 1995).

Weiner's three-dimensional scheme (locus × stability × controllability) became the foundation for a general theory of motivation and emotion. It was later

Table 7.2 A 2×2 scheme for the perceived causes of achievement outcome

	Internal	External
Stable	Ability	Task difficulty
Unstable	Effort	Luck

Source: From B. Weiner et al., *Perceiving the Causes of Success and Failure*, Morristown, NJ: General Learning Press, 1971. Copyright 1971. Reprinted with permission.

extended to classify causes in the social as well as the achievement domain and each dimension was found to be associated with specific affects:

locus → pride, self esteem;
stability → hopefulness, hopelessness;
controllability → shame, guilt [when self-directed] and anger, gratitude, pity [when directed towards others].

Although a considerable body of research has provided support for this theory, it is not without problems. An important concern is whether the everyday perception of causes matches the logical analysis offered by Weiner. This issue can be broken down into at least three questions: do people naturally organize causes using the dimensions postulated? Are the dimensions truly different (orthogonal to each other) or are they correlated, suggesting that fewer than three dimensions are needed? Can specific causes be mapped onto these dimensions or is the perception of specific causes idiosyncratic to perceivers and/or situations?

Fewer studies have addressed these questions than one might expect. However, across the dozen or so relevant studies there is strong evidence that people organize causes along various dimensions. However, they may not be limited to Weiner's three dimensions. For example, several studies distinguish an intentional–unintentional dimension. In one of the few studies examining causes outside the achievement domain, Passer, Kelley and Michela (1978) investigated the dimensions underlying causes given for interpersonal conflict. As shown in figure 7.4, they found evidence of a dimension that reflected the attitude towards the attribution target. Weiner, however, has argued that the bulk of the evidence supports his three-dimensional topology. Although reasonable, this is not an entirely satisfactory argument because of the nature of the available data. It is limited not only by the number of studies conducted but also by the fact that unless a broad sample of causes is investigated, the dimensions that emerge will be constrained by the causes examined. In other words, the structure uncovered by an investigator will depend, in part, on how stimuli are sampled, and the majority of available studies sample stimuli from only one domain, most frequently the achievement domain.

The second question concerning the orthogonality or separateness of causal dimensions is more easily answered. At the empirical level, causal dimensions are intercorrelated (e.g. Anderson, 1983). However, the magnitude of the correlations shows that for any two dimensions there is more unshared variability than shared variability. In addition, it makes conceptual sense to keep the dimensions separate just as it makes sense to keep height and weight separate, even though they are highly correlated.

Turning to the final question, it is clear that there is variability across people and situations in mapping specific causes onto causal dimensions. For example, Krantz and Rude (1984) asked respondents to classify four widely studied causes in the achievement domain (ability, effort, task difficulty, luck) in terms of the three causal dimensions postulated by Weiner. Few respondents classified causes on the dimensions in the expected manner. Just under half, for instance, classified ability as unstable. Individual differences in the perception of supposedly 'stable'

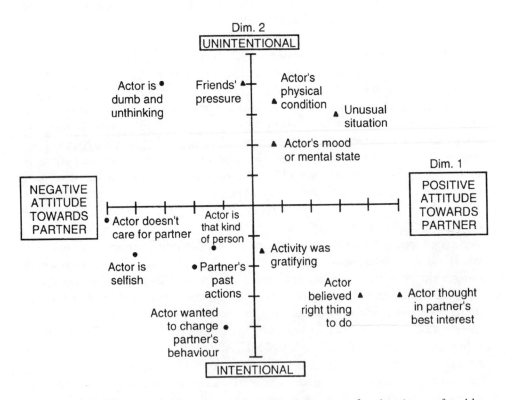

Figure 7.4 Two-dimensional solution for 'actor' condition; the types of explanations preferred by actors are indicated by triangles (from Passer et al., 1978, © 1978 by the American Psychological Association, reprinted with the permission of the publisher and author)

causes (such as intelligence) have subsequently been investigated and given rise to another theory of motivation that divides people into 'incremental' theorists (intelligence/ability can be increased through effort) and 'entity' theorists (intelligence/ability is fixed; see Dweck and Legett, 1988). Such individual differences mean that psychologists cannot always accurately map causes onto underlying dimensions. This does not invalidate Weiner's topology; it simply reminds us that it is important to evaluate the respondent's perception of a cause.

Other objections could be raised about Weiner's application of attribution theory. For instance, most of the research supporting the theory rests on the use of rather 'artificial' procedures (ratings of hypothetical scenarios, impoverished stimuli, laboratory-manipulated success and failure, for example) and assesses respondents' statements about how they will behave (their behavioural intentions) rather than their actual behaviour. However, such concerns should not blind us to the fact that the attributional analysis of motivation has led to the documentation of highly robust and easily replicated phenomena. This alone attests to its usefulness. In addition, it has resulted in important advances in attribution theory. Whatever one thinks of Weiner's theory, one cannot help being impressed by its comprehensiveness. We end this section by outlining briefly a recent development of the theory that increases its scope even further.

In his most recent book, Weiner (1995) demonstrates how judgement of responsibility can be used to generalize theoretical principles initially derived from the study of achievement evaluation to a wide variety of behaviours, resulting in a general theory of social conduct. Although not always cognizant of prior work on responsibility judgements, Weiner now accords responsibility attributions a central role, in that causal attributions are postulated to give rise to judgements of responsibility and it is these judgements that determine affective experience and direct behaviour. Thus, the sequence outlined earlier has been altered to:

Event (exam failure) → outcome-dependent affect → causal attribution →
responsibility judgement → affect (anger, sympathy) → behaviour

The value of this extension lies not so much in its novelty but in the impressive body of evidence marshalled to support it and in the extent to which it offers a comprehensive theory of social conduct.

Attributions and clinical psychology

Since the inception of experimental social psychology there have been attempts to apply social-psychological principles in clinical psychology (Snyder and Forsyth, 1991). Not surprisingly, therefore, applications of attribution theory to clinical problems emerged soon after the publication of correspondent-inference theory and the ANOVA model. Some of the applications, especially early ones, are explicitly related to classic attribution models but many others simply reflect an attributional perspective and are not related to basic attribution research. Indeed, in some applications it is clear that the authors have never read the most basic statements of attribution theory in the social-psychological literature!

Unlike the application to motivation, the attempts to apply attribution theory in clinical psychology are so diverse that it is difficult to do them justice in a brief summary (for an excellent treatment of this topic, see Försterling, 1988). With this caveat in mind, we begin with an actual case-study (published in Johnson, Ross and Mastria, 1977) and derive from it a simple dichotomy that can be used to organize clinical applications of attribution theory.

Case-study

Mr J. came to the attention of psychiatrists when he claimed that he was being sexually aroused and brought to orgasm by a 'warm form'. These experiences were distressing to Mr J. and after disclosing them he was diagnosed as schizophrenic, he was institutionalized, and administered Thorazine, an anti-psychotic drug. Although the psychiatric staff believed Mr J. to be mentally ill, careful observation showed that he was inadvertently stimulating himself through leg movements. The 'delusional behaviour' disappeared when the patient was taught to attribute the cause of his sexual arousal to his leg movements and it remained absent through the six-month follow-up period.

The case of Mr J. illustrates that a client's beliefs about the cause of behaviour can be dysfunctional. In this case the absence of an understandable cause for the erotic experience resulted in misattribution ('delusional thinking') that led Mr J. to be seen as insane. Once the misattribution was diagnosed, appropriate treatment could proceed. In Mr J.'s case, 'reattribution training' took place in that a plausible, alternative cause was offered for his experience. According to the discounting principle, this should have lessened belief in the first cause, which is in fact what happened.

An important distinction illustrated by this case is that between *diagnosis* (determining the nature of the problem) and *treatment* (intervening to bring about more adaptive functioning). Although there is an interplay between diagnosis and treatment, most clinical applications of attribution theory can be classified according to these two categories. However, there is a huge imbalance in the distribution of studies that fall into the two categories. The vast majority analyse problems in attributional terms, with far fewer investigating attributional treatments. Each will be examined in turn.

Misattribution

The phenomenon of misattribution, especially of physiological arousal, was the subject of many of the early attempts to understand clinical problems. For example, Storms and Nisbett (1970) demonstrated that insomniacs who attributed the arousal that kept them awake to a neutral source (a pill), reported a reduction in the time it took to fall asleep as compared with subjects who could not attribute their arousal to the pill. Although plagued by a host of problems (such as difficulty in replicating findings, the absence of attribution measures to support the misattribution interpretation; Fincham 1983), the ideas that prompted research on misattribution are still helpful in understanding clinical problems.

More recent research has focused on multiple attribution dimensions and shown that attributions which do not specifically reflect lack of knowledge about the cause of a problem, as in the case of Mr J., may be maladaptive. For example, there is considerable evidence that seeing oneself as the cause of a negative event, viewing the cause as stable or unlikely to change, and as global or affecting various areas of one's life, is associated with several failures of adaptation (see Buchanan and Seligman, 1995; Peterson et al., 1993).

Learned helplessness and depression

Perhaps the most intensively investigated problem is the phenomenon of **learned helplessness**. Because it has been proposed as a model of depression and has stimulated a great deal of research in its own right, we briefly examine learned helplessness before illustrating applications of attribution theory pertaining to treatment.

LEARNED HELPLESSNESS

Learned helplessness describes the response pattern that often occurs following exposure to noncontingent or uncontrollable outcomes. For example, dogs exposed to uncontrollable shock, compared with animals in a control group, are passive (motivational deficit), unemotional (emotional deficit), and fail to learn when the shock is avoidable (cognitive deficit). This response pattern is similar to the symptoms of depression and has generated considerable interest in learned helplessness. To account for human depression an attributional reformulation of learned helplessness was proposed (Abramson, Seligman and Teasdale, 1978). It was argued that causal attributions determine responses to noncontingent events. The model proposed is shown below:

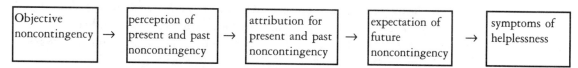

(taken from Abramson et al., 1978)

Again, however, it is the underlying dimensions of the attributions that are considered important. Specifically, the internal–external dimension relates to self-esteem deficits; the extent to which the cause is global rather than specific, or affects many areas of life rather than one area of life, is related to the generality of symptoms; and the stable–unstable dimension affects their chronicity. Even though no attempt was made to link these dimensions to Kelley's (1967) criteria of consensus, distinctiveness, and consistency, they are similar if not identical. What is different, however, is that unlike the ANOVA model, individual differences in responses on the dimensions have become the focus of attention in the attributional reformulation of learned helplessness. **Attributional style** is conceived as a personality trait that mediates between negative events and depression. A 'depressive attributional style' refers to the tendency to view negative events as caused by factors that are internal, stable and global.

As a model of clinical depression, learned helplessness has been controversial. Over 100 studies using some 15,000 participants have firmly established that there is at least a moderate correlation (about +0.3) between attributional style and depression (Sweeney, Anderson and Bailey, 1986). The problem is that such a correlation does not address the role of attributions in producing depression as we cannot infer causation from correlation. There is some evidence that attributions also predict depressive symptoms at a later time (e.g., Nolen-Hoeksma, Girgus and Seligman, 1992) and that attributions predict increases in depressed mood for students who receive bad marks in an exam (Metalsky, Halberstadt and Abramson, 1987). Such data provide stronger grounds for believing that attributions lead to depression but it is still only correlational evidence (albeit longitudinal).

Because it is unethical to induce clinical depression, experimental evidence relating attributions to depression comes from laboratory analogue studies that examine depressed mood. Although they often yield results consistent with the reformulated model of learned helplessness, it is difficult to generalize from temporary mood changes induced in the laboratory to clinical depression. Such a problem is not encountered when therapy-outcome research is examined. In one relevant study (Hollon, Shelton and Loosen, 1991), depressed patients were randomly assigned to receive 12 weeks of treatment comprising cognitive therapy, or tricyclic antidepressant drugs, or both treatments. All groups experienced relief from depression. Interestingly, there was a correlation between change in attribution and change in depression in both the cognitive (correlation of 0.77) and the combined treatments (correlation of 0.55) conditions. Although they are encouraging, there are at least two problems with these results. First, there was no correlation in the drug treatment group. Why would this happen? Secondly even if attributions bring about relief from depression, it does not logically follow that they caused the depression.

What can we conclude about learned helplessness? First, crucial tests of the attributional reformulation of learned helplessness have not been conducted. Even though examination of expectancies, the most direct determinant of helplessness, is considered crucial to testing the validity of the model (Alloy, 1982), such examination has not occurred. Similarly, examination of the *pattern* of attribution responses postulated (internal, stable, global) has been forgone in favour of examining mean scores across dimensions. But mean scores can be generated by many different patterns of responses (Horneffer and Fincham, 1995). Finally, we know very little about the developmental origins of the attributions associated with learned helplessness (Fincham and Cain, 1986), an important omission if we seek to prevent learned helplessness.

Notwithstanding these concerns, several converging lines of evidence suggest that attributions are important for understanding depression, or what is perhaps more likely, a subtype of depression. Although the causal picture is still unclear it seems safe to conclude that the attributions outlined in the model are a vulnerability factor that can lead to depression in the presence of a stressful life event. Perhaps more important is the fact that this work has led to a focus on attributions that have now been associated with numerous problems. In our judgement, the real contribution to emerge from the reformulated model is an increased understanding not of depression but of numerous other problems where application of the causal dimensions postulated in the model have advanced understanding of the problem. Before turning to the example of close relationships, we briefly consider the impact of attribution theory on treatment.

Attributional retraining

Bandura has stated that 'The value of a theory is ultimately judged by the power of the procedures it generates to effect psychological changes' (Bandura, 1977, p. 4). Numerous studies demonstrate convincingly that inducing unstable attributions (such as lack of effort) for failure increases performance and persistence in achievement tasks (see Försterling, 1988, for a review of 'attributional retraining'). Although promising, the generalizability of this finding to many therapy contexts is open to question because of the exclusive focus on changing attributions for academic or experimental tasks in non-clinical, child samples. Perhaps the most significant limitation of this literature is the use of clinically naive interventions in analogue studies. For example, in a widely cited study the 25-session intervention consisted of saying to a child after each experimentally induced failure 'that means you should have tried harder' (Dweck, 1975). An attempt to use this intervention in a clinical context resulted in a child telling the experimenter in no uncertain terms, 'I am sick of you telling me that I'm not trying and don't tell me that again' (Rhodes, 1977, p. 64). Moreover, the relative efficacy of such interventions is misleading because they are often not compared with more common clinical interventions. For example, Dweck (1975) compared the attribution intervention with one in which children received continual success. Thus, the alternative intervention consisted of 'treating' a problem that involved reaction to failure by avoidance of failure!

In retrospect, the claims for an 'attribution therapy' have been overstated and have detracted attention from the legitimate, but more restricted, role of attributions in therapy. With some exceptions (such as the case of Mr J.), the proper role of reattribution in therapy is as a technique utilized as part of a more broadly based intervention (for example, as in cognitive therapy, Beck, Rush, Shaw and Emery, 1979). In particular, clients' attributions for behaviour change require attention if the effect of the change is to be maximized. For example, a depressed client who is induced to establish social contact with others may not change his negative beliefs about himself if he attributes the change to the therapist's skill, luck, or the friendliness of other people.

In view of the above arguments the absence of research on an 'attribution therapy' is less problematic than it might have first appeared to be. Close examination shows that most therapeutic approaches include attention to patient attributions even though they might not discuss attributions explicitly. In fact, it is hard to conceive of a therapy that does not deal with attributions in some form or another. From this perspective, attribution theory appears to be a huge success in terms of Bandura's criterion for a good theory. However, the paucity of research on attribution as an adjunctive therapy technique remains troubling.

Close relationships

Research on close relationships has recently emerged as a specialty area and social psychology has taken its place alongside other disciplines in an attempt to understand such relationships (see chapter 12). Attribution theory has been enormously productive in this field (cf. Harvey, 1987). Most attributional research has focused on understanding partnership/marriage and the findings in this area are among the most robust in the relationship literature (cf. Fincham and Bradbury, 1991).

Stimulated in part by learned-helplessness theory, initial attributional research examined the hypothesis that attributions might help us understand relationship satisfaction and the breakdown of relationships. Specifically, interest in attributions rested on the assumptions that attributions:

(a)   maintain current levels of relationship satisfaction and can initiate changes in relationship satisfaction; and

(b)   mediate or give rise to the response one partner makes to the other's behaviour.

We examine each of these assumptions in turn.

Attributions and relationship satisfaction

In distressed, compared with non-distressed, marriages attributions are hypothesized to accentuate the impact of negative partner behaviour (e.g., 'she was home late because she doesn't care about me') and minimize the impact of positive partner behaviour (e.g., 'he only brought me flowers because he wanted to have sex'). Notice that once again the critical element is the characteristics of the causal attribution (for example, for negative behaviours the cause is located in the partner, is global or influential in other areas of the marriage, and is stable or likely to be present in the future). In contrast to these *distress-maintaining* attributions, satisfied partners are thought to make *relationship-enhancing* attributions that minimize the impact of negative partner behaviours (e.g., 'she was home late because the traffic was heavier than usual') and accentuate positive partner behaviours (e.g., 'he brought me flowers because he really appreciates me').

Although attributions in close relationships usually focus on responsibility and blame, researchers did not initially investigate these constructs and unwittingly followed the practice in basic attribution research where data on causal judgements served as the basis for statements about responsibility and blame. This practice is intriguing because there is a body of attribution research that clearly documents differences in responses to questions regarding cause, responsibility, and blame, and shows that lawful relationships exist between these different judgements (see Fincham and Jaspars, 1980; Shultz and Schleifer, 1983; Shaver, 1985). Briefly stated, causal judgements deal with who or what caused an event (that is, they are primarily descriptive) whereas responsibility and blame deal with accountability for the event and with sanctions (that is, with evaluation) once the cause of the event is known. As noted earlier, this important distinction has now become a central one in Weiner's (1995) latest theoretical writings.

Soon after research on attributions in close relationships began, Fincham (1985) attempted to expand the attributions studied in close relationships. In his research spouses were asked to rate responsibility criteria such as their partner's motivation, intent and blameworthiness (these are called 'responsibility' attributions as partners in close relationships do not appear to distinguish responsibility from blame; Fincham and Bradbury, 1992). Just as in the case of causal dimensions, responsibility attributions can be seen as relationship enhancing (for example, positive partner behaviour is seen as intentional, unselfishly motivated and praiseworthy) and distress maintaining (for example, negative partner behaviour is seen as intentional, selfishly motivated and blameworthy). The attributional hypothesis can therefore be examined in relation to causal and responsibility attributions. The nature of the hypothesis is summarized in figure 7.5

Numerous studies have examined the attributions of distressed and non-distressed spouses, with marital distress being defined by spouses' reports on standard measures of marital satisfaction. Across a variety of attributional stimuli (e.g., couple problems, partner behaviour), attributions have been shown to be related to marital satisfaction (see Bradbury and Fincham, 1990).

An interesting variant of the attribution hypothesis has been less widely examined. This variant states that attributional style or consistency in attribution responses is related to marital distress. Thus interest shifts from mean scores to variability of responses. Such variability can be viewed in two ways: consistency in responding to items assessing the same attribution dimension and consistent use of particular patterns of responses across attributional dimensions (e.g., a partner-stable-global pattern). Baucom, Sayers and Duhe (1989) found some evidence to support the attribution-style hypothesis in that (a) less variable or

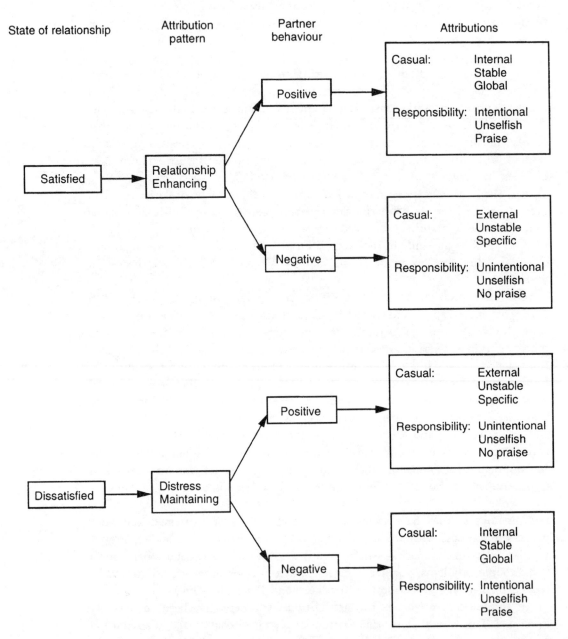

Figure 7.5 The attributional hypothesis in close relationships: attributions vary as a function of the state of the relationship and the nature of partner behaviour

more consistent responses to items assessing the same attribution dimension were associated with marital distress, (b) use of fewer patterns of response across attribution dimensions was associated with husbands' distress, and (c) reliance on a single pattern of response across dimensions was related to wives' distress. Although these results are promising, Horneffer and Fincham (1995) were only able to replicate them in part; they found that the use of theoretically derived benign and non-benign patterns of responding across attribution dimensions was related to marital distress. It therefore remains to be determined whether attribution style, conceptualized in terms of consistency of responses, exhibits as robust an association with marital satisfaction as the attribution mean scores that have typically been investigated.

Although an association exists between attributions and relationship satisfaction, it does not tell us whether attributions initiate changes in marital satisfaction rather than vice versa. This issue is a very difficult one to investigate owing to ethical problems in manipulating the variables involved, and to the fact that marital satisfaction tends to be quite stable over time. Nevertheless, several studies have been conducted in an attempt to address this issue by examining the association between attributions and satisfaction over time.

In an initial study, attributions and satisfaction were assessed at two points in time separated by a 10–12-month interval (Fincham and Bradbury, 1987). Initial causal and responsibility attributions were used to predict later satisfaction, after statistically controlling for initial satisfaction. For wives, both types of attributions predicted later satisfaction. However, earlier satisfaction did not predict later attributions, suggesting that attributions influence satisfaction and not vice versa. Why significant results were obtained only for wives was unclear, though the small sample (39 couples) may account for this finding.

A second 12-month longitudinal study using a larger sample was therefore conducted (Fincham and Bradbury, 1993). Two important improvements were made in this study. The first addressed the possibility that depression and self-esteem might account for the attribution–satisfaction association. Because both depression and self-esteem are related to attributions and to marital satisfaction, it is reasonable to ask whether attributions and satisfaction are related simply because of their association with these variables. Secondly, the study excluded people with chronic depression or marital distress. This is important because depression and distress tend to be quite stable, which can artificially inflate longitudinal relations between them. It was found that attributions were still related to satisfaction even when depression and self-esteem were statistically controlled. Interestingly, a recent study replicated this finding in showing that attributions account for unique variance in marital satisfaction independently of both depression and anger (Senchak and Leonard, 1993). Perhaps more importantly, attributions predicted later satisfaction for both husbands and wives but satisfaction did not predict later attributions.

In a final study using a sample of newlywed husbands, maladaptive responsibility attributions contributed to declines in reported satisfaction 12 months later but not vice versa (Fincham, Bradbury et al., 1995), thereby showing that the longitudinal pattern of findings extends beyond the population of relatively stable and established married couples. The available evidence is therefore consistent with the view that attributions initiate changes in satisfaction.

Attributions and responses to behaviour

What of the second assumption that stimulated interest in attributions and close relationships? Do attributions guide responses to partner behaviour? This question was addressed initially by asking whether attributions correlate with behaviour. Early studies supported such an association for attributions (see Bradbury and Fincham, 1990) but did not show that the attribution–behaviour relation occurred independently of marital satisfaction, a major shortcoming in view of the documented association between behaviour and marital satisfaction. With marital satisfaction partialled from the association, it has recently been shown that (a) wives' distress-maintaining responsibility attributions were related to less effective problem-solving behaviours coded from a marital interaction (Bradbury and Fincham, 1992, study 1); and (b) husbands' and wives' distress-maintaining causal and responsibility attributions were related to increased rates of negative behaviour during a problem-solving discussion (Bradbury and Fincham, 1992, study 2), and to increased rates of specific negative affects (Fincham and Bradbury, 1992).

Finding that spouses' attributions are related to their behaviour is encouraging but does not address whether the attributions guide responses to particular partner behaviours and not others. For example, attributions are thought to be evoked by and guide responses to negative behaviour. Consistent with this view, Bradbury and Fincham (1992, study 2) found that wives' maladaptive attributions correlated with the tendency to reciprocate negative husband behaviour, the hallmark of marital distress. But again, are such relations simply due to the documented relation between marital satisfaction and behaviour? Bradbury and Fincham (1992) ruled out this possibility by showing that the correlations remained significant even when satisfaction was partialled out of the relation. Finally, they also showed that these attribution–behaviour relations are stronger for distressed spouses.

Although impressive, such correlational data can never be as convincing as experimental data for inferring causation. It is therefore worth noting that the data reviewed are consistent with the findings of the one experimental study conducted on this topic (Fincham and Bradbury, 1988). In this study, spouses read an unflattering description of themselves which they thought was either written spontaneously by their partner ('partner locus'), or solicited by the experimenter ('experimenter locus'). In this latter case, they could *discount* the

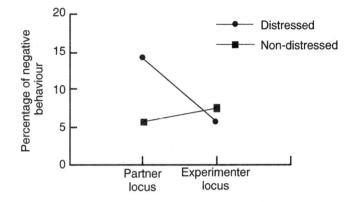

Figure 7.6 Percentage of negative spouse behaviour displayed after reading partner's description

partner's role in producing the negative description and so one might expect that there would be less negative behaviour towards the partner in this condition. Although individually tailored, the descriptions were in fact equally negative across both conditions. But, as figure 7.6 shows, they elicited different reactions in distressed spouses during a five-minute discussion that took place after the descriptions were read. Thus, both correlational and experimental findings are consistent with the view that attributions influence marital behaviour.

Critical issues

Despite the tremendous progress made in the study of attributions in close relationships the research is not without problems. One of the most obvious problems concerns the heavy reliance on self-report. Both attributions and marital satisfaction are usually measured using questionnaires and the relation between them could be inflated by common-method variance. It is therefore worth noting that an attribution–satisfaction association has been obtained using attributions coded from conversations (e.g., Holtzworth-Munroe and Jacobson, 1988; Stratton, Heard, et al., 1986). Such data rule out the idea that the association simply reflects method variance as different methods are used to assess attributions (observation) and satisfaction (self-report). In a similar vein, it is often argued that the use of self-report shows little more than that a person's negativity is expressed consistently across questionnaires. However, Karney, Bradbury et al. (1994) show that the attribution–satisfaction association remains significant even when negative affectivity is statistically controlled.

Perhaps more important than the above considerations is the restricted range of issues in close relationships that have been analysed from an attribution perspective. For example, we know relatively little about the role of attributions in different phases of relationships. Yet we might expect attributions to be more salient in phases of the relationship where there is a lot of change (for example, early in the relationship as partners get to know each other, and in the termination phase of the relationship) than when the relationship is relatively stable. Similarly, little is known about attributions that are communicated between partners. What is the relation between such communicated attributions and attributions that remain private? And how do communicated attributions influence the relationship? Although it has not escaped attention, more also needs to be learned about the conditions which instigate attributions in relationships.

Notwithstanding these and other limitations, available data on attributions in close relationships are quite impressive. There is clearly a robust association between attributions and marital satisfaction, and several artifactual explanations for the association (such as depression, negative affectivity, self-esteem) have been ruled out. Moreover, extant data are consistent with the view that attributions maintain current levels of satisfaction and can initiate changes in satisfaction. Finally, there is an association between attributions and observed relationship behaviour and evidence to suggest that attributions influence a person's response to the partner's behaviour.

Summary and Conclusions

We began this chapter by reviewing the classic attribution theories, which address the kinds of information that people use to determine causality, the kinds of causes that they distinguish, and the rules they use for going from information to inferred cause. We then looked in detail at more recent research on the nature of causal attributions, systematic biases that characterize them, what factors instigate them, and what processes underlie them. These issues revealed the breadth and depth of research in this area, but also yielded a more measured view of attribution research. Specifically, causal attributions do not exhaust the variety of common-sense explanations; far from being scientific, they actually reveal many biases; they are triggered by specific factors rather than being automatic; and they are typically less detailed and more biased than the classic theories imply. In contrast to the measured view that emerged from the first half of this chapter, the second half started with the observation that the emergence of attribution theory was the most important development in social psychology. The attempt to understand this observation led us to explore some of the main applications of attribution theory. In doing so, we could only sample from a large and diverse literature. None the less, research on motivation, clinical psychology, and close relationships demonstrates the continued vitality of attribution research, and the tremendous impact of attribution theory in advancing our understanding of applied problems.

Glossary terms

Actor–observer difference
Attribution theory
Attributional bias
Attributional style
Augmentation principle
Causal attribution

Causal schemata
Correspondence bias
Correspondent inference
Covariation principle
Discounting principle

Fundamental attribution error
Learned helplessness
Normative model
Salience
Self-serving bias

Discussion points

1 To what extent is Kelley's ANOVA model 'idealized', and how has it been improved upon in more recent research?
2 A great deal of attribution research rests on the distinction between internal and external causal attributions. Does this do justice to the rich variety of common-sense explanations?
3 Are causal attributions made 'spontaneously', 'automatically', both, or neither?
4 Evaluate the contribution made by recent linguistic analyses of attribution to our understanding of biases in the attribution process.
5 In what ways do attributions differ in satisfied and distressed relationships?
6 Why has attribution theory been so productive in applied research?
7 How has attribution theory contributed to psychotherapy?

Suggestions for further reading

Fletcher, G. and Fincham, F. D. (eds) (1991) *Cognition in Close Relationships*. Hillsdale, NJ: Erlbaum. A detailed treatment of attributional and other social-cognitive approaches to close relationships by leading scholars in the field.

Hewstone, M. (1989) *Causal Attribution: From cognitive processes to collective beliefs*. Oxford, UK and Cambridge, MA: Blackwell. A comprehensive analysis of theory and research, including intra-personal, interpersonal, intergroup and societal attribution, which reviews both American and European developments.

Jones, E. E. (1990) *Interpersonal Perception*. New York: Macmillan. A personal account of attribution theory, written by one of its major figures. Particularly good on the stategic nature of attributions in interpersonal interactions.

Jones, E. E., Kanouse, D. E., Kelley, H. H., Nisbett, R. E., Valins, S. and Weiner, B. (1971) *Attribution: Perceiving the causes of behaviour*. Morristown, NJ: General Learning Press. A now-classic collection of some of the most important early theoretical statements on attribution, including actor–observer differences, and causal schemata.

Weary, G., Stanley, M. A. and Harvey, J. H. (1989) *Attribution*. New York: Springer-Verlag. This book is concerned with the application of attribution theory, especially in clinical and other settings outside the laboratory.

Weiner, B. (1986) *An Attributional Theory of Motivation and Emotion*. New York: Springer-Verlag. A scholarly monograph outlining the development of Weiner's theory, and detailing the importance of attribution in predicting both motivational behaviour and affective reactions.

Weiner, B. (1995). *Judgments of Responsibility*. New York: Guilford. In presenting a general theory of social motivation this book provides extensive overviews of serveral research areas. It also includes experiments that can be completed by the student to illustrate attributional phenomena.

Key studies

Storms,. M. D. (1973). Videotape and the attribution process: reversing actors' and observers' points of view. *Journal of Personality and Social Psychology*, 27, 165–75.

Bradbury, T. N. and Fincham, F. D. (1992). Attributions and behaviour in marital interaction. *Journal of Personality and Social Psychology*, 63, 613–28.

8 Attitudes: Structure, Measurement and Functions

Dagmar Stahlberg and Dieter Frey

Contents

Introduction

The attitude construct: definitions and conceptual distinctions

Attitude measurement
Self-report measures of attitudes
Attitude measures not based on self-reports

Functions of attitudes
Motivational functions
Attitudes guiding information processing

Attitudes guiding behaviour
Correspondence of attitudinal and behavioural measures
Special characteristics of the attitude
Personality factors
Other factors that influence behaviour – models of the attitude–behaviour relation

Summary and conclusions

Introduction

ATTITUDE

The concept of **attitude** 'is probably the most distinctive and indispensable concept in contemporary American social psychology' (Allport, 1954, p. 43). This was true for the American social psychology of the mid-1950s and is still true for contemporary social psychology (e.g., Eagly and Chaiken, 1993; Olson and Zanna, 1993).

Why is the concept of attitudes so popular in social psychology? Psychology's aim is to explain and predict human behaviour, and attitudes are supposed to influence behaviour. Social attitudes, therefore, serve as indicators or predictors of behaviour. Furthermore, to change attitudes is seen as a meaningful starting point for modifying behaviour, not only in social-psychological research but also in everyday life, as the following examples may show:

1   Politicians try to evoke positive attitudes and opinions concerning themselves as well as their political programmes in order to be re-elected or to realize such programmes.
2   Carefully planned commercials are delivered to potential product consumers to convince them of the merits of a new chocolate bar, a new detergent or a certain car model, so turning potential consumers into real ones.
3   Your partner wants to know whether you like Greece, or her feminist friends, or whether you dislike doing the dishes, in order to predict your behaviour: for example, whether you will readily accompany her on a journey to Greece, whether you will enjoy an evening with her feminist friends, or whether you will always quarrel about which of you is to do the washing-up.
4   Negative social attitudes (prejudices) towards certain groups (like migrant workers, homosexuals, etc.) can lead to behavioural discrimination (for example, refusing to employ members of these social groups).

As can be seen from these examples, the concept of attitudes appears to have a dominant role to play in a social-psychological model of behaviour. Thus there is ample reason for analysing this concept in more detail. First we explain what social attitudes are – that is, how they are defined and what different conceptions of attitudes exist. Then we turn to the question: 'What are the functions of attitudes?' Finally we discuss the relationship between attitudes and behaviour.

The Attitude Construct: Definitions and Conceptual Distinctions

The term 'social attitude' was introduced into social psychology by Thomas and Znaniecki (1918), in order to explain behavioural differences in everyday life between Polish farmers in Poland and in the USA. Since then, many different definitions for the increasingly popular concept of attitudes have been proposed.

Two different approaches to the definition of attitudes can be distinguished. The first view is based on the idea that an attitude is a combination of three conceptually distinguishable reactions to a certain object (e.g., Eagly and Chaiken, 1993; Rosenberg and Hovland, 1960). These reactions are specified as *affective* (concerning emotions such as love and hate, like and dislike), *cognitive* (concerning beliefs, opinions and ideas about the attitude object – the object towards which the attitude is directed), and *conative/behavioural* (concerning behavioural intentions or action tendencies). An example of such a **three-component model of attitudes** was recently proposed by Eagly and Chaiken (1993). They define attitudes as follows: 'Attitude is a psychological tendency that is expressed by evaluating a particular entity with some degree of favor or disfavor . . . Evaluating refers to all classes of evaluative responding, whether overt or covert, cognitive, affective or behavioral' (p. 1). Eagly and Chaiken also stress the status of attitudes as a hypothetical construct that intervenes between certain classes of stimuli and certain classes of observable responses (see figure 8.1 for a summary of the attitude conception of Eagly and Chaiken, 1993).

Sometimes people think or act differently from the way they feel. Because of this lack of consistency between affective, cognitive and behavioural reactions, a second class of definitions of the term attitude has rejected the idea of a multicomponent model of attitudes. These concepts regard the affective

THREE-COMPONENT MODEL OF ATTITUDES

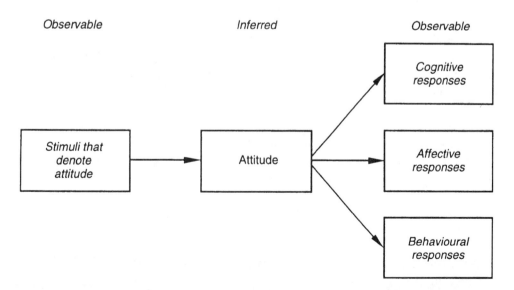

Figure 8.1 Attitude as an inferred state, with evaluative responses divided into three classes (cognitive, affective and behavioural) (figure adapted from Eagly and Chaiken, 1993, p. 10)

component of attitudes as the only relevant indicator of their evaluative nature, and therefore use the terms affect and evaluation interchangeably: 'the term attitude should be used to refer to a general, enduring positive or negative feeling about some person, object or issue' (Petty and Cacioppo, 1981, p. 7; see also Fishbein and Ajzen, 1975). These sorts of definitions are labelled *unidimensional* because they focus on only one attitude component. As a consequence of this restriction, supporters of this model distinguish the attitude concept from the concept of beliefs on the one hand and from behavioural intention or overt action

BELIEFS

on the other (cf. Fishbein and Ajzen, 1975). The term **beliefs** is reserved for the opinions held about the attitude object, or – in other words – for the information, knowledge or thoughts someone has about the attitude object (for example: 'Karl thinks that his old car is still a reliable one'). *Attitudes*, then, stand for the affect which is connected with the attitude object, that is, its positive or negative evaluation (for example: 'Karl likes his old car'). **Behavioural**

BEHAVIOURAL INTENTION

intention, finally, describes some sort of predisposition to a certain kind of attitude-relevant action, i.e., the readiness to behave towards a certain attitude object in a special way (for example: 'Karl decides not to buy a new car').

Although there are other conceptions of attitudes to be found in the literature (see, for example, the differentiation of evaluation and affect by Breckler and Wiggins, 1989, 1991), the three-component and the unidimensional models have received the most attention. An obvious question remains: 'Which of the two positions is most consistent with the empirical evidence?' The three-component model claims that the three defined components described above should be moderately correlated, thus appearing separate but not completely unrelated. Studies in which the correlational structure of the different components has been analysed have yielded contradictory results. Some authors have concluded that the three-component theory received no empirical support, because factor-analytic approaches (methods of analysing basic dimensions in correlational data) were not able to justify the three components: they were often too highly correlated to be conceptually differentiated (see, for example, Hormuth, 1979; McGuire, 1969, 1985). Support for the three-component model of attitudes was reported by Kothandapani (1971). He succeeded in showing that each of the three attitude components was highly correlated with itself when measured with different kinds of scales, but was not highly correlated with the other two components (for contradictory results see Ostrom, 1969). Recent analyses of attitudinal structures using more refined statistical methods (cf. Bagozzi and Burnkraut, 1979, 1985; Dillon and Kumar, 1985) reached equally contradictory conclusions. In an overview of these research findings Chaiken and Stangor (1987) conluded that a definitive judgement of the three-dimensional versus the one-dimensional issue seems premature at present (see also Eagly and Chaiken, 1993).

Moreover, Breckler (1984) assumed that attitude dimensionality might vary with the kind of attitude object studied. This notion was also supported by the work of Schlegel (1975) and Schlegel and DiTecco (1982). They showed that attitudinal structures could be conveyed by a single affective response, as Fishbein and Ajzen (1975) postulated, when relevant beliefs about the attitude object were simple, their number was small, and they did not contradict each other. However, if beliefs are numerous, complicated and at least partly contradictory – for example, if a person has intense personal experiences of the attitude object (in this study, the use of marijuana) – a simple evaluative response will fall short of representing the whole attitude structure. Furthermore, attitude dimensionality may depend not only on the attitude object under scrutiny but also on the person who has formed the attitude. One can assume that cognitive complexity, tolerance of ambiguity, or other individual difference variables may be linked to the structure of people's attitudes.

Attitude Measurement

How do you measure the attitude of a person towards attitude objects as varied as a particular politician, nuclear power plants, or a new consumer product? Obviously, the easiest way to measure these attitudes is to ask for some sort of self-report from the people whose attitudes you are interested in. And indeed, most methods of attitude measurement are based on the assumption that attitudes can be measured by the opinions or beliefs of persons about the attitude object (e.g., Likert, 1932; Thurstone, 1931), whereas other methods try to assess primarily the evaluative character of an attitude (Osgood, Suci and Tannenbaum, 1957). These measurement procedures are therefore called self-report measures or direct measures. On the other hand, with non-direct techniques one tries to measure attitudes without the person holding the attitude being aware of the measurement procedure. The advantage of the latter techniques is that they are less susceptible to social desirability or self-presentational motives. In the following, the most important direct and indirect procedures for attitude measurement in contemporary social psychology will be discussed.

Self-report measures of attitudes

The one-item rating scale
Very often a one-item rating scale is used to measure attitudes. This simple method is an economic way of measuring an attitude in many representative studies, such as opinion surveys and polls. The investigators formulate a single question from which they think a direct estimation of the attitude is possible. This question is then connected with a multi-point rating scale: for example, 'How satisfied are you with your life?' Possible answers are offered ranging from 'not at all satisfied' (= 1) to 'very satisfied' (= 7). The major problem with such a single-item rating scale lies in its potential lack of reliability: the responses to

the items may be influenced by the context (other questions being asked), the order of the items, the mood of the respondent, and other extraneous factors (see Schwartz and Strack, 1991). To overcome this problem of low reliability, other more complex forms of attitude scales can be constructed.

The Likert scale

One of the most popular standard attitude scales was developed by Likert (1932). The great popularity of the **Likert scale** is due mostly to its low costs. Compared with other classic approaches to attitude measurement (such as the Thurstone scale of equal appearing intervals), a Likert scale can be much more easily developed.

A Likert scale is constructed as follows:

1   The first step in constructing a Likert scale consists of the collection of a great number of items (about 100) relevant to the attitude that is to be measured. These items should clearly express positive or negative beliefs or feelings about the attitude object in question.

2   In the next step, a large sample of people representative of the population whose attitudes are to be assessed is asked to assess the collected items on a five-point rating scale. A possible example of such an item to measure attitudes towards nuclear power plants is shown in table 8.1.

3   In the third step, a preliminary attitude score is computed by adding up subjects' responses to the different items. To ensure that all items reflect the single attitude in question, an item analysis is performed, by correlating each item with the total score for all items. Because only items which are highly correlated with the total attitude score can be regarded as indicative of the underlying attitude, all items that do not fulfil this requirement are eliminated in the final scale. Such a final scale then meets Likert's criterion of internal consistency (high correlations of each single item with the total score).

4   The final attitude score is obtained by summing up the responses towards those items left in the scale.

Table 8.1 An example of a possible Likert-scale item to measure attitudes towards nuclear power plants

'I believe that nuclear power plants are one of the great dangers of industrial societies'	
+2	Strongly agree
+1	Moderately agree
0	Neutral or undecided
−1	Moderately disagree
−2	Strongly disagree

Likert scales are very popular in psychological research. One problem with these scales, however, is the fact that they do not strictly fulfil the requirement of equal-interval scales (see Petty and Cacioppo, 1981; Stroebe, 1980). An equal-interval scale would imply that a scale value of 10 would reflect an attitude that was exactly half as positive as an attitude described by the scale value of 20. In actual research, Likert scales are often used as if they do fulfil these assumptions. Another problem can be seen in the ambiguity of moderate test scores. It is unclear how to interpret moderate scores because they could reflect moderate responses to all items as well as very inconsistent response patterns (see, for example, Shaver, 1981; and see also Stosberg, 1980, for a critique of the underlying additivity assumption).

Semantic differential

The problem with scales like the Likert scale is that for each new attitude object a new scale has to be constructed. The **semantic differential**, which was developed by Osgood, Suci and Tannenbaum (1957), offers the possibility of measuring different attitudes with the same scale.

SEMANTIC DIFFERENTIAL

In developing the semantic differential, Osgood and his co-workers confronted their subjects with certain concepts, such as father, politics, self etc. Subjects were then asked to rate each concept on different bipolar rating scales, the endpoints of which were bipolar adjectives such as 'pleasant/unpleasant' or 'hard/soft'. Using factor analysis, Osgood et al. identified three basic dimensions on which concepts could be described. These factors were interpreted as evaluation, potency and activity. The researchers – following a unidimensional attitude concept – assumed that the pairs of adjectives showing high loadings on the evaluation factor (high correlations with the factor) would be appropriate for describing a person's attitude to the object in question. Table 8.2 shows an example of a semantic differential attitude scale which uses some of the adjective pairs that were found, in former studies, to have high loadings on the evaluative factor. The resulting attitude, then, is obtained by summing up the scores from each rating scale, which normally vary between +3 and –3.

According to Osgood et al. (1957), attitude scores obtained by a semantic differential measure are supposed to have the property of an equal-interval scale. The reliability of the scale is, according to Robinson and Shaver (1969), comparable to that of the Likert scale. The main advantage of the semantic

Table 8.2 Examples of evaluative ratings used in semantic differential scales

Good	+3	+2	+1	0	–1	–2	–3	Bad
Pleasant	+3	+2	+1	0	–1	–2	–3	Unpleasant
Valuable	+3	+2	+1	0	–1	–2	–3	Worthless
Clean	+3	+2	+1	0	–1	–2	–3	Dirty
Friendly	+3	+2	+1	0	–1	–2	–3	Unfriendlly

differential is its easy applicability towards different attitude objects. However, this point is also a danger: because of the high degree of abstraction of this instrument, it can be less appropriate for describing behaviourally relevant attitudes. Another – probably more severe – problem is that the factorial structure of a given semantic differential scale varies considerably with the type of the actual concept being rated. This implies that the main advantage of the semantic differential – its universal applicability – cannot be taken for granted.

General problems of these scales

All measures which are based on self-descriptions start from the assumption that the person who responds is able and motivated to disclose his or her true attitudes. However, there is a great deal of evidence that people are often motivated to misrepresent their attitude – for example, to give socially desirable answers. Because self-evaluation data can be easily falsified, or are susceptible to impression-management motives, other instruments have been developed to assess attitudes (see next section).

Another problem can be seen in the reactivity of the attitude-measurement procedure itself. For certain attitude objects, people sometimes do not possess any explicitly or clearly formulated attitude. However, in being asked to make statements about these attitude objects, they are urged to express a certain well-defined position. Sometimes, therefore, the process of attitude measurement itself will develop attitudes which would otherwise not have been formulated. These spontaneous attitudes may be very unstable and therefore rather bad predictors of behaviour. Again, some of the techniques of non-direct attitude measurement mentioned below do not share these problems.

Attitude measures not based on self-reports

Physiological measurements

Emotional reactions are reflected by physiological reactions (skin response, pulse rate, dilation of the pupils etc.). Therefore, it makes sense to look at physiological reactions in order to find more objective attitude indicators.

GALVANIC
SKIN
RESPONSE

The most important objective indicator of attitudes has been the **galvanic skin response** (GSR). The GSR measures the electrical resistance of the skin, which changes when people are emotionally aroused. Hence, the GSR allows the researcher to assess a subject's emotional response towards an attitude object. For example, in an experiment by Porier and Lott (1967), black and white experimenters touched their white subjects with their hand, apparently by accident. The stronger the subjects' racial prejudices were (which was measured beforehand, by a questionnaire), the more the subjects' galvanic skin response changed when being touched by the black experimenter relative to being touched by the white experimenter. As can be seen from this example, the main problem with psycho-physiological indicators of attitudes like the GSR (cf. Petty and Cacioppo, 1981) is that these measures assess the intensity of emotional responses but not their direction. Furthermore, the measures are influenced by many other features of the attitude stimulus presented (such as its novelty and its unexpectedness; cf. Sokolov, 1963).

An objective attitude indicator that can be used to measure the quality or direction of attitude (its positiveness/negativeness) is the facial electromyogram (EMG). Schwartz, Fair, Salt, Mandel and Klerman (1976) showed that with positive affective states, certain face muscles are activated more strongly and others less strongly than with negative affective states. Cacioppo and Petty (1979a) validated this instrument in an experiment concerning reactions to persuasive communications which were pro-attitudinal or contra-attitudinal for the subjects. They showed that the EMG could depict whether subjects had listened to a pro- or contra-attitudinal communication. Petty and Cacioppo (1981) therefore concluded that the EMG measure was sensitive to different qualities (positive or negative) of an affect or emotion. They doubted, however, whether the instrument could also be used successfully to assess the intensity of an emotional reaction.

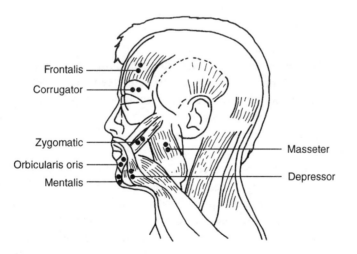

Figure 8.2 The Facial EMG: A Covert Measure of Attitudes. The facial EMG makes it possible to detect differences between positive and negative attitudes. Notice the major facial muscles and recording sites for electrodes. When people hear a message with which they agree rather than disagree, there is a relative increase in EMG activity in the depressor and zygomatic muscles but a relative decrease in the corrugator and frontalis muscles. These changes cannot be seen with the naked eye. [From Cacioppo & Petty, 1981.]

Physiological measures of attitudes are not very often used in practice. One reason may be the above-mentioned insensitivity of most of the instruments towards the quality of an attitudinal response. Another important reason, however, is the necessity of using technical devices, which are not easily applied in field settings.

Behaviour observation and non-reactive measurements

These methods derive attitude measures from open, observable behaviour patterns. In most behaviour observation the subjects know that they are being observed. However, in non-reactive measurement the subjects are observed without their knowledge, or, even more indirectly, some of their behaviour patterns are analysed. These types of attitudinal measures are called behaviour indicators (Petty and Cacioppo, 1981), observation techniques (Calder and Ross, 1976), and unobtrusive measures (Stroebe, 1980; for an overview see Kidder and Campbell, 1970; Selltiz, Wrightsman and Cook, 1976).

Marlowe, Frager and Nuttall (1965) inferred the attitudes of their subjects towards Afro-Americans from their willingness to show Afro-American students around Harvard University Campus. Campbell, Kruskal and Wallace (1966) drew conclusions about racial attitudes from the seating arrangement in college classes, that is, by observing the seating distance between Afro-American and white students. Further indicators of interpersonal attitudes include eye contact (Argyle, 1967) and body posture (Mehrabian, 1968).

LOST LETTER
TECHNIQUE

A good example of an inconspicuous observation technique is the so-called **lost letter technique** described by Milgram, Mann and Harter (1965). To measure the political attitudes of citizens in different parts of a city, the researchers 'lost' postage-paid letters which were addressed to organizations whose ideology was made evident by their names, for example, the Communist Student Organization, UNICEF, and so on. According to the rate at which the letters came back to a certain organization (all letters actually ended up in post-office boxes rented by the researchers), a conclusion was drawn as to the popularity of each organization and thus the ideological orientation that predominated in particular parts of the city.

BOGUS
PIPELINE

Finally, the **bogus pipeline** method has to be mentioned. Jones and Sigall (1971) report that with this technique one can detect attitudes that would otherwise not be disclosed, because they are embarrassing to the individual. Following the bogus pipeline procedure, subjects are connected via electrodes to an apparatus that can allegedly predict exactly their attitudes concerning given objects by means of physiological measurements (a sort of lie detector). The subjects can assure themselves beforehand of the accuracy of the apparatus by thinking about certain attitude objects when (supposedly) being connected to the apparatus. Subjects are then questioned about certain attitudes and requested to answer these questions sometimes correctly, i.e., according to their real attitudes, and sometimes incorrectly, i.e., contrary to their real attitudes. They are then shown that the apparatus is able to detect whether they gave the correct response or whether they cheated. In reality, the apparatus's responses have been manipulated by the experimenter, who could not be seen by the subject and who knew the correct response pattern from a pre-test which subjects had filled out beforehand. When the subjects are convinced of the apparatus's capacity to detect their real attitudes, those attitude questions are asked that are of real interest to the investigator. On the assumption that no one likes to be surpassed by a machine when giving information concerning their own attitudes, truthful answers – even to embarrassing or unpleasant questions – are expected.

Although interesting findings using the bogus pipeline procedure have been documented in the literature (for an overview of this method see Brackwede, 1980), this method seems unsuitable for frequent use because it is very expensive. Moreover, it only works with uninformed persons as subjects; the more the apparatus is used, the more popular and well known it will become, and knowledge of the absence of its supposed capabilities will spread. There are, of course, also ethical issues involved in the crude misleading of the subjects.

Let us summarize the advantages and problems of the non-reactive measurements discussed. Unobtrusive measurement procedures are less liable to conscious distortions than self-report methods; however, this advantage is gained at the cost of enormous ambiguities of interpretation (such as the questionable validity of the attained measures) and ethical problems. It is often difficult to determine what these objective indicators mean exactly with respect to an attitude, and they are often determined by motives or situational constraints other than attitudes.

Functions of Attitudes

Why do people have attitudes? Put less functionally, what are the consequences of holding attitudes? These questions – and especially that of the motivational roots of attitudes – have been addressed by Katz (1967), McGuire (1969) and Smith, Bruner and White (1956) in their *functional attitude theories*. The four motivational functions described below, which were formulated by Katz and others, are still referred to in recent research on attitudinal functions (see, for example, Herek, 1986; Shavitt, 1989).

Motivational functions

Ego-defensive functions
Katz (1967) starts from a psychoanalytical background using concepts of defence mechanisms such as rationalization or projection to describe this attitudinal

function. Attitudes in this function can, for example, protect one from negative feelings towards oneself or towards one's own group by allowing projections of these feelings towards other persons, such as minority groups. People who are threatened by feelings of dissatisfaction with their own marriages could manage these feelings by projecting them on to divorced people, that is, by expressing rather negative feelings towards this group.

The value-expressive self-realizing function

Katz assumed that people have a need to express attitudes that reflect their own central values, or components of their idea of themselves. For instance, it can give you great satisfaction to express your opposition to laws imposing capital punishment, when you believe deeply in the value of human rights. This kind of attitude expression is directed mainly towards confirming the validity of one's own self-concept and less at impressing others. The latter aim, nevertheless, is another important function of attitudinal expression.

The instrumental, adjustive or utilitarian function

Attitudes help people to reach desired goals, such as rewards, or to avoid undesirable goals, such as punishment. It is therefore assumed that people express favourable attitudes towards attitude objects that satisfy their personal needs and negative attitudes towards objects that are associated with frustration or negative reinforcement. Furthermore, the expression of attitudes itself may be rewarding or punishing. For example, most people – not only social psychologists – know that similarity often breeds liking. Therefore, it may be functional or instrumental to adopt similar attitudes to those of someone whom it is desirable to win as a friend.

Knowledge or economy functions

Attitudes also serve the functions of organizing or structuring an otherwise chaotic world. If we tried to deal specifically with every detail of our (social) environment, we would be overcome by complete information overload. Attitudes allow us to categorize incoming information such as new experiences along established evaluative dimensions and can help us to simplify and understand the complex world in which we live. For example, if you like the work of a certain student very much, you will expect him or her to pass their examinations quite successfully. Your attitude, then, tells you what to expect in this situation.

Recent researchers regard this knowledge, economy or schematic function of attitudes as being of central importance. Guiding information processing is seen as a central function of, if not all attitudes, then at least all attitudes that are highly accessible and well established (e.g., Fazio, 1989; Shavitt, 1990). This function will therefore be analysed in more detail in the following section. Before continuing with the question of how attitudes guide information processing it should be added that in the last decade research on attitudes has shown a renewed interest in their functional basis (for an overview see Olson and Zanna, 1993; Tesser and Shaffer, 1990). Although no new functions have been added, the existing concepts have been clarified (for a summary see Eagly and Chaiken, 1993). It has been emphasized that an attitude can serve either one (central) function or multiple functions: for example, a positive attitude towards a certain political programme, such as energy conservation, can serve utilitarian functions (this attitude is approved of by important others); it can be an expression of central values (belief in responsibility for future generations); and it can guide or structure information processing (it may indicate the usefulness of paying close attention to information provided by a certain political candidate).

Furthermore, models of attitudinal functions have been studied on a more empirical basis in the last decade. Katz (1960) noted that there should be variations in attitude functions across persons, attitude domains, and situational contexts. In the last decade all these assumptions have been supported empirically: Snyder and DeBono (1987) showed that the attitudes of so-called high self-monitors (people whose behaviour is primarily oriented to situational cues or to the potential reactions of their interaction partners, cf. Snyder, 1974) are more likely to serve the social adjustive rather than the value-expressive function. The opposite is true for the attitudes of low self-monitors (people whose social behaviour depends greatly upon their internal states, dispositions, attitudes etc.). Variations in the functions of attitudes due to attitudinal domains and the context in which attitudes are presented have also been demonstrated (Sanbonmatsu and Fazio, 1990; Shavitt, 1990).

This research on the motivational/functional properties of attitudes is extremely interesting in the light of research on persuasion, which offers substantial support for the notion that matching the persuasive communication or the persuasive context with the function that underlies an attitude can enhance attitude change (for a summary, see Eagly and Chaiken, 1993; see also chapter 9).

Attitudes guiding information processing

There are three schools of thought on why attitudes should guide information processing. One view is based on the motivational principle of cognitive consistency. **Cognitive consistency theories** are among the most influential approaches in social psychology (see Frey and Gaska, 1993; Stahlberg and Frey, 1987). The principle of consistency was introduced into social psychology by Heider (1944, 1946). All consistency theories assume that individuals strive to have their own cognitions (beliefs, attitudes, perceptions of their own behaviour) organized in a tension-free, that is non-contradictory, way. When people perceive that some of their attitudes are contradictory, they will enter into a state of cognitive imbalance. This state is unpleasant and produces tension. Therefore,

COGNITIVE
CONSISTENCY
THEORIES

they will be motivated to establish a consistent and tension-free relationship between the cognitions by changing one or all of them. If, for example, new information or certain beliefs contradict an existing strong attitude this may lead to a reinterpretation of the incoming information or to a change in beliefs; in this case the attitude guides information processing.

Apart from consistency theories, however, other social-psychological theories exist which assume that attitudes will guide the perception and evaluation of attitude-relevant information. *Social-judgement theories* such as the assimilation-contrast theory (Sherif and Hovland, 1961; Sherif and Sherif, 1967), the adaptation-level theory (Helson, 1964), the variable-perspective theory (Upshaw, 1969) and accentuation theory (Eiser and Stroebe, 1972) also postulate that our attitudes will influence our perception and/or judgement of attitude-relevant information, especially attitudinal positions occupied by other people (for an overview, see Beckmann and Mattenklott, 1985; Stahlberg, 1987). Sherif and Hovland (1961), for example, assume that our own attitude serves the function of a judgemental anchor in comparison with which all other possible attitude positions are judged. More concretely, it is expected that other attitude positions that are relatively close to one's own position on the attitude continuum will be perceived as resembling one's own attitude even more than they actually do (*assimilation*) and will be evaluated very positively (as being fair and objective). Attitudinal positions, on the other hand, which had less in common with one's own would be rejected as unfair propaganda (*contrast*).

To complete our discussion of whether attitudes do influence information processing, *schematic* conceptions of attitudes have to be mentioned. According to the social-cognition approach (see also chapters 5 and 6), social information is not passively received and stored in memory, but is selectively encoded and actively organized in cognitive memory structures, which are generally called schemata (Fiske and Taylor, 1991). Research on schemata in social psychology has shown that social schemata guide the encoding of social stimuli as well as the retrieval of information stored in memory (for an overview of schemata research in social psychology see, for example, Fiske and Taylor, 1991; Schwarz, 1985). For example, people often react faster to schema-relevant information and show a better encoding of and memory for this kind of information. Some authors argue that attitudes can be conceptualized as such schemata and should therefore guide information processing (e.g., Judd and Kulik, 1980; Lingle and Ostrom, 1981).

To summarize, several theoretical models exist to predict that attitudes guide information processing. Let us now look at the relevant empirical data. To analyse the potential of attitudes to guide information processing we have to look at three different components of that process:

1   The active *search* for attitude relevant information.

Plate 8.1 The kind of anti-smoking information that a heavy smoker is likely to try to avoid

2 The *encoding* of the information, i.e., perceptual and judgemental processes.
3 The *retrieval* of such information from memory.

Active search for attitude-relevant information

Dissonance theory (Festinger, 1957) has proved the most successful theory of cognitive consistency for making explicit predictions about selective exposure to attitude-relevant information. In general, dissonance theory predicts that people are motivated to expose themselves to (attitude-) consonant information and to avoid (attitude-) dissonant information in order to stabilize a decision (or an existing attitude), and in such a manner to maintain cognitive consonance or avoid cognitive dissonance. For example, if someone really likes smoking cigarettes she would be expected to avoid information that stressed the negative consequences of smoking, such as cancer and other health problems. On the other hand, she would probably enjoy hearing about very famous people who also like smoking or that smoking prevents people from gaining too much weight. Smoking cigarettes and knowing that smoking causes cancer can be dissonant cognitions, because if smoking causes health problems it may follow that smoking will have to be given up. Therefore, in order not to create tension or dissonance, attitude-dissonant cognitions are avoided and consonant cognitions are selectively sought out.

DISSONANCE
THEORY

This **selective exposure** hypothesis was investigated in an experiment by Frey and Rosch (1984). Subjects had to evaluate the ability of a manager; specifically, they had to decide, on the basis of a written description about the manager's competence, whether his working contract should be prolonged or not. This judgement had to be expressed either in a 'reversibility' or in a 'non-reversibility' condition. Subjects in the first condition were told that they would be able to reverse their judgement later in the experimental session. Subjects in the 'non-reversibility' condition, on the other hand, were explicitly instructed that they had to make final judgements about the ability of the manager, which could not be corrected.

After expressing their judgements, subjects were given the opportunity to receive additional information about the manager. The descriptions were phrased in such a way that it was evident whether they were positive or negative (for example, 'Mr Miller has done a good job and therefore his contract should be extended', or 'There are much more competent managers than Mr Miller and therefore his contract should not be extended'). Of the ten descriptions (five positive and five negative), the subjects could select as many as they wanted. The results of the experiment clearly supported the selective exposure hypothesis, as can be seen in figure 8.2.

In both experimental conditions, judgement-consonant information was preferred over judgement-dissonant information. Moreover, when subjects were told that the judgements were irreversible the selective-exposure effect was stronger than when subjects expected their judgements to be reversible. The

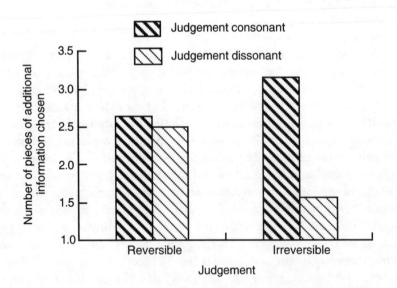

Figure 8.3 Information-seeking as a function of information/judgement consistency and judgement reversibility (figure adapted from data presented by Frey and Rosch, 1984)

latter finding stresses the fact that there must be a certain amount of commitment to one's judgement, decision or attitude in order to produce strong selective-exposure effects. When, on the other hand, a person is not committed to his or her attitude, the latter can be reversed easily and therefore cannot be expected to evoke a significant selective-exposure effect.

Selective-exposure effects have been clearly demonstrated in a research programme by Frey (1986; see also Frey and Stahlberg, 1986; Frey, Stahlberg and Fries, 1986). This research also specifies under what conditions people do not show selective-exposure effects but, on the contrary, selectively look out for dissonant information. Subjects tend to expose themselves to dissonant information when (1) their cognitive system (i.e. their attitude) is relatively strong, so that they will be able either to integrate or to argue against this kind of information; or when (2) the cognitive system is relatively weak, so that the individual prefers in the long run to change it and render it consonant with the existing, perhaps overwhelming, dissonant information.

Imagine, for example, that a politician whom you really like has supported political decisions that you think are clearly wrong, or that he has been accused of telling lies concerning important political facts. If this negative information is overwhelming, it may seem better to reverse your attitude towards this political candidate in order to avoid future dissonance.

Perception and evaluation of attitude-relevant information

We have seen that people often try to avoid attitude-dissonant information. In daily life, however, this sort of information often cannot be easily avoided. But again attitudes exert influence on information processing, this time by biasing the perception and also the evaluation of the attitude-relevant information. Fazio and Williams (1986) demonstrated that people selectively process information about the qualities of attitude objects. They analysed attitudes towards presidential candidates in the 1984 US presidential elections. Later they correlated these attitudes with a measure of people's perception of the presidential candidates Reagan and Mondale, taken after television debates by the candidates. It was shown that how favourable the attitudes were was significantly correlated with the perception of the candidates' performances ('Reagan was much more impressive' or 'Mondale was much more impressive'). Subjects with positive attitudes towards Reagan tended to find him more impressive than Mondale, whereas the opposite occurred for subjects favouring Mondale.

Distortions in perception and evaluation of attitude-relevant information have also been demonstrated in the context of social-judgement theory, for example, by Hovland and Sherif (1952). They showed that white subjects with positive attitudes towards black people, and black people themselves, displaced attitude statements that were unfavourable towards black people, distancing them from their own attitudinal positions. They judged these statements as more 'anti-black people' than did an 'average' white subject control group (for a critical discussion of this and other comparable studies, see Eiser and Stroebe, 1972; see also Judd, Kenny and Krosnick, 1983).

Finally, the research by Petty and Cacioppo (1986a) on biased processing of attitude-relevant information can be interpreted as supporting the assumption that a person's own attitude can schematically affect the perception and evaluation of attitude-relevant information. When recipients of a pro-attitudinal message already possess an organized knowledge structure about the attitude object (attitudinal schema) they will react in a biased way to the message content. Compared with recipients who do not possess a comparable knowledge structure they will judge the message to be more convincing, and report more attitude-supporting thoughts (Cacioppo, Petty and Sidera, 1982).

Research on counter-attitudinal messages also confirms the hypothesis that subjects with attitudes that are based on existing knowledge structures produce more counter-arguments and less attitude-supporting thoughts than do subjects with attitudes based on less elaborate knowledge structures (Wood, 1982). The common idea of both studies is that only certain classes of attitudes may elicit strong selective perception and judgement effects. Only if people possess an organized knowledge structure or a strong schema-like attitude will information be processed in a biased way. This notion is also supported by the work of Houston and Fazio (1989). They showed that the biased evaluation of attitude-relevant information only occurred when subjects' attitudes were strong (highly accessible, meaning for example that people show very short reaction times when asked to make attitudinally relevant judgements).

To summarize, attitudes can affect the perception and evaluation of attitude-relevant information especially if they are highly accessible and based on an elaborate knowledge structure. This biased processing of attitude-relevant information can be explained by all the theoretical positions outlined above (consistency theories, social-judgement theories and schema theory).

Recall of attitude-relevant information

As early as 1932, it was assumed that attitudes guide the retrieval of information that is stored in memory (see Bartlett, 1932). Levine and Murphy (1943) assumed that information that supports social attitudes is better remembered than that contradicting such attitudes. Empirical research conducted to test this hypothesis regularly exposes subjects to information that is either consistent or inconsistent with their attitudes, and after some time asks them to reproduce as much of the information as they can. The results of these studies can be summarized as follows.

The findings are somewhat inconsistent. Whereas different studies can be cited which at least partly failed to verify the hypothesis of attitudinal guidance of the retrieval process, other experiments are more supportive (e.g. Jones and Aneshansel, 1956; Ross, McFarland and Fletcher, 1981). Ross et al., for example, demonstrated that attitudes exert directive influences on individuals' recall of their past behaviour concerning brushing their teeth. The authors first changed or stabilized their subjects' attitudes towards the benefits of frequent tooth-brushing. Afterwards, measures of attitude and behaviour recall (how often, for example, subjects had brushed their teeth in the preceding two weeks) were recorded. Results showed that, for example, subjects who had heard a message derogating frequent toothbrushing reported significantly more negative attitudes towards toothbrushing and at the same time remembered less frequent toothbrushing than subjects who were exposed to a message favouring frequent toothbrushing. Ross et al. therefore concluded that attitudes in this case served as retrieval cues that led to the salience of attitude-consistent behaviour or the reconstruction of actions in the light of the attitude. In an overview of relevant studies, Roberts (1985) comes to the conclusion that the empirical data taken together demonstrate a 'reliable but modest relationship between opinion and recall' (pp. 236–7).

A theoretical model which integrates many of the inconsistent empirical results is the model of bipolar attitudinal effects proposed by Judd and Kulik (1980). They assume that attitudes as schemata induce selective processing of attitude-relevant information in a bipolar manner; that is, they facilitate the encoding and retention of both attitude-consistent and attitude-contradicting information and impede the processing of attitude-neutral or irrelevant information. In their research, they demonstrated that attitudes indeed facilitated recall of attitude statements that were strongly agreed *or* disagreed with, compared with statements that elicited more moderate responses on the agreement scale (see also Hymes, 1986; Lingle and Ostrom, 1981).

Other authors emphasize the necessity of further isolating variables which may be responsible for enhanced memory for attitude-consistent or attitude-inconsistent information (see Eagly and Chaiken, 1993). In this context research has shown that individual differences exist regarding the better recall of attitude-congruent or incongruent information (cf. open- vs. closed-mindedness, Kleck and Wheaton, 1967). Furthermore, Pratkanis and Greenwald (1989) found that the structure of attitudes determined memory for attitude-supporting or contradicting information: unipolar attitudes towards music produced selective memory for consistent information. On the other hand, bipolar attitudes towards nuclear power elicited a heightened recall of both consistent and inconsistent information. Eagly and Chaiken (1993) expect that studying these mediating variables will enable future research to illuminate the role of special processes in the attitude–memory relationship, such as selective storage, selective retrieval or even selective reconstruction of attitude-relevant information that was never really stored in the memory (see Ross, 1989).

To summarize, attitudes can affect the selection, perception and evaluation of attitude-relevant information, especially if they are highly accessible, highly resistant to change and based on an elaborate knowledge structure. Attitudes can also influence memory for attitudinally relevant information. This biased processing of attitude-relevant information can be explained by all the theoretical positions outlined above (consistency theories, social-judgement theories) or on a purely cognitive basis (schema theory).

Attitudes Guiding Behaviour

We have seen that attitudes influence information processing. Now we turn to the equally important question of whether they also guide behavioural decisions. One of the most frequently described studies in the literature addressing the question of the attitude–behaviour relationship is that of LaPiere (1934). In the early 1930s, LaPiere travelled with a Chinese couple throughout the USA. At the beginning of this journey, LaPiere himself was quite sceptical of whether or not the three travellers would be accepted in hotels and restaurants, owing to the widespread anti-Asian prejudices at that time. However, to his surprise, service was refused to him and the Chinese couple in only one out of over 200 establishments. Six months after this unexpectedly positive experience, LaPiere wrote a letter to all the hotels and restaurants he had visited during the journey, and asked them whether they would 'accept members of the Chinese race as guests in their establishments'. In line with the assumed prejudice, but discrepant with their actual behaviour, 92 per cent of the hotels and restaurants which responded answered with a clear negative reply. In the following years, LaPiere's finding has often been cited as evidence for the lack of correlation between attitudes and other verbal responses on the one hand and overt behaviour on the other hand. Together with other studies (Ajzen and Fishbein, 1970; Corey, 1937) that also failed to find a strong relationship between attitudes and behaviour, LaPiere's findings led to a rather pessimistic view about predicting behaviour from attitudes (see, for example, Wicker, 1969).

This pessimistic view is not, however, supported by all studies of the attitude–behaviour relationship (e.g. Fishbein and Coombs, 1974; Newton and Newton, 1950; see also, for an overview, Ajzen and Fishbein, 1977). To summarize, all these empirical data show that the question 'Are attitudes and behaviour correlated?' is not a very fruitful one, because it turned out to be too global or undifferentiated. Therefore, some authors in the late 1960s started to ask new questions like: 'When are attitudes and behaviour correlated?', 'What factors affect the size of the correlation when and if it is found?' and 'By which processes do attitudes influence behaviour?' (Zanna and Fazio, 1982).

In the following section, some of these factors which qualify the attitude–behaviour relationship will be discussed.

Correspondence of attitudinal and behavioural measures

One of the most frequently addressed methodological criticisms of attitude and behaviour measurement is that of the low correspondence of both measures in terms of their specificity. Ajzen and Fishbein (1977) pointed out that both attitudes and behaviour can be characterized by considering four different elements:

1   The *action* element (what behaviour is to be performed: for example, voting behaviour, helping someone, or buying something).
2   The *target* element (at what target the behaviour is to be directed: for example, a certain political candidate, a close friend, or a new product).
3   The *context* element (in which context the behaviour is to be performed: for example, in a totalitarian or democratic political system, publicly or privately, and with a full or empty wallet).
4   The *time* component (at what time the behaviour is to be performed: for example, in spring 1998, at once, or during the next two years).

Many studies failed to ensure a close correspondence between the specificity of the attitude and behaviour measurements concerning the four elements just mentioned. For example, the attitude measurement has often been taken in a very global way, specifying only one (mostly the target element) or two of the above elements: for example, 'Do you like a certain political candidate or not?' The behaviour measure, on the other hand, has often been a very specific one (characterized along all four dimensions above): for example, 'Will you be voting for John Major in the 1992 British general election?'

A close relationship, following Ajzen and Fishbein's argument, can only be found when both measures correspond in their degree of specificity. In their review of studies addressing the attitude–behaviour relationship, Ajzen and Fishbein (1977) found strong support for this notion: substantial correlations between attitudes and behaviour had only been found when both measures showed high correspondence. Davidson and Jaccard (1979) performed a more direct test of the correspondence hypothesis by analysing women's attitudes and behaviour (use of birth control pills during a two-year period). A general measure of attitude towards birth control turned out not to be substantially related to the behaviour measured (r = +0.08), but when the attitude measure became more specific this correlation increased (up to a correlation of +0.57 for the attitude towards using birth control pills during the next two years).

At this point, however, it is necessary to mention that Ajzen and Fishbein's (1977) argument does not imply that global attitudes (for example, when only specified in terms of a certain target) are useless in predicting behaviour. As long as the behaviour is conceptualized in a comparably global way, there can be a quite substantial relationship between global attitudes and behavioural acts. For example, there may be high correlations between global attitudes towards energy conservation and a behavioural measure which is composed of different behaviours in different contexts, like preferring to ride a bicycle instead of driving a car for short distances, lowering the average room temperature, etc. (multiple acts), and/or a repeated observation of behavioural acts (preferring the bicycle in different seasons, etc.; see, for example, Fishbein and Ajzen, 1974; Liska, 1978; Weigel and Newman, 1976).

Other forms of correspondence have also been discussed in recent literature on the attitude–behaviour relationship. Some authors have shown that attitudes and behaviour correlate more strongly when the attributes or functions (see motivational functions of attitudes) of the attitudes that are salient at the time attitudes are assessed match the attributes or functions salient at the time the behaviour is performed (Shavitt and Fazio, 1991; Tesser and Shaffer, 1990). For example, Shavitt and Fazio (1991) compared attitudes and behavioural intentions with regard to two different beverages: '7-Up' and 'Perrier' mineral water. They assumed that attitudes towards '7-Up' would be based primarily on the attribute of taste, whereas 'Perrier' would be evaluated primarily on the basis of self-presentational concerns because of 'its prevalent social definition as a favorite drink of trend-conscious, upwardly mobile individuals' (Shavitt and Fazio, 1991, p. 509). Before measuring attitudes towards one of the two beverages, Shavitt and Fazio made either taste or social-impression attributes salient. This procedure meant that for each beverage either attributes consistent with the typically salient attribute for this product ('7-Up' – taste, or 'Perrier' – social impression) or inconsistent attributes ('7-Up – social impression, or 'Perrier' – taste) were made salient. Taste was made salient by an initial questionnaire that asked subjects to judge the goodness of taste of 20 food items. The salience of the attribute 'social impression' was heightened by a comparable questionnaire that asked for the social impression 20 different actions might create (e.g., driving a BMW car). These salience manipulations directly preceded the attitude measurement.

Later on in the experiment subjects were asked to express their intentions of buying or drinking the beverage in question in different situations. The authors hypothesized that at this point the intentions should be formulated on the basis of the naturally salient attributes. As a consequence the relationship between attitudes and behavioural intentions was expected to be stronger when the attributes made salient before the attitude measurement corresponded to the attribute naturally salient, when expressing behavioural intentions. Indeed, Shavitt and Fazio were able to show that attitudes and behavioural intentions were more strongly related when taste was made salient for the product '7-Up' and impression-management concerns were made salient for the mineral water 'Perrier' (see figure 8.3).

Other research findings indicate that thinking about a special attitude can either enhance or reduce the attitude–behaviour correspondence (Wilson and Dunn, 1986; Wilson, Dunn, Kraft and Lisle, 1989). In the research by Wilson and colleagues subjects were asked to think about their reasons for expressing the attitude in question. This procedure reduced the attitude–behaviour consistency, which was measured afterwards. Thinking about reasons made cognitive aspects of the attitude salient which otherwise would not have been considered when expressing an attitude and when translating attitudes into behaviour. On the other hand, if thinking about one's attitude leads to reflection about feelings related to the attitude, or if thinking about both the attitude and the behavioural decisions focuses on cognitive aspects, the attitude–behaviour relationship is strengthened (e.g., Snyder and Swann, 1976; Wilson and Dunn, 1986).

As a more general consequence of these findings Millar and Tesser (1989) formulated the hypothesis that attitudes and behaviour will show high correspondence whenever the salient aspects of both concepts, in terms of cognitive or affective focus, match. To test this hypothesis, Millar and Tesser carried out an experiment in which they made either the cognitive or affective aspects of the subjects' attitude towards some puzzles and the relating behavioural choice (working on the different puzzles) salient. These puzzles had allegedly been designed to increase analytic ability. As in the experiments described above, the affective or cognitive components of the attitude were made salient by asking the subjects either to think about *how* they felt about the different puzzles (reflection on feelings – affective focus) or to think about *why* they felt the way they did about the puzzles (reflection on reasons – cognitive

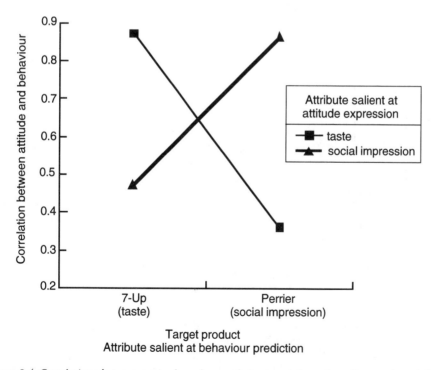

Figure 8.4 Correlations between attitude and mean behavioural intentions (figure adapted from data presented by Shavitt and Fazio, 1991, p. 510)

focus). This salience manipulation was directly followed by the attitude measurement. Independently, the affective or cognitive focus of the behavioural choice was varied by defining the behaviour as instrumental (cognitive focus) or consummatory (affective focus). In the instrumental behaviour condition subjects were led to expect that working on the puzzles would improve their analytic ability in a later test. On the other hand, subjects in the consummatory behaviour condition expected that working on the puzzles would be an end in itself and would not be instrumental in improving future test performance.

The results supported Millar and Tesser's hypothesis that attitudes and behaviour based on the same cognitive or affective components were more strongly related than attitudes and behaviour with a non-matching focus (see also Millar and Tesser, 1986; see figure 8.4).

To summarize, a high correspondence between the attitudinal and the behavioural measures is an important prerequisite for finding high attitude–behaviour correlations. However, whereas Ajzen and Fishbein (1977) defined correspondence concerning the action, target, context and time components in both measures, more recent contributions have added some other features of correspondence, such as the function of attitudes and behaviour or the cognitive–affective focus of both elements.

Special characteristics of the attitude

As mentioned above, some authors conceptualize attitudes as possessing affective, cognitive and conative components (e.g., Eagly and Chaiken, 1993; Rosenberg

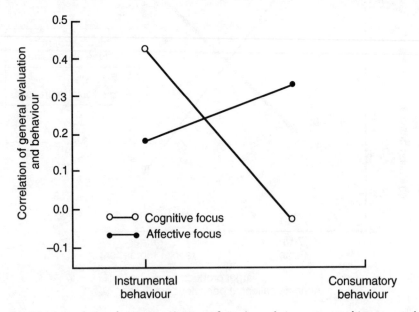

Figure 8.5 Mean correlations between evaluation of puzzles and time spent working on puzzles in free-play period (Millar and Tesser, 1986)

and Hovland, 1960). However, most research on attitudes and behaviour has reduced attitudes to their affective component. This reduction of the attitude concept has been motivated economically, because evaluative statements are easily measured, for example by a semantic differential (see above). Moreover, in cases where the affective component gives quite a good summary of the whole complex attitude (where, for example, the cognitive and affective components are consistent with each other), measures of only the affective component may be sufficiently good predictors of behaviour. But sometimes cognitive and affective components can be inconsistent (a person may be convinced of the harmful effects of smoking on health yet still enjoy smoking). According to Rosenberg (1968), attitudes which have a low affective–cognitive consistency are relatively unstable over time. This instability is mediated by the following process: when persons become conscious of the inconsistency of their attitude components they will be motivated to change one or both components in order to re-establish affective–cognitive consistency.

Research by Rosenberg (1968) supports the assumption that the affective–cognitive consistency of an attitude correlates with its stability and resistance to attitude change. It seems reasonable to anticipate that attitudes characterized by affective–cognitive consistency, and therefore stability, will have greater validity as predictors of subsequent behaviour. In research by Norman (1975), the relationship between attitude and behaviour was investigated with subjects who were differentiated according to the high or low affective–cognitive consistency of their attitudes. In three experiments the relationship between the measured affective component and the investigated behaviour was higher for subjects whose attitudes showed affective–cognitive consistency than for those who had attitudes low in affective–cognitive consistency.

Findings of Bagozzi and Burnkraut (1979) also show that affective reactions to an attitude object do not always represent the complete cognitive content concerning the object. A single affective response alone cannot always adequately represent the universe of beliefs related to a given attitude object. This being the case, since attitudes are very complex and differentiated, one can assume that behaviour will be better predicted when, in addition to the affective attitudinal response, the complex belief system of a person regarding the attitude object (cognitive component) is also considered. That is, it is better to take the whole structure of an attitude into account.

Schlegel (1975) assumed that the more direct experience subjects had of an attitude object, the more hierarchical and complex the organization of their attitude structure would be and the less the structure could be illustrated by a single affective factor. This hypothesis was confirmed in his research on attitudes towards the consumption of marijuana. On the basis of these research findings, Schlegel and DiTecco (1982) were able to show that for attitudes which were not based on direct experience (again with marijuana consumption) an affective-response measurement gave a sufficiently good summary of the whole attitude structure. Behaviour prediction in this case could be based entirely on those affective components; further measurement of cognitive structures did not improve the behaviour prediction substantially. With attitudes based on direct experiences, the picture changes. Predictions of behaviour (marijuana use) simply on the basis of affective responses towards this attitude object were not very successful, but could be substantially improved by introducing variables based on the cognitive structure of the attitude – that is, beliefs about the attitude object.

The question of whether attitudes based or not based on direct experience of the attitude object are better predictors of behaviour is also addressed in a research programme by Fazio and Zanna (1981). To begin with, there exists a contradiction between the findings of Schlegel and DiTecco (1982) and the research programme of Fazio and Zanna (1981) concerning the effects of direct experience on the attitude–behaviour relationship. Schlegel and DiTecco argue that the behavioural repertoire of persons who have had direct experience of an attitude object is greater. Therefore, the knowledge about this attitude object is greater and the attitude structures are more complex. These complex attitude structures cannot be integrated into a single affective attitude judgement, and therefore the latter is only a poor predictor of behaviour. On the other hand, Fazio and Zanna (1981) postulate that attitudes that are acquired by direct experience have a greater clarity (can be better discriminated from other possible attitude positions) and increased stability over time, and people are more strongly committed to those attitudes. Attitudes that are based on direct experiences are, therefore, more easily available and produce a stronger attitude–behaviour relationship.

In an extensive research programme, Fazio and his colleagues (see for example, Fazio and Zanna, 1981) demonstrated that direct experience with an attitude object strongly affects the relationship between attitudes and behaviour. For example, Regan and Fazio (1977) analysed students' attitudes and behaviour directed towards the severity of and possible solutions to a housing shortage on the campus. They showed that behaviour could be more accurately predicted on the basis of attitudes when the attitudes were acquired by direct experience of the housing shortage. These findings were supported in more experimentally controlled studies (Regan and Fazio, 1977). It was also shown that the higher availability of attitudes based on direct experience (owing to their clarity, stability over time etc., as mentioned above) was responsible for their greater potential to predict behaviour (see Fazio et al., 1982).

The contradiction between the results and theoretical reasoning of Schlegel and DiTecco (1982) on the one hand, and Fazio and his colleagues on the other, can be resolved by assuming some curvilinear relationship (see figure 8.5). In the first stages of direct experience, attitudes based on more direct experiences are better predictors of behaviour (owing to the mediating mechanisms such as better availability postulated by Fazio et al., 1982). With increasing direct

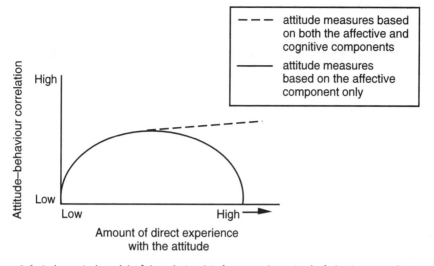

Figure 8.6 A theoretical model of the relationship between the attitude–behaviour correlation and the amount of direct experience with the attitude object

experience, however, attitude structure becomes more and more complex and, finally, cannot be sufficiently integrated into one single affective response. From then on, more direct experience will result in a decrease in behavioural predictability on the basis of the affective component of an attitude. Nevertheless, as shown by Schlegel and DiTecco (1982), this decline in behavioural predictability can be fully compensated when a cognitive attitudinal measure is added. Then, indeed, attitudes based on direct experiences remain better predictors of behaviour than other attitudes.

The way in which attitudes are formed is also a central topic of Petty and Cacioppo's (1986b) elaboration likelihood model and Chaiken's (1987) heuristic–systematic model (see chapter 9; and also Eagly and Chaiken, 1993). In the elaboration likelihood model Petty and Cacioppo assume that there exist two distinct routes to attitude formation and attitude change: the central and the peripheral routes (a similar distinction is made by the heuristic–systematic model, Chaiken, 1987). Attitudes are formed or changed via the central route whenever the (potential) holder of the attitude is motivated and capable of processing attitude-relevant information in an extensive and elaborate way. In this case the content of the attitude will primarily be a function of reliable and valid information about the attitude object. However, if the (potential) holder of an attitude is either not motivated and/or not capable of processing the relevant information intensively, attitudes are formed or changed via the peripheral route. Under these conditions attitudes are not formed or changed by considering convincing attitude-relevant information but by relying on certain peripheral cues such as the trustworthiness of the source of information or the number of people who advocate a certain attitudinal position. Concerning the attitude–behaviour relationship Petty and Cacioppo assume that attitudes formed or changed via the central route are better predictors of behaviour than attitudes formed via the peripheral route. This hypothesis was supported by Petty, Cacioppo and Schumann (1983) and Cacioppo, Petty, Kao and Rodriguez (1986).

Personality factors

The notion that some people show greater attitude–behaviour consistency than others has been tested in several studies which focus on different personality characteristics. We now give brief examples of this research.

Self-monitoring and objective self-awareness

Low self-monitors – people whose social behaviour depends greatly upon their internal states, dispositions, attitudes etc. (cf. Snyder, 1974) – show a higher correspondence between attitudes and behaviour than do high self-monitors. High self-monitors are primarily oriented to situational cues or to the potential reactions of their interaction partners when making behavioural decisions. Their behaviour does not reflect internal states such as emotions or attitudes, and varies greatly across situations. The higher attitude–behaviour correspondence of low self-monitors could be partly due to their preference for situations in which existing attitudes can be openly expressed and therefore easily translated into action (Snyder and Kendzierski, 1982).

A higher attitude–behaviour correlation has also been reported for persons who are highly 'objectively self-aware' (cf. for example, Carver, 1975; Gibbons, 1978). Self-awareness can be a trait or a variable internal state (Duval and Wicklund, 1972; Wicklund, 1975). The attention of a person who is highly self-aware (by trait or owing to certain situational cues) is primarily focused on the self, that is, on his or her own feelings, emotions, norms, attitudes and other internal states, whereas the attention of a person low in self-awareness is directed at other people, the personal or impersonal environment.

Self-consistency

According to Bem and Allen (1974), one can argue that only for those persons who define themselves as relatively self-consistent over different situations does a high correlation between attitudes and behaviour exist. For those subjects who define themselves as relatively inconsistent, there exists a relatively low correlation between attitude and behaviour. Zanna, Olson and Fazio (1980) presented support for this hypothesis that behavioural consistency in the past leads to higher attitude–behaviour covariation than does past behavioural variability.

Other factors that influence behaviour – models of the attitude-behaviour relation

Of course, attitudes will be weak predictors of behaviour when the situational constraints are so strong that no individual behaviour is possible. One of the most frequently discussed situational constraints is that of a strong social norm in the specific situation in which an attitudinally relevant behaviour has to be performed. Fishbein and Ajzen (1975) proposed a model of attitudes and behaviour which incorporates the component of social norms as a major factor. This model, called the **theory of reasoned action**, and its extension – the **theory of planned behaviour** (Ajzen, 1991; Ajzen and Madden, 1986) – are presented in figure 8.6. It is the most influential and popular model of the attitude–behaviour relationship. Ajzen and his colleagues assume – as shown in figure 8.6 – that the immediate determinant of behaviour is a person's intention to perform (or not to perform) this behaviour. *Behavioural intention*, then, is first determined by the person's positive or negative evaluation of performance of this behaviour, or in other words the *attitude* towards the behaviour. A person's attitude towards the behaviour (for example, saving energy) is a function of the expectation or *belief* (the subjective probability) that this behaviour will lead to a

THEORY OF
REASONED
ACTION

THEORY OF
PLANNED
BEHAVIOUR

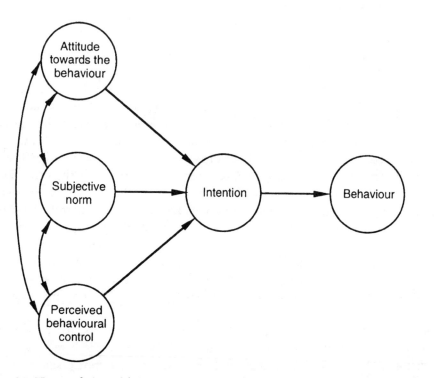

Figure 8.7 Theory of planned behaviour (the theory of planned behaviour extends the theory of reasoned action by adding the new factor 'perceived behavioural control') (Ajzen, 1991)

certain consequence (for example, 'Saving energy results in a loss of comfort' or 'Saving energy contributes to environmental protection') and the *value* ascribed to these consequences ('A loss of comfort is bad' or 'Environmental protection is good'). An attitude is predicted by multiplying the value and expectancy components associated with each behavioural consequence and summing up these products. The theories of reasoned action and planned behaviour are therefore also described as **expectancy-value models**.

The second determinant of behavioural intention is called the *subjective norm* (the person's judgement of the likelihood that relevant others, such as friends, partner and so on, expect him or her to show the behaviour in question). Again, the subjective-norm component is determined by two factors that are multiplied and added together: *normative beliefs* (what relevant others expect the person to do) and the person's *motivation to comply* with these expectations.

In the original theory of reasoned action, attitudes and subjective norms were the only two factors to influence behavioural intentions and thereby also behaviour. The extended theory of planned behaviour added another factor called 'perceived behavioural control'. This extension became necessary because the original model led to a good prediction of behaviour only in those cases in which this behaviour was under a high degree of volitional control. However, whenever people perceived that they had, or actually had, incomplete volitional control the extended model led to much better predictions of behaviour. Perceived behavioural control was conceptualized as a person's expectancy of the ease or difficulty of performing the intended behaviour. A person's confidence of being able to perform a certain behaviour may be low, for example, when he or she expects events to happen that would conflict with this behaviour (for example, the fact that the person might break his/her leg or be under extreme time pressure could conflict with his/her intention to conserve energy by riding a bicycle). Perceived behavioural control should, on the one hand, affect intentions (if people do not expect to be able to carry out a certain behaviour successfully they will probably not be highly motivated even to try). On the other hand, perceived behavioural control should exert a direct influence on the behaviour itself if perceived control is related, to some extent, to actual control (if a person lacks the ability to be a good tennis player, he or she will probably fail to win a match even if the intention to do so is strong). Ajzen and Madden (1986) confirmed the hypothesis that the incorporation of the 'behavioural control' component allows for more accurate prediction of behaviour such as students' class attendance and course achievements, compared with the original version of the theory of reasoned action.

As an illustration, the model of planned behaviour predicts that persons will engage in energy conservation when they believe: (1) that there is a strong probability that conserving energy will result in positive consequences such as guaranteeing the energy supply for future generations, or preventing negative consequences like environmental damage (the attitude component); (2) that their friends, family and colleagues at work expect them to conserve energy, and they are motivated to comply with this expectation (the subjective norm component); and (3) that they will be able to overcome all possible problems that could prevent them from saving energy (perceived behavioural control).

The predictions of the theory of reasoned action as well as of the theory of planned behaviour have been tested in many empirical studies and have received considerable empirical support (for an overview, see Ajzen, 1991; Eagly and Chaiken, 1993). The work of Fishbein and Ajzen also stimulated research which led to findings that are not consistent with these models, showing that other factors besides attitudes, social norms and perceived behavioural control can influence behaviour. For example, Bentler and Speckart (1979, 1981) showed that habits exert a direct influence on behaviour which is not mediated (contrary at least to the model of reasoned action) by social norms or attitudes (see also Echabe, Rovira and Garate, 1988; Mittal, 1988). Other variables which account for significant parts of the behavioural variance, apart from attitudes and social norms, are the experienced moral obligation to show a certain behaviour or the relevance of this behaviour for self-identity outcomes (see, for example, Gorsuch and Ortberg, 1983; Granberg and Holmberg, 1990).

On the basis of these and other research findings the general validity of the models of reasoned action and planned behaviour has been questioned by several authors, and alternative or enlarged models have been proposed. A composite attitude–behaviour model that summarizes several of the variables of the model of reasoned action and other variables mentioned above, such as habits, attitudes towards targets (besides attitudes towards behaviour) and self-identity outcomes, was proposed recently by Eagly and Chaiken (1993).

Simon (1981) questioned the assumption of human rational decision-making which underlies the model of reasoned action. He assumed that because of the capacity limitations of human information processing, people do not try to 'optimize' outcomes through their behavioural decisions but are in general 'satisfied' with any outcome that is above a subjective level of aspiration. Individuals strive not for maximum utility but for satisfying outcomes that can be far short of a theoretically achievable maximum. For example, most women may marry men with whom they are by and large satisfied but whose attractions are far below those of the more ideal partner whom they might have found had they continued their search process.

Frey, Stahlberg and Gollwitzer (1993) also emphasized that the assumption of intensive elaboration of alternative behavioural options (see Ajzen and Fishbein, 1980; Davidson and Morrison, 1983; Fishbein, 1980) covers only a limited sample of human behavioural decisions. All situations in which people are not motivated or capable of intensively processing the pros and cons of specific behavioural alternatives are not covered. For example, people may be unwilling to engage in extensive cognitive elaboration whenever they are pessimistic about whether they can achieve an optimal behavioural decision with justifiable costs (amount of time or cognitive effort invested). Elaboration may also be avoided because people are afraid that the result will be an affectively undesirable behavioural alternative. The latter may be the case whenever the attitude in question possesses an inconsistent structure (affective–cognitive inconsistency of the attitude, but also any inconsistency between attitudes and social norms).

Fazio (1990) also criticized the model of reasoned action for being limited to behaviour in situations where people are highly motivated and capable of thinking deliberately about the attitude and/or the behaviour relevant to this **MODE MODEL** attitude. In his **MODE model** (motivation and opportunity as determinants of how attitudes influence behaviour) he added the idea that whenever motivation or opportunity for reasonable decisions on attitude-relevant behaviour is missing, highly accessible attitudes may automatically guide behaviour because they influence the perception and judgement of the situation (see also Doll and Ajzen, 1992).

Eagly and Chaiken (1993) further criticized existing models of the attitude–behaviour relationship for not clarifying the exact nature of the relation between intentions and behaviour: 'the concept of intentions remains underdeveloped in the reasoned action model. Intention might ... be conceptualized as a continuum running from vaguely formulated thoughts about future behaviour to clear-cut plans that one is going to engage in a particular behaviour at a particular point in time' (p. 185). Research which fills this gap has recently been carried out by Heckhausen (1990) and Gollwitzer (1990, 1991; for a summary **RUBICON** see Frey, Stahlberg and Gollwitzer, 1993; Gollwitzer, 1993). In their **Rubicon** **MODEL** model they differentiated four distinct, sequential action phases which are characterized by specific mind-sets. Important for the development of the intention concept are the first two phases described in the model. In the *pre-decisional phase* of action people deliberate on specific action goals out of their numerous preferences and wishes. This pre-decisional phase is presumed to be accompanied by a deliberative mind-set where the person's thinking is directed towards the expected values of potential action goals. In the *post-decisional (pre-actional) phase* the decision to pursue a specific action goal has been made and the person is now concerned with the implementation of this goal. The corresponding implemental mind-set is directed towards concrete prerequisites for implementing the selected action goal. The borderline between the pre-decisional and the post-decisional phase (the Rubicon) is characterized by selection of a specific action goal or, in the terminology of the models of reasoned action or planned behaviour, by formulating a clear behavioural intention. In order to translate the formulated behavioural intentions into actions the Rubicon model postulates a different kind of intention that is formulated in the post-decisional phase (behavioural plans): the person must deliberate on the questions of when, where, and how to realize the selected behavioural goal (Gollwitzer, 1993). The concept of behavioural plans can therefore be a valuable supplement to the attitude–behaviour models described above.

In summary, factors such as social norms, moral norms and habits evoked in a certain situation can exert strong influences on behaviour and strengthen or attenuate the attitude–behaviour relationship. However, behavioural decisions are not always a consequence of rational and extensive information processing, as some of the most popular attitude–behaviour models, for example the theory of planned behaviour, assume. Sometimes behaviour may be guided by the automatic activation of attitudes or other affective preferences. Finally, even explicitly formulated behavioural intentions may not guarantee that the overt behaviour will be shown in reality: only if a person makes concrete plans about where, when and how to realize the behaviour, is the probability that the behaviour will actually be shown maximized.

Summary and Conclusions

In this chapter the structure, measurement and functions of attitudes and the relationship between attitudes and behaviour have been discussed. Research interest in all of these topics has been strongly renewed in recent years following the decline in interest in the late 1960s and 1970s. This decline in interest in attitude research was basically due to the pessimistic view of the attitude–behaviour relationship that was widely shared at the end of the 1960s. Not surprisingly, the renewal of interest is also related to the more optimistic perspective that was developed at the beginning of the 1970s and which was connected with the work of Fishbein and Ajzen. Furthermore, a lot of work in the field of applied social psychology is based on these refined models of behavioural prediction (see the fields of energy conservation, consumer decision-making, health psychology). Moreover, there are enough compelling future perspectives – such as the discussion of more 'cognitive' versus more 'affective' models of behavioural prediction – to ensure the persistence of this 'comeback' of theorizing and empirical work on attitudes for some years to come.

Glossary terms

Attitude	Expectancy-value models	Selective exposure
Behavioural intention	Galvanic skin response	Semantic differential
Beliefs	Likert-scale	Theory of planned behaviour
Bogus pipeline	Lost letter technique	Theory of reasoned action
Cognitive consistency	MODE model	Three-component model of
theories	Rubicon model	attitudes
Dissonance theory		

Discussion points

1   Characterize the three-component and the unidimensional models of attitude structure. Discuss the relationship between the complexity of an attitude and the adequacy of the two models of attitude structure.
2   What are the advantages and disadvantages of attitudinal measures based on self-reports and other sorts of attitude measures such as physiological indicators or the bogus-pipeline procedure?
3   Some authors argue that attitudes guide information processing (e.g., recall of attitude-relevant information) in a bipolar manner. What does this mean?
4   How has cognitive dissonance theory contributed to our understanding of the functions of attitudes?
5   The most popular models of the relationship between attitudes and behaviour are the theory of reasoned action and the theory of planned behaviour. In what respect can one argue that these models are based on the idea of human rational decision-making?
6   How do recent models of attitude clarify the processes linking attitudes to behaviours?

Suggestions for further reading

Eagly, A. H. and Chaiken, S. (1993) *The Psychology of Attitudes*. San Diego, CA: Harcourt Brace Jovanovich. This book provides a comprehensive review of attitude research in recent decades, including the latest theoretical developments in that field.

Fazio, R. H. (1990) Multiple processes by which attitudes guide behaviour: The MODE model as an integrative framework. In M. P. Zanna (ed.), *Advances in Experimental Social Psychology* (vol. 13). San Diego, CA: Academic Press, pp. 75–109. This article deals with the very important question of how attitudes guide behaviour; that is, what different processes might be involved.

Fazio, R. H. and Zanna, M. P. (1981) Direct experience and attitude–behaviour consistency. In L. Berkowitz (ed.), *Advances in Experimental Social Psychology* (vol. 14). New York: Academic Press, pp. 161–202. An interesting research programme (with laboratory and field studies) which deals with the effect of direct experience of an attitude object on attitude–behaviour consistency.

Fishbein, M. and Ajzen, I. (1975) *Belief, Attitude, Intention, and Behaviour*. Reading, MA: Addison-Wesley. This book gives a detailed introduction to one of the most popular theoretical models concerning the attitude–behaviour relationship: the theory of reasoned action. Other important attitude theories and relevant empirical findings are also discussed.

Frey, D. (1986) Recent research on selective exposure to information. In L. Berkowitz (ed.), *Advances in Experimental Social Psychology* (vol. 19). New York: Academic Press, pp. 41–80. Hypotheses concerning selective exposure to information derived from dissonance theory are presented and discussed in the light of relevant research findings.

Olson, J. M. and Zanna, M. P. (1993) Attitudes and attitude change. *Annual Review of Psychology*, 44, 117–54. An update of research developments in the area of attitudes can be found in the reviews which appear every three years in the *Annual Review of Psychology*.

Roberts, J. V. (1985) The attitude–memory relationship after 40 years: a meta-analysis of the literature. *Basic and Applied Social Psychology*, 6, 221–41. This paper presents an analysis of the available research on the selective-recall hypothesis, that is it tries to give an answer to the question of whether attitudes selectively guide the recall of attitude-relevant information.

Schlegel, R. P. and DiTecco, D. (1982). Attitudinal structures and the attitude– behaviour relation. In M. P. Zanna, E. T. Higgins and C. P. Herman (eds), *Consistency in Social Behaviour: The Ontario Symposium* (vol. 2). Hillsdale, NJ: Erlbaum, pp. 17–49. This article presents a fascinating analysis of attitude structures, stressing the fact that the complexity of attitudes has to be taken into account when predicting behaviour.

Key studies

Breckler, S. J. (1984). Empirical validation of affect, behavior, and cognition as distinct components of attitude. *Journal of Personality and Social Psychology*, 47, 1191–1205.

Ajzen, I. and Madden, T. J. (1986). Prediction of goal-directed behavior: Attitudes, intentions, and perceived behavioral control. *Journal of Experimental Social Psychology*, 22, 453-474.

9 Principles of Attitude Formation and Strategies of Change

Wolfgang Stroebe and Klaus Jonas

Contents

Introduction

The notion of using social-psychological knowledge to change attitudes and to influence behaviour conjures up visions of advertising executives planning mass media campaigns to sell cars, refrigerators or margarine. And yet, probably one of the most effective campaigns in recent times, achieving substantial changes in attitudes and behaviour, has been the campaign against smoking. It began in 1964 with the publication of the report of the United States Surgeon General's Advisory Committee on Smoking and Health (USDHEW, 1964). The persuasive information on the substantial health impairment suffered by smokers contained in this report was quickly adopted by newspapers and magazines and thus reached a very wide audience. The material not only persuaded many smokers but it also convinced politicians that it was time to act, and, some years later, compulsory health warnings were introduced on tobacco advertisements and cigarette packets. Finally, in the eighties, Federal cigarette tax was doubled and various states introduced additional excise taxes on cigarettes, thus substantially increasing the financial cost of smoking. Largely as a result of this anti-smoking campaign, smoking is now generally recognized as a health risk and an addiction. Moreover, especially in the USA, smoking has declined substantially.

This chapter examines the psychological processes which mediate the impact of mass media campaigns like the 'war against smoking' on attitudes and behaviour. The first part of the chapter discusses attitude formation in terms of principles of learning, such as classical and instrumental conditioning. The second part focuses on the attitudinal impact of persuasive communications and on the processes which mediate this impact. In the third part we review incentive-induced strategies of change.

The Role of Reinforcements in Attitude Formation and Change

In line with the classic definitions of attitude as learned predispositions (e.g., Allport, 1935; Campbell, 1963), early theorists of attitude formation have argued that attitudes are learned according to the same principles as other learned responses. Influenced by the then still dominant behaviourist learning theories, these theorists believed that attitudinal responses are automatically strengthened through processes of **classical and instrumental conditioning** (e.g., Staats and Staats, 1958; Verplanck, 1955). However, with the emergence of cognitive theories of social learning (e.g., Bandura, 1986), psychologists began to suggest that the impact of reinforcements on behaviour is mediated by their informative and incentive functions.

CLASSICAL AND INSTRUMENTAL CONDITIONING

Plate 9.1 Anti-smoking campaigns, like this poster, have helped to increase the perceived health risks of smoking and led to a decline in this habit

Classical conditioning of attitudes

Through classical conditioning, a neutral stimulus initially incapable of eliciting a particular response gradually acquires the ability to do so through repeated association with a stimulus that has already evoked this response. A well-known example of such an initially neutral stimulus is the tone which Pavlov's dogs heard before receiving food. After these two stimuli had been paired for several trials, the tone began to evoke salivation, a response previously elicited only by the food. It is likely that this tone not only became the elicitor of a salivating response but also acquired a positive evaluation. If one could have asked these dogs to rate the tone on a number of semantic differential scales before and after it had been paired with the food stimuli, ratings would probably have improved over the trials. This is, at least, what one could infer from the findings of experiments on classical conditioning of attitudes (e.g., Berkowitz and Knurek, 1969; Kuykendall and Keating, 1990; Staats and Staats, 1958; Zanna, Kiesler and Pilkonis, 1970).

Instead of food or electric shocks, Staats and Staats (1958) used words that elicited positive affect (such as gift, sacred, happy) or negative affect (such as bitter, ugly, failure) as unconditioned stimuli. These words were presented auditorily immediately after the visual presentation of the name of a nationality in what was ostensibly an experiment testing whether subjects could separately learn verbal stimuli presented in the two different ways. For half the subjects (American college students) Dutch was consistently paired with positive and Swedish with negative adjectives, while the pairing was reversed for the other half. Other nationality names were always paired with neutral words. When the target nationalities were later rated on semantic differential scales, the nationality that had been paired with positive words elicited a more positive rating than the nationality that had been paired with negative words.

That attitudes acquired through classical conditioning can affect behaviour was demonstrated by Berkowitz and Knurek (1969), who used Staats and Staats's (1958) procedure to condition negative attitudes to a critical name. When subjects, in what was ostensibly a second experiment, were engaged in a discussion with two fellow students, one of whom had the critical name, they generally acted in a more unfriendly manner towards the negatively named person than to the discussion partner who had a neutral name.

Mediating processes. Whereas it is generally accepted that evaluative responses can be attached to formerly neutral stimuli through procedures of classical conditioning, there has been a great deal of discussion about the processes which mediate this association. It is important to note that Staats and Staats do not assume that the attitude towards the target nationalities changed because the association of positive (or negative) adjectives with a nationality name led to a change in the traits attributed to these people. According to classical conditioning, the change in evaluation is due to the fact that the positive evaluative reaction initially evoked by the adjectives has now also been passed on to the nationality name by mere association. Such processes could play an important role in the formation of ethnic and national attitudes.

The viability of this interpretation has been challenged by researchers (e.g., Insko and Oakes, 1966; Page, 1969) who argued that subjects had recognized the systematic relationship between the adjectives and the nationality names and were merely responding to demand characteristics by telling the experimenter what they thought he or she wanted to hear. An explanation in terms of *demand characteristics* suggests that subjects realize that there is a contingency between certain nationality names and positive or negative evaluative words.

Page (1969) conducted a number of studies in which subjects were extensively questioned, after conditioning experiments, about their awareness of the association of the unconditioned and the conditioned stimulus (e.g., nationality name and positive or negative evaluative words). Page could indeed demonstrate that subjects who showed conditioning effects had also been aware of the contingencies. But Staats (1969) argued that the awareness was created after the conditioning through the questionnaire. Once subjects were made aware of the contingency, those who had shown the conditioning effect were most likely to realize that there had been an association. Furthermore, it would be difficult to attribute the findings of Berkowitz and Knurek (1969) to demand characteristics.

244 Wolfgang Stroebe and Klaus Jonas

In a recent relevant experiment Krosnick, Betz, Jussim and Lynn (1992) obtained results which also cannot be explained by demand characteristics. Krosnick and colleagues demonstrated changes in the evaluative ratings of a target in two experiments in which the unconditioned stimuli were presented subliminally. Subjects viewed slides of a female target person going about normal daily activities (such as getting into a car). Immediately preceding each slide was a subliminal exposure of an affect-arousing photograph (e.g., a flash of 13-m.s. or 9-m.s. duration). Half the subjects were subliminally exposed to positive-affect-arousing photos (such as a bridal couple) and half to negative-affect-arousing photographs (such as a were-wolf). As the results showed, the subliminal photographs influenced evaluations of the target in accordance with the valence of the unconditioned stimuli. Additional measures revealed that subjects were not able to detect the affective content of the affect-arousing slides at better than chance levels. Thus, since subjects were unaware of having been exposed to the unconditioned stimuli, they could not be aware of the contingency between the unconditioned and the conditioned stimulus.

In conclusion, the findings of research on classical conditioning suggest that our attitudes may unwittingly be coloured by the context in which an object has been experienced. This process is quite functional when the relationship between stimulus and context is a stable one. Thus, it is healthy to develop an aversion to certain types of alcohol because their taste has been associated with terrible hangovers in the past. It is less desirable, however, when children develop negative attitudes towards members of other nationalities or races because the significant people around them make negative remarks or show their distaste whenever certain outsiders are encountered or when their name is mentioned (see chapter 3). Classical conditioning also offers an explanation for the effectiveness of advertising practices that pair brand names with positive but seemingly irrelevant stimuli.

Instrumental conditioning of attitudes

With classical conditioning, the organism plays a passive role. It has no control over the response which is originally elicited through the unconditioned and later through the conditioned response. With operant or instrumental conditioning, on the other hand, the organism has to first produce a response before it can be reinforced. In this paradigm, the frequency with which a specific response occurs increases because it is followed by positive consequences or decreases because it is followed by negative consequences. The response to be conditioned must be part of the organism's behavioural repertoire.

The majority of studies on instrumental conditioning were conducted with animals, which on responding correctly were typically rewarded with food pellets. Obviously, such food pellets are not appropriate for research with humans. Even if food pellets are replaced by sweets, the use of such reinforcers is rather limited. Verplanck (1955) solved this problem by reinforcing human behaviour with recognition or positive regard. The students who served as experimenters were instructed to involve other students in planned conversations. During the first ten minutes, the experimenters would behave neutrally and simply note down the number of opinion statements made by their subjects. In the following ten minutes they would reinforce any opinion statements made by their subjects by enthusiastically agreeing. During the final 10 minutes experimenters would either not agree with any opinion statement or even show disagreement. As expected, agreement acted as a positive reinforcer. During the second period of ten minutes all subjects increased the number of opinion statements they expressed. During the last period, where the expression of opinion statements was no longer reinforced, or even punished, 21 of the 24 subjects reduced the number of opinion statements.

Whereas Verplanck merely influenced the frequency of the expression of opinion statements, Hildum and Brown (1965) were the first to demonstrate that (stated) attitudes could be changed through differential reinforcement. Students of Harvard University were interviewed about their position regarding the Harvard philosophy of offering a broad and general course of study. Subjects had to answer a set of attitude questions by responding in terms of Likert-type answer categories which reflected different degrees of agreement or disagreement. Half of the subjects were reinforced with the word 'good' for agreement with favourable statements or disagreement with unfavourable statements. The other half were reinforced in the opposite direction. As expected, subjects who had been reinforced in the positive direction ended up showing a more positive attitude than subjects who had been reinforced in the negative direction.

In a later study, Insko (1965) had students of an introductory psychology class interviewed by telephone about some issue of local interest. Again, half the subjects were reinforced for favourable attitudinal responses to a certain topic, the other half for unfavourable attitudinal responses. One week later, subjects were given an attitude questionnaire during the introductory psychology class, assessing, among other issues, their attitude to the issue used in the reinforcement study. It could be shown that the groups who had been differentially reinforced differed in their attitude even one week later.

Mediating processes. Although these studies demonstrate that verbal reinforcement can result in attitude change, it remains unclear whether these effects occur automatically and below the level of awareness or are mediated by cognitive processes. As an alternative to an interpretation in terms of automatic conditioning effects, where the 'good' response of the experimenter acts like a food pellet in a Skinner Box, Cialdini and Insko (1969) suggested a two-factor theory of verbal reinforcement. According to this hypothesis, the 'good' response by the experimenter has two functions: (1) it serves as a cue about the attitudinal position held by the interviewer; (2) it creates a rapport between interviewer and respondent. Thus, one factor is information, the other sympathy. Subjects' friendly feelings towards the interviewer then motivate them to conform with the interviewer's position.

Cialdini and Insko (1969) examined their hypothesis in a study which capitalized on the animosity that exists in many psychology departments between clinical and experimental psychologists. Psychology students were interviewed about their attitude towards clinical and experimental psychology by an experimenter who pretended to be a Ph.D. student either in experimental or in clinical psychology. Cross-cutting this manipulation, the experiment would reinforce agreement with either pro-clinical attitude statements or pro-experimental statements. Afterwards, subjects' attitudes towards clinical and experimental psychology were assessed by a second experimenter. If it is the information that the reinforcement gives about the attitude position of the experimenter which is responsible for the impact of the reinforcement, then such reinforcement should be less effective when this information is in conflict with other information that subjects have about the attitude of the interviewer. Consistent with this hypothesis, Cialdini and Insko (1969) observed the reinforcement effect mainly when the reinforcement direction agreed with the professional identity of the interviewer.

Summary

There is conclusive evidence that attitudes can be formed through procedures of classical and instrumental conditioning. However, the mechanisms accounting for this relationship are still unclear. Although behaviourist and cognitive interpretations of conditioning were hotly debated during the 1970s, this controversy has never been resolved. Existing empirical evidence does not rule out the possibility that attitudinal conditioning may sometimes influence attitudes without mediation by higher-order cognitive processes (see Eagly and Chaiken, 1993).

Persuasion and the Role of Information in Attitude Formation and Change

With the cognitive revolution of the sixties and seventies, cognitive approaches increasingly dominated attitude research (see chapter 8). Cognitive theories have proved particularly useful in the analysis of the processes or variables which mediate the impact of persuasive appeals on attitudes. They describe how attitudes form and change in response to complex verbal messages, which typically consist of an overall position that is advocated and one or more arguments designed to support the position. Whereas some persuasion theories focus on **systematic processing** by emphasizing the importance of the message-recipients' detailed assessment of argument content, the **dual-process models of**

SYSTEMATIC
PROCESSING

persuasion take a broader perspective. These approaches take into account systematic processing but they consider in addition the idea that individuals adopt attitudes on the basis of other factors than their understanding and evaluation of the semantic content of a persuasive communication.

Theories of systematic processing

An information-processing model of persuasion

The information-processing paradigm proposed by McGuire (1968, 1969, 1985) provides a useful framework for thinking about the stages involved in the processing of persuasive communication. He proposed that the persuasive impact of a message is the product of at least five steps: (1) attention, (2) comprehension, (3) yielding, (4) retention and (5) behaviour (see figure 9.1). For example, the ultimate objective of a speech given on television by a political candidate before an election is to get the members of the audience to vote for his or her party. In terms of McGuire's framework, the candidate's first problem is to reach the audience. If viewers use this opportunity of a break between programmes to fetch a drink (failure to attend), the appeal will not result in attitude change. However, even if viewers attend to the communication, it will have little impact if they do not understand the arguments because these are too complex (failure to comprehend) or if they do not accept the communicator's conclusions (failure to yield). But even if the candidate manages to persuade the audience, this will be of no use if viewers change their attitudes again before election day or if extreme weather conditions keep them away from the ballot box (failure to act). Since the receiver must go through each of these steps if the communication is to have an ultimate persuasive impact, and since it is unlikely that the probability of any given step will be maximal, McGuire's framework explains why it is often difficult to induce behaviour change through information campaigns.

In social-psychological studies of persuasion, the impact of a communication is typically assessed immediately following exposure to the message. Thus, our

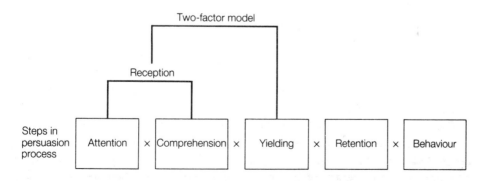

Figure 9.1 The information-processing paradigm of McGuire

analysis is restricted to the first three steps of the chain. Furthermore, since attention and comprehension have usually been combined into a single step of reception of the message content in order to simplify measurement, McGuire's model can be reduced to a two-step version, which states that the probability of a communication resulting in attitude and opinion change is the joint product of the probability of reception and acceptance (yielding).

Individual differences in persuasibility. According to this two-step model, factors which are positively related to both reception and yielding should also be positively related to persuasion. However, the more interesting prediction of the model is for cases where a given determinant of persuasion has opposing effects on reception and yielding. McGuire (1968) suggested that this is the case for many individual-difference variables. For example, it is plausible to assume that people are more likely to understand a message the more intelligent they are. Thus one would expect that intelligence was positively related to reception. One would also expect that people who are intelligent are more critical and therefore less likely to accept a message. If intelligence is positively related to reception but negatively related to yielding, the two-step model would predict a curvilinear relationship between intelligence and attitude change: individuals who are highly intelligent (zero yielding) or exceedingly unintelligent (zero reception) should be least influenceable, whereas individuals of moderate intelligence should be most easily influenced.

Such curvilinear predictions are difficult to test. In order to allow for more exact predictions, McGuire (1968) introduced the 'situational weighting principle', which postulates that the relative importance of reception and yielding varies with the nature of the persuasion context. For example, reception is assumed to be a more important mediator of persuasion for complex, well-argued messages whereas yielding is assumed to be more important than reception for simple messages supported by few arguments or in simple conformity situations. By taking into account such changes in the relative importance of reception and yielding, more refined predictions can be derived. For example, if complex, well-argued messages make reception the major mediator of attitude change, the model predicts that more intelligent recipients should be more easily persuaded than less intelligent recipients. For unsupported recommendations, on the other hand, for which yielding should be the major mediator of change, a negative relationship between intelligence and attitude change would be expected. An experiment by Eagly and Warren (1976) supported these predictions (for a recent meta-analytic review of individual differences in influenceability see Rhodes and Wood, 1992).

Reception as mediator of change. Few studies have provided support for the assumption central to the McGuire model, that the reception of message arguments determines attitude change. In general, message reception, when measured by the recall of message arguments, is not found to correlate significantly with attitude change (for a review see Eagly and Chaiken, 1993).

There are a number of reasons why such correlations are often not obtained. One reason is that, according to the situational weighting principle, reception should be related to persuasibility only for complex but not for simple messages. Another reason likely to reduce the correlations between argument recall and attitude is that if individuals form spontaneous impressions during exposure to the message (i.e., on-line), they might forget the information and not store it in memory. Correlations between argument recall and attitude are most likely to occur if individuals are prevented from forming an attitude as the message is received, but must express an opinion at a later time. In support of this assumption, Mackie and Asuncion (1990) demonstrated that subjects whose capacity for on-line judgement was reduced by distraction, evidenced memory-based attitude change, that is, a high correlation between argument recall and attitude change. No such correlation was found for subjects whose capacity for on-line judgement had not been constrained.

On a more general level, it could be argued that factors which increase a person's motivation or ability to think about and elaborate information at the time of message exposure should reduce the correlation between attitudes and information recalled from the message (Petty, Priester and Wegener, 1994). As will become evident in the next section, the more individuals are able and motivated to think about a communication, the more strongly should attitude change be determined by the cognitive responses stimulated by the message. Thus, although the model developed by McGuire provides a useful heuristic framework for the study of factors which influence attitude change in a persuasion context, there is limited empirical support for the central assumption of the model that attitude change is determined by the reception of the arguments contained in a message. Furthermore, the model lacks specific theoretical principles that would allow one to predict the factors that affect acceptance and to understand the processes which mediate the relationship between acceptance and attitude change.

The cognitive-response model

The **cognitive-response model** of persuasion was developed by Greenwald (1968). Unlike McGuire's model, which emphasized the role of message comprehension in attitude change, the cognitive-response model stresses the mediating role of individual thoughts or 'cognitive responses' that recipients generate – and thus rehearse and learn – as they receive and reflect upon persuasive communications (Greenwald, 1968; Petty, Ostrom and Brock, 1981). By also developing a measure of cognitive responses (i.e., thought listing), Greenwald (1968) enabled researchers to assess more directly the processes assumed to mediate attitude change. With this thought-listing task, subjects are asked to list their thoughts or ideas relevant to the message topic. These thoughts are later categorized into those which are typically favourable to the

COGNITIVE-
RESPONSE MODEL

overall position advocated by the message and those thoughts which are generally unfavourable.

According to the cognitive-response model, listening to a communication is like a private discussion where the listener argues with (or against) the arguments presented in the communication. The model assumes that these cognitive responses mediate the effect of persuasive messages on attitude change. Messages should be persuasive to the extent that they evoke favourable thoughts but not persuasive to the extent that they evoke unfavourable thoughts. Moreover, these effects of favourability of recipients' thoughts should be greater, the more recipients engage in message-relevant thinking.

The cognitive-response perspective stimulated a great number of persuasion experiments, each of which manipulated a variable assumed to influence the extent of message processing (such as distraction, message repetition, issue involvement) and crossed this variable with a variable which reliably affects the favourability of the recipients' message-relevant thinking, namely the quality of the arguments presented in the communication. Consistent with expectations, the favourability of recipients' thoughts (as influenced by argument quality) affected persuasion only to the extent that recipients processed the message relatively carefully and therefore reacted to argument quality (for a review see Eagly and Chaiken, 1993).

DISTRACTION   **Distraction** was the first major persuasion variable to be investigated from a cognitive-response perspective. In this research, individuals who were exposed to a counter-attitudinal message were distracted by having to perform an irrelevant activity or by experiencing sensory stimulation irrelevant to the message (such as listening to a radio-transmitted speech which was heavily masked by static). Since a pioneering experiment conducted by Festinger and Maccoby (1964), results of studies on the role of distraction in persuasion have been controversial (for reviews see Baron, Baron and Miller, 1973; Eagly and Chaiken, 1993), with some studies finding attitude change to increase with increasing distraction (e.g., Festinger and Maccoby, 1964) whereas others observed the opposite relationship (e.g., Haaland and Venkatesan, 1968).

According to the cognitive-response model, such discrepant results are to be expected. Distraction reduces the recipients' ability to generate cognitive responses to a message. The impact of distraction on attitude change should therefore depend on the favourability of the thoughts produced by a message (Petty, Wells and Brock, 1976). If these dominant thoughts are mainly unfavourable, distraction should enhance persuasion. However, for messages which elicit predominantly favourable thoughts, distraction should work to inhibit persuasion.

In a classic study which replicated the distraction findings of Festinger and Maccoby (1964), Osterhouse and Brock (1970) exposed subjects to a message which contained seven low-quality persuasive arguments. Low-quality arguments were chosen to encourage counter-arguing. Half of the subjects could attend to the task without disturbance, whereas the other half were distracted from listening by having to monitor a series of flashing lights. By varying the rate at which these lights flashed, three levels of distraction could be created. Results were consistent with predictions. As distraction increased, persuasion increased, whereas both the number of counter-arguments that subjects generated and their recognition memory for persuasive arguments decreased significantly. Additional analyses indicated that there was a significant negative correlation between agreement and counter-arguing. Furthermore, if counter-arguing was held constant by means of a statistical procedure (analysis of covariance), the impact of distraction on attitude change became smaller.

Petty, Wells and Brock (1976) showed that the impact of distraction on attitude is dependent on the nature of the dominant thoughts stimulated by a communication. These authors conducted two experiments in which distraction was manipulated by having subjects record visual stimuli while listening to a message. The favourability of recipients' cognitive responses was manipulated by using either strong arguments (that is, arguments likely to elicit favourable thoughts) or weak arguments (i.e., arguments open to refutation and counter-argumentation). The results of both experiments supported the predictions derived from the cognitive-response model (see figure 9.2). Increases in distraction enhanced persuasion for the message which consisted of low-quality arguments, but reduced persuasion for the message containing exclusively high-quality arguments. Additional support for the assumption that both the increase and the decrease in persuasion was due to thought disruption comes from subjects' retrospective reports on their thoughts while listening to the

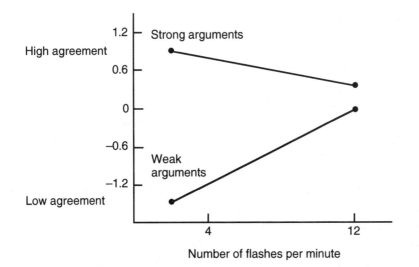

Figure 9.2 Mean attitude scores in relation to argument quality and level of distraction (Petty, Wells and Brock, 1976, expt 2)

communication. The distraction manipulation seems to have decreased recipients' counter-arguments for the low-quality argumentation and reduced the number of favourable thoughts for the high-quality version of the message.

Dual-process models of persuasion

Although the two models of persuasion discussed so far differ in the extent to which they emphasize reception of the arguments contained in a communication or the cognitive responses stimulated by these arguments, they agree in making attitude change dependent on the systematic processing of persuasive communications. For recipients unable or unmotivated to process the persuasive communication, little attitude change is expected to occur. In contrast, the dual-process theories discussed in this section incorporate the idea that under certain conditions people will adopt attitudes on bases other than their systematic processing of the arguments contained in the message. In this section two dual-process models will be discussed, namely the **elaboration likelihood model** of Petty and Cacioppo (1986a,b; Petty et al. 1994) and the **heuristic–systematic model** of Chaiken and her colleagues (e.g., Bohner, Moskowitz and Chaiken, 1995; Chaiken, Liberman and Eagly, 1989).

ELABORATION
LIKELIHOOD
MODEL

HEURISTIC-
SYSTEMATIC
MODEL

The elaboration likelihood model

When people receive a communication and are faced with the decision whether to accept or reject the position it advocates, they will try to form an opinion of its validity. This assessment may be arrived at by two different modes of information processing. According to what has been called the '**central route to persuasion**' by Petty and Cacioppo (1986a, b), recipients spend considerable time and effort on a critical evaluation of the message content. They scrutinize the message, they try to remember what they already know about the issue and then relate this knowledge to the arguments contained in the message. This mode of information processing is identical to the processes assumed in the cognitive-response model. However, sometimes recipients may be unwilling or unable to engage in this extensive process of message evaluation. Under these conditions attitudes will be formed according to the **peripheral route to persuasion**. This type of persuasion is conceptualized as the product of a variety of mechanisms which cause persuasion in the absence of argument scrutiny, such as classical or instrumental conditioning, or of heuristic processing, to be discussed below.

CENTRAL
ROUTE TO
PERSUASION

PERIPHERAL
ROUTE TO
PERSUASION

ELABORATION

Petty and Cacioppo (1986a,b) use the term '**elaboration**' to denote the extent to which a person thinks about the issue-relevant arguments contained in a message. At one end of the elaboration continuum message recipients rely on processes that characterize the peripheral route to persuasion. At the other end, they engage in a great deal of argument evaluation and issue-relevant thinking ('central route' to persuasion). The probability that a recipient will critically evaluate the arguments contained in a message (i.e., the 'elaboration likelihood') is determined by both motivation and ability. Motivation is important because such elaboration requires time and effort. Ability is important because a certain amount of intelligence, specific knowledge, or time is needed to appraise the validity of arguments contained in a message.

The heuristic–systematic model

Like the elaboration likelihood model, the heuristic–systematic model postulates two modes of information processing (e.g., Bohner et al., 1995; Chaiken, 1980; Chaiken and Eagly, 1993; Chaiken et al., 1989). One mode, called systematic processing, is identical to what Petty and Cacioppo termed the central route to persuasion. Individuals engage in systematic processing when they are motivated and able to judge the validity of a message's advocated position by scrutinizing persuasive argumentation and by thinking about the information in relation to other information they may possess. However, when individuals are unable or unmotivated to engage in systematic processing, they might base their decision to accept the message on some peripheral aspect such as the source's credibility or other non-content cues. This has been called '**heuristic processing**' by Chaiken and her colleagues.

HEURISTIC
PROCESSING

According to the heuristic–systematic model, people often use simple schemata or decision rules (i.e., cognitive heuristics) to assess the validity of a message and to decide whether they are willing to accept it. For example, people may have learned from previous experience that statements by experts tend to be more veridical than statements by non-experts. They may therefore apply the rule 'statements by experts can be trusted' in response to indications that the communicator is an expert (Eagly and Chaiken, 1993). Or they may have learned to trust people they like, and on finding a communicator likeable, they will apply the 'liking–agreement' heuristic, such as, 'people agree with people they like' or 'people I like usually have correct opinions on an issue' (Eagly and Chaiken, 1993). In terms of the elaboration likelihood model, heuristic processing involves one of many different strategies that form the 'peripheral route to persuasion' (Petty and Cacioppo, 1981, 1986; Petty et al., 1994).

Ability to process and attitude change

Much of the research on the impact of processing ability on attitude change has focused on two variables, namely distraction and message repetition. Since distraction research has already been reviewed earlier, we will restrict our discussion here to the role of message repetition. In contrast to distraction, which reduces processing ability, (moderate) argument repetition should provide recipients with more opportunity for cognitively elaborating a communication. Thus, repetition should enhance attitude change for strong messages but reduce it for weak ones. This hypothesis was tested by Cacioppo and Petty (1985), who exposed subjects either one or three times to a message that contained either strong or weak persuasive arguments. Consistent with their predictions, agreement with high-quality messages increased with increasing exposure, whereas agreement with the low-quality message decreased. However, the positive impact of repetition of high-quality messages seems to be limited. When messages are repeated too often, boredom appears to occur, which may result in rejection even of high-quality arguments (Cacioppo and Petty, 1979b).

Motivation and attitude change

The most influential determinant of a person's motivation to think about the arguments contained in a message is the perceived *personal relevance* of the communication. One important line of studies assessing the influence of motivation on acceptance has therefore manipulated the personal involvement of recipients. Only when highly involved, should recipients of a communication be motivated to assess the validity of the position advocated by critically evaluating the arguments contained in the message. With low involvement, when the issue of the communication is of little relevance, the recipient should rely on peripheral cues to evaluate the validity of the position advocated by the communicator.

These predictions were tested in an experiment by Petty, Cacioppo and Goldman (1981), who exposed college students to an attitude-discrepant communication (advocating a major change to the student examination system). This communication, on a topic of which American college students have a great deal of knowledge, contained either strong or weak arguments and was either attributed to a source of high expertise (the Carnegie Commission on Higher Education) or to one of low expertise (a class at a local high school). Subjects' involvement was manipulated by informing them either that the changes advocated in this message were going to be instituted the following year and would thus affect the subjects themselves (high involvement) or that they would take effect only in ten years' time (low involvement). Petty and colleagues (1981) predicted that argument quality should have a stronger effect on subjects of high rather than low involvement. Source credibility, on the other hand, a peripheral cue, should result in more attitude change with low rather than high involvement. Thus, when subjects believed that the changes would affect their own fate, they should be motivated to scrutinize the arguments and to engage in issue-relevant thinking. With them, argument quality would be a major factor in persuasion. Students who believed that these changes would only be instituted long after they had left the university would not be motivated to think a great deal about the communication. They would assess the validity of the advocated position by using heuristic rules such as 'the experts will know best'. The results strongly supported these predictions (figure 9.3). Similar findings were reported by Chaiken (1980).

The mood state experienced by recipients is another factor which influences their motivation to elaborate on the content of a message. When in a good mood, individuals seem to be more likely to engage in simplified, heuristic processing, whereas in a bad mood they may engage in more effortful systematic processing strategies, perhaps because their negative feeling informs them that their current situation is problematic. This was demonstrated in a laboratory experiment in which good or bad mood was induced in subjects by having them dwell on either a positive or a negative life event (Bless, Bohner, Schwarz and Strack, 1990). When these subjects were subsequently exposed to a communication consisting of either high-quality or low-quality arguments, argument quality affected attitude change only for subjects who were in a bad mood (figure 9.4). Conceptually equivalent findings were obtained in a number of other studies

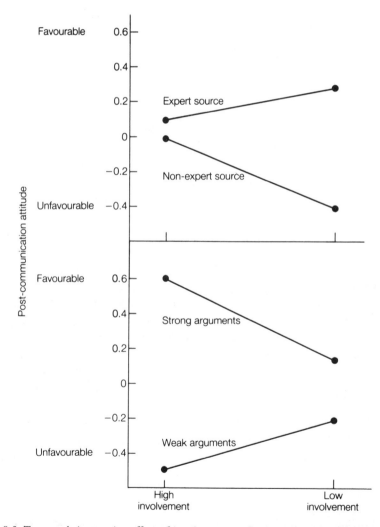

Figure 9.3 Top panel: interactive effect of involvement and source expertise on post-communication attitudes. Bottom panel: interactive effect of involvement and argument quality on post-communication attitudes (Petty, Cacioppo and Goldman, 1981)

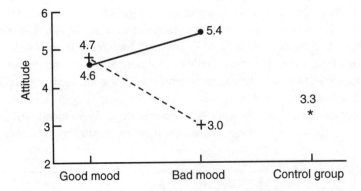

Figure 9.4 Attitude change as function of mood and message quality. (●······●): strong message quality; (+——+): weak message quality. (Adapted from Bless, Bohner, Schwarz and Strack, 1990, expt 1)

(e.g., Mackie and Worth, 1989; for a review see Schwarz, Bless and Bohner, 1991).

In addition to factors associated with the persuasive message or the persuasion context, there are also individual differences in people's motivation to think about persuasive communications. For example, people who enjoy thinking (that is those high in **need for cognition**; Cacioppo and Petty, 1982) should be more likely to form attitudes on the basis of the arguments contained in a communication than people who are low in need for cognition. Cacioppo and Petty (1982), who constructed a scale to measure need for cognition, supported this hypothesis in a study in which subjects high or low in need for cognition were exposed to either high-quality or low-quality arguments. Consistent with expectations, argument quality affected attitude change mainly for subjects who were high in need for cognition. Further evidence that individuals with a high need for cognition are more motivated to think about arguments contained in a communication comes from a recent experiment by Haugtvedt and Petty (1992). These authors demonstrated that, compared to individuals with a low need for cognition, attitude change in subjects with a high need for cognition was more persistent and more resistant against counter-argumentation. In line with Cacioppo and Petty's assumption that need for cognition reflects individual differences in motivation rather than ability, only low correlations have been observed between need for cognition and intelligence (Cacioppo, Petty, Kao and Rodriguez, 1986).

Co-occurrence of processing modes
Since the information contained in peripheral cues may often be quite valid, it would seem a waste of easily accessible, useful information, if individuals engaged in systematic processing were unable to use these non-content cues. It is

important to note, therefore, that dual-process models do not totally exclude the possibility of central and peripheral processing occurring *at the same time*. Although they assume that systematic processing predominates when motivation or ability to scrutinize information is high, they suggest certain conditions under which individuals might also use peripheral cues. For example, when the scrutiny of the arguments in a message does not result in clear-cut positive or negative conclusions, individuals might resort to using heuristic cues in their evaluation of the validity of a message. In support of this hypothesis, Chaiken and Maheswaran (1994) recently demonstrated that when the arguments in a message were ambiguous, source credibility (a peripheral cue) influenced attitudes even under conditions of high task importance.

Objective versus biased information processing

So far we have described the information processing underlying attitude change as a relatively objective and unbiased activity. The elaboration likelihood model as well as the original version of the heuristic–systematic model postulate a single motive: people are motivated to hold correct attitudes. This *accuracy motivation* determines the processing goal, namely to assess the validity of persuasive messages.

More recently, Chaiken and her colleagues (1989; Bohner et al., 1995) have extended the heuristic–systematic model and incorporated two further motives or goals for heuristic and systematic processing. Whereas accuracy motivation encourages objective and unbiased information processing, the other two motives are assumed to bias the processing of attitudinal information, that is to induce individuals to hold particular preferred attitude positions. One class of motives likely to bias information processing has been labelled *defence motivation*. The processing goal of defence-motivated individuals is to confirm the validity of particular attitudinal positions. A number of conditions can motivate individuals to defend their present attitudinal position, such as vested interest, attitudinal commitment, or a need for consistency. Defence-motivated processing can be either heuristic or systematic. The defence-motivated perceiver is assumed to use the same heuristics as somebody who is accuracy-motivated, but to use them *selectively* so as to support preferred attitude positions. Defence-motivated systematic processing is similarly selective. Attitude-relevant information that supports favoured positions or opposes non-favoured ones should receive more attention and be more positively interpreted than information that supports positions which are not favoured by the recipient.

A second class of motives likely to bias information processing has been termed *impression motivation*. This motive refers to the desire to express attitudes that are socially acceptable. It is assumed to be aroused in influence settings, in which the identities of significant audiences are salient or when people must communicate their attitudes to others who may have the power to reward or punish them. The processing goal of impression-motivated perceivers is to assess the social acceptability of alternative positions in order to accept attitudinal positions which will please or appease potential evaluators. Like accuracy- and defence-motivated processing, impression-motivated processing can be both heuristic and systematic. Impression-motivated heuristic processing is assumed to involve the use of simple rules to guide one's selection of socially acceptable attitude positions (for example, moderate positions minimize disagreement). In impression-motivated systematic processing the same task is achieved by scrutinizing the available information in terms of its acceptability to the social influence context.

By incorporating into their model the idea that recipients of communications may not always be striving for an attitude which is valid, but may simply want to defend the positions they are holding or hold positions which are socially acceptable, Chaiken and her colleagues (1989) have linked their model to other important theories of attitude change and social influence, such as dissonance theory (Festinger, 1957) or the social influence model of Deutsch and Gerard (1955). For example, one reason why people may resist change and defend their present attitude position may be the motive to maintain consistency among attitudes, beliefs, and behaviours. Thus, one derivation of dissonance theory discussed earlier (chapter 8), the selective-exposure hypothesis, states that people are motivated to expose themselves to 'attitude-consonant' information and to avoid 'attitude-dissonant' information in order to stabilize an existing attitude in such a manner as to maintain consonance or to avoid dissonance. Dissonance theory would further suggest that if people are unable to avoid dissonant information they should be expected to evaluate and process it in a way which would make it consistent with their attitudes.

The incorporation of impression motivation links the heuristic–systematic model to theories of social influence such as the model of Deutsch and Gerard (1955) discussed in chapter 16. This model postulates that group members may accept opinions from other members either because they believe them to be valid reflections of reality (informational social influence) or because they think that acceptance of these beliefs will raise their status within the group (normative social influence). Informational social influence should predominate in settings which arouse accuracy motivation, whereas normative social influence should occur under conditions which arouse impression motivation.

By incorporating the notion of multiple processing goals, Chaiken and her colleagues have managed to integrate the notion of biased processing systematically into their revised dual-process model. We have therefore focused our discussion on the work of Chaiken and colleagues (1989) even though Petty, Cacioppo and their colleagues (e.g., Petty and Cacioppo, 1986; Petty et al. 1994) have also discussed the idea of biased processing in the context of the elaboration likelihood model.

The persistence and resistance of attitude change

Dual-process theories predict that persuasion induced by systematic processing, or the central route, is more persistent than persuasion induced by peripheral or heuristic processing. High levels of issue-relevant cognitive activity are likely to require frequent accessing of the attitude and the related knowledge structure (Petty et al., 1994). This activity should therefore increase the number of linkages between structural elements, making the attitude schema more internally consistent, enduring, and also more resistant to counter-arguments. Since examination of persistence requires a second, delayed point of attitude measurement, only a few studies have addressed this issue. These studies support the conclusion that attitude changes which are accompanied by high levels of issue-relevant cognitive activity are more persistent than changes that are accompanied by little issue-relevant thought (e.g., Chaiken, 1980; Haugtvedt and Petty, 1992; Petty and Cacioppo, 1986). However, as Eagly and Chaiken (1993) pointed out, heuristic processing could also result in enduring attitude change, if the cue became associated with the attitude and remained salient over time (for example, I might persistently recall that my drinking two glasses of wine a day was recommended by a physician whom I have great trust in). None the less, such an attitude would be vulnerable to counter-propaganda because it lacks elaborate cognitive support. Beyond the fact that my physician recommended it, I would have no rationale for supporting the habit.

Summary

This second part of the chapter has reviewed the theoretical developments which have substantially increased our understanding of the cognitive processes which mediate the impact of persuasion. Whereas McGuire's model illuminated some of the processes involved in message reception, the cognitive-response model provided powerful insights into the processes underlying the acceptance of a message. However, both theories still maintained that persuasion had to be the outcome of a systematic processing of the semantic content of a message. Only with the emergence of dual-process theories was it finally accepted that people adopt attitudes on bases other than their systematic processing of arguments. When individuals are either unable or unmotivated to assess argument quality, they may, for example, engage in 'heuristic processing' and rely on simple decision rules to decide on the acceptability of a communication. However, even though this type of 'peripheral processing' can result in substantial attitude change, empirical evidence suggests that this change is generally less enduring.

Despite their similarities, there are a number of differences between the two dual-process theories discussed in this chapter, most apparent in the broader definition of peripheral processes in the elaboration likelihood model. By incorporating into the 'peripheral route' all mechanisms of attitude change which do not involve message-relevant thinking, the elaboration likelihood model is able to integrate a larger number of situational and individual difference variables than the heuristic–systematic framework. But there are also costs in terms of predictive power. The 'peripheral route to persuasion' does not reflect a specific mode of information processing, but a collection of different mechanisms ranging from classical conditioning to self-persuasion. Therefore, although the elaboration likelihood model enables one to predict when peripheral-route persuasion is likely to occur, it fails to explain what kind of peripheral process has operated or why it has operated (Eagly and Chaiken, 1993). By focusing on only one mode of peripheral processing, the heuristic–systematic model has been better able to elaborate the motivational processes that underlie information processing in persuasion and to suggest ways in which heuristic and systematic processing can serve motivational concerns other than the accuracy motive.

Incentive-induced Attitude Change

Powerful institutions often influence behaviour through incentives, social norms or legal sanctions rather than relying on the uncertain effects of persuasion. For example, when Swedish drivers could not be persuaded to use their seat belts, the government introduced a law that made seat-belt use compulsory for front-seat passengers in private cars. Introduction of this law increased the frequency of seat-belt use from 30 per cent to 85 per cent within a few months (Fhanér and Hane, 1979). Similarly, in New York, where seat-belt use ranged from 10 to 20 per cent prior to the introduction of a seat belt law in 1984, it increased to 45 to 70 per cent after the law entered into force early in 1985. The introduction of these laws also resulted in substantial reductions in the deaths of vehicle occupants (Robertson, 1986).

Governments can also use taxation to reduce the occurrence of undesirable behaviour patterns. Thus, there is ample evidence that the demand for alcoholic beverages and cigarettes, like the demand for most commodities, responds to changes in price and income (see Stroebe and Stroebe, 1995). A review of econometric studies conducted in several countries concluded that, everything else remaining equal, a rise in alcohol prices generally led to a drop in the consumption of alcohol, whereas an increase in the income of consumers generally led to a rise in alcohol consumption. There is similar evidence for smoking, although less research seems to have been conducted on this issue.

The usefulness of strategies which influence behaviour via changes in the incentive structure seems limited owing to the tendency for changes in the 'price' of a given behaviour to influence mainly the attitude towards purchasing the product. Because the attitude towards a given behaviour reflects the perceived consequences of engaging in that behaviour, changes in the price of alcoholic beverages should influence one's attitude towards buying alcoholic beverages but not one's attitude towards the critical behaviour itself (that is, drinking them).

Consequently, although a marked increase in the price of alcoholic beverages is likely to induce people to buy fewer of them, they might drink at their old level of consumption when not constrained by price (such as at a party where drinks are freely available).

Despite the narrow impact of such incentive-based programmes, there are conditions under which incentive-induced behaviour change could produce more general attitude change. In the following, we will discuss two such conditions, namely the experiences gained (or not gained) by engaging in certain behaviours, and the attitudinal consequences of engaging in behaviour which is counter-attitudinal.

Incentive-induced behaviour and experience

Consider, for example, the use of incentives to induce individuals to engage in behaviour from which they anticipate negative consequences. Should these expectations be unrealistically negative, their experience with the behaviour would allow them to view it more positively. For example, many individuals did not use their seat belts because they expected these belts to restrict their freedom and to be generally oppressive. Whereas this might have been true for seat belts of the first generation, it is certainly not true for the modern belts which have been installed in cars during the last few decades. Thus, people who were induced to use seat belts might have found the experience much more pleasant than they had anticipated. This might account for findings of Fhanér and Hane (1979) that the introduction of the law about seat-belt use in Sweden brought about more positive opinions regarding the wearing of seat belts in those who complied.

Similarly, high prices might prevent individuals from engaging in a new form of behaviour found enjoyable by those who perform it. For example, after initially negative reactions, young adults who experiment with smoking often enjoy the experience. Since it is very difficult to give up smoking once one has adopted the habit, strategies which would prevent young adults from beginning to smoke would seem most effective. On average, teenagers have less disposable income than adults, and are therefore more likely to be deterred from smoking by marked increases in the price of cigarettes, particularly if they have not yet started the habit or are still in a phase of experimenting. According to one estimate, a 10 per cent increase in the price of cigarettes would result in a 14 per cent decrease in demand for cigarettes among adolescents as compared with a 4 per cent decrease among adults (Lewitt and Coate, 1982).

Counter-attitudinal behaviour and attitude change

What happens when people are induced to engage in a behaviour from which they expect negative consequences and these consequences do indeed occur? One would be tempted to argue that no attitude change should result under these conditions. However, this is not what has been found in studies on the attitudinal impact of **counter-attitudinal behaviour**. Most experiments on this issue found that people were likely to change their attitudes if they had freely chosen to perform a counter-attitudinal behaviour which resulted in negative consequences (e.g., Linder, Cooper and Jones, 1967). Since this issue has been discussed in the context of dissonance theory, it will first be necessary to describe this theory to provide an answer to this question.

An analysis in terms of dissonance theory

Whenever an individual chooses between alternative courses of action, there is some information (dissonant cognitions) that would have justified a different decision. For example, if Carol, a first-year student, attends class on a beautiful day, the knowledge that she is missing a lot of fun at the swimming pool is a dissonant cognition, whereas the knowledge that she is increasing her chances of getting a good grade would constitute a consonant cognition. Having these dissonant cognitions leads to an aversive emotional state called dissonance (see also chapter 8). The magnitude of dissonance (and thus the motivation to reduce it) will be the greater, the greater the number and/or the importance of the dissonant cognitions. Thus, if Carol knows that this would have been her last chance to spend an afternoon with her friend before he leaves town, her dissonance will be greater than if she is just missing a swim and a bit of sun.

There are various strategies available to Carol to reduce her dissonance. For example, she could increase the perceived importance of the consonant cognitions by persuading herself that the material covered this afternoon was not only vital for the examination but was also really fascinating. She could also reduce the importance of the dissonant cognitions by telling herself that it would not really have been any fun at the pool.

When a person is induced by monetary incentives or by the threat of negative sanctions to say or do something which runs counter to his or her firm convictions, the monetary incentive or the legal sanction are 'consonant cognitions' because they justify the chosen action. For example, a businessman who files an incorrect tax return to gain a tax benefit (or to avoid paying a fine) will feel that gaining the benefit (or avoiding the fine) justifies his behaviour. Obviously, this justification will be greater if the benefit gained (or the fine avoided) was large rather than small. Thus, if an individual behaves counter-attitudinally to gain some benefit (or to avoid a penalty), dissonance will be greater if the benefit (or the penalty) is small rather than large.

Festinger and Carlsmith (1959) tested these predictions by having subjects first perform two dull motor tasks. After subjects had worked on these tasks for an hour, they were asked, under some pretext, whether they would be willing to tell the next subject that the experimental task was rather interesting. Subjects were either offered $20 or $1 for telling the lie. How did subjects feel after having actually told another (confederate) subject that the experiment was interesting? According to dissonance theory, their feelings should depend on the amount of money they had been paid. Subjects in the $20 condition should feel very little dissonance, because earning this amount of money should amply justify deviating from the truth. Subjects who had earned only $1 should feel a great deal of dissonance since the money did not really justify telling a lie. One way to reduce dissonance is for subjects to persuade themselves that the experimental task had in fact been quite enjoyable. Consistent with these predictions, Festinger and Carlsmith found that subjects in the $1 condition reported a more favourable attitude towards the experimental task than subjects who had been paid $20.

Festinger and Carlsmith intuitively built two features into their experimental situation which, though not specified in the original version of the theory, turned out to be essential for dissonance arousal. First, since the experimenter's request was not ostensibly part of the experiment, subjects were free to refuse the request and thus experienced high freedom of choice. Secondly, since the (confederate) subject indicated that she had intended not to participate in the experiment until the subject told her that the experiment was interesting, the subject's behaviour led to negative consequences (that is, it misled the second student and made her participate in a very dull experiment).

The importance of freedom of choice for dissonance arousal was later demonstrated by Linder, Cooper and Jones (1967), who reasoned that if subjects believed that by signing up for the experiment they had committed themselves to comply with any demand made during the experimental session, they would feel that they had no choice but to perform the counter-attitudinal behaviour requested by the experimenter. Under these conditions, the counter-attitudinal behaviour should not arouse dissonance. Instead, being offered a reward (e.g., money) for behaving counter-attitudinally should act as a reinforcement, and attitude change would be expected. Linder and colleagues conducted two experiments in which they manipulated freedom of choice in addition to the size of the reward. In line with their expectation, the dissonance-predicted inverse relationship (i.e., less change of attitude with high than with low incentive) was only found under conditions of high choice. When subjects were given little choice to refuse to perform the counter-attitudinal task, more attitude change was observed if the incentive was high rather than low (figure 9.5).

The importance of negative consequences of counter-attitudinal behaviour for the arousal of dissonance was first demonstrated by Nel, Helmreich and Aronson (1969) and later by Cooper and Worchel (1970). Cooper and Worchel (1970) replicated the Festinger and Carlsmith (1959) experiment, adding conditions in which the confederate subject was apparently not persuaded by the real subject. Consistent with predictions, the inverse relationship between size of incentive and attitude change could only be observed in the conditions with negative consequences. In the conditions where the confederate was not convinced and

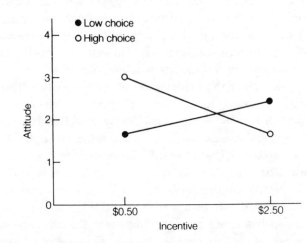

Figure 9.5 Mean attitudes towards the essay topic under different choice and incentive conditions (based on Linder, Cooper and Jones, 1967, expt 1)

thus evaded the dull experience, size of incentive had no effect on attitude change.

Thus, the answer to the question about the relationship between compliance and attitude change is not a simple one. Persons who are induced to behave counter-attitudinally may change their attitudes, but the magnitude of change will depend on their freedom of choice, the size of the incentive, and on the consequences of the behaviour. For individuals who felt free to refuse the counter-attitudinal task, most attitude change will result when the incentive was minimal and the behaviour led to negative consequences. With little freedom of choice, on the other hand, more attitude change will result if large rather than small incentives were offered for compliance.

An analysis in terms of self-perception theory

SELF-PERCEPTION
THEORY

The dissonance interpretation of attitude change following counter-attitudinal behaviour was soon challenged by **self-perception theory** (Bem, 1965, 1972). This theory assumes that since internal cues are often weak, ambiguous or uninterpretable, when asked to indicate their own attitude, people are frequently in the same situation as outside observers. Like outside observers, they infer their attitudes from relevant instances of past behaviour. Thus, when asked to state their attitude towards the motor task, subjects in the Festinger and Carlsmith experiment remember that they have told another subject that the task was interesting. They will use this knowledge as information about their own attitude towards the task, unless there are reasons to devalue their behaviour as a source of information. Being paid a large sum of money to behave in a certain way is one good reason to devalue one's behaviour as a source of information about one's attitudes. Self-perception theory can thus account for the Festinger and Carlsmith findings without referring to aversive states and clashing cognitions. According to self-perception theory, subjects in the $1 condition will infer from the fact that they told another subject the experiment was interesting, that they must have found the task quite interesting. After all, what other reason could they have had to make this statement. Subjects who have been paid $20, on the other hand, will attribute their behaviour to the money and will thus not use it in inferring their attitude towards the experimental task. They will therefore indicate a less favourable attitude towards the task than subjects in the $1 condition.

To demonstrate the viability of his position, Bem (1965) replicated the findings of dissonance experiments in 'interpersonal replications' of forced compliance experiments. In these replications, the different experimental conditions were described to subjects, who then had to infer the attitude of an individual who had complied with the experimenter's demand. These observers were usually quite able to replicate the findings of the original studies (e.g., Bem, 1965; Calder, Ross and Insko, 1973). However, such studies can only show that subjects could have inferred their attitudes from their own behaviour, they cannot prove that subjects actually did go through such an inference process.

With two theories as different as dissonance and self-perception theory, a decision about their relative validity should be easy. However, since the two theories differ only in their assumptions about the processes that mediate attitude change, it turned out to be rather difficult to devise some 'crucial experiment'. Such an experiment was finally conducted by Zanna and Cooper (1974), who used 'misattribution' processes to demonstrate the presence of an aversive state. Subjects were given a placebo pill (a pill which has no effect) and were told either that this pill had no effect (placebo instructions) or that it would lead to some aversive feeling of arousal. Then subjects wrote a counter-attitudinal essay under high – or low – choice conditions. According to dissonance theory, writing a counter-attitudinal essay under high choice should lead to aversive arousal, which subjects would normally attribute to the writing of the essay. However, subjects who had been led to believe that the pill would cause an aversive arousal should misattribute the tension to the pill. Thus, there should be attitude change only under high choice and with placebo instructions. According to self-perception theory, giving the pill should not affect attitude change. The results supported dissonance predictions (figure 9.6). These findings were replicated in later studies (e.g., Cooper, Zanna and Taves, 1978; Higgins, Rhodewalt and Zanna, 1979; Pittman, 1975). Croyle and Cooper (1983) managed to demonstrate such arousal differences directly through physiological recording.

The controversy was finally resolved by suggesting that the two theories should be regarded as complementary formulations with each theory being applicable to its own specialized domain. Fazio, Zanna and Cooper (1977) argued that self-perception theory accurately characterizes attitude change in the context

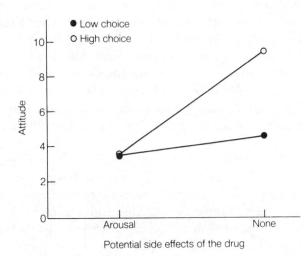

Figure 9.6 Mean attitudes towards the essay topic under different conditions of choice and misattribution (based on Zanna and Cooper, 1974)

of attitude-congruent behaviour while dissonance theory explains attitude change in the context of counter-attitudinal behaviour. An attitude-congruent position is defined as any position that is still acceptable to an individual, even though it may not be in accordance with his or her actual attitude. For example, people who believe that all atomic power stations should be closed down immediately would probably find the position that no new nuclear reactors should be built and that the existing ones should be phased out within a period of ten years also acceptable, while they would find the argument that we need more atomic power stations to ensure future energy needs completely unacceptable. Thus, arguing the former position would be attitude-congruent while arguing the latter would be counter-attitudinal. Again using misattribution processes as an indicator of the presence of dissonance, Fazio et al. (1977) could show that attitude change due to counter-attitudinal behaviour was mediated by dissonance while attitude change due to pro-attitudinal behaviour was not. Since it can be assumed that subjects are motivated to put forth considerably more cognitive effort in order to justify their action if it is counter-attitudinal rather than **pro-attitudinal behaviour** (Stroebe and Diehl, 1988), this integration is consistent with expectations from dual-process theories that under low involvement inviduals predominantly rely on peripheral processes.

PRO-
ATTITUDINAL
BEHAVIOUR

IMPRESSION
MANAGEMENT
THEORY

An analysis in terms of impression management theory
Another major challenge to the dissonance interpretations of forced compliance research was posed by **impression management theory** (Schlenker, 1982;

Tedeschi and Rosenfeld, 1981; Tedeschi, Schlenker and Bonoma, 1971). Impression management refers to the behavioural strategies that people use to create the social images or identities they desire (Tetlock and Manstead, 1985). Inverting a basic assumption of dissonance theory, Tedeschi and colleagues suggested that individuals have a social concern with appearing consistent to others. Thus, a subject's score on an attitude scale after a forced-compliance experiment is assumed to be motivated by a need to appear, rather than to be, consistent. The apparent attitude change of subjects in low-incentive conditions is a tactic to feign consistency between behaviour and subsequent attitude expression. The subject in the low-incentive condition, who has been given insufficient reason to tell another subject that the experiment was interesting, will now pretend that he or she really found the task interesting, in order to appear consistent. Subjects in the high-incentive condition, on the other hand, have been paid a reasonable sum of money to make their statement. They can therefore honestly report their real attitude, because they have no identity problem: the experimenter can attribute their counter-attitudinal behaviour to environmental factors (Tedeschi and Rosenfeld, 1981). Since impression management theory assumes that the apparent attitude change in the low-incentive condition has been feigned for the benefit of the experimenter, counter-attitudinal behaviour must be public for a manifestation of attitude change to occur. More specifically, the theory implies that subjects must believe that the experimenter is able to connect them to both their counter-attitudinal behaviour and their marks on the attitude scale.

It is difficult to test these assumptions because in this type of deception experiment one never knows what subjects really believe. For example, in the Festinger and Carlsmith experiment, the attitude measure was taken by an interviewer who was ostensibly a representative of the psychology department and had no direct connection with the experimenter. Thus, the fact that there was attitude change in their low-incentive condition would tend to disconfirm impression management theory. But can we be sure that subjects really accepted this story? It is conceivable that subjects suspected that the experimenters would come to know their ratings (as in fact they did). Similar objections were raised against the findings of Hoyt, Henly and Collins (1972), who obtained attitude change from subjects even though their counter-attitudinal essays had not been signed. Thus Gaes, Kalle and Tedeschi (1978) speculated that subjects may have felt that they could have been identified by their seats or through their handwriting. However, as Cooper and Fazio (1984) commented, with 'such tortuous logic, it is very difficult indeed to accept any reasonable test that would support the notion that only feigned attitudes are involved in the induced-compliance paradigm' (p. 251).

The use of the 'bogus pipeline' (see chapter 8; Jones and Sigall, 1971) presents a more promising approach to pitting the two theories against each other. If the attitude change observed in forced-compliance experiments was only due to a need for self-presentation, then no attitude change should occur when the bogus pipeline is used to measure attitudes. The bogus pipeline procedure was developed by Jones and Sigall (1971) as a procedure to establish in subjects the belief that their 'real' attitudes could be monitored by an apparatus more sensitive than a lie detector. Since feigning consistency would make no sense under these conditions, there should be no attitude change in the low-incentive condition when subjects expect that their attitude will be assessed through the bogus pipeline. In a series of studies which compared the bogus pipeline procedure with normal attitude assessment, Tedeschi and his collaborators (Gaes et al., 1978; Riess, Kalle and Tedeschi, 1981) generated evidence that supported the impression management position.

The failure of these studies to find attitude change with the bogus pipeline is not necessarily inconsistent with dissonance theory. The bogus pipeline equipment may have functioned as the environmental equivalent of the arousal evoking pills in the arousal attribution studies described earlier. Thus, Stults, Messé and Kerr (1984) demonstrated that subjects who were attached to a bogus pipeline exhibited attitude change if given the opportunity to get accustomed to the equipment, but showed no attitude change if no habituation experience was provided. Since the opportunity to get accustomed to the bogus pipeline equipment should make the attribution of arousal to the equipment less plausible, these findings tend to support the misattribution interpretation of these bogus pipeline experiments.

After a thorough evaluation of the evidence from studies pitting impression management against dissonance theory, Tetlock and Manstead (1985) concluded that neither side emerged as a clear winner. They further argued that impression management and dissonance theory should not be viewed as mutually exclusive but that the two theories should be regarded as complementary formulations. Thus, instead of searching for crucial experiments, researchers should examine the conditions under which concerns for self-presentation or internal consistency are likely to become dominant.

Pro-attitudinal behaviour and attitude change

There are certain conditions, however, under which the introduction of incentives to motivate individuals to engage in a particular behaviour could have negative consequences on their attitudes. Paradoxically, this is most likely to happen when individuals have already engaged in this behaviour even before incentives were introduced, because they found it enjoyable. Thus, if governments, persuaded by evidence that physical exercise extends life expectancy, were to introduce a law making jogging obligatory, this might induce many people to jog who would never have done so otherwise. But it might also corrupt the motivation of the jogging addicts. At least this is the prediction one would derive from research on the effects of extrinsic incentives on intrinsic motivation and performance. This research has demonstrated that performance of an intrinsically enjoyable task can decrease, once people have been given some reward for performing that task (Deci, 1975; Lepper and Greene, 1978).

One of the early investigations of this hypothesis was conducted by Lepper, Greene, and Nisbett (1973), who introduced an attractive drawing activity during the free-play time of nursery school children. After the baseline interest of children had been observed during free play, children who showed an initial intrinsic interest in the activity were chosen as subjects and asked to perform the activity under one of three conditions: in the Expected Award condition, children were promised a reward for the performance; in the Unexpected Award condition, children were unexpectedly given a reward afterwards; in the No Award condition, children were neither promised nor given a reward. Two weeks later, the material was again provided in the classroom and the interest in the activity was unobtrusively observed. As predicted by the authors, Expected Award subjects showed a significant decrease in interest in the activity from the baseline to post-experimental observation, whereas subjects in the No Award or Unexpected Award conditions showed no significant change in overall interest. Similar findings were reported in a set of studies conducted by Deci (1971, 1972) with adult subjects, who were either paid or not paid to work on puzzle tasks that they had found intrinsically interesting.

Lepper and colleagues (1973) interpreted these findings in terms of self-perception theory. To the extent that the extrinsic incentives are sufficiently salient, the individual will attribute his or her behaviour to these compelling extrinsic contingencies rather than to an intrinsic interest in the task. After having been rewarded for performing a task, subjects would be less likely to consider the activity interesting in itself (that is, they would have a less positive attitude towards the task). Thus, an expected and contingent reward leads to a shift in the subject's self-perceived motivation from intrinsic to extrinsic. An activity that was originally approached as an 'end in itself' is now seen as a 'means to an end' (Kruglanski, 1975). Lepper and colleagues (1973) called this interpretation the '**over-justification hypothesis**'.

OVER-
JUSTIFICATION
HYPOTHESIS

These findings have intriguing implications for the impact of the introduction of monetary incentives on attitudes towards activities which are already consistent with an individual's attitudes. It is not quite clear, however, whether the threat of legal sanctions will have the same impact as a monetary incentive in such a case. After all, individuals have to see their own behaviour as under the control of the external incentive for the 'over-justification effect' to occur. At least with pro-attitudinal behaviour, legal sanctions seem to be somehow less salient than monetary incentives. Thus, although most of us will neither steal nor murder, we are unlikely to attribute our abstention to the threat of legal sanctions.

Summary

In our discussion of the attitudinal consequences of compliance, we distinguished between counter-attitudinal and pro-attitudinal behaviour. When individuals are induced to behave counter-attitudinally, the magnitude of attitude change will depend on their freedom of choice, the magnitude of the incentive offered for the behaviour and the negativity of the consequences of the behaviour. With high choice and negative consequences, more attitude change will result when the incentive is small rather than large. When individuals feel little freedom of choice, there will be more change with large rather than small rewards.

These findings were discussed in terms of three theories: according to dissonance theory, counter-attitudinal behaviour produces dissonance, an aversive tension which individuals reduce by making their attitudes more consistent with their behaviour. Since counter-attitudinal behaviour that can be justified because of low freedom of choice and high incentives should result in less dissonance than behaviour that cannot be so justified, dissonance theory is consistent with the pattern of findings reported above.

Both self-perception theory and impression management theory offer alternative interpretations to that of dissonance theory. According to self-perception theory, individuals infer their own attitude from their past behaviour, unless there are obvious non-attitudinal causes for their actions (such as high incentives or low freedom of choice). According to impression management theory, on the other hand, a subject's mark on the attitude scale in a forced-compliance experiment is assumed to be feigned in order to manage the impression that is given to the experimenter. The apparent attitude change of subjects in low-incentive conditions is a tactic to feign consistency between behaviour and subsequent attitude expression. After decades of attempts to pit these theories against each other, a consensus seems to have emerged (e.g., Fazio et al., 1977; Tetlock and Manstead, 1985) that they should be regarded as complementary rather than mutually exclusive formulations. Thus, instead of attempting to conduct 'crucial' experiments, researchers have begun to develop and explore possible conceptual frameworks that would integrate the psychological processes described in these different theories (e.g., Schlenker, 1982).

Strategies of Change: An Evaluation of their Relative Effectiveness

Since people are rarely interested in attitude change as an 'end in itself', but as a means to changing behaviour, influencing behaviour through monetary incentives or legal sanctions would seem to be the most effective of the strategies discussed in this chapter. And indeed, there is evidence to support this notion. For example, after campaigns that pointed out the great safety advantage of using seat belts had been fairly unsuccessful in Sweden, the country introduced a law that made seat-belt use compulsory. Within a few months, the frequency of seat-belt use increased considerably. Furthermore, an assessment of the attitudes of a sample of Swedish car users before and after the introduction of the law indicated that the law had brought about more positive opinions regarding seat-belt use at least in those who complied (Fhanér and Hane, 1979). In view of the overwhelming success of strategies of incentive-induced behaviour change, one wonders why people still bother with persuasion.

There are actually a number of considerations to be taken into account. The most obvious is lack of power. Only governments have the power to enact laws and even they are constrained in the use of this power. For example, although the behavioural factors contributing to coronary risk (e.g., smoking, eating fatty food, over-use of alcohol) are well known, governments rely on persuasion rather than legal action to change behaviour. A law that would forbid smoking, or reintroduce prohibition, would be unpopular enough to lead to a change in power at the next election. Furthermore, most governments recognize that changing behaviour by persuading people rather than forcing or bribing them is more consistent with present-day ideals of self-determination and democracy.

An additional constraint on strategies of influence based on the use of monetary incentives or legal sanctions is that these strategies can only be used for behaviour that can be monitored. Thus, while efficient for publicly identifiable behaviour such as seat-belt use, speeding, or the use of catalytic converters, positive or negative incentives are difficult to apply if the behaviour that one wishes to influence is difficult to monitor objectively. For example, in the area of race relations, governments can eliminate some of the objective and observable instances of discrimination (for example, by introducing quotas for employment of members of racial minorities) but they cannot force people to be nice to members of outgroups, to invite them to their homes or let their children marry one of them. This is one of the reasons why the American Supreme Court mandated the end of segregated schooling. Since they could not outlaw prejudice, they attempted to reduce it by increasing interracial contact.

A further disadvantage which is inherent in the use of legal sanctions to induce behaviour changes is that once behaviour is under the control of some extrinsic incentive, it will not only be necessary to monitor the behaviour continually but it will also be difficult if not impossible to return to internal control. Thus, speed limits become ineffective unless they are continually monitored and seen to be monitored. And even though laws like the one making seat-belt use compulsory seem to result in attitude change, one wonders what would happen if such laws were to be revoked. Extending notions of self-perception theory, one would expect that individuals would now attribute their past behaviour to the law. They would therefore be likely to change their behaviour if the laws were to be changed.

Thus, the great advantage of influencing behaviour through persuasion is that the behaviour remains under intrinsic control and thus does not need any monitoring. Furthermore, at least for attitude change brought about by the 'central route', the change should be fairly persistent. And yet, if behaviour change is deemed important, such considerations may often be outweighed by the greater effectiveness of direct strategy.

Finally, the effectiveness of legal sanctions is likely to depend on the acceptance of the law and on individual perception that violation of the law is associated with a high risk of sanction. For example, it is quite likely that the introduction of a law making seat-belt use compulsory would not have been as effective as it was if people had not accepted that such a law was in their own best interest. In fact, without the persuasion campaign that made it widely known that the wearing of seat belts substantially reduced the risk of injuries in traffic accidents, it is unlikely that such a law would have been introduced.

In conclusion, it should be pointed out that changing the incentive structure or using persuasive appeals should not be seen as competing strategies of attitude and behaviour change. On the contrary, since changes in the incentive structure are unlikely to affect behaviour unless people are made aware that monetary inducements or legal sanctions have been introduced to encourage a given behaviour, governments typically rely on mass-media campaigns to inform the population of these changes.

Summary and Conclusions

This chapter has discussed strategies of attitude formation and change from three different theoretical perspectives. The first part focused on principles of learning such as classical and instrumental conditioning. We reviewed a number of studies that demonstrated that attitudes can be acquired through processes of classical conditioning. Studies of attitude change have also repeatedly demonstrated that attitudes can be changed by positively reinforcing individuals whenever they have expressed an attitude that was favourable (or in another condition unfavourable) towards some attitude object. However, as with classical conditioning studies, the behaviourist explanations of this relationship are now generally questioned.

With the cognitive revolution in the sixties and seventies, cognitive approaches increasingly dominated attitude-change research. Cognitive theories have proven particularly useful in the analysis of processes or variables which mediate the impact of persuasive appeals on attitudes. Whereas early theories focused on persuasion resulting from systematic processing of the semantic content of persuasive messages, more recent dual-process theories have accepted that, in addition, people adopt attitudes on bases other than their systematic processing of arguments. For example, when individuals are either unable or unmotivated to assess argument quality, they often engage in heuristic processing and rely on simple decision rules to decide on the validity of an argumentation.

Rather than relying on the uncertain effects of persuasion, powerful institutions often influence behaviour through incentives, social norms, or legal sanctions. Thus, governments may use taxation or legal sanctions to make certain behaviours like smoking, drinking alcohol or non-use of seat belts more costly to the individual. Such strategies have not only been successful in affecting the targeted behaviour, they have also often resulted in substantial changes in attitudes. Since changes in incentive structure are unlikely to affect behaviour unless people are made aware that monetary inducements or legal sanctions have been introduced to encourage a given behaviour, and since acceptance of these government strategies is likely to aid compliance, we argued that the use of incentives and of persuasive appeals should be considered as complementary rather than competing strategies of attitude and behaviour change.

Glossary terms

Central route to persuasion
Classical conditioning
Cognitive-response model
Counter-attitudinal behaviour
Distraction
Dual-process models of persuasion

Elaboration
Elaboration likelihood-model (ELM)
Heuristic processing
Heuristic–systematic model
Impression management theory

Instrumental conditioning
Need for cognition
Over-justification hypothesis
Peripheral route to persuasion
Pro-attitudinal behaviour
Self-perception theory
Systematic processing

Discussion points

1   Under which conditions is recall of message arguments likely to be related to attitude change?
2   What are the similarities and differences between the cognitive-response model and the dual-process models of persuasion?
3   What is the relationship between argument quality, processing motivation, and processing ability as determinants of attitude change in dual-process models?
4   What are the differences and similarities between the concepts 'central and peripheral route' on one hand, and 'systematic versus heuristic processing' on the other?
5   Under what conditions is counter-attitudinal behaviour assumed to result in attitude change according to recent formulations of dissonance theory?
6   Compare the different theoretical interpretations of attitude change resulting from counter-attitudinal behaviour discussed in this chapter.
7   Discuss the advantages and disadvantages of persuasion versus incentive-induced change as strategies of attitude and behaviour change.

Suggestions for further reading

Bohner, G., Moskowitz, G. B. and Chaiken, S. (1995) The interplay of heuristic and systematic processing of social information. In W. Stroebe and M. Hewstone (eds), *European Review of Social Psychology* (vol. 6, pp. 33–68). Chichester: Wiley. This chapter describes the revised multi-motive version of the heuristic–systematic model and demonstrates the power of this extended model as a general theory of social influence.

Eagly, A. H. and Chaiken, S. (1993) *The Psychology of Attitudes*. Fort Worth, TX: Harcourt, Brace, Jovanovich. A well-written and comprehensive book on attitudes and attitude change.

Petty, R. E. and Cacioppo, J. T. (1986) *Communication and Persuasion: Central and peripheral routes to attitude change*. New York: Springer. This book still contains the best discussion of the elaboration likelihood model and the classic studies conducted to test this model.

Petty, R. E., Priester, J. R. and Wegener, D. T. (1994) Cognitive processes in attitude change. In R. S. Wyer Jr and T. K. Srull (1994), *Handbook of Social Cognition* (vol. 2, pp. 69–142). Hillsdale, NJ: Lawrence Erlbaum Associates. This chapter describes the elaboration likelihood model and summarizes the research which was conducted to test this model.

Stroebe, W. and Stroebe, M. S. (1995) *Social Psychology and Health*. Buckingham: Open University Press. This book applies principles of attitude and behaviour change to the area of health behaviour.

Key studies

Linder, D. E., Cooper, J. and Jones, E. E. (1967). Decision freedom as a determinant of the role of incentive magnitude in attitude change. *Journal of Personality and Social Psychology*, 6, 245–54.

Petty, R. E., Cacioppo, J. T. and Goldman, R. (1981). Personal involvement as a determinant of argument-based persuasion. *Journal of Personality and Social Psychology*, 41, 847–55.

PART III

Emotion,
Communication and
Relationships

Contents

10   Emotion

Klaus R. Scherer

Contents

Introduction

Imagine strolling through a park on a sunny Sunday afternoon in May. The first flowers are out, the birds are chirping, and you are feeling great – particularly given the fact that a very special person is walking hand-in-hand with you. All of a sudden you notice a man emerging from behind some bushes along the trail. He is holding a knife and there seems to be blood on his hands . . .

EMOTION

The chances are that you would experience what is commonly called an **emotion**. But what seems a straightforward, albeit highly aversive, reaction turns out to be a major problem for social psychologists. For example, what exactly is *the* emotion? The quickening of your heartbeat? Your mouth and eyes opening widely? Your gasp? The sudden urge to run away? Or the feeling that you are in danger – something you will call *fear* when interrogated about your state of mind at the time? Or a combination of all of these different aspects? We will have to discuss different views as to how to define the phenomenon.

Another issue of debate is the question of why we have emotions. Are they really irrational passions that often prevent us from being reasonable human beings? What is their function? Are they present in animals? Are there differences between cultures? How would an Eskimo react if a man with blood on his hands appeared from behind a snowdrift? All of these questions are linked to the issue of the social nature of the human species and thus a proper topic for social-psychological investigation. But even apart from such fundamental issues, social psychologists stumble across emotion at many points in the study of social cognition and behaviour. If the sight of the man with the knife has frightened you out of your wits your judgement as to the likelihood of his attacking you and the person next to you may be impaired. You may overreact. The event, if traumatic, may affect your memory of park strolls with a significant other for years to come. You may change your opinion about certain races or nationalities, if the man should happen to be a member of a social group different from your own. Major effects of emotion on social cognition have been demonstrated in the literature: perception, judgement, memory, problem solving, task performance, and many other aspects of individual functioning can all be strongly affected by different emotions (Forgas, 1991; and see chapter 6 in this volume). Emotion has also been shown to play an important role in attitude change (Breckler, 1993; for a review, see chapter 10 in this volume).

Emotion also strongly affects social interaction. Your interaction with the man will be very different depending on whether you are frightened or angry. Of particular importance is *emotional signalling*, via expressive behaviour. The process and outcome of negotiations and social encounters heavily depend on the exchange of such signals, such as of threat or appeasement (see chapter 14). The reaction of the knifeman towards you will be determined in large part by the emotional signals you are providing.

In general, the phenomenon of aggression is closely tied to emotion, particularly frustration and anger (Averill, 1982; Berkowitz, 1962). If your partner has frustrated you just before your encountering the man, and if you feel strong enough to deal with the person, you are more likely to attack than to flee. Emotions also influence the opposite pole, prosocial behaviour. A number of studies have shown that the likelihood of someone behaving in an altruistic manner is dependent, in a complex manner, on mood and emotion (Isen, 1990; see also chapter 13).

As one might expect, emotions play a major role in the establishment and management of social relationships, such as in friendship and marriage (Berscheid, 1991; Gottman, 1993; Gottman and Levenson, 1983) as well as in the case of the loss of a partner (Stroebe and Stroebe, 1987). But emotions also play a role in more mundane social encounters. One of the most surprising results of a recent series of studies by Rimé and his collaborators (Rimé, Mesquita, Philippot and Boca, 1991) on the social sharing of emotion is that people like to talk about their emotional experiences to others and do so very frequently indeed (see chapter 12).

One of the areas of social psychology for which emotion is of major relevance is group dynamics (see Heise and O'Brien, 1993) and collective behaviour. Le Bon's (1895/1960) early work on mass behaviour relied strongly on the mechanism of *emotional contagion*, which he used to explain the irrationality of much of the behaviour in large crowds (see chapter 18). To use our park example as an illustration: if you show a fearful response upon seeing the knifeman, it is likely that you will *infect* your partner – who might at first have reacted in a rather cool fashion – with your fright. This interesting phenomenon, after having been neglected for decades, is now finding renewed interest from social psychologists (see Hatfield, Cacioppo and Rapson, 1994).

Little wonder that emotion is central to social-psychological analysis. This chapter will summarize some of the current debates and illustrate some of the research efforts in this area.

What is an Emotion?

This was the title of one of the most influential journal articles ever written in psychology. It appeared in 1884 and its author was William James, Professor of philosophy and psychology at Harvard University, one of the founding fathers of modern experimental psychology. In this essay, James defended what he considered a revolutionary thesis concerning the nature of emotion: namely 'that the bodily changes follow directly the *perception* of the exciting fact, and that our feeling of the same changes as they occur *is* the emotion' (James, 1884/1968, p. 19, emphases in the original).

The James–Lange theory

James illustrated his point of view with an example that has become a classic: we meet a bear in the forest, our heart races, our knees tremble and, because we are *perceiving* these physiological changes, we *feel* afraid. A year after the appearance of James's seminal article, the Danish physiologist Carl Lange (1885) proposed a model of emotion which, in spite of many minor differences, suggested the same basic mechanism with respect to the causal sequence as James. Because of this similarity, we traditionally speak of the James–Lange theory of emotion, also referred to as a peripheral position (since it focuses on the peripheral, i.e. the autonomous and somatic, rather than the central nervous system). According to this view, then, an emotion is elicited by a person's awareness of a specific pattern of bodily changes.

The James–Lange position is compared with the established view of emotion at the turn of the century in the first two rows in figure 10.1 (which we will keep returning to for comparisons with more recent theories). Since the likelihood of encountering bears has steadily decreased since 1884, our more realistic example of an eliciting situation for the experience of fear in the modern world is used.

Obviously, there is quite a large amount of overlap between the 'pre-James' and 'James' views. Both positions agree on the 'components' of the phenomenon: an event, the perception/evaluation of the event, a wide variety of bodily reactions and action tendencies, and a characteristic feeling state. Both positions use the term *emotion* to refer to the *feeling state* component of the total phenomenon. Furthermore, both positions agree on the existence of a process, a sequence of events, and on the differentiation of causes and consequences. The disagreement concerns precisely the status of 'emotion-in-the-sense-of-feeling' (henceforth referred to as 'emotion/feeling'): is it a cause of characteristic bodily reactions and action tendencies or rather their consequence? This issue has been at the root of a lively controversy that still persists today. How can modern social psychology settle this classic dispute?

Emotion as a social-psychological construct

We first need to have a working definition of what we mean by emotion and/or feeling. Unfortunately, there seem to be as many definitions of emotions as there are theories of emotion (Kleinginna and Kleinginna, 1981). Like many other psychological terms, in both lay and scientific psychology, emotion is a *hypothetical construct*, which is not directly observable as such, but which is inferred from a number of indices and their interaction. There is a growing consensus that the construct *emotion* should not be used as a synonym for **feeling**, as is often the case. Feeling is now generally considered to be just one of several *components* of the total emotion construct. Other components are neurophysiological response patterns (in the central and autonomous nervous systems) and motor expression (in face, voice and gesture). Social psychologists often refer to

FEELING

Pre-James	perception of an event	elicitation of an 'emotion=feeling' ⇑	'emotion/feeling'	elicitation of a specific reponse ⇑	differentiated pattern of physiological arousal and appropriate action tendencies
Example:	seeing a man with a knife	⇑	feeling afraid	⇑	heart racing, knees trembling; wanting to run
James	perception of an event	elicitation of a specific response ⇑	differentiated pattern of physiological arousal and appropriate action tendencies	perception of bodily change ⇑	'emotion/feeling'
Example:	seeing a man with a knife	⇑	heart racing, knees trembling; wanting to run	⇑	feeling afraid
Schachter	perception of an event	elicitation of non-specific arousal ⇑	general activation of the sympathetic branch of the ANS (autonomic nervous system)	cognitive explanation, based on event and situational cues ⇑	'emotion/feeling'
Example:	seeing a man with a knife	⇑	heart racing, knees trembling, face flushing	⇑	feeling afraid
Modern	perception and appraisal of an event	initiation of changes in all major subsystems of the organism ⇑	differentiated and adaptive changes in physiology, expression, motivation	reflection of these component changes in a monitoring system ⇑	changes in feeling state (one component of the total emotion process)
Example:	seeing a man with a knife and evaluating the potential consequences given one's own resources	⇑	heart racing, knees trembling, face flushing; eyes, mouth wide open; wanting to run	⇑	feeling afraid (in a manner that reflects the situation and the bodily changes)
Continuous process	⇐	⇓	⇓	⇓	⇒

Figure 10.1 The sequence of the emotion process as seen by different theorists

EMOTIONAL
REACTION
TRIAD
these three components – feeling, physiology, expression – as the **emotional reaction triad**.

Another component seen as an essential part of the emotion construct is the *action tendency* resulting from the evaluation of the eliciting event – such as wanting to run away or to hide, out of fear of attack by a bear or a thug. Some authors have argued that the action-tendency component is in fact the most important aspect of an emotion in the sense that it defines its specificity – *wanting to flee* being specific to fear, or *wanting to attack* being specific to anger (Frijda, 1986, 1987; Plutchik, 1980). It is important to note that most emotion psychologists distinguish action tendencies from overt instrumental behaviour. The actual running or hitting are not generally considered to be *components* of emotion but rather are seen as *behavioural* consequences of emotion.

It seems reasonable to assume that the emotion construct should also include a *cognitive* component. Clearly, mental processes must be part of the adaptive reactions of the organism to an emotion-eliciting event since the latter always requires some kind of evaluative information processing, no matter how rudimentary, to make sense of what happens. Thus, a bear hunter will evaluate the appearance of James's bear very differently from how a picnicker would. You might react quite differently to the knife-brandishing man if you were a member of the national karate team. The cognitive activity of evaluation often changes rapidly when new information becomes available. For example, we will evaluate the man with the knife very differently once we notice that he has carved a stick for a little boy playing nearby and has inflicted a minor cut on himself. In
APPRAISAL
consequence, one might argue that cognitive evaluation, or **appraisal**, is also one of the components of the emotion construct, a point that is indeed argued by several emotion psychologists. This cognitive perspective on emotion fits the strong rise of cognitive approaches in social psychology (see chapters 6 to 9).

The number of emotion components enumerated so far – feeling, physiological changes, motor expression, action tendencies, and cognitive processing – include most if not all aspects of psychological functioning. How can we distinguish emotion from other kinds of psychological processes?

To define the term more precisely, we suggest using *emotion* as a shorthand for a *process* that involves fairly massive, interrelated changes in several organismic subsystems, occurring in response to an eliciting event of major significance to the individual. Rather than talk about *emotional states*, we should refer to *emotion episodes* to underline the fact that emotion is a dynamic process which has a beginning and an end and is of relatively brief duration. This allows us to
MOOD
differentiate emotion from other psychological constructs such as **mood** (generally considered to be more diffuse, to last much longer, and not necessarily to be elicited by a concrete event) (for discussions of mood aspects see chapters 6
EMOTIONALITY
and 13). We also distinguish emotion from **emotionality** (a relatively stable personality trait; see Ekman, 1984, 1992; Frijda, 1993a).

One way to highlight the special nature of emotion as a *crisis response* (in a positive or a negative sense) is to postulate that the various psychological and physiological components interact in a very specific way during the emotion episode. Scherer (1984, 1993) has suggested that the subsystems of an organism, which normally 'do their own thing', become *synchronized* during the emotion process in order to allow the organism to cope with the emergency situation created by the eliciting event. For example, while you are strolling peacefully through the park with your friend, the vegetative part of your autonomous nervous system is slowly digesting lunch, your respiration and heartbeat are optimally tuned to provide the required oxygen for your strolling and speaking pace, your facial muscles are involved in sending smiles of various sorts, and your thoughts revolve around the conversation and further planning of the afternoon's activities. As soon as you see the man, the knife, and the blood, digestion stops, your respiration and heartbeat change dramatically, your facial muscles tense, your eyebrows rise, your mouth opens, the conversation stops, and your thoughts are frantically concerned with making sense of the situation and deciding what to do next. The regional blood supply to your lower body increases, preparing your leg muscles for vigorous running. Thus, all of your bodily and mental systems are being co-ordinated and synchronized to deal with what might be a major emergency situation, recruiting all organic resources available to deal with the emergency – a situation threatening one of your major goals in life: to stay alive and unhurt.

Summary

We have reviewed the classic controversy around the James–Lange theory of emotion, which focuses on the causal sequence of bodily changes and emotion in the sense of a feeling state. Part of the dispute is taken care of by more precise definitions. *Emotion* is currently seen as a superordinate *hypothetical construct* which includes *feeling* as one of several components (motor expression, physiological changes, action tendencies, and cognitive processing). If *emotion* is defined as an *episode* of interrelated, synchronized changes in these components in response to an event of major significance to the organism, the sequence problem becomes an issue concerning the dynamic interrelationships between the components in a particular emotion episode.

Why do we have Emotions?

Obviously, the synchronization of psychological and physiological processes in an attempt to mobilize all the resources of an organism to face a significant event is a rather costly affair. Not only are some of the subsystems involved prevented from carrying out their normal function (for example, we cannot digest or think very well when we are in the grip of a powerful emotion), but there is also a strong mobilization of energy, which constitutes a drain on the organism's resources (this is why very prolonged emotional arousal can be considered as *stress*). What is the reason for the existence of such a costly mechanism?

The evolutionary significance of emotions

As with other phenomena in social psychology, the question concerning the 'why' or 'what for' (i.e., the *function* of a particular mechanism) is often best answered by turning to the *phylogeny* of the process or behaviour in question (i.e., its evolution). The human mind and behaviour, just as the morphology of the human body, are the product of *evolution*. Psychobiologists have demonstrated the continuity of many psychological and behavioural principles across different species. Emotion is no exception. Some of psychology's most important insights about emotion are due to comparative analysis – determining how emotional processes are similar and different for different species of animals including man (see also chapter 2). For example, Hebb and Thompson (1968), in an in-depth analysis of the significance of animal studies for social psychology, have shown humans to be the most emotional of all animals. This is surprising given the established idea of humans as the first truly rational beings. How can we understand this paradox?

One answer comes from a milestone monograph written by Charles Darwin, the father of evolutionary theory (see chapter 1). In *The Expression of the Emotions in Man and Animals* (1872/1965) Darwin argued that the emotions serve useful functions for the organism, with respect both to the preparation of adaptive behaviour and to the regulation of interaction in socially living species. Focusing on the functionality of emotional expression, Darwin attempted to show for each of the major emotions how the different features of expression, particularly in the face and the body, could be analysed in terms of adaptive behaviour patterns, of which they were considered to be the rudiments. For example, raising the eyebrows in order to increase the acuity of vision, pulling up the nose to avoid exposure to unpleasant odours. While not all of Darwin's speculations about the functionality of particular types of expressive patterns are supported by empirical evidence (see Ekman, 1979), the major tenet of his argument, the notion that emotional expression has evolved out of adaptive behaviour patterns, is still accepted by many emotion psychologists. Also, the idea that we can find precursors of human emotional expressions in animal signalling is supported by ethological research (see figure 10.2 for an illustration of the relationships between chimpanzee and human facial expression).

Emotion as a social signalling system

Most influential has been Darwin's claim that emotional expression serves as a complex signalling system in animal and human communication. The expression of an organism's emotion not only allows others to infer the reaction of the expressor to a particular event or action, it also signals a particular action tendency (e.g., aggression in the case of anger) which can strongly determine the subsequent interaction process. Let us assume that the knife-wielding man in the park is an apprentice mugger and you are his first 'case'. Much of the interaction will depend on the emotional signals you are sending. If you are freezing while uttering a fearful scream the man will see that he has frightened you and, if he can prevent you from running away, that it is safe to demand your wallet. If you shout angrily at him and move forward (since you are a karate champion), he will probably see that you are angry and likely to attack. Obviously, then, the consequent interaction depends strongly on the emotional signals sent by the interaction partners. The social psychology of human social interaction also

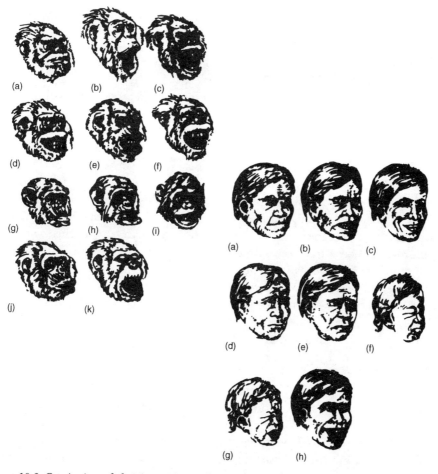

Figure 10.2 Continuity of facial expression from chimpanzees to humans (reproduced from Chevalier–Skolnikoff, 1973)

demonstrates the importance of **affect** signals in the delicate business of dealing with our fellow men and women in establishing relationships, interacting in groups, and in many other social domains (see contributions in Feldman and Rimé, 1991). A particularly interesting case is provided by negotiation situations, where emotion signals are often sent for tactical reasons (for example, trade union officals' feigned anger at a 'ridiculously low' pay rise offer by the management). A nice demonstration of the way in which the emission of emotion signals may be motivated by social communication is provided by a field study that Kraut and Johnson (1979) conducted in a bowling alley, in which they videotaped bowlers' smiling behaviour. The study showed that the commonly observed joyful or triumphant smiles following a good throw did not appear at the moment the skittles fell – they only appeared when the bowlers turned round to look at their fellow players. Clearly, then, one of the major functions of emotional expression is *communication* – often in the service of social bonding or interactional strategy (see also chapter 2).

Emotion affords behavioural flexibility

As we have seen, Darwin claimed that emotion signals are rudiments of formerly adaptive behaviour patterns. This points to another major aspect of the functionality of emotions: they are in the service of adaptive behaviour, but they are not quite yet behaviour itself.

In recent years, social psychologists have suggested that we view the emotions as quasi-automatic response mechanisms, which we are not totally free to switch on and off at will, but which do not blindly execute simple stimulus–response chains (S–R chains). Whereas in S–R chains a specific response is directly coupled or linked to the eliciting stimulus, emotions *decouple* stimulus and response, that is, they separate event and reaction by replacing the automatism of instinctive reactions with a preparation for several reaction alternatives. In other words, the organism can choose from several possible responses to a given event. This is a much more flexible mechanism, providing the organism with greater choice in its behavioural reactions. Yet, a certain automatism remains – the emotions do prepare us, whether we want to or not, for particular types of adaptive behaviour (Scherer, 1984).

Let us take our concrete example. If I were a karate champion and if I were exclusively governed by a stimulus–response mechanism, I would immediately attack the man with the knife. Being endowed with the emotion of anger rather than a simple insult–aggression chain, I would immediately get angry, which, among other things, would prepare my organism for aggressive action by providing the necessary activation, optimal blood circulation in the areas of the body likely to be involved, and preparatory muscle tension. However, since anger decouples the stimulus and the response, I do not hit the person right away. While the emotion has prepared a response that could be considered evolutio- narily adaptive, I have now gained some *latency time*, which permits me to choose an optimal reaction from a large repertoire of possible behaviours. For example, I might not want to hit the man if he appeared to be much stronger than me, or if I discovered, a split-second after first seeing him come out of the bushes, that he had just carved a stick for a child. Thus, the latency time that intervenes between the elicitation of the emotion and the execution of an actual reactive behaviour pattern allows further evaluation of the situation, including an appraisal of the likelihood of success and the seriousness of the consequences of a particular action.

This decoupling of stimulus and response, providing time for further situation and response evaluation as well as for behavioural negotiation and social interaction, would seem to be the most important function of emotion. But, as mentioned before, evolution in its wisdom also provides a specific preparation for action that the organism can fall back on, particularly when there is great urgency and when too much further evaluation and exchange of signals might have negative consequences, as in the case of imminent danger. These built-in provisions for preparation and direction for appropriate action have been described by a number of psychologists (Frijda, 1986; Plutchik, 1980).

An interesting related function, the *amplification of motives*, has been described by Tomkins (1984), whose work contributed much to the revival of the social psychology of emotion. According to his view, emotions tell us what is important to us at a particular time. Similarly, Frijda (1986) proposed that the action tendency produced by a particular emotion gives absolute priority to the underlying motive or goal. Thus, emotion is strongly linked to motivation (see also Buck, 1985).

Information processing

At the same time, emotion is also strongly linked to cognition or information processing. Once we can no longer rely on innate S–R mechanisms, we need criteria to evaluate the massive information that constantly impinges upon us. Cognitive social psychologists increasingly realize that human information processing does not work in the same rule-governed, 'cold' information sifting and sorting fashion that is typical of computers (see chapter 6). Human information processing, particularly in the social domain, often consists of 'hot cognition' (emotional reactions helping us to sort the relevant from the irrelevant, the important from the not so important; see Frijda, 1986, 1993b; Lazarus, 1991). As already mentioned by the early philosophers, valence (that is, pleasure and pain, agreeableness and disagreeableness) plays a major role in turning cold cognitions into hot ones. Some of the criteria used to evaluate incoming information are based on innate preferences. For example, newborn infants will react with positive affect to sweet and with negative affect to bitter tastes (Chiva, 1985; Steiner, 1979). However, many of the criteria that we employ in stimulus evaluation are acquired or learned during socialization, and represented by needs, preferences, goals, and values.

Regulation and control

What is the function of feeling as one of the most prominent components of human emotions? James's idea that 'emotion/feeling' *is* the perception of bodily changes in an emotional episode suggests a type of *monitoring*. Rather than limiting the monitoring only to the physiological changes, we propose that feeling is a reflection of everything that goes on in the process of synchronization of different organismic subsystems in an emotional episode (Scherer, 1984, 1993). Thus, our feeling state serves to reflect and integrate all the components of the emotional episode, such as our evaluation or appraisal of the situation, the bodily changes occurring in our nervous system, the action tendency or preparedness for particular behaviours, and the expressive signals that we are giving off to the social environment. Since, in the process of emotion, the state of all these components and their synchronization or desynchronization changes constantly, our feeling, as an integrated reflection of all of these sub-processes, would allow us a constant monitoring of what goes on. This is, of course, a fundamental requirement for being able to *regulate* or *control* the emotion process.

Virtually all theories of emotion, starting with Aristotle, have assumed that while we are thrown into emotion or passion, we are not totally helpless: we can control, regulate, or modulate the emotion. The feeling component of emotion, which may be the only one absent in the emotional system of the non-human mammals, and even of the higher primates, is precisely what we need as a feedback system for such regulation attempts – often in the service of social norms. The regulation of emotion may be as important to human society as is emotional signalling: the sociologist Elias (1977) has proposed an elaborate theory arguing that the development of civilization is based on an ever-increasing capacity for affect control. Regulation does not necessarily mean suppression or inhibition of emotion. Hochschild (1979, 1983) has shown that there are also positive 'feeling rules' requiring an intensification of appropriate feelings in the service of particular social interests (for example, stewardesses creating positive social affect routines towards airline passengers). The argument is that these rules require not only feigning a particular emotion (by emitting the appropriate signals) but also *actually feeling* it.

We can now return to the sequence issue discussed above. If feeling fulfils a monitoring function, reflecting and integrating all other components involved in the emotion construct, it must indeed be, as postulated by James and Lange, a *consequence* rather than a *cause*. However, rather than assuming simple causal chains, such as 'I tremble therefore I feel afraid', we expect to find a complex dynamic network of interrelationships among the different components. In particular, feelings reflect not only bodily changes but also the individual's evaluation of the emotion-eliciting situation. This may be the key to the problem and it is this issue that we will turn to next.

Summary

Following the pioneering lead of Darwin, social psychologists and ethologists have highlighted a large number of important functions of the emotion mechanism. In the course of evolution, the development of emotion has allowed a decoupling of instinctive stimulus–response contingencies. This provides a latency time during which to chose from a large repertoire of possible responses, but at the same time automatically prepares particular action tendencies to allow adaptive emergency responses. The expression of emotion serves important signalling functions, allowing subtle interpersonal negotiations. Finally, the feeling component of emotion is a powerful mechanism to facilitate regulation and control of emotional behaviour.

How are Emotions Elicited and Differentiated?

Much of the work of social psychologists interested in emotion has been concerned with the question of which situations are capable of provoking emotional responses (elicitation) and which out of the many possible emotions is the one that is elicited by a particular type of situation (differentiation).

Philosophical notions

For most philosophers this question did not constitute a major problem. An insult to our honour would obviously produce anger, an attack by a powerful enemy, fear, and so on. This normative approach, adjudicating the appropriateness of particular emotions to eliciting situations and persons, postulates a clear match between the type of eliciting situation and the type of emotion. Lay people, also, do not quite understand the question: it seems clear to them why someone reacts with a particular emotion in a particular situation – for example, being afraid when encountering a bear or a man with a knife. So what is the problem? The problem lies in the fact that often information about the situation alone does not allow us to predict the ensuing emotion. As we have seen, a hunter might be quite happy to see the bear trot out of the forest. A plainclothes policeman might be relieved to finally happen upon the mugger he has been tracking for days in the park. It seems that one of the decisive factors in emotion elicitation and differentiation is the interaction between the type of situation and the significance of the event to the person experiencing the emotion.

This is why all eminent philosophers who have dealt with emotion in their treatises, have explicitly or implicitly defined the different kinds of emotions in terms of the significance of the events or actions for the person – or, as we might say today, in terms of the person's evaluation of an event with respect to important needs, goals and values. Even James, bent on arguing the revolutionary hypothesis that the type of emotion experienced was determined by the perception of the patterns of bodily changes, had to admit that the nature of these bodily changes, in turn, was determined by the overwhelming 'idea' of the significance of the elements of a situation for the well-being of the organism (e.g., the probability that the bear will kill us or that we will kill it; James, 1894, p. 518). In modern parlance, this sounds suspiciously close to the notion of the *appraisal* of the event in terms of the organism's important needs, goals and values. Nobody had said it in exactly that way, since it was not a major issue of the social psychology of emotion. It seemed trivial. Then non-trivial social psychology came and complicated things.

Schachter's two-factor theory

At the beginning of the sixties, the experimental social psychologist Schachter was one of the first to propose a *cognitive* theory of emotion. While accepting several of the fundamental tenets of the James–Lange theory (such as equating emotion with verbally reported feeling, and assigning a central role to arousal in the peripheral nervous system), he doubted that there could be as many differentiated patterns of physiological changes to account for the great variety of moods and emotion states for which there are verbal expressions (particularly since physiological psychologists seemed to have trouble demonstrating such differences experimentally even between major emotion categories). Thus, contrary to James, Schachter suggested that the perception of heightened *non-specific* arousal (defined in terms of sympathetic **activation**, as indexed by sensations like the heart beating faster, limbs trembling, face flushing, etc.) is sufficient to *elicit* 'emotion/feeling'. With respect to the *differentiation* of the emotion – where James would have answered 'the specific nature of the bodily changes' – Schachter argued for a 'steering function' of cognitions arising from the immediate situation as interpreted on the basis of past experience.

ACTIVATION

According to this view, there are two factors (or elements) that are necessary to elicit and differentiate emotion as feeling: (1) the perception of heightened **sympathetic arousal**, and (2), cognitions concerning the interpretation of the situation in the light of one's past experiences (see sequence diagram in figure 10.1). Schachter acknowledged that 'In most emotion inducing situations, of course, the two factors are completely interrelated. Imagine a man walking alone down a dark alley, a figure with a gun suddenly appears. The perception–cognition "figure with a gun" in some fashion initiates a state of physiological arousal; this state of arousal is interpreted in terms of knowledge about dark alleys and guns and the arousal is labelled "fear"' (Schachter and Singer, 1962, p. 380). Note that, contrary to James–Lange, Schachter does not presume that it is

SYMPATHETIC AROUSAL

differentiated physiological patterning that produces a particular feeling – he assumes, for the 'normal case', that non-specific sympathetic arousal and the simultaneous cognitive interpretation of the eliciting event produce the feeling.

But Schachter was not really interested in the normal case; he focused on situations in which the two factors are *not* linked. What happens, he asked, if a person experiences heightened arousal for which there are neither immediate explanation nor appropriate cognitions? Schachter argued that this situation would elicit an 'information search and self-attribution' process (see chapters 5–7 in this volume). We can state the presumed mechanism in a somewhat simplified manner: if I detect a heightened level of sympathetic arousal that I cannot attribute to an extraneous factor, I know that I am likely to feel an emotion. I will then carefully scrutinize my physical and social environment and, on the basis of all pertinent cues, decide which emotion is appropriate. It is this emotion, then, that I will feel (of course, there is no assumption that any of this is voluntary or conscious).

In a now classic experiment, Schachter and his collaborator Singer tested this notion (Schachter and Singer, 1962). They administered either adrenaline (also known as epinephrine) or placebo injections to subjects who had been told that the experiment was to test the transient effects of a vitamin compound on vision. The subjects in the control condition (placebo injection) were just told that the injection would have no side effects whatsoever. Subjects in the adrenaline condition were divided into three experimental groups: (1) the *adrenaline ignorant* group (subjects were told that the injection had no side effects); (2) the *adrenaline informed* group (subjects were told that the injection was likely to make their hands shake, their hearts race, and their faces flush – all of which are common effects of adrenaline); (3) the *adrenaline misinformed* group (subjects were told that after the injection it was likely that their feet would feel numb, their body would itch, and a slight headache would develop – none of which is a common effect of adrenaline. This was intended as a control group to check on the effect of telling subjects something about the possible effects – it was run only in one experimental condition).

What are the predictions so far? Subjects in the placebo condition should not feel much of an emotion since their non-specific arousal has not increased. Subjects in the *adrenaline informed* group should not feel much of an emotion either – while their arousal has increased, they have been given a perfectly plausible explanation for this state – the side effects of the injection. Only the subjects in the *adrenaline misinformed* and the *adrenaline ignorant* groups should feel an emotion – they are highly aroused, have no good explanation for why this is the case, and thus presumably attribute their state of arousal to some underlying affect state. But which emotion will they feel?

This is where the second part of the experimental manipulation comes in. After subjects had received the injection they were asked to wait about 20 minutes until the 'vitamin compound' had taken its effect (at which point the vision tests would be performed). Subjects waited in a room together with another subject who had supposedly also received an injection. In fact, this 'subject' was a confederate of the experimenters, who had been trained to act either in a very joyous and playful manner (*euphoria condition*, engaging himself in buoyant games like flying paper planes) or in a wrathful, infuriated manner (*anger condition*, irritated and aggressive reactions such as ripping up a questionnaire and leaving the room). Given the researchers' expectation about the role of a given situational context in interpreting non-specific arousal, the hypothesis was that subjects spending 20 minutes in the company of a euphoric-acting confederate should feel more euphoric, while those exposed to the angry-acting confederate should feel more angry. However, this should only be true for the subjects in the *adrenaline misinformed* and the *adrenaline ignorant* groups. Only these subjects should be scanning their environment for plausible cues for their presumed emotional arousal; the subjects in the *adrenaline informed* groups should not be affected by the confederate's behaviour since they have had a perfectly satisfactory explanation for their state of arousal. Subjects in the placebo condition should be unaffected because they have not experienced heightened arousal and are thus unlikely to feel emotional.

Figure 10.3 shows the results of the experiment, and compares them to the hypotheses. Two dependent measures were used: (1) asking subjects to rate their feeling state on two five-point scales for happy (euphoric) and angry mood respectively, and (2) observing the subjects' behaviour through a one-way mirror and coding it for the presence of behavioural signs of euphoria or anger. While the authors interpreted these results as supporting their hypotheses, it has since been pointed out that the effects were very small and that only parts of the predictions were supported. Take a few minutes to look at figure 10.3 and try to discover why the data are less than perfect in supporting the authors' hypotheses (note that the *adrenaline misinformed* group was only run in the *euphoria* condition).

Do not read on before having tried to make sense of the data in figure 10.3!

You will probably have noticed that only the behaviour-observation variable supports the hypotheses for both emotions studied. As far as the subjects' own ratings of their emotional state were concerned Schachter and Singer found only a slight effect for euphoria and actually the opposite of what was expected for anger.

Apart from the weak results, the methods used in this study have been strongly criticized. Furthermore, attempts at replication have been generally unsuccessful (see Gordon, 1987; Reisenzein, 1983, for a review of these issues).

In spite of these shortcomings, the experiment has had an enormous influence on the social psychology of emotion, as it demonstrated the possibility that in a

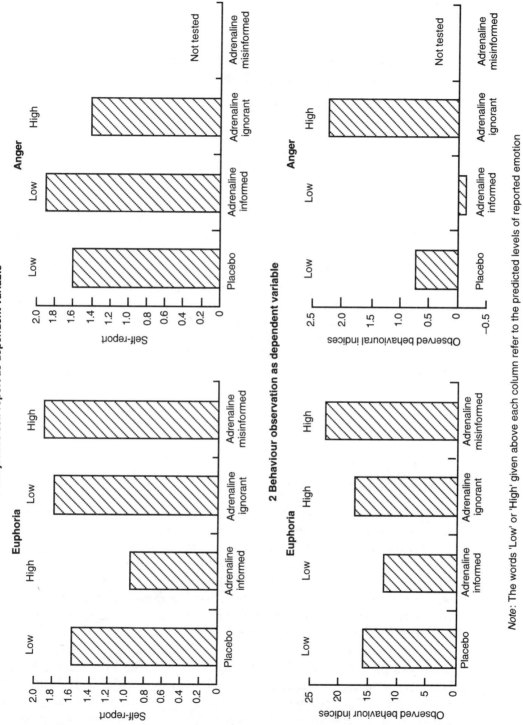

Figure 10.3 Hypotheses and results of the Schachter–Singer experiment

case where we cannot easily account for an abnormal degree of arousal, we will turn to the social environment to find cues that might explain this internal state. It is by now an established finding in social psychology that we use information from the social environment (particularly other people) as a guide to judgement and choice in situations of uncertainty (see chapter 16 in this volume). Schachter and Singer were among the first to point to the possibility that our emotional experience, which had always been thought to be a very private domain and directly linked to the intricate goings-on in the body, is also subject to a multitude of social influences, and, under certain conditions, might even be completely open to manipulation.

Unfortunately, rather than treating the Schachter–Singer 'information search and self-attribution' paradigm as a special case, as the authors had themselves suggested, many subsequent authors, including Schachter himself, used it as the basis for what has become known as the *Schachter–Singer theory of emotion*, the only theory of emotion to be covered in most textbooks of social psychology in the past 30 years. (At this point, please refer back to the diagram in figure 10.1 to recall exactly what the Schachter–Singer emotion *theory* is all about.) Clearly, as a *general theory* of emotion, trying to explain how emotions are *typically* elicited and which factors determine their differentiation, the Schachter–Singer approach seems not only of limited value but actually misleading. While it was a clever idea to induce arousal via adrenaline injection and to manipulate attributions about its effects, it was in no way an operationalization of how emotional arousal is produced under normal circumstances. This issue is addressed by what seems to be the majority view on emotion elicitation and differentiation today – *appraisal theories*.

Appraisal theories

Arnold (1960) was among the first psychologists to formally propose that the significance of an emotion-eliciting event to the experiencing person (as had been implied by all major thinkers on emotion) was established through a process of evaluation or appraisal of the event, based on a set of criteria specific to the person. A few years later, Lazarus (1966) made a major contribution in pointing out that there is a *process* of appraisal, with *re-appraisals* often changing and correcting first impressions, and thus changing the resulting emotion. Lazarus also introduced the distinction between what he called *primary and secondary appraisal* of an emotion- or stress-eliciting event: while the primary evaluation deals with the pleasantness and unpleasantness or the goal conduciveness of the event, the secondary appraisal determines to what extent the person will be able to cope with the consequences of an event, given his or her competencies, resources, or power. Lazarus calls his model 'transactional' – the significance of the event is determined not only by the nature of the event but also by the needs, goals and resources of the person. These two determinants interact or transact and it is the result of this transaction that will determine the nature of the emotion, or the amount of stress suffered (Lazarus, 1966, 1991).

One of the major advances due to the recent proliferation of appraisal theories is the detailed specification of appraisal dimensions or criteria. Appraisal theorists have established lists of such criteria, which are assumed to be used in evaluating emotion-antecedent events. Examples for such criteria are the novelty or expectedness of the event, its pleasantness, whether it helps or hinders reaching one's goals, and how well one can cope with the consequences (see Frijda, Kuipers, and ter Schure, 1989; Scherer, 1988, for details). Let us return to our park example. When you see the man with the knife emerge from the bushes a very rapid process of cognitive evaluation of the significance of this event for your own personal well-being will ensue – utilizing some of the central appraisal criteria suggested by emotion theorists: what is the intention of that man (causality, agency, responsibility)? Will his actions affect my own plans and goals, such as survival, remaining unharmed, enjoying myself (goal conduciveness)? Will I be able to deal with an attack, i.e., am I stronger, would it be promising to call for help (coping potential, power)? The outcome of the event appraisal using these and other evaluation criteria will determine your emotional reaction.

Many appraisal theorists have ventured predictions as to when particular types of emotion should occur as the result of particular patterns of appraisal results. The first column in figure 10.4 shows some examples of concrete hypotheses about antecedent appraisal patterns for some of the major emotions.

Much of recent social-psychological research on emotion has been directed at testing some of these predictions or studying the relationships between appraisal results and emotional responses in a more inductive fashion. Generally, subjects are asked to *recall* episodes of typical emotions, such as anger, fear, or shame, and are then asked to respond to questions about the underlying cognitive appraisal processes (Gehm and Scherer, 1988; Mauro, Sato and Tucker, 1992; Roseman, Spindel and Jose, 1990; Smith and Ellsworth, 1985).

An alternative strategy is to systematically construct scenarios or vignettes on the basis of the predicted appraisal profiles and to ask subjects to *imagine* experiencing this situation and to indicate their probable emotional reactions. For example, Weiner (1980) presented students with a scenario describing a fellow student asking to borrow the subject's class notes since he had missed the previous week's class. The reason given by the student to justify the demand was varied for different groups of subjects, on the basis of theoretical predictions with respect to *controllability* as an appraisal factor: (1) having gone to the beach (high control); (2) having had reading problems because of a change in glasses (medium control); and (3) having had eye problems – and the person is described as wearing an eye patch and dark glasses (low controllability). Figure 10.5 shows the results. As predicted, the affective reaction reported by the subjects was more negative, involving mostly anger, the more controllable the causal factor was.

Verbal label	Appraisal profile	Facial expression	Vocal expression	Physiological symptoms
Happiness/Joy	Event seen as highly conducive to reaching an important goal or satisfying a need		Increases in pitch level, range and variability as well vocal intensity	Heart beating faster, warm skin temperature
Anger/Rage	Unexpected event, intentionally caused by another person, seen as obstructing goal attainment or need satisfaction; subject judges own coping ability as high, considers action as violating norms		Increase in pitch level and intensity level. Increase in high-frequency energy in the spectrum	Heart beating faster, muscles tensing, changes in breathing, hot skin temperature
Sadness/Dejection	Event that permanently prevents need satisfaction, seen as uncontrollable by human agency, person feels totally powerless with respect to consequences		Decrease in pitch level and range as well as intensity level. Decrease in speech rate	Lump in throat, crying/sobbing, muscles tensing
Fear/Terror	Event occurring very suddenly, uncertain consequences threatening fundamental goal of survival or bodily integrity, urgent reaction required, person uncertain about ability to master the situation		Strong increase in pitch level and range. Increase in high-frequency energy in the spectrum. Increased speech rate	Heart beating faster, muscles tensing, change in breathing, perspiring, cold skin temperature, lump in throat

Figure 10.4 Illustrations of differentiated appraisal and response profiles for four major emotions, based partly on theoretical predictions and partly on results of empirical studies using verbal report data (see Scherer, 1984, 1986; Scherer and Wallbott, 1994; facial expressions reproduced from Ekman and Friesen, 1975)

Their readiness to help varied correspondingly (see also chapter 7 for a more detailed discussion of *controllability* in Weiner's theory of attribution).

Such studies have generally provided strong support for the theoretical expectations formulated by appraisal theorists (Parkinson and Manstead, 1992; Roseman, 1991; Smith and Lazarus, 1993). Yet another empirical approach consists of choosing a particular emotion-inducing event that affects many people at the same time, such as term examinations for students, and then obtaining information about both the differential appraisals of the situation and the type of emotional response. Such studies, in addition to providing evidence for the predicted appraisal–emotion links, have shown the importance of *emotion blends*, the fact that the complex appraisal of a given situation by a particular person is likely to give rise to a mixture of several emotions rather than only one specific emotion (Folkman and Lazarus, 1985; Smith and Ellsworth, 1987).

A major methodological problem for empirical tests of these appraisal theories is the difficulty of assessing the nature of the emotion-antecedent cognitive appraisal processes independently of the underlying feeling state (Parkinson and Manstead, 1992). Most of the research described above has relied on retrospective

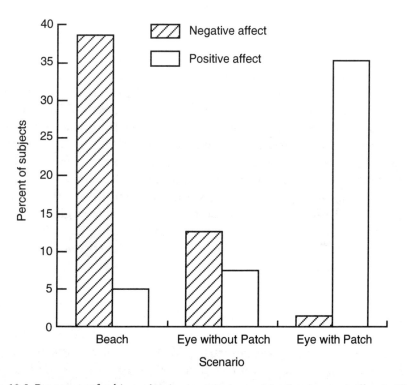

Figure 10.5 Percentage of subjects showing negative or positive interpersonal affect in Weiner's class notes study (after Weiner, 1980)

verbal self-report as to the nature of the evaluation that has preceded the emotional experience. Obviously, this kind of evidence is very imperfect since one cannot rule out that the respondent may construe the likely appraisal antecedents on the basis of culturally shared ideas (social representations) about which types of events produce particular emotions. One way to avoid the danger of circularity in this kind of approach is to manipulate situations in such a way that one can expect the appraisal process to produce certain types of results. Such studies are not only difficult to carry out, but also run into the problem that some subjects may not evaluate the situation as the experimenter expects them to, particularly if their needs, goals, and resources differ greatly from those of other subjects in the experiment. Thus, the only long-term hope is to be able to monitor evaluation processes independently of the conscious recall and verbalization of the subjects. While this may be a long way off, modern techniques in neuropsychology might one day allow at least a rudimentary analysis of what goes on inside our head just before the onset of an emotional reaction (see Scherer, 1993).

Current controversies

Appraisal theories are rarely challenged with respect to their basic assumptions. Most scholars interested in emotion seem to accept that, in many cases, emotions are elicited when events are appraised as being of major significance to the organism. The nature of the emotion depends on the detailed results of an evaluation guided by criteria having to do with the nature of the event and the needs, goals, values and resources of the organism. However, there are some issues that are quite hotly debated in this area. One of these concerns what is often considered to be an excessive cognitivism of appraisal theories. The very terms *evaluation* and *appraisal* imply that there is high-level cortical and possibly conscious activity which precedes emotional arousal. There are many cases where this is manifestly not the case. A fairly intense emotion can be produced by an immediate, almost automatic reaction that seems to preclude much conscious thinking and evaluation. In consequence, there is some debate as to *how much* cognition is really necessary for emotion and whether there might be an 'affect system' that is quite independent of any cognitive processes.

This issue has been at the centre of a lively debate between Zajonc (1980, 1984), whose work on the effect of mere exposure (see chapter 9, this volume) demonstrated effects of preference that seemed quite independent of higher cognitive activity, and Lazarus (1984), one of the pioneers of the appraisal approach. Once one looks at the neurological and psychological details of the information processing that is invariably involved in any kind of reaction, the issue becomes much less controversial. While the words 'evaluation' and 'appraisal' sound highly analytical (in terms of cortical, conscious processing), this is not implied by most appraisal theorists (see Leventhal and Scherer, 1987).

Another issue which is still quite controversial is the number of appraisal criteria likely to be used and the nature of the appraisal process. Some theorists propose a very small number of criteria and try to explain the different emotions on this basis alone. Others have suggested a much larger set of criteria, attempting a more fine-grained differentiation of the various emotions. This, of course, is linked to the question of how many emotions there are. Is there just a limited number of basic or fundamental emotions (see Ekman, 1984, 1992; Izard, 1991, 1992) and/or a limited number of emotion circuits in the brain (Gray, 1990, Panksepp, 1982), or are there as many different emotions as there are results of the appraisal process (Scherer, 1984)?

For social psychologists, the emotion-antecedent appraisal mechanism is of particular importance since it may help to explain cultural differences in eliciting situations and emotional experience. As mentioned before, while there may be some innate or universally acquired appraisal criteria, in most cases the appraisal criteria will depend on acquired needs and to a large extent on culturally defined goals and values (see Mesquita and Frijda, 1992; Shweder, 1993). For example, Wallbott and Scherer (1995) found that for respondents in individualistic cultures (highly valuing the rights and interests of individuals), there was relatively little difference between shame and guilt; in both cases, the behaviour that had elicited the emotion was considered to be highly immoral. In collectivistic cultures (giving priority to the interests of the family and of social groups), on the other hand, guilt experiences were provoked more frequently by events that were judged to be much more immoral than those that produced shame. Consistent with these different appraisal tendencies in collectivistic and individualistic cultures, the data showed rather striking differences in the other components of these two emotions. Shame experiences in collectivistic cultures were intense but brief, without major consequences. In contrast, in individualistic cultures, the reaction profiles for shame experiences were very much like those of guilt experiences (involving long-term effects on self-evaluation).

The way in which socio-cultural value systems affect emotional life is as yet little studied. Most of the work on cross-cultural differences in emotion experience are focused on differences in the words available in different languages to express emotion (see below). Much more fruitful for a social-psychological analysis would be a comparative study of the importance of values, goals, person schemata, causal attributions, and other constructs that play a role in emotion-antecedent appraisal processes.

Are there Specific Response Patterns for Different Types of Emotions?

The James–Lange theory postulated the existence of specific response patterns as a prerequisite for differentiated emotions. Theorists like Schachter and others have doubted the existence of such patterns and relied on cognitive interpretation of *non*-specific arousal to explain emotion differentiation (look back again at figure 10.1). What is the evidence? We shall deal with each of the three major components constituting the so-called response triad of the emotions – physiological changes, motor expression, and feeling states – separately.

Motor expression

If emotional **expression** in face, body and voice is to serve a major function in communication and social interaction, there must be clearly differentiated signals corresponding to different types of emotion.

Facial expression

The empirical evidence available suggests that this is indeed the case. The expression modality studied most intensively in the century after Darwin's pioneering work has been the face. Tomkins (1984) postulated the existence of a limited number of basic discrete emotions (as amplifiers of motives, as we have seen) and suggested that innate neural motor programmes are executed when the respective emotion has been induced by appropriate stimulation. These programmes are expected to produce, in addition to typical facial expressions, differentiated reaction patterns in the voice as well as in physiological response systems.

If one assumes that innate neural motor programmes produce specific response patterns for primary emotions, the facial expressions of emotion should be very similar across cultures (as shown in figure 10.4). Ekman and Izard showed that subjects from widely different cultures were able to identify rather accurately the emotions facially expressed by American encoders in series of photographs (for overviews see: Ekman, 1972; Ekman and Friesen, 1971; Izard, 1971). Critics were quick to point out, of course, that this procedure may not have been the correct way of investigating the universality of facial expression of emotion since the wide distribution of Hollywood films all over the world may have taught people in other cultures to identify American facial expressions reliably. In response to these criticisms, Ekman, Sorenson, and Friesen (1969) conducted a study which showed that members of a tribe in a remote area of New Guinea, who had had very little contact with the outside world, identified Western facial expressions relatively accurately. They also produced expressions of specified emotions that were similar to those seen in the West when asked to show a face typical for specific emotion-eliciting situations (Ekman, 1972).

Since then, there have been quite a number of studies in this area, with respect to both decoding and encoding of the different primary emotions (see Camras, Holland, and Patterson, 1993; Manstead, 1991). The bulk of the evidence indicates that actor-portrayed facial expressions can be decoded rather accurately by judges from different cultures (Ekman, 1982; 1989; Oster, Daily, and

Goldenthal, 1989). This generally supports the Darwinian notion of facial expression having evolved from formerly 'serviceable habits', which in principle should be the same for all cultures in the world. Comparative studies (Redican, 1982; van Hooff, 1972) show that there are a number of elements that can be traced back to functional behaviour patterns, and which we find in similar forms in other animals as well as in young babies. However, these studies also show that there are features that are specific to human facial expression and for which it is difficult to find functional explications in a biological sense. Furthermore, while the intercultural studies of facial expression have demonstrated considerable universality, there has also been evidence for cultural specificity. This is true for decoding, where cultural influences on emotion perception in the face have been demonstrated (Matsumoto, 1989), as well as for encoding. For example, contrary to the claim for a pan-cultural facial expression of contempt (Ekman and Friesen, 1986), Ricci-Bitti, Brighetti, Garotti, and Boggi Cavallo (1989) compared contempt expression in the United States and Italy and found quite marked *differences* in the facial patterning of this emotion.

What could be the origins of such cultural differences in expression? Wundt (1900), one of the pioneers of experimental and comparative psychology, has pointed out very early on that emotional expression is subject to cultural control and that many cultures sanction explicitly or implicitly what expressions can be legitimately shown under particular circumstances (something Ekman and Friesen, 1969, have called **display rules**).

DISPLAY RULES

Much of the work reported above is based on the recognition of emotions facially expressed by actors. Obviously, these expressions are likely to be very typical and pure, produced specifically for easy communicability. How well does the face communicate emotions under more normal circumstances? There are now quite a few studies in which the ability of judges to decode spontaneously-occurring facial expressions (for example, while the persons whose faces are observed view disgusting slides, receive shocks, etc.) is examined. Most of these studies find better-than-chance recognition (see Buck, 1984) although the overall amount of accuracy is not impressive, particularly when several negative emotions are to be distinguished (Wagner, MacDonald, and Manstead, 1986). It must be noted, however, that the emotion-eliciting stimuli were quite weak in many of these studies. Therefore, the results are not quite representative of the communicative power of facial expressions of strong emotions.

Vocal expression

Can judges recognize an emotion expression on the basis of voice and speech cues alone, that is, without pertinent verbal information? Many such studies have been conducted (mostly using actor portrayals of vocal emotion expressions), and reviews of the studies in this area have reached the conclusion that judges in these studies are correct about 50 per cent of the time (Pittam and Scherer, 1993) – far beyond what one would expect by chance (since judges generally choose from between 5 and 10 alternative responses the chance rate amounts to 10 to 20 per cent, depending on the study). Although only a few cross-cultural studies have been done in this domain, the data that do exist strongly point in the direction of the recognizability of vocally expressed emotions across language and culture boundaries, rendering the hypothesis likely that vocal expression, like at least some facial expression, is partly biologically based (Frick, 1985).

This is supported by strong comparative evidence pointing towards the evolutionary continuity of vocal emotion expression. Behavioural biologists, studying vocal animal communication, have pointed to important similarities in the vocal expression and communication of motivational–emotional states in many different species. Thus, angry, hostile, dominant states are generally expressed by harsh, loud vocalizations, whereas states of fear and helplessness give rise to high-pitched, thin-sounding vocalizations. To a large extent, this also seems to be true for equivalent human vocalizations (Scherer, 1985). However, as for facial expression, there are sizeable differences between species and cultures due to the constraints of the demands exerted by communication systems and cultural expression norms.

In fact, these influences on the voice are even more pronounced than those on the face, since the voice has also become the carrier signal for speech in the course of the evolution of language. Thus, while the facial muscles do serve other functions related to vision, eating, and speaking (see Ekman, 1979), one of their major functions seems to be the facial expression of affective states. In contrast, except in the case of brief non-linguistic affect vocalizations or interjections, the voice does double duty in carrying linguistic (phonological and morphological) and extra-linguistic meaning (related to the speaker's state). Since different languages with widely different phonological and syntactical structures are spoken in different cultures, we might expect a high degree of cultural diversity of emotion signalling in the voice.

Unfortunately, the study of the objective characteristics of emotional expression, including a comparison between different languages, is not very advanced. In recent years, researchers using digital speech analysis have attempted to determine the prototypical acoustical profiles for the major emotions. Some results of this research tradition (see Scherer, 1986; Pittam and Scherer, 1993; Scherer, Banse, Wallbott, and Goldbeck, 1991) are shown in figure 10.4.

Gesture and posture

Whereas facial and vocal expressions have been studied quite extensively, gesture and posture have received little attention. Yet, we are all familiar with typical emotion gestures such as hiding one's face behind one's hand or wringing one's hands, many of which are quite similar across cultures (La Barre, 1947; Eibl-Eibesfeldt, 1972). Most of the empirical studies on gestures have focused on speech-related hand movements (see Feyereisen and de Lannoy, 1991; Rimé and

Schiaratura, 1991), only very few have examined the way in which emotions affect gesturing (Ekman and Friesen, 1969, 1971; Wallbott, 1985).

Ever since Darwin there has been the idea that there are specific 'motor attitudes' for particular emotions (Bull, 1951). Functionally, it obviously makes a lot of sense to reduce one's size in conditions of fear and submissiveness and to appear bigger than one really is in situations where one is threatening an adversary. In triumph, one expects to see an erect posture, in defeat, a slumped one (see Riskind, 1984).

Summary

On the whole, then, empirical evidence suggests that there are specific expression patterns in the face and the voice (as well as in gesture and posture) for many of the major emotions. This is as we would expect if emotional expression is to provide unambiguous signals in social communication informing the social environment about an organism's emotional reaction and consequent behaviour intention.

Physiological changes

Throughout the centuries, the notion of emotion has implied the presence of sizeable physiological upheaval. As we have seen, one of the central issues that has been hotly debated concerns the *specificity* of this upheaval or arousal for discrete emotions.

Changes in physiological state do not primarily serve communicative purposes (although blushing, increased respiration rate, general muscle tension, etc. can be quite obvious signs of emotional arousal and can be used as a basis for emotion attribution by observers). A primary function of the physiological changes is the provision of energy and the preparation for specific action. This was the main thesis of Cannon (1929), a physiologist who was one of the main adversaries of James and Lange. Contrary to their *peripheralist* position (see also Schachter, 1970), he took a *centralist* viewpoint, assuming that for each major emotion special mechanisms in the central nervous system produce physiological changes appropriate for adapted action in the different subsystems of the organism.

Unfortunately, empirical studies in this domain suffer from a major methodological difficulty. For both ethical and practical reasons, it is almost impossible to induce strong, realistic emotions in the laboratory using systematic manipulation. Consequently, emotion-specific differences have rarely been demonstrated empirically, at least for humans. Because of this lack of evidence, some psychologists have argued that the notion of physiological differentiatedness should be replaced by an assumption of generalized non-specific arousal or activation (see Duffy, 1941; Schachter and Singer, 1962).

This corresponds to throwing the baby out with the bath water. It is certainly the case that the methods actually used for emotion induction in laboratory studies (such as imagination and film viewing) are unlikely to produce very powerful emotions, but they may nevertheless help to settle the issue. A review of the pertinent studies to date, by Cacioppo, Klein, Berntson and Hatfield (1993), shows that the evidence for complete autonomic differentiation of each of the major emotions (that is, a specific, typical configuration of physiological symptoms for each emotion) is inconclusive, but that there seem to be consistent patterns of differences between specific pairs of emotions on some physiological parameters. For example, one finds consistent differences between fear and sadness with respect to heart-rate across different studies (see figure 10.4). If even weak emotions, as generated in the laboratory, yield discernible physiological response patterns, one might expect that stronger emotions will show more strongly differentiated patterns.

Subjective feelings

In some ways, this may be the most important component of emotion. We could indeed ask whether we can speak about having an emotion at all if we do not have a conscious experience of it, a specific feeling that we can then label with an appropriate verbal concept. Not surprisingly, throughout the history of the study of emotion, many theorists have tended to *equate* emotion with feeling (see page 282). It seems more reasonable, however, to view the feeling component as a reflection of the changes occurring in *all* other components (see Scherer, 1993). This proposal maintains the important role assigned to the conscious experience of what is happening in our body but situates the experience in the *total context* of our particular self with its history, its preferences, and its present state being affected by a particular event.

Dimensions of feeling

Throughout the history of philosophy it has been claimed that the major dimension of feeling is linked to pleasure and pain, agreeableness and disagreeableness, or, as it is often glossed in modern social psychology, positive or negative *valence*. In fact, quite a few modern social psychologists believe that feeling can be quite conveniently reduced to the valence aspect (positive or negative affect) with respect to persons, objects or events. This position, however, does not acknowledge major advances in our understanding of feeling states that were made during the final part of the nineteenth century. Wundt (1874) proposed a tri-dimensional system to characterize the specific nature of these complex emotional feeling states by adding *excitation vs depression* and *tension vs. relaxation* to the classic *pleasantness vs. unpleasantness* dichotomy.

  Much of the modern work has relied on short-hand descriptors of the felt experience – in particular, emotion words and photographs of facial expressions. An almost countless number of studies has shown that subjects are able to judge the similarity of verbal emotion concepts or to evaluate the emotion words on relevant rating scales. The data consistently confirm two of Wundt's dimensions, pleasantness/unpleasantness and excitation/depression (the latter being more often described as high/low activation, or active/passive, in subsequent research). Not only do these two dimensions emerge from dimensional analyses of similarity judgements, the relative locations of particular emotion concepts within the two-dimensional space are also fairly stable. This is true independently of the language or culture in which these studies have been conducted (Davitz, 1964; Fillenbaum and Rapaport, 1971; Osgood, May and Miron, 1975). Circular or circumplex models of emotion have been proposed, based on such findings, (Plutchik, 1980; Russell, 1980, 1983). However, these models have been criticized on both conceptual and methodological grounds (Larsen and Diener, 1992). The third dimension defined by Wundt, tension/relaxation, has not been consistently found in subsequent empirical research.

While the individual emotions can be projected into a two- or three-dimensional scheme, this is always a simplification. The enormous number of verbal labels for emotions, particularly subjective feeling, that exist in virtually all the languages in the world, indicate that much more subtle differentiations of emotional processes are possible. Depending on the criteria used by the individual researcher, between 200 and close to 1,000 such terms have been identified for some of the languages studied. The use of such emotion labels may well be our major access to feeling states. If subjective feeling is restricted to the conscious experience of emotion, then it would seem that the verbal expression that we use to describe this state is the closest we can come to defining it.

Verbal labelling of feeling states

Not surprisingly, then, words have consistently been one of the major manifestations of emotions studied. In recent years, anthropologists have relied heavily on the use of emotion labels to discuss similarities and differences in the emotions experienced in different cultures. Generally, these researchers find informants in the culture they are studying and elicit from them the terms that are currently used to describe affective states. They then try to establish the equivalence of such terms to the emotion vocabulary in Western languages.

For example, Levy (1984) found that Tahitian islanders had very few words for sadness-related emotions, talking mostly about 'feeling heavy or fatigued' or 'not feeling a sense of inner push' in such cases, whereas they had a much richer set of terms for other emotions such as anger. He concluded that cultures may be more or less prone to perceive and talk about particular types of emotions. Similar studies, conducted in a number of non-Western cultures (see Lutz and White, 1986; Mesquita and Frijda, 1992; Russell, 1991; Shweder, 1993), have shown a large cultural diversity of emotion vocabularies and ways of talking about emotional phenomena. This has led some anthropologists to conclude that there is little universality of emotion. Rather, according to this view, emotions are mainly determined by culture-specific values and modes of interaction.

This anthropological evidence as well as indications of historical changes in emotion concepts have served as bases for the claim that emotions are a **social construction**. Social psychologists proposing this view (see Averill, 1980; Harré, 1986; see also Oatley, 1993) presume that emotions have no reality other than that which is culturally created, or socially constructed. This idea is of course partially consistent with the concept of subjective feeling states as reflecting the total context of the emotional episode – the appraisal of the eliciting event or situation and the nature of the response. Obviously, the cultural context, the values with which the event is concerned, and the role of the individual in the situation will all differentially affect the particular feeling state likely to result. Cultural differences in value systems, social structures, interaction habits, and many other factors may thus influence emotion experiences and be reflected in cultural specificities of feeling states. These differences are likely to be most pronounced with respect to the labelling of specific aspects of the emotional experience, given the effect of cultural evolution on language.

However, such cultural differences in feeling states and ways of talking about them do not necessarily invalidate the notion that the basic *emotion mechanism* is common to the human species. In order to argue that all of emotion is socio-culturally constructed and that there is little or no **universality**, one would need to show strong differences in appraisal processes, expressive behaviours, physio-logical reaction patterns, and action tendencies in different cultures. The evidence so far points in the opposite direction. Large cross-national studies involving several thousand subjects in over forty countries on all five continents (Scherer, Wallbott, and Summerfield, 1986; Scherer and Wallbott, 1994) found cultural differences in reported profiles of different feeling states, but these were rather minor in comparison with a massive effect of universal differences between emotions. We may conclude then that feeling, as expressed by verbal emotion labels, is more likely to be affected by socio-cultural variation than are other components of emotion. This makes sense because the subjective feeling state represents both the cultural and situational context as well as all of the other components of the emotion process.

Summary

The empirical evidence shows fairly consistent emotion-specific profiles for facial and vocal expression and recent data suggest that at least pairs or groups of emotions can be differentiated with respect to specific physiological parameters. Feelings have been exclusively studied through verbal labels. A large number of studies have shown that a small number of superordinate dimensions are sufficient to summarize these feeling labels. Cross-cultural studies have shown strong cultural differences in emotion terminology, possibly reflecting differences in feeling state. On the whole, the evidence supporting differentiation of the emotions in the process of appraisal and response leads us to view the sequence issue in a new light.

Given that there is some evidence for emotion-specific response profiles, what is the conclusion with respect to the sequence issue that has haunted us from the outset of the chapter? The last sequence diagram at the bottom of figure 10.1 suggests how one might envisage the problem. Clearly, the assumed mechanism is much more complex than envisaged in the earlier models. The basic assumption is that differentiation is produced by the results of an evaluation or appraisal of the eliciting event, and that this differentiation concerns several subsystems of the organism, directed toward an adaptation to the situation created by the event. Subjective feeling as one of the components of the emotion process reflects these changes, and is thus necessarily a consequence. However, feeling in itself serves as a stimulus, which is perceived and appraised by the individual and may thus in turn influence the nature and direction of the total emotion process.

How do the Emotion Components Interact?

Catharsis

One of the major functions of Greek tragedy was supposed to be *catharsis*: the spectators, in the process of observing the strong emotions displayed on the stage, were supposed – via a process of empathy – to drain or cleanse their own affective states and thus achieve a serene state. In subsequent thinking one often finds the idea that strong emotional arousal can be drained by violent motor expression and acting out (see chapter 14). The mechanism of catharsis supposedly involves the interaction of the expression, physiology, and feeling components of emotion. By amplifying expression, one is supposedly able to soothe the organism, reduce arousal and, at the same time, change or de-amplify the subjective feeling state.

Proprioceptive feedback

The mechanism postulated here is quite the opposite from that of catharsis. Increased physiological activity or strong expressive behaviour is expected to *amplify* the subjective feeling state. The most recent version of **proprioceptive** feedback notions, studied extensively in social psychology, has been the so-called **facial feedback hypothesis**. Following Tomkins's (1984) postulate of the central role of the face in emotion regulation, it is assumed that facial expressions of emotion consistent with a particular state will enhance the respective feeling, whereas a de-amplification or incompatible facial expressions would de-emphasize the accompanying feeling state.

PROPRIOCEPTIVE FEEDBACK

FACIAL FEEDBACK HYPOTHESIS

Lanzetta, Cartwright-Smith and Kleck (1976) asked different groups of subjects to either amplify or suppress their facial expression while receiving electric shocks during an experimental procedure, supposedly to fool observers. As predicted, subjects attempting to suppress or inhibit their expressiveness rated the shocks as less painful than those asked to exaggerate expressions. This type of result has been found repeatedly in studies using an amplification–suppression paradigm.

Another paradigm for the study of facial feedback uses an artificial induction of muscular activation patterns. Under the guise of studying psychomotoric co-ordination, Strack, Stepper, and Martin (1988) asked subjects to hold a pen in their mouths in ways that either inhibited (holding with the lips only) or facilitated (holding with teeth only) the muscles typically associated with smiling (see plate 10.1). In two studies, subjects using their 'smiling muscles' to hold the pen reported more intense humour responses to cartoons presented during the experimental procedure. Laird (1974), who also found effects of facial feedback manipulations in a number of different studies with his collaborators, emphasized the strong individual differences present in the data. He argued for a self-perception approach, assuming that facial feedback effects are only found in individuals paying attention to their self-produced cues. In addition, one could evoke a Schachterian kind of information search and attribution process, on the assumption that subjects try to find an explanation for the particular sensation that is normally associated with an emotion.

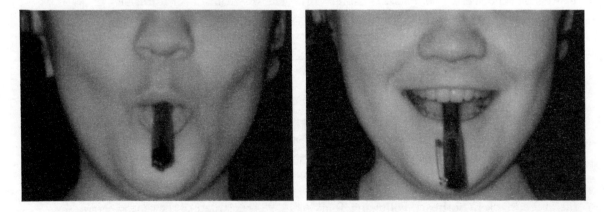

Plate 10.1 Facial configurations used in the facial feedback experiment by Strack, Stepper and Martin (1988)

While the strength of the facial feedback effects and the nature of the mechanism are still hotly debated (Cacioppo, Uchino, Crites, Snydersmith, Smith, Bernston and Lang, 1992; Izard, 1990; Matsumoto, 1987; Zajonc, Murphy, and Inglehart, 1989), the finding that feelings elicited by particular stimuli can be amplified or de-amplified by appropriate or inappropriate muscular innervation (muscular activation) in the expression component of emotion seems quite logical within a componential view of emotion. If feeling is a reflection of all the other components, then, by definition, feelings would monitor the states of the other subsystems of the organism and thus be more intense if there were strong rather than weak expression. Unfortunately, the issue is more complicated. If feelings really reflect all of the components of emotion, then they will also reflect voluntary or involuntary efforts to hide or de-amplify emotional expression. One could imagine that being forced to show a friendly smile while experiencing intense anger would actually increase the feeling of anger rather than decrease it.

While many of the effects postulated by a weak version of the facial feedback hypothesis (amplification or de-amplification of feelings elicited by appropriate stimuli) can still be accounted for by the notion that feeling state is a reflection of whatever goes on in other parts of the body as well as in our head, this is not true for the strong version of the hypothesis. The latter is based on the idea that there may be hard-wired connections between emotional-reaction components (possibly due to innate neuromotor programmes for basic emotions), permitting the artificial induction of emotion by appropriate manipulation of one of the components.

In a widely discussed paper, Ekman, Levenson and Friesen (1983) reported evidence that the induction of particular motor expressions may not only amplify the feeling state but actually create a specific emotion, as indexed by differential physiological responses and verbal feeling reports, *without* any other kind of stimulation. These researchers asked actors to produce combinations of facial muscle movements on the basis of detailed coaching as to how and when to move particular parts of the face. At the same time, their physiological responses were measured. After completion of the so-called 'directed facial action task', the actors were asked to rate their feeling state. The combination of facial action units that the actors were requested to make were those theoretically predicted to be characteristic for fundamental discrete emotions (Ekman, 1989). Although ostensibly the task had nothing to do with emotion and the actors had not been told that this was the purpose of the study, the results did show a clear differentiation of the physiological response patterns for the different facial combinations, largely corresponding to theoretical expectations. Furthermore, there was a tendency for the actors to feel the emotion the facial signs of which they had unwittingly produced in their face. The study has been repeatedly criticized with respect to possible experimental artefacts. For example, the actors might have noticed that the facial configuration shaping up in their faces as a result of the instructions formed the expression of a particular emotion, which may suggest other emotion-induction mechanisms such as imagination or subject-compliance factors. Also, some configurations might have required more effort and thus have affected psychophysiological responses. However, the authors have since replicated the results with both North American and Sumatran subjects (Levenson, Ekman, and Friesen, 1990; Levenson, Ekman, Heider, and Friesen, 1992), providing some evidence against the suggestion of artefacts raised by critics.

If findings such as these can be replicated reliably and the detailed patterns of connections between emotional reaction components uncovered, it would seem fruitful to study whether the emotion process can be triggered by activating any one of the contributing components. In particular, feeling state should be readily influenceable by making use of internal feedback mechanisms. Unfortunately, the study of the relationships and interactions between emotion components has barely begun. Such studies would evidently have important implications for application, for example in therapy. There is, however, the danger, as in the Schachter/Singer experiment, that the ecological validity of the phenomenon will be lost from sight as it is unlikely that our emotions are frequently elicited by systematic manipulations of our facial muscles or other peripheral body organs.

Summary

The interrelationships between the different emotion components have not yet been studied extensively. Most of the research to date has been directed at the effects of motor expression on feeling state. There is some evidence for both *catharsis* and *proprioceptive feedback* effects. While these may seem contradictory at first sight, a process perspective may help to accommodate both mechanisms in naturally occurring situations: uncontrolled motor expression after elicitation of an emotion episode is likely to intensify the respective feeling (proprioceptive feedback) but the more rapid depletion of the arousal elicited by the respective event (as predicted by catharsis notions) may reduce the intensity of the feeling more quickly than would be the case if the expression had been partially suppressed.

Summary and Conclusions

Emotion is an ubiquitous phenomenon in human social behaviour. As a mechanism selected in the course of evolution it subserves adaptation to significant changes in the physical and social environment by allowing a flexible choice of response alternatives against a background of automatically produced action tendencies. The signalling function of emotional expression is of particular importance for species that live socially, as is the role of feeling states for monitoring and regulating emotional reactivity. Given its key function in adaptation, it is not surprising that emotion involves virtually all organismic subsystems, which are synchronized during an emotion episode to muster all the resources of the organism in an effort at adaptation. The complex interrelationships between the different components of emotion are currently under study. Recent social-psychological work has shown the importance of the individual's appraisal of potentially emotion-eliciting events with respect to major needs, goals, and resources available for coping. Owing to the strong cultural influences on the definition of goals and values, one can expect important effects of social groups and cultural variability on emotional experience. This is also true for different ways of labelling and regulating particular feeling states in different cultures.

Research on emotion is currently mushrooming in social psychology. While recent theorizing and empirical work have greatly expanded our knowledge of the phenomenon and have allowed us to formulate powerful hypotheses, future research needs to be directed towards the study of strong, real-life emotions rather than focusing exclusively on laboratory induction (via film-viewing or imagery techniques) of relatively weak and non-specific emotional processes. Otherwise, the central issue of the existence and the nature of emotion-specific response profiles in the motor expression and autonomous nervous systems cannot be directly addressed.

It will be important to overcome the widening gulf between a psychobiological approach, being mostly interested in the emotion-specific efference or externalization of internal states, and a socio-anthropological approach, postulating the primacy of a social and cultural construction of emotional experience. There is much evidence that emotion is the result both of phylogenetically continuous, psychobiological mechanisms as well as of social and cultural factors that determine both the elicitation, the type of response, the regulation, and in particular, the verbal and non-verbal communication of the feeling component.

Another major issue concerns the dynamic interrelationships of the different emotion components, in particular the relationship of subjective feeling state to the physiological emotion components. Since feeling state is necessarily measured (and communicated) via verbal report, the issue of labelling, and particularly the role of culture in the total context of the emotional experience, should occupy a major place in social-psychological research on emotion.

This concludes the review of the emotion mechanism and its role in social psychology. As mentioned in several places in this chapter, scholars from many different disciplines have wrestled with the complexity of this phenomenon in the course of the last two millennia. Students of human behaviour, particularly social psychologists, increasingly find that emotion plays a central role as a mediating mechanism between motivation, cognition, and behaviour – especially in social contexts. As a consequence there has been an explosion of interest in affective phenomena during recent years and there is hope that it may not take another two millennia to advance our understanding of emotion.

Glossary terms

Activation	Emotional reaction triad	Mood
Affect	Emotionality	Proprioceptive feedback
Appraisal	Expression	Social construction
Display rules	Facial feedback hypothesis	Sympathetic arousal
Emotion	Feeling	Universality

Discussion points

1　As mentioned repeatedly in the chapter, emotion plays a major role in many social-psychological phenomena. Look at some of the other chapters in the textbook – for example, those on attitudes, social cognition, group dynamics – and discuss how various types of emotions might affect the phenomena described.

2　Take an emotion-eliciting event that happened to yourself and try to remember all the details. Now look again at figure 10.1 and analyse how each of the theoretical positions described there might explain what you experienced. Elaborate the criteria you use in deciding to prefer one of the explanations.

3　Think of a very typical emotion-producing event, such as failing an important examination, or the death of a close friend or relative, and discuss how various social-psychological processes described in this textbook might account for differences between cultures in their reactions to such events.

4　Look again at the Schachter–Singer experiment that was described in much detail in this chapter. How would you, after having read the chapter, reconceptualize and re-do the experiment if you wanted to examine the rare case where there is no link between cognitive evaluation of an event and the subject's physiological arousal.

Suggestions for further reading

Clark, M. S. (ed.) (1992) *Review of Personality and Social Psychology* (vol. 13). Newbury Park, CA: Sage. A collection of chapters written by social psychologists currently working on emotion. The volume provides critical insights and ideas for further study.

Frijda, N. H. (1986) *The Emotions*. Cambridge and New York: Cambridge University Press. In addition to presenting Frijda's own theory, this book contains a wide-ranging and learned discussion of relevant theory and research.

Izard, C. E. (1991) *The Psychology of Emotions*. New York: Plenum Press. Based on Izard's theory, the book attempts to integrate many of the major aspects of emotion.

Lazarus, R. S. (1991) *Emotion and Adaptation*. New York: Oxford University Press. A highly readable account of Lazarus's theoretical approach, cross-referencing many major approaches and highlighting possible applications of emotion research, particularly in the health area.

Lewis, M. and Haviland, J. M. (eds) (1993) *Handbook of Emotions*. New York: Guilford Press. A comprehensive overview of the major aspects of research on emotion in several disciplines.

Scherer, K. R. (ed.) (1988) *Facets of Emotion: Recent research*. Hillsdale, NJ: Erlbaum. A series of chapters presenting empirical data on different aspects of emotion such as appraisal, response characteristics, and communication. The annex contains useful materials for further study.

Scherer, K. R. and Ekman, P. (eds) (1984) *Approaches to Emotion*. Hillsdale, NJ: Erlbaum. A collection of original chapters presenting some of the major theoretical approaches in the field.

Shaver, P. (ed.) (1984) *Review of Personality and Social Psychology* (vol. 5). Beverly Hills, CA: Sage. A classic collection of theoretical and research papers written by social psychologists working on emotion.

Strongman, K. (ed.) (1991, 1992) *International Review of Studies on Emotion* (vols 1 and 2). Chichester: Wiley. A recent collection of contributions highlighting current theorizing and research on emotion.

Key studies

Schachter, S. and Singer, J. E. (1962). Cognitive, social and physiological determinants of emotional states. *Psychological Review*, 69, 379–99.

Ekman, P. and Friesen, W. V. (1971). Constants across cultures in the face and emotion. *Journal of Personality and Social Psychology*, 17, 124–9.

11 Communication in Interpersonal and Social Relationships

John M. Wiemann and Howard Giles

Contents

Introduction

Let us not under-estimate one fact, from the outset of this chapter: the quality of
life can depend, to a large extent, on the nature of one's **communication** with
other people! High-quality communication leads to satisfying, productive
relationships with work-mates, friends, lovers, and family. The physician who
uses 'baby talk' to her elderly patient and ignores the latter's complaints,
demeans the patient and diminishes the patient's ability to cope. Communication
can have dire consequences.

COMMUNICATION

As we will argue, the quality of communication and relationships does not
depend solely on just one individual (that is to say, it is determined
interactionally), but each of us is, at least partially, responsible for this quality.
Thus, the selection of messages is, of necessity, strategic (Daly and Wiemann,
1994). With an increasing variety of modes and media of communication
available to us in the pursuit of our various personal and relationship goals, often
the choice between them for delivering a particular kind of message is
consequential for our (and our partner's) well-being and for our success in
achieving a particular goal (Furnham, 1986).

Undeniably, a lack of satisfying and good-quality communication can have
serious implications for our psychological well-being and physical health, with
chronic loneliness leading to depression, alcoholism and drug abuse, resulting in
a negative spiral of unsatisfactory communication and poor health (see McCann
and LaLonde, 1993). Moreover, one of the few agreed causes of marital discontent
and divorce is a breakdown in communication between spouses, sometimes
resulting in severe clinical conditions, negative consequences for the couple's
social networks, and lowered productivity at work (e.g., Kitson, Babri and
Roach, 1985; see chapter 12).

Communication: its characteristics

Communication itself can be a most effective way of easing psychological
suffering, such as for those who have cancer (Dunkel-Shetter and Wortman,
1982) or have recently been bereaved (Lehman, Ellard and Wortman, 1986). Yet
many of the victims' close contacts may find themselves unwilling or unable to
provide effective communication, perhaps owing to ill-managed cues from the
afflicted themselves. Indeed, both aging and death itself have been shown to have
been accelerated by a lack of communicative opportunities (e.g., Blazer, 1982).

The focus of this chapter is on the way verbal and non-verbal behaviour
function in the service of interpersonal communicative goals. The communication discipline has a long tradition. Its first treatise – Aristotle's *Rhetoric* (1932
edn) – was concerned with public persuasion in the service of democratic
government; indeed, it is still in use today as a text. Interestingly, social

psychology's first major involvement with communicative needs also arose out of real, practical matters (Hovland, Janis and Kelley, 1953), namely, the Allies' concerns about the influence of German propaganda during the Second World War and their desire to sharpen their own persuasive line.

Communication is, of course, much more than 'attitude change', the continuing importance of which is well documented in chapter 9. And although there are a multitude of competing definitions of communication (Dance and Larson, 1976), we would prefer to emphasize two characteristics which distinguish it from mere behaviour. First, in order for elements of a message to be encoded, the producer must be operating at *some level* of consciousness and therefore with some degree of intentionality (see, for example, Blakar, 1985). Admittedly, people typically do not think much about greeting friends on the street; they just do it. Yet such routines were, at some point, consciously learned, practised and stored in memory for retrieval. Hence, in this case, only a very low level of consciousness and intentionality are necessary.

A second characteristic of communication is that it is an interpersonal process in the sense that it is a system requiring more than one actor in an ongoing series of events. Here, we focus attention on *interaction* rather than on thinking or talking to oneself, on a set of *shared* symbols, and on the *dyad* as the basic unit of analysis, which has a past (memory), a present and a (potential) future. Crucially, the *pattern* of participants' behaviour is arguably more important than outcomes measured at some specified point in time (Watzlawick, Beavin and Jackson, 1967). For example, who got his or her way can ultimately be *less* important to the future prospects of a marriage than precisely *how* a couple came to their decision (Krueger, 1982).

Unfortunately, research strategies for studying communication in this way still lag behind our understanding of the phenomenon, although they have changed over the years. Earlier, scholars tended to classify communicative behaviour according to the 'channel' in which information was conveyed. The simplest distinction was – and for some still is – between verbal content (language) and everything else (non-verbal behaviour), including body movements (**kinesics**) and voice qualities and intonation (**paralinguistics** and **prosodics**). Traditionally, such work focused on a single channel, the eyes, for example, with other aspects of the message either controlled for or ignored. This distinction between verbal and non-verbal communication has become blurred with the realization that 'utterances' (verbal *and* non-verbal) emerge developmentally from the same central processing unit (Bates, 1979; Kendon, 1983); consequentially, it is now the *relationships* between verbal and non-verbal communication that are taken more seriously and explored more systematically (e.g., Cappella and Palmer, 1993).

We do not find the verbal/non-verbal dichotomy particularly useful, either for our research, or for the summary we are undertaking here. For instance, the manner in which a person discloses some past tragic event can only be interpreted

KINESICS
PARALINGUISTICS
PROSODICS

adequately if we are aware of the whole array of extra-contextual factors simultaneously operating, including gestures, previous discourse, and vocal quality. Otherwise we cannot decide (or guess) whether the revelation was meant as a cry for help, a request for sympathy, an indication that the discloser had transcended the trauma, or what. For us, then, *a functional approach* to communication more fully captures the complexity of the literature as well as the experiences of ordinary communicators who send, receive, process and negotiate intricate messages with each other. After all, communicators are attempting not only to transmit information but also to craft (and continually reshape) their messages in such a manner as to create and maintain (usually) positive self-esteem. Communication, then, can be a multifunctional 'game', sometimes highly emotionally charged, at other times tactically ingenious, often quite unsuccessful (Coupland, Wiemann and Giles, 1991).

We turn now to one of the earliest functional studies, which was conducted by Argyle and Dean (1965), although we doubt whether it was seen as such by the investigators involved at the time. While it has since been criticized (e.g., Patterson, 1984), it is still widely cited in the social psychology of communication and has been an important stimulus for more recent theorizing (Street and Cappella, 1985).

Eye contact, distance and affiliation

Argyle and Dean recognized that eye contact (that is, the meeting of two people's gaze or their looking into each other's eyes) serves many functions, such as gathering information and controlling intimacy. Conversational intimacy can be communicated in a number of ways, such as talking about personal issues, standing very close and being amenable to touch, smiling and, of course, eye contact. These authors concluded that the amount of eye contact in any given conversation is the product of a variety of approach and avoidance forces. The former include the need for feedback and **affiliative messages**, while the latter include the fear of being seen or of revealing some inner state, the avoidance of the other's responses, and the like. Using Miller's (1994) conflict theory, Argyle and Dean reasoned that these approach–avoidance forces work to produce a desirable level of intimacy by means of the communicational resources one has to hand; in other words, an 'equilibrium' is engineered that is appropriate to the context, developing relationship, and message. Hence, if one increases intimacy by means of one communicational element (such as standing a little closer), then the system will be adjusted so as to compensate by means of other elements (for example, reducing other-directed gaze).

AFFILIATIVE
MESSAGES

These researchers conducted a series of experiments to test aspects of this model dealing with eye contact and physical proximity. Before running the main experiment, they had to determine the distance that constitutes the equilibrium point for conversation 'for local subjects and conditions'. As frequent travellers to other countries will appreciate, this distance varies dramatically from culture to culture. Argyle and Dean accomplished this by having 12 subjects (6 adults and 6 children) approach: a man whose eyes were open on one occasion but closed on another, and a life-size photograph of the same person. The results were consistent with their theorizing: subjects stood closest to the photograph (26.3 in), not so close to the actual person with eyes shut (30.8 in), and furthest away from him with his eyes open (37.1 in). This final distance was interpreted as the equilibrium point for conversation during eye contact in this kind of setting.

The study proper employed 24 subjects (12 of each sex), who were asked to discuss with a confederate researcher (either a man or a woman) a card depicting an ambiguous scene and to make up a story about it. Subjects sat across the corner of a table from the confederate at distances of 2, 6 and 10 ft. The table was placed in a laboratory so that observers behind a one-way mirror could record the frequency and duration of glances into the confederate's eyes. Since the confederate was briefed to gaze steadily at the subject, the subjects' glances brought the pair into eye contact.

Three main results emerged (see figure 11.1). First, and as predicted by the so-called equilibrium hypothesis, eye contact decreased as proximity increased for all four combinations of subjects and confederates according to sex. Moreover, as distance increased, glances became longer. Secondly, there was a significant interaction between sex of subject and sex of confederate, with much less eye contact and shorter glances in mixed-sex dyads; these differences were most pronounced at 2 ft. Thirdly, subjects in the 2 ft condition showed 'signs of tension' even with reduced eye contact. This was probably because other forces (such as politeness) prevented them from reducing eye contact to zero in order to restore equilibrium. Hence the authors point to some qualification of their model, but the results clearly support the equilibrium hypothesis.

A Functional Approach to Communication

Argyle and Dean's study called attention to the fact that any single communicative behaviour can serve a variety of functions and, by implication, the function is more interesting than the behaviour *per se*. More importantly, they illustrated that these functions are served by clusters of behaviours used in concert. By *function*, we mean the inevitable, natural and unavoidable consequence of communicative behaviour. Neither purpose nor intention is implied, although these may be present (Dance and Larson, 1976). Reference to the COMMUNICATIVE CONTROL **communicative control** function means that every message contains informa tion about the distribution of control between or among the people conversing (or, at least, about the message sender's desired distribution of control). This META-COMMUNICATION characteristic of communication has been called **meta-communication**, referring to the fact that messages have both relational-level and content-level meaning

(Watzlawick et al., 1967), with the former providing guidance about how the content is to be taken or how it is to be understood. A sarcastic tone of voice, for example, indicates that the positive content of an utterance should not be understood as such.

We are discussing here *general* rather than contextually bounded functions. As the term implies, these are relevant trans-situationally and usually subsume more context-specific functions. For example, telling your lover to bring you a beer functions as a means to get the other to perform a service for you *now*; this is a context-bound function. Yet, at a more general level, you are asserting that you have the right to make such requests and expect them to be carried out. You are then, by your discourse, expressing your view of the control you have in the relationship; it is this kind of general function in which we are most interested here.

There is substantial agreement in the literature that there are two primary functions of communication: determination of (1) the distribution of communicative *control* in a relationship, and (2) the level and valence of *affiliative*

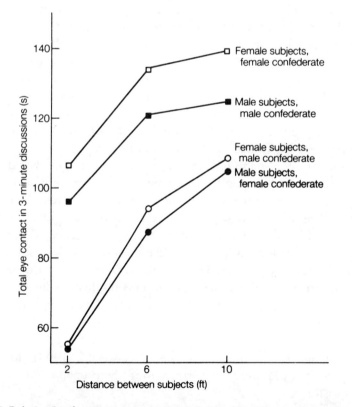

Figure 11.1 Relationship between eye contact and distance for different combinations of subjects and confederates (Argyle and Dean, 1965, p. 300)

messages which will characterize it. Other functions have been identified (see W. P. Robinson, 1972), for example, the expression of empathy or task orientation; yet, whilst important, they have received less attention in the research literature and seem subordinate to control and affiliation. That is to say other functions are either context-specific (e.g., 'I feel sad now and would like someone to feel sad with me', that is, to be empathic) or can be analysed in terms of control and affiliation (e.g., by showing support for another you show that you like them).

Control

Control: its features

Control has long been considered an important, if not the most important, construct in social science and communication studies (Berger, 1994). Control can be conceptually differentiated from power. Depending on the specific interests of researchers, when power is used it is (theoretically at least) used up, whereas control is ongoing and is distributed (but not necessarily evenly) in relationships. We use 'control' here because it has come to mean the actualization of power or the outcome of an influence attempt, whilst 'power' more commonly refers to the potential of an individual or social group to influence, control or coerce (see Ng and Bradac, 1993). More specifically, control is the constellation of constraints people place on one another by what they say and how they structure conversation, which in turn limits the options available to participants (Wiemann, 1985). To the extent that one person can limit what another can do next and still be seen as acting in an appropriate, logical, coherent and sane manner, that person has control over the other(s).

Such control can be approximately mutual or it can be distributed asymmetrically, as, for example, in parent–child communication, and if expectations are in line with the apparent control distribution then relational satisfaction will ensue. Because control distribution is seldom a topic of conversation – and indeed it may be a taboo topic because of the negative cast the term itself has when applied to social relationships (Bradac, Wiemann and Schaefer, 1994) – the negotiation referred to above takes place at the relational or meta-communicative level. Here the negotiation is implicit, rather than explicit. Control is not discussed, but is acted out. This is accomplished through manipulations of various:

- linguistic choices, including silence (Jaworski, 1993), for example referring to you and your partner using the pronoun 'We' rather than 'You and I';
- non-verbal behaviours and conversational structures, such as maintaining or averting partner-directed gaze.

Your behaviour can be seen as control 'moves' or 'bids', which are responded to by your partner, or as responses to your partner's moves, which may be accepting or challenging the bid(s) you have just made.

This negotiation is usually casual in dyads where a low level of intimacy is anticipated, but it increases in intensity and seriousness in relationships where stability, high intimacy and dependency are anticipated or desired. Hence, we might expect a couple to pay more (non-conscious, perhaps) attention to control issues when they move from a casual to an exclusive dating contract. (In relationships where institutional authority specifies control relationships, as, for example, in the military, then of course little negotiation is needed.) It may well be, then, that moves and counter-moves eventually lead to the establishment of an equilibrium for control distribution in much the same manner as Argyle and Dean claim exists with regard to intimacy. Further, it is likely that communicators seek optimal control distribution rather than maximal control (or dominance) for one or the other. Partners, in other words, tend either to give up some control (across the spectrum of mutual activities or in specific contexts) in order to satisfy the other's desire for control, and/or to take control in order to satisfy their partner's desire to be submissive.

Control: communication correlates

Control moves can be constructed from a variety of discrete behaviours, including talking more than one's partner; talking less but self-protectively questioning more; formal terms of address and pronoun usage (e.g. *tu* versus *vous* in French) (Brown and Gilman, 1960); staring; and exhibiting a relaxed posture (arms akimbo, reclining or backward-leaning posture, open legs, etc.) (see, for example, Argyle, 1975). Control appears to be a major factor in a short dyadic encounter, which can sometimes be of crucial importance, for example, in the doctor–patient consultation. Here 'good' communication is obviously vital for effective health care, as the physician must be able to develop rapport with patients and draw them out in order to gain as much information as possible in order to provide appropriate diagnosis and treatment. To do this, a doctor's best bid would seem to be to encourage patients to open up by being a good listener, allowing them the ideal empathic context in which to express themselves. However, findings from American research (see Fisher and Todd, 1983; West, 1984) present a rather contrasting profile of doctor–patient communication. This shows that physicians do most of the talking, interrupting, questioning, agenda-setting and terminating of consultations. The conversational *imbalance* displayed creates the risk of a physician 'not getting to the bottom' of the problem by not letting patients frame it in their terms, or not allowing them their own interpretations of events.

One of the major control features mentioned above, *interruptions*, has received widespread empirical attention in other social contexts, given that it is an integral element of the turn-taking system (Duncan and Fiske, 1977; Wiemann and Knapp, 1975). For instance, Zimmerman and West (1975) report, in a controversial study, that in mixed-gender dyads men interrupt women more than vice versa; in fact, 98 per cent of the interruptions were male initiated. They concluded that this behaviour is one of many indicators of unequal control distribution in US society (and by implication, many other societies) which favour males (see, for example, P. M. Smith, 1985). Other such indicants may include the frequent use by women of *intensifiers* ('so', 'very', 'really'), *hedges* ('sort of', 'kind of', 'well', 'you know'), *polite forms*, *intonations* (using a rising pattern in declarative statements), and *tag questions* ('This is an interesting area, *isn't it?*') (Lakoff, 1975).

However, the supposition that women use this so called 'powerless speech style' has been questioned in several studies which show, for instance, that interruptions (at least on some occasions) can serve predominantly positive functions (such as expressing support, showing interest) whether used by women or by men, and that women interrupt as much as, if not more than, men (Dindia, 1987; Kennedy and Camden, 1983). Further, speaking turns in discussion groups which were gained by interruptions were superior predictors of the influence rankings of group members as compared with number of speaking turns gained

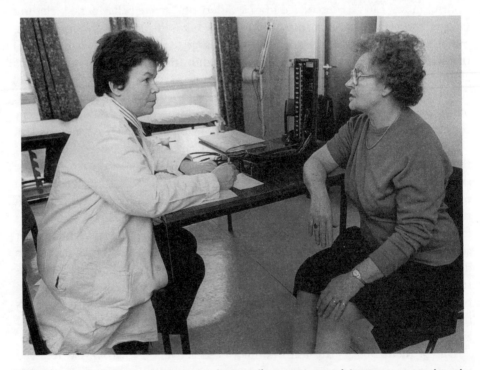

Plate 11.1 In medical consultations, the doctor talks, questions and interrupts more than the patient

by non-interruptive means (Ng, Bell, and Brooke, 1993). Hence, while it would be an error to conclude that interruptions and similar conversational devices are never used as indices of control distribution, it would be an error of equal magnitude to see them only in that light.

However, use of this powerless speech is not in any case confined to women, or even necessarily related to sex (Brouwer, Gerritsen and DeHaan, 1979; Leet-Pellegrini, 1980), but seems to correspond generally with low-status speakers, as shown by Lind and O'Barr (1979) in their research on courtroom language. They found that law students reacted less favourably to witnesses' attractiveness and credibility, not to mention their advocated position, when they spoke to a supposed lawyer using linguistic intensifiers, hedges and rising intonation than when they did not incorporate these features into their testimony. Interestingly, Scherer (1979) showed that 'the voice of social influence' varies cross-nationally. In a role-playing study in the United States and West Germany, he found that individuals who were consensually agreed to be the most influential in various decision-making groups adopted different conversational styles in the two countries. This 'conversational style of influence' includes not only linguistic variations but also variations in non-verbal behaviour, such as specific patterns of gaze (Kalma, 1992) and the ability to take the speaking turn successfully (Ng et al., 1993).

Control features: their social meanings

Scherer's (1979) study also highlights the issue that the social meaning of differing speech styles has considerable significance for person-perception and impression management (Ryan, Giles, and Bradac, 1994). Features such as the diversity of one's vocabulary, a fast speech rate and a prestigious accent can have a very positive effect on a person's perceived control (Ng and Bradac, 1993). Studies all over the world have shown that a standard accent not only conveys impressions of status and perceived competence (Giles and Coupland, 1991), and from a very early age, but also has profound effects on others' tendency to co-operate with such speakers. For example, Giles and Farrar (1979) used an authentic bi-dialectal interviewer to ask housewives to complete a questionnaire; half were approached with the request in a standard British accent, the others in a non-standard but local regional accent. The respondents produced approximately 51 per cent more words to the standard-accented interviewer than when she invited their co-operation, with the same non-verbal manner, in her non-standard accent. Moreover, with regard to job suitability, a series of studies on employment interviews (see, for example, figure 11.2) has shown that a standard-accented speaker induces far more favourable reactions for higher-status occupations than the same person producing the very same message in a non-standard accent (see Kalin, 1982). Similar kinds of findings have also emerged with regard to a speaker's, and more particularly a child's, perceived educational potential (see Edwards and Giles, 1984). Of course, *how* something is said has to

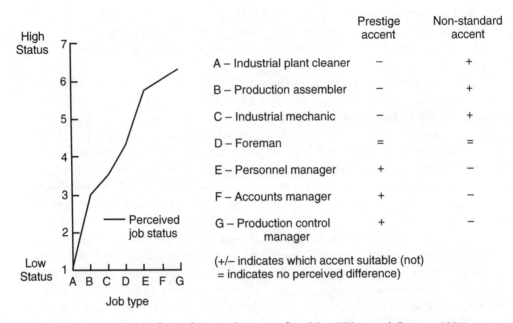

Figure 11.2 Perceived job suitability and accent (after Giles, Wilson and Conway, 1981)

be gauged against other interactional features such as the content of the message (Giles and Johnson, 1986). Yet it is remarkable just how powerful vocal features can be, even when other contextual information such as speakers' socio-economic backgrounds, visual cues and quality of achievements are examined simultaneously (e.g. Elwell, Brown and Rutter, 1984; Seligman, Lambert and Tucker, 1972). Indeed, the same discourse from a speaker can be interpreted in widely different but schema-consistent ways. For instance, selected findings from a recent study showed that some of the very same statements made by an audio-taped speaker talking at length about his car were attributed to his being pompous, arrogant and egocentric when young and with a standard accent, but to his being narrow-minded, obsessed with the past, and out of phase with the present when elderly and with a non-standard accent (Giles et al., 1990).

Control features: their dynamic nature

The above findings notwithstanding, we should not conceive of language features as unchanging or permanent. Often they can be socially constructed, owing to changing environmental conditions. An illustration of this process is provided by findings from Thakerar and Giles (1981). They asked subjects to listen to a tape-recording of a student talking about an intellectual task he had just completed. They were then requested to rate him along a number of personality attributes and speech dimensions. This a control group duly did, but there were two other experimental conditions. Just before rating, the experimental subjects were

Plate 11.2 In employment interviews standard-accented speakers tend to induce more favourable reactions than for non-standard speakers

provided with additional information. One group (high status) were told that the student had done well thus far in his undergraduate studies, whereas the other group (low status) were told that he had done poorly. As figure 11.3 shows, subjects reconstructed their perceptions of his speech in a manner stereotypically consistent with his supposed social characteristics. In the next phase of the experiment, subjects were asked to listen once again to the taped extract and re-rate the speaker, just in case they wished to change their minds after a second hearing; instructions were provided such that they were not compelled to modify. Rather than the two experimental groups re-aligning their speech perceptions in accord with the control groups, these subjects actually *polarized* their ratings.

Individuals can variously perceive the general status of language patterns around them given the prevailing social climate and their group identities (Harwood, Giles and Bourhis, 1994). For instance, and as illustrated in figure 11.4, before the Sino-British Treaty (which gave political sovereignty over Hong Kong to the People's Republic of China in 1997) was signed, Cantonese students perceived the Chinese language to possess a lower status in government services, the mass media, schools and religious contexts than English. However, after

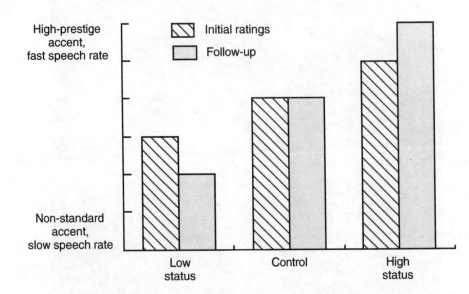

Figure 11.3 The perception of speech characteristics as a function of speaker's competence (based on Thakerar and Giles, 1981)

signing, the Chinese language was perceived to assume the higher-status position on these dimensions, whilst the status of English had correspondingly declined. As the authors pointed out, since the social fabric of Hong Kong had changed little between the first and the second data collection, these findings can be seen as a reflection of the weakened position of Westerners through the process of socio-political negotiation.

Control: communicative management

Such studies have implications at the *behavioural* level, too. It is a well-established finding that people have beliefs about the social meanings of various language features appropriate for certain settings (Brown and Fraser, 1979). Hence, we tend to speak more prestigiously and in a grammatically more sophisticated way in more formal situations (Labov, 1966). Indeed, in certain bilingual and multilingual settings *diglossia* operates, wherein people use the high-status language or dialect in public settings (such as in education, or the media) and the lower-status or vernacular in more private ones (in the home, or the neighbourhood; Fishman, 1972). But besides these prescribed norms we can, of course, modify our communicative styles so as to achieve the impression we wish to make at a particular moment. We can, therefore, linguistically shape our perceived identities in the ears of others and thereby attempt to control the kinds of attributions they make about us (see Giles and Street, 1994). The extent to

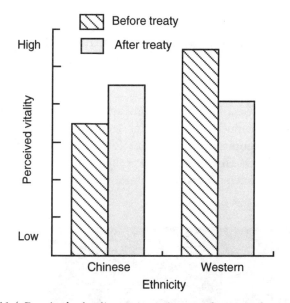

Figure 11.4 Perceived ethnolinguistic vitality as a function of political events

which we can succeed as linguistic chameleons is a complex issue, as we often hypercorrect our speech and 'leak' contradictory (Noller, 1982) and/or 'giveaway' information by means of other modalities and features (DePaulo, Stone and Lassiter, 1985). Nevertheless, our communicative performances in search of social control (Tedeschi, Lindskold and Rosenfeld, 1985) are fashioned to some extent by the perceived features of our interactants.

This is neatly demonstrated by a series of studies by Caporeal, Lukaszewski and Culbertson (1983) on the institutionalized elderly in California. They found that certain nurses would use a kind of 'baby talk' to their elderly patients, irrespective of the latter's functional autonomy. Needless to say, some elderly people may resent what they perceive to be 'put-downs'. It appears that young people's tendency to fashion their communicative behaviour not to where the elderly actually are, but to where they *stereotype them to be*, might sometimes be in part a function of their need to induce dependency in their elders (Ryan et al., 1986). In other words, it is a resource for establishing social control, and such 'over-accommodative' behaviour can sometimes be directed towards other socially stigmatized groups (for example, the visually handicapped; Coupland, Coupland and Giles, 1991; see also Coleman and DePaulo, 1991).

Whatever the function of such over-accommodations for varying people, the net effect can be one of reducing the social control of those who are recipients of it (Taylor, 1992). Furthermore, it is our contention that when sufficient people in differing settings address an elderly person in such a communicative style, evoking images that suggest they are 'past it', there comes a time when even the most resilient will begin to take on the characteristics they believe to be elderly. Therefore language can trigger a response of talking, looking, thinking and feeling older, and in due course may be a long-term constituent element in the social construction of death.

Summary

We have in this section provided a flavour of the many ways in which different aspects of communicative behaviour can be used for social control interactively, and in contexts which have significant implications for our health, wealth and stealth. We should, however, emphasize the point that while we have distinguished conceptually between context and communication, there is no such

Plate 11.3 Care assistants to elderly people may, unwittingly, talk down to them with a kind of 'baby talk' which is resented

fine dividing line in most of social reality. Very often our language patterns are those which principally define what a situation is – for example, as formal, tense and emotional (see Giles and Coupland, 1991). Indeed, those in control – be they parents, media programmers, teachers, politicians or whoever – can (consciously or non-consciously) act as linguistic machiavellians to the extent that their (even supposedly objective and descriptive) communicative choices can dictate to us our understanding of social events and objects (Robinson, 1993).

Affiliation

Affiliation: its features

As alluded to above, communicative control and interactive affect are interdependent forces; mutuality does not necessarily imply relational satisfaction, any more than asymmetry inevitably implies antipathy. Indeed, whereas the social meaning conveyed by a non-prestige accent is unfavourable in many formal contexts, it has on the other hand far more positive connotations with respect to social attractiveness and integrity (Giles and Powesland, 1975). In other words, a stereotyped picture of a standard-accented speaker often exists as an educated, competent and ambitious person, yet one who is interpersonally cold and untrustworthy. And it is to this latter constellation of attributes that we now turn, in terms of our second fundamental communication function – affiliation, or the love–hate dimension of communication relationships.

Affiliation is similar to and related to intimacy (e.g., Argyle and Dean, 1965) but, we believe, is a more precise term. Affiliation is concerned with expressed affect (positive *and* negative), while intimacy refers primarily to knowledge about another that is of a personal nature. Intimacy is frequently displayed by the use of affiliative behaviours, of course. Further, intimacy is almost always used in conjunction with positive (approach–approach) relationships.

The negative side of the affiliation continuum is important if we wish to understand the maintenance of unsatisfactory, unhappy, even hostile relationships and the decline of those which once prospered (see chapter 12). Interestingly, there has been an overwhelming bias towards studying only the positive communicative patterns and to examining strategies which enhance 'appropriate', 'open', 'honest', 'truthful', 'effective', 'efficient' and 'successful' exchanges (e.g. Grice, 1975; Higgins, 1980). Messages which lead to and maintain negative relationships are treated typically as somewhat psychopathological. Yet, there are many relationships which are characterized by ongoing hostility, deception or antagonism but where abnormal behaviour (in the clinical sense) is not manifest, and we will examine these later. Further, it is our contention that problematic talk, communicative dilemmas and outright miscommunication are *regular* features of social interaction – as much between friends as between strangers or enemies (Coupland, Wiemann and Giles, 1991).

Affiliation: its positive aspects

Affiliation is expressed by increased proximity (closer than situationally normative), other-directed gaze, eye contact, touching, open posture, intimate topics, **self-disclosure**, and the offer of general support for the presented self-concept of one's partner (e.g., Altman and Taylor, 1973; Cushman and Cahn, 1985). Interestingly, research has shown that people can decode the social meanings of these cues in others' non-verbal displays (Forgas, 1978). For instance, how many times have you made (probably accurate) guesses about the relational status of a couple in a bar or restaurant (for example, whether they are on a first or second date versus whether they have been married for a long time), and also guessed which of them is the more involved with or committed to the relationship on the basis of communicative cues? Doubtless we use others' language behaviours and monitor our own in ongoing interaction in order to display our desired level of affiliation.

Of course affiliative expression is a varied and complex process. Alberts (1986), in an analysis of the conversational features accompanying the development of heterosexual relationships in certain romantic novels, found that the initiation of them was characterized (somewhat counter-intuitively) by teasing, anger and conflict. A particular feature discovered here was 'face-threatening' acts, as illustrated by this example of a man and woman meeting. The man's opening bid is:

> Business or pleasure? No don't tell me, let me guess. For you business only. You hate to fly and you don't look like you've had a day's pleasure in your life.

A feature of such (fictional anyway) initial exchanges which lead to relational involvement is counter-banter or the use of reciprocal face-threatening acts. Hence, the woman retorted in this particular case:

> I don't talk to strange men. Especially rude, conceited men with corny come-ons who dress like refugees from the sixties and look old enough to know better.

Alberts argues that this kind of discourse generates attributions and may possibly lead to potential romanticism. We conjecture that it is the *counter* that is of crucial importance here. In other words, it could be the sequential negotiation, or proliferation, of face-threatening acts that *really* make the interaction special; after all, this is a deviation from a conversational norm. Whatever it be, Alberts (1986) is fascinating reading in terms of how we may construct our discourse ingeniously to intensify the development of romantic encounters (but see, however, Ulrich, 1986, for a critique of generalizing ordinary language use from literature).

Affiliation: its management

Interlocutors may desire different levels of affiliation, and this has to be negotiated (albeit a not particularly romantic view) in much the same way as was control. Indeed, a man who desires more affiliation than his date appears willing to give will have to work to keep the expression of his affiliation within tolerable limits for her; he will have to accept those limits (temporarily, at least, and possibly while attempting to modify them) or terminate the relationship.

This process is quite complex, as, like control, people seldom discuss affiliation issues until a point of imminent change or crisis has been reached (Baxter and Wilmot, 1985). (When was the last time you ended a conversation with someone you had just met in a lecture by saying, 'Let's be friends'?) The working out or negotiation of affiliation level takes place over time and is guided by cultural expectations of how fast relationships should progress (e.g., prolonged courtship in some cultures, injunctions such as 'no kissing on the first date' in others) and is sometimes mediated by instrumental purposes far removed from affiliation (as romantic involvements revealed in spy trials often attest).

We would like to suggest that the negotiation process can be modelled by using Argyle and Dean's equilibrium hypothesis, with only slight modification. Assume that each person's equilibrium point for affiliation in a specific budding relationship is the point at which he/she begins the negotiation of how much affiliation (affection) will be displayed in the relationship. This initial negotiation will lead to an implicitly agreed upon affiliation level which will optimize the desires of each party. That is, they will arrive at a level that allows each to be satisfied as much as possible given the other's desired level of affiliation. While the equilibrium point for the relationship could theoretically range anywhere between the desired affiliation levels of the two participants, we speculate that it is most likely to approximate the level of the *least* affiliative partner.

Attempts to increase or decrease the affiliation level are based on the desire by one partner to have the relational level most closely approximate his or her desired level. Since some subset of the possible 'intimacy' behaviours is likely to be used to propose increased affiliation (e.g., attempting to hold the date's hand while maintaining other related behaviours at the current level), one's partner (the 'target', if you like) can accept the bid, attempt to maintain the current level of affiliation, or even lower that level. Most difficult for a partner is to decline the bid for increased affiliation without rejecting the bidder outright. Argyle and Dean's framework suggests that this might be accomplished by accepting one affiliation gesture, but reducing affiliation communicated in another channel so that the total expressed affiliation does not change (for example, allowing hand to be held, but reducing intimacy of topic or reducing partner-directed gaze).

When an intimacy level is consistently expressed by both partners, stability reigns and communication between them feels and seems 'natural' and 'normal'. Atypical behaviour, especially if it is frequent and persistent, is taken as an attempt to reopen the negotiation process, which frequently occurs prior to one partner actually verbalizing his or her feelings. In other words, one acts out 'I love you' before saying it, in order to make sure that the pronouncement will be greeted with the desired response and to minimize the risk of rejection (that is, to have the partner say 'I love you too' rather than yawn or laugh).

Affiliation: its communicative development

Which combination of affiliative behaviours will be seen as 'normal' will depend on the nature of the relationship (e.g., parent–child, lecturer–student) and the level of affiliation achieved. Knapp (1983) proposed eight dimensions along which communicative behaviours so vary (see figure 11.5). He pointed out that behaviour along each dimension will move towards greater affiliation until an 'optimal level' is reached. At that point it will stabilize, but fluctuations (sometimes sizeable) will occur from time to time on one or several of the dimensions.

Knapp (see Knapp and Vangelisti, 1992) developed a communication model of relational development and deterioration composed of ten 'interaction stages'. The relational stages that are characterized by increasing intimacy and (usually) increasing positive affiliation include, progressively, (1) initiating, (2) experimenting, (3) intensifying, (4) integrating, and (5) bonding. The initiating stage, for example, is the time in a relationship when partners are just getting to know each other, and includes assessing the attractiveness and availability of a prospective partner. In the experimenting stage, partners are exploring each other, reducing uncertainty, finding points of common ground and topic areas that should be avoided. At this stage, communication is relaxed and uncritical; commitments are few and not strong. As relationships progress, they intensify, in that self-disclosures of personal information become more intimate (see below), partners increase commitment to each other, and the communication between

---

Less Intimacy – – – – – – – – – – – – – – – **More Intimacy**

Narrow .... Broad
Stylized .... Unique
Difficult .... Efficient
Rigid .... Flexible
Awkward .... Smooth
Public .... Personal
Hesitant .... Spontaneous
Overt judgement suspended .... Overt judgement given

---

Figure 11.5 General dimensions of communication associated with relationship development (Knapp, 1983)

partners becomes increasingly unique. Partners reach the integration stage when they begin to share various aspects of their lives, including social circles, private and public intimacies (tokens of intimacy such as rings, for example), and a 'couple' identity. Verbally, 'you and I' become 'we', and 'pet' names come into use. Bonding is the public declaration that commitments have been made and accepted; a contract is entered into. Marriage is the most public and official of bonding rituals (for heterosexual couples, at least), but bonding can take many forms and can mark different stages of a relationship (e.g., engagement prior to marriage). A relationship can, of course, slow down, stall or stabilize at any of these stages.

With regard to the decline or coming apart side of relationships, Knapp described the stages of (6) differentiating, (7) circumscribing, (8) stagnating, (9) avoiding, and (10) terminating. These stages can be thought of as roughly parallel to the first five stages. Each is characterized by decreasing affiliation and attention to the other's feelings. As the relationships declines, the 'we' becomes 'you and me', the quality and quantity of information exchange decreases, and communication becomes more difficult, stylized, awkward and the like. Partners avoid each other when possible, either by physical separation or by ignoring each other when physical separation is impossible. Termination is the more or less formal announcement that the relationship is over. The most clear exemplar is the proceeding (legal and otherwise) in the run-up to a divorce decree.

Knapp's premise is that movement from stranger to intimate is both accomplished and characterized by specific types of communication strategies. Movement is generally systematic and sequential, but it can be either forward or backward; and while it can occur within stages, it is always to a new 'place' (that is, the relationship changes as a result of communication even though it may not get more or less intimate). At any step, the relationship can be stabilized. For example, a relationship can reach the experimenting stage, where partners are learning about each other and the 'fit' between them ('Do you like sailing? So do I!'), but may not progress beyond that. Such relationships can be happy and satisfying because the partners do not wish to increase the affiliation level. According to this model, a relationship that had at one time been stabilized at the experimenting stage of interaction and then began to deteriorate would move laterally to stagnating – the negative side of this level of affiliation.

Relational decline is not simply the reverse of its development, as argued by a number of scholars: breakup differs from buildup because of shared knowledge and the mutual history of the partners (see, for example, Baxter, 1983). But the import of Knapp's model for our purposes is that it associates types of messages, or more generally *communication* strategies, with the level of affiliation characteristic of a relationship at any given time. And while Knapp sees a variety of verbal and non-verbal communicative behaviours contributing to maintenance or change (see, for example, Knapp, Ellis and Williams, 1980), *self-disclosure* is clearly the most potent strategy available (Altman and Taylor, 1973; with respect to marital communication, see Gottman and Levenson, 1983).

Self-disclosure and positive affiliation

Self-disclosure is the voluntary making available of information about one's self that would not ordinarily be accessible to the other at that moment. It typically consists of information verbally revealed by one person to another, but can also be information that one allows the other to learn, for example, by spending time with the other or permitting the other into a private place. It serves to escalate a relationship towards positive affiliation because of the operation of what Gouldner (1960) called the *norm of reciprocity* (that is, the 'demand' for an equivalent response from one's partner to a variety of social behaviours, particularly self-disclosures: see Holtgraves, 1993). Thus, one disclosure is thought to beget another of approximately equal valence (positive or negative information) and depth (of intimacy), and in this way, step by step, relationships become more intimate (Altman and Taylor, 1973).

Of course, the process is not quite this simple. The likelihood of reciprocity and thus relational development is influenced by several variables. The nature of the relationship between the discloser and his or her target, the target's perception of why he or she was selected for the disclosure, timing (in terms of relational development and context) of the disclosure, and the goal of the target, all mediate reciprocity (see Derlega, Metts, Petronio and Margulis, 1993).

Some types of disclosures are responded to more positively than others. Positive information of low intimacy is most effective in producing positive affiliation in initial interactions (Gilbert and Horenstein, 1975), but this relationship varies with knowledge of the partner, content of the disclosure, perceived rewardingness of the partner, and characteristics of the discloser (e.g., Bradac, Tardy and Hosman, 1980). Importantly, the process by which self-disclosures are made is crucial to how they are received. Revelations that come 'out of the blue' are received very differently from those which are or which can be attributed to some previously stated propensity. This is so not only in terms of the recipients' evaluations of the discloser, but also consequentially in terms of how best to respond next (e.g. express empathy, question further, change topic). For example, in intergenerational first encounters, the elderly often divulge quite 'painful' information about themselves that causes their younger interlocutors some communicational difficulties (Coupland, Coupland, Giles and Wiemann, 1988). People do vary in their criteria for deciding when and how to disclose (Petronio, Martin and Littlefield, 1984) as well as in the ability to induce their partners to 'open up' (Miller, Berg and Archer, 1983).

Further, valence and level of self-disclosure are judged appropriate in the context of the current state of the relationship. A potential relational partner would predictably be 'put off' by too intimate disclosures in an initial interaction, because these put great demand on the partner also to reveal intimate information about him or herself. Indeed, Berger (1979) suggested that self-disclosure is often the next phase after biographical exchange of non-intimate information in pursuit of social knowledge about the other. Similarly, intimate positive revelations early on are usually seen as 'coming on too strong' or bragging, and thus deter relational development (Knapp and Vangelisti, 1992). Self-disclosure is, then, a powerful tool in the affiliation negotiation process.

Lies and deception: dangers to affiliation?

In pursuit of affiliative goals, people also lie about their aspirations, intentions and credentials (Buller and Burgoon, 1994; Burgoon, 1994), as well as about their group's capabilities, attributes and potential (Bradac, Friedman and Giles, 1986). They also evade difficult questions and keep secrets, although sometimes, of course, they must tell the truth. We, as hearers, often second-guess the lies, evasions and secrets of others (Hewes et al., 1985). As we have argued elsewhere, communication can sometimes be complex and exhausting work as we attempt to 'pull the wool over the ears of others' while debugging their messages at one and the same time (Giles and Wiemann, 1987).

Not all 'non-truths' are, of course, maliciously motivated. Camden, Motley and Wilson (1984) have provided a list of the types of social motivations underlying 'white lies', including saving listeners from embarrassment, avoiding conflict or being overly-controlled, and presenting a positive self-image. To us, and despite the fact that these motives exude a sense of creating, maintaining or repairing a positive self-esteem, they none the less appear too 'socially agreeable'. Surely, many of us can recount instances when we or others have deceived or lied so as to be, for example, *mean*, or have tried to create *instability* in a particular relationship (see Baxter, 1985)? In this vein, O'Hair and Cody (1994) propose a taxonomy of motives for deception based on the 'target' or beneficiary (self, other or relational) of the deception and its valence. Positively valenced motives include *egoism* (self-protective deceptive strategies), *benevolence* (other-protective strategies), and *utility* (strategies that will improve, escalate or repair a relationship). Negatively valenced strategies are *exploitation* (strategies that manipulate or harm another for one's own gain), *malevolence* (harming another for revenge, sabotage, sadism and the like), and *regress* (strategies to harm a relationship).

In a study demonstrating a regress deception, Ragan and Hopper (1984), after an analysis of the way lovers are seen to *exit* from their relationships in novels, show that one partner often uses a 'suspension of the let-it-pass rule' (e.g., 'What do you mean by that? I haven't a clue as to what you're getting at!') so as to underscore strategically the apparent lack of mutual understanding that now exists between them. In other words, people can use communication subtly so as to achieve negative affiliation levels, and paradoxically (as these authors claim), it takes co-ordination to accomplish 'consensus about dissensus'.

O'Hair and Cody (1994) present a three-stage model of the deception process (see figure 11.6). In the first stage, deceivers make decisions about lying, based on their motives, on the predicted consequences and on ethical/moral considerations. Then they select a strategy for the deception. In the third stage, deceivers produce the deceptive behaviour they feel will be most successful – that is, they have to appear to be telling the truth (honesty profile) and not look as if they are lying (controlling cues that might give the deception away, while acting 'naturally').

Negative affiliation: personal versus social identities

But why didn't more negative motives surface in the study by Camden et al.? One answer may lie in the particular methodology used. Informants were asked to uncover *others'* lies to them personally, some of which may have escaped them entirely, and others of which may have produced misattributions. An equally plausible, if not more significant, answer might rest in the fact that the students' diaries were 'inter-individual' and did not reflect the full range of self-presentation strategies, and attributions of these strategies. Following on from Tajfel and Turner (1986), much of our social life is spent in *intergroup* encounters (which may be dyadic) between individuals from different socio-economic classes, age groups, occupational categories and so forth (see chapter 17). In such

Critical/Ethical Analysis	Strategy Selection	Behavioural production
Motives 1 Exploitation 2 Egoism 3 Benevolence 4 Malevolence 5 Utility 6 Regress	**Deceptive Act** 1 Lies 2 Evasion 3 Overstatement 4 Concealment 5 Collusion	**Strategic Deception** 1 Behavioural presentation 2 Leakage control
Predicted Consequences 1 Detection potential 2 Harm to target/third party 3 Loss of trust and respect 4 Relational costs 5 Positive consequences		**Honesty Profile** 1 Friendliness 2 Attentiveness 3 Precision 4 Low drama
Ethical/Moral Considerations 1 Deception is unethical 2 Means of survival 3 Situational determination		

Figure 11.6 Deception process

encounters our social group identities can be of supreme importance, and we then use language to create, maintain or bolster our sense of distinctive and valued ingroup identity (Giles and Coupland, 1991). In other words, we *communicate* with each other, not always as individuals with unique temperaments and personalities, but sometimes as undifferentiated representatives of social groups, using language to stereotype other relevant outgroups in a negative fashion (see Semin and Fiedler, 1992). Under these circumstances, it would seem that tactless lies and deception which 'put down' linguistically an outgroup and/or elevate an ingroup are rational choices for maintaining a favourable group identity, or for 'winning' a point in public discourse (Robinson, 1993). Much then of what is supposedly, and so-called, 'interpersonal' communication is actually *intergroup* (see, for example, Gudykunst, 1986). In this regard, group membership and intergroup attitudes are not always self-evident (see Potter and Wetherell, 1987); they are often highly creative processes in which linguistic 'work' must be accomplished to construct and/or sustain them. Indeed, the very natures of group memberships and identities are negotiated and displayed in discourse (see Hecht, Collier and Ribeau, 1993; Potter, Edwards and Wetherell, 1993). Moreover, intergroup communication can of course involve multiple categories, as shown in Ting-Toomey's (1986) analysis of conflict between black male and white female interactants.

But given that communication features (such as dialect, jargon, slang, body movements) are very often valued dimensions of group identity, the desire for positive differentiation is likely to manifest itself along *communicative* dimensions (Giles, 1977). A compelling illustration of this, termed *ethnic affirmation*, is provided empirically by Yang and Bond (1980). They found that when 'forcing' Chinese bilingual students to complete a value survey in English rather than in Cantonese, respondents compensated for this by becoming more Chinese in their values in the former than in the latter condition.

When relations between social groups are co-operatively stable and intergroup stereotypes are complementary and positive (Taylor, 1981), then Gudykunst and Kim's so-called 'communicative distance of sensitivity' will obtain when speakers from the two categories interact. Herein, speakers may accommodate various facets of their speech, non-verbals, and discourse towards each other (Giles, Coupland and Coupland, 1991), as illustrated in a study by Mulac et al. (1988) where males and females attenuated their distinctive linguistic styles from intra- to intergender encounters (see also Hogg, 1985). However, as relations between social categories become more conflictual, communicative patterns may be mediated by socio-linguistic stereotypes in an increasingly negative affiliative manner. This can be reflected in *speech divergence* (such as the accentuation of a Welsh speaker's accent, or even a shift into the Welsh language itself, when talking with an English person: see Bourhis and Giles, 1977), *behavioural confirmation* (for example, the communicative tactic of inducing people, perhaps by asking 'impossible' questions, to act in a stereotype-consistent manner; see

Word, Zanna and Cooper, 1974) and *verbal derogations* (or ethnophaulisms), respectively.

Of course, the achievement of negative affiliation in dyads need not be so consciously fashioned in all cases. For instance, Schaap, Buunk and Kerkstra (1988) have shown that a feature of unhappy married couples is the inability of husbands to recognize discontent or negative affect in their wives. As a consequence, the latter feel neglected, misunderstood and uncared for, thereby prompting them into a verbalized expression of this unfortunate state of affairs. In turn, husbands withdraw emotionally, inducing wives to get them involved again (Watzlawick et al., 1967). Such a destructive communication cycle is naturally enough the breeding ground of relational discontent (Noller and Fitzpatrick, 1988).

Summary

In this section, we have shown how communication can serve affiliative functions at the relational (including both interpersonal and intergroup) level. Communication can be used craftily in building up relationships through patterns of appropriate self-disclosure. It is also an effective mechanism for maintaining harmony. Gottman (1982) argued that an important feature of happily married couples is the ability of one partner to defuse negative affect once it has been expressed by the spouse. Whilst we have observed that communication functions in pursuit of positive and of negative affiliation, we should emphasize that the latter need not always be psychologically debilitating, as, for example, in its capacity to sustain group identity. Furthermore, it is possible that the communication of negative affiliation has actually very positive outcomes under certain circumstances.

The Goal: Communicative Competence

Throughout this chapter, we have presented an analysis of interpersonal communication from a functional perspective. These functions are general in that they are inevitable characteristics of every message exchange – they are simultaneously the driving force and the products of our messages. They are the vehicles people use to define, change and stabilize relationships. Our analysis illustrates how people get things done through communication; and how communication not only reflects our social world, but builds upon it and helps determine it (Giles and Wiemann, 1987). By focusing on relationships, we have attempted to call attention to the fact that the work of communication is a *joint* activity (see Potter et al., 1993). But it is also important to keep in mind that individuals are separate from the several relationships and groups in which they are simultaneously involved. What is good for one relationship may have a negative impact on another, or on the individual apart from relational considerations. People face the general communication problem of balancing competing demands for affiliation, and for the ability to control and to be controlled in a variety of relationships, with finite interpersonal resources. They must use these resources to relate with their environment, including other people, by both adapting to the environment and attempting to adapt it to them. How do we understand and explain the success and failure of individuals as they attempt to cope with this difficult problem?

A theory of *communicative competence* (Wiemann, 1977; Wiemann and Bradac, 1989) offers a framework for examining effective interpersonal communication. The position we adopt is *relational* and pragmatic. It is relational in that the primary level of analysis is that of interactants in relationships. Indeed, when we listen to a couple conversing we can form judgements not only about the individuals separately involved but also about the communicational style and language features used by them *as a pair* (Giles and Fitzpatrick, 1984). Our position is also pragmatic in that what communicators actually do and how they do it is the focus of analysis. Hence, **communicative competence** here is defined as the appropriate pragmatic use of social knowledge and social skill in the context of a relationship (Wiemann and Kelly, 1981).

COMMUNICATIVE
COMPETENCE

This definition implies several characteristics of communicative competence. First, behaviour must be appropriate to the context in which it is displayed, the primary context usually (but not always) being the relationship with those present. In this latter respect, Giles and Fitzpatrick (1984) argued that a speaker could effect 'couple talk' even when separate from his or her partner. Here, couple identity can mediate individual linguistic choices through 'we'-related topics, references to 'our' activities, and an 'us' focus manifesting expressedly shared attitudes and couple (rather than self-) disclosures. Secondly communicative competence for us means that both knowledge of communication rules and the accommodative skills and flexibility to implement that knowledge are necessary for the ongoing achievement of a competent (and sometimes perhaps, deliberately *in*competent) relationship.

Finally, a third feature of communicative competence is that it is in the relationship, not the individuals. Thus, we refer to *relationships* as competent — and *individuals* as socially skilled. This conceptualization challenges the 'disease' metaphor of interpersonal behaviour implied in much social-science literature, wherein a person below some skill threshold is seen as inadequate (incompetent) and therefore not a particularly desirable relational partner. While a number of skills may enhance one's opportunity to enter into competent relationships (see, for example, Check, Perlman and Malamuth, 1985), it does not guarantee them. (Even the best, most skilled communicators have negative relational experiences.) Neither does a repertoire of relatively few skills preclude successful relationships. (Even the most unskilled interpersonal bumblers find people with whom they are congruent and form happy relationships.) Communicative competence does not refer to approaching perfection or achieving excellence. Rather, we feel that communicative competence is doing well enough to preserve a relationship with a desired definition (Wiemann and Bradac, 1989). In other words, it is being able to avoid relational traps and pitfalls and to repair damage when avoidance tactics fail. Indeed, relationships are naturally fraught with complications and tensions which must be worked out communicatively (Brown and Rogers, 1991), the productive working out of which creates the competent relationship.

Thus we have a model of interpersonal communicative competence that directs our scrutiny to individuals, with varying levels of communication-relevant knowledge and skill, interacting in the context of relationships which they create or achieve by their ongoing communication. Communication outcomes can only be fully understood at the *relational level* (whether between or among individuals or groups) and in terms of patterns of interlocking behaviours which serve to define the relationship as a specific type of system. The primary dimensions along which competence is assessed by both participants and observers are control and affiliation levels. A relationship is seen as competent to the extent that the individuals who compose it either (1) are sufficiently satisfied with the control and affiliation definition they jointly create to maintain it, or (2) when dissatisfied, are able and willing to work towards a redefinition or termination of it. Individuals negotiate relational definitions by employing a variety of communication strategies and tactics along the lines suggested throughout this chapter. There is no implication that there are universal 'good' or 'moral' relational definitions that all should work towards in order to be considered competent. Note that under specification (1) above, a long-term, hostile 'enemies' relationship is competent if both parties are satisfied with that relational definition and both are sufficiently attracted to it to remain in the relationship.

Summary and Conclusions

Our intent has been to highlight the *social dimension* of interpersonal communication in the main by discussing its relational character *within* the dyad and between groups. Communication is a strategic behaviour through which people not only convey content (referential messages), but also negotiate and display definitions of their relationships. These definitions are construed along the dimensions of control distribution and displayed affiliation. Understanding how these meta-messages are created and processed helps individuals to create the kinds of relationships they want, to stay in the relationships successfully, and, when desirable, to get out of relationships that are no longer satisfying or productive. The goal of this sort of analysis of interpersonal communication is competent communicative relationships.

Glossary terms

Affiliative messages   Communicative control   Paralinguistics
Communication   Kinesics   Prosodics
Communicative competence   Meta-communication   Self-disclosure

Discussion points

1   What features of another's speech style or non-verbal behaviour are socially diagnostic for
    you, and why? Perhaps you might like to focus on the communicators in some applied
    context such as a medical interview, commercial transaction, or legal interrogation.
2   How, when, and why do you think you change your communicative patterns to be more
    affiliative or controlling of particular others? What *other* social functions or interactional
    goals affect your communicative choices?
3   Think of some social groups to which you belong and with which you identify strongly
    (e.g., cultural, gender, political). Now consider dyadic interactions with members of the
    contrasting groups. In what situations do you feel such 'intergroup' encounters have
    consequences for your communicative style?
4   What are the characteristics of communication in your best, most satisfying relationships?
    How do they differ from those of unsatisfying or negative relationships? How do you think
    changing your communication patterns would influence the course of these relationships
    (both positive and negative)?

Suggestions for further reading

Canary, D. J. and Stafford, L. (eds) (1994)
Communication and Relational Maintenance.
San Diego, CA: Academic Press. Essays
address the question of how people maintain their personal involvements. Communication action, social-psychological and
dialectic perspectives are discussed in this
innovative collection.

Cupach, W. R. and Spitzberg, B. H. (eds)
(1994) *The Dark Side of Interpersonal Communication*. Hillsdale, NJ: Erlbaum. Essays
in this book examine seemingly negative
aspects of interpersonal relationships, including messages that hurt, deception,
conversational dilemmas and predicaments,
consequences of privacy violations and
physical and psychological abuse.

Daly, J. A. and Wiemann, J. M. (eds) (1994)
Strategic Interpersonal Communication. Hillsdale, NJ: Erlbaum. A collection of essays
covering a wide range of communication
phenomena focusing on how people go
about achieving their social goals through
strategic symbolic interaction. Topics include how people acquire social information, gain compliance, seek affinity, and use
language to control and comfort.

Giles, H. and Coupland, N. (1991) *Language:
Contexts and Consequences*. Milton Keynes:
Open University Press. Provides an account
of the relationships between language and
situation, attitudes, and ethnic identity,
bilingualism and aging, integrating them
from the perspectives of communication

accommodation and ethnolinguistic identity theories.

Giles, H. and Robinson, W. P. (eds) (1993) *Handbook of Language and Social Psychology* (paperback edn). Oxford: Pergamon. A comprehensive volume which provides numerous critical and readable analyses of many areas of communication from the interpersonal to the more social.

Knapp, M. L. and Vangelisti, A. L. (1992) *Interpersonal Communication and Human Relationships*, 2nd edn. Boston: Allyn and Bacon. A very readable introduction to the role interpersonal communication plays in the development and maintenance of social relationships, integrating a variety of communication and social-psychological perspectives into a coherent view of day-to-day experience.

Knapp, M. L. and Miller, G. R. (eds) (1994) *The Handbook of Interpersonal Communication*, 2nd edn. Thousand Oaks, CA: Sage. An invaluable sourcebook for those with particular interests in virtually all aspects of interpersonal communication phenomena and processes and/or for those students requiring an in-depth knowledge of the area.

Key studies

Caporeal, L. R., Lukaszewski, M. P. and Culbertson, G. H. (1983). Secondary baby talk: judgments by instititionalized elderly and their caregivers. *Journal of Personality and Social Psychology*, 44, 746–54.

Noller, P. (1982). Channel consistency and inconsistency in the communications of married couples. *Journal of Personality and Social Psychology*, 43, 732–41.

12 Affiliation, Attraction and Close Relationships

Bram P. Buunk

Contents

Introduction

Affiliation – the need for social contact
Situations fostering affiliation: when do people affiliate?
Motives for affiliation: why do people affiliate?
Stress does not always lead to affiliation
Effects of affiliation

Attraction and the development of friendships
The physical environment
The similarity of attitudes
Friendship as a relationship

Romantic attraction
The physical attractiveness stereotype
Gender differences in preferences for physical attractiveness
Equity and choice of partner

Close relationships: satisfaction, commitment and dissolution
Relationship satisfaction
Commitment
The consequences of breakups

Summary and conclusions

Introduction

Carl is in general a happy man. He enjoys having fun and playing with his best friends. Recently, he fell in love with Carin, a beautiful woman whom he had known for some time; however, Carin does not reciprocate his feelings. Since then, Carl has felt quite unhappy and at times lonely. Although he needs company because of his unhappiness, even being with his friends hardly improves his mood. Carin likes Carl, but just does not have romantic feelings for him. She feels that Carl lacks ambition, and is not the type of man she is looking for. Her closest girlfriend, with whom she discusses everything, agrees that Carl is not right for her. Carin wants a close relationship, though, but still feels a little sad because a former relationship ended through a lack of commitment by the other.

Humans are a very social breed. They seek each other's company in a variety of situations, they make friendships with other people, and they seem to find their ultimate happiness and despair in their intimate relationships. But what is it that drives us to engage in contact with others? What determines the fact that we often find ourselves quite rapidly liking some people more than others? Why do we fall in love with that particular person? Why do some relationships end quite quickly, and why do others remain close throughout a life-time? Such issues are dealt with in the present chapter. We begin with a discussion of *affiliation*, the motives for and consequences of seeking out the company of other people, followed by a section on *attraction and friendships*, that focuses on the factors that make individuals take a liking to other people and become friends with them. Next, the nature of *romantic attraction* is dealt with, and finally, processes in the development of *close relationships* are discussed.

Affiliation – The Need for Social Contact

Situations fostering affiliation: when do people affiliate?

Although humans have a general inclination to affiliate with others, there are certain circumstances that seem to make this inclination particularly salient. For example, Fox (1980) asked his subjects to indicate, for a number of situations, whether they preferred to be alone or in the company of other people. The desire for company was higher than the desire to remain alone in *pleasant and enjoyable conditions* (for example, when happy, engaging in sports, doing your daily work) and in *threatening conditions* (such as, in dangerous situations, when alarmed, when afraid). However, the desire to be alone was higher in *unpleasant circumstances* (when nervous, when tense, after failing a test at work) and in *conditions that require concentration* (such as trying to solve a difficult problem, making important decisions). Hill (1987) suggested that people affiliate basically for four reasons: to reduce uncertainty by comparing oneself with others, to obtain positive

Plate 12.1 Why do we fall in love?

stimulation through interesting and lively contact with others, to gain praise and attention, and to get emotional support.

Affiliation as a response to a threat has received special attention from social psychologists, beginning with the pioneering work of Schachter (1959), who studied the importance of affiliation by confronting subjects with a novel and frightening situation, and offering them the opportunity to be with other people (Jones and Gerard, 1967). In Schachter's experiments, female students in the experimental condition were welcomed by someone who introduced himself as Dr Gregor Zilstein of the Medical School's Department of Neurology and Psychiatry. He had the outward appearance of a doctor, with a white coat and a stethoscope, and behind him was an impressive array of electrical equipment. Dr Zilstein gave a lecture on the importance of research on the use of electroshock therapy, and told the subjects that they would receive a series of painful electric shocks that would hurt, although there would be no permanent damage. In the control condition, the same experimenter appeared, but without all the electrical equipment, and the subjects were told that they would receive a series of very mild shocks, which would not be at all painful, and that they would in fact enjoy the experiment. Next, all subjects were told that they had to wait 10 minutes, and they were asked to indicate whether they wanted either to wait alone, or to wait in the company of others. As predicted, the results showed that about twice as many subjects wanted to be in the company of others in the high-anxiety condition (63 per cent) than in the low-anxiety condition (33 per cent). The results of this pioneering research have recently been followed up by studies in

AFFILIATION

more natural settings. For instance, in a study among Dutch nurses, Buunk and Schaufeli (1993) showed that those who were feeling burned out as a result of emotionally taxing work with patients had a higher desire to seek out others to discuss their problems at work.

Motives for affiliation: why do people affiliate?

But why do individuals affiliate when confronted with a stressful situation? Although one can think of various reasons, such as seeking reassurance, looking for support, simple curiosity, and expressing one's emotions to obtain relief, research has indicated that three motives especially play a role in this regard: *social comparison*, *anxiety reduction*, and *information seeking*.

Social comparison

SOCIAL
COMPARISON
THEORY

According to Schachter (1959), when individuals are confronted with the prospect of receiving an electric shock, they may not know how to feel and respond: 'Am I too worried?', 'Should I be really nervous?', 'Am I the only one who is afraid?'. According to **social comparison theory** (Festinger, 1954), in such an ambiguous situation affiliation with others facing the same situation would give one the opportunity to compare one's responses with those of others, and thus to assess the appropriateness of one's feelings. In line with social comparison theory, Schachter found that individuals under threat of an electric shock preferred to be in the company of someone also waiting to undergo the same experiment, rather than in the company of others who were in a quite different situation, such as waiting for a professor. As Schachter concluded: 'Misery doesn't love just any kind of company, it loves only miserable company' (p. 24).

Additional evidence supporting the social-comparison interpretation comes from experiments showing that, as Festinger's (1954) theory would predict, it was especially *uncertainty* about one's responses that enhanced affiliative desires. For example, Gerard (1963) had bogus electrodes attached to subjects' hands and forearms, and induced fear in the way Schachter had done. Subjects had a so-called 'emotionality index' in front of them that supposedly recorded their emotional responses. In the certainty condition, the subjects saw that their response was quite stable, whereas in the uncertainty condition the needle on the index made rather erratic movements. Subjects who were made uncertain about their responses had a stronger desire to wait with others than those in the certainty condition. Similar findings have been obtained in more natural settings. For instance, in a study among married individuals, Buunk, VanYperen, Taylor and Collins (1991) found that the more uncertain individuals were about how things were going in their marriage, the more they preferred to talk with others in a similar situation, especially when they felt their marriage was dissatisfying.

Anxiety reduction

In addition to a desire to reduce uncertainty through social comparison, a desire for anxiety reduction may also play an important role in affiliation under stress. For example, in the study by Gerard (1963) mentioned above, subjects were most inclined to affiliate with others who appeared less emotional than they were themselves, supposedly because they sought reassurance that the prospects were not as bad as they anticipated. In a similar study, Rabbie (1963) found that high-fear subjects preferred to affiliate with a moderate-fear companion, and not, as social comparison theory would predict, with a high-fear companion. A host of more recent evidence indicates that individuals in threatening and stressful circumstances do often turn to sympathetic others who might offer them reassurance and emotional support (e.g., Wills, 1991).

Information seeking

Shaver and Klinnert (1982) presented a perspective on affiliation under stress based upon *attachment theory*. They pointed to the fact that just as young children look to their parents for guidance when confronted with a new stimulus, adults faced with a threat will seek out someone knowledgeable who may provide information to enable them to assess the danger implied in this threat. Schachter (1959) had argued against such an interpretation by showing that affiliation with others who also faced a severe shock was preferred above affiliation with subjects who had already undergone the experiment, and who could provide information about the severity of the threat. Kulik and Mahler (1989) examined this issue in an interesting natural setting, that is, among patients who had to undergo an operation – a situation usually evoking a considerable amount of anxiety. Contrary to what Schachter would have predicted, and in line with the analysis of Shaver and Klinnert (1982), most patients preferred on the night before their operation to be with someone who had already had an operation – thus with someone who could provide information about the exact nature of the threat, rather than with someone who was also about to undergo an operation.

The three motives discussed here are not mutually exclusive: it seems quite likely that in many situations all three motives are present. Thus, individuals under stress may affiliate with similar others, who may provide them with social comparison information with which to evaluate their emotions; with calm others, who may reduce their anxiety; and with well-informed others, who may provide objective information about the nature of the threat. Moreover, affiliation under stress may also stem from the desire to obtain instrumental support, in the form of concrete help and assistance.

Stress does not always lead to affiliation

Although humans tend in general to affiliate when under stress, there is also evidence that stress may reduce rather than enhance affiliative tendencies. The first type of situation in which this might occur is one in which the stress is *embarrassing*. In an early study, Sarnoff and Zimbardo (1961) showed that subjects who learned that, as part of the experiment, they would have to suck bottles and other infantile objects for two minutes apiece, preferred much less often to wait with others than subjects who would supposedly have to suck on neutral objects such as whistles and balloons.

Extremely strong feelings of fear and emotional upset are a second situation in which individuals may prefer to be alone rather than with others. For example, Molleman, Pruyn and van Knippenberg (1986) found among cancer patients that strong feelings of anxiety lowered affiliative desires. In fact, there was a curvilinear relationship between anxiety and desire for affiliation: those with a low level of anxiety, as well as those with a very high level of anxiety, felt a lesser need to interact with other patients than those with an intermediate level of anxiety (see figure 12.1). Probably, extreme forms of anxiety and upset lower the

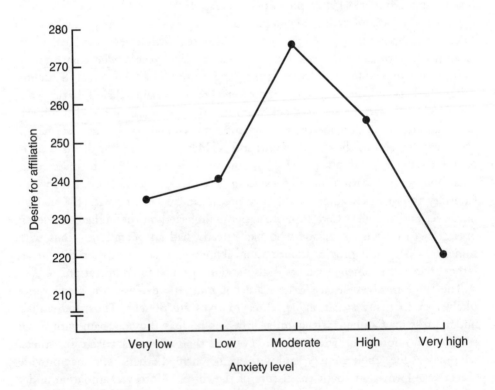

Figure 12.1 Anxiety and desire for affiliation among cancer patients (based upon Molleman, Pruyn and van Knippenberg,1986)

desire for affiliation because individuals are worried that by talking about their feelings with others their fears may be increased.

Effects of affiliation

Do people under stress find what they are looking for? Does affiliation help in reducing uncertainty and stress? Do people who are under stress change their feelings as a consequence of social comparisons? Is the avoidance of affiliation better for those experiencing strong anxieties and embarrassing stress? Such questions have been addressed by many different disciplines and from divergent theoretical perspectives, a few of which will be discussed below.

Affiliation and anxiety reduction

Various experiments have provided evidence for the beneficial effects of affiliation on anxiety. In a well-known study (Amoroso and Walters, 1969), subjects received electric shocks as part of a learning experiment, resulting in increased heart-rate. When they were told to wait a while until the next trial, those who were joined for eight minutes by three other subjects who were confederates of the experimenter, showed a dramatic decrease in heart-rate and in subjectively reported anxiety, even though no talking was allowed. These effects were much stronger than those in the control condition, in which subjects had to wait alone. In particular, the presence of liked and familiar others has positive effects upon stress and anxiety. For example, Kissel (1965) found that the mere presence of a friend, who neither said nor did anything, had a stress-reducing effect when working on a difficult task, compared with the presence of a stranger.

Despite the evidence for a stress-reducing effect of affiliation, in some cases affiliation may enhance rather than reduce anxiety and distress, especially in the case of embarrassing stress. For example, in a study by Glass, Gordon and Henchy (1970) in which subjects watched a film depicting an aboriginal puberty rite involving mutilation of the genitals of adolescent boys, the presence of a friend led to *higher* nervousness than seeing the film alone or with strangers present. Supposedly, the film evoked embarrassment because it stimulated repressed motives, such as castration anxiety and homosexuality, and this stress was augmented by the fact that a friend was present.

Social support and stress reduction

The literature on **social support** provides a great deal of evidence for the stress- reducing features of affiliation. Social support refers to the feeling of being supported by others, and is usually divided into four components: *emotional* support (feeling cared for, loved and appreciated); *appraisal* support (feedback and social comparison on how to evaluate things); *informational* support (such as information about how to handle things); and *instrumental* support (receiving concrete aid and help) (House, 1981). The first three of these components

SOCIAL SUPPORT

correspond to the three functions of affiliation under stress that were mentioned earlier: anxiety reduction, social comparison, and information seeking. In numerous studies, social support has been found to be beneficial in terms of stress reduction, an effect that has been observed with respect to such divergent stressors as the transition to parenthood, financial strain, health problems, and work stress (e.g., Buunk, 1990; Cutrona and Russell, 1987; Wills, 1991). Emotional support occurring in the context of close relationships appears to be especially helpful, because persons under stress can talk to someone who is accepting, can receive negative feedback without feeling rejected, and can be reassured about their worth as a person (Wills, 1991).

BUFFER EFFECT OF SOCIAL SUPPORT

Social-support researchers have been particularly interested in the so-called **buffer effect of social support**, that is, those instances where people who feel supported are less affected by stressful events and conditions than those who feel unsupported. An example of the buffering role of social support comes from a study by Cohen and Hoberman (1983). As figure 12.2 indicates, this study showed that individuals who felt their life was very stressful, had many more physical symptoms such as headaches, insomnia and weight loss when they perceived low support from others than when they perceived high support. There is also experimental evidence for a buffer effect of social support. For instance, Sarason and Sarason (1986) found some evidence that subjects who were informed that they *could* turn to the experimenter for help (but actually never did) were

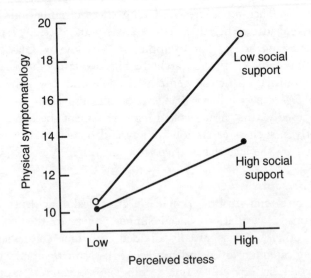

Figure 12.2 The relationship between perceived stress and physical symptomatology for individuals low and high in social support (based on Cohen and Hoberman, 1983)

able to perform better on a task that required considerable cognitive effort than subjects who did not have this opportunity.

Although there is substantial evidence that discussing one's feelings with others may be good for one's health (Pennebaker, 1989), in some cases sharing one's feelings may enhance one's fears. In an interesting experiment by Costanza, Derlega and Winstead (1988), subjects were asked to engage in a brief discussion with other subjects, before they had to guide a tarantula through a maze. Subjects who were instructed to talk about their fears, feelings and anxieties experienced *more* negative affect, and kept the spider at a greater distance than subjects who had been instructed to engage in problem-solving conversation.

The dramatic effect of discussing one's fears too much was also shown in a study by Hobfoll and London (1986) conducted during the war between Israel and Lebanon in 1982. Remarkably, among the women with strong coping traits (that is, those having high self-esteem, and a sense of mastery), those who had more intimacy with their friends (such as feeling appreciated and feeling free to discuss important things), and more support (including emotional support and advice), appeared to experience *more* emotional strain and stress than those with less intimacy and support. Hobfoll and London attributed this to what they called a 'pressure cooker' effect, whereby rumours were spread rapidly, probably exaggerated, and the war became the main topic of conversation. This is in line with social-comparison theory, which would predict that individuals who engage in a discussion of their fears in a group in which most others are also afraid will develop more fears after the discussion.

Lack of affiliation, and loneliness

One of the most direct and obvious signs of a lack of affiliation or of satisfying social relationships is **loneliness**. Loneliness is a complex affective response stemming from a felt deficit in the number and nature of one's social relationships. In a study by Shaver and Rubinstein (1980), loneliness was found to constitute four clusters of feelings and experiences: (1) *desperation* (feeling desperate, panicky, helpless and abandoned); (2) *depression* (feeling sad, depressed, empty, sorry for oneself and alienated); (3) *impatient boredom* (feeling uneasy, impatient, and bored; unable to concentrate); and (4) *self-deprecation* (feeling unattractive, stupid and insecure). Loneliness is in general more common among people living alone, especially among those without a satisfying intimate relationship (DeJong-Gierveld and van Tilburg, 1987).

Not only the absence of an intimate relationship, but also the absence of friendships may foster feelings of loneliness. In fact, according to Weiss (1975), two basic forms of loneliness exist: *emotional* isolation, which results from the absence of an intimate partner, and *social* isolation, which is a consequence of the absence of supportive friends and ties to a social network. Russell, Cutrona, Rose, and Yurko (1984) found that social loneliness was more often accompanied by depression, and was particularly related to the quantity and quality of friendship

LONELINESS

relations, a lack of casual contact with others, a lack of reassurance of worth by others, and a lack of friendships. In contrast, emotional loneliness was accompanied more by anxiety, and was particularly related to a lack of intimate contact, a lack of romantic relationships, and a lack of attachment.

Lack of affiliation and health

A lack of involvement in relationships not only leads to loneliness, but may also have serious health consequences. In a well-known study, Berkman and Syme (1979) examined which individuals of a sample that had been questioned first in 1965 had died nine years later. Those who had passed away appeared to have been socially isolated: they were more often unmarried, had fewer good and frequent contacts with friends and families, and were less often members of church and other organizations. Whereas for men, being married was more important for survival, for women, having intense relationships with friends and family played a larger role. These differences in mortality were directly due to effects of affiliation as such, and not caused by the fact that those less socially connected lived more unhealthily, or that those with a disability were less well able to establish and maintain social ties. Since this pioneering study, there have now been at least 10 different epidemiological studies showing similar effects of affiliation (Atkins et al., 1991). For example, in one study among elderly people, those who had more interaction with others were nearly twice as likely, and those who perceived their supportive environment to be adequate were 3.4 times as likely, to survive for the next 30 months (Blazer, 1982).

Attraction and the Development of Friendships

In many situations we affiliate without making a conscious choice of the company of specific others. For example, we may join a sports club without feeling particularly attracted to the members of that club, and we usually move to a new neighbourhood without even knowing who our neighbours will be (Berscheid, 1985). Interestingly however, there is ample evidence that affiliation and physical proximity may foster friendship. We will first discuss how this might occur, and next we will deal with the important impact of attitude similarity upon **attraction**. Finally, attention will be paid to the fact that attraction does not necessarily lead to friendship, but that friendship implies more, that is to say, an interdependent relationship that includes a willingness to co-ordinate actions and to take the interests of the other into account.

ATTRACTION

The physical environment

We like those we are with – many studies have shown that simply being in the physical presence of another individual will enhance the probability of becoming friends. The pioneering study on this issue was done over forty years ago by

Festinger, Schachter and Back (1950) in Westgate West, a housing complex for student couples, consisting of seventeen buildings, each with ten apartments on two floors. Couples were assigned to them on the basis of a waiting list. As figure 12.3 shows, after a number of months, *more than ten times as many* friendships had developed with others within the same building as with others in different buildings. But even within one's own building physical propinquity appeared to play a major role. More friendships had been formed with others on the same floor than with others on different floors, and the more doors away another couple lived on the same floor, the less often a friendship had developed with the other couple!

A number of other studies have produced similar findings, even when physical propinquity was assessed in quite different ways. For example, Segal (1974) asked students in the Training Academy of the Maryland State Police Force to name their three closest friends in the force. There appeared to be an extremely high correlation (r = 0.91) between the place of the student's surname in the alphabet, and the mean alphabetical place of the surnames of the men chosen as friends. This was due to the fact that rooms and seats in the classroom were assigned on the basis of alphabetical order.

There may be several reasons why propinquity leads to attraction. First, there are simply fewer barriers to developing a friendship with someone close by. Even climbing a stairway to see someone on a different floor is more trouble than just seeing the people next door. Secondly, by being regularly in the company of another, we obtain more information about the other person and have the opportunity to discover mutual interests and common attitudes. For example, in

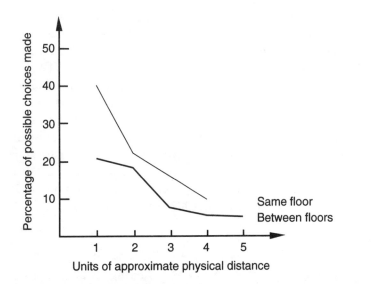

Figure 12.3 Propinquity and friendship choice (based on Festinger, Schachter and Back, 1950)

a study carried out in a housing project, Athanasiou and Yoshioka (1973) found that those living close to each other often formed friendships on the basis of similarities in leisure-time interests. Thirdly, propinquity may lead to attraction through the so-called *mere exposure* effect. This was shown by Saegert, Swap and Zajonc (1973), who presented their experiment as a study on the perception of different tastes. For each trial, subjects had to go into a different room to taste a certain substance. Frequency of exposure was manipulated unobtrusively by having each subject spend a different number of trials of about 40 seconds with each of five other subjects. The more often one subject had been together with another in the experiment, the more the other was liked. That mere exposure may indeed lead to the development of friendships was shown in a study by Yinin, Goldenberg and Neeman (1977) in an Israeli university, where the dormitories differed in the amount of interaction they allowed the participants, from low to very high. For example, in the dormitory providing low interaction, rooms had private showers and sinks, whereas very high interaction was provided in an isolated unit with all facilities communally shared, including toilet, showers, sink, and kitchen. The higher the level of interaction allowed, the higher the proportion of friends chosen within the living unit.

It must be noted that the impact of environmental propinquity upon attraction may depend on various other factors. First, the effects of propinquity are especially pronounced when the subjects are quite similar. For instance, in the Festinger et al. (1950) study, all subjects were war veterans or students. Secondly, propinquity may also decrease attraction by making the unpleasant character-istics of others more noticeable. For example, in a study in Southern California, Ebbesen, Kjos and Konečni (1976) found that not only the most liked others lived close by, but also the most *dis*liked others. These others were disliked because they exhibited annoying behaviour such as parking in front of the driveways, and making noise at night. Thirdly, the mood induced by the environment may determine whether propinquity enhances attraction (see also chapter 10). For instance, a study by Kenrick and Johnson (1979) showed that when subjects were confronted with intermittent, unpredictable bursts of very loud noise they felt more attracted to another individual who was also present than under more normal conditions. According to Kenrick and Johnson, this was due to *negative reinforcement*: the other acted as a generalized reinforcer who reduced the impact of the aversive arousal, and the positive affect due to this led to a liking of the other. In general, aversive environmental conditions such as heat, noise and atmospheric electricity seem to *intensify* our positive as well as our negative feelings for others (Baron, 1987).

The similarity of attitudes

Similarity is in general a potent factor fostering attraction and friendships. Friends have been found to be more similar to one another than non-friends in age, sex, marital status, race, personality traits and intelligence (Hays, 1988). *Attitude similarity*, in particular, appears to lead to attraction. In Byrne's (1971) well-known *attraction paradigm*, subjects fill out an attitude questionnaire, and a few weeks later they learn about the attitudes of another individual – for example, by receiving the filled-out questionnaire of another, such as the one presented in figure 12.4. Such experiments consistently show that attraction is a direct linear function of the proportion of similar attitudes (that is, the number of similar attitudes divided by the total number of similar and dissimilar attitudes). This so-called *law-of-attraction* has also been found to occur when one meets the other in person. For example, Griffit and Veitch (1974) studied the development of attraction among male volunteers who were confined to a simulated fallout-shelter environment for a period of ten days. Before the beginning of the experiment, attitudes towards 44 topics were assessed. During and at the end of the stay, subjects were asked to indicate the names of three people they would like to keep in the shelter, and three names of people they would like to be evicted. Those who were chosen to stay had attitudes more similar to the attitudes of the subjects than those chosen to be removed.

Although the law-of-attraction is well-established and has a wide applicability, two factors have been found to influence the relationship between attitude similarity and attraction. First, the *discrepancy* between one person's attitudes and those of the other play a role: the larger the discrepancy, the less the attraction appears to be. Thus, if I agree only slightly with the statement that abortion should be a matter of personal choice, but another individual agrees very much with this statement, I will like the other less, other things being equal, than when he or she also agrees only slightly with it. Secondly, the more *important* the attitude is for an individual, the more attitude similarity will affect attraction. For example, Byrne, London and Griffitt (1968) induced two levels of attitude similarity: high (75 per cent similar attitudes), and low (25 per cent similar attitudes). This similarity concerned either the topics most important to the subject, or the least important topics. Only with respect to important topics did attitude similarity affect attraction.

But why is attitude similarity so important? According to social comparison theory, when comparing our opinions on new issues, we might benefit more from talking to others who hold the same attitudes as we do than from talking to others who hold quite different views. Although this process undoubtedly plays a role, the major explanation given by Byrne (1971) is based upon *classical conditioning*. Byrne showed that hearing someone express similar attitudes evokes positive affect, and that hearing someone express dissimilar attitudes evokes negative affect. Next, Byrne showed that such affective responses can be conditioned to other persons. A person whose picture was present was liked more when subjects were simultaneously listening to the expression of similar attitudes to their own than when they were listening to someone expressing dissimilar attitudes. Of course, one could argue that this could be the result of thinking

Classical Music (check one)
- − I dislike classical music very much.
- − I dislike classical music.
- − I dislike classical music to a slight degree.
- − I enjoy classical music to a slight degree.
- − I enjoy classical music.
- ✗ I enjoy classical music very much.

Sports (check one)
- − I enjoy sports very much.
- − I enjoy sports.
- − I enjoy sports to a slight degree.
- − I dislike sports to a slight degree.
- ✗ I dislike sports.
- − I dislike sports very much.

Welfare Legislation (check one)
- − I am very much opposed to increased welfare legislation.
- ✗ I am opposed to increased welfare legislation.
- − I am mildly opposed to increased welfare legislation.
- − I am mildly in favour of increased welfare legislation.
- − I am in favour of increased welfare legislation.
- − I am very much in favour of increased welfare legislation.

War (check one)
- ✗ I feel strongly that war is sometimes necessary to solve world problems.
- − I feel that war is sometimes necessary to solve world problems.
- − I feel that perhaps war is sometimes necessary to solve world problems.
- − I feel that perhaps war is never necessry to solve world problems.
- − I feel that war is never necessary to solve world problems.
- − I feel strongly that war is never necessary to solve world problems.

Strict Discipline (check one)
- − I am very much against strict disciplining of children.
- − I am against strict disciplining of children.
- − I am mildly against strict discipline of children.
- − I am mildly in favour of strict disciplining of children.
- ✗ I am in favour of strict disciplining of children.
- − I am very much in favour of strict disciplining of children.

Divorce (check one)
- − I am very much opposed to divorce.
- − I am opposed to divorce.
- ✗ I am mildly opposed to divorce.
- − I am mildly in favour of divorce.
- − I am in favour of divorce.
- − I am very much in favour of divorce.

Figure 12.4 Profile of attitudes of stranger (based on Byrne, 1971)

that the person in the picture was the one expressing the attitudes. However, in a subsequent experiment, Byrne showed that conditioning also occurred when the statements could not be attributed to the person in the picture, because he or she was of the opposite sex from the person expressing the attitudes.

Although the link between attitude similarity and attraction is a very robust one, there are some qualifications to this general pattern. First, it is not attitude similarity as such, but rather, similarity in preference for free-time activities, that may be important for friendship (Werner and Parmalee, 1979), casting some doubt upon the assumption of Byrne (1971) that attitude similarity leads to attraction because it is intrinsically rewarding. Secondly, under certain circumstances, especially high uncertainty and confusion, individuals may feel more attracted to a dissimilar other, because such a person can supposedly provide more new information, and give a different perspective (Kruglanski and Mayseless, 1987; Russ, Gold and Stone, 1979), indicating that cognitive needs are sometimes more salient than the affective value of attitude similarity assumed by Byrne (1971).

Friendship as a relationship

Even when the environmental factors are conducive, and when a high degree of attitude similarity exists, a friendship between two people may still not come into existence. According to **social exchange theory** (Thibaut and Kelley, 1959), reciprocity of liking is an important condition for a stable relationship. Therefore, characteristic of the beginning of a friendship is that there is *mutuality* of attraction. In general, knowing that someone likes us will increase our liking for that person, although when someone tells us things about ourselves that are completely incongruent with our self-concept, we find it hard to believe them, and will not return their liking (Berscheid and Walster, 1969; Stroebe, 1977). Mutual attraction may give rise to the *voluntary interdependence* that is characteristic of friendships (Hays, 1988). Individuals involved in such relationships are willing to co-ordinate their behaviour to some extent, and to take the interests of the other into account. In contrast to, for example, kin or work relationships, this interdependence is voluntary, and primarily based upon mutual attraction. The enjoyment of each other's company is indeed a central criterion for labelling someone as a friend, although intimacy, affection and mutual assistance are also characteristic of friendship (Wright, 1974). The movement towards intimacy may occur quite fast: in one study, after just six weeks the number of intimate behaviours had reached their peak, and the friendships had started to stabilize (Hays, 1988).

Friendship is characterized by certain norms and rules. According to Argyle and Henderson (1985), rules are shared opinions or beliefs about what should, and what should not be done. These authors identified as the most important rules in friendship: volunteering help in time of need, respecting the friend's

SOCIAL EXCHANGE THEORY

privacy, keeping confidences, trusting and confiding in each other, standing up for the other in his or her absence, and not criticizing each other in public. According to a study by Argyle and Henderson, transgression of these rules played an important role in the breakup of friendships, although the most important factor was that the former friend had been jealous or critical of the person's other relationships.

Gender and friendship

There are important differences between male and female friendships. In general, women want others as friends to whom they can talk about intimate issues such as feelings and problems, and women disclose more intimate things in their relationships with friends than men do. In contrast, men look for friends with similar interests, emphasize more the joint undertaking of activities, and do not give a high priority to discussing feelings (Sherrod, 1989).

Why are friendships between men less intimate than those between and with women? Reis, Senchak and Solomon (1985) examined a number of different explanations, and showed that most explanations could be excluded. First, the difference is not due to the fact that men apply different *criteria* for intimacy than women, because men appeared to judge video fragments showing differing degrees of intimacy in the same way as women did. Secondly, the difference appeared not to be due to a reluctance of men to *label* their interactions as intimate, because conversation narratives that could not be identified as having been written by a man or by a woman were judged as more intimate when they

Plate 12.2 Friendships between women tend to be more intimate than those between men. Why?

came from a female than when they were written by a male. Finally, and perhaps most importantly, the gender differences in intimacy in friendship are not due to *social skills*, because when men are asked to have an intimate conversation with their best friend, they are, according to judges, just as able to do so as women. Reis et al. concluded that the main reason men have less intimate interactions with their friends is not because they cannot do so as a result of their socialization, but because they simply *prefer* not to have intimate interactions on many occasions, even though they know quite well how to have these. But why do these differences then exist? Socio-evolutionary theorists point to the similarities between gender differences in friendship found among humans and among primates such as chimpanzees. They argue that evolution has favoured a male preference for instrumental friendships in groups, because men had to collaborate in hunting and fighting. In contrast, women had to establish and maintain a network of nurturing relationships aimed at taking care of and raising children (de Waal, 1983; see also chapter 2).

Romantic Attraction

No one will doubt that feeling sexually attracted to someone and falling in love with him or her is experienced quite differently from liking someone and developing a friendship with him or her. Many romantic relationships are, especially in the beginning, characterized by a sexual attraction that feeds feelings of **passionate love**. This experience includes a strong longing for union with the other, and is characterized by high arousal and an interplay between intense happiness and despair. Furthermore, passionate love is usually accompanied by a preoccupation with the partner and idealization of the other, and by the desire to know the other, as well as the desire to be known by the other (Hatfield, 1988).

PASSIONATE LOVE

Basing their idea on *cognitive emotion theory*, Berscheid and Walster (1978) proposed that passionate love requires two components: first, a state of physiological *arousal*, due to either positive emotions such as sexual gratification and excitement, or negative emotions such as frustration, fear and rejection. The second component of passionate love consists of *labelling* this arousal as 'passion', or 'being in love'. Whether such labelling occurs depends on a number of factors, including general notions about what one should feel in the case of passionate love, beliefs about what constitute appropriate partners and circumstances, knowledge about which situations produce which emotions, and self-perceptions as a romantic person.

Most research in this tradition has focused upon the non-obvious prediction that negative emotions may fuel passion. For example, White, Fishbein and Rutstein (1981, experiment 2) showed that not only seeing a comedy, but also watching a movie depicting killing and mutilation, enhanced men's romantic attraction to a woman seen subsequently on a video recording (see also chapter 10). In an experiment by Dutton and Aron (1974), men who had been frightened, by giving them the prospect of receiving an electric shock, found a woman with whom they were supposed to participate in a learning experiment much sexier and more attractive than did men who had been told they were just going to receive a barely perceptible tingle of a shock. Walster (1965) found that a woman whose self-esteem had been temporarily lowered, responded much more positively to a friendly stranger who had expressed romantic interest in her, than did women whose self-esteem had been raised. Not only arousal due to negative feelings, but also neutral arousal has been found to be linked to passionate attraction. In one experiment, White et al. (1981, experiment 1) showed that men who had been involved in two minutes of exercise found an attractive woman on videotape, whom they expected to meet, more attractive, and an unattractive woman less attractive, than did men who had only been involved in fifteen seconds of exercise.

According to Kenrick and Trost (1989), the fact that passionate love is such an intense emotional experience is due to the evolutionary importance of sexual reproduction. Although affiliation and friendship may also have fostered survival, had sexual attraction between males and females not existed we would not have been on earth (see also chapter 2). Nevertheless, to some extent the chances of developing a romantic relationship with someone else are determined by the same factors that are important for the development of friendship. Propinquity makes the beginning of romantic attraction more likely, and perceived attitude similarity is also important for love relationships (Buunk and Bosman, 1985). For example, Byrne, Ervin and Lamberth (1970) administered an attitude–personality questionnaire to a large group of students, and selected from this group 24 pairs of a male and a female who were very similar in attitudes, and 20 pairs who were very dissimilar (with the restriction that the male had to be as tall as or taller than the female). The subjects were asked to go on a 'coke date' of about 30 minutes, and even after this brief encounter, attitude similarity appeared to have a clear effect upon attraction, including perceived desirability as a date and as a marriage partner. However, in this experiment, the *physical attractiveness* of the 'partner' was as important in determining attraction as the proportion of similar attitudes. In a similar vein, Walster et al. (1966) invited students for a 'computer dance', in which they were paired with another individual of the opposite sex. Physical attractiveness, as assessed by independent judges, had a strong effect upon attraction for men as well as for women.

The physical attractiveness stereotype

Physical attractiveness affects romantic attraction through a positive stereotype: when someone is beautiful, we automatically attribute, in general, many other positive characteristics to him or her (Feingold, 1992). Although attractive people are viewed as somewhat less modest, they are especially perceived as sexually warmer and more socially skilled than unattractive people, but also as more sociable (e.g., more extrovert and friendly), more dominant (e.g., more assertive), and mentally healthier (including happier and emotionally more stable). Both male and female attractive targets are viewed in a more positive light than unattractive ones, although there is a stronger tendency to attribute sexual warmth to attractive women than to attractive men.

These stereotypes are not completely unfounded. Although the personality and behavioural characteristics of attractive people are in general not very different from those of unattractive people, attractive people have been found to be less lonely, less socially anxious, more socially skilled, and more popular with the opposite sex. Among women attractiveness is, more than among men, correlated with self-esteem, popularity with the opposite sex, and sexual permissiveness (Feingold, 1992). Probably, from the beginning of their lives, attractive people receive more positive attention, and will, through a so-called **self-fulfilling**

Plate 12.3 The physical attractiveness stereotype: we attribute many positive characteristics to someone who is beautiful

prophecy, become more self-confident in their social life. This process was shown on a small, though quite decisive scale in an experiment by Snyder, Tanke and Berscheid (1977). These investigators led male subjects to believe that they were conducting a 'getting acquainted' telephone conversation with an attractive versus an unattractive woman. Remarkably, the women who were *believed* to be attractive (though they were not actually judged more attractive by independent raters) became, as a consequence of the positive behaviours of the males, more friendly and sociable, whereas the women assumed to be physically unattractive became cool and aloof during the conversation.

Gender differences in preferences for physical attractiveness

Although both men and women value physical attractiveness, this is in general a somewhat more important determinant of romantic attraction for males than it is for females. In an experiment by Stroebe, Insko, Thompson and Layton (1971), subjects were shown attitude profiles of others varying in degree of similarity to the subjects, combined with pictures varying in attractiveness. The results showed that subjects liked more, and would consider further as a dating and marriage partner, those similar to themselves rather than dissimilar, and those attractive rather than those unattractive. The effects of physical attractiveness were somewhat stronger for males than for females. Buss (1989) found, in a study in 37 cultures, that although both genders rated physical attractiveness as important, in most cultures men found this more important than women did.

The higher value placed by males upon physical attractiveness is in line with **socio-evolutionary theory,** which maintains that individuals act largely unconsciously through mechanisms that were selected in the course of human evolution because they helped to maximize the likelihood of our ancestors being able to produce and to raise viable offspring (Buss, 1994; see also chapter 2). According to this perspective, males have been selected to prefer women who are likely to produce healthy babies and who are likely to successfully raise such children. Therefore, men would have become particularly sensitive to signs of youth, health and reproductive value. Signs of youth are indeed, in all cultures, important cues for female attractiveness. For instance, Cunningham (1986) showed that males are attracted more to females possessing young-looking, so-called *neonate*, features – large eyes, a small nose area, a small chin, and widely spaced eyes. Furthermore, in line with the evolutionary perspective there is the fact that the small waist–hip ratio preferred by men in women is related to the likelihood of conception and to general health (Singh, 1993).

According to the socio-evolutionary perspective, it is crucial to take into account the fact that human offspring are helpless at birth and continue to be dependent upon parental care for years. During most of our evolutionary history, particularly while breast-feeding, females had more chance of having their offspring survive if they were choosy in selecting male partners, that is, selecting males who would provide the necessary resources during the long period that the children needed care, and women would thus have become particularly sensitive to signs of status and dominance (Buss, 1994). Therefore, the cues women use to assess attractiveness are in part different from those of males. Women, more than men, are attracted to others of the opposite sex who display non-verbally dominant behaviour (for example, not sitting on their own, gesturing a lot, and not nodding their head too much) (Sadalla, Kenrick and Vershure, 1987); tall (but not too tall) men with athletic features are considered especially attractive (Hatfield and Sprecher, 1986); and the attractiveness of males, more than that of females, is related to mature features such as prominent cheekbones and a long and wide chin, a large smile area, and a higher-status clothing style (Cunningham, Barbee and Pilkingham, 1986).

Equity and choice of partner

Although in general the most attractive people are preferred as a partner, in line with **equity theory** (Walster, Walster, and Berscheid,1978), individuals realize that they cannot expect more than they have to offer themselves, and adapt their standards for a partner to their own level of attractiveness. Indeed, physically attractive individuals judge their dates more harshly (Walster et al., 1966), and are more likely to consider dating attractive others, and less likely to consider dating unattractive others; whereas less attractive individuals will probably be more willing to date less attractive others (Stroebe et al., 1971). Because of this process of adapting one's criteria to one's own 'market value', individuals will tend to end up with partners of approximately their own attractiveness level. This is referred to as the *matching hypothesis*. When there are differences in the level of attractiveness, according to equity theory these will be compensated for by other assets. For instance, in line with the socio-evolutionary perspective, women may become involved with higher-status men who are less physically attractive than they are themselves (Buss, 1994). Moreover, individuals who believe that their partners are more attractive than themselves, tend to love their partners more (Critelli and Waid, 1980).

EQUITY THEORY

Attractiveness is not a completely fixed characteristic: in their attempts to obtain as attractive a partner as possible, men and women will aim to enhance their attractiveness to those they would like to become involved with. This can be achieved through two strategies. In the first place, one can work on making oneself more attractive. For instance, Buss (1988, study 2) found that men said more often that they had displayed and bragged about resources, and had displayed sophistication, strength and athleticism, whereas women said more often that they had worn sexy clothes and make-up, had kept clean and groomed, had altered their appearance, had worn stylish clothes and jewellery, and had acted coyly. The second strategy for making oneself more attractive is through derogation of competitors. For example, Buss and Bedden (1990) found that males said that they would derogate a competitor's achievements and strength, and try to defeat him physically and in sports. Women indicated that they would be more likely to call their competitor promiscuous, and derogate her appearance.

Because beginning and developing a romantic relationship is – just as friendship – contingent upon reciprocity of liking, individuals face not only the task of enhancing their attractiveness, but also the task of finding out whether the other is interested in them. Douglas (1987) examined the strategies of *affinity testing* in situations in which the likelihood of subsequent interaction was ambiguous, and discovered a number of different strategies, such as *confronting* (e.g., 'asking if she liked me'); *withdrawing* (actions that required the partner to sustain interaction, for example, 'I would be silent to see if he would start the conversation again'); *hazing* (actions that required a partner to provide a commodity or service at some cost to him or herself, e.g., 'I told him I lived 16 miles away . . . I wanted to see if he would try and back out'); *diminishing* (lowering one's own value: 'I told him I wasn't very interesting. Waiting for him to say "Oh, no" '); and *networking* (including third parties to acquire or transmit information, e.g., 'I went over and asked his friends about him').

Close Relationships: Satisfaction, Commitment and Dissolution

Once the beginning of a relationship is established, partners may begin to develop an interdependent relationship by increasing their mutual involvement. Various processes play a role in this regard, including showing a willingness to take the interests of the other into account (Rusbult and Buunk, 1993), and building intimacy by revealing one's personal desires, anxieties, fantasies and emotions (Reis and Shaver, 1988). Some relationships will become happy, satisfying and stable; others will be filled with conflicts and problems, and are likely to end sooner or later. One of the most prominent features in which happy and distressed couples appear to differ is the way they *communicate* with each other (see also chapter 11). For example, couples are happier when their interaction is characterized by problem-solving and open communication. Thus the more they disclose their thoughts, the more directly they express their feelings, the more they show affection and understanding, the more they let the other know that they empathize with his or her feelings, and the better they are in taking the perspective of the spouse – the happier they are. In contrast, couples are less happy the more they show conflict-avoidance (for example, not wanting to discuss problematic issues, making indirect references to a conflict issue), soothing (ignoring and covering up differences), and destructive communication (for example, criticizing, disagreeing, complaining, and sarcastic remarks) (see Noller and Fitzpatrick, 1990; Schaap, Buunk and Kerkstra, 1988). Negative reciprocity, that is reacting to a negative remark by the partner with a negative remark, is especially characteristic of distressed couples, and is predictive of a future decline in satisfaction (Levenson and Gottman, 1985).

Happy couples also differ from unhappy couples in the way marital problems are attributed (see also chapter 7). In line with attribution theory, those low in satisfaction tend to engage in maladaptive attributions. They tend to blame the problems in the relationship on their partner, and to see their own and their partner's problem-related behaviour as global (also affecting other behaviours in their marriage), as well as stable (likely to occur in the future). Put differently, individuals in distressed relationships do not see problems arising as issues that should be resolved in their own right, but as issues typical of severe and stable problems in their relationship. Research has shown that such a maladaptive attributional pattern predicts a decline in marital satisfaction (Fincham and Bradbury, 1991). Furthermore, partners in happy couples tend to see their partner's behaviour as more positive than their own behaviour, whereas partners in unhappy couples tend to see their own behaviour as more positive than that of their partner. For example, individuals satisfied with their relationship tend to give the partner more credit for resolving conflict, and tend to blame themselves more for inconveniencing the other (Thompson and Kelley, 1981).

Relationship satisfaction

Even couples who experience many conflicts and problems will not necessarily evaluate their relationship as bad. According to social exchange theory (Thibaut and Kelley, 1959), the satisfaction of individuals in a relationship is dependent upon the **comparison level (CL)**: the level of outcomes they believe they deserve from the relationship. One important determinant of the comparison level is *relational* comparisons, that is comparisons with the partner (Buunk and VanYperen, 1991). As predicted by equity theory, individuals in close relationships will feel distressed when the proportion of inputs and outcomes is not the same for both partners. Distress will occur for the over-benefited, who feel guilty because they receive more from the relationship than they believe they deserve, as well as for the under-benefited, who feel sad, frustrated, angry and hurt because they receive less than they believe they deserve (cf. Sprecher, 1986). Not surprisingly, the under-benefited will feel more distressed since they receive fewer rewards from the relationship than do the over-benefited. In many studies, support has been obtained for these assumptions. For instance, as shown in figure 12.5, Buunk and VanYperen (1991) found that those perceiving equality in the distribution of inputs and outcomes were most satisfied, followed by those feeling advantaged, with those feeling deprived experiencing the lowest level of satisfaction. Furthermore, equity theory predicts that individuals will aim to restore the balance. Prins, Buunk and VanYperen (1992) found that women (but not men) in inequitable relationships were inclined to engage in a rather extreme form of equity restoration, i.e., extramarital relationships. Not only had such

COMPARISON
LEVEL (CL)

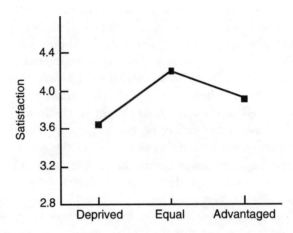

Figure 12.5 Equity and satisfaction in intimate relationships (based on Buunk and VanYperen, 1991)

women a stronger desire to engage in such relationships, they had also actually been involved more often in such relationships than women in equitable relationships.

Despite the importance of equity for satisfaction in close relationships, its role should not be over-estimated. First, according to Clark and Mills (1979), romantic relationships are not *exchange* relationships with an expectation of reciprocation of things done for each other, but rather, *communal* relationships in which the partners respond to each other's needs. Research by Clark and Mills has shown that individuals interpret a strong inclination of the other to reciprocate favours as a sign that the other person is not interested in a romantic relationship. Secondly, the level of rewards seems a better predictor of satisfaction in love relationships than fairness: it is more important to feel that our partner is rewarding us by providing love, status, information, and sexual satisfaction, than to perceive perfect equity in the exchange of rewards (Cate, Lloyd and Long, 1988). Furthermore, recent research suggests that the effect of equity upon relational satisfaction is mainly found for individuals high in *exchange orientation*. Such individuals are strongly oriented to direct reciprocity, expect immediate and comparable rewards when they have provided rewards for others, and feel uncomfortable when they receive favours they cannot reciprocate. As figure 12.6 shows, only for individuals high in exchange orientation was relationship satisfaction related to the degree of equity. For those low in exchange orientation it did not seem to matter whether they felt deprived, equitably treated or advantaged (Buunk and VanYperen, 1991). Finally, there is little evidence that equity predicts the quality of the relationship in the future (e.g., Lujanski and Mikula, 1983; VanYperen and Buunk, 1990).

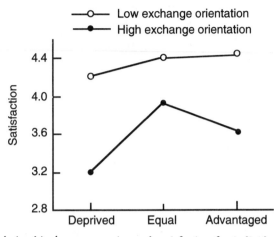

Figure 12.6 The relationship between equity and satisfaction for individuals low and high in exchange orientation (based on Buunk and VanYperen, 1991)

Satisfaction is related not only to what one sees one's partner as getting, but also to the outcome of comparisons with other individuals in one's reference group. Buunk and VanYperen (1991) designated this type of comparison as *referential* comparisons. Those who perceive their own input–outcome ratio as better than that of comparable same-sex others appear to experience the highest level of marital satisfaction. Furthermore, a study by Buunk, Collins, Taylor, VanYperen and Dakoff (1990) showed that those with an unhappy marriage tended to interpret both upward *and* downward comparisons in a negative manner more often than happily married individuals. Unhappily married individuals felt envious when they saw others enjoying a better marriage, and when they encountered couples with more serious marital problems than they had, worried that the same might happen to them.

Commitment

Although it would seem self-evident that people who are satisfied with their relationship will also stay with their partners, social scientists have long observed that happy relationships are not necessarily stable relationships, and that stable relationships are not necessarily happy relationships (Rusbult and Buunk, 1993). Rusbult (1983) has proposed the **investment model** to explain what makes people motivated to maintain their relationships, that is to say, what factors enhance *commitment* to these relationships. According to Rusbult, commitment refers to the individual's tendency to maintain a relationship and to feel psychologically attached to it. Commitment is in the first place supposed to be directly affected by *satisfaction*: the higher the satisfaction, the higher the

INVESTMENT MODEL

commitment. However, in line with social exchange theory (Thibaut and Kelley, 1959), the investment model supposes that a second factor affecting commitment is the perceived quality of *alternatives*, in other words, the individual's judgement of the attractiveness of alternative options to being in this relationship. The **comparison level for alternatives (CLalt)** constitutes the lowest level of outcomes someone will accept in the light of available alternative opportunities. These opportunities include the best imagined alternative relationship to the present relationship, the appeal of living alone, the availability of rewarding options besides the present relationship (such as an interesting job, or good friends), and the actual presence of an alternative partner.

COMPARISON LEVEL FOR ALTERNATIVES (CLALT)

When developing a relationship, individuals will gradually close themselves off, behaviourally and cognitively, from attractive alternatives. For instance, Simpson, Gangestead and Lerma (1990) found that individuals involved in dating relationships, as compared to those not involved in them, tended to perceive persons of the opposite sex as less attractive. Johnson and Rusbult (1989) found that derogation of alternatives was particularly manifest among highly committed individuals, who perceived an outside individual as a serious potential threat because he or she was attractive, and because they had to engage in interaction with him or her as part of a study on computer dating. Nevertheless, an attractive outside partner is one of the major factors fostering a breakup (Buunk, 1987).

Many relationships suffer unhappy periods and, even when the alternatives are quite attractive, that does not necessarily mean they fall apart. Therefore, the investment model proposes a third variable: *investment size*. This refers to the variety of ways in which individuals become linked to their partner, by investing time and energy, by making sacrifices, by developing mutual friends, by developing shared memories, and by engaging in activities, hobbies and possessions that are an integral part of the relationship. According to recent research, during the course of a relationship the selves of both partners begin to overlap and become interconnected. Benefiting the other is seen as benefiting oneself, and through identification, the traits and abilities of the other become vicariously shared (Aron, Aron, Tudor and Nelson, 1991; Aron, Aron and Smollan, 1992).

A substantial number of studies have provided support for the investment model and have shown that all three factors – satisfaction, alternatives and investments – are independent predictors of commitment, and in the long run of the likelihood of breaking up a relationship (Rusbult and Buunk, 1993). Despite this empirical support, however, some limitations of the investment model must be noted. First, the three determinants of commitment are not independent of each other, and often a change in one determinant may lead to change in another. For example, finding an attractive alternative partner may foster a decrease in investment size. Secondly, most research on the model has been conducted on short-term relationships in student samples, and much less on long-term marriages in community samples. Finally, the model says little about individual differences in the willingness to commit oneself. For instance, individuals who, because of experiences in their youth, have problems with trusting others, and with accepting love from others, will less easily develop a committed relationship than those who feel confident about themselves and others in relationships (Shaver, Hazan and Bradshaw, 1988).

The consequences of breakups

The breakup of a relationship, and especially a divorce, may have serious consequences. The mental and physical health of divorced people has been found to be worse than that of married individuals, and even worse than that of widowed and never-married individuals. One of the reasons for this is that getting divorced may in some cases be a consequence, instead of a cause, of mental problems (Buunk and Van Driel, 1989; Stroebe and Stroebe, 1986). Nevertheless, ending a marriage through divorce is in itself a stressful experience. Usually, divorced people have to go through a grief process, and are confronted with the transition from being married to being single. Living alone, after having lived with a partner for a long time, usually requires considerable adjustment. It is often difficult to maintain earlier, couple-based friendships and consequently new relationships have to be initiated and built. Moreover, adapting to a different, lower social status can be a painful process, especially because there is still some stigma attached to being divorced; also divorcees usually receive less support than widowed people, because friends may side with the former spouse. Furthermore, divorcees often have to deal with feelings of failure and rejection. Nevertheless, adjustment to divorce and breakup causes less distress for some individuals than for others. For example, individuals who had a less close relationship with their former partner, who took the initiative to break up or divorce, who are embedded in social networks, and who at present have a satisfying, intimate relationship, are relatively better off. In addition, certain personality characteristics, including high self-esteem, independence, tolerance for change, and egalitarian sex-role attitudes, facilitate coping with the situation of being divorced (e.g. Price-Bonham, Wright and Pittman, 1983; Simpson, 1987).

Summary and Conclusions

This chapter has dealt with core aspects of human social behaviour, i.e., the basic needs for the company of others, for friendship, for intimacy, for passion, and for a stable romantic relationship. The material presented in this chapter testifies how, through the course of evolution, humans have developed to become extremely social animals, who need relationships with others, to ward off anxiety, to obtain support, to survive, to evaluate their responses, and to raise their offspring. We have seen that when these needs are frustrated, the consequences can be rather serious, including depression, anxiety, despair, loneliness, health complaints, and finally death. Such findings illustrate, maybe more than anything else, the crucial importance of the issues studied by a truly *social* psychology.

Glossary terms

Affiliation
Attraction
Buffer effect of social
  support
Comparison level (CL)
Comparison level for
  alternatives (CLalt)

Equity theory
Investment model
Loneliness
Passionate love
Self-fulfilling prophecy

Social comparison theory
Social exchange theory
Social support
Socio-evolutionary theory

Discussion points

1 How could one design an appartment building in such a way that interaction and the development of friendships within the building would be stimulated?
2 In what different ways may social support foster survival? Why may support be related to health?
3 Can you think of as many conditions as possible under which talking to others will reduce stress?
4 What could people do to alleviate loneliness without seeing others?
5 Think of as many features as possible that make a friendship different from a love relationship.
6 Derive from the findings in this chapter a situation in which there would be a strong likelihood that a man and a woman would become romantically attracted to each other. Think, among other things, of the spatial context, the characteristics of the two people, and the activities they might engage in.
7 Think about a possible cross-cultural study that would test socio-evolutionary notions about physical attractiveness.
8 Come up with a number of ways in which individuals who feel they give more time and attention to their partner than they get in return could restore equity.
9 Suppose a couple feels they are not as committed to their relationship as they were before. What can you suggest, on the basis of the investment model, they could do to enhance commitment?

Suggestions for further reading

Buss, D. M. (1994) *The Evolution of Desire. Strategies of human mating*. New York: Basic Books. An interesting, well-written book on the socio-evolutionary approach to romantic attraction and close relationships.

Buunk, B. P. and Van Driel, B. (1989) *Variant Lifestyles and Relationships*. Newbury Park: Sage. Deals with close relationships outside marriage, including relationships of singles, unmarried cohabitation, extramarital relationships, homosexual and lesbian relationships, and communal groups.

Hatfield, E. and Sprecher, S. (1986) *Mirror, Mirror . . . The importance of looks in everyday life*. New York: SUNY Press. A somewhat dated, but good review of research on physical attractiveness.

Hendrick, C. and Hendrick, S. (1993) *Loving, Liking and Relating*. Pacific Grove, CA: Brooks/Cole. A recent review of the literature summarized in the present chapter.

Lerner, M. J. and Mikula, G. (eds) (1994). *Entitlement and the affectional bond: Justice in close relationships*. New York: Plenum. A useful reader on equity, social exchange and justice in dating, marital and family relationships.

Noller, P. and Fitzpatrick, M. A. (eds) (1988) *Perspectives on Marital Interaction*. Clevedon/Philadelphia: Multilingual Matters. A well-composed reader of chapters dealing particularly with marital communication.

Sarason, B. R., Sarason, I. G. and Pierce, G. R. (eds) (1990) *Social Support. An interactional view*. New York: Wiley. An excellent volume on all aspects of and approaches to social support.

Sternberg, R. J. and Barnes, M. L. (eds) (1988) *The Psychology of Love*. New Haven: Yale University Press. A book with chapters on various approaches to love.

Key studies

Hazan, C. and Shaver, P. (1987). Romantic love conceptualized as an attachment process. *Journal of Personality and Social Psychology*, 52, 511–24.

Rusbult, C. E. (1980). Commitment and satisfaction in romantic associations: a test of the investment model. *Journal of Experimental Social Psychology*, 16, 172–86.

13   Prosocial Behaviour

Hans W. Bierhoff

Contents

Introduction

Examples of prosocial behaviour

Why do people help one another?
Sociobiology
Individualistic approach
Interpersonal approach
Studying prosocial behaviour in social systems

Emergency intervention: when do we help?

The consequences of receiving help
Social support

Summary and conclusions

Introduction

Today's altruist may be tomorrow's passive bystander; it all depends on the social situation. This is the message in Latané and Darley's (1969) well-known article on bystander apathy. For example, if another person acts altruistically or egoistically the chances are high that observers will do the same (Rushton, 1980). A host of additional situational variables (such as the number of bystanders, and time pressure) exert powerful influences on altruistic behaviour. In this chapter, the terms *altruism, prosocial behaviour* and *helping behaviour* are used inter-changeably.

In general, social psychologists have suggested two different types of definitions of prosocial behaviour. Some have excluded egoistically motivated behaviour (for example, **reciprocity**) and emphasized empathically motivated behaviour (such as the termination of the victim's suffering). Others have argued that it is impractical to define altruism on the basis of an assumed motivational state because it seems to be impossible to decide in each individual case whether the behaviour was empathically motivated or not. In line with the second approach, Bierhoff (1990) has specified two conditions that define prosocial responses: (1) the *intention to benefit* another person, and (2) *freedom of choice* (e.g., lack of professional obligations).

RECIPROCITY

Examples of Prosocial Behaviour

ALTRUISTIC
BEHAVIOUR

The parable of the Good Samaritan is an excellent example of **altruistic behaviour**. While the altruistic behaviour of the Samaritan was not observed by bystanders, other forms of altruism do take place in public. Consider, for example, the emergency aid for Africa organized by Bob Geldorf, or 'ferry aid' as a response to the ferry disaster in Zeebrugge. These modern examples of altruism make it clear that altruistic responses need not be without personal gain. For example, pop stars like Tina Turner or Paul McCartney might gain an advantage by sacrificing time and money for people in need, because by acting altruistically they might promote their records. In addition, many people will admire them for their unselfishness. Altruistic behaviour is not necessarily unselfish behaviour. In many cases, rewards – subtle or obvious – accrue (cf. Snyder and Omoto, 1992).

Prosocial behaviour is determined to a large extent by rewards and costs. This is not to deny that truly selfless altruists live among us, who act altruistically without taking the (negative) consequences into account. In fact, such interventions are most likely in emergency situations which demand immediate action. For example, when an aeroplane crashed into the Potomac near Washington National Airport, television cameras showed that a bystander jumped into the river and saved one of the survivors even though the water was freezing and frostbite was a likely consequence of this heroic deed.

A central question for research on altruism is related to the motives underlying such responses. Research has found a number of altruistic motives (such as, moral obligation, **empathy**, reciprocity, enhancement of self-esteem, and a desire for recognition). In an empirical study using a representative sample of 2000 German respondents we tried to learn something about the motives for prosocial behaviour (Bierhoff, Klein and Kramp, 1990). The content analysis of answers in response to five written accident scenarios read by our respondents showed that self-esteem enhancement and moral obligation were the most often mentioned motives for altruistic behaviour on behalf of road-accident victims. In addition, motives such as empathy and reciprocity were frequently mentioned.

It is especially interesting to consider the results showing the motives which may impede altruistic responses. The factors mentioned (e.g., stress, danger, time and material losses) can nearly all be subsumed under the category *costs of helping*. Therefore, people tend to think that the anticipation of negative consequences

Plate 13.1 'Live Aid' – the global concert in aid of the starving in Ethiopia – is a modern example of altruism (Wembley Stadium, London, 14 July 1985)

reduces altruism. This is especially true for loss of time, which was the most often mentioned reason for not helping. Other frequently mentioned inhibiting factors were danger, stress, and lack of competence. Confirming these results, Snyder and Omoto (1992) report in their study on AIDS volunteers that the psychological costs of volunteer work (such as stigmatization and embarrassment) determine the decision to quit.

Loss of time is a good example because it illustrates the inhibiting influence of negative consequences on altruism. The assumption that loss of time reduces altruism is plausible because a basic rule of our daily life is that 'time is money'. In many real-life situations people are in a hurry. Waiting is a frustrating experience. Therefore, a willingness to sacrifice time for a person in need can be understood as generosity (Levine, 1987).

Darley and Batson (1973) conducted an experiment which fits nicely into this framework. Their subjects were students in a theological seminary. While some of the students were instructed to think about professional problems, others were asked to think about the parable of the Good Samaritan. As they left, the experimenter indicated either that they would be late ('Oh, you're late; they were expecting you a few minutes ago'), on time ('The assistant is ready for you, so please go right over') or early ('If you would like to wait over there, it shouldn't be long').

On their way, students met a 'victim' who ostensibly had fallen to the floor. The percentage of subjects who offered help constituted the dependent variable of the study. The results are summarized in figure 13.1. While the instruction to the students had a slight effect on altruism – those who were instructed to think

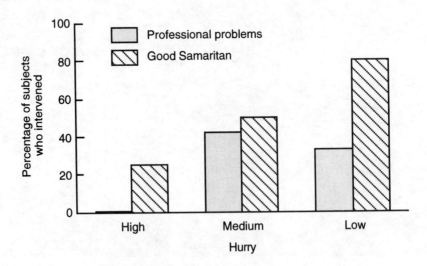

Figure 13.1 The effect of instruction and degree of hurry on altruistic responses in an emergency situation (based on Darley and Batson, 1973; and Greenwald, 1975a)

about the parable tended to help more – the 'hurry' variable exerted a much stronger influence. In general, subjects were less helpful when they were in a hurry. This result is remarkable because the reason for the hurry was not very serious.

This experiment shows that seemingly trivial variables can exert a profound effect on altruistic responses. The results of the Darley and Batson experiment also illustrate what levels of altruism may be expected in emergency situations when only a single bystander is involved. The 42 per cent of subjects in the neutral, medium-hurry condition who helped may be more or less representative of the level of altruism which might be expected in comparable real-life situations (cf. Latané and Nida, 1981).

The general level of altruism may also be inferred from another study (Bierhoff, 1983), in which students were asked to volunteer for a reaction-time experiment. They were informed that if they participated in the experiment without payment the money would be sent to children in need. The choice was between 0 and 12 half-hour sessions. On average subjects volunteered 3.71 sessions. In a replication of the study the mean value of altruism was 4.40 sessions. In summary, these results indicate that the general level of helpfulness is higher than some pessimists might have assumed. The willingness to work 2 hours for people in need is a substantial contribution, which should be taken as an indication that people tend to be altruistic in many situations.

As an example, the TV-reports about starving children in Ethiopia elicited an enormous amount of help. In an era of egoism, such overwhelming generosity all over the world seems surprising. Another area where prosocial behaviour is very important is blood donation. It is well known that the need for blood products in blood banks is increasing. The recent scandals concerning AIDS-infected blood in France and Germany attest to the sensitivity of the issue. A highly important question for society is what causes blood donors to donate blood for the first time and what factors contribute to the continuity of their prosocial commitment? From several empirical studies of first-time and regular blood donors the conclusion was drawn that first-time donors are motivated primarily by external motives (such as peer pressure), while regular donors are relatively more influenced by internal factors such as moral obligation, self-definition and self-based altruistic concerns (Piliavin, Evans and Callero, 1984; see also the research on bone-marrow donors by Sarason et al., 1993). Obviously, the issue of medical donor attitudes in general is very important for the future development of medical services.

Why do People Help One Another?

How can the phenomenon of altruism be incorporated into theories such as sociobiology or interdependence, which are based on egoistic motives? Is helping others for no immediate reward not inconsistent with the basic assumptions of these theoretical approaches? These are the leading questions of the theoretical debate on altruism. In the following section, the discussion is structured in terms of the level of analysis: biological level, individualistic level, interdependence level, and social-systems level. In the context of these theoretical analyses, a number of important issues in altruism research are discussed: Reciprocity in the context of the sociobiological approach; the role of moods in the context of

SOCIAL
RESPONSIBILITY

individualistic approaches; norms of fairness and **social responsibility** in the context of the social-systems approach. In addition, the distinction between egoistically and altruistically motivated prosocial behaviour is taken into account. Is there an empathy-based altruism which might be contrasted with a more selfish prosocial motivation?

Sociobiology

Natural selection is guided by reproductive success (Voland, 1993; see also chapter 2 of this volume). A key insight is that altruism might be understood as the result of natural selection if it increased rather than decreased the chance of the individual (or of her relatives) to reproduce. Two general processes may have contributed to the development of altruism: kin selection and reciprocity.

Consider kin selection first: the reproductive success of the individual (that is, the inclusive fitness) is dependent on the distribution of his or her own genes in the next generation. Inclusive fitness is the sum of an individual's own reproduction success (direct fitness) and the proportion of the reproduction success of relatives that is elicited by the altruistic behaviour of the individual (indirect fitness; Hamilton, 1964). For example, the relatedness coefficient between siblings is 1/2. Therefore, one's own genes can be favoured by increasing the survival chances of brothers or sisters. Self-sacrifice for the benefit of relatives might reduce direct fitness yet increase the fitness of others.

But prosocial behaviour is not limited to relatives. The theory of reciprocal altruism by Trivers (1971) explains prosocial behaviour among non-relatives. The basic tenet of the theory is that prosocial behaviour is favoured by natural selection if it follows the principle of reciprocity and if the costs for the helper are lower than the benefits for the help-recipient. The principle of reciprocal altruism is based on the fact that it is worthwhile for Tania to protect Steffi if it means that other persons (like Steffi) protect Tania.

If the costs to the helper are low and the benefits to the help-recipient are high, reciprocal altruism may be advantageous. The problem with this type of altruism is that it might not be reciprocated by the help-recipient. For example, the help-recipient might be interested in exploiting the altruistic intentions of others. Therefore, reciprocal altruism may be limited to certain circumstances

(Voland, 1993): a high level of trust between helper and help-recipient, stability of group membership, longevity of the group, and a high degree of recognizability among the group members. In general, these are conditions which increase the likelihood of mutual support and decrease the danger of exploitation of altruistic responses.

Individualistic approach

The individualistic approach to prosocial behaviour is represented here by theories and research on the relationship between mood states and helping. In general, the effects of good mood and of sad mood on helping are quite different.

Empirical studies show that helping is fostered by a *positive mood*, which is induced by success or by thinking about happy experiences. For example, children who are in a happy mood tend to contribute more to charity (Isen, Horn and Rosenhan, 1973, experiment 1) or share more with others (Rosenhan, Underwood and Moore, 1974) than children in a neutral mood. The positive relationship between good mood and helping was confirmed in a meta-analysis by Carlson, Charlin and Miller (1988).

The effects of good mood on helping are relatively short-lived. In a field experiment (Isen, Clark and Schwartz, 1976), subjects received a packet of stationery as a gift at home. Shortly afterwards they received a telephone call which was apparently misdirected. Subjects were asked to help the caller by making a phone call. The telephone rang 1, 4, 7, 10, 13, 16, or 20 minutes after the first contact. Results, which are illustrated in figure 13.2, indicate that the request was highly successful if it was made 1, 4 or 7 minutes after the presentation of the gift (on average, 83 per cent of subjects performed the task). With a time delay of 10, 13 or 16 minutes the response rate decreased to about 50 per cent. Finally, in the 20-minutes condition, only 12 per cent of subjects made the phone call requested, a response rate which comes close to the results in the control conditions, in which no gift was received.

These results might be explained in terms of an affect-priming model which was developed by Bower (1981) and Forgas (1992). In this model the informational role of mood is explained as the selective activation and enhanced accessibility of mood-congruent memory contents. The good mood may arouse positive thoughts which include positively toned activities such as prosocial behaviour.

A second approach which focuses on the informational role of moods is the affect-as-information model developed by Schwarz (1990; see also chapter 6 of this volume). In this approach it is assumed that subjects follow a 'How do I feel about it?' heuristic, in the sense that the current mood is used as a piece of information which is integrated into the overall judgement. In contrast to the affect-priming model, the mood-as-information model is primarily applied to

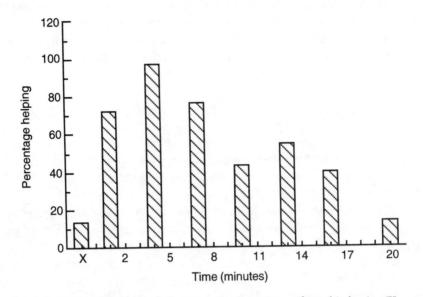

Figure 13.2 Percentage of subjects helping, depending on timing of mood induction (X = control group without mood induction) (based on Isen, Clark and Schwartz, 1976)

simplified information-processing on the basis of heuristics. For example, if a person is asked to evaluate another person she might simply refer to her feelings about the other person.

From this perspective, feelings carry an informational value which might substitute for careful analytic reasoning. Specifically, positive feelings might inform the person that the current environment is a safe place (Schwartz, 1990). It is understandable from this perspective that subjects respond more altruistically in a positive mood because the mood may signal that the situation is safe and under control. The feeling-as-information model simply implies that actors take their mood as an index of the safety of the given situation. Since altruistic responses are suppressed by danger signals (Cacioppo and Gardner, 1993), the relative absence of danger inferred from being in a good mood may encourage altruism.

Forgas (1992) summarizes relevant research by pointing to an asymmetry of research findings with respect to positive and negative mood influences. The effects of a positive mood seem to be stronger and more consistent than the effects of negative moods. From an evolutionary perspective it might be argued that a *bad mood* signals problems and possibly danger (Schwartz, 1990). Therefore, the conclusion is justified that bad mood when in a state of high self-focus undermines altruistic intentions by increasing the perceived cost of intervention. Some of the empirical results agree with this prediction. For example, Underwood, Froming and Moore (1977) found that children in a 'think fun' condition donated more money than children in the control condition. In contrast, children in a 'think sad' condition donated less than children in the control group. A linear increase in altruism from sad to control to happy children was observed.

In contrast, subjects who take the perspective of another person who is sad (empathic concern) are quite helpful (cf. Rosenhan, Salovey, Kárylowski and Hargis, 1981). Why are these subjects who vicariously experience bad mood helpful? A possible answer is that the unhappy fate of others elicits social comparison processes which indicate the relative well-being of the potential helper.

In their meta-analysis comparing negative and neutral mood conditions Carlson and Miller (1987; see also Miller and Carlson, 1990) found that **interpersonal guilt**, as a special negative emotion, consistently increased helping (cf. Bierhoff, Lensing and Kloft, 1988, who reported corroborating evidence from studies conducted in Germany). In summary, the rate of helping is highest if the actor has harmed another person (interpersonal guilt), while it is lowest if another person harms the actor (victimization).

INTERPERSONAL GUILT

Interpersonal approach

Helping behaviour is embedded in interpersonal relations. The question arises as to whether the interpersonal perspective may offer new insights into the motives of prosocial behaviour. For example, does it make a difference whether helping takes place between friends or strangers?

From the viewpoint of exchange theory, people are motivated to maximize the positive consequences to themselves. According to interdependence theory, people are mutually dependent. In addition it is assumed that they enter exchange relationships in order to try to gain rewards. In their theory of interdependence Kelley and Thibaut (1978) allow for the possibility that interdependent persons transform the exchange relation, which is based on the given rewards and costs, into a prosocial relation. Kelley and Thibaut explain that it might be mutually desirable for interdependent persons to perform *prosocial transformations*. The likelihood of prosocial transformations depends on many factors. In the following, three issues are considered: the distinction between exchange and communal relationships, the role of empathy as an altruistic emotion, and the development of a prosocial self-concept on the basis of attributional retraining.

Interpersonal relations may be close or superficial. In close relationships (such as between friends), but not in superficial relationships, people emphasize solidarity, interpersonal harmony, and cohesiveness. In addition, in close relationships rewards for successful performance of a task are distributed according to the equality norm, while in superficial relationships rewards are distributed according to the contributions of each person to the task (on the basis of the equity norm; cf. Bierhoff, Buck and Klein, 1986).

A similar distinction has been drawn by Mills and Clark (1982; see also Clark and Mills, 1993), who contrasted *exchange* and *communal* relationships. Examples of *exchange relationships* are those between strangers or acquaintances, while *communal relationships* are exemplified by relationships between friends, family members, or romantic partners. In exchange relationships people strive for maximal rewards, while in communal relationships people are concerned with the other's welfare. Therefore, it is plausible to assume that in exchange relationships people are motivated by egoistic motives, while in communal relationships they are motivated by the desire to alleviate the suffering of the victim.

In *exchange relationships* people try to achieve a reward–cost balance. They are attracted by rewards and avoid incurring costs. In accordance with this description, empirical studies show that people in exchange relationships respond positively to repayments for benefits given and carefully keep track of individual inputs into joint tasks (Clark, 1984). For *communal relationships* a different pattern of results emerges. In an experiment students were led to believe that another student might need their help. Students who were in a communal relationship with the other student gave more attention to the other's need when no opportunity to repay was expected (in comparison with students who were in an exchange relationship; Clark, Mills and Powell, 1986). In contrast, when subjects expected an opportunity to repay the other person in a later part of the experiment, keeping track of the needs of the other person was equally careful in exchange and in communal relationships.

This pattern of results seems to indicate that people in communal relations are more helpful than in exchange relations if no mutual give-and-take is expected. This conclusion is supported by the results of additional studies which show that people are more helpful in communal than in exchange relationships and that this effect is stronger when the help-recipient is in a sad mood (Clark et al., 1987).

Why does the recipient's sadness increase helping among potential donors with a communal orientation? Clark et al. (1987) suggest that communal observers are prone to attend to others' sadness (because they are disposed to keep track of others' needs) and, as a consequence, experience more feelings of empathy. The concept of empathy plays an important role because it may represent a genuinely altruistic motive which goes beyond egoistic aims. While developmental psychologists are interested in the origins and socialization of empathic concern for others (Zahn-Waxler and Radke-Yarrow, 1990), social psychologists are primarily interested in the issue of empathy-based altruism.

Empathy-based altruism
Much of the research by Batson (1987) has concentrated on the question of whether prosocial behaviour is motivated by altruistic or egoistic motives. The

altruistic motive is equated with empathy, which elicits concern for the other's welfare. Empirical evidence indicates that empathy and prosocial behaviour are positively correlated (Eisenberg and Miller, 1987).

How might an experiment offer an answer to the question of whether prosocial behaviour is motivated altruistically or egoistically? The basic idea is to confront subjects with a victim and to offer them the possibility of leaving the situation. If people are egoistically motivated they might prefer the escape alternative because it allows them to reduce any negative arousal which may have been elicited by the presence of the victim. In contrast, people who are motivated by empathy are not as likely to leave the situation since their desire to alleviate the suffering of the victim would still exist after they had left. In an experiment by Batson et al. (1981), female introductory psychology students observed Elaine, an experimental confederate, who was apparently receiving electric shocks. In the second trial she behaved as if she was suffering very much from the shocks, as a result of which, the experimenter asked her whether she would be able to continue with the experiment. Next, the experimenter asked the observer – the real subject of the experiment – whether she would be willing to continue with the experiment in which Elaine was participating, by taking over the role of the shock victim.

In one condition subjects believed that Elaine shared many attitudes with them. In another condition, subjects were induced to think that Elaine held dissimilar attitudes. Batson et al. assumed that *high attitude similarity* would heighten altruistic motivation while *low attitude similarity* would foster an egoistic motivation. (Another common manipulation of empathy rests on the instruction to empathize with the victim, which is contrasted with the instruction to observe the victim; see Fultz et al., 1986; Toi and Batson, 1982). In addition, difficulty of escape was manipulated. In the *easy escape condition* subjects knew that they could leave the observation room after the second trial, which meant that they would not be forced to continue observing Elaine's plight if she continued with the experiment. In the *difficult escape condition* subjects were instructed to observe the victim through to the end.

The hypothesis was that subjects would be reluctant to help Elaine if they were in the easy escape–dissimilar attitude condition. In all other conditions, the rate of helping should be high. The results confirmed this 'one to three' prediction: while the helping rate was 18 per cent in the easy–dissimilar condition, the proportion of helpers was much higher in the three other conditions (see figure 13.3). This pattern is representative of several experiments conducted by Batson and his co-workers (e.g., Toi and Batson, 1982).

The central idea behind Batson's argument is that subjects who report that they feel primarily personal distress in response to an emergency are acting in a situation-specific manner, while subjects who report that they feel predominantly empathic concern act altruistically, independently of situational constraints (Batson et al., 1981). This pattern of results agrees with the empathy-altruism

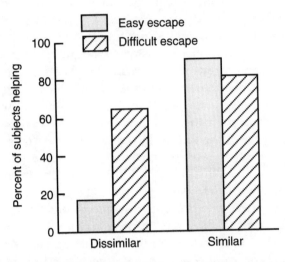

Figure 13.3 Percentages of subjects who helped Elaine, depending on her similarity and their own ease or difficulty of escape (based on Batson et al., 1981, expt 1)

hypothesis, which states that empathy motivates altruism (Batson, 1987). Empathic concern as a personality variable might be equated with chronic altruistic motivation, while the habitual prevalence of personal distress might be considered as an enduring egoistic orientation.

Two studies by Cialdini et al. (1987) which are partial replications of the Batson et al. (1981) experiments elicit doubts with respect to the generalizability of the results. They found that subjects in the high-empathy condition showed a low rate of helping if they received an additional financial incentive. Evidence to the contrary was provided by Batson et al. (1989), who showed that empathic subjects who expected their mood to improve did not reduce their readiness to help Elaine.

It seems that the 'one-to-three' pattern of results emerges only under specific conditions and that the theoretical distinction between egoistically and altruistically motivated helping is hard to verify empirically (cf. Batson et al., 1988). Empathic concern certainly presupposes taking the perspective of the victim and sharing her suffering. But at the same time, reduction of the victim's suffering reduces negative feelings in the helper, who typically experiences relief.

Attribution and prosocial self-concept

What happens if someone tells you that you are a 'real contributor to the community' and someone 'who really wants to help others'? Such messages are part of strategies for attributional retraining which focus on changing the self-concept of the target person (Försterling, 1985). While attending to the plight of others may increase empathic concern, strategies which focus on attributional style may foster an altruistic self-concept. It is well known that attribution retraining can increase the willingness of people to engage in socially desirable activities (Miller, Brickman and Bolen, 1975). This possibility of modifying attributional style is especially relevant for strategies for increasing altruistic behaviour in an applied context.

In a study of potential bone-marrow donors it was found that persons who had received positive feedback for participating in blood donation (the blood centre had expressed appreciation and recognition in a brochure) *and* had answered a questionnaire related to altruism, were more willing to place their names in a bone-marrow registry than people who received no feedback for donating blood, but who had read the brochure containing the positive feedback, or who did not answer the questionnaire (Sarason et al., 1993; see figure 13.4).

A social-learning account (cf. Rushton, 1980) might argue that the appreciation received for their altruistic behaviour and the completion of the questionnaire might have strengthened the belief in blood donors that they were part of a special group of people who were 'real contributors to the community'. This

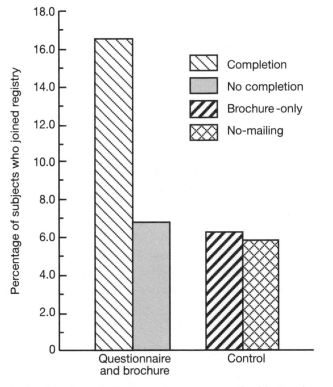

Note: Total No. = 3495: overall percentage of subjects who joined the bone-marrow registry = 8.5

Figure 13.4 Percentages of subjects who joined the bone-marrow registry (adapted from Sarason et al., 1993)

explanation comes close to a self-perception analysis (Cacioppo and Gardner, 1993). By receiving positive feedback stating that 'blood donors are special people who are greatly valued by the blood centre', and by returning the questionnaire, people were induced to think of themselves as helpful and responsible citizens. Research indicates that, following altruistic responses, internally focused feedback which describes the target person as helpful induces the self-concept of an altruistic person, which in turn increases future altruistic responses (Grusec and Redler, 1980).

Piliavin (1989) has pursued the hypothesis that the motives and self-identities of blood donors might be different depending on the social context. She compared the United States's 'community responsibility' system, in which donors are not motivated by any kind of material reward, with the Polish voluntary system, in which participants are not paid, although they receive other privileges (such as a day off work with pay), and with the Polish paid system, in which participants are paid for blood donation. In general, results indicated that the psychological determinants of intention to donate blood are quite similar for the American system and for the Polish voluntary system. For example, for voluntary donors, self definition as a regular donor and motivation to give were significant predictors of intention to donate blood in the next six months. In addition, self-salience of the blood-donor-role identity (measured by items like 'To me, being a blood donor means more than just giving blood') is a significant predictor of intention to give in the future. Finally, actual donation behaviour within the following six months was strongly influenced by intention (data on the intention–behaviour link were only available for American respondents).

In contrast, the pattern of results for participants within the Polish paid system was quite different. They placed more emphasis on external motives, including social pressure and social approval. In addition, the motivation of Polish and US voluntary donors became more internal as the number of prior donations increased, while the motivation of paid donors became more external among those who reported a high number of prior donations.

In summary, these results indicate that only *voluntary donors* develop a donor self-identity and a strong internal motivation to help. Therefore, the conclusion is justified that prosocial behaviour in an applied context might be fostered by attributional retraining which focuses on the self-concept of an altruistic person.

Studying prosocial behaviour in social systems

Prosocial behaviour frequently takes place within social systems. In a social system there is a shared set of beliefs and convictions governing the behaviour of individual participants. The social-systems view has a parallel in Batson's altruistic-motivation approach and in Piliavin's donor self-identity approach because it is assumed that individual responses are not completely determined by individual costs and rewards. Instead, it is expected that individuals respond by reference to consensually shared norms in social settings (cf. Milgram et al., 1986; Schmitt, Dube and Leclerc, 1992).

Fairness norms

People follow normative expectations about the level of rewards and costs that they themselves deserve. In addition, people subscribe to the *belief in a just world*, which states that people get what they deserve (Lerner, 1980). As a result, fairness norms are applied to one's own and to others' benefits and deprivations. Specifically, it is assumed that viewing the deprivation of others elicits observers' empathic affects (Hoffman, 1990).

The relation between fair payment, overpayment, and altruism towards deprived people was studied in an experiment by Miller (1977), which is also interesting because it sheds new light on the issue of altruistic motivation. Subjects had the opportunity to earn money by signing for experimental hours in four conditions. (1) Each hour was paid at $2 (this payment was equivalent to the department norm and therefore appropriate within the given social system). (2) Each hour was paid at $3 (which amounted to relative overpayment compared with the norm of two dollars). (3) Each hour was paid at $2: but $1 was paid to the student and $1 was donated to a needy family which was short of money (therefore, the student received less than the norm prescribed while acting altruistically). (4) Each hour was paid at $3: but $2 were paid to the student and $1 was donated to a needy family (in this condition, the student got what s/he deserved according to normative standards; at the same time she acted altruistically). The mean response on the dependent variable – the number of hours for which the students volunteered – was significantly different in the four conditions: while willingness to co-operate was quite low in the first condition, it was quite high in the last condition (see figure 13.5).

These results lead to several conclusions: first, the additional incentive of one dollar in the overpayment condition increased the rate of co-operation only minimally. Secondly, the additional one dollar increased the co-operation rate considerably if it served as an altruistic inducement which did not threaten the subject's personal standard of deserving – altruism is a strong response if it does not violate the personal norm of fair payment for one's own efforts. Thirdly, altruism was suppressed if it meant violating personal standards of deservingness. Getting only one dollar for one's work seems to reduce co-operation even if the second dollar goes to people in need.

Miller's (1977) results might be summarized in a two-stage model of egoism–altruism. People consider what is their own fair share. In addition, people experience empathic affect and act altruistically (on the basis of fulfilled personal fairness) if the fate of others seems to be unjustly bad. Obviously, it is hard to act altruistically while one's own fair treatment is jeopardized. In contrast, people who perceive their own outcomes as fair seem to be very sensitive with respect to

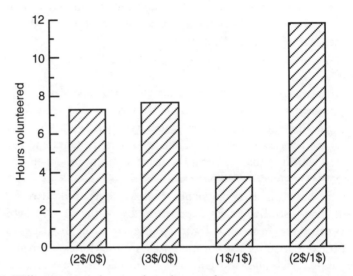

Figure 13.5 Willingness to volunteer, depending on fair payment, overpayment, and altruism (based on Miller, 1977, experiment 2). In the 2$/0$ condition and the 3$/0$ condition each hour volunteered was paid at 2$ and 3$, respectively. In the 1$/1$ condition and the 2$/1$ condition each hour volunteered was paid at 1$ or 2$ for the subject and 1$ for a needy family

the perceived unfairness of that of others (cf. Hoffman, 1990). This model has important implications in applied settings. For example, willingness to be an unpaid blood donor should be higher among subjects who perceive their own fate as fair compared with subjects who believe that they are treated unfairly.

In addition, theoretical implications with respect to the issue of altruistic motivation suggest themselves. A genuinely altruistic motivation comes into play after the fulfilment of egoistic aspirations related to the fairness of one's own position in the social system. Outcomes which fall beyond the level of the personal fairness standard elicit an egoistic orientation which dominates altruistic inclinations.

From a social-systems viewpoint, facilitating and inhibiting influences on prosocial behaviour are taken into account. Inhibiting influences refer to norms which foster an egoistic orientation. For example, in many situations normative barriers against helping are present. Gruder, Romer and Korth (1978) describe a norm of self-sufficiency which implies that victims should have taken care of themselves in the first place. If victims act negligently, helping responses may be suppressed. In many public places the norm of self-sufficiency seems to prevail.

Several other social norms tend to inhibit altruistic behaviour. For example, intergroup researchers have reported that in many societies a strong ingroup/outgroup bias exists (see chapter 17). People usually contrast their own-community solidarity with attitudes towards people who are members of outgroups and who seem to deserve less help (Hoffman, 1990). A large body of research exists which indicates that helping is dependent on the race and appearance of the victim (cf. Köhler, 1977). The typical result is that more help is offered if the victim is of the helper's race and if the victim seems to be a high-status person.

Although empathic concern and prosocial behaviour seem in general to be stronger towards ingroup members, this limitation might be eliminated if empathic affect is based on justice principles, especially the need principle. The results of a study by Montada and Schneider (1991) indicate that people who endorsed the *need principle*, which states that needy people should be supported, reported more perceived injustice with respect to unemployment and a stronger link between one's own advantage and the disadvantage of others, and expressed greater prosocial commitment. In contrast, people who endorsed the *equity principle* expressed less prosocial commitment.

Social responsibility

Many societal institutions encourage prosocial behaviour. Religion's prosocial preaching emphasizes the idea of charity and 'brotherly love'. Batson (1983) points out that religion's prosocial preaching might widen altruistic tendencies, which are described by sociobiologists and which are quite narrow in their scope (excluding non-relatives). Religion widens the ingroup beyond the family and offers the possibility of experiencing a 'we-feeling' and solidarity with other members of society.

Prosocial behaviour is also fostered in the family. Empirical studies indicate that prosocial behaviour in children is related to parents' socialization practices. For example, Bar-Tal, Nadler and Blechman (1980) found that children's prosocial behaviour was positively correlated with the use of support practices by the parents, including helping to prepare homework. In contrast, the use of discipline (for example, physical punishment, social isolation) was negatively related to prosocial behaviour.

On the basis of these socialization influences (including school and children's television) children acquire generalized feelings of social obligation and responsibility. The norm of social responsibility prescribes that individuals should aid other people who are dependent on their help. Berkowitz (1978) assumed that prosocial behaviour was a direct function of felt responsibility in a social situation. Earlier research had indicated that subjects worked harder on behalf of their partner the more dependent the partner was. It was assumed that perceived dependency elicited the norm of social responsibility, which in turn motivated prosocial responses. But prosocial activities require sacrifices, which might be avoided by passing the responsibility to others. The presence of other workers offers the possibility of **diffusion of responsibility**.

DIFFUSION OF RESPONSIBILITY

These predictions were tested in an experiment which, subjects were told, concerned a study of worker–supervisor relationships. They were told that they would play the role of the worker. Their task was to produce paper boxes on the basis of the instructions of the supervisor. The success of the supervisor was said to be in part dependent on the performance of the subject. In the high-dependency condition, it was announced that the success of the supervisor would be heavily dependent on the worker (80 per cent dependency). In the low-dependency condition, the dependence of the supervisor was described as 20 per cent. In addition, the number of workers was varied. The subject worked either alone or together with two other workers. The results are illustrated in figure 13.6. The highest level of productivity was observed in the high-dependency–one-worker condition, while the lowest level occurred in the low-dependency–three-workers condition. The results are explained by referring to the different levels of personal responsibility that are experienced in the four experimental conditions.

Normative beliefs are learnt during the socialization process (see chapter 3). In an attempt to differentiate between cultural rules and individual feelings, Schwartz (1977) contrasted social norms with personal norms. Because individuals differ with respect to their social learning of cultural values and rules, each person is characterized by a unique set of individual values and normative beliefs. Norms are based on values which have several facets. Schwartz and Bilsky (1987, p. 551) define values as beliefs which pertain to desirable end states, transcend specific situations, guide selection and evaluation of events and are ordered by relative importance. On the basis of data from seven countries Schwartz and Bilsky (1990) derived seven types of social values including the

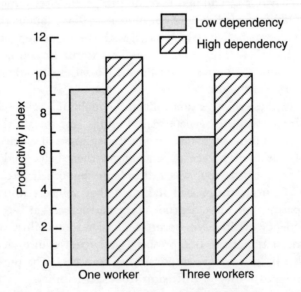

Figure 13.6 The effects of dependency and diffusion of responsibility on productivity (based on Berkowitz, 1978)

prosocial domain. In a later analysis by Schwartz (1992), the prosocial value type was subdivided into benevolence and universalism: 'Benevolence focuses on concern for the welfare of close others in everyday interaction' (p. 11), while universalism refers to 'understanding, appreciation, tolerance, and protection for the welfare of *all* people' (p. 12). While benevolence refers to close relationships, universalism includes social justice and prosocial commitments on a wider social dimension. For example, while research on social responsibility might be subsumed under the benevolence value, research on fairness and **existential guilt** is closely related to universalism.

EXISTENTIAL GUILT

How are prosocial actions instigated? What is the process which translates values into actions? The activation of prosocial behaviour is described by Schwartz and Howard (1981), who propose a process model of altruism, which specifies five successive steps:

attention → motivation → evaluation → defence → behaviour

The first step of the process occurs when the person becomes aware that others need help. The attention phase includes recognition of distress, selection of an effective altruistic action, and self-attribution of competence. The next phase is related to the construction of a personal norm on the basis of social values (such as benevolence, responsibility, and fairness) and the subsequent generation of feelings of moral obligation (motivation phase). The third phase (evaluation of anticipated consequences of altruistic responses) centres around an assessment of potential costs and benefits. The expected costs include social costs (such as social disapproval), physical costs (pain, for example), self-concept distress (violation of the self-image) and moral costs (which result from violating personal norms).

An example might clarify this model. People were asked to read schoolbooks to blind children (Schwartz, 1977). The recognition of the unfulfilled needs of blind children is the first part of the attention phase. Next, the question of whether effective actions to remove the problems are available and whether the potential helper feels competent to execute these actions (such as reading to blind children) is considered. If the answer is affirmative, feelings of moral obligation are generated on the basis of relevant values of benevolence and universalism (motivation phase). If strong feelings of moral obligation are generated, the potential helper will consider the expected consequences of helping (such as how much time must be invested, how much approval is gained by acting altruistically). If the evaluation is inconclusive (if the pros and cons are in balance) the potential helper may be inclined to deny his personal responsibility or he may deny the seriousness of the needs of the blind children (defence phase). Only if the anticipatory evaluation yields a positive result is a decision to read to the blind children likely (behaviour phase).

Although normative beliefs about altruistic behaviour seem to be a standard lesson of socialization (Batson, 1983), norm-inhibiting processes, which include threats to perceived freedom of choice and denial of responsibility, are also important. Individuals tend to act against reductions of their behavioural freedom by denying their responsibility to act altruistically.

Emergency Intervention: When do we Help?

Numerous studies indicate that the willingness to intervene in emergencies is higher when a bystander is alone than when she is in the company of other bystanders (Latané and Nida, 1981). In one of the first experiments that showed this effect (Latané and Rodin, 1969), students overheard that a woman working next door in her office had climbed onto a chair, fallen on the floor and lay moaning in pain. In one condition the student was alone. In a second condition

Plate 13.2 After the bomb explosion in Oklahoma (19 April 1995) there was no shortage of help-givers to rescue survivors. But helpers are not always so forthcoming

another student (a confederate of the experimenter) was present, who was instructed to be passive. In a third condition two strangers were present at the time of the accident. Although two persons could have intervened in this case, in only 40 per cent of dyads did at least one student intervene. In this condition the *individual* likelihood of intervention can be calculated as 22.5 per cent. This percentage is lower than in the alone condition, but higher than in the passive-confederate condition (see figure 13.7).

What are the processes which inhibit helping in groups of bystanders? Empirical evidence indicates that three processes cause the effect (Latané and Darley, 1976; Schwartz and Gottlieb, 1976):

1. A single bystander feels that the responsibility for intervening is focused on her. With other bystanders present the felt responsibility is attenuated. The *diffusion of responsibility* leads to less altruism. This effect increases with the number of bystanders (Latané, 1981).

2. High situational ambiguity elicits feelings of uncertainty in the bystander. Because each bystander hesitates and tries to work out what is going on, the bystanders are models of passivity for each other. This social-comparison process leads to the erroneous conclusion that the other bystanders interpret the event as harmless. Thus a social definition of the situation emerges which hinders altruistic responses. This process of **pluralistic ignorance** is more comprehensively discussed by Miller and McFarland (1991).

PLURALISTIC
IGNORANCE

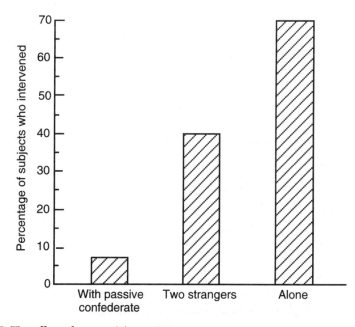

Figure 13.7 The effect of a second bystander on emergency intervention (based on Latané and Rodin, 1969)

3.   A third factor which presumably reduces the willingness to help is **evaluation apprehension**. The presence of the other bystanders elicits feelings of uneasiness because the others are observers of a potential intervention. These anxieties exert their inhibiting influence especially in situations in which the bystander is in doubt about whether she will be able to intervene successfully. But it is also possible that the process of evaluation apprehension increases the likelihood of an intervention. If a bystander believes that she is competent and able to perform very well, the presence of others may possibly be an incentive for intervention. Under these special conditions the bystander may feel that she is showing her superiority and strength by intervening.

Prosocial responses in emergency situations do occur in real life. For example, Steven Spielberg's film *Schindler's List* describes the true story of the dramatic rescue of more than 1000 Jews in Nazi Germany. In this endeavour Schindler invested a lot of time, money, and creativity and was confronted with dangerous risks. Nevertheless, his involvement as a rescuer of Jews constantly grew over time. Oliner and Oliner (1988) interviewed rescuers of Jews in Nazi Europe. Compared with a control group of people who had not intervened on behalf of Jews, the rescuers were characterized by higher expressions of social responsibility and a tendency towards more internal control. These results were replicated in a study of first-aiders who intervened on behalf of injured traffic-accident victims (Bierhoff, Klein and Kramp, 1991). Compared with a matched control group of potential non-helpers, helpers scored higher on a social responsibility scale, lower on a scale measuring hostile and selfish intentions, and higher on an empathy scale. These three scales were positively correlated with each other and could be considered to measure an underlying value-dimension of 'concern for others' which is close to the prosocial value domain described by Schwartz and Bilsky (1990).

The Consequences of Receiving Help

The interpersonal relationship between donor and recipient can be defined in different terms. Gergen and Gergen (1983) argue that donor and recipient negotiate about the meaning of their interpersonal relationship. For example, the relationship might be interpreted as a mutual exchange. On the other hand, the relationship might be understood as a long-lasting dependency of the help-recipient. If the altruistic act is defined as an instance of mutual exchange, the help-recipients might infer that they are mutually dependent on each other. If, on the other hand, the altruistic act is defined as evidence for the dependence of the help-recipients, they might infer that they are weak and passive persons.

Donors and recipients have different perspectives in the relationship (Dunkel-Shetter et al., 1992). The donor profits from the fact that giving help is regarded as desirable and fair. Although she has to incur costs (time, money and effort, for example), the positive consequences of giving help may outweigh the negative consequences. The recipient wants to prevent the conclusion that she was unable to master her fate. Because of the negative implications of weakness and inferiority associated with the role of help-recipient, the recipient will be inclined to redefine the altruistic relationship by emphasizing his or her own contributions.

The aid relationship comprises *four basic components* (Fisher, DePaulo and Nadler, 1981). Donor characteristics (e.g., manipulative intent) and recipient characteristics (e.g., self-esteem) exert a modifying influence on the consequences of receiving help. In addition, aid characteristics (e.g., amount of help) and context characteristics (e.g., opportunity to reciprocate) influence feelings of indebtedness, evaluation of the donor, and self-attributions by the recipient.

These components of the aid transaction influence the magnitude of the self-threat and self-support inherent in the aid for the recipient (Nadler and Fisher, 1986). Negative responses by the recipient are predicted if self-threat prevails. Negative responses comprise negative feelings, negative evaluation of the donor and aid, and a high motivation for future improvement. On the other hand, positive responses are predicted if self-support prevails. Situational variables and dispositional factors exert an influence on the magnitude of self-threat and self-esteem, which in turn determines whether the negative reactions or positive reactions of the recipient prevail.

Situational cues which emphasize the negative implications of receiving help (such as scornful comments) are especially threatening for recipients with a high self-esteem. In one study, self-threatening aid elicited a large degree of subsequent self-help when the recipient's self-esteem was high (DePaulo et al., 1981). In this study subjects received help which was accompanied either by a positive comment ('Good luck on the next task') or by a negative comment ('I guess this [task] is [too] hard for you'). High self-esteem subjects worked especially hard on a difficult task when they had received the negative message instead of the positive one. In general, receiving help is more threatening for persons with high self-esteem than for persons with low self-esteem (Nadler and Mayseless, 1983). In addition, the *willingness to seek help* depends on the self-threat associated with receiving help, and this effect is especially pronounced for high self-esteem individuals (Nadler, 1987). In general, people who might seek help with solving a problem have exaggerated fears because they expect rejection from potential helpers even if such rejections are an exception (Engler and Braun, 1988). Seeking help is more common in reciprocal relationships (such as between friends; Wills, 1992).

These results may be interpreted as a plea for more reciprocity in altruistic relationships, especially with regard to high self-esteem recipients. Altruistic responses which are embedded in a mutual give-and-take may have more desirable effects than one-sided aid which offers no opportunity for repayment. A warning should be added: this plea should not be understood as an argument in favour of the norm of self-sufficiency. Long-lasting discrimination against the underprivileged requires efforts to improve their fate. This includes aid from professional services (e.g., social workers) and from non-professional donors. Professional and non-professional helpers may be equally successful (Wills, 1982).

The most adequate model for altruistic relationships was described by Brickman et al. (1982), who introduced the notion of *responsibility attribution* as a key concept. They distinguished between responsibility for the *cause* of a problem and responsibility for the *solution* to the problem. Their *compensatory model* relieves the person of the responsibility for the origin of his problem but holds the help-recipient responsible for the solution to his problem (cf. chapter 18). According to this model, help-recipients are seen as innocent victims of deprivation who are capable of profiting from temporary aid. After the elimination of the deprivation, recipients are considered to be responsible for their own future and to be competent enough to help themselves (Bierhoff, 1991).

Social support

Social support focuses on giving and receiving help that relationships offer when coping with stressful life events and daily troubles (Morgan, 1990). In general, a distinction between the perceived availability of social support (cognitive social support) and received support (behavioural social support) is drawn (Schwarzer and Leppin, 1992). Three conceptualizations of social support are distinguished by Pierce, Sarason and Sarason (1990): the social-network, or structural approach; the social-support-as-helping, or functional approach; and the general-perception approach. The functional approach is of special importance for research on altruism since it allows for an integration of theories and studies on social support and prosocial behaviour (Bierhoff, 1994).

Does social support protect the individual against the disadvantageous consequences of negative life events? To answer this question with respect to mental health, data on general well-being and negative affects such as depression and sadness are obtained. In general, social support seems to result in a certain amount of protection when stressful life events occur (Cohen and Wills, 1985). In addition, social support exerts a generally positive effect on psychological well-being, which is not confined to stressful life events (Stroebe and Stroebe, 1992). In a meta-analysis of 70 studies on the relation between social support and depression, a moderately high negative correlation of −0.22 was obtained (Schwarzer and Leppin, 1992). Cognitive social support was a stronger predictor of depression than behavioural social support. Further research is needed to clarify the differential effectiveness of cognitive and behavioural social support. In addition, more research is needed on the buffering hypothesis, which states that social support is especially effective when stressful life events occur (see chapter 12).

Social support may have positive as well as negative effects on the recipient (Nadler and Fisher, 1986). For example, it is important that the help given matches the needs of the recipients. In a study on the long-term effects of losing a child or a spouse in a road crash, respondents identified giving advice and encouraging recovery as unhelpful (Lehman, Ellard and Wortman, 1986). In addition, Wortman and Conway (1985) mention several problems that arise in social support relationships: supporters feel insecure about how to implement their help appropriately, they usually have a short-term perspective, and if some kind of negative feedback from the recipient occurs, they may feel a threat to their positive self-esteem.

In general, a perceived reciprocity of the relationship between provider and recipient is less likely to elicit negative responses on the part of the recipient, especially in exchange relationships. Social support could be understood from an exchange perspective since it is exchanged in interpersonal relations (Dunkel-Shetter et al., 1992). In social relationships which are not communal, people keep track of inputs and rewards (Clark and Mills, 1993). In an exchange context, one-sided support might have a negative impact. In contrast, in a communal context high solidarity is congruent with one-sided help and the potential negative consequences of receiving help tend to be minimized.

Summary and Conclusions

Finally, some general statements regarding the most important determinants of altruism in everyday situations are appropriate. What are the factors which presumably exert the largest effects on prosocial behaviour? Such summarizing statements should be considered with caution, but a first sketch of important determinants is useful. A first factor consists of social institutions (family, school, religion, television). For example, the use of supportive socialization practices in the family fosters a prosocial orientation in children. In general, social models who act altruistically contribute heavily to the socialization of altruism in children (Rushton, 1980). In addition, the phenomenon of pluralistic ignorance, which was observed in emergency situations among groups of passive bystanders, is an example of inhibiting influences of social models on observers. Developmental psychologists have accumulated a lot of evidence which indicates that social models (in the family, in the school, on television) exert a strong influence on the socialization and performance of prosocial behaviour.

Secondly, after the elicitation of prosocial norms or mood states that facilitate prosocial behaviour, people consider the pros and cons of available prosocial action alternatives. *Positive consequences* which facilitate prosocial activities include self-esteem enhancement and positive feedback. In addition, *negative consequences* which inhibit prosocial action – especially loss of time, danger and embarrassment – explain a notable amount of variation in altruism.

A third influential factor which seems to be very important in emergency situations is diffusion of responsibility. This factor contributes decisively to the inhibition of intervention in groups of bystanders. Processes of responsibility denial are also involved in defence mechanisms against normative obligations, which can render prosocial behaviour rather unlikely.

A fourth general principle is based on mutual give and take. A person who reciprocates a favour follows a normatively prescribed sequence of behaviour. Therefore, the perceived legitimacy of such behaviour sequences is relatively high and negative implications for the help-recipients (threats to themselves) are avoided.

In addition, individual differences in altruism must be taken into account (Rushton, 1980). In particular, the work on rescuers of Jews and on first-aiders shows that in naturalistic situations individual variations with respect to prosocial orientation make a difference and explain some additional portion of the variance above that explained by situational factors.

Glossary terms

Altruistic behaviour	Evaluation apprehension	Pluralistic ignorance
Diffusion of responsibility	Existential guilt	Reciprocity (norm of)
Empathy	Interpersonal guilt	Social responsibility (norm of)

Discussion points

1 The effects of bad mood on helping are intriguing. Why does it make a difference whether the potential helper is in a bad mood or vicariously takes the perspective of another person who is sad?
2 Is prosocial behaviour motivated by altruistic or egoistic motives? Is it possible to conduct empirical studies which might answer this question?
3 To what extent is it possible to enhance prosocial behaviour by attributional retraining which focuses on the self-concept of the potential helper?
4 How do you explain the fact that altruism is reduced if personal standards of deservingness are violated?

5 In what ways do situational factors increase or decrease prosocial behaviour which is under the control of the norm of social responsibility?

6 Is it possible to reduce the diffusion of responsibility which has often been observed in emergency situations?

7 Why does social support make help-recipients feel under threat in many applied situations? Is it appropriate to emphasize the reciprocity norm in altruistic relationships, especially with regard to help-recipients who express a high self-esteem?

Suggestions for further reading

Batson, C. D. (1991) *The Altruism Question. Toward a social-psychological answer.* Hillsdale, NJ: Lawrence Erlbaum. On the basis of a historical overview of the altruism question the empathy–altruism hypothesis is developed and research is presented which supports the hypothesis.

Eisenberg, N. (1986) *Altruistic Emotion, Cognition, and Behavior.* Hillsdale, NJ: Lawrence Erlbaum. Origin and development of empathy and prosocial moral reasoning are emphasized.

Hunt, M. (1990) *The Compassionate Beast. What science is discovering about the human side of humankind.* New York: Morrow. On the basis of the relevant literature and interviews with a number of distinguished researchers a journalist describes the main topics and controversies of altruism research.

Montada, L. and Bierhoff, H. W. (eds) (1991) *Altruism in Social Systems.* Lewiston, NY: Hogrefe. A collection of empirical studies and theoretical contributions which are written from the social-systems perspective.

Spacapan, S. and Oskamp, S. (eds) (1992) *Helping and Being Helped. Naturalistic studies.* Newbury Park, CA: Sage. A collection of chapters examining altruistic behaviour in everyday life.

Staub, E., Bar-Tal, D., Karylowski, J. and Reykowski, J. (eds) (1984) *Development and Maintenance of Prosocial Behavior: international perspectives on positive morality.* New York: Plenum. Covers psychological approaches to social development and social determinants of prosocial behaviour. In addition, applied research on prosocial behaviour (for example, on blood donation) is included.

Wills, T. A. (ed.) (1982) *Basic Processes in Helping Relationships.* New York: Academic Press. The helping relationship – especially in a therapeutic context – is the focus of this book. The relevance of social-psychological theories for client–clinician interactions is demonstrated.

Key studies

Darley, J. M. and Batson, C. D. (1973). From Jerusalem to Jericho: a study of situational and dispositional variables in helping behavior. *Journal of Personality and Social Psychology*, 27, 100–8.

Latané, B. and Rodin, J. (1969). A lady in distress: inhibiting effects of friends and strangers on bystander intervention. *Journal of Experimental Social Psychology*, 5, 189–202.

14　Aggressive Behaviour

Amélie Mummendey

Contents

Introduction

In 1990 alone there were 2,467 cases of actual or attempted murder or manslaughter in what was then West Germany; this represents four or five victims of extreme violence for every 100,000 inhabitants. The number of victims of serious and dangerous physical injury in the same year was 67,095 – about the number of inhabitants of a medium-sized town. Unfortunately, there is nothing special about West Germany in having such statistics; the figures of other European countries are comparable, and those for the United States even higher. Of course, these figures do not reflect the full spectrum of human aggression; everyday cases of less extreme physical or psychological injury are innumerable, and death or serious injury in the course of war are often not even included in these statistics.

Thankfully, the probability that any of us will be victims or uninvolved witnesses of extreme violence is – at least in Europe – small. But we are daily witnesses of such events, as mediated by the newspapers and, especially, television. The more spectacular the event, the more insistently we ask 'why?' What causes someone to insult, threaten, hit, torture or kill another person? We are particularly interested in the causes, because we hope that by identifying them we may find a means of controlling and reducing aggressive behaviour.

In the course of 75 years of social-psychological research on aggression, different theories have been developed as to its causes. A great number of experiments have been carried out to investigate which factors or conditions increase or limit the extent of human aggression.

In this chapter we first present some of the most influential theoretical attempts to explain aggressive behaviour: aggression as instinct; frustration and aggression; and aggression as learned behaviour. In the third section we consider the main variables that mediate aggression – such as arousal, the social construction of aggression, and norms. In the course of the chapter we will review a selection of empirical research on factors which influence aggression. We will also deal with some of the problems inherent in classical aggression research – problems which in recent years have led to a number of changes in how aggression is both perceived and researched as a social-psychological problem.

Theories of Aggression

Consider the following episode, which takes place in a bar in an unidentified German city but could just as easily have happened in many other European or North American cities. A crowd of young people are there, some sitting at tables, most crushed against the bar. Among them a group of Turkish youths, whose parents came to Germany as migrant workers (*Gastarbeiter*). The bar is cramped, hot and loud. Two young men, Thomas (who is German) and Özal (who is Turkish), get involved in a heated discussion. Suddenly the German springs to his feet, shouts at the Turk and punches him on the chin. The Turkish youth stumbles, smashes his head against the edge of a table and falls to the ground. Blood pours from his mouth.

To what theories can we turn to identify the causes of the young German's aggressive behaviour? We will first look more closely at the major theoretical approaches to aggression; later we will try to analyse the episode from these different theoretical perspectives.

In psychological research on aggression, there are two basic and influential positions: One of them sees aggression as a form of behaviour which is governed by innate instincts or drives; the other sees aggression as a form of behaviour which, like other behaviour, is acquired through individual experience. There is also a third, intermediate position, which integrates the concept of drive and learning – the frustration–aggression hypothesis. We shall deal with each approach in turn.

Aggression as instinct

At the beginning of the twentieth century William McDougall wrote in his *Introduction to Social Psychology* (1908) that the whole spectrum of human behaviour, including hostile and aggressive behaviour, was under the control of 18 different instincts. However, the assumption that behind hostile behaviour lies a hostile **instinct** does not help to explain the occurrence of such behaviour.   INSTINCT
One concept, namely observed behaviour, is simply replaced by another, namely the assumed basic drive. It is for this reason that such simple concepts faded quickly into the background. In the place of instinct, it was psychoanalysis on the one hand and ethology on the other that had the most influence, especially on everyday ideas about the causes of aggression.

The psychoanalytic approach

In the framework of *psychoanalysis* Freud first developed a conception of aggression as a servant of the 'pleasure principle'. Aggression was seen as a reaction to frustration experienced in the pursuit of 'pleasure' or the satisfaction of *libido* (the sexual energy of the 'life instinct'). After 1920, with the publication of *Beyond the Pleasure Principle*, and possibly influenced by his experiences during the First World War, Freud gave up this conception of aggression in favour of a *dual instinct theory*. Alongside the desire for self-preservation (the life instinct, *Eros*), Freud conceived a second instinct (the 'death instinct', *Thanatos*), a tendency towards death and a return to the state of the inorganic. The destructive energy associated with this second instinct must continuously be turned away from the individal, to the outside, in order to prevent self-destruction. Just as sexual energy is used up and tension reduced through sexual activity, Freud assumed that aggressive behaviour diverts destructive energy and also reduces tension. This led to the idea of **catharsis**, which was important for later research: hostile and aggressive tendencies can be expressed in non-destructive ways, such as in biting humour or fantasy, thereby diverting destructive energy and weakening the tendency towards actual aggressive behaviour. Thus Freud viewed the primary function of an instinct as the reduction of a 'tension of needs'. The need for destruction generates tension, which is reduced by aggressive behaviour, but which builds up again during a 'rest period' without aggressive behaviour. Therefore Freud viewed human aggression as inevitable.

This short summary of the orthodox psychoanalytic theory of aggression raises the general problem of how to test these assumptions empirically. Essential concepts such as that of destructive energy are so global and inexact that one can derive no precise predictions or hypotheses that can then be tested. The psychoanalytic approach is really only able to attempt an explanation of events or behaviour that have already taken place. Needs usually have identifiable causes and can be evoked: thus, hunger arises as a need for nutrition following food deprivation. It is doubtful whether, in a similar manner, an individual would experience a greater need for aggression because deprived of the opportunity to aggress against others.

For these reasons, the psychoanalytic instinct theory of aggression has no real influence on contemporary aggression research. However, independent perspectives generated from this theory have led to central concepts in empirical research on aggression. This can be seen in the case of the frustration–aggression hypothesis, which we consider later. First, we deal with an alternative approach to aggression as instinct.

The ethological approach

Some ethological, just like psychoanalytic, approaches postulate the existence of instinctive, aggressive energy. Unlike the psychoanalytic concept of drive, the ethological approach to aggression accords it a species-serving function (Lorenz, 1963; see also chapter 2 of this volume). Aggression is an innate behavioural disposition arising from natural selection; like other dispositions – such as looking after the young – aggression increases the chances of the survival and successful conservation of the species. Aggression ensures that members of the same species do not live too close to each other, but rather, disperse over a wide territory, thus developing greater resources for future generations. Fights between rivals serve to select the strongest and healthiest leaders of the herd. Through within-species aggression, a hierarchy is established within a social unit which places the best individuals in the highest ranks. The following assumptions about the occurrence of aggressive behaviour are made: within each individual there is a potential for behaviour-specific energy (i.e., aggression), which is automatically stored up. The probability and intensity of aggressive behaviour depend on the actual strength of this potential.

For each domain of behaviour there are *fixed action patterns*. These action patterns are fed not through external stimuli but by an internal, central arousal potential, and they are stimulated by this behaviour-specific energy. This stimulation requires an external 'eliciting stimulus', then aggression may build up to a point where it spontaneously 'explodes' without obvious external stimuli (Lorenz, 1963).

These basic assumptions were visualized in the form of a hydraulic model similar to a continuously heated steam boiler: as pressure builds up, so steam must be continuously released. If the safety valve for releasing steam is blocked, pressure buildup is too high and steam escapes spontaneously. Lorenz and Freud agree on the assumption that human aggression is inevitable. However, Lorenz draws rather different conclusions about the possibilities for controlling violence. To avoid the spontaneous explosion of the 'steam boiler' in the form of uncontrolled aggression, he recommends the continual and controlled discharge of small amounts of energy through socially acceptable forms of aggression. Active, or even passive, participation in competitive sports is given as an example of an acceptable form of aggression.

This assumption has been criticized and refuted by many. The familiar scenes of fights between opposing football fans, as well as the results of empirical studies, show that sporting competitions often have the effect of escalating violence rather than controlling or weakening it (see Gabler, Schultz and Weber, 1982). In general, hydraulic models of motivation or behaviour have been rejected as mistaken analogies. Thus Hinde (1960) criticized the way in which psychological or behavioural energy was confused with physical energy; the former is a hypothetical construct, while the latter has characteristics that can actually be investigated. This mistaken analogy gives a totally false impression of the exactness of the model. Unlike the case of physical energy, there is no empirical basis to Lorenz's idea of a spontaneous build-up of aggressive energy.

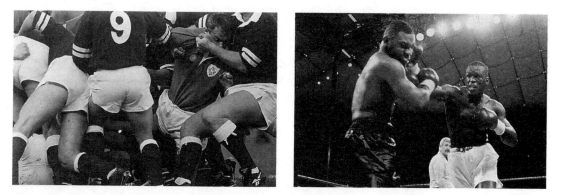

Plate 14.1 Is active, or even passive, participation in competitive sports an acceptable form of aggression?

Let us return to Thomas and Özal, and the question of what caused the aggressive outburst in the bar. If we take aggression as an instinct then we must assume that, at the time of his aggressive act, Thomas had built up a sufficient potential (energy) for aggressive behaviour; Özal functioned simply as a suitable 'eliciting stimulus'. This interpretation might seem plausible at first. But we are left in the dark if we look more closely and ask: why did Thomas become violent in exactly this situation; why was it Özal who elicited the aggression; and why did Thomas show exactly this form of aggressive behaviour?

Frustration and aggression

The frustration–aggression hypothesis

In 1939 five authors, the so-called Yale Group, published a book with the title *Frustration and Aggression*, which initiated experimental research on aggression within social psychology (Dollard et al., 1939). For several decades their **frustration–aggression hypothesis** was the theoretical core of research in this area.

FRUSTRATION–
AGGRESSION
HYPOTHESIS

These authors rejected the concepts of a death instinct and of specific innate instincts as drives towards aggression. They leaned far more on the older ideas of Freud, but also emphasized the formulation of operational concepts and of empirically tested assumptions. Their energy model of aggression assumes that a person is motivated to act aggressively, not by innate factors, but by a drive induced by **frustration**. By frustration they mean the condition which arises when goal attainment is blocked while aggression is an action aimed at harming another organism. These two concepts are linked to the following two statements: frustration always leads to some form of aggression; and aggression is always a consequence of frustration.

FRUSTRATION

Aggression is not always directed towards the cause of frustration. If, for example, a person is physically strong or socially powerful, then this frustrated individual can turn his or her aggression towards another, less dangerous person. The target of aggression can be replaced. One form of reaction can also be replaced by others. Target substitution and response substitution are forms of **displacement** of aggression. This concept, like catharsis, is borrowed from psychoanalysis: aggression, whether directed at the target or displaced, discharges the aggressive energy produced by frustration. Through this catharsis the readiness for aggression disappears.

DISPLACEMENT

Immediately following the publication of the Yale Group's book, the simple hypothesis concerning the causal relationship between frustration and aggression was questioned. Critics argued that frustration did not always lead to aggression, and that other reactions – such as crying, fleeing or apathy – were also observed. In addition, while frustration may lead to aggression, it is not always necessary; aggression often occurs without any preceding frustration. A paid assassin, for example, often carries out his task without knowing his victim, let alone being frustrated by him.

Given these objections, the authors quite soon changed their original assumptions. Frustration was seen only as a stimulus to aggression, which took its place in an individual's hierarchy of possible response tendencies; none the less, aggression was seen as the *dominant* response tendency following frustration (Miller et al., 1941). Thus frustration creates a readiness for aggression, but whether this is expressed in actual behaviour depends on additional conditions.

This question of the specific stimulus conditions that bring about aggressive behaviour leads us to the work of Berkowitz, and his revision of the frustration–aggression hypothesis.

Cue–arousal theory

As an answer to the question of the causes of aggression, it is unsatisfactory to say that frustration *sometimes* does (and therefore sometimes does not) lead to aggression. This 'sometimes' must be incorporated into our theoretical assumptions, and it is exactly this that Berkowitz (1964, 1969, 1974) does. Between the concepts of frustration and aggression he inserts an intervening concept – that of appropriate environmental conditions (or *cues*) for aggression. Frustration does not immediately evoke aggression, but generates in the individual a state of emotional arousal, namely *anger*. This aroused anger generates an inner readiness for aggressive behaviour. But this behaviour will only occur if there are stimulus cues in the situation which have an aggressive meaning: that is, cues which are associated with anger-releasing conditions, or simply with anger itself. Stimuli acquire their quality of being aggressive cues through processes of **classical conditioning**; in principle, any object or person can become an aggressive cue in this way.

CLASSICAL CONDITIONING

Thus an aggressive act has two distinct sources: the aroused anger within the harm-doer, and the cues within the situation. Berkowitz and his colleagues carried out a series of experiments to test these assumptions of **cue–arousal theory** systematically (see Berkowitz, 1974; also Gustafson, 1986, 1989). One experiment in particular aroused considerable interest, generating extensive criticisms and both successful and unsuccessful replications of what has become known as the *weapons effect*.

CUE–AROUSAL THEORY

According to Berkowitz, through experience certain objects become associated with aggression; these objects have a high value as aggressive cues. Weapons, especially revolvers, are a prime example. Revolvers, unlike knives or sticks, are objects which have a clear and limited function. The presence of revolvers, as objects with aggressive meaning, should, then, lead in general to more extreme aggression than the presence of objects with neutral connotations.

Berkowitz and LePage (1967) tested exactly this hypothesis, asking: if weapons function as aggression-arousing cues, do frustrated or angered people show more aggression in the presence of weapons than when they are absent or when only aggression-neutral objects are present? The subjects (male college students) had to perform a task, and had their performance evaluated by an experimental confederate. This evaluation, consisting of a number of electric shocks, was independent of the actual performance, and served the purpose of generating different strengths of aroused anger. As expected, the subjects who received a higher number of shocks reported more anger than those who had only received one shock. In a second phase of the experiment, the recipients of both high levels ('angered' subjects) and low levels ('non-angered' subjects) of shock had to evaluate the performance of the confederate, also by means of giving electric shocks.

At this stage the various experimental conditions were manipulated, in terms of aggression-arousing cues. In one condition, a shotgun and a revolver were placed on a nearby table; the subjects were told that the weapons belonged to the confederate, and that they should pay no attention to them. In this way the weapons were associated with the opponent. In a second condition, the same weapons were visible, but not linked to the opponent (unassociated condition). In a third (control) condition, no objects were present. Finally, an additional control condition was arranged for the angered subjects only. Some badminton rackets – aggression-neutral objects – were placed on a nearby table.

The results are shown in figure 14.1. For non-angered subjects there was no significant effect of the aggressive cues on the number of shocks given to the confederate. For the angered subjects, in contrast, there was a clear effect: angered subjects gave more shocks in the presence than in the absence of weapons; the

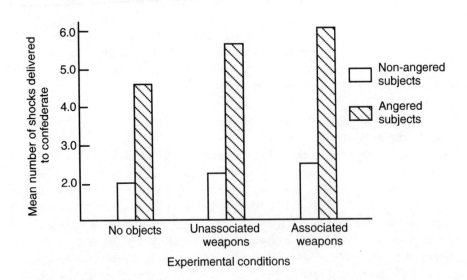

Figure 14.1 The 'weapons effect' (Baron, 1977, p. 165; based on Berkowitz and LePage, 1967)

level of aggressive behaviour was not significantly different in the associated and unassociated weapons conditions. Finally, the angered subjects also gave more shocks in the presence of weapons than in the presence of badminton rackets.

These results support the hypothesis concerning the role of aggression-arousing cues in eliciting aggression. This weapons effect has since been replicated in naturalistic situations (Simons and Turner, 1976), using slides instead of actual weapons (Leyens and Parke, 1975), with knives (Fischer, Kelm and Rose, 1969), and with toy weapons in a study using children (Turner and Goldsmith, 1976).

Nevertheless, a number of experiments have not managed to confirm Berkowitz's assumptions, either finding no weapons effect (e.g. Turner and Simons, 1974), or finding an effect without first arousing anger in the experimental subjects (Fraczek, 1974; Schmidt and Schmidt-Mummendey, 1974). Thus there seems to be a weapons effect in the sense of an aggression-intensifying effect of situational characteristics, but it is questionable whether this effect should be understood in Berkowitz's sense as a classically conditioned cue. One also has to take account of the perceived costs of attacking an opponent – such as punishment from a third party, or the revenge of the victim. According to some critics, the intensifying effect of aggressive cues may be, rather, that they signal to the individual that aggression is an appropriate form of behaviour in that situation (see Page and Scheidt, 1971; for a review, see Carlson, Marcus-Newhall and Miller, 1990).

If we apply the perspective of the frustration–aggression hypothesis, in its broadest sense, to our example of Thomas's aggressive act towards Özal, then our interpretation of what happened in the bar will be somewhat different. Thomas must have been frustrated; we could imagine him getting upset about what Özal said during their discussion, perhaps he felt insulted, and then he reacted to this frustration with aggression. It is also conceivable that Thomas's anger stemmed from something else that happened, but that Özal was the most suitable target for his aggression. Likewise, we might ask about the potentially aggressive cues which transformed Thomas's anger into actual aggressive behaviour. For example, some Germans hold a stereotype of Turks as 'given to violence'. In this way Özal, as a Turk, may have been associated with violence and thus functioned as an aggressive cue for Thomas; or this cue may have signalled the appropriateness of aggression in this situation. But why did Thomas show this particular form of aggression, rather than one of the many imaginable alternatives? How did he acquire his repertoire of behavioural alternatives, and his expectations about which action would be most expedient?

The expected consequences of aggressive behaviour receive attention in the third theoretical perspective on aggression, to which we now turn. This social-learning approach deals in the most detail with the environmental conditions that lead people to acquire and maintain aggressive behaviour.

Aggression as learned behaviour

In the approaches sketched above, aggression is seen as the inevitable and necessary consequence of increased drive or energy, brought about by factors either within the person or in the external environment. A historically more recent view sees aggression rather as a specific form of social behaviour, which is acquired and maintained in the same way as any other form of social behaviour. From the perspective of learning theory, the following questions arise. How does an individual acquire aggressive forms of behaviour? Under what conditions do they become a part of the behavioural repertoire? Which factors determine whether such available forms of behaviour actually occur? Which factors are responsible for the fact that aggressive behaviour is enacted not once but repeatedly, thus becoming habitual?

With regard to the relevant conditions, we have already looked, for example, at eliciting stimuli and the link between frustration and aggression. Now we turn to the question of how aggressive behaviour is acquired and maintained.

Instrumental conditioning

How is aggressive behaviour acquired? Individuals behave in particular ways in order to reach desired goals. If a child really wants that gleaming, bright-red fire-engine standing on the table, then it will go to the table and get it. But the situation becomes complicated if another child is playing with the toy. Somehow this other child must be made to give up the fire-engine. One possibility is direct: simply grab the toy. Different consequences can ensue from this behaviour. If the aggressive behaviour is successful (with the result that it is seen as a useful way of obtaining an attractive object), then the child will use the same means in other, comparable situations. By means of positive reinforcement, the tendency to behave aggressively will be strengthened. Indeed, it has been shown that people acquire different forms of aggressive behaviour through this process of **instrumental conditioning**. Quite different forms of positive reinforcement can be effective in this way: receiving attractive objects like toys, money or sweets (Walters and Brown, 1963); winning social approval or increased status (Geen and Stonner, 1971); and avoiding pain (Patterson, Littman and Bricker, 1967).

INSTRUMENTAL
CONDITIONING

Social modelling

In order to generate rewarding experiences through behaviour, the individual must know not only how to behave in the required way, but also how to use the behaviour in this way. Bandura (1973) proposed that the first step towards acquiring a new form of aggressive behaviour was the process of **modelling**: individuals acquire new and more complex forms of behaviour by observing this behaviour and its consequences in other people – or models. A typical experiment on modelling was carried out by Bandura, Ross and Ross (1961, 1963), in which children observed an adult playing with some toys. This adult showed very

MODELLING

unusual, and for the children quite new, behaviour: he marched into the playroom, hit a large inflated toy (a 'Bobo doll') with a rubber hammer, and then kicked and yelled at it. Children in the control condition saw an adult who played quietly with the toys. In a second phase of the experiment, the model was either rewarded by the experimenter or experienced no positive consequences. Then the children had a chance to play with the same toys. It was found that the children imitated the model's behaviour when they had seen it rewarded. The effect was found whether the model was seen in real life or only observed on video. Further, either a realistic or a comic figure could serve as a model. While many studies with children have emphasized the acquisition of new forms of behaviour (see Bandura, 1977; Baron and Richardson, 1994), similar studies with adults have shown how a model could reduce inhibitions about behaving aggressively in certain situations (Baron, 1971; Epstein, 1966).

Recall our example: Thomas punches Özal in the face. It does not take us long to find models for this sort of behaviour. At least in Western cultures we can hardly avoid seeing such behaviour, if not at first hand then at least through the mass media. It is not only the behaviour of the model that is observed, but the way it is anchored in a social context. The observer learns that in many cases it is exactly these forms of behaviour that have positive consequences.

Violence on television: the impact of mass-media models on aggression

Bandura and his co-workers planned their provocative Bobo-doll studies to test hypotheses about imitation which were derived from social-learning theory. These results seem directly relevant to the important general question: does the presentation of violence on television encourage viewers to act aggressively? However, there are several grounds for caution in generalizing directly from Bandura's studies: the films used were not realistic television films; the measured behaviour had little to do with realistic attacks on other people; and in real life we are unlikely to find the same absolute similarity between the situation observed and the one in which the viewer later acts. For these reasons a great many studies were later conducted which bore a closer resemblance to realistic television viewing (see Comstock and Paik, 1991, for a review).

A series of correlational studies agree that there *is* a positive association between viewing violent television programmes and behaving aggressively (e.g. McCarthy et al., 1975). Of great interest here is the *direction* of this effect. To address this question, a series of three field experiments were carried out in the United States and Belgium (Leyens et al., 1975; Parke et al., 1977). Juvenile offenders were shown exciting films (with or without violence) five nights running in the hostels in which they lived. Trained observers coded the actual amount of violence shown by the boys in the course of a normal day. The boys who had viewed violent films showed more aggressive behaviour than those who had viewed non-violent but still exciting films. In a subsequent laboratory experiment, the same boys were given the opportunity to give electric shocks to

Plate 14.2 Violence on the screen: does it lead to catharsis, or imitation?

an opponent (actually a confederate) who had provoked them. The boys who had viewed violent films also gave more electric shocks than did those who had seen non-violent films.

These findings are corroborated by the results of other field and laboratory studies. For example, Liebert and Baron (1972) showed that boys and girls (aged 5–6 and 8–9) who had previously viewed film extracts with violent scenes gave more severe punishments to a pretend opponent than did children who had viewed a film of an exciting race. These consistent results might give the impression that independent individuals are directly influenced by television. But this conclusion has been criticized by Leyens, Herman and Dunand (1982), who point out that it is not independent but *interdependent* individuals who sit together in front of the television or go to the cinema. Television viewing – like almost all social behaviour – takes place in a social context. Individuals interact with one another, and talk about the films they see or want to see. They can also influence each other to behave aggressively. As a meta-analytic overview of 23 experimental studies shows, aggression seems to increase after the experience of filmed or televised violence (Wood, Wong and Cachere, 1991).

Overwhelmingly, laboratory and field studies show only short-term effects of media violence on viewers' aggressive tendencies (see Huesmann and Miller, 1994; Leyens and Herman, 1979). To learn something about the possible long-term effects of viewing televised violence, longitudinal studies have measured both viewing habits and observed aggression at several points in time. For example, Eron et al. (1972) tested their sample at the age of 8 years and then at the age of 18. The pattern of correlations obtained supported the hypothesis that relatively high aggressivity at the age of 18 was related back to relatively frequent viewing of violent films at the age of 8. Other longitudinal studies, albeit over a shorter period, report similar results (Eron and Huesmann, 1980; Huesmann, Lagerspetz and Eron, 1984; Singer and Singer, 1979). These studies are critically reviewed by Friedrich-Cofer and Huston (1986) and by Freedman (1984, 1988). On the basis of a previous analysis by Hearold (1986), Comstock and Paik (1991) present a meta-analysis of more than a thousand comparisons of the effects of media violence presented in experiments, field studies and longitudinal studies. They conclude that the picture is rather unequivocal: there is a pervasive short-term effect of TV-violence on the behaviour of recipients and, concerning long-term effects, at least significant positive correlations are shown between the amount of TV-violence viewed and the extent of tendencies to behave aggressively. Comstock and Paik summarize the various factors that, according to the studies reviewed, play a role in the effects of TV-violence on aggressive behaviour (pp. 255f). They suggest that these factors can be grouped along four different dimensions. Positive effects of media violence on viewers' aggressive tendencies are more likely if:

(1) *Efficacy* is given: aggression in the media is presented as an efficient instrument through which to achieve one's goals, and/or remains unpunished.

(2) *Normativeness* is given: physical violence or intentionally hurtful actions are shown without also presenting their consequences for the victim, the induced suffering, sorrow or pain. Thus aggression is presented as 'consequenceless' on the victim's part; moreover it is often shown as being justified, for example, if the 'good guys' such as police officers are the perpetrators.

(3) *Pertinence* is given: the perpetrator is portrayed as similar to the viewer, who could imagine herself in the perpetrator's place. Aggression is presented in a realistic manner, rather than as fantasy or fiction-like.

(4) *Susceptibility* is given: the viewer watches the portrayal of violence in a state of emotional excitement such as pleasure or anger and frustration. In any case, the emotional arousal prevents a more distant or critical attitude on the viewer's part.

Frequent viewing of televised violence not only has a direct impact on the viewer's readiness to behave aggressively; it also influences attitudes towards aggression. People who learn from television that conflicts are often violently resolved, and that one aggressive act tends to be followed by another, also overestimate the likelihood that they themselves will be victims of violence, are suspicious of others and demand more state funding and harsher sentences in the fight against crime (Gerbner et al., 1980). As a rule, such attitudes are associated with a conservative outlook. But interestingly, one study showed no difference between liberals and conservatives when they were both 'heavy' consumers of television violence (Gerbner et al., 1980).

A three-year longitudinal study of children in West Germany also showed long-term effects of viewing violence on attitudes towards aggression (Groebel and Krebs, 1983; Krebs, 1981; Krebs and Groebel, 1979). Boys and girls who preferred and watched more violent television, later judged aggressive retaliation more positively.

Summary

The assumptions about the causes of aggressive behaviour postulated by the theories discussed in this chapter can be placed on a continuum from internal to environmental. At one extreme, the instinct theories developed by Freud and Lorenz conceive of aggressive behaviour as motivated by an aggressive instinct. Using hydraulic systems such as the steam boiler as a metaphor, these instinct theories assume that from time to time the individual has to release the aggressive energy continually produced by this instinct and behave aggressively (that is, 'let off steam') in order to avoid damaging consequences for the organism.

Social-learning theory represents the other extreme of the continuum. According to this position, aggressive behaviour, like most forms of behaviour, is learned through instrumental conditioning and/or modelling. It is thus under the control of environmental reward contingencies.

Frustration–aggression theories take an intermediate position. Like instinct theories they conceptualize aggressive behaviour as motivated by a need to release aggressive energy. However, this aggressive energy is not automatically produced by some internal process but results from an environmental event, the frustration of some goal-directed behaviour. Since the original hypothesis that frustration is both a necessary and a sufficient cause of aggression could not be supported empirically, more recent versions of this theory have abandoned this assumption, and attempt to specify the conditions under which frustration leads to aggression.

These theories have important implications for the social control of aggression. While the environmental control of aggressive behaviour should be difficult or even dangerous according to theories that attribute aggression to internal causes such as instincts or drives, learning theory suggests numerous strategies for aggression control.

Mediating Variables in Aggression: from Internal States to Socio-cultural Factors

Research into the factors which mediate aggressive behaviour focused initially on internal states such as aversive arousal or pain. However, although frustration, anger or pain are important elicitors of aggressive behaviour, it soon became obvious that whether individuals responded to such stimuli with aggressive behaviour depended largely on their own *interpretation* of the other person's behaviour. Thus people are more likely to behave aggressively if they interpret a given action as aggressive rather than as unintentional or even benevolent. This discussion of social construction, social interpretation and attribution as modifiers of aggressive behaviour will lead us, finally, into the analysis of the role of social norms in aggression.

The role of arousal in aggression

Aversive arousal and aggression

Let us imagine that someone experiences frustration: perhaps because despite hours of trying he cannot mend his tape-recorder; perhaps because, as a result, his girlfriend teases him publicly about how impractical he is. We would also expect that, as this aroused anger increases, so will the readiness to respond aggressively – perhaps by throwing his tape-recorder at the wall, or insulting his girlfriend.

Thus the experience of negative arousal seems to be an important factor in the readiness to respond aggressively. Alongside frustrations, there are many other experiences which can heighten an individual's level of aversive arousal and increase the probability of aggression. In particular, research has looked at environmental influences on aggression, such as noise, crowding and heat.

Donnerstein and Wilson (1976) planned the following experiment to investigate the influence of noise on aggression. In phase 1, half the male subjects were angered by having some written work negatively evaluated by a confederate (the other subjects had the work judged positively). In phase 2, the subjects had the opportunity to give this same confederate (who had judged their work) electric shocks of varying intensity when she made mistakes in a learning task. The strength of shock delivered served as the measure of aggression. During this phase of the learning task the subjects wore headphones, by means of which slightly or extremely unpleasant levels of noise were transmitted. The results were clear (see figure 14.2). Noise, as an aversive stimulus, only increased aggression when the subjects had previously been angered.

Other experiments supported these findings (Geen and O'Neal, 1969; Konečni, 1975): noise can make people more aggressive, but only when this aggressive behaviour (either through provocation or by watching aggressive models on film) has become the individual's dominant response tendency, that is, when the individual is already prepared to behave aggressively.

Studies on the influence of crowding look, at first sight, less consistent. Correlational studies on the relation between density of housing and violent crime showed negative results (e.g., Altman, 1975). Although there was more violent crime in densely populated than in less crowded residential areas (Scherer, Abeles and Fischer, 1975), this effect disappeared as soon as additional variables

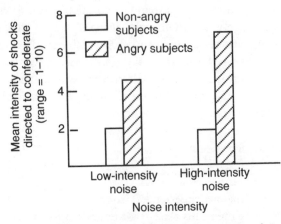

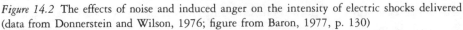

Figure 14.2 The effects of noise and induced anger on the intensity of electric shocks delivered (data from Donnerstein and Wilson, 1976; figure from Baron, 1977, p. 130)

such as income or education were controlled for. Laboratory experiments showed both increased (Freedman et al., 1972) and decreased (Hutt and McGrew, 1967) effects of crowding on the extent of aggressive behaviour. Of great importance here is whether spatial density is subjectively perceived as unpleasant (a crowded underground train) or pleasant (a disco) (see Stokols, 1972). When crowding interferes with what a person wants to do, then it is perceived as unpleasant. In this case aggressive tendencies can be intensified, but so too can the tendency to leave the situation (see Baron and Richardson, 1994; Geen, 1990; Kruse, 1975, for reviews).

Our own experience, as well as expressions like 'the long hot summer', support the assumption that the number and intensity of violent acts, especially in cities, increase as the temperature rises. In order to substantiate this plausible everyday

Plate 14.3 Spatial density (or crowding) may be perceived as unpleasant or pleasant

impression, and to provide systematic evidence about the nature of the temperature–aggression link, a considerable number of investigations, laboratory experiments as well as statistical analyses of archival data, have been conducted (see Anderson, 1989; Baron and Richardson, 1994, for reviews). Archival studies provide statistical data on the frequencies of different kinds of aggressive crimes (such as homicide, rape, and aggravated assault) and the monthly distribution of these crimes, on the one hand, and climatological data (such as number of hot days per year, temperature differences between different geographical regions) on the other. In particular, more recent analyses provide careful control for possible confounding variables such as socio-demographic factors (unemployment, income, education, age, racial composition). Reviewing a considerable range of archival studies, Anderson (1989) feels ready to conclude: 'Clearly, hot temperature produces increases in aggressive motives and tendencies. Hotter regions of the world yield more aggression . . . Hotter years, quarters of years, seasons, months, and days all yield relatively more aggressive behaviors such as murder, rapes, assaults, riots and wife beatings, among others' (p. 93).

People are presumed to be negatively aroused by high temperature. This negative affect leads to aggressive behaviour; as the temperature increases, the intensity of aggressive response increases as well. This assumption relating aggression to heat has been tested directly in a series of experiments. Here too it was proposed that a heat-induced state of arousal would intensify aggressive tendencies if the individual was already prepared to act aggressively owing to previous provocation. Interestingly, Baron and Bell (1975, 1976) found different results in a series of experiments. Contrary to the hypothesis, aggressive behaviour (duration and intensity of electric shocks) actually decreased, as the temperature increased from 20° to 30°C. People who had previously been provoked behaved *less* aggressively under 'heat' conditions, while people who had previously been treated in a friendly manner behaved *more* aggressively. Baron and Bell therefore proposed a curvilinear relation between temperature and aggression (see figure 14.3).

According to Baron and Bell, the influence of temperature on aggression is mediated by the level of negative affect, and not just the general arousal, that a person experiences. For people in a neutral mood, an unpleasant temperature can worsen their mood and increase aggressive tendencies; such people's readiness to behave aggressively is similar to that generated by provocation and its resulting negative affect. If unpleasant temperature brings an additional negative experience to this degree of negative affect, then maximal readiness to respond aggressively will be exceeded. Under these conditions individuals feel so bad that all they want to do is get away. Bell and Baron (1976) tested this idea experimentally. They allocated subjects to experimental conditions that were ordered in terms of aroused negative emotions. This was done using hot and cold temperatures, linked to positive or negative evaluation by a confederate. The data revealed the predicted curvilinear picture; the highest intensity of aggressive

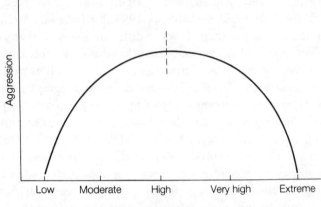

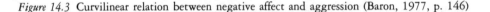

Figure 14.3 Curvilinear relation between negative affect and aggression (Baron, 1977, p. 146)

behaviour was shown by subjects who experienced mild negative affect. In conditions of both extremely positive and extremely negative affect, there was significantly less aggressive behaviour.

Archival studies and experimental studies thus provide an inconsistent picture concerning the relation between uncomfortable temperature and aggression. Is there a simple linear relation, i.e., the greater the heat, the more intense or severe the aggression; or is there an interplay between aggressive and escape tendencies leading to a curvilinear relation between temperature and aggression? Geen (1990) offers a solution. In real-life situations, unlike laboratory ones, people might not see or may not actually have the possibility of escaping, so there, the relation between temperature and aggression appears to be linear.

But, even if we follow the conclusion drawn by Anderson cited above, does this allow us to infer a direct relationship between aggression and uncomfortable temperature? We suggest not. We need to look at the particular aspects of the situation which are associated with high temperature in the environment and which might have directly affected people's behaviour – they may operate as third variables mediating the relation between temperature and aggression. People might have more free time during summer months, they spend more time outdoors – both perpetrators and victims. So it sounds reasonable when Baron and Richardson (1994) as well as Geen (1990) conclude that the relationship between heat and aggression is far more complex; we need to identify specific conditions mediating or moderating the relation between ambient temperature and aggressive behaviour.

Non-specific arousal and excitation transfer

Because provocation, heat and noise are conditions normally experienced as aversive, one would expect them to be perceived as direct sources of increased aversive arousal, which influence readiness for aggression. The extent of general physiological arousal is, however, also influenced by other activities such as physical exertion, sensational news stories, thrillers or erotic films. Can such non-specific sources of arousal complement the arousal experienced from sources which are clearly associated with aggression? Can people, in this way, experience a heightened general level of arousal and, as a result, behave more aggressively?

Influenced by Schachter's (1964) two-factor theory of emotion (see chapter 10), Zillmann (1971, 1979) developed his **excitation-transfer theory**. According to this theory, people can transfer residual arousal produced by one source to a new arousing condition; that is, arousal left over from a previous situation can be added to arousal produced in a new situation. The conditions under which such excitation transfer and, accordingly, increased aggression are found, are clearly of interest.

EXCITATION-TRANSFER THEORY

First of all, a series of experimental results shows that the transfer of residual excitation to a new situation only increases aggression when aggression is the dominant response tendency in the new situation. Thus when an individual is already primed to act aggressively, the transferred residual arousal may increase the likelihood of an aggressive response. In one experiment, Zillmann, Katcher and Milavsky (1972) induced conditions of provocation using a confederate, and arousal by means of physical exertion or no exertion. Subjects had either to pedal on a cycling machine for 2.5 minutes, or to view a series of slides. Subsequently they had the opportunity to give the confederate electric shocks. Consistent with the hypotheses, the additional arousal only increased the level of shocks delivered by subjects who had previously been provoked.

There also seems to be a second factor that influences the conditions under which increased physiological arousal leads to more aggression – namely, how the arousal is interpreted or labelled. If, in response to a disparaging comment or an unjustified accusation, we feel our blood pressure and respiration rate increase and our face blush, we interpret this state of arousal as anger. Arousal *interpreted* as anger increases the probability of an aggressive response. But the same signs of physiological arousal can also be felt in a situation where we are, quite unexpectedly, asked to deliver a short talk in front of a seminar group. Now, the obvious interpretation is embarrassment or fear, and an aggressive response is less likely.

Zillmann, Johnson and Day (1974) created experimental conditions which led subjects to attribute the cause of general arousal either to a neutral or to an aggression-relevant source. It was expected that only in the latter case would the transfer of residual arousal increase aggression. Once again male subjects were provoked by a confederate, and then later had the opportunity to give him different levels of electric shock. Between these two phases, they pedalled a cycling machine for 1.5 minutes to generate an increased state of arousal. In addition, a 6-minute rest period was arranged, which for one group of subjects was before, and for the other group after the cycling exercise. Zillmann, Johnson and Day predicted that in the sequence exertion–rest–reaction, the residual arousal felt in the reaction phase would be interpreted as anger, because the rest period had provided the opportunity to recover after the exercise. In the sequence rest–exertion–reaction, however, the arousal should be traced back to the exertion, and thus no increase in aggression was expected. The results showed exactly this pattern (see figure 14.4). We should here emphasize that there were clear differences in aggressive behaviour, although all subjects were provoked and physically aroused to the same extent.

In answer to the question as to under which conditions general arousal is related to an increase in aggression, we can conclude that such an increase is to be expected when the individual lacks clear information about the causes of arousal. Given clear information, the arousal will be correctly interpreted and will have no effect on the extent or the probability of aggressive behaviour (see Rule and Nesdale, 1976; Tannenbaum and Zillmann, 1975).

Aggression as pain-elicited behaviour

The theoretical position described above sees the relation between arousal and aggression as a *sequence*: different conditions lead to general arousal; depending on its perceived causes, this arousal is then labelled and leads to a specific emotion,

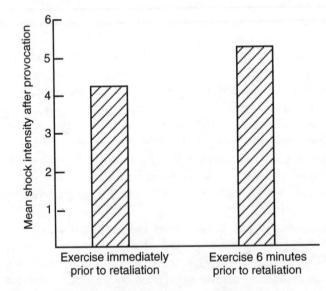

Figure 14.4 Arousal by physical exercise and aggression (based on data from Zillmann, Johnson and Day, 1974)

such as anger. The kind of behaviour that is expected depends, in turn, on the type of emotion.

Berkowitz (1983, 1989, 1990) criticized this view and proposed an alternative theory which he calls the **cognitive–neoassociationistic approach**: there is no such thing as unspecific or neutral arousal. Aversive events have a direct negative effect and lead directly to the instigation to aggression (or to flight); subjective emotional experiences in the form of anger or fear may or may not accompany these forms of behaviour (see figure 14.5). Anger and aggression are, then, *parallel* and not sequential processes: '. . . aversive events produce a negative affect, this affect, regardless of its source, tends automatically to activate both flight tendencies and their associated physiological reactions, expressive-motor responses, thoughts, and memories' (Berkowitz and Heimer, 1989, p. 31).

COGNITIVE–NEO-
ASSOCIATIONISTIC
APPROACH

The more unpleasant the event, the greater the individual's readiness for aggression. Whether aggression is actually shown depends on situational cues. In principle, a diversity of conditions can become aversive events, depending on individual experiences: insults, attacks and provocations are usually seen as unpleasant. *Physical pain* is a prototypical condition for the triggering of negative affect. Berkowitz, Cochran and Embree (1981) allocated subjects either to painful or to pleasant conditions, in which they supervised confederates working on a task and gave them feedback in the form of rewards or punishments. During the study all subjects had to hold their hand in a container of water for 7 minutes, twice in succession. In the painful condition the water was an icy 6°C; in the pleasant condition it was between 18 and 23°C. A second factor, orthogonal to the first, consisted of informing the subjects either that punishment had a positive, helpful influence on performance or that it disturbed and injured the

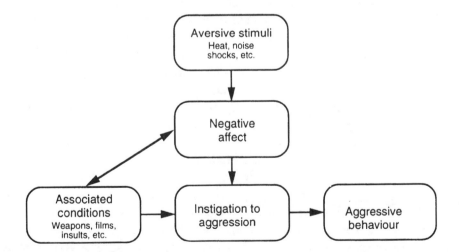

Figure 14.5 A schematic model of Berkowitz's (1992) cognitive–neoassociationist approach (Tedeschi and Felson, 1994)

partner. It was found that, in the painful condition, the subjects made use of the opportunity to treat their partner harshly. But note that the cause of the painful sensation, and thus the negative affect, had nothing to do with the person who became a target for aggression.

If we now try to apply what we have learned to the example involving Thomas and Özal, we come to the following conclusion: Thomas was probably in a state of aversive arousal, he felt angry. The surroundings of the bar – crowded, hot and noisy – probably further heightened his arousal. Thomas saw Özal's behaviour in the course of their discussion as the cause of his anger. Very probably, Özal was not the first person whom Thomas had punched on the chin. Indeed, Thomas had probably learned to react in this way.

The social construction of aggression

Frustration, anger, aggressive cues and experience with aggressive models, whether direct or channelled through the media, are clearly important conditions for the occurrence of aggressive behaviour. In our considerations thus far we have implicitly assumed a definition of aggression which without doubt defines as aggressive both Thomas's behaviour and that brought about in experiments such as those involving the delivery of painful electric shocks. Let us compare this implicit definition of aggression with the one suggested by Baron (1977) and again by Baron and Richardson (1994): 'Aggression is any form of behaviour directed toward the goal of harming or injuring another living being who is motivated to avoid such treatment' (1977, p. 7; 1994, p. 7). From what we know, Thomas's behaviour satisfies these implied criteria, namely, intention to harm and (potential) injury to the victim. At issue here is not the kind of behaviour in itself. Almost every behaviour, even a failure to act (as in the case of giving help), can become aggression if someone judges that the actor intended to harm the victim. Conversely, even cases of extreme brutality need not be identified as aggression: if asked, Thomas would describe his behaviour as necessary self-defence because he felt threatened by Özal. More extremely still, members of institutions that torture other people describe their cruelty not as aggression but as necessary means for the defence of their system and its values.

When we appraise a behaviour as aggressive, we go beyond a simple description to make an evaluation: the behaviour is bad and inappropriate, and it violates a norm; the perpetrator deserves to be punished for it. Being judged by an observer or even by a participant has, then, social consequences; if a form of behaviour is judged to be aggressive, a negative sanction seems appropriate. If the same behaviour is judged to be morally justified, positive sanctions are even possible. Clearly, when asking about the causes of aggression, more is of interest than simply the conditions for the occurrence of that behaviour. Of even greater importance are the conditions for judging individual behaviour as 'aggressive'.

The interpretation of individual behaviour as aggressive

Blumenthal et al. (1972) carried out a large-scale study of American men's attitudes to different forms of violence. The results show clear differences between social groups. Students with negative attitudes towards the police judged police behaviour during student demonstrations (e.g., assaults on students) to be violent; but the behaviour of positively perceived student demonstrators (e.g., 'sit-ins') was judged non-violent. Conversely, for people with positive attitudes to the police, the behaviour of student demonstrators was negatively evaluated: for them, sit-ins were violent acts deserving arrest, and they supported the use of firearms by the police against demonstrators who damaged property. These authors conclude that the same behaviour can be seen as necessary and good, or as abhorrent and punishable, depending on whether the precipitating action is seen as legitimate or illegitimate.

Alongside large-scale studies, many experiments have also been carried out to investigate the influence of various criteria on whether a behaviour is judged to be aggressive. These studies conclude that *intention to harm*, *actual harm* and *norm violation* are the main criteria for labelling an act as aggressive (Ferguson and Rule, 1983; Löschper et al. 1984).

If we agree that aggression is an interpretative construct rather than a descriptive one, then looking for the factors influencing or determining the interpretation becomes interesting. What are the conditions for the perceiver to judge that an action is 'aggressive'? First, the particular social-normative context embedding the critical action will be of importance. Depending upon the context-specific validity of norms, a particular behaviour may be norm-violating or not. Secondly, attribution theory (especially Jones and Davis's, 1965, theory of correspondent inferences) provides a viable line of thinking about what leads people to infer intent from action performed by another person (see chapter 7). Thirdly, this attributional perspective, specific to the key positions in an aggressive interaction (i.e., actor and recipient, harm-doer and victim or outside observer), may play an important role in determining the interpretation and evaluation of a critical action. Several studies performed by Mummendey, Linneweber and Löschper (1984a, 1984b; and also Felson, 1984) clearly show a perspective-specific divergence: actors evaluate their own actions far more positively than recipients (and observers) do (see figure 14.6). This divergence occurs irrespective of whether the actor initiated the interaction sequence or only reacted to behaviour by the opponent. In a further study, Mummendey and Otten (1989) demonstrated that this divergence was not due to perspective-specific differences in the perception or segmentation of the interaction sequence, but was clearly produced by a disagreement in evaluating own versus other's actions. Recent studies performed by Mikula that were concerned with determinants of everyday experience of injustice showed similar effects. Looking at descriptions and evaluations given by both partners in close relationships, about a joint event

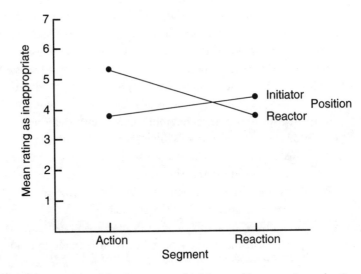

Figure 14.6 Perspective-specific divergence of initiator and reactor in evaluating an aggressive action (Mummendey, Linneweber and Löschper, 1984)

of injustice, the perspective-specific differences in evaluating own versus other's actions became obvious (Mikula, 1994).

Social influence and coercive power

Aggression is, then, as we have seen, not purely a descriptive but also an evaluative concept. It involves subjective judgements about the actor's intentions and whether the behaviour is normatively appropriate. Tedeschi and co-workers suggested that aggression should be analysed by separating behaviour from evaluation. When viewed in an evaluatively neutral manner, aggressive behaviour involves a special form of social influence: an individual coerces another person to do something which that person would not have done without that coercion.

COERCIVE
POWER

Aggression thus consists of the application of **coercive power**, whether in the form of threat or of punishment. By means of threat, we make clear that we want something special from someone, and that punishment will follow non-compliance. A punishment is any form of treatment that is aversive for the victim. The interesting research question is to define the conditions under which people seek to use this coercive form of influence.

SOCIAL
INTER-
ACTIONIST
THEORY OF
COERCIVE
ACTION

Tedeschi and Felson (1994) have developed a **social interactionist theory of coercive action** in order to clarify this problem. On the basis of concepts of rational choice theory they postulate that the performance of a coercive action has to be seen as resulting from a decision process: the actor, before using a threat or a punishment, will have examined alternative means to achieve the relevant goals. Three major goals can be differentiated by which the choice of coercion is motivated: (a) to control others, (b) to restore justice, and (c) to assert or protect identities. The actor decides whether to choose a coercive or a non-coercive alternative. If coercion, then which kind and which intensity, and finally, at what moment in social interaction? The decision to coerce or not, is influenced by the *expectancy* (how likely it is that the particular goal will be achieved by this means), the *value* attached to the respective goal, and the estimation of *utilities* and *costs* associated with the behavioural alternatives. Above all, the performance of a coercive action is preceded or guided by a rational process. Rationality may vary with respect to the amount of elaboration and extension of thought; it may be strong or weak, especially if the situation is rather emotional, or if quick decisions have to be made. But rational decision is the fundamental principle. According to the three different goals which are pursued by coercion, the outcomes of coercive actions gain different values. If the goal is to achieve some positive resource, compliance by the target might be the intended outcome; if, however, the goal is to restore justice or to restore identity, the goal might be to harm or injure the target (see figure 14.7). There may be cases of actions serving several goals at the same time. This would lead to an increase in the tendency to choose a particular action alternative.

In this sense, Thomas's behaviour towards Özal could be described as the subjectively optimum alternative in order to achieve situationally relevant goals, possibly protection of his own identity as strong, powerful and dominant, against a foreigner, possibly restoration of justice, or possibly both. The question of

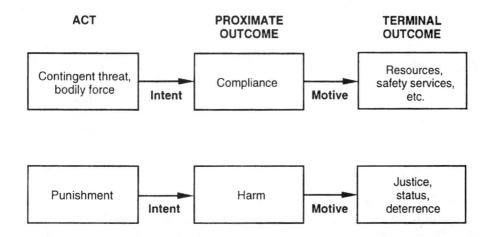

Figure14.7 The components of coercive actions (Tedeschi and Felson, 1994)

whether this form of coercive action is evaluated as *aggression* is quite independent of this description. This question has less to do with the conditions for the occurrence of the behaviour, than with the conditions under which certain behaviours are consensually *interpreted* as 'aggressive'. As we have seen, exactly the same behaviour is labelled as aggressive when perceived as illegitimate and as violating norms; but as non-aggressive when there is no norm violation.

Attribution and aggression

Actions in themselves do not contain the defining criteria mentioned above – intention to harm, actual harm and norm violation – but are actively constructed in these terms. That does not mean, however, that these perceptions happen by chance. On the contrary, everyday interactions are regulated by an impressive social consensus. Herein lies an important task for social psychology, namely to discover the cognitive and normative factors that influence interpretation and evaluation. Thus Rule and Ferguson (1984) ask about the conditions under which people react to aversive events *as if* they were aggressive ones. In other words, we are talking about the nature and process of causal attributions for aversive events (see chapter 7), and their influence on emotional and behavioural reactions. Rule and Ferguson highlight two aspects of these causal attributions. First, there are the factors that determine who, or what, is perceived as *responsible* for an aversive event. Secondly, there are the determinants of an *is–ought* discrepancy with respect to the behaviour in question; that is, a perceived discrepancy between what the actor actually did, and what he should have done in a given situation. In our example, we would perceive a large is–ought discrepancy if Thomas had punched Özal for no reason, such as, in the absence of a previous insult. The discrepancy would be smaller if the action had been a *reaction* to a verbal provocation; and there would be almost no discrepancy if Thomas had merely replied with a verbal insult instead of a punch.

The is–ought discrepancy is, then, particularly important when the actor is held responsible for having caused the aversive consequences. To attribute responsibility, we must decide whether the aversive consequences were *intended* or not; if unintended, the perceiver must decide whether the consequences were, for the actor at least, *foreseeable* or not. If the consequences were intended, the perceiver must decide whether the actor's motives were malevolent or not. Depending on this decision process, the perceiver classifies the aversive consequences as accidental, or foreseeable, and as arising from either malevolent or well-meaning motives. The more aversive the consequences, and the greater the is–ought discrepancy perceived by a victim or an observer, the more angry and revengeful she will be. The results of various studies based on self-descriptions indicate that people become angry when they feel that they are victims of wilful and/or unjustified aversive actions performed by others (Averill, 1982; Mikula, 1994; Torestad, 1990), and that, if this is the case, they retaliate more severely (Ohbuchi and Kambara, 1985).

Norms as regulators of aggression

Perceived injustice and the norm of reciprocity

Parents typically tell their children that they should not hit, scratch or kick other children, and that if found behaving in these ways, they will be punished. But if their little son comes home in tears, claiming that someone took away his bike, or kicked him, the same parents typically tell him to stand up for himself: 'If someone kicks you, then kick them back!' A high percentage of voters throughout the world ardently support the death penalty: someone who kills, or tries to kill, another person deserves to die. Gouldner (1960) proposed that the *norm of reciprocity* ('tit for tat') is a socially shared prescription that operates in many different societies. If someone thinks they are a victim of aggression, then, following the reciprocity norm, they can feel justified in retaliation, seeing it as just and appropriate.

Experimental studies support this observation. When students watch actors on the stage, the initiator of a hostile act is perceived as aggressive, offending and behaving unfairly. An actor who physically attacks another in response to provocation is, however, judged to be acting defensively and fairly (Brown and Tedeschi, 1976).

As we have seen, certain information increases the probability that an action will be labelled as aggressive and that, as a consequence, the violence will be reciprocated or escalated. In the same way, information that weakens the attribution of responsibility or the perception of norm violation can have exactly the opposite effect on the unfolding of an interaction: the perpetrator is judged less negatively, and the tendency to retaliate is weaker (Ohbuchi, Kameda and Agarie, 1989). We might learn, for example, that Thomas had drunk too much alcohol, that he was tired or under stress; in other words, he was not fully in control of his actions, and he neither desired nor could have foreseen the consequences of his behaviour. Such additional information can be used to *excuse* the actor. Another possibility is that the consequences of behaviour might be re-evaluated, the act being seen as justified, appropriate, unavoidable or even necessary: 'Finally, Thomas showed Özal what for! That's the way to treat people like him.' These kinds of accounts are classified as *justifications* (Tedeschi, Lindskold and Rosenfeld, 1985; and see Schönbach, 1985, for an alternative classification of accounts).

This information can be used deliberately, as an *account*, to influence another person or the public in how they interpret an event. Or it might be available for witnesses to the event to choose from. In either case, the information affects how the behaviour is evaluated, and seems to reduce both the anger felt by the victim, and the tendency to retaliate (Rule, Dyck and Nesdale, 1978; Zumkley, 1981).

Zillmann and Cantor (1976) reported that excuses given *before* a provocation, prevented anger from being aroused and reduced the tendency to retaliate against the provoking other. When excuses were given *after* the provocation, the victim also expressed less anger than when no mitigating information was offered, but the tendency to take revenge was not reduced (see also Johnson and Rule, 1986; Zillmann, 1988).

The role of norms in intergroup aggression and collective violence

The scene is what at that time was West Berlin. About 30 young people – including youths, students and former tenants – have occupied a large, still-habitable house to prevent its demolition. The police, having in vain asked the squatters to leave the house, are preparing to evict them. The police break down doors, storm into the flats and try to drag the occupants out of the building. The squatters throw stones and set about the police; sympathizers in the street set cars alight, tear up the cobblestones and build barricades to prevent police reinforcements from getting through.

COLLECTIVE
VIOLENCE

The people involved in this **collective violence** are behaving in ways which, as individuals, they would probably never dream of doing. Experimental studies confirm the impression gained from everyday observations: individuals in groups

Plate 14.4 People involved in collective violence sometimes behave in ways which, as individuals, they would probably never dream of doing

show much more aggressive behaviour than they do when acting as individuals (Jaffe and Yinon, 1983; Mullen, 1986). The group situation seems to produce more explosive outbursts, while those involved are prepared to accept worse consequences for themselves. In the tradition of early mass psychology, associated with LeBon, Tarde and Sighele, this group influence was analysed as follows: individuals in groups or masses behave more irrationally, more impulsively and less normatively than they do as individuals (see chapters 1 and 17). A modern version of this perspective is found in work on **deindividuation** (Diener, 1980; Zimbardo, 1969). Deindividuation refers to a special individual state in which control over one's own behaviour is weakened, and there is less concern about normative standards, self-presentation and the later consequences of one's behaviour. Various factors contribute towards deindividuation, such as anonymity, diffusion of responsibility, the presence of a group, and a shortened time perspective. When individuals become deindividuated – and this may be produced by a group situation – then it is predicted that the usual inhibitions will be lowered, and impulsive behaviour, such as violence or vandalism, becomes possible.

DEINDIVIDUATION

However, empirical findings do not give unconditional support to these assumptions. Thus, anonymity may increase (Donnerstein et al., 1972), reduce (Baron, 1970), or have no effect on (Lange, 1971) the aggression. In general, however, there is support for the idea that being in a group or crowd has a deindividuating effect on individuals, and that such individuals are less conscious of their identity, less attentive to their personal norms and internal thoughts, losing their usual inhibitions about aggressive behaviour (Prentice-Dunn and Rogers, 1983, 1989; Spivey and Prentice-Dunn, 1990).

In opposition to the basic assumptions of deindividuation theory stands *emergent-norm theory* (Turner and Killian, 1972). According to this view, conspicuously extreme forms of behaviour are more likely in group or crowd situations, *not* because individuals lose their inhibitions or care less about norms, but because new norms arise in groups, which are adhered to by all concerned and are shared in specific situations. In situations of confrontation between the police and demonstrators, norms may develop that people should defend themselves against the police. Aggressive forms of behaviour such as stone-throwing become possible not because individuals conform *less* to norms, but, on the contrary, because they conform *more* to norms in this situation. Thus, in group or crowd situations it is not necessarily the extent of normative control that changes but rather *the norms themselves*, to which behaviour is oriented. If the function of anonymity is to weaken the pressure to conform to norms, then from emergent-norm theory one should predict the following: under conditions of anonymity, aggressive behaviour in a group situation should be weakened *if* the situational norms demand aggression. Behaviour that conforms to norms, in this case aggressive behaviour, would be most likely *not* when individuals were anonymous but when they were identifiable and could be called to account for norm violations (see Reicher, 1982).

Mann, Newton and Innes (1982) designed a study to decide between the competing approaches of deindividuation and emergent norms. Their results supported both theories: anonymous subjects were more aggressive, but especially when aggressive behaviour was normative, and less so when it was normatively inappropriate. Rabbie, Lodewijkx and Broeze (1985) clarified the picture a little further: their male subjects behaved more aggressively under conditions of anonymity, while female subjects were more aggressive when identifiable.

Alongside anonymity, deindividuation is also promoted by the presence of others or a group; thus more, or more intense, aggression is expected in groups than in individual situations. However, here too the experimental findings are not clear-cut (Rabbie, 1982; Rabbie and Horowitz, 1982; Rabbie and Lodewijkx, 1983). It depends on which norms are dominant within the group. In particular, group members clearly react more extremely towards an opponent than they would as individuals. Studies by Rabbie and colleagues support this *norm-enhancement hypothesis*: groups behave more aggressively than individuals when such behaviour can be defined as legitimate and normatively appropriate.

In group situations, individuals are provided with information about the appropriateness and legitimacy of possible forms of behaviour. Thus, aggressive interactions seem, in both interpersonal and intergroup contexts, to be guided by the same principles. It is just not convincing to explain observable differences in interpersonal and intergroup aggression in terms of inner states and loss of rationality. In both individual and group situations, actors seem to see their own behaviour as quite appropriate. If more extreme forms of aggression characterize group situations, then this seems to be due to the fact that group members mutually reinforce each other in the view that they are all behaving appropriately (Mummendey and Otten, 1993).

Summary and Conclusions

At the beginning of this chapter we asked: what can cause a person to insult, hurt or even kill another person? Why is it that people will treat others in ways that they would certainly never wish to be treated themselves?

We have looked at a number of theoretical approaches and a variety of empirical findings in the field of aggression. We can summarize the picture as follows: aggressive behaviour can be learned through instrumental conditioning or modelling. The readiness actually to use this behaviour arises when it is seen as a useful means to an end – terminating a situation which is physically or psychologically aversive, and for which another person is held responsible. Under these conditions, there is a good deal of evidence that the use of aggressive means is socially acceptable and normatively appropriate – provided that the aggression takes the form of reciprocal retaliation or reaction.

We have also seen that the same behaviour may or may not be judged aggressive, depending on relevant norms and on how the aggressive behaviour is attributed. The same behaviour can also be judged from different *perspectives*. In particular, there are clear differences in the evaluation of identical behaviour from the perspective of harm-doer and of victim.

Aggressive behaviour, whether between individuals or groups, is – like other forms of social behaviour – regulated by socially accepted and situationally relevant norms. In looking for the cause of aggression, therefore, we should not concentrate on the conditions that energize individual drives or reduce the rational control of behaviour. Rather, we should look for the conditions (at least from the actor's point of view) which make intentionally harming another person seem both situationally appropriate and justified.

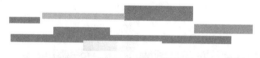

Glossary terms

Catharsis
Classical conditioning
Coercive power
Cognitive–neoassociationistic
   approach
Collective violence
Cue–arousal theory

Deindividuation
Displacement
Excitation-transfer theory
Frustration
Frustration–aggression
   hypothesis

Instinct
Instrumental conditioning
Modelling
Social interactionist theory of
   coercive action

Discussion points

1 Discuss the explanatory function of classical conditioning for the theoretical analysis of aggression.
2 Is catharsis a useful concept with which to analyse and explain effects of media violence on the likelihood of aggression?
3 'Clearly, hot temperature produces increases in aggressive motives and tendencies' (Anderson, 1989, p. 93). Discuss and evaluate this statement.
4 In what ways do attributional processes influence aggressive tendencies and actions?
5 Discuss the function of anger emotions as conceptualized in Berkowitz's versus Zillmann's approach.
6 Discuss the relation between aggression and coercive action.
7 'Collective aggression is irrational, impulsive and lacks normative concerns.' Discuss this statement in the context of current theoretical positions.

Suggestions for further reading

Averill, J. R. (1982) *Anger and Aggression: An essay on emotion.* New York: Springer. Detailed, high-level approach to the social construction of anger.

Baron, R. A. and Richardson, D. R. (1994) *Human Aggression*, 2nd edn. New York: Plenum. Readable, wide-ranging introductory overview.

Berkowitz, L. (1993) *Aggression: Its causes, consequences, and control.* New York: McGraw-Hill. Comprehensive synopsis of the psychology of aggression, with main focus on the author's cognitive–neoassociationistic approach.

Felson, R. B. and Tedeschi, J. T. (eds) (1993) *Aggression and Violence. Social interactionist perspectives.* Washington, DC: American Psychological Association. Collection of chapters representing current areas of aggression research in psychology and also sociology which all share a social-interactionist perspective on the topic.

Geen, R. G. and Donnerstein, E. I. (eds) (1983) *Aggression: Theoretical and empirical reviews.* New York: Academic Press. A two-volume work presenting the most important theories of aggression, as well as empirical research, at an advanced level.

Staub, E. (1989) *The Roots of Evil. The origins of genocide and other group violence.* Cambridge: Cambridge University Press. Characterization of conditions and processes underlying various forms of mass violence (e.g., mass murder and genocide).

Tedeschi, J. T. and Felson, R. B. (1995) *Aggression and Coercive Actions: A social interactionist perspective.* Washington, DC: American Psychological Association. A comprehensive monograph on the current state of psychological research on aggression, a critical review of influential theoretical approaches and an outline of a new social-interactionist perspective on aggression and violence.

Key studies

Berkowitz, L. and LePage, A. (1967). Weapons as aggression-eliciting stimuli. *Journal of Personality and Social Psychology*, 7, 202–7,

Zillmann, D., Johnson, R. C. and Day, K. D. (1974). Attribution of apparent arousal and proficiency of recovery from sympathetic activation affecting excitation transfer to aggressive behavior. *Journal of Experimental Social Psychology*, 10, 503–15.

PART IV
Social Groups

Contents

15   Group Performance

Henk Wilke and Ad Van Knippenberg

Contents

Introduction

A large portion of student life is spent in groups. Participation in courses, workgroups and tutorials involves group activities. Group activities also play a large role in other stages of life. Most of us are brought up in families; classroom and club experiences are very often coloured by interaction with other people. Having a profession quite often implies working with others. For these groups the common denominator is interaction and this interaction is assumed to give rise to certain outcomes for each of the group members. In their turn these outcomes motivate people to join and to stay within a group.

Several kinds of outcomes may be distinguished. Take a workgroup, for example. One may want to join a workgroup because one's friend is already a member of it, – that is, outcomes derived from interpersonal attraction are involved. Another good reason for joining or remaining within a workgroup is that the aims of the group coincide largely with one's personal aims – that is, group performance benefits individual group members. This is the case when interaction within the workgroup helps someone to pass his or her final examination. Also, interaction as a process may be perceived as rewarding in itself. These outcomes are involved if one wants to get to know other people or if one enjoys interacting with other people. Lastly, external outcomes may also be at stake. For example, a student may join a specific workgroup because being a member of it enhances one's status on the campus or because this membership makes a good impression on the teaching staff.

Thus, we may be attracted towards a group for several reasons: because of the people who are in it; because the group task is important to us; because we like interacting; and because an external agent rewards us. Needless to say, these reasons may act in combination. In this chapter we primarily focus on the task performance of individuals and groups. However, as we shall see, performance also brings incidental outcomes that may be provided by other participants or which may be experienced during the process itself, such as satisfaction.

Determinants of Productivity

What determines the actual performance of an individual or group? Consider the following problem.

> A man bought a horse for $60 and sold it for $70. Then he bought it back for $80 and again sold it for $90. How much money did he make in the business?

According to Steiner (1972) the way in which an individual or a group performs a task depends primarily on two elements, namely task demands and human resources. In this section we will turn to these two elements and indicate how they are related to potential and actual performance.

Task demands are the resources required to perform a task. In order to solve the horse-trading problem one has to split the problem into two negotiations, namely one in which $70 is compared with $60 and another one in which $90 is compared with $80. One has to realize that in both instances a gain of $10 is made and that the gains add up to $20.

Human resources include all relevant knowledge, abilities, skills or tools possessed by the individual or group attempting to solve the problem. In the case of the horse-trading problem, the individual or group may or may not possess the needed analytical and computational resources to meet the demands of the task. Thus, task demands specify the kinds and amounts of resources that are needed, whereas the human resources specify whether the individual or the group possesses these resources.

Potential productivity of an individual or a group refers to the extent to which the available human resources suffice to meet the task demands. When an individual or group potentially possesses all the necessary skills to solve the horse-trading problem, then this individual or group has a greater potential productivity than a group or an individual lacking some of the human resources to meet the task demands.

Actual productivity. Suppose we have an individual with high potential productivity, because she possesses the necessary human resources to meet the task requirements. Does this guarantee a high actual performance? From everyday life we may observe that a high potential productivity may not always be attained. In our example, an individual may be able to distinguish between the two negotiations. However, the positions of seller and buyer may be mistaken: thus one may end up with a wrong answer; one might make some unexpected computational errors; or one might make the right computations but nervously write down a wrong answer. In these cases actual productivity (actual performance) fails to equal potential productivity: one possesses the human resources needed to perform the task, but something in the *process*, consisting of the actual steps taken by an individual when confronted with the task, may go wrong.

The above reasoning suggests the following relation between actual performance, potential performance, and process losses (see also Steiner, 1972):

$$\text{actual performance} = \text{potential performance} - \text{process losses}$$

Not only intrapersonal but also interpersonal processes may affect actual performance and may keep a group below its potential performance. Thomas and Fink (1961) allowed college students one minute to solve the horse-trading problem. Thereafter they formed groups of two to five members and asked them to discuss the same problem, and it was explicitly stated that this discussion did not have to lead to consensus. In spite of these instructions the results indicated that most groups actually reached consensus. When, in one of these groups, the majority of its members initially had the wrong solution, the final consensus tended to be incorrect, suggesting that consensus involved a process loss for groups having a majority of participants who had initially failed to achieve the right solution.

A main weakness of consensus is that it tends to neglect minority opinions (see chapter 16). Research done by Maier and Solem (1952) demonstrates how this process loss may be overcome. In their research, subjects individually had to come to a solution for the horse-trading problem. Thereafter they were randomly allocated to groups. In half of these groups procedural instructions to a leader were given: the leader had to refrain from expressing his or her own judgement, and his or her function was merely to monitor the discussion time. In the other half of the groups the leader was instructed to stimulate active participation of all members. It appeared that incorrect group solutions did occur more frequently in *procedural* leadership groups than in *participatory* leadership groups, suggesting that, by encouragement of uniform participation, process losses may be avoided. When procedural instructions were given, single individuals who had already achieved the correct solution were sometimes persuaded to accept the wrong solution, in other words, a process loss occurred.

This chapter deals with a class of phenomena having to do with *group performance* in a broad sense. We start out with the problem of the effect of the presence of others on individual task performance. Next we discuss group productivity of small interacting groups. Finally, the relatively more complex problems of the development of group structure and the effects of variations in group structure on task performance will be analysed.

Task Performance in the Presence of Others

How the presence of others affects an individual's task performance was one of the earliest research interests in social psychology. As early as 1898 Triplett observed that cyclists rode faster when racing together than when racing alone. In the years that followed, numerous experiments were carried out in which the effect of the presence of others was investigated on a wide variety of tasks. Some studies showed performance improvement as a result of the presence of others, that is, **social facilitation**; others showed performance impairment, that is **social inhibition**. Probably because of a lack of theoretical progress, the interest in *social facilitation and inhibition* (SFI) research suddenly dropped in the late 1930s. The issue was neglected until Zajonc (1965) published an article which represented a major theoretical breakthrough in understanding social facilitation and inhibition phenomena. Zajonc's work inspired social psychologists to resume the study of the effects of the presence of others on task performance, and since

SOCIAL
FACILITATION

SOCIAL
INHIBITION

then social facilitation and inhibition has constituted a lively research area in social psychology once again.

Early social facilitation and inhibition studies

SFI has traditionally been studied in two broad categories of social situations: audience presence and co-action. The first type of study deals with the question of how the *presence* of a passive audience influences individual performance. Co-action studies focus on the question of how the presence of someone else performing the same task affects an individual's task performance. In both research areas, the results seemed contradictory. For instance, Travis (1925) found that, when working in front of an audience compared with working alone, well-trained subjects clearly improved their performance on a pursuit-rotor task measuring eye-hand co-ordination. An opposite audience effect was shown by Pessin (1933). He found that subjects needed fewer trials to learn a list of nonsense syllables when practising alone than when facing an audience. When, however, subjects were later asked to recall the list of syllables, their performance was better with than without an audience. Similar patterns of results were found in co-action studies. Sometimes co-action seemed to facilitate performance (e.g. Triplett, 1898), particularly the quantitative aspects of performance, while in other studies the quality of performance was impaired in co-action settings (e.g. Gates and Allee, 1933).

CO-ACTION

Zajonc's explanation of ambiguous SFI results

In his classic article, Zajonc (1965) noted a distinct regularity in SFI research which had been only tacitly understood so far. Furthermore, Zajonc proposed a set of ideas which could account for the observed results.

Zajonc suggested that the presence of others led to improved performance (social facilitation) if subjects were working on easy, well-learned tasks. However, the presence of others led to impaired performance (social inhibition) when subjects were engaged in difficult tasks which were not (yet) well learned. This simple distinction between easy and difficult tasks could account for many seemingly conflicting results of audience as well as of co-action studies. It explains, for instance, the results of Triplett (1898), Travis (1925), Pessin (1933) and Gates and Allee (1933) mentioned above.

Zajonc not only observed these regularities but also proposed a theoretical explanation. His crucial suggestion is that audiences enhance the emission of dominant responses. **A dominant response** is described as the response which prevails, that is, which takes precedence in a subject's response repertoire in a given stimulus situation. In easy tasks, Zajonc argues, the correct responses are

DOMINANT
RESPONSE

dominant, and therefore audiences facilitate performance on easy tasks, such as pedalling a bicycle. However, in complex tasks (like reasoning or learning) the wrong answers tend to be dominant, and therefore audiences give rise to performance deterioration on such difficult tasks.

Why do audiences elicit dominant responses? According to Zajonc, audiences create arousal in subjects, that is, they enhance their general drive level or activation level. In Zajonc's view, the mere physical presence of others suffices to induce arousal in the subjects. As an innate response, some sort of preparedness results from the presence of others and leads to a readiness to respond to whatever unexpected action the other might undertake (Zajonc, 1980b). Furthermore, according to Zajonc, enhanced drive or arousal leads to an increased emission of dominant responses, a notion Zajonc derives from Hull–Spence drive theory (see Spence, 1956; Zajonc and Nieuwenhuysen, 1964).

In figure 15.1 (panel a), Zajonc's explanation of SFI phenomena is presented schematically. According to Zajonc, the presence of others (conspecifics) leads to an increased arousal or drive level which, in turn, elicits an enhanced emission of dominant responses. Since dominant responses tend to be correct in easy tasks, performance on easy tasks will be facilitated. Performance on difficult tasks, where dominant responses tend to be incorrect, will be impaired.

Zajonc's explanation seemed to account for many of the observed effects in the SFI literature. In subsequent literature, alternative explanations were suggested for the relationships between the presence of others and arousal, and between arousal and task performance, and in fact some entirely different models were proposed. A brief outline of some of these alternatives is presented below.

Alternative explanations of SFI

Cottrell (1968, 1972) was among the first to criticize Zajonc's approach. He suggested an alternative explanation for the connection between the presence of others and arousal. In Cottrell's view, increased arousal constitutes a learned response to the presence of others, and not an innate one. Subjects tend to be aroused by audiences because they have learned to associate the presence of others with performance evaluation, which, in turn, is linked to positive or negative outcomes. Thus audiences produce 'evaluation apprehension', which enhances drive (or arousal). The mere physical presence of others is not sufficient to elicit arousal and the concomitant increased emission of dominant responses (figure 15.1, panel b).

Several experiments yielded support for Cottrell's view (e.g., Henchy and Glass, 1968; Paulus and Murdoch, 1971). The former experiment may serve as an example. Henchy and Glass assigned subjects to one of four conditions: 'alone'; 'expert together' (i.e., task performance in the presence of two others, explicitly introduced as experts); 'non-expert together' (i.e., task performance in the presence of two non-experts); and 'alone recorded' (in which the subject performed the task alone, but was filmed for later evaluation by experts). As predicted by Cottrell's approach, facilitation of dominant (well-learned) responses only occurred in the expert-together and in the alone-recorded conditions, while task performance in the non-expert-together condition was similar to that in the alone condition. These results thus seem to demonstrate that some concern about being evaluated is necessary for the enhanced emission of dominant responses.

Recently, Sanna (1992) further elaborated on the role of evaluation in the explanation of SFI phenomena. Sanna distinguished between *efficacy expectancy*, that is the expectation as to whether one will be successful on the task or not, and *outcome expectancy*, i.e. the degree to which one expects favourable or unfavourable outcomes contingent upon performance. In Sanna's view the crucial variable is not task difficulty *per se*, although it may affect efficacy expectancy, but the

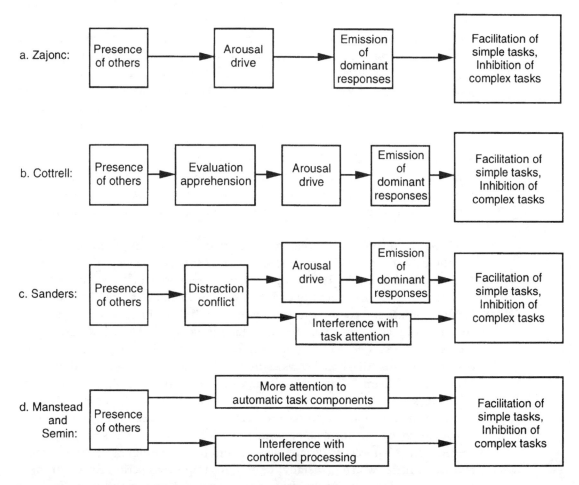

Figure 15.1 Explanations of SFI by (a) Zajonc; (b) Cottrell; (c) Sanders; and (d) Manstead and Semin

subjective sense that one will perform well (poorly) on the task and the attendant expectancy of favourable (unfavourable) outcomes, that enhances (reduces) task performance. In line with these ideas, Sanna (1992; Sanna and Shotland, 1990) demonstrated that subjects who expected to perform well also expected a positive evaluation from the audience and improved their performance, while subjects having negative performance and outcome expectations showed impaired performance in front of an audience.

Another explanation of why audiences are arousing was suggested by Sanders, Baron and Moore (1978; see also Sanders, 1981). In their view, the simple physical presence of others serves as a distracting stimulus (for example, because of noises or gestures, anticipated approving or disapproving reactions, the tendency to make social comparisons). The presence of others leads to increased drive because it brings about a 'response conflict between attending to the task at hand and attending to the distracting stimuli' (Sanders, 1981, p. 233). Two distinct effects of the presence of others on task performance may then be noted. First, because the presence of an audience is distracting, one may expect a general impairment of task performance. That is, performance on both complex and simple tasks may suffer because some of the attention needed to carry out the task will now be directed at the audience. Secondly, Sanders posits that the distraction-response conflict enhances the performer's drive, which, just as in Zajonc's view, will result in the enhanced emission of dominant responses. The latter implies improved performance on simple tasks and worsened performance on complex tasks. Taking these two effects together, both obviously lead to worse performance on complex tasks, while on simple tasks the positive effect of increased drive will generally outweigh the negative effect of the somewhat distracting audience, the net result being improved performance (see figure 15.1, panel c).

While the theoretical alternatives put forward by Cottrell, Sanna and Sanders mainly pertain to why the presence of others elicits arousal in individuals, Manstead and Semin's (1980) approach focuses on the information-processing aspects of the explanation of SFI phenomena. In Zajonc's theory, the distinction between simple and complex tasks plays a central role. This distinction, however, appears to be an uneasy one, because there is no solid theoretical basis for an independent assessment of which tasks are easy and which are difficult (or, for that matter, for the *a priori* assessment of which responses are dominant). Manstead and Semin suggest an elegant alternative by referring to Shiffrin and Schneider's (1977) two-process (automatic versus controlled) theory of human information processing. Automatic, routinely processed tasks tend to be characterized by suboptimal performance. The presence of a social-evaluative audience leads subjects to devote more attention to the progress of the automatic task sequences, which generally results in improved performance. In more complex tasks, that is tasks which require cognitively controlled processing, the presence of an evaluative audience tends to impair performance because the audience places further attentional demands upon the individual, which subtract from the already demanding task requirements (figure 15.1, panel d). This explanation of SFI phenomena substantially modifies Zajonc's model in that it avoids the somewhat strained assumption of arousal-induced emission of dominant responses by introducing more advanced information-processing views on activation level and on (competitive) allocation of attention.

Summary

In the past decade, the idea that one single explanation might account for SFI effects seems to have been abandoned in favour of a multifaceted view of these phenomena. In current views (see, for example, Geen, 1991), Zajonc's suggestion that arousal leads to enhanced emission of dominant responses no longer plays a role. Instead, it is argued that, given complex tasks or tasks on which the subject is not well trained and expects to be unsuccessful, audiences may evoke uncertainty and anxiety over potential negative evaluation. This is accompanied by an aversive affective state (arousal) which, on complex tasks, will create or increase 'cognitive overload', which will worsen task performance. Conversely, on simple or well-learned tasks, the expectation of success and favourable evaluation by an audience may motivate subjects to improve their performance.

Performance in Interacting Groups

Having described how individual performance may be influenced by the presence of others, we now take one step further and pose the question of how interacting groups perform. Steiner (1972, 1976) has convincingly argued that this question can only be answered if the nature of the task involved is taken into account. In order to make predictions about group performance he developed an interesting classification of tasks, which is summarized in the first three questions in table 15.1. We have extended the classification by adding a fourth question concerning outcome interdependency.

Steiner's classification of tasks

The first question – Can the task be broken down into subcomponents, or is division of the task inappropriate? – compares divisible and unitary tasks. Reading a page of a book is essentially a one-person job; having two persons read alternate lines would serve no purpose. Thus reading a page or solving an arithmetic problem are *unitary* tasks; splitting up a unitary task makes little sense. *Divisible* tasks, however, can be broken down into subtasks and assigned to different people. Playing a football game, building a house and planting a garden are tasks which can be broken down into subtasks. Thus for unitary tasks mutual

Table 15.1 Summary of an extended version of Steiner's typology

Question	Answer	Task type	Examples
Can the task be broken down into subcomponents, or is division of the task inappropriate?	Subtasks can be identified	Divisible	Playing football, building a house, preparing a six-course meal
	No subtasks exist	Unitary	Pulling a rope, reading a book, solving a problem
Which is more important: quantity produced or quality of performance?	Quantity	Maximizing	Generating many ideas, lifting the greatest weight, scoring the most runs
	Quality	Optimizing	Accurate book-keeping, estimating temperature in a room, writing a term paper
How are individual inputs related to the group's product?	Individual inputs are added together	Additive	Pulling a rope, filling envelopes, shovelling snow
	Group product is average of individual judgements	Compensatory	Average individuals' estimates of the number of beans in a jar, weight of an object, room temperature
	Group selects product from pool of individual members' judgements	Disjunctive	Questions involving 'yes–no, either–or' answers, such as maths problems, puzzles, and options
	All group members must contribute to the product	Conjunctive	Climbing a mountain, eating a meal, relay races, soldiers marching in file
	Group can decide how individual inputs relate to group product	Discretionary	Deciding to shovel snow together, opting to vote on the best answer to a maths problem, letting leader answer question
How are group members interdependent as to their outcomes?	Commonality of interests	Co-operative	All examples above
	Conflict of interests	Competitive	Status struggle
	Both common and conflicting interests	Mixed motive	Social dilemma

Source: Adapted from Steiner, 1972; Forsyth, 1983

assistance is impractical, whereas for divisible tasks a certain division of labour is feasible. In this view, pulling a rope is a unitary task. To be sure, Steiner remarks that it can be conceived of as involving a number of subtasks such as grasping the rope, bracing one's feet, contracting one's biceps and so on, but all phases have to be performed by a single individual. Several people may pull on the same rope but when this occurs, Steiner maintains, we have an instance of parallel performance rather than a division of labour.

The second question – Which is more important: quantity produced or quality of performance? – compares maximizing and optimizing tasks. When tasks entail doing as much as possible of something, or doing it as rapidly as possible, then we call this a maximizing task. For example, if an individual or group is requested to exert maximum force on the rope or if a group of mountaineers is asked to ascend a cliff as rapidly as possible, we call this a quantitative task, since the criterion of success is to complete the task in a maximum way. In contrast, optimizing tasks have as their criterion the production of some specific preferred outcome. When individuals or groups are asked to exert a force of exactly 100 pounds we speak of an optimizing task, since success is determined by the extent to which the specific criterion of 100 pounds will be approximated.

The third question – How are individual inputs related to the group's product – gives rise to five possible answers:

1 *Additive tasks* permit that the contributions of various members are combined. For example, when several people shovel snow from the pathway, each performs the same act while taking care to stay clear of the closest co-workers. In this case, group task performance can be expressed as the total surface cleared of snow.

2 *Compensatory tasks* require a group decision based on the average of individual members' solutions. Group members' estimates of the temperature of the room, the number of beans in a jar, or the number of cars in a car park may be averaged so that over-estimations are pitted against under-estimations and finally the right answer may be achieved.

3 *Disjunctive tasks* require that the group selects one specific judgement from the pool of individual members' judgements. The horse-trading problem dealt with earlier is a disjunctive task, since in a group several judgements may arise and one answer has to be selected.

4 *Conjunctive tasks* require that all group members act in unison. The speed at which a group of mountain climbers can ascend a cliff is determined by the slowest member.

5 *Discretionary tasks* are tasks which leave it to the group to decide how the task will be performed. For example, the group's estimation of the temperature of the room can be made in several ways. One person, the leader, may decide and the other group members will be bound by this

decision; some but not all members may come to an agreement; the final group judgement may also be the average of all individual members' judgements. Thus discretionary tasks are involved when the group has the freedom of choice to select its own decisional procedures.

A fourth question – How are group members interdependent as to their outcomes? – may be answered by describing a range of interdependence situations that vary from pure co-operation, via a mixture of co-operation and competition, to pure competition:

Pure co-operation can be said to take place when all group members share equally in group success and group failure and when it is in the interest of the group members to pursue the collective goal. This situation can be characterized as one in which individual interests completely coincide with the group interests.

Pure competition in groups exists when group members do well if they manage to obtain more behavioural outcomes than any of the other group members. In this case group members are engaged in a struggle for outcomes, such as status or rewards to be gained when the group succeeds.

SOCIAL
DILEMMA A *mixture of co-operation and competition* is coined a **social dilemma**. In this case individual group members are better off if they personally do not pursue the group goal (for example, by working not for the group, but for themselves); however, together as a group they are better off if they pursue the group goal, by

Plate 15.1 Mountain climbing as a group is a *conjunctive* task: the speed of the party is determined by the slowest member

pursuing collective goals rather than their individual goals. In practice it is not always easy to determine beforehand the interdependence situation that group members are in. Also, pure cases of co-operation or competition are rarely found in everyday life, but the following examples illustrate how various interdependence situations may arise, for instance, in soccer teams. If all members of a soccer team A believe that the best thing each individual group member can do is to work hard to win the match, then they are involved in purely co-operative interdependence. If the players of a soccer team B are keen on drawing the attention of officials from other clubs, who might be interested in buying one or two of the best players, they are engaged in pure competition: those players who succeed in getting a transfer do benefit from their actions, but they may damage the interests of their fellow players. A mixture of co-operation and competition exists if members of team C try to perform beautiful individual actions to win the admiration of the crowd. However, if all team members do so they may not operate as a coherent and efficient team. As a consequence they may lose the match and in that case all group members would have been better off if they had suppressed their personal desire to excel and had worked harder for the team as a whole.

Predicting group productivity

Steiner's ingenious classification has two attractive properties. First, with the help of this classification many tasks can be classified. Three examples may demonstrate this. A tug-of-war contest involves a task that is unitary, maximizing and additive. Assembling a car is divisible, optimizing and conjunctive. Solving the aforementioned horse-trading problem is a unitary, optimizing and disjunctive task.

Secondly, Steiner's classification of tasks allows us to make predictions about group performance. In the following we will show how group performance for a specific task is dependent on the group members' resources to deal with the task. This approach is in agreement with what we tried to demonstrate in the introduction to this chapter, where we stated that group productivity is equal to potential productivity minus process losses. The different classes of tasks demand different sorts of resources: skills, abilities and tools. If group members possess these human resources, the task demands will be met and the task may be fulfilled successfully. If, in contrast, the group does not possess those necessary resources, group failure may be observed. In the following section we will demonstrate the predictive value of Steiner's classification for additive, compensatory, disjunctive and conjunctive tasks.

Additive tasks

For additive tasks the individual contributions are added together, therefore it is not surprising that it has been established that the more persons in a group, the better the group performance. Especially for unitary tasks such as pulling a rope or clapping after a concert, the old saying 'many hands make light work' applies. Steiner (1976) remarks that the recipe for group success is quite simple: each group member should do as much as he or she can while maintaining the necessary co-ordination with the other group members. However, although this recipe is simple, adhering to it may not be.

This fact was acknowledged by Ringelmann, who carried out his research between 1882 and 1887 (see Kravitz and Martin, 1986). Ringelmann was a professor of agricultural engineering at the French National Institute of Agronomy, who investigated the relative efficiency of work furnished by horses, oxen, men and machines in various agricultural applications. He had young men pull a rope, either alone or in groups of two, three or eight members. He measured the momentary force exerted by means of a recording dynamometer. When subjects worked alone, they pulled with an average force of 63 kilograms. But two men did not pull with a force of 126 kilograms, three with a force of 189 kilograms, and so on. The two-person group had an average pull of only 118 kilograms (with a loss of 8 kilograms); three-person groups pulled with an average of 160 kilograms (showing a loss of 29 kilograms); and the eight-person group exerted a force of 256 kilograms below its potential. Thus the production loss per subject increased with group size. This inverse relationship between the number of people in the group and individual performance is termed the *Ringelmann effect*.

Why do individuals reduce their performance when group size increases? Ringelmann explains this result in terms of *co-ordination losses*. According to Steiner (1972, 1976), group productivity is not equal to potential productivity because losses owing to faulty processes must be taken into account.

Stroebe and Frey (1982) point out that the production losses of the Ringelmann group may be ascribed to at least two sorts of losses:

1   *Motivation losses*, that is, the tendency to let the others do the work, while taking advantage of the fact that one's own contribution is not identifiable and that one shares in the total group product, which makes it profitable to each of the group members to withhold part or all of their own contribution. Incidentally, this type of motivation loss is also at the root of many public-choice problems. For example, for each of us it is most attractive to let others pay the taxes or to let others take care of the environment, because while doing so one profits in two ways: one withholds one's contributions to the public good, and one profits from the public good (e.g., the welfare state and the clean air) when it is provided. In the area of public goods this motivation loss is dubbed the **free-rider effect**. Each individual is faced with a social dilemma: it is in any one person's interest not to contribute to a public good, but, if nobody contributes, everyone is worse off than if all had contributed.

FREE-RIDER
EFFECT

2 *Co-ordination losses*, for example, group members might not have pulled in the same direction or, when they did, they might not have exerted their potential force at the same moment.

Extending Steiner's original approximation of group performance we are now in a position to become more specific:

group productivity = potential productivity − motivation losses − co-ordination losses

And indeed, from results of subsequent experimental studies (e.g., Ingham et al., 1974), in which researchers tried to distinguish the two kinds of productivity losses, it appears that, as well as co-ordination losses, motivation losses play an important role in rope-pulling groups.

Production losses have also been demonstrated with other tasks such as shouting, pumping air and brainstorming (see Jackson and Harkins, 1985). In a study on **social loafing**, Latané, Williams and Harkins (1979) requested subjects to cheer or clap as loudly as they could, and recorded their performance (in dynes/cm^2). It appeared that the production loss for two-person groups was 29 per cent, for four-person groups 49 per cent and for six-person groups 60 per cent. In a second experiment they tried to disentangle production loss into two components, namely motivation and co-ordination losses. Subjects were asked to participate in a shouting task and the cheering was again measured by a sound-level meter. Each subject was asked to shout by himself or herself, in actual groups of two or six, and in pseudo groups of two or six, where subjects were led to believe that others shouted with them, but actually they were shouting alone, thus preventing co-ordination losses.

SOCIAL LOAFING

The results are depicted in figure 15.2. The broken line along the top represents potential productivity to be expected if no co-ordination and motivation losses occur. The dark area at the bottom shows the obtained productivity per person in actual groups. Group productivity is obviously lower than the potential productivity, and this decrease can be considered as representing the sum of the losses due to co-ordination and motivation losses. Figure 15.2 also shows the productivity of pseudo groups. By inference, motivation losses can now be estimated. The lightly shaded area in figure 15.2 represents motivation losses (reduced effort). The area representing co-ordination losses is inferred by subtracting the productivity of pseudo groups, in which only motivational losses were incurred, from the productivity of actual groups which did incur both co-ordination as well as motivational losses. These results demonstrate that half of the productivity losses may be ascribed to motivation and the other half to co-ordination losses. This suggests that actual productivity in real groups is equal to potential productivity of group members minus co-ordination and motivational losses.

The subsequent question is how these losses may be prevented. Research (e.g., Harkins and Jackson, 1985) suggests that when participants have the idea that their contribution can be evaluated through comparison with the contributions of others, the Ringelmann effect disappears, that is, group productivity is then equal to the potential productivity of group members.

In sum, for additive tasks group performance is equal to the potential performance of group members minus process losses. Two kinds of process losses seem to be involved, namely losses due to faulty co-ordination and losses due to decreased motivation. The Ringelmann effect – the fact that rope-pulling group members do not live up to their performance potential – is due to these two types of losses. In the remainder of this section, a specific type of additive task is

BRAINSTORMING   discussed, namely **brainstorming**, in which motivation losses appear to play a minor role while co-ordination losses, in the form of what is called 'production blocking', contribute strongly to reduced performance.

'Brainstorming' is a group technique originally suggested by Osborn (1957), having as its aim the improvement of group productivity. To facilitate productivity, members of groups receive instructions, before they start, to generate ideas about a certain topic within a limited time. The participants are encouraged to generate as many ideas as possible, but they are not allowed to

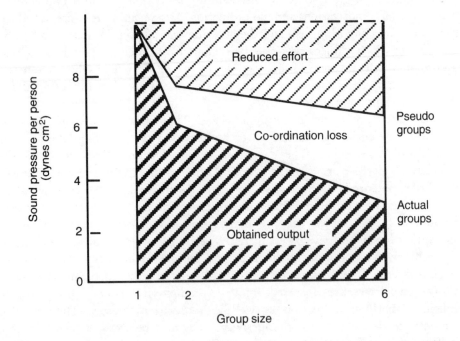

Figure 15.2 Intensity of sound produced per person when cheering in actual or pseudo groups of 1, 2 and 6, as a result of reduced effort and faulty co-ordination of group efforts (based on Latané, Williams and Harkins, 1979, expt 2)

evaluate or to be critical of the ideas expressed by themselves or others, although they may offer ideas that build upon previous suggestions. Evaluation and selection of ideas is to be done later. Osborn claimed that groups which followed these instructions generated more ideas, and that the (subsequently assessed) quality of these ideas was also superior. However, the empirical evidence does not support this claim.

McGrath (1984, p. 131) is quite explicit in this respect: 'Individuals working separately generate many more, and more creative (as rated by judges) ideas than do groups.' This conclusion has been corroborated in a recent meta-analysis of the results of 20 separate studies (Mullen, Johnson and Salas, 1991). In their meta-analysis Mullen et al. compare real brainstorming groups with nominal groups. Nominal groups consist of individuals who do not interact and whose performances are added, to compare their performance with the performance of real groups. They distinguish between two types of nominal groups – 'together': that is individuals performing individually while sitting together; versus 'alone': individuals performing in isolation. Mullen et al. conclude that, if one wants to employ brainstorming techniques – despite the fact that it generally does not enhance the quality and the quantity of performance – it would be best to use small groups who are not under the surveillance of an expert (such as the experimenter) and whose members write down their ideas rather than vocalize them.

Bond and Van Leeuwen (1991) have criticized the meta-analysis performed by Mullen et al. (1991). Their re-analysis of the same 20 studies shows that only two factors contribute to production losses in brainstorming groups: group size, and type of nominal group (together versus alone). According to their analysis, response mode (taped versus written) and the presence of an authoritative outsider (experimenter present versus absent) had no effect.

Diehl and Stroebe (1987; see also Stroebe and Diehl, 1991) have made a more thorough effort to explain why production losses in brainstorming groups occur. They identified three distinct hypotheses, which were tested in a series of experiments. We will discuss these hypotheses together with the corresponding empirical evidence in the following sections (for a review, see Stroebe and Diehl, 1994).

Free-riding

The free-riding explanation (see also Stroebe and Frey, 1982) suggests that members of brainstorming groups expect that their individual ideas will be pooled, whereas in nominal groups it is believed that each person will be individually credited for any idea proposed. The fact that individual contributions are pooled in brainstorming groups evokes the temptation to free-ride, that is, to let the others do the work, a motivation loss which is unlikely to occur in nominal groups, where each person's contribution remains visible.

To investigate the plausibility of this explanation, Diehl and Stroebe (1987) instructed nominal and brainstorming groups either to expect *individual* assessment or to expect *pooled* assessment. The results indicated that assessment indeed had an effect: there was greater productivity among subjects who had been led to expect individual as opposed to pooled assessment. However, the explained variance – a statistic that reflects the impact of the effect – was only 8 per cent. Most of the variance was explained by type of group (80 per cent): brainstorming groups produced less than nominal groups. Having thus discarded the idea that the free-rider explanation is a very important one, Diehl and Stroebe (1987) proceeded to test another hypothesis.

Evaluation apprehension

The evaluation-apprehension explanation proposes that in brainstorming groups – despite the instructions not to evaluate the ideas that are put forward – the fear of negative evaluations from other group members prevents subjects from presenting their ideas, an explanation which is consistent with the social facilitation literature (Cottrell, 1972, and Sanna, 1992); presumably the tasks given to brainstorming groups are difficult ones that lead to negative perceptions of self-efficacy. In the study by Diehl and Stroebe (1987), nominal and brainstorming groups either followed the usual procedure or were video-taped, ostensibly for the purpose of presentation to a social psychology class which was attended by most of the subjects. Moreover, pooled and individual assessment instructions were provided in this experiment. It appeared that the prospect of being evaluated indeed reduced group productivity, but again the type of group explained most of the variance (70 per cent): nominal groups outperformed brainstorming groups. From their study Diehl and Stroebe (1987) concluded that 'although assessment expectations and evaluation apprehension have been shown to affect brainstorming productivity and can thus be assumed to contribute to productivity loss in brainstorming groups, their impact has been minor when compared to that of type of group' (p. 505). Having discarded the idea that assessment and evaluation apprehension are crucial to explaining production losses in brainstorming groups, Diehl and Stroebe investigated the production-blocking explanation.

Production blocking

The production-blocking explanation proposes that the most important cause of the inferiority of real brainstorming groups is the rule of etiquette that only one group member may speak at a time, which induces non-participation by other group members, who may possibly forget their ideas or who may be prevented from developing new ideas. The production-blocking explanation was also investigated by Diehl and Stroebe (1987). They reasoned that because production blocking cannot be eliminated in real brainstorming groups, its role can only be examined by introducing blocking in nominal groups. Four subjects worked in individual rooms. In front of each subject there was a display of four lights, each light belonging to one specific group member. The subjects were instructed to express their ideas vocally. As soon as one person started to speak, a voice-activated sensor switched his or her light to green. The green light switched off when the person did not say anything for 1.5 seconds. In the meantime all other lights were red. Three experimental conditions were realized in which these light displays were used. In addition, the usual real-group and nominal-group conditions were run.

In condition 1 (blocking, communication) subjects could hear the ideas expressed by other subjects, which was not possible in condition 2 (blocking, no communication). In condition 3 (no blocking, no communication) subjects were informed about the function of the lights, but they were encouraged to disregard these lights and talk whenever they wanted to do so. The results, which are summarized in figure 15.3, indicated that quantitative production was lower in the conditions with blocking (real groups, condition 1 and condition 2) than in the two conditions without blocking (condition 3, nominal groups), suggesting that blocking is a major factor explaining production losses in brainstorming groups. While discussing the practical implications of the result showing that blocking caused production losses in brainstorming groups, Diehl and Stroebe (1987, p. 508) remark: 'Because blocking slows down the generation of ideas in groups, it might be more effective to ask subjects first to develop their ideas in individual sessions and next have these ideas discussed and evaluated in a group

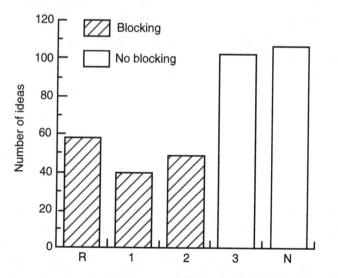

Figure 15.3 Brainstorming in real (R) groups; in condition 1: blocking plus communication; in condition 2: blocking – no communication; in condition 3: no blocking – no communication; and in traditional nominal (N) groups (after Diehl and Stroebe, 1991)

session. The task of the group would then consist of evaluation rather than production of ideas.'

It should be noted that these recommendations are already fulfilled in another technique, namely the Nominal Group Technique (NGT; see Van de Ven, 1974). NGT involves a two-stage process. Individuals first work separately in a generation stage and subsequently work as an interacting group in an evaluation (choosing) stage. This technique has been employed for the generation and evaluation of ideas (as in brainstorming), of goals to be set and of decisions to be made.

Thus, brainstorming tasks are usually additive and difficult tasks, and it appears that with increasing group size, fewer ideas are produced, a finding which is consistent with the social loafing literature. It is not easy to explain why brainstorming groups are less productive than individuals acting alone. The free-rider explanation and the evaluation apprehension explanation have received some support, with suggestions that motivation losses such as the tendency to let others do the work and the fear of negative evaluation by others do reduce group productivity. However, the most prominent reason why production losses occur in brainstorming groups seems to be the rule that as long as one member speaks other group members have to listen. According to Diehl and Stroebe (1987), blocking also leads to motivation losses, since by the co-ordination rule of only one speaker at a time, other group members may forget their ideas or be discouraged from presenting them. From this perspective it may be argued that the blocking rule, as such, brings about co-ordination loss, which presumably is detrimental to the motivation of group members to produce new ideas.

Stroebe and Diehl (1994) wonder why the brainstorming method of generating ideas is still so popular among academics, politicians and businessmen despite the overwhelming evidence that brainstorming groups are inferior in performance as compared with nominal groups. Stroebe and Diehl (1991) ascribe this to the 'illusion of group effectivity'. Why are members of brainstorming groups under the illusion that they are more productive? Stroebe and Diehl (1994) suggest two related reasons.

First, in brainstorming groups members do correctly observe that, in the group, in total more ideas are generated than they could imagine on an individual base, i.e., 'two heads are better than one'. Secondly, in brainstorming groups members are unable to differentiate between their own ideas and those suggested by others. Because contributing more ideas is more desirable than contributing fewer ideas, they may be inclined to claim some of the proposed ideas as having been generated by themselves, while their ideas have actually been proposed by another group member, resulting in an over-estimation of ideas that have been proposed by themselves. Support for the latter explanation comes from a study by Stroebe, Diehl and Abakoumkin (1992).

It was found that the performance of nominal groups was superior. However, the satisfaction of members with their performance was greater for real groups than for nominal groups, a result that supports the 'illusion of group effectivity' hypothesis. Stroebe et al. also collected data about the ideas generated during the session by each group member. In a second session conducted two weeks later, subjects were presented with their own ideas and those of the other members of their real or nominal groups and asked to indicate whether each idea had been (a) suggested by them, (b) suggested by another group member but it had also occurred to them, or (c) suggested by another group member and it had not occurred to them. Stroebe and colleagues found that subjects in real four-person groups claimed that 61 per cent of the ideas had occurred to them at the first session (a, b), whereas those in nominal groups made such a claim for only 47 per cent of ideas. Since subjects in real groups had stated at the end of their brainstorming session that they had reported practically all the ideas which had occurred to them during the session, their claims at the second session are highly unrealistic. Furthermore, Stroebe and colleagues could also show that compared with subjects who had worked individually (nominal groups), members of real groups did significantly worse in identifying ideas which they had actually suggested and also felt significantly less confident of the validity of their decisions.

It is worth noting that, although social loafing and free-riding are used in the foregoing as interchangeable terms, there is a tendency in recent literature (e.g., Baron, Kerr and Miller, 1993) to ascribe specific connotations to these concepts. Although both concepts refer to group members' tendency to let others do the work, the underlying motivation for *social loafing* is that one can get away with it in situations in which individual contributions are not identifiable or cannot be evaluated. In contrast, *free riding* is assumed to be motivated by the subject's view that it does not really make much difference for the group performance as a whole if one refrains from contributing; that is, one tends to see one's own contribution as dispensable because one expects others to take care of a sufficiently high level of group performance, or because one expects that others will contribute so little that the group would fail anyhow (see also, the section below on co-operative, mixed-motive and competitive interdependence).

Compensatory tasks

For compensatory tasks the group product is the average of individual judgements. In a series of early studies (Gordon, 1924; Knight, 1921) individuals were asked to make private estimates of the temperature of a room, the number of beans in a jar and the number of buckshot in a bottle. It appeared that the statistical average of the many judgements came closer to the correct value than the estimates rendered by most of the individuals. Shaw (1981) concluded that the bulk of evidence indicates that – for compensatory tasks – the average of judgements is more accurate than are the judgements of individuals. Steiner (1972, 1976), however, is more critical of this conclusion. He points out that 'statisticized' groups occur quite rarely in daily life and they may not be recognized as such when they do occur. Moreover, the average of all judgements only leads to a superior group performance when no information is available about the competence of members and when individual prejudices may be presumed to generate errors that cancel one another out. When some individual judgements have more influence than others, or if some members abstain from expressing their judgement, the average judgement is less likely to be correct.

Disjunctive tasks

In our introduction we discussed the horse-trading problem in some detail. This is a unitary, optimizing and disjunctive task. It is a disjunctive task because the group has to select one judgement from the pool of individual judgements. Groups are very often confronted with disjunctive tasks, for example: should a student pass or fail? Should a certain investment be made or not? Should NATO invade Yugoslavia or not?

Interest in disjunctive tasks arose in the early 1930s (Shaw, 1932). Besides the horse-trading problem, the so-called missionary/cannibal problem was quite often employed. This disjunctive task has the following content:

> Three missionaries and three cannibals are on one side of the river, and want to cross to the other side by means of a boat that can only hold two persons at a time. All the missionaries but only one cannibal can row. For safety reasons, the missionaries must never be outnumbered by the cannibals, under any circumstances or at any time, except when no missionaries are present at all. The question is: how many crossings will be necessary to transport the six people across the river?

The correct answer is 13 crossings. Shaw (1932) observed that, overall, groups outperformed individuals. These results were explained by referring to the enhanced opportunity of groups for correcting errors and rejecting incorrect suggestions.

Later on, successful and failing groups were compared more closely. Another explanation was then proposed: the so-called *truth wins* rule. This rule says that if there is one group member who proposes the correct answer then it is likely that the group will succeed. This explanation did not always hold either. For some problems the truth wins rule does apply, such as for the cannibal/missionary problem. However, for others, such as for the horse-trading problem, it appeared quite often that having one successful member was no guarantee of group success.

This result was explained by pointing out that the missionary/cannibal problem has a very appealing solution – it has *eureka* appeal – while other tasks have a less obvious solution. The consequence is that if, in a *eureka* task group, one member has the correct solution the other group members more or less automatically adhere to this solution, which is not the case for problems which do not have such an obvious and insightful solution. For non-*eureka* tasks it can easily occur that a correct solution by one member will not be supported by the other group members or that a group member with a wrong solution will dominate the solution process. For non-*eureka* problems it is not the truth-wins rule, but the *truth-supported wins* rule that explains group success.

Thomas and Fink (1961) described a three-step model which appears to encompass the critical aspects of group success for disjunctive tasks:

1 *Potential performance*: do group members possess the necessary resources to solve the problem?
2 *Motivation*: do group members, possessing the correct solution, actually propose this solution?
3 *Co-ordination*: do correct solutions elicit support more often than incorrect solutions?

In the same vein, Steiner (1972) summarizes the findings as follows. For disjunctive tasks a group's potential productivity is determined by the resources of its most competent member. However, even when there is a very competent member, process losses may prohibit the group from producing the correct solution. This is the case when the most competent member does not employ his or her resources or when other group members do not adhere to her solution. The latter seems to be very likely, (a) when the most competent member has a low status in the group, and (b) when the most competent member is not confident enough either to communicate the solution or to persuade the other group members.

In decision-making bodies, such as committees and boards of directors, there are quite often explicit rules for making decisions. For example, in parliament there is the democratic rule that the majority wins; in some boards of directors of organizations this may also be the case, but in others the explicit rule is that the president makes the final decision. In problem-solving groups, quite often there are no explicit rules by which to make the group decision. How to establish what decision rule has been followed is usually not easy for group members. They know the problem, they may observe the group members' preferences for certain solutions, they have a vague impression about the discussion and they know what the group has decided.

An interesting approach to determine which rule or decision scheme a group has conformed to is proposed by Laughlin (1980; see also Davis, 1973; Stasser et al., 1989). The **social decision scheme (SDS)** model defines a social decision scheme as a 'probabilistic rule which specifies the likelihood that a group will reach any particular decision given that it begins discussion with any particular distribution of member opinion' (Kerr, 1992, p. 69). In a non-technical sense this means that the model predicts how likely it is that group members having initial preferences for a certain solution will reach a group solution when they follow a

SOCIAL DECISION
SCHEME (SDS)

Plate 15.2 Decision-making bodies, including political cabinets, often have explicit rules for how to make decisions

specific rule, or social decision scheme. Several of these rules have been distinguished. The most prominent decision schemes are the 'majority wins', 'truth wins' and 'equiprobability' decision schemes. The *majority wins* social decision scheme predicts that the group choice should correspond with the initial preferences of the majority in the group. This decision scheme appears to be followed in groups having to make attitudinal judgements and in jury decision-making (Stasser et al., 1989). Laughlin and Ellis (1986, p. 177) suggest that this decision scheme is followed in case of 'evaluative, behavioral or aesthetic judgments for which there does not exist a demonstratably correct answer'.

The *truth wins* social decision scheme predicts that the group choice may be determined by one group member or by a small faction; that is, the group choice may correspond with the initial preference of one group member or a minority of group members. This scheme appears to predict rather well for intellectual tasks for which there is a demonstrably correct answer, such as *eureka* problems.

The *equiprobability* social decision scheme holds that any group choice is possible when initially there is at least one advocate in favour of that choice, or anything may happen as long as there is at least one group member who wants it to happen. This scheme is followed when group members experience an extremely high task uncertainty, that is, in tasks for which it is almost impossible to come up with a correct group solution (Davis, 1982). This scheme is also highly probable if all group members consider the group decision unimportant (Laughlin and Ellis, 1986). This implies that conforming to a specific decision rule is dependent not only on the specific task (e.g., judgemental and intellectual), but also on specific task conditions. For example, Kerr (1992) suggests that the same task (e.g., judgemental task), may lead to conforming to the *majority wins* decision scheme when presented in an ego-involving way, but to conforming to the equiprobability decision scheme when the task is presented in a fairly unimportant way.

Conjunctive tasks

For conjunctive tasks it is necessary that all members contribute to the task. For tasks such as climbing a mountain and for soldiers marching in file the criterion is that all group members make the proper response. When conjunctive tasks are unitary it has been observed that each member must contribute, lest the group fails (Steiner, 1972), i.e., group process depends on the competence of the least proficient member. Because the chance of having an incompetent member increases with group size, it is logical that as the number of group members increases the group productivity will diminish. In everyday life, however, many conjunctive tasks are divisible; subtasks are then allocated to individual members. For example, climbing a mountain can be divided into several subtasks, such as rope leader and followers, where the followers are connected with a rope to the rope leader, who takes the lead. If the most able climber performs the most difficult subtask, that is, when she is made rope leader, and when the easiest subtasks are performed by the less able climbers, the group productivity is higher than the potential productivity of the least able group member. In sum, performance of unitary conjunctive tasks depends on the least able group member. However, for divisible conjunctive tasks the group performance can be raised above the potential productivity of the least able group member, if the abilities of the group members coincide with the difficulty of the specific subtasks involved.

Co-operative, mixed-motive and competitive interdependency

How will co-operation and competition affect group performance? Deutsch (1949) argued that in situations in which a group member's locomotion towards a goal (success on a task) has positive consequences for other group members (co-operative tasks; positive interdependency), group members will be motivated to help each other, they will like one another, and the group as a whole will be strongly propelled towards the group goal. In groups faced with a competitive task, group members will hinder each other, they will learn to dislike each other, and the group as a whole will be less likely to produce a good group product.

These conjectures were confirmed in Deutsch's experiment and in a large number of other studies (see Johnson et al., 1981), suggesting that co-operative groups are more productive, they show more co-ordination and greater mutual attraction among group members than competitive groups. In a review of these studies, Brown (1988) remarks that 'This apparently unassailable superiority of cooperation should cause us to question seriously the overwhelming emphasis on competitive arrangements in our educational institutions and workplaces. The evidence is that such arrangements are quite literally counterproductive' (Brown, 1988, p. 32).

A mixed-motive situation is one which contains competitive and co-operative elements. A well-known example is the social dilemma faced by group members who are each individually better off by producing as little as possible, but who as a group are better off when each contributes to the group task. Kerr (1982; Kerr and Bruun, 1983) has shown that the social-dilemma analogy is of relevance for our understanding of task performance. He reasoned that as groups increase in size, group members' behaviour becomes less identifiable, and group members' task efforts usually have less effect on the total group performance. As a consequence, motivation losses in larger groups are larger than in smaller ones. In one of his experiments (Kerr and Bruun, 1983, expt 2), subjects in two-person or in three-person groups had to perform an additive, a disjunctive or a conjunctive task. Each member of the most productive group would receive a prize.

Before performing the task, group members were informed of how much they had to produce in order to be successful. Subsequently, various task instructions were given. In the additive condition the number of successful members counted. In the conjunctive condition every member had to succeed for the group to succeed, that is, group performance was dependent on the performance of the least able group member; in the disjunctive condition the group was successful if at least one member was successful, that is, group performance was dependent on the most able group member. Success or failure in comparison with other groups was established in several trials. For all conditions, the performance of individual group members showed that task performance was higher for two-person than for three-person groups. So, increasing group size enhances motivation losses, or, in other words, the larger the group, the more social loafing.

In another experiment (Kerr and Bruun, 1983, expt 1), group members received information about their relative ability (allegedly assessed in a previous session), and about the size of their group. Each group had one member with a high ability score and one member with a low ability score. Subjects were randomly assigned to one of these ability positions. Two-person, four-person and eight-person groups were introduced. Besides ability positions and the size of the group, task demands also varied. Additive, conjunctive or disjunctive task instructions were provided. Kerr reasoned that in a disjunctive task group, in which only the best member's performance mattered, the less able members would become free-riders because their efforts would be dispensable. In contrast, in a conjunctive task group, in which the least able group member's performance mattered, he expected that high-ability group members would become free-riders, i.e., would tend to reduce their efforts.

As predicted, the ability of the group members had opposite effects for the conjunctive and disjunctive tasks. When only the best individual score counted (disjunctive task), the low-ability member performed less well, but when the group score was defined by the worst individual score (conjunctive task) the high-ability member worked less hard. The subjects' responses to the question 'how much did the success of the group depend upon you, personally?' indicated that the effects reported above reflected the extent to which group members considered themselves dispensable. The reduced efforts of low-ability subjects in a disjunctive-task setting and of high-ability subjects in a conjunctive-task setting were labelled 'free-rider effects'.

Besides 'social loafing' and 'free-rider' effects, Kerr (1982) found evidence for the 'sucker effect'. A sucker in a social dilemma situation can be described as a person who contributes to the group goal and later on learns that other group members have not contributed, but nevertheless profited from the contribution of the sucker. Kerr (1982) demonstrated that group members with a capable partner who 'free-rode' on their efforts, that is, a partner who could have contributed but refrained from doing so, reduced their efforts in order to escape the role of sucker.

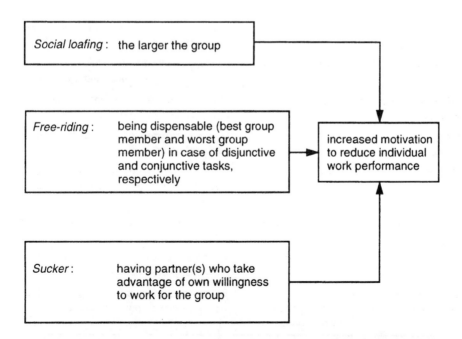

Figure 15.4 Three motivations for reducing individual contribution to group tasks

As figure 15.4 illustrates, Kerr's research shows that performing group members take into account forthcoming behavioural outcomes. As a consequence, they reduce their efforts if the group size is larger (the social loafing effect), if their own efforts are considered dispensable (the free-rider effect) and if they are afraid of becoming suckers (the sucker effect).

Summary

From the foregoing, two conclusions may be drawn. First, Steiner's classification allows us to make a set of predictions for the tasks under consideration. These predictions are summarized in table 15.2. Secondly, the basic idea that group productivity is equal to the extent to which group members succeed in meeting the demands of the tasks minus eventual process losses appears to offer a deeper understanding of the nature of the tasks. Moreover, it has been suggested that process losses may be specifically ascribed to motivation and co-ordination losses.

Table 15.2 Performance of groups working on various types of tasks

Task/motivation	Group productivity	Description
Additive	Better then best	Group out-performs the best individual member
Compensatory	Better than most	Group out-performs a substantial number of members
Disjunctive (*Eureka*)	Equal to the best	Group performance matches the performance of the best member
Disjunctive (non-*Eureka*)	Less than the best	Group performance can match that of the best member, but often falls short
Conjunctive (unitary)	Equal to the worst	Group performance matches the lowest performance of a member
Conjunctive (divisible with matching)	Better than the worst	If subtasks are properly matched to ability of members, group performance can reach high levels
Co-operative	Facilitates group performance	Depends on the cognitive rules of the task (see above)
Competitive	Worsens group performance	Group performance hampered by competing individual group members
Mixed motive	Group performance less than optimal	Better than under pure competition, but worse than with pure co-operation

Source: Adapted from Steiner, 1972; Forsyth, 1983

Group Structure

In the preceding sections we explained how group members' resources may meet task demands. Most of the tasks we dealt with were unitary tasks – tasks which cannot be broken down into subtasks. In the present section we extend our analysis of group behaviour by describing the behaviour of groups faced with tasks that can only be solved when the overall task is divided into several subtasks, and in which the subtasks are assigned to different group members – in other words, we are dealing with divisible group tasks. An example is playing a game of soccer. Several subtasks, like defence and attack, may be distinguished and assigned to specific players. However, a soccer team cannot easily win a match when the subtasks are not well integrated into a convincing overall conception of how the team as a whole should perform its overall task.

Group structure pertains both to the differentiating elements as well as to integrating mechanisms. The elements are persons and positions, while the *integrating mechanisms* are communication, attraction, status, control and roles (see Collins and Raven, 1968). Before we go into more detail about the ways in which those elements of social structure are interconnected, we will give an example of how a group structure may develop over time.

Development of structure

Whyte (1948) illustrates the development of structure in his well-known story of Tom Jones's restaurant. Tom Jones starts his restaurant with two employees. There is almost no division of labour; all three cook, serve and wash dishes. After some success, Jones is able to hire new personnel and divides the labour into service employees, kitchen employees and dish washers. Co-ordination is done by Tom Jones himself. The relationships remain close and personal: the formal control is low. After further expansion Tom Jones introduces supervisors for service, food production and washing up. Also a checker is introduced. This person has to add up the bills for his waiters and to see that food is served in a correct style and in the right portions. With increasing numbers of customers, Jones cannot be personally in touch with his customers any more and contact with his employees becomes formal. He supervises the organization from a distance.

The foregoing story illustrates the development of structure within a restaurant setting. In the initial phases, all employees perform more or less the same job. Through informal communication among the three of them, mutual adjustments can take place so that the total job may be done. Important for this implicit adjustment is that personal relations are good, i.e., mutual attraction should be high. There is no formal control. Being part of the group, Jones can follow minutely and correct the course of affairs. Although there is almost no division of labour it is clear that Jones is in charge. He fulfils the leadership role and his position is evaluated as higher than those of his co-workers. In the final stage of the restaurant a division of labour has taken place. A formal network of supervisors and workers has evolved while Jones supervises the organization as a whole.

ROLE

This structure, once established, is largely independent of the persons who occupy the various positions. Each participant – boss, supervisors, cooks and waiters – plays his **role**, and the behaviour of each is determined by certain rules, standards of conduct or norms, which specify acceptable behaviour. Moreover, an organizational structure develops, and is subsequently maintained, because the role behaviours are under control: the boss controls the supervisors, and the supervisors control the waiters, dish washers and kitchen personnel.

It may be assumed that these positions are evaluated differently by personnel and customers. Presumably Jones has a higher status than the supervisors, while the position of a supervisor is evaluated more highly than that of a waiter. These status differences, i.e., evaluations of positions in the group, may reinforce the established structure of the group. The structure has emerged and is maintained by communication. By communication, positions and roles are defined and assigned to certain persons. Moreover, communication enables the organization to maintain and change the pattern of roles and norms.

COHESION

Lastly, attraction among group members may strengthen or weaken the informal **cohesion** of the group. In sum, this example demonstrates how the elements of group structure (persons and positions) are integrated by roles, norms, status, control, attraction and communication. In the following we will deal with the formation of status, with roles, norms and communication networks.

Status

STATUS

An example of how **status** differences may arise in the laboratory is provided by a classic observation study by Bales (1950a), who observed problem-solving groups consisting of unacquainted persons. The interactions within three-person to six-person groups were observed by means of Bales's **interaction process analysis (IPA)**. This observation system specified four broad behavioural categories, namely positive and negative socio-emotional behaviours, task behaviours and behaviours referring to exchange of information. For each of these behaviours, the observation system coded members initiating such behaviours and group members being the recipients (or target) of such behaviours. Patterns of observations revealed that one could distinguish between members specializing in task behaviour and other members specializing in socio-emotional behaviour. Task behaviour refers to all activities directed at task completion, while socio-emotional behaviour is directed towards interpersonal relations.

INTERACTION PROCESS ANALYSIS (IPA)

Task and socio-emotional specialists

Bales and Slater (1955) trained their assistants to observe the behaviour of groups. These observers became practised at listening to a group discussion, breaking down the verbal content into the 'smallest meaningful units' that could be distinguished (Bales, 1950a) and, subsequently, classifying these units into observation categories.

From the study by Bales and Slater (1955) it appears that group members vary widely in terms of the behavioural categories of Bales's observation system. Moreover, this study suggests that within a group two kinds of leaders tend to operate: a *socio-emotional* and a *task* leader. In terms of Bales's observational categories, summarized in table 15.3, more often than other group members, socio-emotional leaders initiate positive socio-emotional behaviours (categories 1 to 3) and information exchange (categories 7 to 9), and they are also the prime recipients or target of information provided by other group members (categories 4 to 6). In contrast, task leaders more frequently initiate task behaviours (categories 4 to 6) and they are more often addressed by other group members to provide information (categories 7 to 9). At the same time, they are often the recipients of negative socio-emotional behaviours (categories 10 to 12). Bales and Slater (1955) indicate that these two kinds of specialists arise quite often in discussion groups. The two functions – task and socio-emotional expertise – are rarely fulfilled by one and the same person. They give two reasons for groups having two leaders. First, the same person rarely has the ability to fulfil both functions. Secondly, as noted above, a task leader arouses considerable hostility, that is, very often other group members express negative socio-emotional behaviour towards the task leader.

Burke (1967, 1974) has since reported evidence that the two functions may be performed by a single person during a one-hour discussion meeting, provided that members of the group are convinced from the outset that good task performance, rather than harmonious interpersonal relationships, is the ultimate aim. Under these circumstances disharmonious group tensions may be kept at a minimum or, if they do arise, may be tolerated more easily by group members.

Additional questionnaire data collected by Bales and Slater (1955) indicated that the socio-emotional specialist was liked more than any other group member, while the task specialist was perceived as the group member who contributed most to task achievement. The latter findings demonstrate that status differences in groups do appear. However, the question is how do these status differences arise in groups of which the members were previously unacquainted with one another?

Emergence of status

Expectation-states theory (Berger, Rosenholtz and Zelditch, 1980) assumes that in Bales's study *a priori* status expectations were involved. Status differences are

Table 15.3 Bales's observation system, 'Interaction Process Analysis' (IPA)

IPA categories

Socio-emotional behaviour (positive)
 1 Shows solidarity
 2 Shows tension release
 3 Agrees

Task behaviour
 4 Gives suggestion
 5 Gives opinion
 6 Gives orientation

Information exchange
 7 Asks for orientation
 8 Asks for opinion
 9 Asks for suggestion

Socio-emotional behaviour (negative)
10 Disagrees
11 Shows tension
12 Shows antagonism

Source: after Bales (1950a); Bales and Slater (1955)

likely to emerge in groups that are working on a co-operative task, such as the problem-solving groups used by Bales and Slater (1955).

Because the group hopes it can successfully complete its task, the group members become aware of the possibility that some members possess superior skills and abilities that will favour goal attainment. This is, then, the beginning of the status-organizing process. One tries to identify those individuals who are expected to contribute most to goal attainment. These group members are addressed more often and are encouraged to take more initiatives. Moreover, other group members are most likely to comply with their influence attempts. The theory also points out which characteristics may give rise to status differentials. Specific status characteristics refer to the abilities and skills which are of direct relevance to goal attainment, such as mathematical abilities when the task calls for this ability. In the absence of specific status information, groups may still develop expectations by considering diffuse status characteristics – any quality a person has that one may think is relevant to goal attainment. Sex, age, wealth, ethnicity and status in other groups may serve as diffuse status characteristics if group members associate these qualities with goal attainment (for a recent review, see Berger and Zelditch, 1993).

Empirical support for expectation-states theory has been found by Berger, Rosenholtz and Zelditch (1980) and others. For example, Greenstein and Knotterus (1980) observed that a person who had greater ability was more influential than a person with a lower ability; Torrance (1954) reported that in airforce crews working on the horse-trading problem a person higher in military rank was able to exert more influence than persons lower in rank; Ofshe and Lee (1981) found that someone who showed more assertiveness was more influential than someone who was less assertive in his behaviour; Ridgeway (1978) found that a person who showed the strongest group orientation was more able to influence other group members than another person who apparently pursued his own self-interest. It has also been shown that males, whites and older people are more influential than females, blacks and younger people (at least in contemporary Western cultures; see further, De Gilder and Wilke, 1994).

A summary of these findings may be found in figure 15.5. This figure demonstrates why in initially leaderless groups, like those investigated by Bales and Slater (1955), a group structure may emerge. By matching each person with the subtasks that each one is most qualified to perform, group structure does arise. Because some qualifications give rise to higher expectations of successful task contribution than others, status and influence-differentiation in groups do occur. That status differences do not always lead to a better group performance appears from the study by Torrance (1954), who employed pilots, navigators and gunners as subjects. The group-discussion data indicate that of the pilots who had reached the correct answer before group discussion, one-tenth failed to persuade their associates to accept it, while one-fifth of the navigators and one-third of the gunners failed to do so. Thus a correct solution is more likely to

Plate 15.3 In hierarchies, such as the military, persons with higher rank exert greater influence than those of lower rank

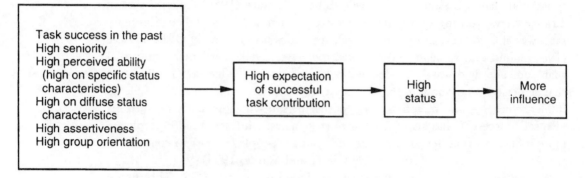

Figure 15.5 Characteristics which give rise to high status and more influence

prevail when it is offered by a high-status person than when it is offered by someone having a lower status. However, Torrance's results suggest that this also holds for higher-status members who advocate the wrong solution, that is high-status members appear to be more successful in persuading the other group members to accept the wrong solution than are low-status members. Thus a high-status person who is on the wrong track is a bigger obstacle for group success than an equally mistaken low-status person.

The leadership role

One of the most salient distinctions between roles is that of leader and followers. A leader guides the group and facilitates the group's behaviour, while the followers are likely to accept the suggestions of the leader. The followers expect the leader to lead the group to group achievement. The leadership role is a position that may be occupied by any of the group members. Why is it then that a certain person becomes the leader? In this section we will deal with several possible answers, namely: (1) the leader is born to leadership; (2) a leader should exhibit certain behaviours; (3) a leader should exhibit certain behaviour in specific situations (see also Smith and Fritz, 1987).

The great-man theory of leadership

What are the characteristics of a successful leader? Until 1950 this so-called trait approach was very popular. Reviewing studies in which characteristics of leaders were compared with those of non-leaders, Stogdill (1948) found that leaders are more intelligent, have more education, are more inclined to take on responsibilities, are more active and have a higher socio-economic status. He concluded that the trait approach yields interesting data, but that dependence on situational factors seems to be of major importance in determining who will become leader.

The behaviour approach

Another approach to leadership focuses on the behaviour of leaders. Several methods of investigation have been used to establish how leaders behave. In the previous section we have already seen that Bales and Slater (1955), employing observation methods, discovered that leaders score higher than their followers on task and socio-emotional activities. Consequently two kinds of leaders can be distinguished: the best-liked person, or *socio-emotional leader*, who takes care of harmonious group atmosphere, and the best-idea person, or the *task leader*, who more than any other follower contributes to task achievement.

The questionnaire method was employed in the Ohio State University leadership studies. The following steps were taken. First, researchers developed a list of nine key types of behaviour that seemed to characterize military and organizational leaders. Secondly, a questionnaire was constructed and submitted to subordinates in all kinds of organizational settings, asking them to rate leaders. Thirdly, correlations between these ratings were calculated and these correlations were compared via factor analysis – a method used to trace salient patterns of correlations. Two factors explained 83 per cent of the variance in the followers' evaluation of their leaders (Halpin and Winer, 1952): these factors were consideration and initiating structure. *Consideration* refers to the degree to which the leader responds to group members in a warm and friendly fashion, and involves mutual trust, openness and a willingness to explain decisions. This factor represents what is called socio-emotional leadership. *Initiating structure*, representing the task-leader factor, is defined as the degree to which the leader organizes, directs and defines the group's structure and goals, regulates group behaviour, monitors communication and reduces goal ambiguities (Halpin and Winer, 1952; Lord, 1977).

Other questionnaire studies have also revealed two broad categories of leader behaviour. Most notable are the investigations performed at Michigan. Likert (1967) employed similar steps to those taken in the Ohio State University leadership studies. His results also revealed two factors, namely *employee-centred* and *production-centred* behaviour; these seem to match the aforementioned factors, consideration and initiating structure, respectively.

Thus in a group there seems to be a need for two kinds of leadership style, each having its own impact on group productivity. Steiner (1976, p. 418) summarizes these findings as follows:

$$\text{actual productivity} = \text{potential productivity} - \text{unrealized productivity}$$

In his view, task leaders bolster the group's potential productivity. They take care that as many as possible of the social resources of the group are mobilized. Socio-emotional leaders serve to minimize unrealized productivity. They prevent the accumulation of tensions that might undermine harmonious group relations, as these may be detrimental to actual group productivity.

The behavioural approach is currently no longer popular. The main reason is that observational studies (e.g., Lord, 1977) often found little support for the consideration factor, which may partially be ascribed to the fact that emotional behaviour is less easy to observe than task behaviour. In an observational investigation, Couch and Carter (1952) reported a low correlation between leadership ratings and the consideration factor. They even found that consideration and initiating structure together explained less variation than a third factor, *individual prominence*, which refers to the leader taking the leadership role by proposing himself or herself as leader.

Ilgen and Fujji (1976) have pointed out that the main weakness of questionnaire studies is that researchers ask respondents for desirable conceptions about their leaders, instead of for realistic ones. Observational studies, on the other hand, are performed by trained outsiders who are less sensitive to such biases.

Contingency of behaviour and situation

One of the main reasons why the behavioural approach was abandoned was that it appeared that the behaviour of leaders differed across situations and that leadership behaviour which was successful in one situation failed in other situations. Several models have been proposed to predict the effectiveness of the leader's behaviour in specific situations (e.g., Bass, 1985; Fiedler, 1978; Field and House, 1990). Below, we will explain Fiedler's model, since this contingency model has evoked the most empirical attention of all contingency models put forward so far. According to Fiedler (1978), studies of leadership have failed to acknowledge that the effect of the behaviour of the leader is contingent on characteristics of the situation involved. His so-called contingency model assumes that group productivity can only be predicted when one knows both the leader's style and his or her situational control; that is, the specific leadership style and the situational control together determine a leader's effectiveness.

LEAST
PREFERRED
CO-WORKER
(LPC) *Leadership style* refers to the extent to which a leader is either relationship or task motivated, and is based on the leader's ratings of the **least preferred co-worker (LPC)**. The *high-LPC leader* or *relationship-motivated leader* perceives this co-worker in a relatively favourable manner – even the *least* preferred co-worker is perceived quite favourably. This type of leader derives major satisfaction from successful interpersonal relationships. The *low-LPC leader* or *task-motivated leader* rates her least preferred co-worker in a very unfavourable way and is described as a person who derives most satisfaction from task performance.

As well as the leadership style, *situational control* is of importance. A leader's situational control refers to the degree to which the leader feels secure and confident that the task may be accomplished. The leader's situational control is dependent on the degree to which (1) the leader–member relations are conceived as supportive, loyal and reliable; (2) the task is structured, because the task contains clear-cut goals and detailed methods of solution; and (3) leaders are in

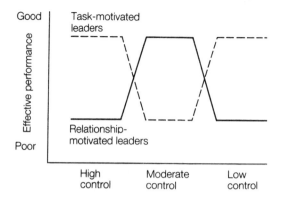

Figure 15.6 Situational control and performance of leaders (Fiedler and Potter, 1983)

a position to supervise their workers and to reward or punish their subordinates.

According to Fiedler, leadership style and situational control determine leadership effectiveness as measured by group performance; that is, one has to know the interaction of leadership style and situational control to be able to predict the effectiveness of the leader. Figure 15.6 summarizes the results of numerous investigations (see Chemers, 1983; Fiedler and Potter, 1983). The effectiveness of relationship-oriented (high-LPC) leaders is represented by the solid line, and that of task-motivated (low-LPC) leaders by the broken line. We observe that task-motivated leaders perform best in situations of high and low control, whereas relationship-oriented leaders are most effective in moderate-control situations (see, for reviews, Chemers, 1983; Fiedler and Potter, 1983; Hosking, 1981; Schriesheim and Kerr, 1977).

Situational demands for leadership

The example of Jones's restaurant demonstrates that in the beginning Jones's leadership was fairly implicit, but that it became more explicit as his restaurant increased in size and complexity. Many groups start in a leaderless way. Committees and clubs quite often start as leaderless groups, and the leadership role emerges later. The question to consider is: when does a group require the instalment of an explicit leader?

As is suggested by the example of Jones's restaurant, the size of the group is an important reason to introduce explicit leadership. Large groups seem to have a greater need for explicit leadership than small groups. This appears from a study by Hemphill (1961). He compared the behaviours of large-group leaders with those of small-group leaders. He observed that large groups rely more often on a leader to make rules clear, keep members informed and make group decisions. In his review of situational factors affecting the need for leadership,

Hemphill (1961) suggested that other factors also facilitate the emergence of explicit leaders in groups, namely the *nature of the task* and the *availability* of a group member who has experience in the leadership role. He specified the following task circumstances promoting the emergence of a leader:

1   Groups must have the feeling that task success is possible.
2   Group members must attach a great value to task success.
3   The task itself must require co-ordination and communication.

These task requirements are clearly involved in social dilemmas task structures in which it is in any individual's interest to behave selfishly (see Dawes, 1980). We have already met this dilemma in the context of the free-rider. All group members are inclined to keep their task expenditure at a minimum; however, when all group members do so, the group as a whole fails.

Other illustrations can also be given. For example, students in a hall of residence may be inclined to heat their own room to a maximum, because it is known that the price of heating is to be shared anyway; however, if all students behave likewise, the collective bill may be extremely high. Dawes (1980) refers to societal problems such as over-population, energy depletion and pollution as social dilemmas. Rutte and Wilke (1984) considered the question of under what circumstances group members will opt for a leader in a social dilemma. Two factors appeared to be of relevance: (1) when the group failed to maintain the collective resource; and (2) when large differences in outcomes between group members emerged. Under these circumstances the group was more inclined to install a leader in the future than when the leaderless group did succeed and distributed the outcomes equally. The first factor refers to task success: if *task success* is *in danger* one opts for a leader. The second factor pertains to equity: when the outcomes are *inequitably allocated* group members prefer a leader, who will take decisions on behalf of all group members.

Three additional results seem to be of importance. First, Rutte and Wilke (1984) investigated subjects' preferences for other decision structures as well: unanimity, large majority, small majority, and each for himself or herself. It appeared that over all conditions of the experiment the preference for a leader was lower than for any other decision structure, suggesting that group members have a strong reluctance to opt for a leader, who takes away their own decisional freedom. Secondly, when asked which group member they would like to choose as a leader, most subjects were likely to prefer themselves, indicating that holding such a powerful position is very attractive, and that being powerless is a demotivating factor. Thirdly, when elected leader, subjects took care of group success and allocated the outcomes in a fair way (Steiner, 1972, 1976).

These findings may be related to Steiner's ideas about group productivity, i.e.

$$\text{group productivity} = \text{potential productivity} - \text{motivation losses} - \text{co-ordination losses}$$

The instalment of a leader is a means by which to increase the co-ordination of group efforts, which obviously reduces co-ordination losses. In turn, improved co-ordination may motivate group members to contribute to the group's success. However, motivational losses may still play a role. The loss of subordinates' freedom to take decisions may induce them to minimize their efforts, and to leave it to the leader to take care of group productivity.

By implication, the results of the experiment by Rutte and Wilke (1985) suggest that group members in a leaderless group have no need to install a leader if the group acts successfully without a leader and when the outcomes of the group's performance are allocated in a fair way, indicating that in some groups co-ordination by a leader is considered superfluous (see also Kerr and Jermier, 1978). In fact it may be argued that the need for, and the effectiveness of, leadership depends on the characteristics of the group and the situation. According to Kerr and Jermier (1978) a group's need for relationship-oriented or task-oriented leadership depends on features of the group's members, the task at hand, and the organization of the group.

When a group is composed of competent group members who have a great need for independence and a sense of professional identity, then task-oriented leadership is unnecessary. It may be assumed that without the intervention of a task leader the group will be able to mobilize sufficient potential productivity to co-ordinate its efforts and to motivate its members. In addition, the properties of the task may make a leader superfluous. When the task itself automatically controls the behaviour of the group members, such as in an assembly line, then a task or co-ordinating leader is not necessary. In that case there is more need for relationship-oriented leadership, which keeps the group members' motivation at a satisfactory level. Lastly, the type of organization also dictates whether a task leader is necessary. When the organization is highly formalized then task leadership is unnecessary, because leadership has been built into formal rules. In that case there is a greater need for relationship-oriented leadership, which humanizes the rigid organizational environment. Moreover, when group members are indifferent towards organizational rewards, when the group is very cohesive and when the leader has neither the means nor the abilities to motivate his subordinates, both relationship- and task-oriented leadership seem to be inadequate.

In sum, these findings suggest that there is a greater need for leadership as groups increase in size. In large groups co-ordination and motivation of group members may become a problem, which may be solved by the instalment of a leader. Two other circumstances seem to lead to the introduction of a leader, namely endangered task success and an unfair allocation of outcomes among group members. By implication, these data suggest that leadership is unlikely when a leaderless group achieves task success and when the group outcomes are allocated in a fair way. Other circumstances, referring to the persons involved, the task, and the type of organization, also indicate when having a leader may be ineffective.

Norms

NORMS

Every group develops certain collective views and standards of conduct – **norms**– which regulate the interaction among group members. For example, in Tom Jones's restaurant certain rules came into being which specified acceptable behaviours in the interaction between the boss, the cooks and the waiters. Quite often these rules of behaviour are fairly *implicit*, and one becomes aware of them only when they are broken. Rules of behaviour may also be fairly *explicit* and laid down in formal rules. When, in a students' residence, informal rules do not suffice to provide regular meals or a clean kitchen, one may decide to draft formal regulations, with punishments for contraventions.

In this section we will sketch how implicit and explicit group norms affect the behaviour of groups. The main question is: what constitutes a normal production level for a group? In answering this question we will focus on how, in groups, a certain standard comes into being, and how these standards are maintained during subsequent interaction. By way of a summarizing statement we will argue that these norms or standards promote the survival of any group, because group norms help a group to accomplish its goals and to maintain itself as a group.

Development of norms

Suppose you and two other people are forming an investors' club. One of the questions which arises is: how much gain on the invested capital may be considered normal, that is, a standard worth achieving? The work of Sherif (1935) – described in more detail in chapter 16 – demonstrates that group members tend to converge towards a common norm, which is the average of their *a priori* individual judgements. This suggests that an investors' club will be likely to reach a common standard of gains which is equal to the average of the individual preferences beforehand. This co-called *convergence* pattern in norm formation is a widely established phenomenon. For example, Hoekstra and Wilke (1972) analysed wage recommendations made by managers, who first had to make recommendations on an individual basis and thereafter in groups consisting of five to seven managers. They observed that for the 432 managers who participated (see Bass, 1965), the mean of individual recommendations was equal to the average of group recommendations. From this study two other results are noteworthy. First, it appeared that the managers took into account the specific characteristics (notably performance) and circumstances of the employees for whom they had to make wage recommendations. These differences between the employees concerned resulted in differential wage recommendations. Secondly, in this cross-cultural study it was established that the national origin of the managers played an important role: (groups of) managers from Belgium, the US and Holland were less generous in their wage recommendations than (groups of) managers from Great Britain, Greece, Spain and Italy. These results make it plausible that groups having to make decisions converge towards a common norm, and that circumstances such as the experiences of group members and their analysis of the problem at hand determine to a large extent the establishment of the specific standard. Thus, group norms may vary as a consequence of the information available to the group members.

Zander (1971) investigated how norms may be changed as a consequence of feedback about the success and failure of the actual group performance. He asked group members to perform a ball-propelling task which requires that all group members stand in a single file, grasp a long pole and swing it in unison so that the end of the shaft strikes a wooden ball and rolls it down an extended channel. The ball stops next to one of several numbers painted on the side of the channel, providing a score for that shot. Five shots make a trial, and the group may achieve up to 50 points on each trial. Zander observed that the group's aspired norm (agreed upon by the group members) tended to be close to the immediately preceding score. If the performance improved, the aspired group performance went up. Zander also detected that aspired levels of group productivity changed more after an improvement than after a deterioration of group performance; that is, production norms were raised more often when the performance increased than they are lowered when the performance decreased. Zander showed that norm formation is dependent on the previous success and failure of the group: norms change more easily after success than after failure of the group.

Maintenance of group norms

Norms concerned with an acceptable production level are rather resistant to change. In the pioneering research by Roethlisberger and Dickson (1939) at the Western Electric Company, it was observed that the workers in a 'bank wiring' section consistently produced below their capacities and below the goals set by the management. Results of interviews showed that older workers adhered to the norm of a limited production, because they saw this norm as essential for group survival, e.g. fairness and job tenure. The results of this study also showed how workers who tried to perform above the informal work norm were discouraged. These 'rate busters' were exposed to sanctions in the form of 'binging' (hitting the arm of the rate buster to indicate disapproval and to disrupt work) and psychological isolation in the group (by not talking to the violator).

The use of communication to affect the behaviour of norm violators has been demonstrated by Schachter (1951), who asked groups to decide on what should be done with a delinquency case. In each experimental group, confederates of the experimenter performed three different roles: (1) the *mode*, who accommodated to the average judgement; (2) the *slider*, who initially adopted an extreme position but moved towards the group norm during the discussion; and (3) the *deviate*, who chose and maintained an extreme position throughout the discussion. The results indicated that initially the group discussion was primarily directed towards the two persons with a deviating point of view, the slider and the deviant. After it became apparent that the deviant would not change, the influence attempts subsided. The group eventually excluded the deviant from discussion by not asking her questions and by ignoring her contributions.

That norms are highly resistant to change has also been demonstrated by Coch and French (1948). They found that workers in the Harwood Manufacturing Corporation showed a strong resistance to a change in the methods of doing their jobs. This resistance expressed itself in grievances about the piece rates that went with the new methods, high turnover, low efficiency, restriction of output and marked aggression towards management. By varying the degree of participation, Coch and French carried out a field experiment. In a no-participation group, workers were merely notified about the introduction of the new work methods, which were said to be no more difficult than the former methods. This group improved little and resistance developed almost immediately after the change occurred. Marked expressions of aggression towards management occurred, such as conflict with the methods engineer, the expression of hostility towards the supervisor, deliberate restriction of production, and lack of co-operation with the supervisor. In the participation group, workers participated in the decisions necessary to carry out the work transfer. In this condition the workers raised their production rates, and the other measures also showed that the participation groups responded in a favourable way to the induced change. In sum, the results of the Coch and French study show that group norms are very difficult to change. However, when more persuasive techniques are introduced, this resistance to the change of group norms may be weakened and a certain openness to new standards may be realized.

Functions of group norms
In the previous paragraphs we have indicated that group norms are developed and maintained. In this perspective, norms are co-ordinating devices (see Steiner, 1972) that contribute to the survival of groups. This proposition has been elaborated by Cartwright and Zander (1968) in dealing with the functions of group standards or norms. They distinguish four functions:

1   *Group locomotion* Norms help groups to accomplish their goals. If an executive committee is to make workable plans, it is necessary that members of the committee all believe in the same policy for the organization.
2   *Group maintenance* Norms help groups to maintain themselves as a group. For example, the requirement that members regularly attend meetings or wholeheartedly support the party platform serves to ensure that the group will continue to exist as an entity.

3 *Social reality* Quite often there is no objective reality. Norms help the group to create and maintain a commonly shared frame of reference, which serves as a social reality. For example, a curriculum committee of psychologists having to decide upon minimum requirements for graduation in psychology has to face questions such as what type of work graduates face, what skills they need, how much practical experience is necessary, and how much statistics they need. Shared agreement about these matters creates a certain standard of conduct, which is necessary to design a comprehensive plan.

4 *Defining relationships to social surroundings* Norms help group members to define their relationships to social surroundings, such as other groups, organizations, institutions and other components of society. The aforementioned curriculum committee, for example, needs to define the relationship of psychologists to other social scientists, to other educational programmes, to research, to industrial and mental health organizations and to society at large, without which the designing of a programme is insufficient.

Wilke and Meertens (1994) argue that group norms solve two kinds of conflicts within a group: cognitive conflicts and conflicts of interest. In the case of *cognitive conflicts*, norms resolve problems as captured by Cartwright and Zander, where they point out that convergence of group members' cognitions is necessary for group locomotion, social reality assessment, and establishing a collective view on the group's surroundings.

The second function of norms is the resolution of *conflicts of interest*. In groups, several outcomes are available, such as privileges, status positions and financial compensation. Severe competition may arise in the group so that the group falls apart (see also the section above, on maintenance of group norms) if all group members strive for more rather them fewer outcomes for themselves, unless the group is able to develop and maintain collective rules on how to solve such a conflict of interest. Many rules have the function of preventing potential conflicts of interests. For example, differentiation in financial compensation in groups may be based on effort expenditure, on seniority and/or on educational background. If all group members agree on one of these criteria, or some combination, a conflict of interest is prevented. It should be noted that this function involving the distribution of scarce resources is captured by Thibaut and Kelley (1959), who maintain that through norms a competitive interdependence relation may be transformed to a co-operative one (Kelley and Thibaut, 1978).

Communication networks

Many tasks are fulfilled by groups which have to communicate. As an example, in the study by Bales and Slater (1955) group members addressed the task leader more than they communicated with other group members, suggesting that there was a tendency to assign a central position to that person. Such a systematic pattern of communication is called a **communication network.**

In the study by Bales and Slater the task groups developed a communication network over time; that is to say, in this study the communication network was a dependent variable. However, equally important is the question of how a communication pattern as such, that is, as an independent variable, affects group performance, and members' satisfaction, since in everyday life groups co-ordinate their communication by pre-established norms about who should communicate with whom. In the next section we will describe how specific communication networks affect group productivity and group members' satisfaction.

Group performance

Leavitt (1951) asked whether communication patterns in groups affect their efficiency. In his experiments subjects were seated around a circular table, separated by vertical partitions. Slots, which could be opened and closed by the experimenter, allowed the subjects to pass certain messages to certain other group members. Figure 15.7 shows a number of communication networks. The networks become increasingly centralized from right to left. The wheel is most centralized since any group member in the periphery must send messages through the single central person. In contrast, in the all-channel network no one controls the distribution of messages and any person may communicate with any other person without having to rely on someone else. Employing fairly simple tasks, which merely required the gathering of information, Leavitt (1951) found that wheels were more efficient than circles. Shaw (1964), however, using more complex tasks which required mathematical operations, found the reverse: circles appeared to be more efficient than wheels. In an experiment in which complex tasks were employed he demonstrated that for the first in a series of problems, circle groups were indeed superior to the more centralized wheel groups. However, for the fifth problem wheels were superior to circles. Thus, after some

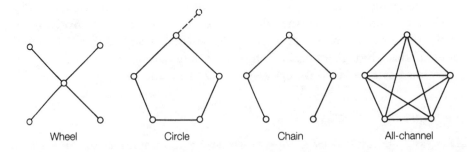

| Wheel | Circle | Chain | All-channel |

Figure 15.7 Some communication networks (based on Leavitt, 1951)

time, more centralized networks perform better on complex tasks than less centralized networks (see also MacKenzie, 1976).

Steiner's ideas (Steiner 1972, 1976) suggest that both simple and complex tasks require co-ordination. Groups working on simple tasks merely have to gather information. This is also necessary for complex tasks. However, groups performing complex tasks also have to perform rather complex operations using this information. Thus complex tasks are relatively more discretionary than simple tasks, that is complex tasks leave it more to the group to decide how to perform the task. Because of the rather undiscretionary nature of the simple task, simple task groups immediately profit from the introduction of a co-ordinating, centralized network of relations. For complex-task groups these co-ordination advantages only begin to pay off after a while, since initially the group has to pay attention to the complex operations of the task itself. It is even possible that initially the introduction of a centralized network may impair group productivity, because of the high co-ordination losses involved. Being confronted with the double task of solving a problem and organizing the group may be too heavy a task. However, as soon as these groups have discovered the operations necessary to perform the task, complex-task groups may also profit from the advantages that a centralized network offers.

Group motivation

In many network studies (see Shaw, 1981, p. 154) subjects are requested to indicate their satisfaction, i.e., how much they enjoyed the task. Two related research findings may be noted. First, satisfaction in decentralized networks is greater than in centralized networks. Secondly, in centralized networks the person in the central position is more satisfied than subjects in the periphery. The explanation of the latter finding is that the central group member is more able to determine the behaviour of the peripheral group members than the peripheral group members are able to determine the behaviour of the central group member. That is, the central group member has more power and, according to Mulder (1960), having more power leads to more satisfaction. In decentralized networks subjects have equal power and the satisfaction of the members is greater than the satisfaction of peripheral group members in the centralized network. As a consequence of sheer numbers, the total satisfaction or group morale in decentralized networks is greater than in centralized networks. These findings suggest that in the long run having a centralized network reduces co-ordination losses. Simultaneously, however, the danger of increased motivation loss arises.

Summary and Conclusions

This chapter has provided a tour through the area of group performance. We have been influenced mainly by Steiner's view that actual performance is equal to potential productivity minus process losses. We looked at group performance from two perspectives.

From the perspective of an individual as a social being, we indicated how individual task performance is affected by the presence of others. Process losses appear to have two components. First, the presence of others evokes task-irrelevant processing – which may be viewed as intrapersonal co-ordination loss. Secondly, the presence of others increases effort; in other words, motivation losses are smaller than when individuals work alone. The combined effect of these two processes is that the presence of others facilitates performance on simple tasks and inhibits performance on complex tasks.

Subsequently, from the perspective of the group we considered how freely interacting group members perform a task. There we established that process losses imply again the same two components, but now on an interpersonal level, that is, interpersonal co-ordination and interpersonal motivation losses which may facilitate or inhibit group performance.

In the last part of the chapter we dealt with group structure. We indicated how and why group structure develops over time, and that two critical group functions operate – task and socio-emotional leadership. We suggested that leaders in successful groups are able to reduce co-ordination and motivation losses. However, having a leader as such may enhance motivational losses, and in some circumstances the instalment of a leader is therefore neither preferred by regular group members nor necessary, given the characteristics of group members and the task and type of organization. Subsequently we argued that norms are essential for any group to accomplish its goals and to maintain itself as a group. Lastly, we elucidated how Steiner's model of group performance may be applied to explain productivity and satisfaction in so-called communication networks. As for group performance in the long run, centralized networks are superior. However, although co-ordination losses may be minimized, enhanced motivation losses may be incurred.

Glossary terms

Brainstorming	Interaction process analysis	Social decision scheme (SDS)
Co-action	(IPA)	Social dilemma
Cohesion	Least preferred co-worker	Social facilitation
Communication network	(LPC)	Social inhibition
Dominant response	Norms	Social loafing
Free-rider effect	Role	Status

Discussion points

1 The strength of Manstead and Semin's model of social facilitation is that it explains rather well the difference between performance on easy and complex tasks. What is its weakness compared with other models?

2 The 'Ringelmann effect' is explained as being due to co-ordination losses. Explain how motivation losses are involved in rope-pulling.

3 Baron et al. (1993) make a distinction between 'social loafing', which is due to the fact that one's own contribution cannot be identified, and 'free-riding', referring to one's belief that one's own contribution is dispensable. Show that, in these terms, Diehl and Stroebe (1987) investigated social loafing. How would you investigate 'free-riding' in brainstorming sessions?

4 Explain that part of the 'Ringelmann effect' might be due to the 'sucker' and 'free-rider' effects as distinguished by Kerr (1983).

5 Evaluate Bales's research findings concerning task and social-emotional leadership in view of expectation states theory.

6 Why is Fiedler's leadership theory so popular in applied research?

7 Discuss why, in crisis situations, a need for centralized leadership quite often emerges. What are the consequences for peripheral group members?

Suggestions for further reading

Baron, R., Kerr, N. and Miller, N. (1992) *Group Process, Group Decision, Group Action*. Buckingham: Open University Press. This book gives an excellent review of theory development and empirical studies in the area of group dynamics.

Baron, R. A. and Paulus, P. B. (1991) *Understanding Human Relations*. London: Allyn and Bacon. A practical guide to people at work in organizations.

Cartwright, P. and Zander, A. (1968) *Group Dynamics: Research and Theory*, 3rd edn. New York: Harper & Row. This volume of collected papers presents much of the classic seminal research and thinking in the area of group dynamics. The introductory chapters provide excellent summaries of the basic ideas.

Forsyth, D. (1990) *An Introduction to Group Dynamics*, 2nd edn. Monterey, CA: Brooks/Cole. A well written, up-to-date and comprehensive introduction to group dynamics.

Liebrand, W., Messick, D. and Wilke, H. (1992) *Social Dilemmas*. Oxford: Pergamon Press. A collection of papers about factors affecting the choices of group members in social dilemmas.

Paulus, P. B. (1983) *Basic Group Processes*. New York: Springer. A collection of sophisticated reviews on group dynamics.

Worchel, S., Wood, W. and Simpson, J. A. (eds) (1992) *Group Process and Productivity*. London: Sage. This collection includes papers on small-group decision-making, status processes, group development and group norms.

Wilke, H. A. M. and Meertens, R. W. (1993) *Group Performance*. London: Routledge. An up-to-date and comprehensive text on group performance. It shows that cognitive, reflective and communicative processes affect group performance.

Key studies

Latané, B., Williams, K. and Harkins, S. (1979). Many hands make light the work: the causes and consequences of social loafing. *Journal of Personality and Social Psychology*, 37, 822–32.

Diehl, M. and Stroebe, W. (1987). Productivity loss in brainstorming groups: toward the solution of a riddle. *Journal of Personality and Social Psychology*, 53, 497–509.

16   Social Influence in Small Groups

Eddy Van Avermaet

Contents

Introduction

Conformity, or majority influence

Innovation, or minority influence

Decision-making in groups

Obeying immoral orders: the social influence of an authority

Summary and conclusions

Introduction

Imagine you are one of a group of seven people who represent the student body at departmental meetings. The forthcoming meeting will discuss and take a vote on a proposed change in the curriculum: several applied courses are to be dropped and replaced by more theoretically oriented subjects. Before the meeting the student representatives get together to try to reach a common position on the issue. You have given the issue a lot of thought and you favour the departmental proposal. At the student meeting you then learn that some people share your view but that others do not. You try to convince them of your viewpoint and they try to convince you of theirs. What will be the outcome? Most probably you will reply: it all depends on the circumstances! In giving that reply, you concur with social psychologists, who for many years now have been systematically studying the factors that determine social influence in small groups.

SOCIAL
INFLUENCE

Broadly speaking the study of **social influence** coincides with social psychology itself, because the entire field deals with the influence of social factors on behaviour. Typically, however, the concept of social influence is given a more restricted meaning: social influence refers to a change in the judgements, opinions and attitudes of an individual as a result of being exposed to the judgements, opinions and attitudes of other individuals (de Montmollin, 1977). With this restricted definition in mind, the present chapter will introduce you to some of the more important phenomena that have been studied concerning social influence in group settings. One should keep in mind that this restricted definition also covers the area of persuasive communication and attitude change, described in chapter 9. It would appear instructive for the student of this book to search explicitly for elements of similarity and integration between these two separate chapters.

CONFORMITY

MAJORITY
INFLUENCE

The first topic is **conformity**, or **majority influence**. Do individuals change their opinions when they learn that the majority of the members of a group to which they belong hold a different opinion? Do they perhaps only give in overtly, yet maintain their own conviction in private, or does majority influence really change people's minds? Under which conditions do individuals manage to resist majority influence? Next we turn our attention to the reverse phenomenon, namely **innovation**, or **minority influence**. Can a minority in a group bring about changes in the opinions of a majority? Which characteristics should a minority have in order to produce an effect? Do minorities exert their influence through the same mechanisms as majorities? Do they have more or less influence? Is there only a difference in quantity of influence, or do majorities and minorities produce qualitatively different effects?

INNOVATION

MINORITY
INFLUENCE

The third and fourth sections will deal respectively with the phenomena of group polarization and obedience. **Group polarization** refers to the fact that, under certain conditions, the outcome of a group discussion is more extreme than

GROUP
POLARIZATION

Plate 16.1 Twenty-five dead bodies of members of a cult were found in these burned-out Swiss chalets: an apparent mass suicide. Is this an example of obedience, majority influence, or minority influence?

the initial average position of the individual group members. We will look into some of the theories and experiments that have been set up to account for this most remarkable phenomenon. Finally, we will pay attention to a special case of social influence: when and why will individuals, merely at the persistent request of an authority, show obedience to orders which they themselves consider unethical and which they are, in principle, unwilling to execute?

Conformity, or Majority Influence

Sherif and the autokinetic effect

In an early social-influence experiment Muzafer Sherif (1935) placed subjects, alone or in groups of two or three, in a completely darkened room. At a distance of about 5 metres a single, small stationary light was presented to them. As you may already have experienced yourself, in the absence of reference points a stationary light appears to move rather erratically in all directions. This perceptual illusion is known as the **autokinetic effect**. Sherif asked his subjects to give a verbal estimate of the extent of movement of the light, obviously without informing them of the autokinetic effect. Half of the subjects made their first 100 judgements alone. On three subsequent days they went through three more sets of trials, but this time in groups of two or three. For the other half of

AUTOKINETIC EFFECT

the subjects the procedure was reversed. They underwent the three group sessions first and ended with a session alone. Subjects who first made their judgements alone, quite quickly developed a standard estimate (a personal norm) around which their judgements fluctuated. This personal norm was stable, but it varied greatly between individuals. In the group phases of the experiment, which brought together people with different personal norms, subjects' judgements converged towards a more or less common position – a group norm. With the reverse procedure this group norm developed in the first session and persisted in the later session alone. Figure 16.1 illustrates both kinds of findings. The funnel effect in the left panel reveals the convergence in the (median) judgements of three subjects who judged first alone (I), and later in each other's presence (II, III, IV). The right panel shows the judgements of a group of three subjects who went through the procedure in the reverse order. Here the convergence is already present in the first group session and there is no sign of funnelling out in the final 'alone' session.

This famous experiment shows that, where confronted with an unstructured and ambiguous stimulus, people nevertheless develop a stable internal frame of reference against which to judge the stimulus. However, as soon as they are confronted with the different judgements of others they quickly abandon this frame of reference so as to adjust to that of others. On the other hand, a joint frame of reference formed in the presence of others continues to affect a person's judgements when the source of influence is no longer present.

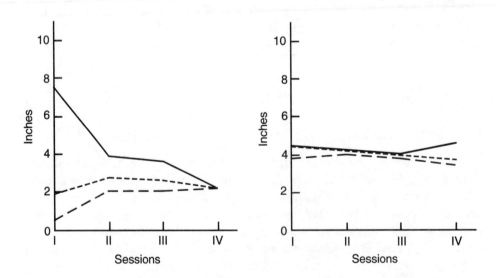

Figure 16.1 Median judgements of movement under alone (I) or group (II, III, IV) conditions (left), and under group (I, II, III) or alone (IV) conditions (right) in Sherif's (1935) study on norm formation

In the introduction, conformity was described as a change in an individual's judgement in the direction of the judgements expressed by the majority of the members of a group to which the individual belongs. Strictly speaking Sherif's study is not a conformity or majority-influence experiment because he merely brought together two or three people who held different opinions. To turn it into a conformity study one would have to replace all the subjects but one with confederates, who would unanimously agree upon a particular judgement. Jacobs and Campbell (1961) did just that and, in addition, after every 30 judgements they replaced a confederate with a naive subject until the whole group was made up of naive subjects. Their results indicated that the majority had a significant effect on the subjects' judgements, even after they had gradually been removed from the situation.

Up to this point you may not be too surprised. After all, it is normal and even adaptive that people are influenced by or conform to the judgements of others when the judgemental stimulus is ambiguous or when they feel uncertain about their own judgement. But would you also conform to the judgements of others when they appear to be patently wrong, when their judgements are completely at odds with what your senses and physical reality tell you? Would social reality prevail, or would you, as the saying goes, 'call them as you see them'?

The surprise of Solomon Asch

The question raised above constituted the starting point of a series of famous conformity experiments conducted by Solomon Asch in the early 1950s (Asch, 1951, 1956). In his first study Asch invited seven students to participate in an experiment on visual discrimination. Their task was simple enough: 18 times they would have to decide which of three comparison lines was equal in length to a standard line. On each trial one comparison line was, in fact, equal in length to the standard line, but the other two were different (for an example, see figure 16.2). On some trials these were both longer or shorter, or one was longer and the other shorter. Also, trials differed in the extent to which the two incorrect lines were different from the standard line. All in all the task was apparently very easy, as is shown by the fact that in a control group of 37 subjects, who made their

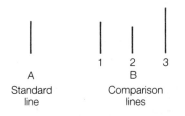

Figure 16.2 An example of the stimuli presented in Asch's experiment

judgements in isolation, 35 people did not make a single error, one person made one error and one person made two errors. Hence, in total over subjects and trials, a negligible 0.7 per cent errors were made in the control condition. In the experimental condition, subjects, who were seated in a semicircle, were requested to give their judgements aloud, in the order in which they were seated, from position 1 to position 7. Actually there was only one real subject, seated in position 6. All the others were confederates of the experimenter and, on each trial, they unanimously gave a predetermined answer. On six 'neutral' trials (the first two trials, and four other trials distributed over the remaining set) the confederates gave correct answers. On the other 12 'critical' trials they unanimously agreed on an incorrect line. The neutral trials, particularly the first two, were added to avoid suspicion on the part of the real subject and to avoid an attribution of poor vision as the cause of the responses of the confederates. It should be pointed out that, throughout the experiment, both the experimenter and the confederates acted in a rather impersonal and formal manner, not showing any surprise or negative reaction to the answers given. As a matter of fact, as you might expect, only the real subjects showed various signs of non-neutral behaviour.

The results reveal the tremendous impact of an 'obviously' incorrect but unanimous majority on the judgements of a lone subject. In comparison with the control condition, which you will remember yielded only 0.7 per cent errors, the experimental subjects made almost 37 per cent errors. Not every subject made that many errors, but it is instructive to observe that out of Asch's 123 subjects only about 25 per cent did not make a single error (compared with 95 per cent in the control condition), another 28 per cent gave eight or more (out of 12) incorrect answers, and the remaining subjects made between one and seven mistakes. From a methodological point of view, it is important to grasp clearly the distinction between percentage of errors and percentage of influenced subjects. Students (and even textbooks) sometimes confuse the two measures by asserting that 37 per cent errors means that 37 per cent of the subjects were influenced. The above distinction is also important from an interpretational viewpoint, because just by itself the error percentage presents only an incomplete picture of the amount of influence exerted (it says nothing about the distribution of this influence).

Essentially similar results have been obtained on numerous occasions, using different subject populations and different judgemental tasks. For those who might feel that the Asch effect reflects only the conformist attitude of a specific time in history or of a specific culture and is therefore a thing of the past, later replications of the Asch study in Belgium (Doms and Van Avermaet, 1982) and in the Netherlands (Vlaander and Van Rooijen, 1985) have obtained essentially comparable results (but see Perrin and Spencer, 1980 for a negative finding). Asch's experiment, with its astonishing results, provided the groundwork for a rich tradition of theoretical speculation and empirical studies directed at determining the boundaries of the phenomenon, the conditions under which conformity increases and decreases, and whether conformity is only public or also private. We now present a selection of this research against the background of the major theoretical perspective within which it can be situated. Most of this research has made use of a paradigm, modelled on Asch's, but far more economical. Using the so-called 'Crutchfield' technique (1955), subjects are typically placed in separate cubicles where they see the responses of (simulated) confederates appear electronically on a panel. The savings in time and confederates are great, but some of the realism of the original Asch procedure is lost in the process.

Why people conform: normative and informational influence

When people have to express a judgement about some aspect of reality in the presence of others they have two major concerns: they want to be right, and they want to make a good impression on the others. To determine what is right, individuals have two sources of information: what their perceptions of physical reality indicate, and what others say. Throughout their lives individuals have learned to appreciate the value of both sources of information. On numerous occasions they have experienced the adaptive value of founding their judgements and behaviours on their own view of reality. On the other hand, a lot of what they have learned about reality has been based on information provided by others, and in their experience relying on others' judgements has proved adaptive as well. Moreover, in most instances both their own judgements and those of others have coincided, providing people with a stable view of their environment. The conformity situation, however, opposes these two sources of information and confronts the individual with the conflict of choosing between two – in principle – reliable bases of information. If, in this perspective, individuals conform, they are said to have undergone **informational influence**: they yield to others because they trust the others' judgement more than their own. There is, however, also another reason why a person might yield to group pressure. Because we are dependent on others for the satisfaction of a variety of needs, it is important that we maximize their liking for us. To the extent that disagreeing with others can be expected to lead to dislike or even outward rejection, and that agreeing will lead to more positive evaluations and continued group membership, people are induced to conform to others' judgements for normative reasons. Hence, conformity caused by the desire to be liked and by the aversion to being disliked is due to **normative influence**.

INFORMATIONAL INFLUENCE

NORMATIVE INFLUENCE

Informational and normative influence (Deutsch and Gerard, 1955) are, then, the major general mechanisms through which groups have an impact on their members. Of course, the relative weight of these two mechanisms varies from situation to situation. In some instances, people will conform more because of the information others provide, whereas in others they will conform mainly for normative reasons. Moreover – and this is an equally important distinction – normative and informational influence processes can be expected to produce effects at different levels. If a person conforms mainly because of what others will think of her, she will change her overt behaviour while privately maintaining her prior conviction; but if she trusts the information provided by others she will, in addition, also change her private opinion. Hence a distinction should be made

COMPLIANCE

CONVERSION

between public conformity, or **compliance**, and private conformity, or, **conver sion**. As a matter of fact, researchers in this field have used public and private response modes in conformity settings as a means of assessing whether normative or informational influence is the more important change mechanism. Results of these experiments have shown that, at least as far as the original Asch experiment is concerned, normative influence is more important than informational influence. This can be inferred from the observation that public responses are far more influenced by the group's judgement than are responses given in private (for a review see Allen, 1965).

In a more general sense, and through manipulation of various characteristics of the influence situation, social psychologists have attempted to collect evidence for the theoretical proposition that conformity will increase or decrease according to the amount of informational and/or normative dependence of an individual on the group.

Normative and informational influence: experimental evidence

Beginning with normative influence, Endler (1965) showed that direct reinforcement for conforming responses leads to an increment in conformity. Deutsch and Gerard (1955) increased the interdependence of the group members by promising a reward (tickets to a Broadway play) to the five groups that made the fewest errors of judgement. Setting this goal for the group, which clearly made the members very dependent on each other for obtaining a desired effect, produced twice as much conformity as a baseline condition. Thibaut and Strickland (1956) described the setting as a test of co-operative ability and told the subjects that groups would be compared on this dimension. Subjects in this condition of competition between groups conformed more than subjects for whom accuracy of individual judgement was emphasized. As a final example of the role of normative influence, Dittes and Kelley (1956) varied the subjects' status within the group. They observed more conformity in subjects of medium status than in subjects of either very low or very high status. High-status subjects can afford to deviate, low-status subjects have nothing to lose (they may not even care about the group); but medium-status subjects have most to gain by conforming and most to lose by not conforming.

Turning to the role of informational influence, it has been shown that the subject's perceived competence at the judgement task relative to others, as well as his self-confidence, determine the amount of conformity (e.g., Mausner, 1954).

Di Vesta (1959) showed that more conformity occurred on later trials if the early trials had contained many neutral trials (where the majority gave correct answers), because under these conditions the subject was more likely to attribute competence to the other group members. Task difficulty or stimulus ambiguity is another variable which, through the informational mechanism, influences conformity. These factors contribute to more uncertainty in a person and to a heavier reliance on the unanimous judgements of others (e.g., Asch, 1952; Crutchfield, 1955).

The size of the majority is yet another example of a relevant variable in this context. Asch (1951) ran groups in which the size of the 'majority' varied from one to sixteen. One person had no effect, but two persons already produced 13 per cent errors. With three confederates the conformity effect reached its full strength with 33 per cent errors. The addition of even more confederates did not lead to further increments in conformity. Later studies by Gerard, Wilhelmy and Connelly (1968) and by Latané and Wolf (1981) have questioned this conclusion and suggest that adding more members to the majority will, in effect, lead to more conformity but with diminishing increments per added member. On the other hand, the degree of perceived independence of the influence sources is also important. Adding more members to the majority will only lead to more influence if the majority members are perceived as independent judges and not as sheep following the others or as members of a group who have arrived jointly at a judgement. Wilder (1977) showed that two independent groups of two people have more impact than four people who present their judgements as a group, and three groups of two have more effect than two groups of three, who in turn yield more conformity than one group of six. Clearly, independent sources of information are thought to be more reliable than a single aggregated information source.

Finally, a fascinating series of studies, excellently summarized by Allen (1975), has looked at the effects of replacing one of the confederates with another person who deviates from the majority position. When Asch gave the subject a 'supporter', in the form of a confederate who answered before the subject and who gave correct answers on all trials, the conformity of the real subject dropped dramatically to a mere 5.5 per cent. In trying to find out whether the reduced conformity was caused by the break in the unanimity of the majority or by the fact that subjects now had a social supporter (for their own private opinion), Asch added a condition in which the confederate deviated from the majority but gave an even more incorrect answer than they did. Hence the majority was not unanimous, but the subject received no social support either. The results showed that the extreme dissenter was nearly as effective in reducing conformity as the social supporter. Breaking the unanimity would therefore appear to be crucial but, as Allen and Levine (1968, 1969) later showed, this conclusion only holds with respect to unambiguous stimulus situations, as in Asch's experiments. With opinion statements, only a genuine social supporter will lead to reduced conformity.

The role of social support is further demonstrated in studies where the subject has a partner for the first part of the experiment, who then ceases to respond owing to an alleged breakdown in the equipment (Allen and Bragg, 1965), or who then leaves the room (Allen and Wilder, 1972). Even under these non-responding-partner or absent-partner conditions people continue to resist influence, at least as long as they are assured that the partner had responded in the same setting (under pressure) as they do. Merely knowing that another person thinks as you do is not sufficient! Also, when a subject is originally given a partner who then deserts by switching to the incorrect majority responses, she will not maintain her prior 'independence'. Rather, she will conform as if she had never had a partner (Asch, 1955).

Although the social-support effects can also partially be interpreted in terms of normative influence, it is instructive to look at them from an informational point of view. Looking at the desertion effect first, it is understandable that a person, upon learning that someone whose judgements he trusts (because they coincide with his own) changes sides, will be strongly influenced by that person's behaviour. 'Here is an intelligent person changing his position; I'd better do as he does because he can be relied on!' In a similar vein the other social-support effects would tend to indicate that the subject's refusal to conform is caused by the fact that, as Allen puts it, the social supporter provides an independent assessment of reality, which is sufficient to outweigh the potential informational value of the majority's responses. This interpretation is strongly supported by the data of an experiment by Allen and Levine (1971). Here too the subject was given a supporter, but in one of their two support conditions the social support was invalid. The supporter, although giving correct answers, could not possibly be perceived as a valid source of information because the subject knew that the supporter had extremely poor vision (as was evident from a pre-experimental eye examination and from his eyeglasses with thick lenses). The results, shown in figure 16.3, indicate that, although invalid social support is sufficient to reduce the amount of conformity significantly when compared with a unanimous majority condition, the valid social supporter has much more impact. One lesson to be learned from all these studies is obvious: if you are afraid of being influenced by a group (at least publicly – and that is often what counts!), make sure you bring a partner along, and preferably one you can count on to stick by your position!

The joint effects of normative and informational influence

As was briefly suggested earlier, in most situations both normative and informational factors play a role in determining the amount of conformity. The studies reviewed above focused on one or the other, because they wanted to illuminate their unique effects. A study by Insko et al. (1983) looked at their joint effects. In this study the subjects, in groups of six, had to judge whether a colour, shown on a slide, was more similar to another colour shown to the left or to another colour shown to the right. On the critical trials four confederates who answered before the subject, and another who answered last, gave responses that deviated from those given by most subjects in a control condition where they were alone. Two variables were manipulated: the subject had to respond either publicly or privately, and was told that the experimenter either could or could not determine which response was more correct. In the 'determined' condition the experimenter referred to an apparatus through which he could accurately measure which response was more correct; in the 'undetermined' condition this was said to be impossible. Insko anticipated more influence in the public than in the private condition because of normative influence (the concern with being liked), and he also anticipated more influence in the determined than in the undetermined condition because of informational influence (the concern with being right). The latter prediction becomes understandable when you realize that not only will you try harder to be correct in the determined condition, but you have every reason to assume that the others too will try harder. The results were

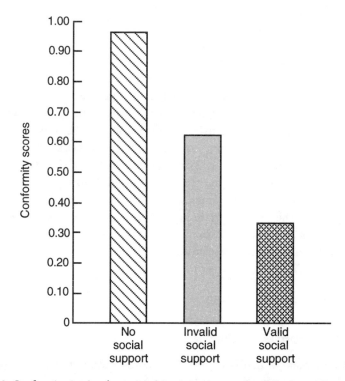

Figure 16.3 Conformity in the absence and in the presence of social support (based on Allen and Levine, 1971)

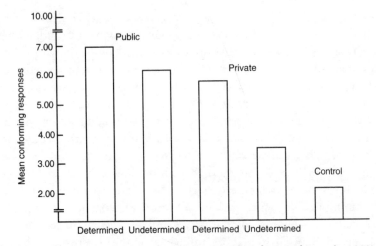

Figure 16.4 Mean conformity data on 10 critical trials (data from Insko et al., 1983)

completely in line with the predictions. Both manipulations yielded a clear main effect and no interaction. As figure 16.4 indicates, in the determined and undetermined conditions public responding led to more conformity than private responding, and at the same time the determined condition produced stronger influence effects than the undetermined condition, in the public but also in the private condition. In addition, all means differed significantly from the no-influence control condition. Hence, even with 'objective' stimuli, informational influence can add to the effect of normative influence!

To conclude, literally hundreds of studies have demonstrated the impact of a majority on isolated individuals, although – as we saw – the addition of a person sharing their viewpoint makes them resist that influence. But is resistance the only behavioural option open to the individual (and his or her supporter)? Can he or she not try actively to attempt to persuade the majority that they might be wrong and that he or she is right? Just look around and you will say 'yes'. However, it was not really until the late 1960s that social psychologists, mainly under the impetus of the French psychologist Serge Moscovici, began seriously to study the conditions under which a minority can do more than merely resist, and can itself become an active source of influence.

Innovation, or Minority Influence

The power of a consistent minority

In 'Twelve Angry Men', a brilliant film directed by Sidney Lumet, twelve jurors have to decide over the guilt or innocence of a young man charged with the murder of his father. At the outset of the deliberation all but one are convinced of the youth's guilt. Does the lone juror (Henry Fonda) yield to the unanimous majority? No! Does he only passively resist their influence attempts? No! Instead he actively attempts to persuade the others of the correctness of his own position, standing firm, committed, self-confident and unwavering. One by one the other jurors change sides, until in the end they all agree that the accused is not guilty. History and present-day social life provide ample examples of minority influence: Galileo, Freud, new forms of art, the growing impact of the ecological movement, and the women's movement are but a few examples.

In his book '*Social Influence and Social Change*', Moscovici (1976) argues that most instances of minority influence or innovation cannot be accounted for by the mechanisms which have traditionally been proposed to explain majority influence. Indeed, if you think about it, minorities do not have a lot going for them: they are few in number; they often do not have normative control over the majority; at first they are more often ridiculed than taken seriously; they are perceived as 'dummies' and 'weirdoes'. In other words, they do not seem to have access to the informational and normative means of control, explicitly or implicitly available to a majority. How can they then have influence? Moscovici answers that the core of their impact is to be found in their own *behavioural style*. A minority has to propose a clear position on the issue at hand and hold firmly to it, withstanding all the time the pressures exerted by the majority. The most important component of this behavioural style is the **consistency** with which the CONSISTENCY minority defends and advocates its position. This consistency entails two components: intra-individual consistency or stability over time (diachronic consistency) and inter-individual consistency within the minority (synchronic consistency). Only if minority members agree amongst themselves and continue to do so over time can they expect the majority to begin to question its own position, to consider the correctness of the minority position, and eventually to be influenced.

The key role of consistency has been demonstrated in many experiments, only two of which shall be described in detail here (for overviews see Maass and Clark, 1984; Wood, Lundgren, Ouellette, Busceme and Blackstone, 1994). In what is essentially a reversed Asch experiment, Moscovici, Lage and Naffrechoux (1969) had subjects participate in a study on colour perception in groups of six. Subjects first underwent a test for colour blindness. Upon passing this test they were then shown 36 slides, all clearly blue and only differing in intensity. Their task was simply to judge the colour of the slides by naming *aloud* a simple colour. Two of the subjects, seated in the first and second position, or in the first and fourth position, were actually confederates of the experimenter. In the consistent condition they answered 'green' on all trials, which made them diachronically as well as synchronically consistent. In the inconsistent condition they answered 'green' 24 times and 'blue' 12 times. The experiment also contained a control condition, where the groups were made up of six naive subjects. As figure 16.5 shows, in the control condition only 0.25 per cent green responses were given, revealing the obviousness of the correct response. Out of 22 naive subjects only one person gave two green responses. In the inconsistent minority condition, 1.25 per cent responses were green, only slightly and insignificantly more than in the control condition. In the consistent minority condition, however, green responses were made 8.42 per cent of the time, which is significantly more than in either of the other two conditions. In terms of the number of subjects who said

Plate 16.2 Henry Fonda wins over a previously unanimous majority of other jurors in the film *Twelve Angry Men*

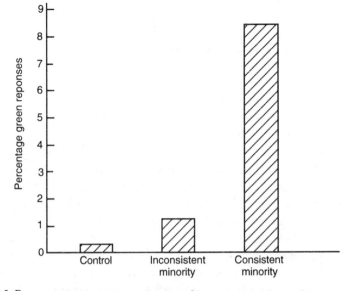

Figure 16.5 Percentage green responses given by majority subjects in the experiment by Moscovici, Lage and Naffrechoux (1969)

green, 32 per cent of the people gave at least one green response. This should not be taken to imply that the overall effect was a consequence of isolated individuals who were each influenced independently by the minority. On the contrary, the effect was the result of a change of the responses within the respective groups, as can be inferred from Moscovici's observation that there were really two categories of groups: those in which nobody was influenced, and those in which several people were influenced. It should also be noted that the minority's seating position made no difference.

This experiment clearly shows that a consistent minority can have a distinct effect on the public judgements of the members of a majority group. Before proceeding it is instructive to compare Moscovici's setting with that of Asch. In the Asch study one subject is opposed by a consistent majority of six; in Moscovici's experiment a group of four naive subjects stands against a consistent minority of only two confederates. In Asch's study the conflict confronting the subjects is induced by the majority; in Moscovici's experiment a similar conflict is induced by a minority. Although the minority does not have 'the numbers', its consistent behavioural style makes it influential – at least after a while, when the majority subjects begin to observe that the minority maintains its position in spite of their opposition. It is indeed a typical observation that, in contrast to conformity studies, the minority effect only begins to show after a certain period (Nemeth, 1982). The impression of potential correctness of the minority position is further advanced when majority members notice that one or more of their own group members begin to answer like the minority – a finding reminiscent of what happens in a conformity setting when a social supporter of the subject deserts to the majority. The picture that begins to unfold, then, is that a consistent minority sets in motion a variety of intra- and interpersonal processes in the majority which ultimately result in influence.

Before discussing these processes, however, let us look at a second experiment, which demonstrates that consistency need not necessarily take the form of repetition of the same response, but can also be expressed through a clear pattern in the responses of the minority. Nemeth, Swedlund and Kanki (1974) essentially replicated Moscovici's earlier experiment, but they added two conditions in which the confederates said 'green' on half of the trials and 'green–blue' on the other half. In a random condition the green and green–blue responses were randomly distributed over the trials, but in a correlated condition the confederates said green to the brighter slides and green–blue to the dimmer slides (or vice versa). In the latter condition the confederates were definitely not repetitive in their answers, yet they were consistent in that their responses were patterned after a characteristic of the stimulus (its brightness). The results showed that, compared with a no-influence control condition, the random condition had no effect. The correlated condition, on the other hand, produced almost 21 per cent influenced responses. Interestingly, and in contrast to Moscovici's findings, a repetitive and consistent 'green' minority did not significantly affect the subjects' responses. Nemeth gives an interesting clue as to why this happened. Her subjects were allowed to respond with all the colours that they saw in the slides, whereas Moscovici's subjects could only respond with a single colour. If a minority does not show any flexibility in its behaviour (when the context allows for it) it has no effect in spite of its consistency, because under these circumstances it also tends to be perceived as rigid and unrealistic. A series of studies by Mugny and Papastamou (Mugny, 1982) provides direct evidence for this interpretation. Using opinion statements rather than a perceptual task, they observed that minority proposals presented to subjects in written form were far less effective in inducing change when they were formulated in slogan-like and uncompromising terms than when expressed in a more moderate language. Importantly, the rigid and the flexible messages were perceived as equally consistent. Mugny feels that a minority will only be effective if it consistently provides a distinct alternative perspective on reality and yet shows its willingness to negotiate a kind of compromise. Of course, beyond a certain point this willingness to compromise may take away some of the perception of consistency and result in less influence (Turner, 1991).

Nemeth's and Mugny's experiments again show that consistency is a necessary condition for minority influence, but at the same time they indicate that whether or not consistency leads to effective influence depends on how it is interpreted by the majority. The image one forms of the minority and the nature of the attributional processes activated jointly by the minority's behavioural style, by the context in which it emits these behaviours, and by the behavioural reactions of the members of one's own group, appear crucial mediating variables in determining the minority's ultimate effect on the judgements of a subject.

Why does consistency lead to influence: an attributional account

In their very perceptive analysis of the minority influence literature, Maass and Clark (1984) start with the plausible assumption that majority members, upon confronting a minority position, will ask themselves: 'Why do they respond as they do?' Their unexpected behaviour sets in motion an attributional search for the causes of their behaviour. By applying Kelley's (1967) *covariation* principle (see chapter 7) one should expect a person attribution, because we are dealing with a configuration of low consensus and high consistency over time (distinctiveness information is usually absent). Research does indeed support this reasoning, because consistent minorities tend to be perceived as certain and confident. This attribution is further enhanced when one observes that the minority maintains its position in spite of the opposition from the majority group. If the social pressure emanating from the majority is conceived as an inhibitory cause, the *augmentation* principle (Kelley, 1973) indeed dictates an even stronger person attribution. This attribution should lead majority members to take the minority position seriously, induce them perhaps to start looking at reality from its perspective and – as a result – to be influenced. Things are more complicated, however, because an attribution of confidence and certainty does not necessarily lead to an inference of competence. A person can be perceived as certain and confident, but if this confidence is viewed as an expression of dogmatism, craziness or some other idiosyncratic characteristic of the minority, no influence should obtain. Generally speaking, and in terms of Kelley's *discounting* principle, in the presence of other plausible causes, consistent behaviour of a minority should be less likely to have much impact. As a matter of fact, it can be postulated that majority members would first look for such alternative interpretations – in view of the unexpected nature of the minority's behaviour – and only take its position seriously after these alternative interpretations have been ruled out.

A number of experiments are consistent with the above line of thought. As pointed out earlier, Mugny and Papastamou have conducted a variety of studies in which they show that a consistent minority which behaves in a very rigid, extreme and dogmatic manner is less influential than an equally consistent minority which uses a flexible negotiation style (Mugny, 1982). Similarly, if through instructions the majority members' attention is focused on the minority's psychological characteristics rather than only on their position, the minority produces less influence (Mugny and Papastamou, 1980). Idiosyncratic attributions are also more likely if the minority consists of only one person (Moscovici and Lage, 1976) unless that person shows other behaviours that can counter such attribution (e.g. Nemeth and Wachtler, 1974). Also, if the minority appears to have something to gain from the position it takes, self-interest becomes a plausible alternative cause of their behaviour (Maass, Clark and Haberkorn, 1982).

In spite of the apparent coherence and elegance of the above attributional account, and in spite of the overall fit of empirically observed influence effects with this account, theoretical arguments as well as some data indicate that the picture is yet far from complete. At the theoretical level and on the basis of Kelley's original covariation analysis Chaiken and Stangor (1987) are surprised that Maass and Clark focus on a dispositional person attribution as a first step in the attributional chain. They argue that the effectiveness of a persuasive communication depends more on whether or not an entity attribution is made; that is, whether the message is perceived to reflect a statement about the true state of affairs. This attribution would appear to require not only high consistency, but also high rather than low consensus and strong distinctiveness. Although we are sympathetic towards Chaiken and Stangor's point at a general level, in the specific case of a minority opposing a majority (low consensus), a person attribution of confidence, certainty and commitment might be a precondition for an ultimate entity attribution. One cannot expect people to accept a minority position as true if the minority itself is perceived as wavering and uncertain in the first place.

At the empirical level direct evidence for the mediational role of confidence, certainty and commitment attributions is mixed. A meta-analysis of all the available studies, including such measures, showed that perceived consistency does act as a significant predictor of influence, but none of the measures of the assumed influence mediators showed a significant relation to the dependent variables (Wood et al., 1994). Wood et al. speculate that the effectiveness of perceived consistency may, rather, derive from its interpersonal consequences. Consistency may have its effects through its impact on attention. Beyond that, a consistent minority also places the responsibility for resolving an ingroup conflict on the majority. More generally, we should perhaps also focus on other cognitive processes, not just attributions (see later sections), and on other motives besides the validation of one's opinions (Chaiken and Stangor, 1987).

Finally, the impact of a consistent minority will of course also depend on the strength of the prior conviction of the majority members and on how they perceive each other. Paicheler (1976, 1977) showed that a minority defending a position in line with the *Zeitgeist* (the direction in which social norms are changing) had more impact than a minority opposing it. If (owing to the *Zeitgeist*) majority members have already become uncertain with respect to their opinions, then a consistent minority which explicitly defends the new norm provides a clear anchor towards which to move. Moscovici's observation that the minority effect is often a group effect (nobody moves or everybody moves) suggests that as the perceived confidence of one's own group decreases, the minority gains in impact. This so-called *snowball effect* was nicely demonstrated by Kiesler and Pallak (1975). After learning an initial distribution of opinions on a discussion topic (with two people deviating strongly from six others), subjects were later informed that one majority member had either moved even further away from the minority (reactionary condition), or moved towards the minority (compromise condition), or completely defected to the minority (defection condition). Compared with a control condition, where the distribution of opinions remained identical, and with the reactionary condition, the compromise condition produced more and the defection condition yielded most influence. Conversely, if majority members stick to their guns and display the same consistency as the minority, minority influence disappears. As Doms and Van Avermaet (1985) have shown, when a subject can enjoy the consistent refusal of fellow majority members to give in, the minority effect disappears completely. Even when people can observe the majority's behaviour only temporarily before being confronted alone by the minority opposition, they resist its influence to a sizeable degree.

Majority and minority influence: compliance and conversion

At this point you might raise the important question: at which level does this influence occur? Perhaps under certain conditions a minority may not lead to public influence (because of normative pressures from the majority), but it could still be influential at a more latent, private level. In our discussion of majority influence we argued that in a conformity setting the normative pressures lead to public influence and that informational pressures lead to public and private influence, but do not forget that in that setting all others are opposed to the subject. In the minority setting, on the other hand, subjects have to deal with two groups – the opposing minority and their own majority group. It is plausible to assume that the minority has less normative control over the subject than does a majority. As a matter of fact, research shows that minorities are strongly disliked (Moscovici and Lage, 1976). For this reason one might expect minorities to have less public influence on a subject, at least when other resisting majority members are also present. But how about private influence? Could it be that a minority has a more profound impact on one's private opinion than a majority, whose answers one might simply accept because 'if so many people agree, they must be right and I must be wrong' without really having given a lot of thought to the issue at hand?

Precisely these thoughts have led Moscovici (1980) to formulate some very striking propositions about the *differences* in process and effect between majority and minority influence. These propositions have generated a lot of research and quite a bit of controversy, because other researchers have emphasized the *similarities* between the two influence modalities (Latané and Wolf, 1981; Tanford and Penrod, 1984; Kruglanski and Mackie, 1990). The question itself is

506 *Eddy Van Avermaet*

fascinating and yet very complicated, and we can therefore only present you with an introduction to it (for an excellent discussion see Maass and Clark, 1984; and Wood et al., 1994). Before doing so, it is perhaps helpful to keep in mind that Moscovici essentially deals with the contrast between a situation in which a unanimous majority confronts a single person and a situation where a minority group stands against a majority group. You should be careful not to generalize from this situation to all conceivable minority–majority interaction settings, where the impact of intra- and interpersonal processes and the direct versus indirect effects of minorities and majorities might be different.

SOCIAL
COMPARISON

Moscovici proposes that the majority, in the conformity paradigm, activates a **social comparison** process in which the subject compares his response with that of others, 'concentrates all his attention on what others say, so as to fit in with their opinions and judgements' (1980, p. 214), without giving a lot of attention or thought to the issue itself. Add to that the role of the normative pressures exerted by the majority, and only public compliance in their presence is expected. Any private effects would be short-lived because once the person, freed from the presence of the majority, focuses again on the issue at hand, he will return to his prior opinions.

In contrast a minority will evoke a validation process – cognitive activity aimed at understanding why the minority consistently holds on to its position. Attention will be focused on the object, and in the process the subject – to some extent without even being aware of it – may begin to look at the object as the minority does and become privately (or latently) converted to its position. The majority's normative pressures (at least if they overtly resist) will however prevent this effect from being shown publicly. Therefore, relatively speaking, minorities will lead to conversion (without compliance) and majorities will lead to compliance (without conversion).

AFTER-IMAGE

To test this theory, various kinds of experiments have been designed. As an example we will describe one very ingenious and provocative experiment conducted by Moscovici and Personnaz (1980). Subjects, participating in pairs, were first shown a series of five blue slides. In private they wrote down the colour of the slide as well as the colour of the after-image of the slide (on a rating scale going from 1 = yellow to 9 = purple). The **after-image** is what one sees on a white screen after having fixed one's gaze on a colour for a while, and it is the complementary colour of the original one. The after-image of blue is yellow–orange, and the after-image of green is red–purple. Next, subjects were informed that their colour response was shared by 81.8 per cent (or by only 18.2 per cent) of the people who had previously participated. The other 18.2 per cent (or 81.8 per cent) had judged the slides as green. During the next phase (15 trials) the colour responses had to be given publicly, but no judgements of the colour of the after-image were asked for. The first subject to respond, a confederate, always said green. In view of the information received prior to this phase, the real subject perceived this green response either as a minority or as a majority response. The third phase (15 trials) was again private, the confederate and the subject writing down both the colour of the slide and the rating of the after-image. The experiment concluded with a fourth phase in which the subject answered, again in private, but in the absence of the confederate. Moscovici felt that if the influence source had brought about a real change in the subject's perception this ought to result in a shift of the judged colour of the after-image towards the complementary colour of green (the higher end of the response scale), even though there had never been a direct attempt by the confederate to influence this judgement. The results, shown in figure 16.6, indicate that, compared with a no-influence control condition, the majority source produced no changes in this judgement, whereas the minority source did.

Using a somewhat different methodology – 'a spectrometer' on which subjects had to adjust the colour so that it matched the slide and the after-image they had previously seen – Personnaz (1981) replicated this differential effect of a majority and a minority influence source. Other replications were less successful however. Sorrentino, King and Leo (1980) failed to find overall evidence for a conversion effect. Doms and Van Avermaet (1982) did find a conversion effect, but this effect was as strong in the majority as in the minority condition. To account for their findings they argued that under certain conditions majorities too may be capable of focusing subjects' attention on the stimulus and that they can therefore induce private change as well.

Another interesting perspective on the comparison between majority and minority influence was offered by Latané and Wolf (1981). In contrast to Moscovici, they view influence as a unitary process regardless of its source. Social

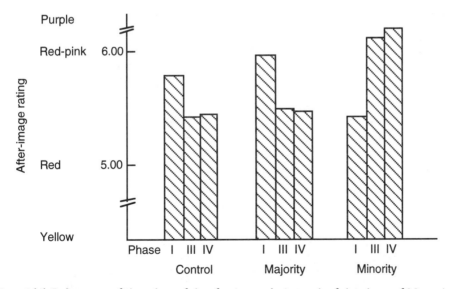

Figure 16.6 Judgements of the colour of the after-image during each of the phases of Moscovici and Personnaz's experiment (data from Moscovici, 1980)

influence, or social impact as they call it, is a multiplicative function of the strength (power, expertise), immediacy (proximity in space and time) and size (number) of the influence source. This implies that the effect of any one of these variables will be greater as the value of another variable increases. Regarding the effect of size, the variable of most interest to them, they postulate a *power function*, with each additional influence source having less impact than the previous one. Fifty people have more impact than five people, but adding one extra person will make less of a difference in the first case than in the second. This principle of marginally decreasing impact is expressed through the equation

$$\text{impact} = sN^t$$

where s is a scaling constant which reflects the impact of a single source, t is an exponent with a value of less than one, and N is the number of influence sources (people). This implies that impact increases as some power of the size of the influence source. Against this background it is already understandable why Latané and Wolf expect minorities, in general, to have less impact than majorities. In addition, in the case where an individual stands with others as the object of social influence, the source's impact will be divided over the target members. Each target will experience less impact than when it is alone. As the size of the target group increases, the source's impact on each target member will decrease. There are therefore two major reasons why minorities are less powerful than majorities as influence sources: they have smaller numbers, and their impact is divided (diffused) over more targets. Latané and Wolf cite research consistent with their major predictions as well as with other implications of their theory. Tanford and Penrod (1984), who proposed a refinement of Latané's social-impact theory, reached basically similar conclusions.

An interesting characteristic of Latané and Wolf's model is that it clearly views social influence as a mutual and reciprocal process, and it should therefore stimulate research in which both minorities *and* majorities can be active sources of influence. As you may have noticed, in most studies either the majority or the minority is essentially a group of frozen confederates. A lot could be gained by paying more attention, not only theoretically but also empirically, to reciprocal influence effects. On the other hand, as Maass and Clark (1984) have remarked, the social-impact models (and the studies cited in their support) deal mainly with public influence and have little to say about the processes through which the antecedent factors of strength, immediacy and size operate. It is precisely to the process and to the level of influence that Moscovici's model speaks the most.

In assessing the relative value of dual process (Moscovici, 1980) versus single-process models of influence (Latané and Wolf, 1981; see also Turner, 1991, for another example), a number of other important points should be kept in mind. First, at the level of research designs, studies cited in support of either kind of model use widely discrepant operationalizations of the majority and minority status of the source (in terms of sheer numbers or in terms of the societal dominance of a position). The majority/minority variable is manipulated on a between-subjects or on a within-subjects basis, and subjects participate in actual groups or as individuals who learn about majority and minority positions only through written or taped accounts. Dependent measures of influence vary from public compliance, to private change on direct measures, to change on indirect measures (such as on a related topic). Secondly, at the level of process analysis the evidence should be judged not only by the extent to which the actual influence effect is in line with the predictions of a given model but also by the presence or absence of direct evidence for the assumed mediators of the effect. Thirdly and most generally, the evidence should be judged by a set of commonly agreed criteria for deciding between a two-process versus a single-process model.

With respect to the conceptually important second point, a number of studies have in effect looked for direct evidence of differential cognitive activity in reaction to minorities and to majorities and have tested its role as a mediator of influence effects. On the basis of conceptual similarity between Moscovici's validation versus social-comparison models of processing information and the distinction between systematic and heuristic processing (Eagly and Chaiken, 1993), or between central and peripheral processing (Petty and Cacioppo, 1986), described in chapter 9, a number of authors measured the number and kinds of thoughts elicited by minority and majority messages (Maass and Clark, 1983; Mackie, 1987). By and large the results of these studies indicate that cognitive activity mediates the influence effects, but differences between majority and minority source conditions are minor or even absent.

As to the third and most general point made above, in a very insightful theoretical analysis Kruglanski and Mackie (1990) argue that more or less stringent criteria can be distinguished to determine whether majority and minority influence differ *per se*. At the most stringent level they can only be considered as different if an antecedent factor, that can be manipulated independently of the nature of the source, shows a statistical interaction with the nature of the source and/or if the nature of the source interacts with the nature of the influence measure. At a somewhat less stringent level, majority and minority influence can be considered different to the extent that different effects are caused by a factor which covaries with the status of the source 'on intrinsic grounds'. To clarify, if a minority by definition always elicits more involvement, this latter factor may be the ultimate reason for differential effects. If one could somehow manage to produce the same amount of involvement with a majority standpoint, the same effect might obtain. At an even less stringent level one might already agree on differences if they were caused by a factor which 'typically' covaried with the nature of the source. Perceived extremity of position is a good example. Although minorities may take more extreme stands typically, in instances where a majority takes a comparably extreme stand it may produce the same effect.

Their own analysis led Kruglanski and Mackie to conclude that there are few cogent theoretical reasons to expect much evidence for the strongest version of the dual-process model, but they are willing to accept a weaker version. They doubt whether variables such as consistency, extremity, involvement, and the like operate differently in the majority and minority cases *per se*, but think it plausible to argue that they are often correlated with source status. In line with this perspective an empirical evaluation of the available evidence by means of a meta-analysis (Wood et al., 1994) shows that, compared with a control condition, minorities *and* majorities can in effect produce influence at *each* of the three levels of public change, direct private change and indirect private change. This fact argues against an exclusive relationship between the nature of the source and the kind of influence effect. At the same time, however, this same meta-analysis shows stronger overall public and direct private effects for majorities, but stronger indirect private-influence effects for minorities, be it only under some conditions. According to Wood et al., the latter effect obtained especially when minority and majority identity were defined in terms of membership of social groups (for example, Greenpeace vs the Environmental Protection Agency), rather than by other means (the distribution of opinions within a small group), when there were few minority members rather than many, and when perceived consistency was very high. It may come as somewhat of a surprise that the overall dichotomy with respect to the influence effects is between the direct public/ private effects and indirect private effects rather than between public effects and the combination of direct and indirect private effects. Apparently, and contrary to Moscovici's original ideas, normative considerations influence public and private direct judgements alike. Not only does one not want to be publicly aligned with a minority (for fear of losing face), one does not even want to face a private alignment with this group. Again, this is especially true when the influence situation is experienced face-to-face and when minorities and majorities are defined in terms of real social groups.

To conclude, there do appear to be privileged relationships between the nature of the source and the size (quantity) and kind (quality) of influence effects, but to a large extent this relationship is caused by a natural or typical correlation between the minority and majority status of the source, its other characteristics and/or the influence setting itself, rather than by the minority or majority status *per se*. Moreover, when minorities or majorities have an effect at a given level, essentially identical normative and informational processes seem to be at work.

Majority and minority influence: imitation versus originality

Moscovici's and Latané's models and many of the studies described above depart from the traditional definition of influence in terms of movement towards the position of the influence source. Nemeth has proposed broadening the concept of influence to refer to any change in thought processes, opinions and decisions, independently of the direction of these changes (Nemeth, 1986). Her perspective has led to a refreshing insight into comparing and distinguishing majority and minority influence.

With Moscovici she shares the view that minorities induce more cognitive effort than majorities and that the nature of the thought processes itself is also different. But whereas Moscovici stresses that the message-relevant thoughts concentrate on the position espoused by the minority, which is then eventually adopted, Nemeth proposes that thought becomes issue-relevant rather than position-relevant. The distinction is important, because it implies that minorities would induce more divergent attention and thinking and the consideration of a multitude of alternatives, including alternatives not proposed explicitly by the minority source. As a consequence the presence of a minority viewpoint, even when it is objectively incorrect, would contribute to judgements which are at the same time more original and qualitatively better, because more alternatives are weighed against each other. Majorities, on the other hand, would produce a restriction of attention, convergent thinking, and the mere imitation of the alternative proposed.

A nice illustration of the above perspective was offered in a study by Nemeth and Wachtler (1983). Subjects in groups of six were shown slides which contained a standard figure and a set of six comparison figures (see figure 16.7). Their task was to detect the standard figure in as many of the comparison figures as possible. Either two or four people, confederates of the experimenter, named two of the comparison figures. One of these was easy (U in figure 16.7), the other was difficult (E, for example). The difficult figure indicated was either correct (E)

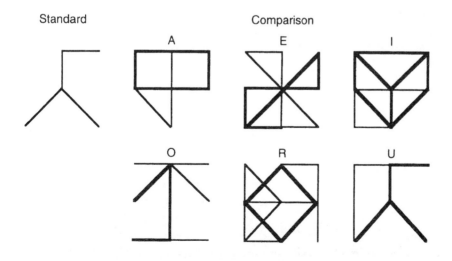

Figure 16.7 An example of the stimuli used by Nemeth and Wachtler (1983)

or incorrect (such as A). Results showed that, regardless of the correctness of the choices made by the confederates, subjects exposed to a majority of four were more likely to imitate responses than those exposed to a minority of two. Most pertinent to Nemeth's thesis, however, was the observation that subjects confronted with a minority, again regardless of the correctness of the proposals, produced a higher percentage of *novel* responses in general and, more specifically, a higher percentage of correct responses (I and R in figure 16.7). It appears therefore that a minority stimulated a more active and differentiated examination of the stimulus field, leading to the detection of novel and correct solutions. More generally, results of this nature (see also Nemeth and Kwan, 1987; Nemeth, Mayseless, Sherman and Brown, 1990) point to the positive contribution of minority viewpoints to creativity in problem solving.

A similar conclusion can be drawn from recent research by Mucchi-Faina, Maass and Volpato (1991). Their research is also interesting in its own right because it shows that the kinds of results obtained by Nemeth and Wachtler are a reflection of the combined impact of the minority status of the influence source and the originality of its proposals. Students at the University of Perugia were asked to indicate their degree of agreement with proposals made by other students on how the international image of the city of Perugia could be promoted. In addition they were asked to generate new proposals themselves. In the experimental conditions two proposals were put before them, one allegedly suggested by a majority of respondents and the other by only a minority. The actual proposals were either conventional (such as a photograph of the 'Palazzo dei Priori', a well-known historical monument) or original (such as a photograph of a famous elevator below the 'Rocca Paolina', a modern touch in an otherwise medieval city). Majority proposals produced a higher degree of agreement, but subjects in the original minority/conventional majority condition generated more new proposals than subjects in the conventional minority/original majority condition. In addition, the proposals in the former condition were more original, more different and more often unique (written by only one subject). Hence, the effect requires a minority status of the source and originality of the proposal. Remarkably, however, an original minority/original majority condition did not yield a similar effect. Apparently, an original minority loses its stimulating impact when presented alongside an equally original majority. Finally, as the authors themselves observe, it is questionable whether the above effects would obtain with minority proposals perceived as eccentric or extravagant. This remark is reminiscent of a general point raised earlier, namely that the impact of a minority influence source is greatly diminished when its opinion is attributed to dogmatism, craziness or some other negative idiosyncratic characteristic (Mugny, 1982).

To conclude, viewed in a broad societal context, it can be argued that social change does owe more to minority influence than to majority influence. Rarely do we find ourselves in an Asch setting (as a matter of fact we avoid it); we are most likely to be part of the majority, feeling at ease with our ways of thinking about reality, and looking at reality as most others do. It takes an active minority to unsettle this equilibrium and to make us really think about why we act as we do: 'Du choc des opinions jaillit la vérité' ('Out of the clash of opinions springs the truth': after the French poet Colardeau, 1732–76)! The effect of minority influence may not always be a change towards the direction of that minority, but it will at least force us to look at things from a different angle, to take on a different and more creative perspective, and perhaps lead us to inherently better solutions of the problems confronting us.

Decision-making in groups

Group polarization

Consider again the hypothetical student meeting we mentioned at the beginning of this chapter. Suppose that at the outset all the student representatives are opposed to the departmental proposal, but with a certain amount of variation as to the extremity of their opposition. In an attempt to reach a consensual position they engage in a discussion, each student presenting his or her own arguments and reacting to those of others. If you guess that the decision will be resolved through a compromise around the average of the initial individual positions, you are probably wrong. In situations of this sort people tend to converge on a position which is more extreme than this average.

Like yourself, for some time social psychologists too held the belief that groups would be less extreme, more moderate and more cautious than individuals. But in 1961 Stoner, a graduate student, ran an experiment – since then followed by more than 300 – that demonstrated the opposite. He presented his subjects in groups of four or five with a choice-dilemma questionnaire. This questionnaire, developed further by Kogan and Wallach (1964), measured a person's tendency towards risk-taking. It consisted of 12 items, each of which described the dilemma confronting a protagonist, who had to choose between an alternative high in probability of success but low in value and another much more attractive path of action but with a lower probability of success. Subjects, acting as imaginary advisers to the protagonist, had to indicate the minimum probability of success under which they would recommend the latter, risky alternative. In Stoner's experiment subjects first filled out the questionnaire in private (pre-consensus), then discussed each item amongst themselves and tried to reach a consensus (consensus), and finally again wrote down an individual judgement (post-consensus). Stoner observed that the achieved consensus and the average of the post-consensus individual judgements favoured a riskier decision than would be expected on the basis of the average of the pre-discussion individual judgements.

Stoner's observation of this 'risky shift' immediately led social psychologists to attempt to replicate and explain the phenomenon. Pretty soon it became obvious that the shift was not always towards more risk, because in a number of cases the shift was in the opposite, 'cautious' direction. Moreover, in 1969 Moscovici and Zavalloni very nicely demonstrated that the decisional shift following a group discussion also obtained with a totally different judgemental dimension. Using Stoner's original procedure they had French high-school students first write down in private their attitudes towards President De Gaulle (or towards North Americans) by indicating the extent of their agreement with statements such as: 'De Gaulle is too old to carry out successfully his difficult political job' (or 'American economic aid is always used to exert political pressure'). Next, as a group, they had to reach a consensus on each item; and finally they made another private attitude rating. With this totally different dimension they observed a shift comparable with Stoner's: as a result of the discussion, subjects became more extreme in their attitudes. As figure 16.8 shows, the attitude towards De Gaulle, which was slightly positive before the discussion, became more positive after the group discussion; this change was maintained during the post-discussion private measurement. The attitude towards the Americans shows a similar polarization pattern but in the negative direction; the original slightly negative attitude became more negative after the discussion.

The phenomenon at hand is therefore much more general than originally assumed. On any judgemental dimension groups tend, on average, to shift in the

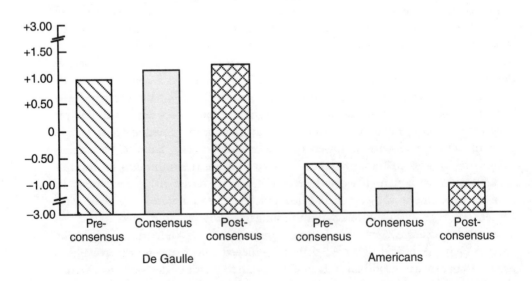

Figure 16.8 Polarization of attitudes towards De Gaulle and towards Americans (data from Moscovici and Zavalloni, 1969)

direction of the pole which they already favour initially. Hence, group polarization refers to an enhancement of an initially dominant position as a result of group discussion (Myers, 1982). An excellent summary by Lamm and Myers (1978) documents this phenomenon in a wide variety of contexts: stereotypes, interpersonal impressions, gambling behaviour, prosocial and antisocial behaviour, negotiations, jury decisions, group counselling and religious social support systems.

Explaining group polarization

As it became apparent that there was more to group polarization than a shift towards risk, many of the early explanations had to be dropped, for the simple reason that they could account only for the risky shift and for none (or too few) of the other instances of polarization.

Among the more general perspectives, for many years explanations in terms of normative and/or informational influence processes dominated the scene. These explanations were very similar to those proposed earlier as underlying the conformity effect. They were later joined by a new contender, self-categorization theory, a general social-psychological theory put forth by Turner (1987). It aspires to account for many group-related behaviours, of which polarization is but one case.

The *normative* or *social-comparison* point of view departs from Festinger's theory of social comparison (1954), which holds that because of a need to evaluate one's own opinions (and abilities) people will compare their opinions with those of others. Furthermore, because people want to have a positive self-image and also want to be perceived positively by others, this comparison process will be biased in the direction of viewing oneself as 'better' or 'more correct' (that is, closer to the norm) than others. The implication of this theory is therefore that when, during the group discussion, you discover that others hold opinions more in the direction of the valued alternative, you will yourself become more extreme in order to differentiate yourself positively from the others. Indirect support for this explanation is found in studies indicating that people indeed think that they are closer to the normative position than others (Codol, 1975), but that at the same time they admire views that are even more extreme than theirs, in the valued direction of course (Jellison and Davis, 1973). Direct support would be obtained if one could show that merely knowing the others' position on an issue, without having heard any of their arguments, would be sufficient to produce a polarization effect. Some experiments have in fact supported that prediction (e.g. Myers, 1978; Sanders and Baron, 1977), but others have not, particularly those that tried to test the social-comparison hypothesis against the informational-influence hypothesis.

The *informational-influence* perspective suggests that group discussion generates a number of arguments, most of which are in support of the position already favoured by the group members. To the extent that these arguments coincide with ones you have already considered yourself, they should serve to strengthen your own position. But the group is also likely to produce arguments you had not thought of before, making your reaction even more extreme. The group-polarization phenomenon basically becomes then a process of *mutual persuasion*, whereby the extent of the shift is a function of the proportion of the arguments favouring one side as opposed to another, their cogency and their novelty (Myers, 1982). In this perspective the arguments presented rather than the communicated positions themselves would constitute the instigating factor of the effect.

One of the many clever sets of studies set up to prove just this point was conducted by Burnstein and Vinokur (1973). They first created a situation in which subjects had no knowledge of each other's position. To this end subjects were told that the experimenter would instruct them individually as to which point of view they should defend. It might or might not be their own, and therefore they would be unclear about each other's position. In fact, half of these subjects were made to argue for their own position (ambiguous–for) and the other half had to argue against it (ambiguous–against). On the basis of the persuasive-information perspective, Vinokur and Burnstein predicted significant shifts (risky or cautious, depending on the kind of item) in the ambiguous–for condition and no shifts in the ambiguous–against condition, because a stronger and more persuasive argumentation can be expected in the first than in the second condition. It is indeed reasonable to assume that, in general, people are better at generating a sizeable number of good arguments *for* than *against* their own opinion. The results, shown in table 16.1, strongly supported these predictions. Vinokur and Burnstein then added a third condition with equally weak arguments to those used in the ambiguous–against condition, but in which subjects would have knowledge of each other's true position. To achieve this goal all subjects were told that everybody had to argue against their own position, which was in fact the case. Weak arguments would be the result, but subjects would be able to infer each other's stand (by reversing the direction in which arguments had been presented). The persuasion perspective predicts no shift in this unambiguous–against condition, but the social-comparison perspective does predict a shift. As table 16.1 shows, the polarization on risky items was

Table 16.1 Opinion shifts in Burnstein and Vinokur's (1973) studies

| Condition | Social comparison? | Strong arguments? | Items | |
			Risky	Cautious
Ambiguous–for	No	Yes	−0.59*	+0.44*
Ambiguous–against	No	No	−0.03	+0.06
Unambiguous–against	Yes	No	−0.25	−0.46*

(* refers to a statistically significant shift)

insignificant. On cautious items, however, a significant shift was observed, but in the risky direction and therefore opposite to the positive, cautious shift expected on the basis of a social-comparison perspective. Although the persuasive-information viewpoint cannot explain this latter effect either (it predicted no shift at all), it explains more of the findings of this study as a whole than does the social-comparison viewpoint.

Although an overall evaluation of the studies aimed at testing a social-comparison/normative explanation versus a persuasion/informational explanation favours the latter (Isenberg, 1986), there is evidence that mere exposure to positions is at least sufficient to produce opinion change (Cotton and Baron, 1980). Moreover, aside from leaving some theoretical questions unanswered (such as, when is an argument persuasive), neither theory can adequately explain the observation that, when holding position information and persuasive arguments constant, either more or less polarization will result depending on the social context within which the information is provided (Wetherell, 1987).

Self-categorization theory, derived from social-identity theory, has emerged as a powerful general approach to group behaviour that does account for these and other observations (Turner, 1987). According to this theory, people use a system of concepts to define themselves. These concepts include self-categorizations as individual persons different from others, and self-categorizations as members of social groups different from other groups. When a social self-categorization becomes salient, it acquires normative properties in that it focuses and orientates people on what binds them together and what distinguishes them from other groups. Turner then advances the crucial assumption that this group norm is not simply the average position of the group members, but rather the prototypical position of the group. The *prototype* is the position that corresponds the best to what the group has in common *and* to what differentiates it from another group. Hence the person who differs the least from ingroup members and the most from outgroup members acts as the group's prototype. This person is the normative reference point, whose arguments will therefore also be perceived as most informational and persuasive. Within this conception the notion of 'norm' is no longer exclusively tied to pleasing others (as in the conformity literature), but rather, it relates to an ideal social self-categorization. The definition of the prototype also implies that its position will vary with contexts, specifically with the distribution of opinions within one's own group and with the differences between one's own group and other groups. Because the ratio between the two is crucial, the prototype will be more extreme when an outgroup is made salient in the first place, but especially when this outgroup is very different from the ingroup. More group polarization can therefore be expected in the presence than in the absence of an outgroup or when a different, as compared with a similar, outgroup is present. The self-categorization perspective on group polarization has many other interesting implications and can account for a variety of findings. As but one example, Hogg, Turner and Davidson (1990) showed that the direction of polarization on an item can actually be reversed by a change in the social context. Their subjects perceived the ingroup norm as more cautious than their pre-test mean upon a confrontation with a riskier outgroup, but they perceived it as riskier when confronted with a more cautious outgroup.

Groupthink: an extreme example of group polarization

In view of the frequency with which, in reality, decisions are made by groups composed of like-minded participants (councils, committees, juries, governments), the research on group polarization has far-reaching implications. The processes involved may indeed lead such groups to advocate decisions which are incorrect, unwise or, in the worst case, disastrous.

Irving Janis (Janis, 1972; 1982) has described a number of instances of political and military decision-making which provide dramatic illustrations of the utmost stupidity shown by groups in spite of the superior 'intelligence' of their members. The Bay of Pigs invasion in 1961 is perhaps the best known example. President Kennedy and a small group of advisers had decided to send a relatively small group of Cuban exiles to invade the Cuban coast with the support of the American air force. Everything went wrong, and within a matter of days the invaders were killed or captured. How, as a group, could Kennedy and his advisers have been so stupid, as they later admitted themselves? As a more recent example, the dramatic explosion of the space shuttle Challenger in 1986 similarly appears to have been the result of a number of ill-made decisions (Esser and Lindoerfer, 1989).

Janis, who undertook a most careful analysis of all the available documents in the Bay of Pigs case and in other similar cases, speculates that the decision-makers became the victims of an extreme form of group polarization, which he GROUPTHINK calls **groupthink**. Groupthink obtains when the decision process of a highly-cohesive group of like-minded people becomes so overwhelmed by consensus seeking that their apprehension of reality is undermined. As Janis contends, this process is encouraged when a number of conditions are fulfilled: when the decision group is highly cohesive; when it is isolated from alternative sources of information; and when its leader clearly favours a particular option. Against the background of these antecedent conditions the group discussions that evolve are likely to be characterized by an illusion of one's own invulnerability, and by attempts at mutually rationalizing actions which are in line with the proposed option while at the same time ignoring or discounting inconsistent information. These processes occur both at the intra-individual (self-censorship) and at the inter-individual (conformity pressures) level. Even though some members of such groups may at one time or another have their private reservations about the proposals made, they are not likely to express them overtly. The ultimate outcome of these processes is a decision endorsed by all, but far removed from what might be expected if rational and balanced information-seeking and

Plate 16.3 The Space Shuttle Challenger exploded 73 seconds after lift-off from the Kennedy Space Center, Florida. All seven crew members were killed. Was 'groupthink' at least a contributing factor?

information-providing processes had operated. Although Janis's analysis is more penetrating than this brief presentation can show, the above material should be sufficient for you to grasp the essentials of this analysis – and to suggest some cures for groupthink. How should the leader behave? What would you think of a devil's advocate in the group? Which benefits can be gained by having the group members write down their personal thoughts and arguments independently and individually?

Undoubtedly the eye-catching characteristics of the groupthink phenomenon itself, combined with Janis's own superb gift at sketching a masterly, vivid account of real-life cases, has contributed greatly to the widespread acceptance of his model. Moreover, other authors have provided similar analyses of other cases (Hensley and Griffin, 1986; 't Hart, 1990). On the other hand, laboratory studies and conceptual analyses of decision-making situations have definitely not confirmed all the links of Janis's model. Amongst other things, the central variable of cohesiveness has not been observed to affect group decision-making in a consistent way. Moreover, many studies fail to make the methodologically wise comparison between the nature and outcome of group functioning in situations where Janis's antecedents are present and those where they are not. On the basis of a critical analysis of the literature, Aldag and Fuller (1993) have proposed a more general group problem-solving model (GGPS-model). Its essential features are that it presents the elements of decision-making processes in less pejorative and value-laden terms (for example, lack of procedural norms is replaced by procedural requirements), and it adds a number of antecedent process and outcome variables. In this latter respect political motives and outcomes play a key role, testifying to the idea that decisions that may be thoughtless and ill-conceived from a rational efficiency point of view can also result from deliberate and planned political strategies.

Obeying Immoral Orders: the Social Influence of an Authority

Milgram's obedience experiment

The various social-influence phenomena described in the previous sections have a number of characteristics in common. The most important of these are that influence sources and targets typically have equal status; the pressure exerted by the influence source is more implicit than explicit; and the source makes no attempt at directly controlling or sanctioning the resistance that targets of influence attempts might eventually show. For example, in Asch's experiment all the subjects were students, the majority only very implicitly exerted pressure by merely stating an opinion that was different from the subject's, and the subject's responses never led to any explicit negative reactions on the part of the majority. An entirely different influence context is created when an influence source has high status, explicitly orders a person to behave in a way which he or she would not spontaneously do or would even have strong feelings against, and continuously monitors whether the person indeed carries out the orders given. Precisely this setting was created in a famous and at the same time notorious series of studies on **obedience** carried out by Stanley Milgram and dramatically captured in his best-selling book *'Obedience to Authority'* (Milgram, 1974). The essential components of Milgram's basic experiment as well as some of its variants have already been introduced in chapter 4. However, for the sake of clarity and vividness in the context of the present chapter, a more integrated and detailed presentation of these studies is necessary.

OBEDIENCE

Through a newspaper advertisement Milgram recruited volunteers to participate, for a payment of $4, in a study on learning and memory. The participants in the experiment were aged between 20 and 50, and they represented almost the entire range of professional levels. Upon arriving at the laboratory the subject was met by the experimenter, actually a biology teacher in his early thirties, and another 'subject', a confederate of the experimenter who in fact was a sympathetic-mannered middle-aged accountant. The experimenter explained that the study dealt with the effects of punishment on learning, and that one of the subjects would be the teacher and the other the learner. Lots were drawn resulting in the subject being the teacher. Teacher and learner were taken to an adjacent room where the learner was strapped into a chair and electrodes were fixed to his wrists – because the punishment to be applied was an electric shock. The experimenter explained that the shocks could be extremely painful, but they would cause no permanent damage.

Next the teacher was taken to his own room, where he received his orders. The learning task was a paired-associates task; each time the learner gave an incorrect answer the teacher had to punish him with an electric shock, beginning at 15 volts (V), and increasing the shock intensity by 15 V with every new mistake. To this end the teacher had to use a shock generator with a row of 30 pushbuttons, each marked with the appropriate intensity (from 15 V to 450 V). Several verbal labels gave the subject a clear sense of the meaning of successive groups of shock levels: the labels went from slight shock (to 60 V), through moderate shock (to

Plate 16.4 At the Nuremberg War Trials, after the Second World War, many prominent Nazis tried to use 'obedience to authority' as a defence. (The front row of defendants shows, left to right, Goering, Hess, Ribbentrop, Leitel and Rosenberg)

120 V), strong shock (to 180 V) and very strong shock (to 240 V), to intense shock (to 300 V), extreme intensity shock (to 360 V) and 'danger: severe shock' (to 420 V). The two final shock levels were marked 'XXX'. Various additional features of the shock generator gave the apparatus a distinctly 'real' appearance. Moreover, to demonstrate the reality of the shocks the teacher received a sample shock of 45 V.

The learning task could then begin. As you probably suspect, the confederate made numerous errors, thereby 'forcing' the subject to administer increasingly stronger shocks. Each time the subject hesitated or refused, the experimenter prodded to go on by means of at most four graded orders: 'Please continue'; 'The experiment requires that you continue'; 'It is absolutely essential that you continue'; 'You have no other choice, you must go on.' The experiment was terminated when, in spite of the experimenter's prods, the subject refused to continue, or when three shocks of the highest intensity had been administered. Before presenting the results we should add that the subject was not only exposed to the explicit influence attempt by the experimenter, but was also confronted with an increasingly explicit appeal by the learner. Whereas at first the subject could hear the victim react with only a minor grunt (from 75 V to 105 V), at 120 V he began to shout that the shocks became very painful. Later in the sequence he started screaming in agony; he shouted to be let out and that he could not stand the pain. From a given point on he refused to provide more answers – but the subject still had to administer shocks because 'no answer is an incorrect answer'.

How did Milgram's subjects, faced with the conflict between the pressures emanating from the authority, from the victim, and from their own inner self, react in this situation? Very much to his own surprise, Milgram observed that 62.5 per cent of his subjects continued to administer shocks to the highest level. The average maximum shock level was 368 V. The authority of 'the man of science', who never threatened with any sanctions let alone held a gun to the subject's head, was sufficient to override the inner (conscience) and outer (the victim's cries) forces that could have made the subject disobey. A frightening perspective. Were Milgram's subjects perhaps 'evil' people? All the evidence speaks against it. For one thing, the subjects' behaviour during the experiment clearly testifies to the strong conflict they experienced: they were extremely tense and nervous, they perspired, bit their lips and clenched their fists. Moreover, a control condition in which subjects were allowed to choose any shock levels they themselves considered appropriate showed that only two out of 40 people exceeded the 150 V level and 28 never even went beyond 75 V. Clearly Milgram's subjects were not sadists; apparently they were caused to behave in the way they did by the powerful role of situational factors. In variations of his basic experiment Milgram has looked at the difference a number of these situational factors make. Some of these variations, as they relate to characteristics of the authority, the closeness of the victim and the behaviour of the subject's peers, are briefly summarized in the next paragraphs.

Situational determinants of obedience

The physical (and emotional) proximity of the victim was manipulated by means of four different conditions. In a first condition the victim pounded heavily on the wall separating his room from the teacher's; in the second he was heard crying and shouting (as described earlier). In two other conditions the subject and the victim were actually in the same room. In one of these the subject not only heard but also saw the victim. In the final condition the subject had to hold the victim's hand on a shock plate. The obedience rates corresponding to these four conditions of increasing contact are shown in figure 16.9. Maximal obedience went from a high of 65 per cent of the subjects to a low (if one can call it that) of 30 per cent. Data such as these should invite you to speculate about the differences between traditional and modern warfare in terms of the differential resistance they would induce towards disobeying military orders.

The authority of the experimenter and the amount of control he had was varied in a number of ways. When the experiment was carried out in a less scientific and prestigious environment – a rundown office building rather than Yale University, where the original study took place – obedience did not drop significantly. However, when – in the original setting – the experimenter was absent from the subject's room and gave his orders over the telephone, maximal obedience

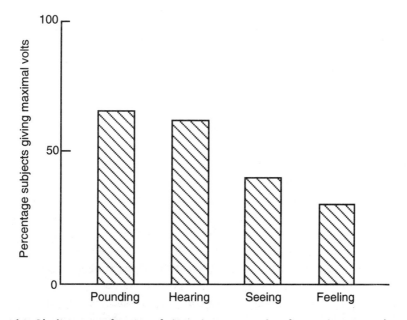

Figure 16.9 Obedience as a function of physical proximity (data from Milgram, 1974)

dropped to 21 per cent (a number of subjects said over the phone that they were giving higher shocks than they in fact did!). The fact that the authority patently violated a promise made to the learner did not reduce obedience greatly. In one of the experimental variations the learner, who had said earlier that he had a heart condition, only agreed to the experiment 'on the condition that you let me out when I say so'. From the tenth shock onwards (150 V) he in effect demanded that the experiment be stopped, but the experimenter ignored him and insisted that the subject had to go on. The percentage of subjects showing maximal obedience in this frightening setting was reduced by only 10 per cent, compared with a baseline condition. A final relevant variation was one in which the experimenter, before (and therefore without) instructing the subject to increase shock levels, had to leave the room. He carried over his authority to a second subject present, who at first would only have to register the learner's reaction times. This second subject then came up with the idea of increasing the shock level with every error and, throughout the learning session, he insisted that the teacher applied his rules. The results speak for themselves. Twenty per cent of the subjects obeyed the equal-status authority to the end. In addition, when a subject refused and the 'authority' decided that he would administer the shocks himself, a number of subjects physically attacked the 'torturer' or pulled out the plug of the shock generator. Such heroism was unfortunately never shown when the authority was 'the man of science in his white coat'!

In a final pair of experimental variations presented here, Milgram investigated the role of peer pressure. In the first there were three co-teachers, the subject and two confederates. The first confederate presented the task, the second registered the learner's responses, and the subject administered the shocks. At 150 V the first confederate refused to continue and took a seat, away from the shock generator. At 210 V the second confederate refused. The effect of their behaviour on the subject was dramatic: only 10 per cent were maximally obedient (see figure 16.10). Rather than interpreting this result to mean that, with peers present, people will listen to the voice of their conscience, it is probably more parsimonious to state that their 'independence' towards the authority-influence source was caused by their 'dependence' on another influence source. The latter's impact was great, particularly when you realize that they only influenced the subject implicitly, through their behaviour. They never said anything to the subject! The subjects' dependence on the behaviour of their peers (rather than on their conscience) was clearly demonstrated in a reversal of the above condition. If the subject, who administered the learning task, was accompanied by a co-teacher, who gave the shocks, 92 per cent of the subjects participated in the experiment to the end. Of course, they did not have to give the shocks themselves; but what kept them from protesting as the confederates had done in the prior condition? In view of the fact that peer behaviour can produce either 10 per cent or 92 per cent obedience, the powerful role of interpersonal rather than intrapersonal factors is distinctly revealed. Again these experiments should make

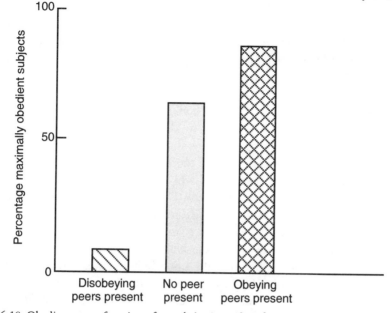

Figure 16.10 Obedience as a function of peer behaviour (data from Milgram, 1974)

you think of real-life examples whereby you protest or do not protest against acts of violence, merely as a function of what others do.

What would you have done?

While reading the above paragraphs you probably constantly said to yourself: 'I would not have obeyed!' For your comfort, that is how most people react upon hearing a description of the Milgram experiments. Milgram himself and others (e.g., Bierbrauer, 1979) asked people from all walks of life, including psychiatrists, how many people would obey the experimenter. Invariably, they all expected low obedience rates (with a maximal average shock of 130 V). Only with a very vivid and lengthy re-enactment of the experiment could Bierbrauer get Stanford students to expect an average maximal shock of 260 V, which is still an under-estimation of what real subjects did. One explanation for the difference between what we think we and others will do and what we in effect do is to be found in the *fundamental attribution error* (see chapter 7) – a tendency to under-estimate the role of situational factors and to over-estimate the impact of personality factors. In the Milgram situation, personality characteristics did not make a lot of difference: his analyses revealed only minor differences between men and women, between people holding different professions or between those scoring differently on personality inventories. Moreover, replications of Milgram's study in different countries and cultures have demonstrated the generality of the effect (e.g., Mantell, 1971; Meeus and Raaijmakers, 1986; Shanab and Yahya, 1978).

The dynamics of obedience

According to Milgram three interlocking factors are at work in these situations. First, subjects in his experiments and people at large have had a life-long history of rewarded obedience to authority and they have come to expect authorities to be trustworthy, credible and legitimate. Secondly, in the experiments and in reality, binding and entrapping factors come into operation. Aside from the fact that there are psychological barriers to disobeying right away, people only gradually slip into committing acts that have graver and graver consequences. The subtle progression and escalation of more and more extreme behaviours plays a crucial role in helping us understand why ethically concerned individuals end up committing unquestionably evil deeds (Darley, 1992; Kelman and Hamilton, 1989). As a third explanatory concept Milgram introduced the notion of agentic shift, to refer to the subjective experience (justification) of: 'I am not responsible, because I was ordered to do so!' These words are reminiscent of the ultimate defence of soldiers, officers and the like upon being brought to trial for acts in which they had been involved. The defence of high Nazi officers after the Second World War, of Argentinian military personnel after the downfall of the junta, and of members of the former East German border patrol after the unification of Germany are cases in point.

As a whole, and as mentioned earlier, the facts themselves and the above conceptual analysis testify to the overriding impact of situational factors, and of how they are perceived by most people, over personality-based determinants. However disturbing, the lessons of Milgram's research cannot be ignored. On the contrary, they should be and are in effect used – unfortunately not always – to interrupt unfolding chains of events before it is too late (Miceli and Near, 1992).

In concluding, Milgram-like experiments raise serious ethical concerns, and they should. Does the scientific benefit and the moral lesson learned from them outweigh the costs and the potential harm to participating subjects (Blass, 1992; Miller, 1986)? Regardless of your answer to this question, however, ask yourself if your ethical concerns would be as great if these studies had shown that people actually disobey the immoral orders given them by an experimenter.

Summary and Conclusions

This chapter has introduced you to various aspects and forms of social influence in small groups. It is perhaps appropriate to conclude with some critical thoughts. First, we started out by giving both a broader and a more restricted definition of social influence. After having read this chapter you may begin to wonder whether the more restricted definition is really more useful. Strictly speaking, the obedience phenomenon studied by Milgram, for instance, does not fall under this definition, although nobody will doubt that this is a clear instance of social influence. To some extent the definition given is perhaps more a reflection of the typical research paradigms used in this area than of the broader phenomenon itself. If you think of the impact others' behaviour has on a person's prosocial or antisocial behaviour (chapters 13 and 14), or if you think of attitude change as it results from exposure to a persuasive message (chapter 9), is there really a fundamental reason to treat these as an entirely different category of phenomena? Would it not be better in the end simply to *define* social influence as the effect of one person's (or several persons') behaviour on another person's behaviour and to analyse *theoretically* all social-influence phenomena from this common and more parsimonious perspective (Nuttin, 1986)?

Secondly, throughout this chapter we may have given the impression that social-influence phenomena are the result of deliberate decisions made by people who know and admit that they have been influenced by the social forces acting upon them. You should know however that, with the interesting exception of Milgram's subjects, who gladly and openly admit that they acted as they did because of the experimenter's request, conformity and minority studies show exactly the opposite. Here subjects frequently categorically deny to the experimenter (and to themselves) that their responses are in any way affected by what others say. In Milgram's experiment with two disobeying confederates, subjects did not attribute their independence to the example set by the behaviour of their peers. This should not necessarily be taken to imply that the information-processing accounts presented in several paragraphs of this chapter are invalid, but at the very least these processes do not necessarily operate at a conscious level. Carried to its extreme, some people might even conclude that, in the final analysis, behaviour comes first and thought follows after!

Although these final critical remarks, as well as the imperfections of some of the 'little' experiments conducted in social-psychological laboratories, may leave you with some doubts and questions, the different lines of research sketched in this chapter offer valuable perspectives towards understanding both everyday and major historical as well as contemporary events. The political landslides during the late eighties in the countries of Eastern Europe, the abolition of Apartheid in South Africa, the mass killings in Rwanda, the group suicide of the members of a sect in Switzerland, are but a few examples of the more dramatic events in which social influence in one form or another played a key role. At the same time, and perhaps less notably so, social influence is an essential ingredient of our everyday social life: what determines which line of clothing we wear, what guides us in our choice of vacation spots, which films do we see? In the final analysis, can you think of any behaviour, thought or feeling which would not be at least partly the result of social-influence processes?

Discussion points

1   Why does normative influence provide only a partial explanation of majority influence?
2   Explain how the social-support effects obtained in conformity studies can be understood in terms of informational influence, as well as in terms of normative influence.
3   Compared with the 37 per cent errors observed by Asch in his conformity study, do you feel that 8 per cent errors observed by Moscovici in his innovation study constitutes a lot of influence or only a little influence?
4   What was the 'after-image' study of Moscovici and Personnaz supposed to show? What conclusions can actually be drawn?
5   If you were to be asked to advise a minority group as to what strategies it might use to exert influence on a majority, what would you tell them?
6   What do you see as the major advantages of Turner's self-categorization explanation of group polarization over earlier theories?
7   How can we explain why Milgram's experimental subjects were so obedient?
8   Do you agree that Milgram's experimental situation captures the essentials of the real-life situations with which it is often compared?

Suggestions for further reading

Allen, V. L. (1975) Social support for non-conformity. In L. Berkowitz (ed.), *Advances in Experimental Social Psychology* (vol. 8). New York: Academic Press, pp. 1–43. A detailed account of theory and research with respect to the factors leading to a reduction in conformity to a majority.

Asch, S. E. (1956) Studies of independence and conformity: a minority of one against a unanimous majority. *Psychological Monographs*, 70, 9, whole of no. 416. This text presents Asch's own account of his famous conformity experiments. The best way to learn about these studies is to read them at first hand.

Janis, I. L. (1972) *Victims of Groupthink*. Boston: Houghton Mifflin. This book contains Janis's theory of groupthink, amply illustrated with case materials.

Milgram, S. (1974) *Obedience to Authority.* New York: Harper & Row. Milgram's own dramatic, best-selling story of his many experiments on obedience to authority.

Miller, A. G. (1986) *The Obedience Experiments: A case study of controversy in social science.* New York: Praeger. An authoritative account of Milgram's obedience research, its impact and the controversy it stirred up.

Moscovici, S. (1980) Toward a theory of conversion behaviour. In L. Berkowitz (ed.), *Advances in Experimental Social Psychology* (vol. 13, pp. 208–39). New York: Academic Press. A presentation of Moscovici's propositions with respect to the relationship between influence source (majority or minority) and level of effect (compliance or conversion), supplemented by an overview of relevant experimental studies.

Turner, J. C. (1991) *Social Influence.* Buckingham: Open University Press. A provocative analysis of a wide spectrum of social-influence phenomena from the perspective of self-categorization theory.

Key studies

Milgram, S. (1963). Behavioral study of obedience. *Journal of Abnormal and Social Psychology,* 67, 371–78.

Moscovici, S., Lage, E. and Naffrechoux, M. (1969). Influence of a consistent minority on the responses of a majority in a color perception task. *Sociometry,* 32, 365–80.

17   Intergroup Relations

Rupert Brown

Contents

Introduction

84 ARRESTS IN MINERS' PICKET BATTLE

Stones, wooden fencing spars, a shovel and a bucket were among missiles hurled at police in riot gear who held back as many as 7000 pickets trying to stop the movement of coking coal from Orgreave to the British Steel works at Scunthorpe, Lincolnshire . . . Violence broke out again when the lorries returned, and pickets scattered across a field as a posse of mounted police pursued them, followed by officers carrying riot shields. (An incident from the 1984–5 British coal strike as reported in *The Times*, 30 May 1984)

41 SOCCER FANS DIE IN STAMPEDE AT EURO CUP FINAL

At least 41 soccer fans died and more than 150 were seriously injured when a six foot concrete wall topped with fencing collapsed at the front of terracing 45 minutes before the scheduled start of last night's European Cup Final in Brussels between Liverpool and Juventus of Turin . . . The disaster occurred when the wall at one end of the stadium gave way during a stampede by Italian spectators after they were charged by a section of the Liverpool crowd. (The Heysel stadium tragedy in 1985 as reported in *The Times*, 30 May 1985)

Even the most casual reader of newspapers cannot help but notice headlines such as these, which frequently appear at our breakfast tables. The events referred to – exactly a year apart in two European countries – are both instances of **intergroup behaviour**: that is, actions by members of one group towards members of another group. It happens that the incidents chosen involved social conflicts of one kind or another, but the definition of intergroup behaviour is by no means so restricted. Many instances of intergroup co-operation and solidarity can be observed in everyday life, even if newspaper editors usually seem to give them somewhat less prominence. Common examples would include acts of solidarity by members of one trade union towards their colleagues in another union in dispute with their employer (during the British coal strike referred to in the first newspaper report, French rail workers and dockers refused to handle coal destined for British power stations), or alliances between community groups or political parties to achieve some common goal.

This chapter will consider some of the ways intergroup behaviour can be understood from a social-psychological perspective. It begins by briefly examining some popular theories which attempt to explain intergroup conflict and prejudice either as the expression of some particular personality type or as the result of temporary or chronic levels of frustration. As will be shown, these ideas are rather limited in their application. A much more fruitful approach is to see intergroup behaviour as a response to real or imagined group interests, and this is the subject of the second section. The third section takes up a question which arises out of the second: namely, does group membership in and of itself give rise

INTERGROUP
BEHAVIOUR

to discriminatory behaviour? As we shall see there are good grounds for thinking that it does; this leads naturally to the fourth section, where the link between group membership and social identity processes is explained. A central idea which emerges out of this is the importance for the individuals of being able to see their group as positively distinct from other groups. Finally, factors likely to lead to a reduction of intergroup conflict are discussed.

Popular Notions of Intergroup Conflict and Prejudice

Prejudice as personality type

PREJUDICE

More common than the outright manifestations of intergroup conflict with which we began this chapter are various forms of **prejudice** – that is, the holding of derogatory attitudes about the members of a social group (racism, sexism and so on). Such intergroup attitudes are commonly associated with the kinds of violent encounters described earlier. The question is: where do these prejudiced attitudes originate? (See also chapter 3).

One popular view is that prejudice is primarily a personality problem; the most influential example of this type of theory was that proposed by Adorno et al. (1950). Their hypothesis was that an individual's social attitudes were 'an expression of deep-lying trends in personality' (Adorno et al., 1950, p. 1). Working from a Freudian perspective, they believed that most people's personality development involved the repression and redirection of various instinctive needs by the constraints of social existence. The parents were considered to be the main agents of this socialization process, and in 'normal' development they usually struck a balance between discipline and allowing the child self-expression. The problem with the bigot, argued Adorno et al., was that this balance was upset by the parents' adopting an excessively harsh disciplinary regime and by their being over-anxious about the child's conformity to social mores. The effect of this, they believed, was that the child's natural aggression towards the parents (an inevitable consequence of being subjected to constraints) was displaced onto alternative targets because of the feared consequences of displaying it directly. The likely choice of targets would be those seen as weaker or inferior to oneself – for example, members of deviant groups or ethnic minorities. The end result, therefore, was someone over-deferential towards authority figures (since these symbolize the parents) and overtly hostile towards non-ingroup members – the so-called **authoritarian personality**.

AUTHORITARIAN PERSONALITY

Adorno et al. developed a personality inventory – the F-scale – which was designed to distinguish between those with potentially Fascist (or racist) tendencies and those with more 'democratic' leanings. High-scoring adults on this scale had rather different childhoods and more dogmatic attitudes than low scorers. The association between authoritarianism and various forms of prejudice has been confirmed in several intergroup contexts: for example, prejudice against ethnic groups in the United States (Campbell and McCandless, 1951), against Muslims in India (Sinha and Hassan, 1975), generalized ethnocentrism in the Netherlands (Meloen, Hagendoorn, Raaijmakers and Visser, 1988), and antipathy towards mentally ill people or sufferers from AIDS (Hanson and Blohm, 1974; Witt, 1985).

In the 1950s this approach attracted much criticism, with the F-scale itself coming under the closest scrutiny (Brown, 1965; Christie and Jahoda, 1954). The various controversies need not detain us here. However, it is important to note the limitations of this kind of 'individual differences' perspective (see also Billig, 1976). First, by locating prejudice in the dynamics of the individual personality, it tends to neglect *socio-cultural factors*, which are often much more powerful determinants. Pettigrew (1958) demonstrated this clearly in his study of prejudice in South Africa. Not surprisingly, he found that white South Africans showed very high levels of anti-black prejudice and yet they did not appear to have particularly high levels of authoritarianism. In other words, in terms of personality type they were rather similar to 'normal' populations; so their overtly racist attitudes probably derived much more from the then prevailing societal norms in South Africa than from any personality dysfunction.

A second problem is the inability of the personality approach to explain the widespread *uniformity* of prejudice in certain societies or subgroups within societies. If prejudice is to be explained via individual *differences* amongst people, how can it then be manifested in a whole population or at least in a vast majority? In prewar Nazi Germany – and in many other places since – consistently racist attitudes and behaviour were shown by hundreds of thousands of people who must have differed on most other psychological characteristics.

A third problem concerns the *historical specificity* of prejudice. As an example, consider the increased incidence of attacks against migrant workers in Germany and against Asian groups in Britain in the early 1990s. These increases in racism took place over the space of just a few years, much too short a time for whole generations of German or British families to have adopted new forms of child-rearing practices giving rise to authoritarian and prejudiced children. Examples such as these strongly suggest that the attitudes held by members of different groups towards each other have more to do with the objective relations between the groups – relations of political conflict or alliance, economic interdependence and so on – than with the familial relations in which they grew up.

The 'scapegoat' theory of prejudice: intergroup aggression as a result of frustration

Between 1882 and 1930 there were nearly 5,000 reported cases of lynchings in the United States. The vast majority of these involved black victims and occurred in southern states. Hovland and Sears (1940), who first brought these gruesome statistics to psychologists' attention, noticed that there was a remarkable correspondence between the annual variation in these killings and various farming economic indicators (farming being the principal industry in the southern states): as the economy receded and times got hard so the number of lynchings increased (see also Hepworth and West, 1988).

What might account for this correlation of economic recession with anti-black violence? Hovland and Sears (1940) believed it was caused by frustration.

FRUSTRATION–
AGGRESSION
Drawing upon Dollard et al's (1939) **frustration–aggression** theory, they hypothesized that the hardships experienced in a depressed economy raised people's levels of frustration, which, in turn, led to increased aggression. According to frustration–aggression theory, aggression is often not directed at the true source of the frustration (such as, the capitalist system which caused the recession), but is often diverted onto vulnerable and easily accessible targets such as members of minority groups.

Attempts to confirm this so-called 'scapegoat' theory of prejudice have met with mixed success. Miller and Bugelski (1948) conducted an experiment in which young men in a camp, eagerly anticipating a night on the town, were suddenly told that their evening out was cancelled. Before this frustrating event the men's attitudes towards two national groups were measured, and again afterwards. These attitudes became significantly less favourable after the frustration, a nice confirmation of the frustration–aggression 'displacement' hypothesis since these two groups could have had no conceivable responsibility for the men's plight. On the other hand, other experiments have yielded more equivocal results (e.g., Burnstein and McCrae, 1962; Stagner and Congdon, 1955).

It was inconsistencies like these, as well as some other conceptual and empirical difficulties, which led to the decline in the popularity of frustration–aggression theory as an explanation of prejudice (Billig, 1976; Brown, 1988). Perhaps the most serious of these problems was the consistent finding that *absolute* levels of hardship and frustration often seemed to be less potent instigators of aggression than a sense of *relative* deprivation. We return to this idea later in the chapter. Another criticism of the frustration–aggression approach is that it assumes that intergroup behaviour is primarily emotionally driven (i.e., by frustration) rather than being goal-directed. As we shall see, this assumption is rather questionable.

Interpersonal versus group behaviour

In attempting to explain intergroup behaviour by means of variations in personality types or levels of frustration, the above approaches make the assumption that people's behaviour in group settings is essentially similar to their behaviour in all other situations. Thus, whether we are alone, or interacting with one or two other close friends, or participating in some event involving a group which is important to us, our behaviour is still seen as being mainly determined by the same psychological variables.

There are, however, a number of difficulties with this hypothesis. First, it cannot easily account for the widespread uniformity of behaviour which is so typical of situations where groups are psychologically salient. This is particularly problematic for any personality-type explanations, as we saw earlier. A second, and closely related, problem concerns situations where several hundred members of different groups are involved – like the two incidents described at the start of this chapter. Here, the number of different possible interpersonal relationships between the protagonists must have been enormous, and yet the behaviour was observably predictable and uniform. Finally, people's behaviour, besides being more uniform in group settings, is also often qualitatively different. For example, in research on bargaining it has been found that during the course of union–management negotiations there are differences between exchanges involving *interparty* interaction and those involving *interpersonal* discussion. In general, the former are characterized by more references to the two groups' objectives, a 'tougher' bargaining stance, and a greater influence of the relative strengths of the two sides' cases. During interpersonal encounters, on the other hand, there are more positive references to one's opponents, the social orientation is of a more 'problem-solving' kind, and the outcome is less predictable from objective features of the groups' negotiating position (Stephenson, 1978). Similarly, the effects of attitudinal similarity, which at the interpersonal level nearly always seem to promote attraction (Byrne, 1971; see chapter 12), are more complex at the intergroup level since both attraction *and* repulsion can result under the appropriate conditions (Brown, 1984; Diehl, 1988).

It was considerations like these which led Tajfel (1978) to suggest that it is important to distinguish between interpersonal and intergroup behaviour and, consequently, led him to argue that theories addressing problems at the one level might not easily be extrapolated to explain phenomena at the other. *Interpersonal behaviour* means acting as an *individual* with some idiosyncratic characteristics and a unique set of personal relationships with others (for example, J. Smith, of a certain physical appearance, intelligence and personality, and with various friendships). *Intergroup behaviour*, on the other hand, means acting as a *group member* (such as, behaving as a *police officer*, or as a *Liverpool supporter*). In the first case the various social categories one belongs to are less important than the constellation of individual and interpersonal dynamics. In the second case the reverse is true; *who* one is as a person is much less important than the uniform one is wearing or the colour of the scarf around one's neck.

What Tajfel proposed, therefore, was that any sequence of social behaviour can be depicted as falling somewhere along a *continuum* defined by the two extremes of interpersonal and intergroup behaviour. Quite where it falls depends on three factors. The first is the clarity with which different social categories can be identified. Where social divisions such as black and white, man and woman, are clearly discernible, this will tend to locate the behaviour towards the intergroup end. Where the category differences are less clear or less relevant, the behaviour is more likely to be interpersonal. The second is the extent to which the behaviour within each group is variable or uniform. Interpersonal behaviour will show the normal range of individual differences; when groups are salient, people's behaviour becomes more similar. The third factor is how far one person's treatment of or attitude towards others is idiosyncratic or uniform and predictable. In our interpersonal dealings we negotiate a variety of ways of responding to those we know; intergroup encounters, on the other hand, are marked by stereotyped perceptions and behaviour.

It is worth noting that these three criteria do not just distinguish interpersonal behaviour from *intergroup* behaviour. Turner (1982) pointed out that behaviour within the group (*intragroup* behaviour) is also often marked by an awareness of category boundaries, uniformity of behaviour and stereotypical perceptions. For this reason, Brown and Turner (1981) proposed that the continuum which Tajfel (1978) had identified should be extended and relabelled as the **interpersonal–group continuum** (see table 17.1).

INTERPERSONAL–
GROUP
CONTINUUM

Intergroup Behaviour as a Response to Real or Imagined Group Interests

Instead of regarding intergroup prejudice as a problem associated with a particular personality type or level of frustration, it may be more useful to view it as the 'normal' response of ordinary people to the intergroup situation confronting them. One factor which seems to be particularly important is the nature of the respective goals of the groups concerned: are the goals *incompatible*, so that what one group is seeking will be at the expense of another; or are they *concordant*, so that both groups are working towards the same objective and may even need each other for its attainment? An example of the former case would be the relationship between workers and their employers where the one's wages are

Table 17.1 The interpersonal–group continuum

Factor	Interpersonal	Group
Presence of two or more social categories?	Obscured or not relevant	Clearly visible and salient
Uniformity of behaviour and attitudes within one group?	Low	High
Stereotyped or uniform treatment of other group members?	Low	High

at the expense of the other's profits. The miners' strike referred to earlier was a classic instance of such an industrial conflict. An example of concordant goals would be when minority political parties form coalitions to achieve political power (such as the right-wing parties in Italy in 1994).

Within social psychology the best known proponent of this approach is Sherif (1966). At the heart of Sherif's theory is the proposition that group members' intergroup attitudes and behaviour will tend to reflect the objective interests of their group *vis-à-vis* other groups. Where these interests conflict then their group's cause is more likely to be furthered by a competitive orientation towards the rival group, which is often easily extended to include prejudiced attitudes and even overtly hostile behaviour. At the same time the success of the **ingroup**   INGROUP
in achieving the goal is likely to be furthered by very positive attitudes towards other ingroup members, thereby engendering high morale and cohesion. Where, on the other hand, the groups' interests coincide then it is more functional for the group members to adopt a co-operative and friendly attitude towards the **outgroup**. If this is reciprocated then a positive joint outcome is more   OUTGROUP
probable.

Sherif's summer-camp studies

To demonstrate the validity of this perspective, Sherif, together with his colleagues, conducted three longitudinal field experiments which have become classics in the literature (Sherif and Sherif, 1953; Sherif, White and Harvey, 1955; Sherif et al., 1961). The full design included three stages: group formation, intergroup conflict, and conflict reduction. To effect this design, Sherif and his colleagues arranged for the experiments to be conducted in the context of a boys' summer camp. The boys themselves, aged around 12 years, had all been carefully screened before being invited to the camp, and only those who seemed to be psychologically well adjusted were accepted. In addition, none of the boys knew each other before coming to the camp. Although this was a highly select and unrepresentative sample it did ensure that any behaviour they subsequently exhibited could not be attributed to a prior history of social or psychological deprivation, or to pre-existing personal relationships between the boys.

Group formation
In the first stage the large group of 22 to 24 children was split up into the two experimental groups of the study. In the first two experiments, in addition to matching on various physical and psychological characteristics, it was also arranged to have the majority of each boy's best friends in the *outgroup* (these friendships had formed in the first few days of the camp). In the third experiment the boys never actually met each other prior to the groups being formed, and were initially camped some distance from each other, unaware of the other group's presence. For some days the children engaged in various activities in

these groups without, however, having much to do with the other group. Although the other group did not figure much in their thinking, it is interesting to note that in the first two experiments the observers did record some instances of comparisons between the groups; in these comparisons 'the edge was given to one's own group' (Sherif, 1966, p. 80). Furthermore, in the third study, where the groups did not know of each other's existence initially, on being informed of the presence of the other group several boys spontaneously suggested that the other group be challenged to some sporting contest. As we shall see, it is significant that these expressions of ingroup favouritism occurred before the intergroup conflict phase of the experiment had actually been introduced.

Intergroup competition

A series of intergroup contests was then announced (softball, tug-of-war etc.). The overall winner of these contests would receive a cup and each member of this successful group would be given a gleaming new pen-knife – just the kind of prize every 12-year-old boy covets. The losers would receive nothing. In this way, an objective conflict of interest was introduced between the groups. In technical terms, they had moved from being independent of one another to being negatively *interdependent*: what one group gained the other lost. With the advent of this conflict stage the boys' behaviour changed dramatically. Whereas in the first stage the two groups had co-existed more or less peaceably, they were now transformed into two hostile factions, never losing an opportunity to deride the outgroup and, in some instances, physically attack it. In a variety of micro-experiments, disguised as games, Sherif and his associates observed consistent ingroup favouritism in judgements, attitudes and sociometric preferences. These behaviours were all the more remarkable when it is remembered that in the first two studies at least, every boy's best friends had been placed in the *other* group. How fragile those initial interpersonal relationships proved to be in the face of the changing intergroup relationship!

Conflict reduction

SUPERORDINATE GOALS

Having so easily generated such fierce competition, the researchers attempted to reduce the conflict by introducing a series of **superordinate goals** for the groups – that is, goals which both groups desired but which were unattainable by one group by its own efforts alone. One such superordinate goal was engineered by arranging for the camp truck to break down some miles from the camp. Since it was nearly lunchtime the children had a clear common interest in getting the truck started to return them to camp. However, the truck was too heavy to be push-started by one group on its own. Only by both groups pulling on the tug-of-war rope attached to the front bumper – the same rope which they had used in *contest* only days earlier! – could the truck be moved. After a number of scenarios like this a marked change was observed in the boys' behaviour. They became much less aggressive towards members of the other group, and on a

Plate 17.1 A tug-of-war *between* groups is an example of negative interdependence

number of quantitative indices showed a clear reduction in the amount of ingroup favouritism.

On the face of it, these experiments seemed to provide strong support for Sherif's theory. The behaviour of these ordinary, well-adjusted children was shown to vary systematically with the changing intergroup relationship. Moreover, the changes in the boys' behaviour were too widespread and too rapid to be attributable to any enduring personality disposition. The intergroup hostility was just as evident in the 'winning' groups as it was in the presumably more frustrated 'losing' groups. Both the popular theories considered earlier, then, were shown up as deficient by these findings. These deficiencies were underlined by later research. In a variety of studies it has invariably been found that groups which either adopt or have imposed on them 'win–lose' orientations show more intergroup discrimination or outgroup aggression than those with more collaborative orientations (e.g., Brown et al., 1986; Ryen and Kahn, 1975; Struch and Schwartz, 1989).

Mere Group Membership as a Source of Intergroup Discrimination

In the previous section we saw how important intergroup goal relationships were in shaping group members' attitudes and behaviour towards both their own

Plate 17.2 An example of a superordinate goal: both groups *pull together* to move a broken-down truck

group and various outgroups. However, an important question remains un-answered from all this research: does the mere fact of belonging to one group have consequences for our attitudes towards other groups? Does being of one nationality (or religion or ethnicity or class), in and of itself, generate predictable orientations towards members from another country (religion and so on)? It is this question we address in this section.

Minimal group experiments

Rabbie and Horowitz (1969) were the first to investigate this. Following Lewin (1948) they reasoned that the essential condition for the arousal of group feelings was the perception of some interdependence of fate amongst the group members. Accordingly, they arranged for schoolchildren who did not know each other to be divided at random into two groups of four persons. Members of the two groups were given identification badges (green or blue) and were initially seated either side of a screen so that they could see only members of their own group. In the control condition, that was the extent of their group experience. In the experimental conditions, on the other hand, the groups further experienced a 'common fate' by being given – or by being deprived of – some new transistor radios. Subsequently, in all conditions, the screen separating the groups was removed and each person was asked to stand up and read out some personal biographical details about himself or herself, while the other children rated him or her on a number of scales. Rabbie and Horowitz (1969) found that in the experimental conditions these impressionistic ratings were markedly affected by the person's group affiliation: ingroup members were consistently rated more favourably than outgroup members. In the control condition, however, no such ingroup bias was observed, although in a subsequent extension of the experiment (which increased the sample size) some biases were observed on two of the scales (Horowitz and Rabbie, 1982). Nevertheless, the conclusion from this experiment seemed to be that classification into a group *by itself* exerted little influence on group members' judgements. But when that classification coincided with some common experience of reward or deprivation, group-related perceptions emerged.

That conclusion proved to be premature, however. Tajfel et al. (1971) took the **minimal group paradigm** one stage further and showed that mere categorization *was* sufficient to elicit intergroup discrimination. Like Rabbie and Horowitz, they assigned schoolboys to one of two groups on a very arbitrary basis – their alleged preference for one of two abstract artists, Paul Klee and Vassilij Kandinsky. However, in this experiment the children knew only which group they themselves had been assigned to; the identities of their fellow ingroup and outgroup members were kept hidden by the use of code numbers. Then, under the general pretext of the experiment ('a study of decision-making'), the children were asked to allocate money to various recipients using specially prepared booklets of decision matrices (see table 17.2 for an example). The identity of the recipients on each page was unknown but their group affiliation was revealed. To eliminate self-interest as a possible motive in the allocations, the children were never able to award money to themselves.

MINIMAL GROUP PARADIGM

The results were clear. Although they made some effort to be fair in their allocations, the children showed a persistent tendency to award more money to ingroup recipients than to those who they believed belonged to the other group. This was true even when, in absolute terms, the ingrouper might be worse off. For example, in the matrix shown in table 17.2 the mean response from people in the Kandinsky group was somewhere between the [11,12] and [13,13] options. Notice that this choice results in the Kandinsky recipient actually receiving 6 or 7 points *less* than he might otherwise have done but, crucially, he thereby receives more than the Klee recipient. The results are rather surprising when one considers how sparse this social setting really was. The children were allocated to two meaningless groups on a flimsy criterion. They never interacted with members of their own or the other group. The two groups had no current or past relationship with each other. And yet, when asked to allocate sums of money to anonymous others, the children consistently favoured ingroup members over outgroupers. Simply being assigned to a group can, after all, have predictable effects on intergroup behaviour.

Table 17.2 A sample matrix from the Tajfel et al. (1971) minimal group experiment

Numbers are rewards for:													
member 74 of Klee group	25	23	21	19	17	15	13	11	9	7	5	3	1
member 44 of Kandinsky group	19	18	17	16	15	14	13	12	11	10	9	8	7

Notes: (a) On each page subjects must choose one box.

(b) This is one of several different types of matrix used. It was designed to measure the tendency to *maximize* the *difference* (MD) between ingroup and outgroup recipients. In the experiment this matrix would be presented to each subject at least twice: once as shown, and once with the group affiliations of the two recipients reversed (i.e. Klandinsky rewards at top, Klee rewards below).

(c) In the original experiments 1 point = 0.1 p. Given that each booklet contained some 16 pages (each with point values ranging from 1 to 29), the total amount of money which each person thought he was dispensing was not inconsiderable. In 1970 this probably amounted to about £0.50, which, at today's prices, is probably equivalent to more than £3.00.

Intergroup discrimination in this minimal-group situation has proved to be a remarkably robust phenomenon. In more than two dozen independent studies in several different countries using a wide range of experimental participants of both sexes (from young children to adults), essentially the same result has been found: the mere act of allocating people into arbitrary social categories is sufficient to elicit biased judgements and discriminatory behaviour (see Brewer, 1979; Tajfel, 1982).

Despite this empirical consensus the minimal group paradigm has attracted controversy. Space does not permit a discussion of all the contentious issues. However, it is worth making the following observations on some of the more important ones. The first concerns whether participants in these experiments are really showing ingroup favouritism or, alternatively, are displaying behaviour better described as some form of *fairness* (Branthwaite, Doyle and Lightbown, 1979; Turner, 1980). It seems clear that people do show a propensity towards equalizing ingroup and outgroup outcomes in these situations. However, it is also true that they are nearly always more 'fair' to ingroupers than to outgroupers. In other words, although people's choices cluster around the centre or 'fair' point (e.g., [13,13] in table 17.2), when an ingroup member is the recipient on the top line the responses tend to be to the left of centre; when an outgroup member is the beneficiary on the same line the responses move to the *right* of centre. Furthermore, the evidence for this persistent bias is derived not just from particular reward-allocation matrices but from a variety of other dependent measures which have also shown that ingroup members or products receive more favourable ratings than equivalent outgroup stimuli (Brewer, 1979; Brown, Tajfel and Turner, 1980).

A second issue concerns whether the pervasive discrimination observed in the allocation of rewards can be generalized to the distribution of penalties or aversive stimuli. Hewstone et al. (1981) modified the normal paradigm by asking group members to *subtract* money from ingroup and outgroup recipients (who had previously been allocated an initial sum). Although some evidence of ingroup bias was observed as a consequence of categorization, the levels were lower than those obtained with the standard measures. Mummendey et al. (1993) extended this principle by asking subjects to distribute (what they thought would be) durations of an unpleasantly high-pitched tone to ingroup and outgroup members. This seemed to eliminate completely ingroup favouritism, and strategies for equalizing outcomes (or fairness) or minimizing the total amount of aversive stimulation were much more in evidence. Intergroup discrimination re-emerged only in certain circumstances – for example, when the subjects were in a subordinate or minority-status group. The explanation for this difference between positive and negative outcomes is still not clear. It could simply be that in the relatively aseptic laboratory conditions in which such experiments are carried out there are strong social-desirability norms against penalizing or harming a fellow subject. This would have the effect of raising the threshold for displaying ingroup favouritism (Mummendey et al., 1993). On the other hand, it could be that *positive* ingroup bias (that is, treating or evaluating the ingroup more favourably than the outgroup) and *negative* ingroup bias (treating the ingroup less punitively than the outgroup) may be controlled by different processes. Other research has found little or no relationship between indices of positive ingroup bias and more obviously negative behaviour (Struch and Schwartz, 1989).

Explanations of intergroup discrimination in minimal groups

It is one thing to establish a phenomenon; it is quite another to explain it. What underlies the apparently gratuitous discrimination in these most minimal of groups? One explanation is in terms of norms (Tajfel et al., 1971). According to this view, being made aware that one is a member of a group may, in most of the cultures in which the experiments have been conducted, evoke associations with teams and team games. These might make a competitive norm highly salient and lead to the unequal allocation of money between the groups in an attempt to 'win'. That this competitiveness is not full-blown might be explained by a countervailing norm of fairness – another value-attribute in Western cultures. This form of explanation is supported by the findings from a cross-cultural study which found variations in the extent of minimal-group discrimination among children of European, Samoan and Maori origin (Wetherell, 1982). All three groups showed clear ingroup favouritism, although the latter two showed somewhat less than the first.

Attractive though such an account may be, it has at least two shortcomings which have inhibited its widespread adoption (Turner, 1980). First, such an explanation needs to be able to predict in advance which of a number of norms will predominate in any particular situation. After all, there are a variety of cultural norms which might be relevant: fairness, as we have seen, is one; profit maximization – surely salient in most Western countries – is another; equity is yet another. Without some theory of norm salience we are only able to explain after the event why a particular pattern of discrimination occurred. A second and related criticism is that normative accounts are, by their nature, rather too general. They do not really permit one to predict the systematic variations in response to the minimal-group situation which it is possible to observe even *within one culture* (Turner, 1981a). For example, introducing group status or size differences, or changing the nature of the recipients, all have reliable effects on levels of discrimination (Brown and Deschamps, 1980–1; Mummendey et al., 1993; Sachdev and Bourhis, 1987).

A second explanation offers some hope of avoiding these problems; this explanation is in terms of categorization processes (e.g., Doise, 1976). Some earlier work had shown that if a non-overlapping classification is imposed on a set of physical stimuli (such as lines of different lengths), then judgements of stimuli falling into different classes will become distorted, with the effect that perceived differences *between* the two categories become exaggerated (Tajfel and Wilkes, 1963). A similar phenomenon has been observed with more social stimuli: attitude statements which are categorized as having come from one of two sources may be seen as more different from one another than those which have not been so classified (McGarty and Penney, 1988). Doise (1976) argues that these judgemental biases are the result of a fundamental cognitive process, that

CATEGORICAL
DIFFERENTIATION

of **categorical differentiation**. He suggests that in order for social categories to be useful ordering and simplifying devices it is important that they discriminate clearly between class and non-class members. Thus, the function of the differentiation process is to sharpen the distinctions between the categories – and, relatedly, to blur the differences *within* them – so as to better organize and structure our mental and social worlds. If we apply this analysis to the minimal-group context it suggests that the situation confronting the experimental participants is sufficiently ill defined for them to latch on to the previously meaningless categories (Klee and Kandinsky) and use them to make sense of it. Once that particular (and only) classification has been adopted the inevitable categorical differentiation occurs, and occurs in the only way possible here – by allocating different amounts to ingroup and outgroup recipients.

Directly related to these categorization processes is another phenomenon, that of perceived group homogeneity (see chapter 6 for a fuller discussion of stereotyping and other phenomena associated with categorization). As noted earlier, categorization does not only result in the accentuation of differences between categories, it also causes members of the same category to be seen as more similar to one another. This perception of homogeneity is often not a symmetrical process: one group is usually seen as more homogeneous than the other. A common finding is that outgroups are seen as more homogeneous than ingroups: 'They' are all the same, but 'We' are all different (Quattrone and Jones, 1980). Why might this be? Linville, Fischer and Salovey (1989) have suggested it is caused by our different knowledge of and familiarity with members of the ingroup and the outgroup: because we are likely to know more ingroup members our perception of the ingroup should be more complex and differentiated. This is unlikely to be the whole explanation however. Greater perceived homogeneity in the outgroup is not always correlated with the numbers of people known (Brown and Smith, 1989; Jones, Wood and Quattrone, 1981) and can also be observed even in minimal group settings where no one is known in the ingroup or the outgroup (Wilder, 1984). An alternative explanation is that it is not the numbers of people known which is important but the nature of ingroup and outgroup categories themselves (Park, Judd and Ryan, 1991). According to this view, perceptions of groups are not based on a tally of specific ingroup and outgroup acquaintances but are derived from the prototypical member of each, and some estimate of variability around this typical person. The reason that the ingroup is sometimes seen as more variable is that it is more important (because it contains the self), more concrete (again because at least one member is very well known), and more provisional (because of a greater need to form an accurate impression about those close to us psychologically).

This explanation cannot be the complete story either because it fails to account for the opposite phenomenon: the perception that the ingroup is more homogeneous than the outgroup (Simon, 1992a). This tends to happen when the ingroup is much smaller than the outgroup (Brown and Smith, 1989; Simon and Brown, 1987), and on judgemental dimensions which are important to the ingroup (Brown and Wootton-Millward, 1993; Kelly, 1989; Simon, 1992b). Underlying this effect may be processes of social identification (Simon, 1992a; see below).

The categorization model offers a simple and powerful explanation of intergroup biases in terms of a single cognitive process. However, there is one important limitation to such an explanation: it cannot readily account for the asymmetry which is such a pervasive feature of intergroup differentiation. In other words, why does the ingroup (and not the outgroup) come off best in intergroup perceptions, judgements and resource allocations? The categorization approach can account for the fact that groups are made more distinctive from one another, but it cannot explain why that distinctiveness is often valued positively for the ingroup and negatively for the outgroup. To understand what underlies that *positive* distinctiveness we need a new concept, that of social identity. This idea will be discussed shortly, but before doing so another explanation for minimal intergroup discrimination will be briefly considered.

Rabbie, Schot and Visser (1989) have suggested that what really motivates subjects' discriminatory behaviour in minimal-group experiments is self-interest. At first glance this seems paradoxical since the paradigm was designed specifically to eliminate self-interest as a possible motive by preventing subjects from ever allocating rewards directly to themselves. However, Rabbie et al. argue that, while such *direct* self-interest considerations may be eliminated, they can still be operative if subjects believe that the members of each group will tend to favour each other. Hence, they too may try to follow this implicit norm so as to maximize the benefits to fellow ingroup members and hence, by reciprocity, to themselves. To test this idea Rabbie et al. (1989) added two variations to the normal minimal group paradigm. In one condition they specified that subjects would only receive what other ingroup members gave them; in another they would only get what *outgroup* members allocated. Altering the subjects' perceived dependence on others in this way had a predictable effect on their own reward distributions: those dependent solely on the ingroup increased their ingroup favouritism somewhat compared with the normal condition, while those dependent wholly on the outgroup sharply decreased it and even showed *outgroup* favouritism. Diehl (1989) also found some evidence that linking subjects' fortunes directly to particular people substantially reduced (though did not eliminate) ingroup favouritism.

These experiments show that people are sensitive to self-interest considerations when these are made more explicit. However, they do not demonstrate conclusively that subjects' expectations of others' behaviour are the sole determinant of their own allocation decisions. Indeed, in a second experiment Diehl (1989) showed that the link between reciprocity expectations and actual behaviour may not be a simple one. In this experiment subjects were given false feedback about outgroup members' *intended* (and not actual) allocation strategies. Subsequently they were asked to indicate their own intentions and then actually distribute the rewards. There was some correlation between subjects' own intentions and their assumptions about what outgroup members would do. However, when it came to their *actual* behaviour there was no reliable difference between those who expected the outgroup to be fair and those who anticipated its being discriminatory. Thus, perceptions of interdependence and mutual reciprocity, while they clearly play a role in guiding group members' behaviour, seem not to provide a complete explanation for intergroup discrimination; other motives seem to be at work too.

Group Membership and Social Identity

Who am I? Who are we?

Segmenting the world into a manageable number of categories does not just help us to simplify and make sense of it; it also serves one other very important function – that of defining who we are. Not only do we classify others as members of this or that group, but we also locate *ourselves* in relation to those same groups. Our sense of identity, in other words, is closely bound up with our various group memberships. As a simple demonstration of this, readers may just ask themselves the following question: 'Who am I?' Analysis of people's answers to that question (repeated a number of times) usually reveal that several (if not the majority) of the self-descriptions refer to group affiliations either explicitly ('I am a member of the Juventus supporters' club') or implicitly, through reference to the occupation of social roles ('I am a miner'), to gender ('I am a woman') or to nationality ('I am German') (Kuhn and McPartland, 1954).

This idea that **social identity** derives from group membership has a long history (e.g., Mead, 1934), but it was not until more recently that it was realized that social-identity processes might have implications for intergroup behaviour (Tajfel, 1978; Tajfel and Turner, 1986). This can happen if we assume, with Tajfel and Turner (1986), that by and large people prefer to have a positive self-concept rather than a negative one. Since part of our self-concept (or identity) is defined in terms of group affiliations, it follows that there will also be a preference to view those ingroups positively rather than negatively. But how do we arrive at such an evaluation? Tajfel and Turner (1986) extend Festinger's (1954) social-comparison theory and suggest that our group evaluations are essentially relative in nature; we assess our own group's worth by comparing it with that of other groups. The outcome of these intergroup comparisons is critical for us because indirectly it contributes to our own self-esteem. If our own group can be perceived as clearly superior on some dimension of value (such as skill or sociability) then we too can bask in that reflected glory. Cialdini et al. (1976) provided a nice illustration of this phenomenon amongst college football supporters. After their college's successes in football matches supporters were more likely to be seen wearing college insignia and clothing than after defeats. Their willingness to be identified as belonging to the group seemed to be associated with the group's fortunes in intergroup encounters (see also Snyder, Lassegard and Ford, 1986). Because of our presumed need for a positive self-concept, it follows that there will be a bias in these comparisons towards looking for ways in which the ingroup can, indeed, be distinguished favourably from outgroups. Tajfel calls this 'the establishment of positive distinctiveness' (Tajfel, 1978, p. 83).

How can this theory – social identity theory, as it is known – help to explain the persistent tendency for people to display intergroup discrimination, even in as barren a context as the minimal group paradigm? Consider again the situation facing the experimental subjects. They have been allocated to one of two equally meaningless groups. Indeed, so meaningless are they that there is literally nothing to differentiate them except the group labels and the fact that they themselves are in one group and not the other. They are referred to by code numbers, thus leading to feelings of anonymity. Given this anonymity the only possible source of identity, primitive though it may be, is their ingroup. However, that group is initially indistinguishable from the other group and hence, according to the theory, contributes little that is positive to its members'

SOCIAL
IDENTITY

self-esteem. Accordingly, the pressures of distinctiveness come into play and the members of both groups seek to differentiate their own group positively from the other by the only means which the experimenters have provided – by allocating more money to fellow ingroupers than to outgroupers. Recall, also, that they will often do this even at the cost of some absolute gain to the ingroup (the maximizing difference strategy).

Social identity theory, then, presumes some direct causal connection between intergroup discrimination and self-esteem. Abrams and Hogg (1988) have pointed out that this link could take either or both of two forms. It could be that people show intergroup discrimination in order to raise their self-esteem, simply on the grounds that positive self-regard is generally to be preferred to a neutral or negative self-concept. Alternatively, it could be that prior low self-esteem, perhaps deriving from membership in a low-status group, causes intergroup discrimination in order to raise it to 'normal' levels. The evidence for both of these processes is equivocal (Hogg and Abrams, 1990). Some studies have found that in minimal-group situations subjects who were denied the usual opportunity to display intergroup discrimination showed lower self-esteem than those who were not (Lemyre and Smith, 1985; Oakes and Turner, 1980). On the other hand, correlations between the amount of discrimination and levels of self-esteem are sometimes close to zero (Hogg and Sunderland, 1991; Hogg and Turner, 1987). Studies which have investigated the opposite direction of causality have produced a similarly confusing picture. Hogg and Sunderland (1991) found that groups deemed to have failed on a task did show lower self-esteem and consequently greater intergroup discrimination. However, other studies have found that it is groups with *enhanced* status or power – and hence presumably higher self-esteem – who show greater ingroup favouritism (Sachdev and Bourhis, 1985, 1987). The more general effects of status on intergroup behaviour will be discussed further below, but, at the very least, the available evidence suggests that the social-identity hypothesis that self-esteem is an important variable controlling or being controlled by intergroup discrimination cannot be unambiguously sustained.

Social identity theory, then, has sought to provide an account of people's readiness to favour these most minimal of ingroups. But its applicability is not limited to these rather contrived experimental situations; part of its attraction has been its ability to make sense of a wide range of phenomena in naturalistic contexts. We shall describe just two examples; for others, see Tajfel (1982) and R. J. Brown (1984).

Intergroup differentiation in naturalistic contexts

There is a common tendency for groups of workers in industrialized countries to be concerned about the size of wage relativities *vis-à-vis* other groups of workers. This was particularly prevalent in the British engineering industry in the 1970s but, historically, examples of disputes centring on differentials go back at least as

Table 17.3 A matrix used to measure intergroup differentiation in wage comparisons (Brown, 1978)

Wages for toolroom group	£69.30	£68.80	£68.30	£67.80	£67.30
Wages for production and development groups	£70.30	£69.30	£68.30	£67.30	£66.30

far as the early nineteenth century. What is interesting about these industrial conflicts is that they may have little 'realistic' basis, in the sense that there is rarely an explicit conflict of interest between the groups concerned. The other important aspect of differentials disputes is – as the words imply – that they are about the *difference* between groups rather than about their levels of wages in absolute terms. These two points were borne out very clearly in a study of an aircraft engineering factory by R. J. Brown (1978). He showed, using matrices adapted from the minimal-group laboratory, that shop stewards from one department in the factory would be prepared to sacrifice as much as £2 per week in absolute terms in order to increase their differential over another group to £1. An example of one of these matrices is shown in table 17.3. When presented with this array of wage relativities, members of the toolroom were virtually unanimous in choosing the extreme right-hand box. That this intergroup differentiation cut across the group's 'real' interests was confirmed in another part of the study, where the same stewards were asked to respond to a hypothetical superordinate-goals scenario involving factory-wide redundancies. Only a minority of those interviewed responded to this scenario by proposing co-operative strategies involving other groups. These findings seemed much more explicable by social identity theory than by the Sherif theory which was described earlier.

A second illustration is provided by the attempts by various ethnic and national groups to maintain the integrity of their language (Giles, 1977). Examples abound. Just in Europe one thinks immediately of the Flemings and Walloons in Belgium, the Catalans in Spain, the Bretons in France, and the Welsh in Britain. In all these cases we see groups trying to make themselves distinctive from other groups in one of the most fundamental ways of all – language. Language is fundamental in two ways. First, our membership of ethnic/national groups is intimately connected with language or dialect use. It is part of our cultural heritage, and indeed may even be a defining attribute for group membership – that is, it can form a part of our social identity. But language is also the prime means of communication with outgroups. Depending on the language, dialect or accent we choose to use we can communicate more or less effectively with members of an outgroup; we can attempt to integrate or cut ourselves off. These considerations have led Giles and his colleagues to explain the behaviour of ethnolinguistic groups in terms of social-identity processes (Giles and Johnson, 1981). Where identity is threatened, efforts to establish distinctiveness may take the form of linguistic divergence. Two experimental studies have found exactly that (Bourhis and Giles, 1977; Bourhis et al., 1978). Both were set in the context of a language laboratory, and in both some language students were confronted with a speaker who threatened their linguistic identities. Clear evidence of language divergence by the students was found, either by broadening their accent or by switching languages altogether. This differentiation is particularly significant since, as some of Giles's earlier work had established, in most *interpersonal* contexts people tend to converge in their language use (Giles and Powesland, 1975). That in intergroup contexts the opposite can happen is further evidence that different (identity) processes may be at work (see also chapter 11).

Ingroup bias and group identification

A central idea in social identity theory is that biased intergroup comparisons are directly linked to social identification. Presumably, the more important a group is to its members the more bias they should show in its favour. This hypothesis was the starting point for two studies which examined the correlation between the strength of group identification and the amount of ingroup bias shown in intergroup judgements (Brown and Williams, 1984; Brown et al., 1986). Both were carried out in industrial settings – one a bakery, the other a paper mill. In both studies the ingroups of interest were the respondents' own workgroup, and the outgroups were other workgroups in the factory, or management. On a variety of indices, clear positive differentiation was observed. The identification with the ingroup was also predominantly positive. And yet, within each group, the relationship between the strength of this identification and the indices of differentiation was very variable, ranging in different groups from positive (as predicted), through non-existent, to negative. A more powerful and reliable predictor of intergroup differentiation in both studies was perceived conflict with the outgroup – a finding more in keeping with the Sherif approach considered earlier.

The rather unstable correlation between group identification and ingroup bias has been confirmed in other studies (Hinkle and Brown, 1990). In an attempt to account for this variability Hinkle and Brown suggested that the psychological processes proposed by social identity theory may not be operative in all groups. They hypothesized that this would depend on two factors: the prevailing level of individualism or collectivism in the group or among group members (Triandis et al., 1988), and their inclination to engage in intergroup comparisons or, instead, a preference for group evaluations of a more abstract or autonomous kind (Hinkle and Brown, 1990). Hinkle and Brown argued that a strong link between group identification and favouritism would only be expected in those groups simultaneously characterized by a *collectivist* orientation – that is, where there was an emphasis on intra-group co-operation and group achievements – and a *relational* orientation – that is, a concern with one's group's standing or performance relative to other groups. In three studies some support was found for this idea: group members classified as collectivist and relational showed positive associations between identification and bias; those designated as individualist and autonomous showed no association at all (Brown et al., 1992).

Subordinate status, intergroup comparisons and social unrest

The examples chosen to illustrate social identity processes had one other feature in common, a feature characteristic of nearly all real-world intergroup relationships: they both featured groups of unequal status. The three groups in the aircraft engine factory formed a clear hierarchy among themselves and, of course, all enjoyed much less power and status than their employers (Brown, 1978). Minority-group languages or dialects are nearly always devalued by the dominant linguistic group (Giles and Powesland, 1975). Let us now consider what the consequences are of belonging to a group of subordinate status.

At first glance these seem negative. Members of such groups will frequently discover that they have lower wages (if they have a job at all), poorer housing, fewer educational qualifications, and are consensually regarded as being inferior on a whole host of criteria. Thus, not only are they worse off in a direct material sense, but psychologically too they may well be disadvantaged. If identity is indeed maintained through intergroup comparisons, as social identity theory suggests, then the outcome of the available comparisons is unremittingly negative for their self-esteem.

Leaving the group

One reaction to this state of affairs is simply to try to leave the group, as Tajfel (1978) has suggested. Examples of members of 'inferior' groups distancing themselves physically or psychologically from their group are not hard to find. In their classic studies of ethnic identification, Clark and Clark (1947) found that black children in the USA showed identification with and preference for the dominant white group – a finding replicated with minority groups in other countries (Aboud, 1988). Disidentification with the ingroup is by no means a phenomenon restricted to children, as Lewin (1948) noted of American Jews who attempt to 'pass' into Gentile society. Ellemers et al. (1988) studied this experimentally by creating high-status and low-status groups between which mobility was either permitted or not allowed. This 'permeability' factor had its effects primarily on the low-status group members: where they saw a chance to escape to the higher-status group, identification with the ingroup decreased. This effect was particularly noticeable amongst the 'more able' members of the subordinate group, presumably because they believed they had a better chance of upward mobility. However, this is not a universal or necessary consequence, as is revealed by studies in different historical contexts which have failed to find such misidentification (Hraba and Grant, 1970; Vaughan, 1978). We return to this point shortly.

Social comparisons

Nevertheless, such individualistic strategies may not always be possible, especially if the group boundaries are relatively fixed and impermeable as is the case with many ethnic and religious groups. In cases like these, Tajfel and Turner (1986) suggest that a number of other avenues may be pursued. One is to restrict the comparisons made to other similar or subordinate status groups so that the outcome of these comparisons is then more favourable to the ingroup. Such was the case in Brown's (1978) factory study mentioned above, where the workers' concern was over differentials amongst themselves rather than with the much larger difference between themselves and management. In another context, Rosenberg and Simmons (1972) found self-esteem to be higher amongst blacks making comparisons with other blacks, than in those who compared themselves with whites. Another strategy is to sidestep the main dimensions of comparison (on which the subordinate group is regarded as inferior) and either invent new dimensions or change the value of those existing dimensions. Thus, Lemaine (1966) found that in a children's camp those groups whose hut constructions seemed poorer than others found new attributes to emphasize (such as the hut's garden). Similarly, the life-style of subcultural groups like the 'punks' of the 1980s or the 'hippies' of the 1970s is characterized by a complete negation of the dominant society's values in fashion, music and morality. Still a third route is to confront directly the dominant group's superiority by agitating for social and economic change. Such were the goals of the black movement in the USA in the 1960s and such are currently the demands of feminist groups in many industrialized societies. These different strategies – the individualistic and the three collective – are summarized in table 17.4.

Cognitive alternatives

Which of these tactics will be chosen may well depend on the prevailing social climate. If it is such that no real alternatives to the status quo may be conceived then the first two options seem more likely; without some sense that the power relations are not immutable, it is difficult for subordinate groups openly to challenge the existing order (the third strategy). Tajfel and Turner (1986) have proposed that for such 'cognitive alternatives' to exist, some perception of instability and illegitimacy is necessary. The system must be seen to be changing and to be based on arbitrary principles of justice. Experimental studies support this idea. Where laboratory groups co-exist in stable and justifiable status relations, subordinate groups show little sign of throwing off their inferiority. If, however, the status hierarchy is implied to be flexible or unfair, subordinate groups respond by displaying strong ingroup identification and favouritism, and hostility towards the dominant group (Brown and Ross, 1982; Caddick, 1982; Ellemers, Wilke and van Knippenberg, 1993). Once again, the likelihood of these reactions translating themselves into collective action aimed at changing the status quo may depend on the permeability of group boundaries. Wright, Taylor and Moghadam (1990) showed that where the latter are completely closed, group members are more likely to respond to disadvantage by some kind of non-normative collective strategy. If, on the other hand, there is the slightest possibility of upward mobility, even if this only results in a few 'token' subordinate group members being allowed to move, then individualistic strategies are more likely.

Relative deprivation

A rather similar conclusion is reached by Runciman (1966) and Gurr (1970). They argue that a key factor in generating social unrest amongst subordinate groups is a sense of relative deprivation. *Relative deprivation* arises from a perceived discrepancy between what one has and what one feels entitled to. This

Table 17.4 Response to a negative social identity

	Individualistic strategy	Collective strategies		
Aim	Change one's personal standing in society	Change standing of one's group in society		
		(1)	(2)	(3)
Method	Leave the group, e.g., blacks attempting to 'pass' as whites	Restrict comparisons to other subordinate groups, e.g., concern by workers over worker–worker wage differences; neglect of worker–employer disparities	Change the dimensions of comparison, e.g., adoption of new cultural and musical forms by 'punks' in Britain	Direct confrontation with dominant group, e.g., demands for social change by feminists in industrialized countries
Possible outcomes	Some individuals may benefit, but many are unable to; position of groups unchanged	Some changes may occur among subordinate groups; major status differences between groups unchanged	May create climate for change if new dimensions achieve social recognition	May lead to change if society is unstable and dominant group's position under challenge from other directions

discrepancy can arise from comparison either with one's own group in the past (Davies, 1969) or, more often, with other groups (Runciman, 1966). Where these comparisons reveal a gap between achievements and aspirations, then people will often feel sufficiently motivated to attempt social change. This will be especially true, as Walker and Pettigrew (1984) have argued, where the comparisons are made on an intergroup basis rather than between oneself and others.

The significance of relative deprivation as a factor generating unrest is supported by a number of studies. Vanneman and Pettigrew (1972) found that amongst whites in the USA the holding of racist attitudes and support for conservative political candidates was related to the white respondents' feelings of relative deprivation, thus showing that relative deprivation can be experienced by dominant groups as well as by subordinate groups. Abeles (1976), similarly, discovered that black militancy in the USA was correlated with relative deprivation and, interestingly, that levels of militancy appeared to be higher amongst blacks of higher economic and educational status – groups who objectively were less deprived (in an absolute sense) than poorer and less well-educated blacks. Finally, Guimond and Dubé-Simard (1983) found that intergroup, but not interpersonal, deprivation was reliably correlated with support for political change in Canada, a finding later replicated by Walker and Mann (1987) amongst young unemployed people in Australia. A recurring theme in all these studies is the importance of the distinction between personal and group deprivation in generating collective dissatisfaction with the status quo.

The Reduction of Intergroup Conflict

Most of the theory and research we have considered thus far has been concerned with what might be termed the negative side of intergroup relations, the processes which give rise to ingroup favouritism, intergroup hostility and the like. What of the other side of the coin, the factors which are likely to facilitate the reduction of intergroup conflict?

Superordinate goals

One obvious strategy, as we saw from the earlier discussion of Sherif's realistic group conflict theory, is to try to arrange for the conflicting groups to co-operate with one another in the pursuit of superordinate goals. As Sherif's own summer-camp studies found, and other research subsequently confirmed, in such circumstances formerly antagonistic relationships can be transformed into something approaching mutual tolerance (Brown, 1988).

However, co-operation over superordinate goals may not always be an effective panacea for the improvement of negative intergroup relations; indeed, it may even increase antagonism towards the outgroup. Worchel, Andreoli and Folger

(1977) noted that in Sherif's studies the co-operation over superordinate goals always proved successful. They showed, in contrast, that when that co-operation did not achieve its aims and had been preceded by a competitive episode, liking for the outgroup diminished. In addition, it may be important for groups engaged in co-operative ventures to have distinctive and complementary roles to play. When this does not occur and the groups' contributions are not easily recognizable, liking for the other group decreases, perhaps because the group members are concerned for the integrity of the ingroup (Brown and Wade, 1987; Deschamps and Brown, 1983). However, the positive effects of distinguishing task roles very clearly may be restricted to co-operative encounters at an intergroup level; when the interaction is more personalized the beneficial effects of clear-cut role assignment may be diminished (Marcus-Newhall, Miller, Holtz and Brewer, 1993).

Redrawing the category boundaries

Social categorization, as we have seen, has the potential to instigate discriminatory behaviour and judgements. But the same processes which are thought to underlie those biases can be harnessed in the service of conflict reduction. Turner (1981) noted that if members of two groups could redefine themselves as belonging to a single superordinate category then the erstwhile 'outgroupers' would be recategorized as fellow members of the new larger ingroup and a more favourable attitude towards them should ensue. An example of this strategy would be when political leaders appeal to societal subgroups to sink their differences in the cause of national unity. The effectiveness of this 'recategorization' approach has been demonstrated by Gaertner and his colleagues. In a laboratory setting they arranged for an intergroup encounter to occur under conditions which led to the perception of participants as belonging to a single group, as two separate groups, or as discrete individuals. As predicted, the 'one group' perception was reliably associated with a more favourable rating of the former outgroup, and more so than in either the 'individual' or 'two group' cases (Gaertner et al., 1993).

Another way in which ingroup biases can be reduced is to arrange for two or more social categories (ethnicity and gender, for example) to cut across one another. Categorization principles would suggest that in 'criss-cross' situations like this the discrimination observed in terms of either of the original categories will be reduced because the simultaneous processes of between-category differentiation and within-category assimilation effectively cancel one another out (see figure 17.1). Deschamps and Doise (1978) and Deschamps (1977) have found evidence of such reduced differentiation when categories (both real and artificial) are crossed. Note, however, that if the two crossing categories result in a double ingroup in juxtaposition with a double outgroup (e.g., in figure 17.1,

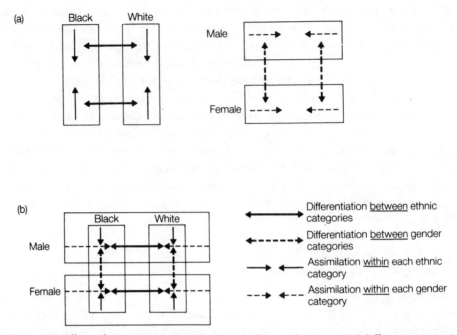

Figure 17.1 Effects of criss-cross categorizations according to the categorical differentiation model: (a) simple categorization; (b) crossed categorizations

black men versus white women), then there is evidence that this results in enhanced rather than reduced differentiation (Brown and Turner, 1979; Vanbeselaere, 1991). Outside the laboratory, where the categories may be psychologically much more meaningful and where they may differ in status and size, such superimposition of categories can have more complex effects. In addition, because of contextual factors, one category dimension can sometimes dominate over others, thus weakening any effects associated with their criss-crossing. This was shown clearly in a study conducted in Bangladesh where the relevant dimensions were religion (Muslim and Hindu), nationality (Bangladeshi and Indian), and language (Bengali and Hindi) (Hewstone, Islam and Judd, 1993). Consistent with an earlier study conducted in India (Hagendoorn and Henke, 1991), Hewstone et al. (1993) found that respondents' intergroup evaluations were strongly determined by religion, rather less so by nationality, and almost not at all by whether the stimulus group spoke the same language or not. The net result of this was that people of a different religion *and* nationality were strongly derogated by respondents, especially in comparison with compatriots of the same religion. Thus, while the crossed categorization strategy clearly has some positive implications for conflict reduction, it cannot be relied on to eliminate all manifestations of ingroup favouritism.

The contact hypothesis

One of the most influential ideas for the reduction of intergroup prejudice is the contact hypothesis. Broadly speaking, this hypothesis suggests that contact between members of different groups, under the appropriate conditions, lessens intergroup prejudice and hostility. This idea has provided the rationale for desegregation policies in housing, employment, and education which have been partially implemented in the USA and elsewhere. Although the contact hypothesis has been proposed in several different forms over the years (e.g., Allport, 1954; Cook, 1962; Pettigrew, 1971, 1986), on one issue these theorists are all agreed: contact between groups by itself, without some co-operation over common goals, will not reduce and may even exacerbate prejudice. The evidence from studies of ethnic relations largely confirms this (Amir, 1976; Hewstone and Brown, 1986; Slavin, 1983).

CONTACT
HYPOTHESIS

The outcome of intergroup contact may also depend on the extent to which the participants from different groups are interacting on an interpersonal or a group basis (Brewer and Miller, 1984; Hewstone and Brown, 1986). Brewer and Miller (1984), mindful of the potentially divisive effects of making social categories salient, have suggested that there are advantages in personalizing intergroup situations by de-emphasizing categorical differences wherever possible. In support of this idea it has been found that instructing people to focus on interpersonal issues in a co-operative group containing both ingroup and outgroup members elicits less ingroup bias than an instruction to focus on the task (Bettencourt, Brewer, Croak and Miller, 1992; Miller, Brewer and Edwards, 1985).

One problem with this approach is that any change of attitude generated by the contact may not generalize to other members of the groups concerned; to the extent that participants are seen as individuals, then, the cognitive link to the prior groups is blocked. In recognition of this, Hewstone and Brown (1986) proposed that there could be some advantages in maintaining the original group boundaries so long as the two groups were still positively interdependent and able to co-operate with one another on an equal footing. In this way the interaction would be of a more intergroup nature, the participants would be likely to be seen as more representative of their groups, and hence any positive change would have more widespread effects. Consistent with this, Wilder (1984) found that contact between members of different college groups who were seen as typical of their group produced more positive intergroup attitudes than contact between atypical members. The beneficial effects of contact with typical outgroup members have been confirmed in the contexts of contact between members of stigmatized and non-stigmatized groups and between members of different countries (Desforges et al., 1991; Vivian, Brown and Hewstone, 1994).

Although the Hewstone and Brown model offers a promising way of tackling the generalization problem it is not without its difficulties. One of these follows from the same argument which provided the rationale for the model in the first place. If intergroup (rather than interpersonal) contact permits greater generalization of attitude change then, in principle, both positive *and* negative attitudes can be generalized. Thus, if the co-operative encounter goes wrong then structuring the interaction at an intergroup level could make matters worse. Furthermore, intergroup interactions may be more anxiety provoking than interpersonal ones and anxiety may not be conducive to harmonious social relations (Stephan and Stephan, 1985). Islam and Hewstone (1993), in a study of Muslim–Hindu contact in Bangladesh, found that features indicative of intergroup relationships were correlated with increased anxiety, which, in turn, was linked with less favourable attitudes towards the outgroup.

There is, then, a fine line to be drawn in designing situations of intergroup contact. Enough category salience must be retained to permit the positive change to be generalized; but not so much as to allow a regression into the familiar and destructive patterns of prejudice which are associated with too firmly drawn category divisions.

Summary and Conclusions

This chapter began with two violent intergroup encounters. In the pages which followed, various social-psychological theories were examined which have been proffered as explanations of scenes such as these. How successful are they in doing this? It is not difficult to see that, taken singly, not one of the approaches can plausibly claim to have provided the whole – or even most – of the answer, if by 'the answer' we mean being able to explain why the events happened where, when and as they did. Mainly this lack of explanatory power has to do with a point which is often overlooked by social psychologists. Social events have historical precursors, and are often controlled by economic and political processes far beyond the reach of any purely social-psychological analysis. This means that, as social psychologists, we ought to be suitably modest in our ambitions to be able to explain them.

But, even with this caveat firmly in mind, it seems that not one of the approaches by itself really provides an adequate explanation of what happened at Orgreave or Brussels. To be sure, some of these protagonists were more involved in the conflict than others, and doubtless there were variations in personality types and levels of frustration which predisposed some individuals to greater outgroup hostility than others. But when one observes the active and simultaneous involvement of such large numbers of people – whether outside that coking depot or in the football stadium – it seems unlikely that everyone involved was so individually predisposed. On the other hand, both events seemed like classic examples of 'realistic conflicts' – the type described by Sherif. The miners and the police were disputing the territory outside the depot and, more generally, engaged in a political struggle over the conduct of industrial disputes. The fighting between Liverpool and Juventus fans, too, could be regarded as reflecting, on the terraces, the objective conflict over European football supremacy to be disputed on the field itself. But even this analysis, useful though it is, takes for granted the groups concerned and the psychological significance of those groups for their members. Being a miner (or a policeman), a Juventus (or Liverpool) supporter, was important for those involved far beyond the immediate context in which they were so tragically participating. For many of them, their whole lives – or, as we might say in psychological language, their whole *identities* – were dominated by the fortunes of their group. What happened to the group mattered to them, and they would have been prepared to risk injury or imprisonment to defend it. In short, therefore, a viable social-psychological explanation of intergroup behaviour is likely to draw on more than one of the theories considered here. On their own, each has its weaknesses; taken together, their strengths provide us with, if not the end of the story, then at least a promising beginning.

Glossary terms

Authoritarian personality
Categorical differentiation
Contact hypothesis
Frustration–aggression
Ingroup

Intergroup behaviour
Interpersonal–(inter)group
  continuum
Minimal group paradigm

Outgroup
Prejudice
Social identity
Superordinate goal

Discussion points

1   How far can intergroup behaviour be explained by personality variables or internal drive states such as frustration?
2   How can intergroup and interpersonal behaviour be distinguished and why is this distinction so important?
3   How far can intergroup behaviour be explained solely by examining groups' material interests?
4   What seem to be the most plausible explanations for discrimination in the minimal group paradigm?
5   Assess the contribution which social identity theory has made to the understanding of the intergroup behaviour of high- and low-status groups.
6   What seem to be the most promising avenues for the reduction of intergroup conflict?

Suggestions for further reading

Abrams, D. and Hogg, M. (1990) (eds) *Social Identity Theory: constructive and critical advances*. Hemel Hempstead: Harvester. Recent theoretical and research contributions to social identity theory.

Brown, R. J. (1988) *Group Processes: dynamics within and between groups*. Oxford: Basil Blackwell. A thorough overview of the field.

Hewstone, M. and Brown, R. J. (eds) (1986) *Contact and Conflict in Intergroup Encounters*. Oxford: Basil Blackwell. A collection of chapters examining the contact hypothesis in several international contexts, and developing a new 'intergroup' approach.

Mackie, D. M. and Hamilton, D. L. (eds) (1993) *Affect, Cognition, and Stereotyping: interaction processes in group perception*. San Diego: Academic Press. A collection of chapters examining the interplay of affective and cognitive processes in intergroup perceptions, concentrating mainly on North American research.

Sherif, M. (1966) *Group Conflict and Cooperation: their social psychology*. London: Routledge & Kegan Paul. A concise account of Sherif's theory and a summary of his summer-camp studies.

Tajfel, H. (1981) *Human Groups and Social Categories: studies in social psychology*. Cambridge: Cambridge University Press. Contains all Tajfel's major theoretical and empirical writing, from his early research on the categorization of physical stimuli to his more recent work on social identity.

Worchel, S. and Austin, W. (eds) (1986) *Psychology of Intergroup Relations*. Chicago: Nelson Hall. A wide-ranging collection of theoretical and empirical chapters covering all aspects of intergroup behaviour.

Key studies

Lemyre, L. and Smith, P. M. (1985). Intergroup discrimination and self esteem in the minimal group paradigm. *Journal of Personality and Social Psychology, 49,* 660–70.

Wilder, D. A. (1984). Intergroup contact: The typical member and the exception to the rule. *Journal of Experimental Social Psychology, 20,* 177–94.

PART V

Epilogue

Contents

18 Applied Social Psychology

Geoffrey M. Stephenson

Contents

Introduction

Application benefits social psychology

It is in the nature of social psychology to be applicable. Many core processes studied by social psychologists – persuasion, communication, intergroup relations, and others – are institutionalized in numerous areas of social, organizational and political life. Hence they offer good opportunities for social psychologists to apply their knowledge and, reciprocally, for social psychology itself to be enhanced directly by study of these phenomena in real-life settings.

It may, for example, be that health campaigns – such as, to induce people to give up smoking – can be improved by the application of social-psychological studies of persuasion, and in turn it may be that the relative effectiveness of different health campaigns can contribute to our theoretical understanding of attitude change (see chapter 9). To take another example, industrial negotiations are not always successful, as the strike record in many industrialized societies indicates: so will laboratory studies of intergroup conflict indicate why things sometimes go wrong, and can an analysis of successful and unsuccessful industrial negotiations enhance our understanding of intergroup relations (see chapter 17)? Hospital and other patients frequently complain of failures in communication: can the social psychologist's knowledge of verbal and non-verbal communication be put to good use in that domain, and what do real-life failures in communication tell us about the processes of interpersonal communication (see chapter 11)? In London, community liaison officers have been appointed by the Metropolitan Police, whose task it is, amongst other things, to improve relations between the police and the black community in London. Can social psychologists who study intergroup relations give those officers any sound advice on how to proceed? And can the officers reasonably be expected to comment on the soundness of principles embodied in that advice (see chapter 17)? On the face of it, social psychology should be applicable. Equally, social psychologists have realized that studies of phenomena in 'the real world', far from threatening the purity of the discipline, are vital to its proper development.

Social psychology's social role

It is to be hoped that a reader who has arrived at this point in the book will have been impressed by the *importance* of the broad social issues which social psychologists address: obedience to authority, social and intellectual development, aggression between groups, the nature of altruism, and so on. Such issues have been topics of philosophical, educational and political debate for centuries, but can now be shown also to be amenable to scientific study. Social psychologists are potentially able to contribute a distinctive viewpoint to the analysis and discussion of important social problems and social issues. At the same time, however, social psychologists are beginning to recognize that the work of other disciplines offers a rich source of material which they can make use of. For example, social psychologists interested in attribution of responsibility may turn profitably to works of legal scholarship as a resource for their own theoretical and experimental work (Fincham and Jaspars, 1980; Lloyd-Bostock, 1984), and social psychologists interested in the interaction of people with their environment find the contributions of architects and planners of fundamental importance in their work (e.g., Bonnes, 1993).

Whilst there is agreement about the principle of the applicability of social psychology, social psychologists differ in the role that they ascribe to application. The difference lies primarily between those who adopt what we may call a natural science model of application, and those who favour a social science model. Let us describe the two approaches in turn.

The Natural Science Model

Solving technical problems

In his forthright defence of the **generalizability** of experimental social psychology, Turner (1981b) sees applied social psychology as a form of 'social engineering':

GENERALIZABILITY

> It [applied social psychology] would not usurp politics in this role but would inevitably be subordinated to it in terms of feasible objectives – which in turn would demand that political and social goals be explicit and acceptable. Its function would be to optimize social institutions and practices by employing specifically social psychological theory to analyse and reconstruct social arrangements to ensure the better achievement of their goals. (p. 31)

In other words, social psychology takes political and social objectives as 'givens', that it accepts uncritically, and by virtue of their expertise, social psychologists rightly criticize the *practices* by which institutions and their representatives in society attempt to implement these objectives. For example, the deterrence or, if necessary, the pursuit and punishment of those who offend against the law are objectives that are taken for granted. Social psychologists may, as social psychologists, merely advise on how *best* to deter, catch or punish: social psychologists are technical advisers.

This **natural science model** is portrayed in figure 18.1. The *practices* by which institutional goals are implemented, but not the *goals* themselves, are open to criticism by social psychologists as likely to be ineffective or inadequate in some respect. Suggested modifications may be accepted, and outcomes influenced

NATURAL
SCIENCE MODEL

Figure 18.1 Natural science model of application as contribution to effective fulfilment of institutional goals

accordingly. This is a process which occurs explicitly as a result of recommendations made by consultant social psychologists. Canter (1982), for example, outlines the technical advisory role of the social psychologist as consultant to architects and administrators in relation to problems of the design of buildings. The process may, however, occur more gradually as knowledge accumulates in a particular domain. For example, there is considerable concern in a number of countries about the dangers of relying exclusively on eye-witness identification of a criminal suspect. Scepticism concerning the relationship between the confidence of an identification and its accuracy (it approaches zero) dates back to the work of Munsterberg (1908), but only recently has an injunction gone out in England that such evidence *should not* be relied upon when it is uncorroborated. More recently, van Koppen (1994), a Dutch social psychologist, has warned of the dangers of 'proactive policing', in which criminals, and not crimes, are investigated. Predicting who will commit future crimes (being proactive) runs the risk that the predictions will become self-fulfilling, and social psychologists are well-equipped to criticize such developments on theoretical grounds. Social psychologists should, in our view, be more prepared to speak forthrightly about the *implications* of their theoretical knowledge.

The natural science model in practice

The natural science model sets the activity of *applying* social psychology apart from 'pure' or 'basic' research. It is a model to which many social psychologists would subscribe, and it is a model which does indeed underlie much research directed to the solution of specific social problems. In such research, an objective (such as to make anti-smoking propaganda more effective) is pursued by asking the social psychologist to suggest the appropriate strategies (for example, to help design films which past research on attitude change suggests will be influential for the target groups concerned). The social psychologist here acts as a consultant to groups, organizations and institutions.

There is one immediate problem with this role: the applied social psychologist must frequently accept institutional goals which reflect an inadequate understanding of the issues. Raven and Haley's (1982) study of infection control in hospitals is a good example of this. Infections acquired by patients whilst in hospital for other reasons (so-called 'nosocomial' infections, from the Greek *nosokomas*, meaning hospital) are an apparently intractable problem; they are estimated to affect 1.6 million people per year in the US, of whom 15,000 will die as a result of the acquired infection. Raven and Haley were called in to improve the effectiveness of infection-control personnel who had recently been appointed to 453 hospitals, and whose job it was to advise, cajole and threaten the staff of the hospitals into obedience to the rules of hygiene. As consultant social psychologists, Raven and Haley's task was merely to help implement the prescribed goal of ensuring the effectiveness of the newly appointed infection-control officers.

The problem as presented to the social psychologists was one of obedience – obedience to hospital rules, and now to the requests of the infection-control personnel. An equally compelling problem, they soon discovered, was that existing authority relationships within the hospital actually encouraged *disobedience*. For example, staff nurses frequently reported that they would be prepared to disobey improper orders from physicians. To give two instances, no less than 40 per cent of the 7,000 or more staff nurses interviewed said they would obey a physician who told them to transfer a patient from isolation whilst that patient was still infectious, and nearly 23 per cent said they would obey an order to continue with a contaminated catheterization. Now, although a clear majority say they would refuse to obey the improper orders, recall that in the Milgram experiment on obedience (described in chapter 16) a large proportion of prospective subject 'teachers' similarly stated that they would refuse to give powerful electric shocks to a 'learner'. In practice, however, the majority of subjects *were* prepared to obey the immoral orders. The numbers of staff nurses reporting compliance – and they are high enough as it is – no doubt underestimate what would happen in practice.

Whilst existing role relationships were clearly the more important problem, Raven and Haley were obliged to direct their attention to the authority and skills of the officers appointed to improve infection control. Had the social psychologists been called in at an earlier stage, the recommended solution to the problem of how to reduce nosocomial infections might well have been different, and based more on an analysis of the existing structure of role relationships within the hospital. The reader, as applied social psychologist, might like to consider to which social-psychological theories he or she would be inclined to turn for assistance in the analysis of this problem of nosocomial infections. There are many that spring to mind: theories of conformity, attribution, social influence, attitude change, attitude and behaviour, group performance, intergroup relations, and no doubt others. The conscientious consultant social psychologist might also wish to make observations in a number of hospitals, using well-established interview and observational techniques, concerning the circumstances in which rules are broken and the understanding which the personnel have of the circumstances. It might also be thought important to consult managerial-psychology colleagues, in order that theories of organizational performance, supervision and product control could be borne in mind: and the relevance of epidemiological and medical literature and background should not be over-looked. As it is, the consultant social psychologists in this instance had to work within the framework imposed by their employer.

The natural science model clearly separates the roles of natural and applied researchers. However, there is quite frequently a closer connection between theory and application than this simple statement of the pure science model immediately suggests. The next section explores this connection further.

Applications may be used to test theory

The results of applications of theory in the real world may act as interesting *tests* of the theories themselves. One of the first pieces of applied social-psychological research was carried out by Lewin and his associates in the 1940s (see Lewin, 1965). Lewin applied his theory of group action to a number of medical problems of the time, including that of persuading young mothers attending health clinics to follow the prescribed feeding instructions for their babies. He hypothesized that, because individuals act always as constituent elements in larger social systems, a decision by a group into which the individual has been incorporated will be a more powerful influence than individual instruction by an expert (see chapter 16).

Lewin compared the relative effectiveness of 20 to 25 minutes individual instruction with the more economical practice of 'group decision'. In the latter the nutritionist discussed the issues with a small group of six mothers, who, as a group, were encouraged to discuss the problem with each other and the nutritionist for the same length of time as the individual instruction took. Group decision was considerably more effective than individual instruction; some 85 per cent of the mothers were following the advice four weeks after group decision, compared with 52 per cent after individual instruction. For other nutrition problems in similar experiments the results were even more dramatic. As pure experiments, these studies were deficient in many respects. For example, it is difficult to say precisely what are the differences between the two techniques, without knowing more than we are given about the content of the instructions and the discussions. Attitudes towards the nutritionist, the amount of information conveyed, relationships with fellow group members, the degree of commitment; all of these might have been 'critical' factors in determining the results. In fact, subsequent work suggested that making a personal decision (especially in the context of group consensus) was the principal factor inducing compliance (Pelz, 1965). The main point, however, is that the results of this piece of application were consistent with Lewin's **field theory** approach in social psychology, and gave encouragement to that viewpoint.

FIELD THEORY

More recently, a similar sequence of events has taken place in relation to applications of *cognitive dissonance theory* in social psychology. Totman (1976), for example, has demonstrated that giving patients the illusion of choice over the medicine they receive, even if that choice is apparent rather than real, has beneficial effects: the medicine is more effective because the individual is more committed to it. Such findings go beyond dissonance theory in that they indicate an interesting effect of mind over body, but they are consistent with the prediction from dissonance theory that individuals committed by their own choice will manifest their beliefs in the medicine to a greater extent than those who are less behaviourally committed (see chapter 9). Attempts to apply the theory of cognitive dissonance in psychotherapy include Cooper and Axsom's (1982) analysis of psychotherapy's benefits in terms of the justification of effort (for example, in the embarrassment and expense of psychoanalytic procedures), and Miller's (1983) formulation of the now-popular technique of motivational interviewing (Miller, 1983). In the course of the former study (Cooper and Axsom, 1982), it was shown experimentally that riding a stationary exercise bicycle to the limits of exhaustion was as beneficial as 'implosive' therapy (a standard behaviour-therapy technique) in the treatment of phobias and it was also shown that those who were given a 'choice' of treatments benefited most of all, in line with predictions from the theory of cognitive dissonance.

Whilst the natural science model as described has many virtues, there are a number of drawbacks. First, by allowing others to establish the goals, it fails – as we have seen in the case of Raven and Haley's nosocomial infections – to ensure that social psychology contributes to the analysis of problems. Social psychologists have both a right and duty to appraise critically the performance of institutions – such as medicine or law – *as social psychologists* and not just as lay critics who happen to be social psychologists. Secondly, by not actively seeking out problematic social issues which might serve to channel their theoretical interests – for example, the effects of increasing divorce rates, the social impact of new technology in work organizations – social psychologists fail to enhance society's ability to cope with change and also fail to exploit the existing possibilities of theoretical development which studying the impact of these changes would yield. There is, in fact, a growing number of scholars who would assign to application a much more fundamental role both in the development of theory in social psychology and in the contribution of social psychology to theory and research in other social disciplines, like law or industrial relations (Stephenson and Davis, 1986). Let us now examine the social science approach in more detail.

The Social Science Model: Addressing Social Issues

Those adopting the social science approach would argue that social psychology provides an indispensable and distinctive dimension in the understanding of society and its institutions. Social psychology's applied role is not, therefore, limited to tinkering, advising or consulting, in order that others – politicians, judges, advertising agencies and so on – may do their jobs more effectively. Rather, the social psychologist is required to work in collaboration with other social scientists in order to ensure that a more complete understanding is achieved of the character and operations of the institutions in question. We cannot, for example, appreciate the significance of criminal statistics, or of police and judicial response to offenders, without some knowledge of the social psychology of crime reporting by victims. More generally, to understand the criminal justice system, we require a social-psychological analysis of decision-making at crucial stages in the career of the criminal – from the decision to commit the crime, through the victim's decision to report, the gathering of evidence, the decision to prosecute, to the trial itself, the sentencing and beyond (cf. Konečni and Ebbeson, 1979). Of course, the system may also be viewed from sociological, legal, economic and political perspectives, but the theoretical perspective of the social psychologist is a vital ingredient.

SOCIAL
SCIENCE MODEL

Figure 18.2 is designed to reflect simply the essence of the **social science model**. Social psychology is portrayed as being *essentially* responsive to social issues, developing theories that are capable of adding a distinctive dimension to the discussion of these issues. Almost certainly this was the motivation underlying many of the major 'discoveries' in our discipline – such as the bases of intergroup prejudice and hostility (Sherif, 1966; Tajfel, 1970), compliance with illegal orders (Milgram, 1974), social-comparison processes in group morale, and persuasion (Stouffer et al., 1949). It is undoubtedly the motivation underlying some theoretical developments in social psychology in Europe, such as the role of minority influence in social change and social movements (see

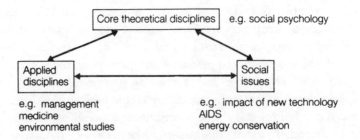

Figure 18.2 Social science model of application as interaction between social psychology, applied disciplines and social issues

Moscovici and Nemeth, 1974), and the role of narrative theory in our understanding of legal and judicial processes (Wagenaar et al., 1993). Researchers concerned with social inequalities – especially sexual inequalities – have contributed to significant advances in our theoretical understanding of the determinants of mental health (Baker-Miller and Mothner, 1981) and academic and occupational success (Kanter, 1977). Moreover, this work frequently challenges the assumptions of conventional theorizing and methodology in social psychology (Wilkinson, 1986). Theories developed in response to social issues enable social psychology to be heard in debates within applied disciplines like medicine, industrial relations and education, regarding what should be done to meet the challenge of social issues. The reciprocal flow of influence between social issues on the one hand, and research and theory in social science on the other, through the elaboration of policy in applied fields is represented in figure 18.2.

One implication of the model is that to contribute effectively the social psychologist working in these fields must become familiar with other disciplinary perspectives. The challenge this presents is increasingly being taken up, and is evident in the publication of journals (e.g., *Law and Human Behaviour*) which have a social-psychological orientation but a strongly interdisciplinary flavour, and in which social psychology helps define and contribute to the critical understanding of social issues.

Health, the criminal justice system, and urban planning have all raised issues which social psychologists have tackled with some degree of success. It is, therefore, appropriate to choose from these areas to illustrate the work that social psychologists are doing broadly within the social science framework.

Social Psychology and Health

The application of social psychology to health exemplifies clearly the contrast between the natural science and social science approaches to application. The main impetus to research has come from the gradual appreciation, over many decades, of the important role of psychological and social factors in health: that is, of health as a social as well as medical problem. Social psychologists have played an important role in developing our understanding of the limits of purely physical explanations of good health. This remains a compelling social issue, and is rapidly taking new forms, as in recent work on the role of social inequalities in health and mental health. Recently, however, the application of social-psychological models of behaviour change has led to the emergence of what is in effect a new discipline of 'health social behaviour': defining what behaviours are desirable and using social-psychological principles to devise ways of encouraging such behaviours. This section of the chapter focuses, although not exclusively, on our understanding of the social-psychological processes that contribute to good health. Readers interested in a more comprehensive coverage, particularly of the technology of applications, are referred to the recent volume by Stroebe and Stroebe (1995; see suggestions for further reading).

A causal model

LIFE EVENTS

Totman (1979, 1982a, 1990) proposes that *social functioning* of the individual is crucial to health. For example, the focus on the importance of **life events** for health, and the role of social networks in sustaining recovery from psychiatric illness, illustrate the importance of adequate interpersonal and social relationships to both physical and mental health (see chapter 11). Life events such as taking a new job or moving house – which are experienced as stressful by the individuals concerned – have been said to be associated with subsequent ill health, both physical (Dohrenwend and Dohrenwend, 1974) and psychiatric (Brown and Harris, 1978). However, there is increasing evidence that the influence of life events and stress depends strongly on their *interpretation* by the individuals concerned. An intriguing study by Peterson et al. (1988) looked at the long-term effects of having a pessimistic turn of mind in young adulthood on how healthy one was thirty-five years later. Of course, health at the outset was taken into account, and even then, men who as young adults explained bad events with stable, global and internal causes at age 25 (a 'pessimistic' attributional style, see chapter 7) were less healthy than were those whose explanatory style was more 'optimistic'. Similarly, Brown and McGill (1989) predicted, and showed, that positive life events only had a negative effect on health in those with comparatively low self-esteem; health improved for those with high self-esteem.

Totman (1979, 1982a) suggests that good health depends upon one's ability to perform appropriately and competently in a social setting. Figure 18.3 tries to portray in a simple way what Totman is trying to say. Within a given social network, people agree on what they would like individually to achieve, and they know in what way it is appropriate for them to attain these goals. This set of knowledge Totman refers to as 'social rules'. However, various physical and personal constraints may prevent our behaving in such a co-operative and productive way, so that our *committed conduct* falls short of what we would intend. We discover this by a comparison process which leads to attempts to achieve consistency by changing the rules, distorting attributions of responsibility and so on. Too great an inconsistency leads to a breakdown in the process, and increases susceptibility to illness. Illness, on this view, is facilitated by *social* breakdown. More particularly, adequate social functioning – and subsequently good health – are undermined if (1) unrealistic standards are set by the individual, (2) the ability to rationalize inadequacies and failure is lacking, or (3) the individual is deprived of others whose performance is complementary to his or her own. What all these circumstances do is detract from the ability to collaborate effectively

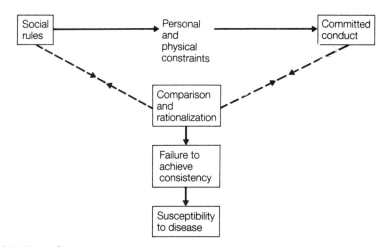

Figure 18.3 View of susceptibility to disease as a product of breakdown in fit between social rules and committed conduct (based on Totman, 1982a)

with others in pursuit of common goals, something which can only be achieved by consistently following rules of conduct which we share with others.

Certainly, there is accumulating evidence that social support does, indeed, act as a 'buffer' against misfortunes of many kinds, and is associated with better functioning of the immune system (e.g., Baron et al., 1990). Experiments with animals demonstrate a 'functional relationship' between experience and the capacity of the immune system (Ader and Cohen, 1993), making it reasonable to speculate about the physiological mechanisms which may explain the associations between social-psychological factors and physical health. However, one should bear in mind more prosaic explanations. Adler and Matthews (1994), for example, suggest that other people in a social network may discourage unhealthy behaviours in response to personal calamities, such as drinking heavily following bereavement. Let us, however, following Totman, examine one particular circumstance in which mismatches between rules and conduct may occur, thereby creating a threat to health.

The example of bereavement

Many attempts have been made to correlate indices of stressful life events with illness, but for a variety of reasons the results have been inconclusive (see Fletcher, 1991, for an extensive review). There are, of course, methodological problems involved: not the least is the tendency for ill people to interpret events in a doleful way (see Schroeder and Costa, 1984, for an analysis of this problem).

Stroebe and Stroebe (1987a, 1987b) argue convincingly that the study of specific life events which can be unambiguously diagnosed, such as divorce or bereavement, overcomes most of the methodological problems associated with the more popular global methods of studying the health–stress relationship. The effects of bereavement have been studied by psychologists mainly in relation to the death of a spouse, but other relationships – the death of a parent, child, or grandchild, for example – have also been examined, though not so extensively as the marital relationship (see Stroebe and Stroebe 1993). The death of a loved one who is genetically related may create grief and psychological pain at least as acute as that experienced when a marital partner dies, so we should expect that the detrimental effects on health of a 'broken heart' are shared by different forms of bereavement. Stroebe (1994) indicates that this is the case. However, over and above the broken heart, the death of a spouse deprives an individual of an important role partner, and a means of social support in the individual's pursuit of social competence. If any life event might be expected to affect the social competence of individuals, then bereavement in marriage is a formidable contender.

Stroebe et al. (1982) elaborate on the likely impact of bereavement from the viewpoint specifically of a social psychologist. The loss of a partner affects four main areas of social-psychological functioning, which we may define in terms of established expectations in the relationship. First, there is what the authors call a loss of 'social validation of personal judgements'. Many processes discussed in earlier chapters testify to the importance of social comparison and validation. Sherif's (1936) experiments on the development of social norms showed how fundamental is the movement towards agreement, and Festinger (1954) postulated that there is a drive towards comparison in human judgement, including those important judgements of self-worth (chapter 16). Tenets of attribution theory suggest that the loss of a partner's viewpoint could make it difficult to behave in a confidently appropriate way (chapter 7), and Schachter and Singer's (1962) socio-cognitive theory of emotion would predict confusion, uncertainty and suggestibility in the emotional life of the bereaved (chapter 10).

The remaining three areas of loss caused by the death of a spouse include loss of 'social and emotional support', loss of 'material and task supports' and loss of 'social protection'. The importance of *emotional* support to the developing organism emerges clearly in chapter 3, and the importance of affiliation in reducing anxiety is apparent from both human and animal studies (see chapter 2). The loss of material and task supports stems especially from role differentiation within marriage, an interesting example of which has been defined by Wegner, Giuliano and Hertel (1985) in the field of memory: married couples specialize in the recall of different classes of event, and are mutually interdependent in that cognitive area as they are in the more obvious task areas, like cleaning the home, repairing the car and changing babies' nappies.

In all these ways the social competence or what we might call the 'social fitness' of the individual is undermined by the loss of a marital partner, thereby jeopardizing emotional and physical health; in consequence, especially in the first six months following bereavement, the risk of dying is heightened, particularly in men. Large-scale cross-sectional data also indicate substantial increases in the mortality ratios of widowed to married people, especially in cases where behavioural factors are paramount, such as homicide, suicide and accidents (including road accidents), but also in those less dramatic cases which account for the larger proportion of deaths overall – coronary heart disease and strokes. As figure 18.4 shows, roughly three widowers die from strokes or heart attacks for every two married men dying from the same conditions. It should also be noted that the increase in susceptibility to heart attacks and strokes is the same for widowers as for widows, and that the greater susceptibility in men is found especially in deaths due to violence (murder and suicide) and alcoholism (as indicated by the figures for cirrhosis of the liver).

The mortality data indicated that age and sex were both significantly associated with susceptibility to illness following bereavement. Let us consider first the effect of age. Would you expect the older or younger bereaved to suffer more or less stress following bereavement? Younger people probably suffer

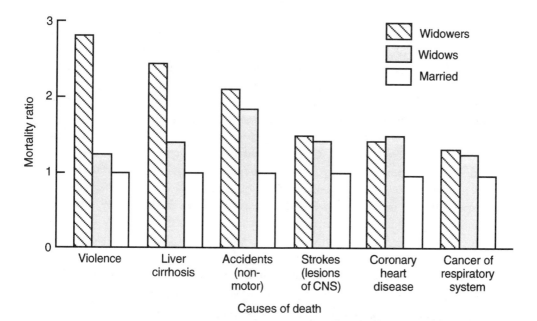

Figure 18.4 Mortality ratios of widowed to married for six causes of death (based on Stroebe et al., 1982)

greater problems of adjustment than older persons. Their expectations are high, set-backs are more problematic, responsibilities are high (large mortgage and young children perhaps) and the dependence upon others is correspondingly greater. However, older married couples have had longer in which to develop a collaborative, interdependent relationship. None the less, one might well expect the younger bereaved to be more 'thrown' and more likely, relatively speaking, to be depressed as a result of bereavement. The results bear out this expectation, and Stroebe and Stroebe (1987b) single out the expectedness of loss and the availability of social support as the most important factors favouring the resilience of the elderly.

Men would appear to be more vulnerable than women to the impact of bereavement. That, it seems, is a more immediately understandable finding, given the known effects of sexual inequality on family life (Williams and Watson, 1988). The social support provided by the partner is probably easier for women to replace than for men, and women are more likely to seek it out. This fact received intriguing support from the finding of a longitudinal study which showed that it was the *more* severely depressed men who refused an interview with the research team but the *less* severely depressed women (see Stroebe and Stroebe, 1987b).

Loss of a spouse clearly disrupts the participative social functioning that Totman's views suggest is crucial to good health (see Totman, 1990). Stroebe (1994) suggests that the concept of 'social integration' may be used to explain why it is that the mortality of bereaved spouses is increased. This interpretation of the findings has been confirmed in more recent studies which have compared the fortunes of those bereaved people who have re-integrated well following bereavement with those who have become more socially isolated. The longitudinal investigations of Gallagher-Thompson et al. (1993) provide a good example. Besides showing the customary enhanced mortality of bereaved widows and widowers compared with married counterparts, Gallagher-Thompson and colleagues also compared the social integration or disintegration of those bereaved persons who died, with a carefully matched group of bereaved persons who survived. The matching in particular took care of physical health variables before bereavement, so that it could not be objected that those who died were an especially frail group to begin with. The results showed that on various measures of social integration and performance the survivors significantly outshone the decedents. The decedents' wives were their main confidante, decedents had smaller social networks, were less involved in socially orientated activities, and moreover expressed regrets about their lack of social involvement.

Recovering from illness: an attributional analysis

It has long been known that the length of time a patient stays in hospital may be affected not only by the recovery process but by organizational and communication problems in the hospital itself (Revans, 1964). Recently, however, studies have shown that the process of recovery from physical illness itself appears to be strongly associated with the patients' understanding of their social role in the aetiology of the illness.

Accidents which result in physical injury are of particular interest in this respect. Such injuries may on occasion have been entirely beyond the ability of the individual to foresee and avoid, but in most cases of, say, injuries sustained in road accidents, games, or in the home, the individual may feel that there was something he or she could have done that might have led to the avoidance of an accident or to a lessening of its impact. An 'accident' is, strictly speaking, an occurrence which was not foreseen, and certainly not intended. Nevertheless, apportioning blame after an accident is an apparently irresistible tendency, a prerequisite of which is the belief that the accident was *avoidable*.

In terms of Totman's model (e.g., Totman, 1982a), the tendency to blame oneself, or to imagine that an accident could have been avoided, might be seen as an attempt to evade facing up to the reality of adjusting to the new circumstances created by the accident; whereas acceptance that it could not have been avoided represents a healthy attempt to rationalize this particular unfortunate set-back in the pursuit of one's goals. One might, therefore, be inclined to predict that successful, speedy recovery from illness should be associated with the 'fateful' rather than the 'remorseful' attribution of responsibility.

Remarkable support for the benefits of fateful attribution comes from studies by Frey and colleagues in West Germany. Frey et al. (1985) were interested in examining the importance of attribution in the process of recovery from physical injuries sustained by victims of accidents – principally accidents at work, road accidents, and accidents sustained at home. Injuries ranged from 'slight' to 'severe' and, of course, severity of injury strongly affected the process of recovery. Within each category of severity, however (severity having been rated independently by a doctor who was unaware of the aims of the study), response to convalescence varied systematically according to the attributions of the patients regarding *responsibility for the accident*, and also regarding *responsibility for the outcome of convalescence*. The investigation was carried out twice, the second time with a larger number of patients (Frey and Rogner, 1987) and controlling for the time of interview (within three days of hospitalization). Let us examine in detail some results from the second study, which replicated and extended the results of the first study.

In order to take into account the effects of severity of injury, all the measures of recovery or response to convalescence were adjusted so as to remove the observed influence of severity. The results showed that those patients who believed that the accident was 'highly avoidable', or that they were much to blame for it, stayed in hospital appreciably longer than those who thought the accident could not have been avoided, or did not accept responsibility for it (see figure 18.5). Ratings of the healing process and subjective ratings of well-being followed the same pattern: an 'unavoidable' accident is much easier to recover from. Patients were also asked a number of questions regarding the importance of their own will in aiding convalescence and their ability to predict their recovery time: the combined index of cognitive control of convalescence indicated that those with a low degree of perceived control spent longer in hospital and felt worse.

Social psychology and health: a model of helping and coping

We have seen that social-psychological processes are important in the onset of a range of medical disorders, and that social perceptions and attributions of patients are very strongly related to their prospects of a speedy recovery in the case of physical injury. At issue in all the instances we have discussed is the

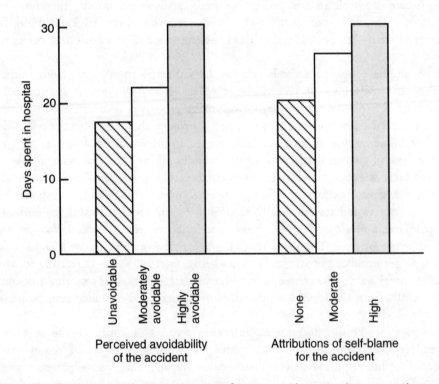

Figure 18.5 Days spent in hospital recovering from an accident according to attributions of responsibility for the accident (all means adjusted to remove the contributions of severity of injury) (Frey and Rogner, 1987)

competence of individuals to respond to stressful crises in a way which maximizes their prospects of healthy psychological and physical survival. Let us now consider an attempt to apply our knowledge to the problem of how to help individuals to survive unscathed.

One reason why women face up to the challenge of bereavement better than men, it is suggested, is because they are more likely to ask for help, and they have more people in their social networks to whom they can turn for assistance. Whilst asking for assistance has been little studied by social psychologists, giving help has been a major topic of research (see chapter 13). Research has concentrated on elucidating the characteristics of the victim who requires assistance, the characteristics of the potential benefactor, and the situational cues which make it more or less likely that help will be given. In addition, the emphasis in research has been on those situations in which help is urgently required, like assisting someone who has collapsed dramatically in public.

Giving help to those who are emotionally distressed, anxious, depressed, or otherwise failing to cope with the problems of life can itself be a stressful experience, leading to what has been termed 'burnout'. This concept was described by Maslach (1982) as a condition in which the professional helper (social worker, psychiatrist, clinical psychologist) feels emotionally exhausted, with little respect or sympathy for clients, and a tendency to attribute blame to the clients for their problems. Whilst social support from colleagues may alleviate the condition (see Russell et al., 1987), Maslach suggests ways in which the client's dependence on the help-giver may be reduced, by stressing the obligations of the client as well as those of the help-giver. The work on 'burnout' raises in an interesting way the whole question of what kind of help it is appropriate to give those whose ability to cope has been undermined (see Schaufeli et al., 1993).

Attribution of blame and responsibility have featured in the broad field of cognitive social psychology, and were considered at length by Brickman et al. (1982) in relation to the question of what is an effective help-giving strategy. They discern four current models of helping and coping in the caring professions, according to (1) attribution of responsibility to the individual client for having the *problem* in the first place, and (2) attribution of responsibility for providing a *solution* to their condition. The four models are presented in table 18.1. We are all most familiar with the *medical* model in which the 'patient' who requires 'treatment' is a passive, helpless creature who is absolved of responsibility for both the problem and the solution. The medical model has, of course, come under consistent attack in all areas of treatment, and there are some instances, for example in the treatment of the elderly, where the denial of the patient's responsibility for the solution exacerbates the very symptoms of mental and physical deterioration that treatment seeks to address. The problem of burnout for those working with clients who have psychiatric, behavioural and personality problems seems to arise at least in part from an unthinking application of the

Table 18.1 Four models of helping and coping

Attribution to self of responsibility for the problem	Attribution to self of responsibility for solution	
	High	Low
High	Moral model (requirement = motivation)	Enlightenment model (requirement = discipline)
Low	Compensatory model (requirement = power)	Medical model (requirement = treatment)

Source: Brickman et al. (1982)

medical model's assumption of the full responsibility of the 'therapist' for treatment and the outcome of treatment.

The *enlightenment model* puts the blame squarely on the shoulders of the patient, a view espoused by a minority in psychiatry (see Mowrer, 1975), and taken up by groups like Alcoholics Anonymous. Responsibility for *treatment*, however, rests with the group or organization, entry into lifetime membership of which requires conversion to a new, prescribed way of life (see Room, 1993).

Neither the moral nor the compensatory models prescribe treatment. However, the *moral model* emphasizes personal responsibility for the problem and suggests that self-discipline is the prerequisite for recovery, a view which is summed up neatly by Glasser's (1975) observation: 'People do not act irresponsibly because they are "ill"; they are "ill" because they act irresponsibly' (p. xvi). This high

COMPENSATORY MODEL

moral tone is absent from the **compensatory model**, which seeks not to blame patients for their condition, but rather to provide them with the necessary equipment, facilities or opportunities which they may use to deal with the problems they face at present (see also chapter 13). In many different spheres of treatment the compensatory model is coming to the fore, from 'treatment' of psychiatric 'patients' in the community, to the treatment of addictions (see Marlatt, 1988; Morojele and Stephenson 1992). Whilst there have been no comprehensive tests of Brickman's model, support for the two key elements of the compensatory model is quite consistent. Victims of rape, for example, who do not blame themselves, either in character or behaviour, for their victimization, recover better following their experiences than do those who do accept some measure of blame (Frazier, 1991; Meyer and Taylor, 1986). Smail (1993) argues that many who suffer personal distress and seek psychotherapy blame themselves inappropriately for circumstances over which they had no control. Moreover, the perception that one has appropriate control over relevant circumstances and conduct is important for recovery not only from accidents, but from a variety of other conditions, such as addictions (Morojele, 1994) and natural disasters (Solomon et al, 1989). Doubtless Brickman's portrayal of the four models is oversimplified, but it provides a convenient, coherent social-psychological framework for interventions by professionals in health and social services, and it provides a useful framework in terms of which past research and experience may be conceptualized and priorities for future work established.

Social-psychological Issues of Criminal Justice

The decision-making sequence in criminal justice

The criminal justice system has been a particular object of study by social psychologists in the United States, in Britain, and also more recently in other European countries (e.g., Wegener, Lösel and Haisch, 1989). Psychologists have studied crime and criminals for a century or more, and also aspects of the legal system – such as eye-witness testimony – for not much less. The concerted contribution of *social* psychologists to these areas is, however, of more recent origin. This is especially so in the field of criminology, where personality psychologists and sociologists have had the predominant influence (see Blackburn, 1993, for a balanced account of different theoretical approaches to the explanation of criminal behaviour).

Figure 18.6 portrays the successive decisions taken by different actors as a 'criminal' passes through the various stages of the criminal justice system, from

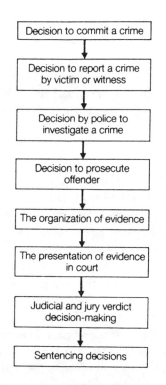

Figure 18.6 Decision-making stages in the process of criminal justice

the initial decision to commit a crime to the sentence he or she receives. In the interests of simplicity it omits a number of areas of decision-making, for example, the decision to grant bail, and plea bargaining before prosecution for an offence. The sequence as portrayed defines broadly the main areas of criminal justice research in social psychology.

The decision-making sequence: brief review of issues and research

Decision to commit a crime
This may be viewed best, at the individual level, as a rational decision, determined by consideration of the likely benefits and costs of transgressing. Certainly much evidence shows that people are opportunistic and do not, for example, steal regardless of how difficult it is to do so without getting caught. We may note that property marking schemes do act as a deterrent (Laycock, 1985), and expert shoplifters are highly and intelligently responsive to adverse conditions (Weaver and Carroll, 1985). Redesigning the layout of stores to increase the visibility to staff of frequently stolen goods does reduce the frequency with which those items are stolen (Farrington et al., 1993). Ehrlich (1982) suggests that there is a 'market' for offences, obeying economic laws of supply and demand. Not only are people directly employed as criminals, for example by drug traffickers; we are all indirectly 'employed' by the decisions of others not to protect their property, like supermarket owners who facilitate theft by permitting easy access to goods. And yet there are problems with such an analysis. For example, why should juvenile crime peak in early adolescence, when the rational arguments in favour of criminal behaviour show no respect for age? Why should boys be much more criminal than girls when the arguments for or against many crimes apply equally to both sexes? We shall return to these questions.

Decision to report a crime
This decision is certainly not taken by every victim of crime. In fact, on average, only about one-third of victims report crimes, rape rarely being reported and car theft nearly always being reported (Hough and Mayhew, 1983; Sparks, Genn and Dodd, 1977). The generally low figure raises some important social issues, given that only a small fraction – varying from one part of a country to another – of *reported crimes* are investigated and result in prosecution. Would resources be more appropriately spent on prevention than on prosecution of such a small minority? Are we justified in destroying the reputation of the one or two shoplifters who do get caught, given the vast majority who escape unnoticed and undetected? Should shops not be obliged to spend more on prevention? Social-psychological studies (e.g., Greenberg et al., 1979) have indicated some of the reasons why people may or may not report: beliefs that the police would not be able to help; discouragement from bystanders and friends; belief that the crime is not serious

enough; and failure to feel angry enough *at the time*. An interesting sidelight from the civil law is thrown on this issue by Lloyd-Bostock's (1979) finding that victims of accidents at work tend not to attribute blame to their employers until persuaded of the feasibility of bringing a prosecution for damages.

Decision to investigate a crime

The broad question of what crimes to investigate and prosecute is beset by social and political controversy, partly because of the class bias arising from prosecution of small-scale property crime (Box, 1972). Only recently have social psychologists begun their contribution to the debate by conducting basic research on what in practice determines the police response to crime. A study in the United States confirmed that the police selectively discourage rape complainants from pressing charges, in line with their perceptions of the resources required and available for investigating a particular complaint (Kerstetter and van Winkle, 1990). Police discretion in Great Britain operates at different levels, from the decision of the individual officer to arrest or not, through the decision of the custody officer to accept a charge, and of a higher officer to recommend prosecution, right through to Chief Constables or Commissioners of Metropolitan Police, who set priorities for their forces each year. The position has now been reached where offences are scaled on a number of dimensions (such as seriousness, prospects of successful detection and prosecution) and ascribed more or less police time in accordance with their priority.

Grant, Grant and Toch (1982) point to the dangers of 'proactive' policing – in which police deliberately maintain a high profile in areas of high crime. Police are likely to arrest 'defiant' individuals who appear to be hostile; such arrests frequently lead to violence and subsequent charges for assault and 'resisting arrest'. Their observations show, however, that this tendency for police to generate offences was remarkably reduced during a sustained campaign to target these police tactics in one US city. When acting collaboratively, police officers are more likely to act in a confrontational way (Decker and Wagner, 1982) and this heightened professional salience is evident also in collaborative testimony, when police composing their notes jointly are more likely than they are as individuals to fill in gaps in their evidence and to have faith in the truth of their embellishments (Clark and Stephenson, 1995; Stephenson et al. 1991).

Social organization of evidence

Social-psychological aspects of police encounters with witnesses and suspects have not featured greatly in research. The interrogation of suspects is, however, an area that has come under a degree of scrutiny in the UK, partly as a result of a number of celebrated cases in which false confessions had been accepted by the police and subsequently the courts, and innocent people had been wrongly convicted. How could that happen? And why is it that about 50 per cent of suspects, under no obligation to say anything, nevertheless do speak when interrogated and do confess fully? Observations suggest that it *is not* necessary for police officers to offer inducements or to oppress suspects physically or psychologically in order to secure a confession (Softley, 1980). Indeed, the rule that confessions should be voluntary is generally observed. However, rather as in the Milgram experiment on obedience (see chapter 16), *the situation* induces suspects to confess. Self-esteem is low; the territory is unfamiliar; there is no accustomed social support; there is an *implicit* threat in the isolation and physical dependence on one's 'captors'; and, finally, officers are perceived to have the authority and right to require compliance (Irving, 1980; Irving and Hilgendorf, 1980). It is not surprising that false confessions *are* sometimes made, and social psychologists are now making a serious attempt to understand that phenomenon (see Gudjonsson and Clark, 1986; Moston et al., 1992).

Procedural justice

ADVERSARY
SYSTEM

We become accustomed to courtroom procedure from books, plays, films and television, if not from direct experience or observations. The tense, emotional drama of the adversary system, in which the *appearance* of truth rather than the

Plate 18.1 Miscarriages of justice (such as Gerard Conlon of the 'Guildford Four', can arise from bad practices in the social organization of evidence

truth itself is the uppermost consideration, is familiar even to those whose legal system *is* inquisitorial, as is the case in most countries in Western and Eastern Europe. Bennett and Feldman (1981) have written one of the most compelling analyses of the adversary system. They suggest that the side that tells the most *coherent* story, regardless of its truth, is the side that will win its case. Indeed, they have experimental evidence that subjects telling coherent but false stories about themselves are more readily believed than those telling less coherent but true stories! However, as Jackson (1990) points out, the story of the crime may be secondary to the story of the trial, or the courtroom drama, in which the interplay of personalities is what crucially affects the decisions of jurors. Opinion in England is beginning to question many aspects of the adversarial system, which encourages deception by police and lawyers, and values winning the case more than establishing the truth. Social psychologists have an important role to play in forthcoming debates on the issues that are raised (Stephenson, 1992, 1995; Williamson, in press).

Eye-witness testimony

No topic has prompted more research, however, than the question of the validity of eye-witness testimony, and eye-witness identification of suspects. This is germane to the more general debate about the propriety of the adversary system because, it is argued (e.g. Loftus, 1984), the results of research run counter to common sense, and juries need special guidance on the acceptability of eye-witness testimony. We shall return to this topic.

Judicial and jury decision-making

Jury decision-making runs eye-witness testimony a close second in terms of its popularity amongst social psychologists. Many experimental studies have been performed, examining in particular how the characteristics of the jurors – their personalities and attitudes – affect their judgements, especially in relation to characteristics of the defendants and of the victims (Dane and Wrightsman, 1982; Hans and Vidmar, 1982). There are not many firm conclusions – possibly because most of the studies have been *simulations*, in which (usually) students individually judge a hypothetical defendant on the basis of an abbreviated description of a trial provided by the experimenter. In such circumstances, quite small differences in the information provided may greatly affect judgements, which, of course, are not constrained by the seriousness of an actual trial, and the social and role expectations impinging on jurors in the real courtroom and the real jury deliberation room. In real trials, as an interesting study by Kerr (1982) demonstrated, many of the factors found to be of importance in *simulations*, such as the ethnic similarity of jury and defendant, have no effect on verdicts, whilst other factors never studied in artificial laboratory conditions, such as the prosecuting lawyers' *respectfulness*, were shown to have a marked effect on verdicts (respectfulness reduces the likelihood of successful conviction). Recent laboratory work, however, has indicated that the search for a plausible story (see Bennett and Feldman, above) is a powerful motive for individual jurors (Hastie et al., 1983; Penington and Hastie, 1993).

One major question – frequently lost sight of – concerns the jury's effectiveness. Do juries make good decisions? The received wisdom, stemming from the American study by Kalven and Zeisel (1966), is that juries' verdicts largely coincide with judges' views, and that, when they err, juries err in favour of the defendant and base their decisions largely on objective evaluation of the evidence. Such a sanguine view does not bear too close scrutiny. Even accepting Kalven and Zeisel's own figures (and the study can be criticized on methodological grounds), more than 13 per cent of those defendants that the judges would acquit are convicted by American juries; another 7 per cent obtain 'hung' verdicts and are retried. Moreover Baldwin and McConville (1979), in a detailed British study which examined not only judges' but also police and lawyers' opinions of the verdicts, found a number of cases of apparently perverse decisions to acquit that startled even the prosecution lawyers and the police. There are many psychological features of groups which could account for bizarre decision-making (see chapters 15 and 16). Cliques may form within the group, and essentially irrational competitive considerations may prevail. Differences in status are associated with power to influence, but not necessarily with intelligence. A dispassionate appraisal of the evidence is unlikely to occur if group tendencies towards polarization and towards consensus prevail in the early stages of discussion; and, when they prevail, processes of both minority and majority influence are unlikely to be consistently associated with truth. None the less, the jury is defended as a democratic bulwark against an overbearing state or judiciary, and undoubtedly there are famous cases where juries have established freedoms by acquitting a defendant who had offended against what the jury – and the public at large – regarded as oppressive laws. The broad political debate about the validity of jury decision-making is one that will no doubt continue.

Given that the jury system will be in existence for some time to come, it is good that social psychologists have made incisive contributions to policy debates regarding key structural and procedural variables in jury performance. For example, we may ask what effect the size of jury will have on the verdicts reached? Is a large jury (e.g., of 12 people) more likely to return a not guilty verdict than a smaller jury (e.g., of six people)? Or, to take a procedural variable, when cases against a defendant are joined (the defendant is tried simultaneously on two or more charges, say, manslaughter and criminal damage), is conviction on either more or less likely than when cases are severed (that is, heard separately)? Or, a related question: does previous experience as a juror change attitudes towards defendants? It seems that the effects of varying jury size depend upon the *decision rule* employed. When decisions are reached by majority vote, convictions are more likely when only a few individuals initially favour a guilty verdict, and the probability of obtaining such unreliable convictions is especially pronounced in small juries (Davis et al., 1975). On the question of joined or severed trials, evidence suggests (e.g., Bordens and Horowitz, 1985) that it is to the disadvantage of defendants for trials to be joined, although this effect is mitigated if the weaker and less serious cases are dealt with first (Davis, 1984). Juror experience was also found, in experiments with students, to be detrimental to the defendant (Davis, 1984), a finding that has been confirmed in real-life jury verdicts. The more juries that jurors have served on previously, the more likely they are to bring in guilty verdicts (Dillehay and Nietzel, 1985).

Sentencing and punishment

These stages lie at the heart of the criminal justice system, but their purpose continues to be debated by lawyers, lay people and (not least) criminals themselves. Questioned recently by a group of long-stay prisoners, visiting social psychologists were asked what 'good' it was doing to keep active, energetic people locked up uselessly in prison when they could be working productively on behalf of their families outside the prison. We fell back upon the classic justifications of punishment: general deterrence, specific deterrence, retribution, incapacitation and reform. This response did not go down well, for the prisoners' view was that for whatever reasons society might want criminals in general to be locked away, it was not appropriate in their particular case, and was serving no useful purpose. Should sentencing be tailored to the needs of individual criminals? Or should 'guidelines' give the judges little discretion to vary sentences?

Having mapped out the field, and some of the principal issues, we now examine aspects of decision-making in just two of the areas we have outlined: the decision to commit a crime by young delinquents; and the testimony of eye-witness observers concerning a violent crime. In all cases the observations of the social psychologists concerned challenge established viewpoints, expose the need for further sustained research, and indicate clearly the contribution to be made to theory in social psychology and to social policy debate.

Juvenile crime as a particular social issue

Juvenile crime has fascinated psychologists for many decades, with Burt's (1925) pioneering study of delinquent boys in London setting the trend. There are good common-sense reasons for the emphasis on youthful crime. In the first place, it preoccupies the criminal justice system in terms of the sheer numbers involved. Moreover, adult criminals have invariably been youthful criminals, so understanding juvenile crime may enable us to take measures which will terminate criminal careers before they become established. Youthful delinquency is also a distressing experience for the families concerned, and may be severely detrimental to the personal and career prospects of the individual, even though he or she does not end up as a 'career criminal'. For good social and humane reasons, then, it is important to understand why young people commit crime. Juvenile crime also presents an absorbing theoretical challenge to society, and to social psychologists in particular. We may well ask why the process of socialization so spectacularly breaks down in adolescence, if indeed it does so.

In the first edition of this book we reported that between 1961 and 1984 the number of adolescent females committing crimes in England and Wales increased from about 0.8 per cent to 1.6 per cent, and the number of adolescent boys from 3.5 per cent to about 8.4 per cent. The equivalent figures for 1992 – 8 years on – were about 2.5 per cent for girls and 10.5 per cent for boys. Crime, and especially crime in adolescence and amongst females, continues to increase.

Let us examine more carefully the figures for 1992 (see figure 18.7, which shows the percentage of persons aged from 10 to 70 who engage in crime). Note first the steep increase in the rate of offending during the adolescent years, peaking for girls at about age 15 (3 per cent criminality) and for boys at age 18 (11 per cent criminality). The fall-off in adulthood is as dramatic as the rise in adolescence, at least for males. For females, the reduction is more gradual.

Figures like these are alarming to politicians and to citizens alike. Citizens fear for their safety, and politicians view with some alarm official projections that now

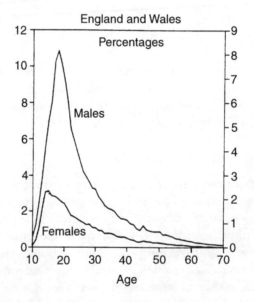

Figure 18.7 Known offenders (persons found guilty or cautioned for indictable offences) as a percentage of the population: by age and sex, 1992 (source: Home Office)

envisage a 20 per cent increase in the prison population by the turn of the century (Dennis, 1993). Six new juvenile prisons are to be built to house English and Welsh children, in an effort to combat the effects of what politicians of all persuasions are apt to see as a breakdown in law and order (Stephenson, 1995). Why is 'socialization' apparently so ineffective? And why in particular should there be so dramatic a rejection of conventional values in the years of adolescence? Social psychology is, of course, unlikely to provide the whole story. Biological, personality and developmental psychology all have something important to say about the association of crime with both age and sex, but social psychology in particular should contribute to our understanding of why adolescents, and especially boys, choose to break the law in a given social environment.

The concept of delinquent involvement
When we ask people at large about their involvement in crime, in the context of research interviews, there is good evidence that individuals are truthful, and that what they say is consistent with what is known officially about their involvement (see Emler, 1984). Adopting this procedure, the myth of the criminal category is soon exploded. What varies is the *extent* of involvement with crime. For example, whilst few people commit armed robbery, about half admit to theft of items from a shop (Hindelang, Hirschi and Weis, 1981), and a large majority to avoidance of fares on public transport (e.g. Shapland, 1978). When a large number of criminal activities are examined, ranging from the relatively trivial to the most serious, studies of normal populations show that a range of scores is obtained whose characteristics indicate that 'delinquency involvement' is a scaleable characteristic. Delinquency, in other words, can be regarded as a generalized behavioural dimension, and self-reports can be used effectively as a research tool to investigate its distribution in different groups. Use of such tests indicates that individual differences are greatest in instances of serious misconduct, and that differences are generalized, with only drug abuse standing out as a distinctive offence. The sex and age pattern found in official delinquency is closely replicated (Emler, 1984).

Delinquency as reputation management
So why are some young teenagers, especially boys, incorrigibly delinquent and involved with fairly serious crime (and some incorrigibly conformist, for that matter), with the majority involved in only petty delinquency to a greater or less extent? The picture that is emerging from social-psychological studies (Emler, 1984) suggests that delinquency is employed strategically, by boys especially, to establish a reputation amongst groups of peers. This view is consistent with the fact that convicted delinquents have been shown in longitudinal studies to have significantly rejected authority in the past, including that of parents, but especially of teachers and police (Farrington, Biron and LeBlanc, 1982). They have also been on the whole less successful at school, and come from relatively

deprived backgrounds. Periods of unemployment *additionally* contribute to their involvement in serious crime (Farrington et al., 1986). The delinquent reputation may be seen as an alternative route to acceptance and prestige from the 'academic' route, and it is one that holds *some* degree of allure to all except the most diehard successful conformists: hence the prevalence of involvement in *some* degree of delinquency (Emler, 1990; Reicher and Emler, 1986).

If delinquency is employed to establish a reputation, we should expect to find that most delinquent conduct has an admiring audience. This is precisely what happens in practice. Emler, Reicher and Ross (1987), in a study of a normal population of boys and girls, found that most classes of delinquent conduct – including drugs offences, theft, aggression, vandalism and status offences (e.g., illegal driving) – were performed almost invariably in the company of others. More importantly the group orientation was particularly characteristic of those activities in the delinquency scale that were statistically most central to the scale, such as gross vandalism, rather than more peripheral activities like truancy. Girls, interestingly enough, were even more likely to commit crimes in groups.

Attitudes to authority are highly correlated with delinquency, a factor that statistically accounts for the difference in delinquency between boys and girls (Reicher and Emler, 1985). Precisely why the gender difference exists is not clear, but one possible explanation lies in the greater academic (or at least career) expectations that boys are subjected to and hence the greater sense of failure amongst those boys who fail to 'make it' at school. School organization certainly contributes in its own right to delinquency (Rutter and Giller, 1983), and Hargreaves (1967) documented neatly how relevant are theories of intergroup relations to the emergence of a delinquent orientation amongst members of the lower streams in a school where streaming was based on academic achievement. In line with Emler's emphasis on 'reputation management', boys who became the influential leaders were those who most blatantly rejected school values, were most disruptive in class and were most delinquent within and outside school. The opposite qualities led to high status in the higher streams. In a neat reversal of the usual procedure, a recent German study sought to discover the characteristics of those adolescents in residential homes who were 'resilient' to delinquency, despite being just as much 'at risk' of delinquency as a 'control' group of adolescents with conduct problems (Lösel and Bliesner 1990). The 'resilient' profile included many factors suggestive of a high conventional reputation, like having a reference person outside the family, a good relationship with the school and realistic conceptions of future performance, together with high achievement motivation and a sense of autonomy.

Just as most children are delinquent to some extent, so are most children non-delinquent most of the time. It is perhaps not surprising that, given opportunities to succeed in work beyond the school environment, and later still in stable sexual and family relationships, involvement in delinquency decreases, and ceases to impress the significant others in one's environment. The finding that unemployment in adulthood in itself contributes to involvement in crime should be understood in both its economic and its social contexts (Farrington et al., 1986). Crime may be relatively more financially rewarding in periods of unemployment, but, equally important, it may again serve, as in adolescence, to enhance social reputation and prestige.

Eye-witness testimony

'Eye-witness testimony is unreliable' has become a well-rehearsed chant in praise of the scientific contribution of psychology to the study of legal procedure. However, neither the legal profession nor all psychologists are certain either that acceptance of eye-witness testimony is a dubious practice, or that psychologists should testify in court as expert witnesses in cases of disputed eye-witness evidence (see the debate between Egeth and McCloskey, 1984; and Wells, 1984). But is eye-witness testimony always so remiss? Do people invariably have to invent, distort, exaggerate and otherwise extend their feeble recollections in order to be able to tell a good story? The assumption that they do is evident in these words of the leading authority on the subject, who, regretting 'that eye-witness testimony will ever be eliminated as a form of evidence', goes on to say:

> We might, then, profitably concentrate our efforts on building a research base to guide us in understanding the errors of eye-witnesses and in developing procedures that produce the least amount of error or distortion in eyewitness reports. (Loftus, 1984, p. ix)

Witnessing a murder: a cautionary case-study

The bulk of the work on which Loftus's gloomy premise about the errors of eye-witnesses is based has been carried out in laboratories, and has concentrated on eye-witness identification of people seen under fairly innocuous conditions, or even of people seen on *films*. The circumstances in which the subjects of Yuille and Cutshall's study (1986) found themselves could hardly have been more different. Let the authors tell the story in their own words:

> The incident involved a gun shooting which occurred on a spring afternoon outside of a gun shop in full view of several witnesses. A thief had entered the gun shop, tied up the proprietor, and stolen some money and a number of guns. The store owner freed himself, picked up a revolver, and went outside to take the thief's licence number. The thief, however, had not yet entered his car and in a face-to-face encounter on the street, separated by six feet, the thief fired two shots at the store owner. After a slight pause the store owner discharged all six shots from his revolver. The thief was killed whereas the store owner recovered from serious injury. Witnesses viewed the incident from various vantage points along the street, from adjacent buildings, or from passing automobiles; and they witnessed various aspects of the incident, either prior to and including the actual shooting or after the shots were fired. (p. 292)

Twenty-one of the witnesses were interviewed by the police shortly after the event, and thirteen of these agreed to take part in a subsequent research interview some four to five months later. In both sets of interviews, verbatim accounts of the incident were obtained, and follow-up questions were asked in order to clarify points of detail. In addition, the researchers asked two misleading questions following Loftus's (1974) well-known procedure, for example, asking half the witnesses whether they had seen 'the' broken headlight and the other half 'a' broken headlight (there was no broken headlight).

Eye-witness accuracy

The sheer volume of accurate detail produced in both the police and the research interviews is truly impressive (see figure 18.8). The researchers obtained much more detail than did the police, because they were concerned with memory for details which were of no forensic interest to the police (such as a description of the blanket covering the thief's body). Witnesses who were central to the drama

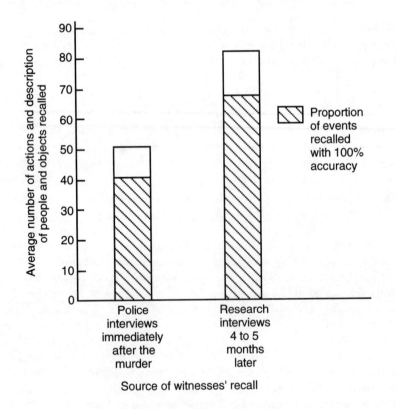

Figure 18.8 Accuracy of recall by witnesses of a murder (based on Yuille and Cutshall, 1986)

gave more details than did peripheral witnesses, but the overall accuracy between the two groups did not differ, and there was virtually no correlation at all between the number of items recalled and their accuracy: more detail does not mean greater inaccuracy.

Figure 18.8 shows the average number of details obtained per witness, with an indication of the number of those details which were entirely accurate. Note the high level of accuracy in both police and research interviews – a level which was maintained throughout, including memory for the *new* material which had not been disclosed to the police but which did emerge four months or so later in response to the more detailed questioning by the researchers. It may also be noted that a number of the errors some four months after the event concerned documented details like time and date of the event, and not the publicly unverifiable details of the events themselves. Many of the errors also concerned details like the number of gunshots (eight in all), which were scored very strictly for accuracy. There were, in other words, few if any *inventions*, and many of those that did occur could plausibly be put down to perceptual distortion stemming from the disadvantageous viewpoint of one or two peripheral witnesses. In further contradiction of laboratory studies, it was found that the wording of the misleading question had no effect (nor were witnesses at all misled by either question form). Moreover, reported stress at the time of the incident was positively related to accuracy. Those witnesses who were deeply affected by the event and, for example, suffered from nightmares following it, were the most accurate of the witnesses – a result which appears to contradict the findings of a considerable body of laboratory research. Interestingly, Smith and Ellsworth (1987) have shown that the distorting effect of misleading questions on memory does not always occur in laboratory studies. Their work indicates that subjects are only affected by misleading questions if they believe that the questioner already knows what actually happened. When subjects believe that the questioner is ignorant of what really happened, misleading questions have no effect at all.

What is becoming clear is that 'typical' distortions arising, for example, from misleading post-event information need not always occur, and probably do not normally occur for information that is of central interest to the perceiver (Toglia et al., 1994). The Yuille and Cutshall case-study by no means undermines all the evidence indicating that in certain circumstances the distorting effects of reconstructive processes in memory may be much in evidence. The extreme unreliability of identification evidence is a case in point. Nevertheless, this unique study demonstrates clearly that it is not easy to ensure that laboratory studies represent 'the task, stimuli and responses in a form that captures the essence of real-world settings', as Wells and Loftus (1984, p. 7) suggest should be the case. Observations in natural environments are surely required. Laboratory studies may, however, be used in a programmatic way to explore critically the implications and potential consequences of procedures employed in the criminal justice system. Two recent examples are the conditions under which reliable testimony may be provided in court by young children (see Dent and Flin, 1992), and the effects of allowing police officers to collaborate in the preparation of their own testimony (Clark and Stephenson, 1995).

Applied Social Psychology of the Environment

There are many 'environments'. There is the built environment of houses, roads, schools and so on; the social environment; the political or economic environment; the cultural environment; the behavioural, the stimulus, perceptual, phenomenological, natural and geographical environments, all of which have been said to contribute to the 'environmental context' of our being in the world. As we have seen, social psychologists have been accused by critics of *neglecting* the environmental context by examining social-psychological processes in only *one* environment – that of the social-psychological 'laboratory' – although critics have not always been clear about just what alternative environments should be the focus of our study. However, whilst acknowledging the ambiguities and confusions which reference to the environmental context engenders, many social psychologists see environmental influences and problems as their main area of research, and view themselves as working in the field of 'environmental psychology' or 'social psychology of the environment'.

The scope of environmental social psychology

The field of 'environmental social psychology', as it is coming to be known (see Canter et al., 1987), is an applied field of social psychology for a number of reasons. First, we have control over many aspects of the physical environment, and the physical environment can be *designed* in the hope of achieving behavioural and social goals. For example, following many instances of disorder and riot at football grounds in England, and a growing reputation for hooliganism amongst English soccer fans, major football grounds have been redesigned in ways which it is supposed will put an end to these behavioural disturbances by requiring seating arrangements which prevent or hinder the movement of fans around the ground, and facilitate separation of rival groups. We shall return to look in detail at one aspect of (urban) environmental design.

Secondly, as Linneweber (1988a) points out, environments are socially meaningful in a number of ways. They provide the context for social activity, they are evaluated by individuals and groups, and they are a source of individual and social identifications. Hence, people have a psychological relationship with their community environment which intimately affects their identity and well-being. Where we live and work is not a trivial matter, and can be a source of utmost pleasure or acute and lasting distress. People differ in what they need and aspire to, and will perceive the same environment in different ways according to

Plate 18.2 Redesign of football grounds – from terraces to all-seater stadium – can help to reduce crowd trouble

how well it 'fits' their requirements. Women with young children, for example, are frequently handicapped by many features of typical urban housing developments: lack of public transportation, and public and cultural meeting places, for example, which have the effect of isolating women socially and work-wise relative to men (Churchman, 1993).

Places are important to individuals and groups because they are inexorably intertwined with autobiographies and shared histories. What pulls together our disparate experiences over time into 'me' as a self-object, is the story we tell of ourselves. That story's continuity – and hence the perception of an integrated self – may be enhanced by the quality and continuity of the environment in which we live, a point accepted long ago by William James, whose view that 'a man's Me is the sum total of all that he can call his' (James, 1890, p. 44) has prevailed in modern-day conceptions of self (Wiley, 1994). The encouragement we are given now to take responsibility for the environment, and to create and preserve it for future generations, serves only to enhance its important role in self-perception. Indeed, Lalli (1992) has recently shown that those who are concerned about environmental issues such as pollution tend to be those who identify strongly with the place where they live.

Linneweber (1988a) demonstrated clearly that not only personal identity, but social identity may be enhanced by perception of one's environment. He examined residents' 'post-occupancy evaluation' of a new housing development, consisting of eight groups of ten or so houses each encircling its own 'village green' area. Individuals in each house were asked to rate their own group of houses, as well as one other group. In addition, occupants were asked to state what would be the rating in an 'ideal' world. Quite consistently, as expected, own-group ratings corresponded more to the ideal than did ratings of the other groups. More impressively, however, there was a strong association between the extent of this own-group bias and the estimated 'relevance' of the dimension concerned: the more relevant a factor, the greater the bias in favour of their own group. For example, the dimensions entitled (in English translation) 'inviting–desolate' and 'accommodating–inelegant' elicited a strong bias in favour of their own group and a high rating as for relevance. At the other extreme, 'accessible–secluded' and 'modern–traditional' showed negligible own-group bias and low ratings of relevance.

The third and perhaps most compelling reason for the applied status of environmental social psychology is that people everywhere are permitting their natural environment to be destroyed. This is arguably the most salient social issue presently facing mankind. Our relationship with the natural environment now assumes *global* proportions, because the deleterious effects of our behaviour are not localized. The problem of global warming is an environmental problem that, if not addressed effectively, will have disastrous consequences for our planet. Stern (1992) indicates that organized human activities in the areas of transportation, building and industry all involve the use of fossil fuels, which in total contributes relatively about 46 per cent to the problem of global warming; use of CFCs in refrigeration, aerosols and industry contributes another 25 per cent, and biomass burning in land-clearance and the like, another 15 per cent, just to list the three main factors contributing to the warming effect. Countless human decisions at the local level have cumulatively distant, and seemingly uncontrollable global effects. Can social psychologists suggest how the behaviour of individual consumers, planners and politicians could be influenced and geared to ameliorating and ultimately solving the problem? The rapid growth in environmental social psychology suggests that the will at least is there.

We have illustrated three main applied aspects of environmental social psychology – the effects of environmental design on social behaviour, the role of place in people's lives, and the growing importance of environmental issues like global warming. In the remaining pages we shall focus on the first of these topics, starting with a brief account of the work of Roger Barker, whose pioneering work on the environmental context of behaviour focused the attention of social psychologists on the role of the physical environment.

Social behaviour in place and time

Roger Barker and his colleagues (e.g. Barker, 1987) have made what may seem the obvious point that different types of social behaviour in public – watching football, singing to God, buying clothes, conducting a business meeting or whatever – regularly occur in defined places at set times. The distinctive patterns of 'place–behaviour–time' relations are termed *behaviour settings*, and Barker's group has sought to define the characteristics and influence of behaviour settings in detail. The important point they make is that social behaviour is *invariably* 'in place' and 'in time'. When behaviour is inappropriate to the setting, it is regarded as a sign of madness or mischief, and it is likely to be ignored, or the perpetrator to be removed to another place, or both. Barker also suggested that particular 'habitats' – for example, the towns or villages in which we live – vary in the extent to which their 'programmes' demand human components, i.e., require any one individual to help create or maintain a setting. The smaller the number of people living in the village, for example, the greater the requirement, other things being equal, to support the local fête, church or dramatic society in order to sustain a comparable number of behaviour settings, and, in consequence the greater the variety of roles that residents will be required to fulfil (see Barker and Schoggen, 1973).

Perhaps Barker under-estimates the extent to which, at the same time, people themselves sustain the setting or system which incorporates them and their behaviour as an essential component. At any rate, mainstream social psychology has responded only fitfully to the naturalistic study of behaviour settings as pioneered by Barker. The focus has largely been on the study of norms and conventions which operate across different behaviour settings, without reference to the culturally determined 'programmes' which more precisely determine behaviour in given settings. However, Linneweber (1988b) provides an inter-esting commentary on Barker and studies of social influence in social psychology more generally. In any given setting three types of norm or expectation may be violated. First, a person may behave *inappropriately towards another individual*, like talking loudly in a library, a flouting of the setting's 'programme' which has a direct impact on the well-being of other users. On the other hand, painting graffiti on buildings is a *violation of the environment* by the individual which may occur independently of the presence of others, although it may also directly affect the comfort of others. Finally, *environments themselves may undermine the purpose of their own settings*, by, for example, not providing adequate visual access to the game at a football match, or physical access to a library for those in wheelchairs. Linneweber shows that these distinctions are clear enough for individuals to be able to make consistent judgements about the content and coding of the different types, and provide a basis for a systematic study of norm violations within the framework of a social psychology of the environment (see also de Ridder and Tripathi, 1992).

Recognition of the interaction between respective components of a behaviour setting raises questions about what Fuhrer (1990) calls the ecological–psychological gap, the reconciliation between the objective environment and its subjective interpretation by individuals who engage in it. These questions will become more acute as we move from studies of relatively simple social behaviour in controlled institutional settings like schools and mental hospitals, to more complex behaviours, such as criminal behaviour, whose environmental context ranges less predictably. So let us now illustrate how the human component of behaviour settings – people and their behaviour – may be affected by manipulating other components, chiefly the physical characteristics of the setting. This has been a long-standing area of research to which social psychologists have made extensive and useful contributions.

Design and social interaction

The growth in *application* of principles derived from Barker's and other social psychologists' detailed observations of environment–behaviour relations owes much to Sommer's book *Personal Space: the behavioural basis of design* (1969), which exerted an immediate and continuing influence.

In that book Sommer emphasized the point that the physical arrangements which attend all our everyday activities seem natural and lawful. Neither the child, nor the teacher, questions that desks are arranged systematically, nor that each child is allocated a regular place in which to sit. We hardly pause to think whether such arrangements might be altered, sensing no doubt that variation would seriously disrupt what has become the natural order of things. It was not surprising, then, to find that residents of an old people's ward in a Saskatchewan hospital in 1957 did not initially take kindly to having their furniture arbitrarily (as they saw it) re-arranged from being 'sociofugal' – chairs backed straight against the four walls of a day room, with additional rows of chairs arranged back-to-back in lines down the centre of the room – to 'sociopetal' – chairs moved away from the walls and grouped around tables placed in various parts of the room. Like it or not, the new arrangements changed the behaviour of the residents, with an increase of 55 per cent in 'brief interactions' and of 69 per cent in 'sustained interactions' (Sommer, 1969, p. 85). Moreover, the magazines that were provided for the use of residents were now left on the tables – rather than being hoarded privately – and were read frequently and openly on the ward. In addition, occupational therapists seemed to be sufficiently encouraged by the transformation in residents' behaviour to introduce craft activities onto the ward.

In Barker's terms, the *programme* of the behaviour setting can be said to have been changed by the introduction of different seating arrangements. The sociofugal arrangements suggested separateness and isolation from others, discouraging eye-contact and preventing interaction with more than one's immediate neighbour, whereas the sociopetal arrangements positively encouraged social interaction. In an experimental follow-up to that study, Holahan (1976) varied the seating patterns systematically, in a hospital setting, across four conditions: sociopetal, sociofugal, mixed and 'free' (in which patients made their own arrangements of chairs). There were significant differences in the distribution of conversations and other social activities across the four conditions, 41 per cent of conversations occurring in the sociopetal, 27 per cent in the mixed, 21 per cent in the sociofugal and 11 per cent in the free. In yet another study, Holahan (1976) indicated how a more extensive re-modelling of the physical arrangements of a ward had major effects not only on interactions between patients but on role relationships between staff, distribution of power, and communication styles of staff.

Sommer's work had extensive consequences in hospital practice, and, as he pointed out later (Sommer, 1983), the scientific impact as measured by citation indexes was also considerable. In the 1990s, some thirty years later, the lessons of his compelling early studies are still being brought home to social and health workers in professional journals (see Gutheil, 1992).

The problem of creating therapeutic environments remains an important social issue, despite the closure of many large institutions and the movement towards community care. However, Sommer's convincing demonstrations in therapeutic and other (e.g., educational) settings that comparatively modest adjustments to the physical environment might result in significant improvements in social behaviour and relationships was not lost on other planners and professionals facing problems of a rather different kind. In particular, problems arising from rapid and extensive urban developments, and an apparently inexorably rising crime rate, attracted the attention of planners and criminologists. The possibility that the built environment itself had inadvertently been designed for crime was one which received increasing attention, and one which we shall now explore.

Settings for crime

Newman (1972, 1980), in his book *Defensible Space*, proposed that people living in properties that were visibly surrounded by indices of ownership – like a private garden overlooked from the house, hedges and fences at the perimeter, a distinctive entrance to the property not used by other residents, and so on – are more likely to be untouched by criminality and vandalism. High-rise blocks of flats represent the antithesis of 'defensible' property; anyone has access to the surrounding territory, which is open to all residents and outsiders, and visitors gaining access to property by the common entrance are no more remarkable than a stranger walking along a relatively busy street. High-rise flats are, in other words, open to invasion; their space is indefensible, and they effectively invite criminality.

Newman contrasted the crime rates of high-rise and low-rise developments, roughly comparable as regards the socio-economic status of their residents, and showed higher figures in the high-rise developments. Moreover, he showed, in another study, that adding further defensible-space features such as boundary fences to existing (low-rise) developments served to reduce the crime rate in those neighbourhoods. In a more recent English study, Coleman (1985) extended Newman's analysis of defensibility to include additional features like the number of interconnecting exits in a block of flats (which would facilitate escape of criminals and vandals), and she showed that, in working-class areas of London, the more 'indefensible' design features that housing projects had, the greater was the vandalism and crime in and about the properties concerned. Sommer (1987)

Plate 18.3 High-rise developments are associated with higher crime ratios than low-rise developments. Why?

DEFENSIBLE
SPACE

extended the application of Newman's idea to the rather different setting of a university campus, and found that university halls of residence with good **defensible space** had considerably lower vandalism and crime rates than halls of residence with poor defensible space.

Not all the evidence has supported Newman, as a recent review by Brantingham and Brantingham (1993) indicates, and as a second study by Newman himself also indicated (Newman and Franck, 1982). The Brantinghams criticize Newman for holding a deterministic view of the impact of the built environment, and they point out that the motivations of both residents and non-residents must be taken into account when predicting the occurrence of so complex a phenomenon as criminal behaviour. Some 'insiders' may be responsible for criminal activity in high-rise blocks, and some people – elderly and infirm folk, for example – may find the physical proximity and accessibility of neighbours in largely communal blocks a feature that alleviates fear of crime.

There is, none the less, strong evidence that objective design features are associated with the emergence of behaviour settings in which criminal activity is more or less 'in' or 'out of' place. In a recent extensive and well-controlled study, Perkins et al. (1993) studied 48 'street blocks' in detail. A 'block' (Taylor, 1987) was defined as the two facing sides of a street, extending between and bounded by cross-streets. Many studies had shown that there was considerable variation between crime rates on seemingly comparable blocks, and this study was carefully designed to evaluate the relative importance of objectively defined defensible-space characteristics. Quite consistently, objective features of the built environment were strongly associated with the considerable variations that were evident in the occurrence of both minor and major criminal activity on the different blocks. The physically *objective* indices were consistently more important than demographics (the socio-economic status of residents, length of residence, age of residents etc.), or the 'transient' environment (e.g., dilapidation of property) or 'territorial functioning' (e.g., neighbours reporting mutual watchfulness). The single most important physical aspect was a narrow, visible street. Wide streets and obstructed views of the street were strongly associated with perceived crime problems and especially with serious crime complaints. Also important in the prediction of serious crime was the existence of non-residential property on the block, for example, shops, schools, churches, offices and parking lots. The implication is clear. Street blocks whose physical characteristics ensure the presence of a large number of residents relative to outsiders, whose watchfulness over the street is facilitated, create settings which discourage those who might otherwise be motivated to commit criminal offences in that area.

Summary and Conclusions

These examples from the applied fields of health, law and the environment have illustrated how social psychology can contribute a distinctive voice in debates about important social issues. The quality of an individual's social relationships may directly affect his or her health, and the ways in which social psychologists are demonstrating this have profound implications for preventive medicine and for our understanding of the healing and therapeutic process. The examples from the legal and judicial fields have indicated, in addition, how important it is to the development of the discipline to employ a range of methods including, fundamentally, naturalistic observation (see chapter 4). The illustrations from environmental social psychology extend this emphasis, and demonstrate very clearly the importance of adopting a thoroughgoing contextual approach to problems of social relationships.

The distinction has been drawn in this chapter between the natural science and social science approaches to application in social psychology. The approaches are illustrative of broad preferences and inclination in the work of different social psychologists. There is no rigid dichotomy, and in particular few social psychologists adhere rigidly to the natural science approach, developing theories independently of their importance for real-world social issues. However, the natural science ethos strongly affects the methods employed by social psychologists, for both good and bad. It is good for a number of reasons. It promotes social psychology's position in the natural sciences, and reminds social psychologists that the issues they deal with are the concern also of colleagues who adopt contrasting perspectives, including the biological perspective (see chapter

2). It is good, too, in its reminder that *evidence for our theories is of paramount importance*. It is sometimes suggested that because our subjects may challenge our theories we should abandon the scientific enterprise and merely *debate* the issues (see chapter 4). On the contrary, our subjects' critical awareness makes the scientific demand for evidence all the more compelling.

Too strict adherence to the natural scientific model, however, would foster an elegantly irrelevant social psychology. This is most surely being countered by recognition of the fundamental role of application in social psychology. Our subjects are indeed our audience – and, rightly and inevitably, the dialogue we establish with them must inform the progress of our discipline. The social science model of application spells out the implications of that dialogue, and the evidence we have reviewed, both in this chapter and throughout the book, testifies to the growing social and community awareness of social psychology – an awareness which augurs well for the future.

Glossary terms

Adversary system	Defensible space	Life events
Behaviour setting	Field theory	Natural science model
Compensatory model	Generalizability	Social science model

Discussion points

1 What evidence is there that 'social fitness' promotes good health?
2 What is wrong with the *medical* model of helping and coping. Which model do you prefer, and why?
3 How valid do you think eye-witness accounts are when presented in court?
4 It has been suggested that some schools may be 'criminogenic'. How do you think schools might cause pupils to be delinquent?
5 What different factors might account for the importance of 'surveillability' in preventing criminal intrusion?
6 Why do you think social psychology has overlooked the importance of the physical environment?
7 How *generalizable* is experimental social psychology?

Suggestions for further reading

Blackburn, R. (1993) *The Psychology of Criminal Conduct*. Chichester: Wiley. The most comprehensive, up-to-date and accurate account available of theories of criminal behaviour, including fair coverage of specifically social-psychological theories.

Bonnes, M. (ed.) (1993) *Perception and Evaluation of Urban Environmental Quality*. Rome: UNESCO Programme on Man and Biosphere. Published conference proceedings including contributions from leading social-psychological researchers in Western Europe.

Canter, D., Jesuino, J. C., Soczka, L. and Stephenson, G. M. (eds) (1987) *Environmental Social Psychology*. London: Kluwer Academic Publishers. This book brings together attempts by researchers in both the US and Europe to adopt a social-psychological approach to environmental problems.

Orford, J. (1992) *Community Psychology: theory and practice*. Chichester: Wiley. A major European contribution to the development of an approach to understanding and helping people which takes as basic the social settings and systems of which they are component parts.

Stephenson, G. M. (1992) *The Psychology of Criminal Justice*. Oxford: Blackwell. This attempts to give an account of decision-making in the criminal justice system, and elaborates many of the issues raised in this chapter.

Stroebe, W. and Stroebe, M. S. (1995) *Social Psychology and Health* Buckingham: Open University Press. An up-to-date and readable coverage of key topics on social psychology and health. The book provides a scholarly analysis of evidence for the impact of behaviour on health, and the role of social psychology in health behaviour, whilst examining one key area in detail: the social psychology of stress and health.

Key studies

Baron, R. S., Cutrona, C. E., Hicklin, D., Russell, D. W. and Lubaroff, D. M. (1980). Social support and immune function among spouses of cancer patients. *Journal of Personality and Social Psychology*, 59, 344–52.

Smith, V. L. and Ellsworth, P. C. (1987). The social psychology of eyewitness accuracy: misleading questions and communicator expertise. *Journal of Applied Psychology*, 72, 294–300.

Glossary

Activation A heightened state of the central and particularly the autonomic nervous system. Some authors use the term to refer particularly to the sympathetic branch of the autonomic nervous system.

Actor–observer difference The claim that actors attribute their actions to situational factors, whereas observers tend to attribute the same actions to stable personal dispositions. The effect is confined to a difference in situational attribution, and appears as a result of differences in information, perceptual focus, and linguistic factors.

Adaptation The possession of characteristics which enable the organism to survive and reproduce better than those with other characteristics. It is implied that these characteristics are better designed for the particular environment than are alternatives.

Additive model A model of impression formation according to which the final impression is a function of the sum of all the points (in terms of positivity) attributed to the various characteristics of the person.

Adversary system The system of criminal and civil justice which prevails in Great Britain, the United States and other (mainly English-speaking) countries. Under the adversary system the conduct of the trial is left to the lawyers who respectively represent the prosecution and the defence.

Affect Often used synonymously with emotion. Some social psychologists restrict the use to the valence aspect, pleasant vs unpleasant or positive vs negative, of feelings.

Affiliation The tendency to seek out the company of others, irrespective of the feelings towards such others.

Affiliative messages Messages concerned with expressed affect, positive (e.g., love) *and* negative (e.g., hate).

After-image The colour seen on a white surface after exposure to another colour; it is the complementary colour of the original colour.

Altruistic behaviour In evolutionary terms this is defined as behaviour which helps another individual's fitness despite a fitness cost for the donor. In social psychology, it refers to behaviour which is undertaken with the intention of benefiting another person where the donor has a choice not to do so.

Analogy Structural similarity guiding an inference from one domain to another.

Anchoring and adjustment Judgemental heuristic that leads to characteristic biases; quantitative tendency to be biased towards the starting value or anchor. The subsequent adjustment process is typically incomplete.

Appraisal Evaluation of the significance of an object, event, or action to a person, including an evaluation of one's coping activities. Can occur at various levels of the central nervous system and need not be conscious.

Assimilation A shift in the frame of reference caused by a context stimulus such that judgements of other stimuli are biased towards the context stimulus (e.g., in the context of humour, other utterances may appear more humorous).

Attachment An enduring emotional tie between one person and another one.

Attitude A psychological tendency that is expressed by evaluation of a particular entity with some degree of favour or disfavour.

Attraction Positive feelings towards another individual, including a tendency to seek out the presence of the other.

Attribution theory The conceptual framework within social psychology dealing with lay, or common-sense, explanations of behaviour.

Attributional bias A bias occurs if the perceiver systematically distorts (e.g., over- or under-uses) some otherwise correct procedure, or indeed if the result of the procedure itself is distorted.

Attributional style The tendency to make a particular kind of causal inference across different situations and across time.

Augmentation principle The augmentation principle (originally invoked in relation to causal schemata) implies that the role of a given cause is increased if an effect occurs in the presence of an inhibitory cause. This idea has also been used to explain the social influence exerted by minorities.

Authoritarian personality A particular type of personality – over-submissive to authority figures – which is also thought to be particularly susceptible to prejudice.

Autokinetic effect The illusion of movement of a stationary point of light when viewed in a totally dark environment.

Availability Judgemental heuristic for judging the frequency or probability of events on the basis of the ease with which relevant memories come to mind.

Averaging model A model of impression formation according to which the final impression is a function of the average of all the points (in terms of positivity) attributed to the various characteristics of the person.

Behaviour setting A small-scale social system, composed of people and physical objects, that is designed to produce a routine programme of actions within specifiable time and place boundaries, e.g., betting shops, classrooms, research seminars, petrol-station forecourts.

Behavioural intention The intention to perform or not to perform an attitude-relevant behaviour.

Beliefs The opinions, knowledge and thoughts someone has about an attitude object.

Bogus pipeline A distortion-immunized method of attitude measurement. The subjects whose attitudes are to be measured are led to believe that the correctness of their responses will be monitored by a sort of lie detector.

Brainstorming A group technique aimed at stimulating group members to generate as many ideas as possible concerning a specified topic.

Buffer effect of social support The effect that those who perceive that they are supported, are less affected by stressful events and conditions than those who feel unsupported.

Categorical differentiation The exaggeration of real differences between two categories.

Categorial information Information concerning the category or group to which a person belongs, often opposed to individuating information.

Category Grouping of two or more distinguishable objects that are treated in a similar way. Classes of objects in the world.

Catharsis Release of aggressive energy through the expression of aggressive responses, or through alternative forms of behaviour.

Causal attribution The inference process by which perceivers attribute an effect to one or more causes.

Causal schemata Abstract, content-free conceptions of the way certain kinds of causes interact to produce an effect (e.g., Multiple

Necessary Cause schema; Multiple Sufficient Cause schema).

Central route to persuasion A person's careful and thoughtful consideration of the arguments presented in support of a position.

Central trait(s) A personal characteristic that strongly influences a perceiver's overall impression of someone possessing that trait (e.g., warm/cold).

Classical conditioning Through classical conditioning some neutral stimulus initially incapable of eliciting a particular response gradually acquires the ability to do so through repeated association with a stimulus that has already evoked that response.

Co-action Two or more individuals performing the same task in each other's presence.

Coercive power The use of threats and punishments in pursuit of social power.

Cognitive consistency theories Theories such as balance theory or the theory of cognitive dissonance, which assume that people strive to organize their own cognitions in a tension-free, i.e., non-contradictory, way.

Cognitive–neoassociationistic approach Theory developed by L. Berkowitz which postulates a direct link between aversion events or negative affects and arousal of fight or flight behaviour. Denies the necessity of cognitive mediators for (emotional) aggression to occur.

Cognitive-response model The cognitive-response model assumes that attitude change is mediated by the thoughts, or 'cognitive responses', which recipients generate as they receive and reflect upon persuasive communications. The model assumes that the magnitude and direction of attitude change obtained by a persuasive communication will be a function of the extent of message-relevant thinking as well as its favourability.

Cohesion The forces that hold a group together.

Collective violence Violence performed simultaneously by a large number of people, groups or masses, either in a spontaneous way like riots or in a planned way like wars.

Communication Message exchange between two or more participants which is characterized by the intentional, conscious (at some level of awareness) use of a mutually intelligible symbol system.

Communication network Pattern of communication channels in a (task) group.

Communicative competence The appropriate pragmatic use of social knowledge and social skill in the context of a relationship.

Communicative control The various constraints people place on one another by what they say and how they structure conversation.

Comparison level (CL) The standard which individuals use to judge whether the outcomes from a relationship are satisfactory or unsatisfactory. It is defined as some modal value of all the outcomes known to the person from previous own experiences in similar relationships and/or from observing the outcomes of comparable others.

Comparison level for alternatives (CLalt) The lowest level of outcomes someone will accept in a relationship in the light of available alternative opportunities.

Compensatory model The view that people who turn to members of the helping professions cope best with stressful circumstances when they are not blamed for their helplessness, but are given the skills which will enable them to accept responsibility for the course of their own improvement.

Compliance A change in overt (public) behaviour after exposure to others' opinions.

Concept Grouping of two or more distinguishable objects that are treated in a similar way. Mental representation.

Confederate An accomplice or assistant of an experimenter who is ostensibly another subject but who in fact plays a prescribed role in the experiment (sometimes referred to as a *stooge*).

Conformity *See* majority influence.

Confounding A variable that incorporates two or more potentially separable components is a confounded variable. When an independent variable is confounded the researcher's ability to draw unambiguous causal inferences is seriously constrained.

Consistency A behavioural style indicative of maintenance of position. Diachronic – consistency over time; synchronic – consistency between individuals.

Construct An abstract theoretical concept (such as social influence).

Construct validity The validity of the assumption that independent and dependent variables adequately capture the abstract variables (constructs) they are supposed to represent.

Constructive memory Intrusions into memory that originate in the subject's imagination or cognitive activities.

Contact hypothesis The idea that contact between members of different groups under certain conditions lessens intergroup prejudice and hostility.

Contrast A shift in the frame of reference caused by a context stimulus such that judgements of other stimuli tend away from the context stimulus (e.g., other people appear rather poor in contrast to an extremely rich person).

Control group A group of subjects who are typically not exposed to the independent variable(s) used in experimental research. Measures of the dependent variable derived from these subjects are compared with those derived from subjects in the **Experimental group** who are exposed to the independent variable, providing a basis for inferring whether the independent variable determines scores on the dependent variable.

Conversion A change in covert (private) behaviour after exposure to others' opinions; internalized change; a change in the way one structures an aspect of reality.

Correspondence bias The tendency to infer an actor's personal characteristics from his/her observed behaviour, even when the inference is unjustified because other possible causes of the behaviour exist (*see* **fundamental attribution error**).

Correspondent inference In Jones and Davis's correspondent inference theory, a correspondent inference refers to the perceiver's judgement that the actor's behaviour is caused by, or corresponds to, a particular trait. Thus the actor's behaviour reflects an underlying disposition.

Covariation principle In Kelley's theory of causal attribution, a perceiver with sufficient time and motivation can make attributions by perceiving the covariation of an observed effect and its possible causes. The effect is attributed to the condition that is present when the effect is present, and that is absent when the effect is absent.

Cover story A false but supposedly plausible explanation of the purpose of an experiment. The intention is to limit the operation of demand characteristics.

Counter-attitudinal behaviour Behaviour (usually induced by monetary incentives or threats) which is inconsistent with the actor's attitudes or beliefs.

Crowd psychology The study of the mind (*cf.* **group mind**) and the behaviour of masses and crowds, and of the experience of individuals in such crowds.

Cue–arousal theory Frustration leads to aggression only in the presence of cues which, through classical conditioning, have become associated with aggression (e.g., weapons) and indicate that aggressive behaviour is situationally appropriate.

Debriefing The practice of explaining to subjects the purpose of the experiment in which they have just participated, and answering any questions the subject may have. It is especially important to debrief subjects when the experimental procedure involved deception – in which case the debriefing should also explain why the deception was considered to be necessary.

Defensible-space (hypothesis) The idea that physical and environmental features of housing facilitate crime deterrence by encouraging actual and perceived influence of its residents into adjacent areas.

Deindividuation An individual state in which rational control and normative orientation are weakened, leading to a greater readiness to respond in an extreme manner and in violation of norms.

Demand characteristics Cues that are perceived as telling subjects how they are expected to behave or respond in a research setting, i.e., cues that 'demand' a certain sort of response.

Dependent variable The variable that is expected to change as a function of changes in the independent variable. Measured changes in the dependent variable are seen as 'dependent on' manipulated changes in the independent variable.

Diffusion of responsibility Social inhibition of helping, caused by a weakened sense of responsibility in a group of bystanders at the scene of an emergency. Each individual member of the group feels less responsibility to intervene in a group than when alone.

Dilution of steoreotypes Tendency to weaken the impact of a stereotype on a judgement, following reception of irrelevant or non-diagnostic individuating information.

Discounting principle The discounting principle (originally invoked in relation to causal schemata) implies that the role of a given cause in producing an effect is decreased if other plausible causes are present.

Displacement Replacing the target of aggression with another target, or substituting one aggressive response for another.

Display rules Modern term denoting the old observation that there are socio-cultural norms that govern the type of emotional expressions that are acceptable in specific situations.

Dissonance theory A consistency theory which assumes that dissonance is an aversive motivational state, which motivates individuals to reduce it. Strategies of dissonance reduction include attitude, opinion and behaviour change as well as the search for consonant or the avoidance of dissonant information.

Distraction While listening to a persuasive communication individuals are distracted by having to perform an irrelevant activity or by experiencing sensory stimulation irrelevant to the message.

Dominant response Response which takes precedence in a subject's response repertoire.

Dual-process models of persuasion Models of persuasion (e.g., elaboration likelihood model; heuristic–systematic model) postulating two modes of information processing, which differ in the extent to which individuals engage in content-relevant thoughts and scrutinization of the arguments contained in a message in order to accept or reject the position advocated in a communication. The mode of information processing used is assumed to depend on processing motivation and ability.

Ease of retrieval Refers to the ease with which raw information for social judgements comes to the judge's mind.

Elaboration Refers to the extent to which a person thinks about the issue-relevant arguments contained in a message.

Elaboration likelihood model The elaboration likelihood model of Petty and Cacioppo assumes that attitude change in response to persuasive communications can be mediated by two different modes of information processing (*see* **dual-process models**). Elaboration denotes the extent to which a person thinks about the issue-relevant arguments contained in a message rather than relying on processes that characterize the peripheral route to persuasion (e.g., heuristic processing, classical conditioning, instrumental conditioning). The probability that a recipient will critically evaluate arguments (i.e., the elaboration likelihood) is determined by both processing motivation and ability.

Emotion Earlier often used synonymously with feeling or affect. Modern usage assumes emotion to be a hypothetical construct denoting a process of an organism's reaction to significant events. Emotion is generally presumed to have several components: physiological arousal, motor expression, action tendencies, and subjective feeling.

Emotional reaction triad *See* emotion; the three response components: physiological arousal, motor expression, and subjective feeling.

Emotionality Relatively stable personality disposition to over- or under-react to specific eliciting situations and to show specific types of response patterns.

Empathy Affective state that corresponds to the witnessing of the emotional state of another person. This feeling state results from taking the perspective of the other and comprehending his or her emotions.

Equity theory Assumes that satisfaction is a function of the proportionality of outcomes to inputs of the person as compared with those of a reference other, and that individuals will try to restore equity when they find themselves in an inequitable situation (*see also* **social exchange theory**).

Ethologist Person who studies animal behaviour from a biological viewpoint: this involves being concerned with a detailed description of behaviour, its occurrence under natural conditions, and its evolutionary significance.

Evaluation apprehension The stressful experience of a person whose behaviour in achievement situations is observed by others. This experience may elicit anxiety and deterioration of performance or high levels of performance,

depending on the familiarity of the task and prior exercise.

Evolution The gradual change of one form of organism into another over succeeding generations.

Evolutionarily stable strategy (ESS) Referring to animal behaviour, this means a consistent set of actions which when followed by all members of a population has a higher fitness than any other alternatives.

Evolutionary psychology An approach to psychology based on the principle of natural selection. The emphasis is placed more on psychological mechanisms and flexibility than is the case for sociobiology (*see* **socio-evolutionary theory**).

Excitation-transfer theory Sources of arousal not directly related to aggression may be added to aggression-specific arousal, thus intensifying aggressive responses.

Existential guilt (see **Interpersonal guilt**)

Expectancy-value models These models assume that decisions between different courses of action are based on two types of cognitions: (1) the subjective probabilities that a given action will lead to a set of expected outcomes, and (2) the valence of these outcomes. According to this approach individuals will choose among various alternative courses of action the one which will be most likely to lead to positive consequences or avoid negative consequences.

Experiment A method in which the researcher deliberately introduces some change into a setting to examine the consequences of that change.

Experimental group A group of subjects allocated to the 'experimental' condition of an experiment, i.e., the condition in which subjects are exposed to that level of the independent variable that is predicted to influence their thoughts, feelings or behaviour.

Experimental scenario The 'package' within which an experiment is presented to subjects.

In field experiments it is, ideally, something that happens naturally. In laboratory experiments it is important to devise a scenario that strikes the subject as realistic and involving.

Experimenter (expectancy) effects   Effects unintentionally produced by the experimenter in the course of his or her interaction with the subject. These effects result from the experimenter's knowledge of the hypothesis under test, and they increase the likelihood that the subjects will behave in such a way as to confirm the hypothesis.

Expression   Muscular actions in the face, the vocal organs, the hands, and the skeletal musculature generally that are linked to internal states of the organism and so provide indices of such states, and thus serve communicative purposes. As a consequence, expression is often manipulated to produce appropriate signals in social interaction.

External validity   Refers to the generalizability of research findings to settings and populations other than those involved in the research.

Facial feedback hypothesis   *See* **proprioceptive feedback**; here specifically the notion that amplification or inhibition of facial expression of emotion will modify the intensity and possibly the nature of subjective feeling.

Factorial experiment   An experiment in which two or more independent variables are manipulated within the same design.

Feeling   Earlier used synonymously with emotion. Modern use restricted to the component of subjective experience of emotional arousal, often conscious and verbalizable by using emotion words or expressions.

Field theory   The framework adopted by Kurt Lewin and other *Gestalt* social psychologists in the 1940s and 1950s, which represented the individual as an element in a larger system of social forces.

Fitness   The ability of an organism to leave a greater proportion of its genes in succeeding generations than other individuals (*but see also* **inclusive fitness**).

Free-rider effect   Strategy of leaving it to other group members to contribute to the collective product.

Frustration   An event that interferes with goal-directed behaviour; and/or the resulting individual state.

Frustration–aggression (hypothesis)   Aggression is always a result of frustration (*see* **catharsis, displacement**).

Fundamental attribution error   The tendency for perceivers to under-estimate the impact of situational factors and to over-estimate the role of dispositional factors in controlling behaviour. This bias can be explained in terms of cognitive, cultural and linguistic factors (*see* **correspondence bias**).

Galvanic skin response (GSR)   The GSR measures the electrical resistance of the skin, which changes when people are emotionally aroused. It can be used as a measure of the intensity of an individual's affective response.

Generalizability   The belief that laboratory-based experimental social psychology can be applied to real-life situations, and is thereby of practical value.

Group mind   The concept of the supra-individual nature and independence of the collective mind of a social group.

Group polarization   A change in the average position of a group, following group discussion, in the direction of the initially dominant pole.

Groupthink   A group decision process, strongly oriented towards consensus, among like-minded and cohesive individuals, resulting in one-sided and incorrect conclusions.

Hawthorne effect   A term used to describe the effect of subjects' awareness that they are being observed, on their behaviour.

Hedonism (psychological)   The doctrine that every activity is motivated by the desire for pleasure and the avoidance of pain.

Helping behaviour In its biological sense this is equivalent to altruistic behaviour.

Heuristics Cognitive devices for quick and economic judgements based on rules of thumb, often at the expense of biases and fallacies.

Heuristic processing Assessing the validity of a communication through reliance on heuristics, i.e., simple rules like 'statistics don't lie', 'expects can be trusted' rather than through evaluation of the arguments.

Heuristic–systematic model The heuristic–systematic model of Chaiken and her colleagues assumes that attitude change in response to persuasive communications can be mediated by two different modes of information processing, namely heuristic and systematic processing (*see* **dual-process models**). When individuals are motivated and able to think about the arguments included in a communication, they are likely to engage in systematic processing. When motivation and ability are low, individuals rely on heuristic cues to decide on whether to accept or reject the position recommended in a communication.

Hypothesis A proposed explanation for an observed relationship between events.

Illusory correlation An over-estimation of the strength of a relationship between two, usually distinct, variables (e.g., 'crime' and 'immigrants'); a possible cognitive basis of stereotyping.

Implicit personality theory General beliefs or theories about the frequency and variability of personality traits for individuals or groups, and also beliefs about the correlations between these traits.

Impression management theory Assumes that individuals have a social concern for appearing consistent to others and may feign attitudinal responses to create the impression of consistency.

Inclusive fitness Refers to the representation of an individual's genes in succeeding generations when help given to relatives is balanced against reproduction.

Independent variable The variable that an experimenter manipulates or modifies in order to examine the effect on one or more dependent variables.

Individualism The doctrine that emphasizes the rights, values, and interests of the individual from which all rights and values of society have to be derived and justified (ethical and political individualism). The doctrine that all explanations of individual or social phenomena are to be rejected unless they are expressed wholly in terms of individuals (methodological individualism).

Individuating information Information concerning a specific individual, often opposed to categorial information.

Individuo-centred approach Any approach to the study of social behaviour and social functions relying exclusively or largely on the study of individual experience and behaviour.

Informational influence Influence based on the informational value of opinions expressed by others, on what they tell a person about an aspect of reality.

Ingroup A group to which a person belongs, or thinks he or she belongs.

Innovation *See* **minority influence**.

Instinct An innate behaviour pattern that appears in response to an appropriate 'eliciting stimulus'.

Instrumental conditioning With instrumental conditioning the frequency with which a specific response occurs increases because it is followed by positive consequences, or decreases because it is followed by negative consequences.

Interaction effect A term used when the combined effects of two (or more) independent variables in a factorial experiment yield a pattern that differs from the sum of the **main effects**.

Interaction process analysis (IPA)   A formal observational measurement system devised by Bales for coding the interactions of members of small social groups. It consists of categories and procedures for coding interaction in terms of these categories.

Intergroup behaviour   Actions by members of one group towards members of another group.

Internal validity   Refers to the validity of the inference that changes in the independent variable result in changes in the dependent variable.

Interpersonal–(inter)group continuum   A continuous dimension of social behaviour distinguishing between actions performed as an individual and actions performed as a group member.

Interpersonal guilt   Negative feelings about oneself which result from the knowledge that one is responsible for the distress or damage of others. **Existential guilt** is a related concept which refers to generalized guilt feelings on the basis of perceived own privileges. A person may feel guilty if he is better off than others although he has done nothing wrong.

Investment model   A theory that assumes that commitment to a relationship is based upon a high satisfaction, a low quality of alternatives, and a high level of investments.

Kinesics   The study and classification of body movements.

Learned helplessness   A state characterized by learning deficits, negative emotion and passive behaviour when organisms learn that their responses are independent of desired outcomes.

Least preferred co-worker (LPC)   In Fiedler's theory of leadership, the individual identified by the leader as 'most difficult to work with'.

Life events   Changes in an individual's circumstances – such as bereavement, moving house, changing a job and getting divorced – which may disrupt social functioning and lead to symptoms of stress and illness.

Likert scale   One of the most popular standard attitude scales. Subjects are presented with a list of attitude-relevant statements and asked to indicate on a five-point scale how strongly they agree or disagree with each statement.

Loneliness   A complex affective response stemming from felt deficits in the number and nature of one's social relationships.

Lost letter technique   An indirect measure of attitudes by the frequency with which apparently lost postage-paid letters addressed to political organizations are mailed by the finders.

Main effect   A term used to refer to the separate effects of each independent variable in a **factorial experiment**.

Majority influence (conformity)   Social influence resulting from exposure to the opinions of a majority, or the majority of one's group.

Manipulation check   A measure of the effectiveness of the independent variable.

Memory-based judgements   Typically, unexpected judgements that have to rely on whatever relevant information can be retrieved from memory.

Mental contagion   The hypothetical mechanism underlying the spread of affect and of ideas in crowds.

Meta-analysis   A set of techniques for statistically integrating the results of independent studies of a given phenomenon in terms of a common metric (effect sizes), with a view to establishing whether the findings exhibit a pattern of relationships that is reliable across studies.

Meta-communication   The use of extralinguistic cues (e.g., smiling) to qualify the referential, verbal content (e.g., 'Oh, I hate you').

Minimal group paradigm   A set of experimental procedures designed to create *ad hoc* groups on essentially arbitrary criteria with no interaction within or between them, and with no knowledge of who else belongs to each group. Once such a situation has been created people's perceptions of or reward allocations to the groups may be measured.

Minority influence (innovation) Social influence resulting from exposure to the opinions of a minority group, or the minority of one's group.

MODE model The MODE (motivation and opportunity as determinants of how attitudes influence behaviour) model assumes that attitudes can influence behaviour either by the deliberate processing of the attitudinal implications for behaviour or by the automatic selective processing of attitude-relevant information.

Modelling The tendency for individuals to acquire new (and more complex) forms of behaviour by observing this behaviour, and its consequences, in real-life or symbolic models.

Mood Affective state, differing from emotion in that moods are of a diffuse origin (rather than a specific eliciting event), a much longer duration, and a lower overall intensity.

Mood congruency The tendency to perceive, encode, store and recall information more efficiently that is affectively congruent with one's emotional state. Also refers to the tendency to give more positive (negative) judgements in positive (negative) mood states.

Natural science model The conception of social psychology as a theoretical discipline whose laws can be effectively applied to the problem of implementing the goals of societal institutions; this model implies that theoretical and applied social psychology are separable endeavours.

Natural selection The process whereby individuals with certain characteristics are more frequently represented in succeeding generations as a result of being better adapted for that environment.

Need for cognition An individual difference variable which differentiates individuals in terms of the extent to which they enjoy thinking about the arguments contained in a communication. When exposed to a persuasive message, individuals high in need for cognition are assumed to engage in more content-relevant thinking than individuals who are low on this dimension.

Normative influence Influence based on the need to be accepted and approved by others.

Normative model Standard, optimally correct way of making an inference or judgement (e.g., Kelley's ANOVA model).

Norms Implicit or explicit rules specifying what one ought to do or to neglect.

Obedience Carrying out the orders given by a person invested with authority.

One-shot case-study A research design in which observations are made on a group after some event has occurred or some manipulation has been introduced. The problem is that there is nothing with which these observations may be compared, so one has no way of knowing whether the event or manipulation had an effect.

On-line judgements Judgements formed immediately upon presentation of stimulus information.

Outgroup A group to which a person does not belong, or thinks he or she does not belong.

Over-justification (hypothesis) Individuals are rewarded for performing a task which they previously found interesting in itself. This over-justification decreases their liking for the task.

Paralinguistics Those vocal characteristics of speech referred to as 'tone of voice' (e.g., pitch, loudness).

Participant observation A method of observation in which the researcher studies the target group or community from within, making careful records of what he or she observes.

Passionate love A state of intense longing for union with another individual, usually characterized by intrusive thinking and preoccupation with the partner, idealization of the other, and the desire to know the other as well as the desire to be known by the other.

Peripheral route to persuasion   Subsumes those persuasion processes that are not based on issue-relevant thinking (e.g., classical conditioning, heuristic processing).

Pluralistic ignorance   A belief that one's perceptions and feelings are different from those of others, while simultaneously one's visible behaviour is identical with others. In groups of bystanders of emergencies: erroneous conclusion of each bystander that the other bystanders interpret the event as harmless.

Polyandry   A mating system comprising one female and several males. It can also refer to human marriages.

Polygyny   A mating system comprising one male and several females. It can also refer to human marriages.

Positivism   The doctrine according to which knowledge should be based on natural phenomena and their temporal and spatial relationships as identified and verified by the methods (methodology) of empirical science.

Post-experimental enquiry   A technique advocated by Orne for detecting the operation of demand characteristics. The subject is carefully interviewed after participation in an experiment, the object being to assess perceptions of the purpose of the experiment.

Post-test only control group design   A minimal design for a true experiment. Subjects are randomly allocated to one of two groups. One group is exposed to the independent variable; another (the control group) is not. Both groups are assessed on the dependent variable, and comparison of the two groups on this measure indicates whether or not the independent variable had an effect.

Prejudice   A derogatory attitude or set of attitudes towards all or most of the members of a group.

Primacy effect   The tendency for information received early to have a stronger influence than later information on one's judgements or memory about persons, objects or issues.

Priming effect   The finding that a *schema* is more likely to be activated if it has recently been presented or used in the past.

Pro-attitudinal behaviour   Behaviour which is consistent with the actor's attitudes or beliefs, although it may not correspond to his or her attitudinal position.

Probability matching   A heuristic tendency to choose different response options in accordance with their reinforcement rates (e.g., to choose an option with a 75 per cent success rate 75 per cent of the time).

Proprioceptive feedback   Proprioception refers to the capacity of internal organs to provide sensory information about changes in the body. Proprioceptive feedback refers to changes in one internal system upon detection of changes in another system.

Prosocial behaviour   In its biological sense this is equivalent to altruistic behaviour.

Prosodics   The melodic aspects of speech, such as intonation and stress.

Prototype   The best exemplar of a given category; an abstract representation of the attributes associated with a category, which is stored in memory and used to organize information.

Quasi-experiment   An experiment in which subjects are not randomly allocated to the different experimental conditions (typically because of factors beyond the control of the researcher).

Quota sample   A sample that fills certain prespecified quotas and thereby reflects certain attributes of the population (such as age and sex) that are thought to be important to the issue being researched.

Random allocation (*sometimes called* **random assignment**)   The process of allocating subjects to groups (or conditions) in such a way that each subject has an equal chance of being assigned to each group.

Reactivity A measurement procedure is reactive if it alters the nature of what is being measured (i.e., if the behaviour observed or the verbal response recorded is partly or wholly determined by the subject's awareness that some aspect of his or her behaviour is being measured).

Recency effect The tendency for the most recent information received to have a stronger influence than early information on one's judgements or memory about persons, objects or issues.

Reciprocal altruism Altruistic behaviour shown by an animal or person when the recipient is likely to behave altruistically to the donor in the future.

Reciprocity (norm of) The norm that we should do to others as they do to us. Reciprocity calls for positive responses to favourable treatment but negative responses to unfavourable treatment. Prosocial reciprocity occurs when people help in return for having been helped. It has been argued that reciprocity is a fundamental principle governing human behaviour.

Reliability A measure is reliable if it yields the same result on more than one occasion or when used by different individuals.

Representativeness Judgemental heuristic used to estimate event probabilities on the basis of crude similarity principles. For instance, a symptom is taken as evidence for a threatening disease even when the objective base-rate of the disease is extremely low.

Risky shift The strengthening of an individual's and a group's tendency towards favouring a risky decision following group discussion.

Role A set of behaviours associated with a position.

Rubicon model This model specifies under which conditions behavioural intentions are actually translated into overt behaviour. In order to translate intentions into behaviour, people have to formulate clear behavioural plans by thinking about when, where and how to realize the selected behavioural goal.

Salience The distinctiveness of a stimulus relative to the context (e.g., a male in a group of females; a group of people, one of whom is in the spotlight).

Sample survey A research strategy that involves interviewing (or administering a questionnaire to) a sample of respondents who are selected so as to be representative of the population from which they are drawn.

Sampling The process of selecting a subset of members of a population with a view to describing the population from which they are taken.

Schema A cognitive structure that represents organized knowledge about a given concept or stimulus, and which influences perception, memory and inference.

Secure base The feeling of security and trust associated with a specific person or place, such as a child's orientation towards his or her primary caregiver.

Selective exposure Dissonance theory assumes that people are motivated to search selectively for information that supports former decisions or existing attitudes, thereby actively avoiding contradictory information.

Self-disclosure The revelation of personal information about oneself to another person.

Self-fulfilling prophecy When an originally false social belief leads to its own fulfilment. Social belief refers to people's expectations regarding another group of people. When a self-fulfilling prophecy occurs, the perceiver's initially false beliefs cause targets to act in ways that objectively confirm those beliefs.

Self-serving bias People are more likely to attribute their successes to internal causes such as ability, whereas they tend to attribute failures to external causes such as task difficulty. This bias appears as a result of cognitive and motivational factors, varying across public and private settings.

Semantic differential   One of the most popular standard attitude scales. The affective or evaluative component of the attitude is measured by subjects' reactions to the attitude object on seven-point bipolar adjective scales such as 'good vs bad'.

Simple random sample   A sample in which each member of the population has an equal chance of being selected and in which the selection of every possible combination of the desired number of members is equally likely.

Simulation heuristic   Outcomes or events are judged to be likely to the extent that they can be mentally simulated or imagined.

Social comparison   The act of comparing one's own attitudes, abilities and emotions with those of others in order to evaluate their correctness and adequacy.

Social comparison theory   A theory that emphasizes that individuals assess their attitudes, abilities and emotions by comparing themselves with similar others, and that they do so especially when they are uncertain about themselves.

Social construction   Notion that social and cultural factors create reality for the individual, independently of biological processes, providing a language for the definition of self and experience in the world.

Social decision scheme (SDS)   A probabilistic rule which specifies the likelihood that a group will reach any particular decision given that it begins discussion with any particular distribution of member opinions.

Social desirability   A term used to describe the fact that subjects are usually keen to be seen in a positive light and therefore reluctant to report on their negative qualities.

Social dilemma   Payoff structure in which it is in the interest of any individual to act selfishly, while it is detrimental to everyone's interests if all do so.

Social exchange theory   A general theoretical model that views relationships in terms of rewards and costs to the participants. It emphasizes that individuals expect certain levels of outcomes on the basis of their standards, that are in part derived from previous experiences, the outcomes of their partners, and the outcomes of comparable others.

Social facilitation   Performance improvement resulting from the presence of others.

Social hypothesis testing   Verifying or falsifying propositions through socially motivated processes of attention, information search, logical reasoning and (often selective) memory.

Social identity   A person's sense of who they are, derived from their group membership(s).

Social influence   A change in the judgements, opinions and attitudes of an individual as a result of being exposed to the views of others.

Social inhibition   Performance impairment resulting from the presence of others.

Social interactionist theory of coercive action   A theory to describe and explain aggression by separating its behavioural and judgemental aspects. In behavioural terms, aggression is defined as a form of **coercive power**. Whether this coercive action is perceived as aggressive depends on evaluative judgements held by the opponents or an outside observer.

Social loafing   Phenomenon occurring when the presence of others results in a decrease of individual effort.

Social representations   Shared social ideas, in the form of common-sense 'theories', whose main functions are to make sense of the world and facilitate communication.

Social responsibility (norm of)   Prescribes that people should help others who are dependent on them.

Social science model   The conception of social psychology as a theoretical discipline whose principles are derived from its distinctive contribution to the analysis of compelling social issues; this model implies that theoretical and applied social psychology cannot be effectively separated.

Social support The feeling of being supported by others, usually divided into four components, i.e., emotional support, appraisal support, informational support, and instrumental support.

Socialization The processes whereby new members of society come to acquire its rules of behaviour and systems of belief.

Sociobiology The application of Darwin's theory of natural selection to explaining the origins and maintenance of social behaviour.

Socio-centred approach Any approach to the study of individual and social behaviour emphasizing the conditioning functions of the social/societal structural context.

Socio-cognitive conflict The communication of discrepancies between the perspectives of two or more participants in a task, which promotes opportunities for the participants to become aware of deficiencies in their individual understanding.

Socio-evolutionary theory A theory that explains human behaviour, including differences in partner preferences according to gender, from their reproductive value, i.e., their value in producing offspring in our evolutionary past (*see* **evolutionary psychology**).

Sociology The social science dealing with social systems/structures such as social relationships, social institutions, whole societies.

Status Evaluation of a role by the group in which the role is contained or defined.

Stereotype Shared beliefs about personality traits and behaviours of group members. By stereotyping we overlook individuality.

Suggestion The technique and/or process by which another person is induced to experience and behave in a given way, i.e., as determined by the suggesting agent, e.g., a hypnotist.

Superordinate goal A goal desired by two or more groups but which can only be achieved through the groups acting together, not by any single group on its own.

Sympathetic arousal *see* **Activation**.

Systematic processing Thorough, detailed processing of information (e.g., attention to the arguments contained in a persuasive message); this kind of processing relies on ability and effort.

Theory A set of abstract concepts (i.e., **constructs**) together with propositions about how those constructs are related to one another.

Theory of planned behaviour The extension of the theory of reasoned action. Besides attitudes and subjective norms, perceived behavioural control is outlined as the third important predictor of behaviour.

Theory of reasoned action The most important classic theory of the relationship between attitude and behaviour. The theory assumes that attitudes combine with subjective norms to influence a person's behaviour.

Three-component model of attitudes This model assumes that an attitude is a combination of three conceptually distinguishable reactions to a certain object: affective, cognitive and conative/behavioural reactions.

True randomized experiment An experiment in which subjects are allocated to the different conditions of the experiment on a random basis.

Universality Psychobiological notion assuming that evolved behavioural mechanisms should be found all over the world, independent of culture (although culturally determined modifications are always considered possible).

Unobtrusive measures (*also called* **non-reactive measures**) Measures that the subject is not aware of, and which therefore cannot influence his or her behaviour.

Utilitarianism The doctrine that the determining condition of individual and social action is the (expectation of the) usefulness of its consequences (psychological utilitarianism). The doctrine that the aim of all social action should be the greatest happiness of the greatest number (ethical utilitarianism).

Validity   A measure is valid if it measures precisely what it is supposed to measure.

Variable   The term used to refer to the measurable representation of a construct (*see also*

independent variable *and* dependent variable, *above*).

Völkerpsychologie   (German = psychology of peoples)   An early (nineteenth- to twentieth-century) form of a historical and comparative socio-cultural psychology dealing with the cultural products (language, myth, custom etc.) resulting from social interaction.

References

Abeles, R.P. (1976) Relative deprivation, rising expectations and black militancy. *Journal of Social Issues*, 32, 119–37.

Aboud, F.E. (1988) *Children and Prejudice*. Oxford: Blackwell.

Aboud, F.E. (1989) Disagreements between friends. *International Journal of Behavioural Development*, 12, 495–508.

Abrams, D. and Hogg, M. (1988) Comments on the motivational status of self-esteem in social identity and intergroup discussion. *European Journal of Social Psychology*, 18, 317–34.

Abramson, L.Y., Seligman, M.E.P. and Teasdale, J. (1978) Learned helplessness in humans: critique and reformulation. *Journal of Abnormal Psychology*, 87, 49–74.

Abric, J.C. (1994) *Pratiques sociales et représentations*. Paris: Presses Universitaires de France.

Ader, R. and Cohen, N. (1993) Psychoneuroimmunology: conditioning and stress. *Annual Review of Psychology*, 44, 53–85.

Adler, N. and Matthews, K. (1994) Health psychology: why do some people get sick and some stay well? *Annual Review of Psychology*, 45, 229–59.

Adorno, T.W., Frenkel-Brunswick, E., Levinson, D.J. and Sanford, R.N. (1950) *The Authoritarian Personality*. New York: Harper.

Agassi, J. (1963) *Towards a Historiography of Science*. The Hague: Mouton.

Ainsworth, M.D.S., Blehar, M., Waters, E. and Wall, E. (1978) *Patterns of Attachment*. Hillsdale, NJ: Erlbaum.

Ajzen, I. (1991) The theory of planned behaviour. *Organizational Behavior and Human Decision Processes*, 50, 179–211.

Ajzen, I. and Fishbein, M. (1970) The prediction of behavior from attitudinal and normative variables. *Journal of Experimental Social Psychology*, 6, 466–87.

Ajzen, I. and Fishbein, M. (1977) Attitude–behavior relations: a theoretical analysis and review of empirical research. *Psychological Bulletin*, 84, 888–918.

Ajzen, I. and Fishbein, M. (1980) *Understanding Attitudes and Predicting Social Behavior*. Englewood Cliffs, NJ: Prentice-Hall.

Ajzen, I. and Madden, T.J. (1986) Prediction of goal-directed behavior: attitudes, intentions, and perceived behavioral control. *Journal of Experimental Social Psychology*, 22, 453–74.

Akhtar, N., Dunham, F. and Dunham, P.J. (1991) Directive interactions and early vocabulary development: the role of joint attentional focus. *Journal of Child Language*, 18, 41–9.

Alba, J. W. and Hasher, L. (1983) Is memory schematic? *Psychological Bulletin*, 93, 203–31.

Alberts, J.C. (1986) The role of couples' communications in relational development: a content analysis of courtship talk in Harlequin romance novels. *Communication Quarterly*, 34, 127–42.

Aldag, R.J. and Fuller, S.R. (1993) Beyond fiasco: a reappraisal of the groupthink phenomenon and a new model of group decision making processes. *Psychological Bulletin*, 113, 533–52.

Allen, V.L. (1965) Situational factors in conformity. In L. Berkowitz (ed.), *Advances in Experimental Social Psychology* (vol. 2, pp. 133–75), New York: Academic Press.

Allen, V.L. (1975) Social support for nonconformity. In L. Berkowitz (ed.), *Advances in Experimental Social Psychology* (vol. 8, pp. 1–43), New York: Academic Press.

Allen, V.L. and Bragg, B.W.E. (1965) The generalization of nonconformity within a homogeneous content dimension. Unpublished manuscript, cited in V.L. Allen (1975).

Allen, V.L. and Levine, J.M. (1968) Social support, dissent and conformity. *Sociometry*, 31, 138–49.

Allen, V.L. and Levine, J.M. (1969) Consensus and conformity. *Journal of Experimental Social Psychology*, 4, 389–99.

Allen, V.L. and Levine, J.M. (1971) Social support and conformity: the role of independent assessment of reality. *Journal of Experimental Social Psychology*, 7, 48–58.

Allen, V.L. and Wilder, D.A. (1972) Social support in absentia: effect of an absentee partner on conformity.

Unpublished manuscript, cited in V.L. Allen (1975).

Alloy, L.B. (1982) The role of perceptions and attributions for response-outcome noncontingency in learned helplessness. A commentary and discussion. *Journal of Personality*, 50, 443–79.

Alloy, L.B. and Tabachnik, N. (1984) Assessment of covariation by humans and animals: the joint influence of prior expectations and current situational information. *Psychological Review*, 91, 112–49.

Allport, F.H. (1924) *Social Psychology*. Boston: Houghton Mifflin.

Allport, G.W. (1935) Attitudes. In C.M. Murchison (ed.), *Handbook of Social Psychology* (pp. 792–844), Worcester, MA: Clark University Press.

Allport, G.W. (1954) *The Nature of Prejudice*. Reading, MA: Addison-Wesley.

Altman, I. (1975) *The Environment and Social Behavior*. Monterey, CA: Brooks-Cole.

Altman, I. and Taylor, D. (1973) *Social Penetration: the development of interpersonal relationships*. New York: Holt, Rinehart & Winston.

Amir, Y. (1976) The role of intergroup contact in change of prejudice and ethnic relations. In P.A. Katz (ed.), *Towards the Elimination of Racism*. New York: Pergamon.

Amoroso, D.M. and Walters, R.H. (1969) Effects of anxiety and socially mediated anxiety reduction on paired-associate learning. *Journal of Personality and Social Psychology*, 11, 4, 388–96.

Andersen, S.M. and Klatzky, R.L. (1987) Traits and social stereotypes: levels of categorization in person perception. *Journal of Personality and Social Psychology*, 53, 235–46.

Anderson, C.A. (1983) The causal structure of situations: the generation of plausible causal attributions as a function of the type of event situation. *Journal of Experimental Social Psychology*, 19, 185–203.

Anderson, C.A. (1989) Temperature and aggression: ubiquitous effects of heat on occurrence of human violence. *Psychological Bulletin*, 106, 74–96.

Anderson, C.A. (1991) Attributions as decisions: a two stage information processing model. In S.L. Zelen (ed.), *New Models – New Extensions of Attribution Theory* (pp. 12–54), New York: Springer-Verlag.

Anderson, C.A., Lepper, M.R. and Ross, L. (1980) Perseverance of social theories: the role of explanation in the persistence of discredited information. *Journal of Personality and Social Psychology*, 39, 1037–49.

Anderson, C.A. and Sedikides, C. (1991) Thinking about people: contributions of a typological alternative to associationistic and dimensional models of person perception. *Journal of Personality and Social Psychology*, 60, 203–17.

Anderson, J.R. (1980) *Cognitive Psychology and its Implications*. San Francisco, CA: Freeman.

Anderson, N.H. (1981) *Foundations of Information Integration Theory*. New York: Academic Press.

Anderson, N.H. and Hubert, S. (1963) Effects of concomitant verbal recall on order effects in personality impression formation. *Journal of Verbal Learning and Verbal Behavior*, 2, 379–91.

Archer, J. (1988) *The Behavioural Biology of Aggression*. Cambridge and New York: Cambridge University Press.

Archer, J. (1994) Violence between men. In J. Archer (ed.), *Male Violence* (pp. 121–40), London and New York: Routledge.

Archer, J. and Huntingford, F.A. (1994) Game theory models and the escalation of animal fights. In M. Potegal and J.F. Knutson (eds), *The Dynamics of Aggression: biological and social processes in dyads and groups* (pp. 3–31), Hillsdale, NJ: Lawrence Erlbaum.

Arcuri, L. (1985) *Conoscenza sociale e processi psicologi*. Bologna: il Mulino.

Argyle, M. (1967) *The Psychology of Interpersonal Behavior*. Harmondsworth: Penguin Books.

Argyle, M. (1975) *Bodily Communication*. London: Methuen.

Argyle, M. and Dean, J. (1965) Eye-contact, distance and affiliation. *Sociometry*, 28, 289–304.

Argyle, M. and Henderson, M. (1985) *The Anatomy of Relationships*. Harmondsworth: Penguin Books.

Aristotle (1932 edn) *The Rhetoric of Aristotle* [335–22 BC] (trans. L. Cooper). Englewood Cliffs, NJ: Prentice-Hall.

Arnold, M.B. (1960) *Emotion and Personality, vol. 1: psychological aspects*. New York: Columbia University Press.

Aron, A., Aron, E.N. and Smollan, D. (1992) Inclusion of the other in the self scale and the structure of interpersonal closeness. *Journal of Personality and Social Psychology*, 63, 596–612.

Aron, A., Aron, E.N., Tudor, M. and Nelson, G. (1991) Close relationships as including the other in the self. *Journal of Personality and Social Psychology*, 60, 241–53.

Aronson, E., Brewer, M.B. and Carlsmith, J.M. (1985) Experimentation in social psychology. In G. Lindzey and E. Aronson (eds), *Handbook of Social Psychology*, 3rd edn (vol. 1, pp. 441–86), New York: Random House.

Aronson, E., Ellsworth, P.C., Carlsmith, J.M. and Gonzales, M.H. (1976) *Methods of Research in Social Psychology*, 2nd edn. New York: McGraw-Hill.

Aronson, E. and Mills, J. (1959) The effects of severity of initiation on liking for a group. *Journal of Abnormal and Social Psychology*, 59, 177–81.

Asch, S.E. (1946) Forming impressions of personality. *Journal of Abnormal and Social Psychology*, 41, 258–90.

Asch, S.E. (1951) Effects of group pressure on the modification and distortion of judgements. In H. Guetzkow (ed.), *Groups, Leadership and Men*, Pittsburgh: Carnegie.

Asch, S.E. (1952) *Social Psychology*. New York: Prentice-Hall.

Asch, S.E. (1955) Opinions and social pressure. *Scientific American*, 193, 31–5.

Asch, S.E. (1956) Studies of independence and conformity: a minority of one against a unanimous majority. *Psychological Monographs*, 70 (9, whole no. 416).

Ash, M.G. (1985) Gestalt Psychology: origins in Germany and reception in the United States. In C. Buxton (ed.), *Points of View in the Modern History of Psychology* (pp. 293–344), New York: Academic Press.

Athanasiou, R. and Yoshioka, G.A. (1973) The spatial character of friendship formation. *Environment and Behavior*, vol. 5, pp. 43–65.

Atkins, C.J., Kaplan, R.M. and Toshiman, M.T. (1991) Close relationships in the epidemiology of cardiovascular disease. In W.H. Jones and D. Perlman (eds), *Advances in Personal Relationships* (vol. 3, pp. 207–32), London: Jessica Kingsley.

Augoustinos, M. and Innes, J.M. (1990) Towards an integration of social representations and social schema theory. *British Journal of Social Psychology*, 29, 213–321.

Averill, J.R. (1980) A constructivist view of emotion. In R. Plutchik and H. Kellerman (eds), *Emotion. Theory, Research, and Experience* (pp. 305–40), New York: Academic Press.

Averill, J.R. (1982) *Anger and Aggression. An essay on emotion*. New York: Springer.

Bagozzi, R.P. and Burnkraut, R.E. (1979) Attitude organization and the attitude–behavior relationship. *Journal of Personality and Social Psychology*, 37, 913–29.

Bagozzi, R.P. and Burnkraut, R.E. (1985) Attitude organization and the attitude–behavior relation: a reply to Dillon and Kumar. *Journal of Personality and Social Psychology*, 49, 47–57.

Baker, N.D. and Nelson, K.E. (1984) Recasting and related conversational techniques for triggering syntactic advances by young children. *First Language*, 5, 3–32.

Baker-Miller, J.B. and Mothner, E. (1981) Psychological consequences of sexual inequality. In E. Howell and M. Bates (eds), *Women and Mental Health*, New York: Basic.

Baldwin, J. and McConville, M. (1979) *Jury Trials*. Oxford: Clarendon Press.

Bales, R.F. (1950) *Interaction Process Analysis: a method for the study of small groups*. Chicago: Chicago University Press.

Bales, R.F. and Slater, P.E. (1955) Role differentiation in small decision-making groups. In T. Parson and R.F. Bales (eds), *Family, Socialization and Interaction Process*. Glencoe: Free Press.

Bandura, A. (1973) *Aggression: a social learning analysis*. Englewood Cliffs, NJ: Prentice-Hall.

Bandura, A. (1977) *Social Learning Theory*. Englewood Cliffs, NJ: Prentice-Hall.

Bandura, A. (1986) *Social Foundations of Thought and Action*. Englewood Cliffs, NJ: Prentice-Hall.

Bandura, A., Ross, D., and Ross, S.A. (1961) Transmission of aggression through imitation of aggressive models. *Journal of Abnormal and Social Psychology*, 63, 575–82.

Bandura, A., Ross, D., and Ross, S.A. (1963) Imitation of film-mediated aggressive models. *Journal of Abnormal and Social Psychology*, 66, 3–11.

Bargh, J.A. and Pietromonaco, P. (1982) Automatic information processing and social perception: the influence of trait information presented outside of conscious awareness on impression formation. *Journal of Abnormal and Social Psychology*, 43, 437–49.

Bargh, J.A. and Thein, R.D. (1985) Individual construct accessibility, person memory, and the recall–judgement link. The case of information overload. *Journal of Personality and Social Psychology*, 49, 1129–46.

Barker, R.G. (1987) Prospecting in environmental psychology: Oskaloosa revisited. In D. Stokols and I. Altman (eds), *Handbook of Environmental Psychology* (vol. 2, pp. 1413–32), Chichester: John Wiley.

Barker, R.G. and Schoggen, P. (1973) *Qualities of Community Life*. London: Jossey-Bass.

Baron, R.A. (1970) *Anonymity, de-individuation and aggression*. Unpublished doctoral dissertation, University of Minnesota.

Baron, R.A. (1971) Exposure to an aggressive model and apparent probability of retaliation as determinants of adult aggressive behavior. *Journal of Experimental Social Psychology*, 7, 343–55.

Baron, R.A. (1977) *Human Aggression*. New York: Plenum Press.

Baron, R.A. (1987) Effects of negative ions on interpersonal attraction: evidence for intensification. *Journal of Personality and Social Psychology*, 52, 547–53.

Baron, R.A., Baron, P.H. and Miller, N. (1973) The relation between distraction and persuasion. *Psychological Bulletin*, 80, 310–23.

Baron, R.A. and Bell, P.A. (1975) Aggression and heat: mediating effects of prior provocation and exposure to an aggressive model. *Journal of Personality and Social Psychology*, 31, 825–32.

Baron, R.A. and Bell, P.A. (1976) Aggression and heat: the influence of ambient temperature, negative affect, and a cooling drink on physical aggression. *Journal of Personality and Social Psychology*, 33, 245–55.

Baron, R.A. and Richardson, D.R. (1994) *Human Aggression*, 2nd edn. New York: Plenum.

Baron, R.S., Cutrona, C.E., Hicklin, D., Russell, D.W. and Lubaroff, D.M. (1990) Social support and immune function among spouses of cancer patients. *Journal of Personality and Social Psychology*, 59, 344–52.

Baron, R.S., Kerr, N.L. and Miller, N. (1993) *Group Process, Group Decision, Group Action*. Milton Keynes: Open University Press.

Baroni, M.R. and Axia, G. (1989) Children's meta-pragmatic abilities and the identification of polite and impolite requests. *First Language*, 9, 285–97.

Barrett, M., Harris, M. and Chasin, J. (1991) Early lexical development and maternal speech: a comparison of children's initial and subsequent uses of words. *Journal of Child Language*, 18, 21–40.

Barrett, M. and Short, J. (1992) Images of European people in a group of 5–10 year old English school children. *British Journal of Developmental Psychology*, 10, 339–63.

Barrows, S. (1981) *Distorting Mirrors: visions of the crowd in the late nineteenth century France*. New Haven: Yale University Press.

Barsalou, L.W. (1985) Ideals, central tendency, and frequency of instantiation as determinants of graded structure in categories. *Journal of Experimental Psychology: Learning, Memory, and Cognition*, 11, 629–54.

Barsalou, L.W. (1991) Deriving categories to achieve goals. In Posner (ed.), *The Psychology of Learning and Motivation* (vol. 27, pp. 1–64), New York: Academic Press.

Bar-Tal, D., Nadler, A. and Blechman, N. (1980) The relationship between Israeli children's helping behaviour and their perception of parents' socialisation practices. *Journal of Social Psychology*, 111, 159–67.

Bartlett, F. (1932) *Remembering – A study in experimental social psychology*. Cambridge: Cambridge University Press.

Bass, B.M. (1965) *A Program of Exercises in Management and Organizational Psychology*. Pittsburgh: Management Development Associates.

Bass, B.M. (1985) *Leadership and Performance Expectations*. New York: Free Press.

Bateman, A.J. (1948) Intra-sexual selection in Drosophila. *Heredity*, 2, 349–68.

Bates, E. (1979) *The Emergence of Symbols*. New York: Academic Press.

Batson, C.D. (1983) Sociobiology and the role of

religion in promoting prosocial behaviour: an alternative view. *Journal of Personality and Social Psychology*, 45, 1380–5.

Batson, C.D. (1987) Prosocial motivation: is it ever truly altruistic? In L. Berkowitz (ed.), *Advances in Experimental Social Psychology* (vol. 20, pp. 65–122), San Diego, CA: Academic Press.

Batson, C.D., Batson, J.G., Griffit, C.A., Barrientos, S., Brandt, J.R., Sprengelmeyer, P. and Bayly, M.J. (1989) Negative state relief and the empathy–altruism hypothesis. *Journal of Personality and Social Psychology*, 56, 922–33.

Batson, C.D., Duncan, B.D., Ackerman, P., Buckley, P. and Birch, K. (1981) Is empathic emotion a source of altruistic motivation? *Journal of Personality and Social Psychology*, 40, 290–302.

Batson, C.D., Dyck, J.L., Brandt, J.R., Batson, J.G., Powell, A.L., McMaster, M.R. and Griffit, C. (1988) Five studies testing new egoistic alternatives to the empathy–altruism hypothesis. *Journal of Personality and Social Psychology*, 55, 52–77.

Baucom, D.H., Sayers, S.L. and Duhe, A. (1989) Attributional style and attributional patterns among married couples. *Journal of Personality and Social Psychology*, 56, 596–607.

Baxter, L.A. (1983) Relationship disengagement: an examination of the reversal hypothesis. *Western Journal of Speech Communication*, 47, 85–98.

Baxter, L.A. (1985) Accomplishing relationship disengagement. In S. Duck and D. Perlmann (eds), *Understanding Personal Relationships* (pp. 243–65), Beverly Hills, CA: Sage.

Baxter, L.A. and Wilmot, W.M. (1985) Taboo topics in close relationships. *Journal of Social and Personal Relationships*, 2, 253–69.

Beale, D.A. and Manstead, A.S.R. (1991) Predicting mothers' intentions to limit frequency of infants' sugar intake: testing the theory of planned behavior. *Journal of Applied Social Psychology*, 21, 409–31.

Beauvois, J.-L. (1984) *La psychologie quotidienne*. Paris: Presses Universitaires de France.

Beauvois, J.-L. and Joule, R.V. (in press) *Dissonance and Rationalization*. Hemel Hempstead: Harvester Wheatsheaf.

Beck, A.T., Rush, A.J., Shaw, B.F. and Emery, G. (1979) *Cognitive Therapy of Depression*. New York: Wiley.

Beckmann, J. and Mattenklott, A. (1985) Theorien zur sozialen Urteilsbildung. In D. Frey and M. Irle (eds), *Theorien der Sozialpsychologie* (vol. 3, pp. 211–37), Bern: Huber.

Bell, P.A. and Baron. R.A. (1976) Aggression and heat: the mediating role of negative affect. *Journal of Applied Social Psychology*, 6, 18–30.

Bellezza, F.S. and Bower, G.H. (1981) Person stereotypes and memory for people. *Journal of Personality and Social Psychology*, 41, 856–65.

Belli, R.F. (1989) Influences of misleading postevent information: misinformation, interference and acceptance. *Journal of Experimental Psychology: General*, 118, 72–85.

Bellis, M.A. and Baker, R.R. (1990) Do females promote sperm competition? Data for humans. *Animal Behaviour*, 40, 997–9.

Bem, D.J. (1965) An experimental analysis of self-persuasion. *Journal of Experimental Social Psychology*, 1, 199–218.

Bem, D.J. (1972) Self-perception theory. In L. Berkowitz (ed.), *Advances in Experimental Psychology* (vol. 6, pp. 1–62), New York: Academic Press.

Bem, D.J. and Allen, A. (1974) On predicting some of the people some of the time: the search for cross-situational consistencies in behavior. *Psychological Review*, 81, 506–20.

Bennett, M. (1985/86) Developmental changes in the attribution of dispositional features. *Current Psychological Research and Reviews*, 4, 323–9.

Bennett, M. (1993) Introduction. In M. Bennett (ed.), *The Child as Psychologist. An introduction to the development of social cognition* (pp. 1–25), New York: Harvester Wheatsheaf.

Bennett, W.L. and Feldman, M.S. (1981) *Reconstructing Reality in the Courtroom: justice and judgement in American culture*. New Brunswick: Rutgers University Press.

Bentler, P.M. and Speckart, G. (1979) Models of attitude–behavior relations. *Psychological Review*, 86, 452–64.

Bentler, P.M. and Speckart, G. (1981) Attitudes 'cause' behaviors: a structural equation analysis. Models of attitude–behavior relations. *Journal of Personality and Social Psychology*, 40, 226–38.

Berger, C.R. (1979) Beyond initial interaction: uncertainty, understanding, and the development of interpersonal relationships. In H. Giles and R. St Clair (eds), *Language and Social Psychology* (pp. 122–44), Oxford: Basil Blackwell.

Berger, C.R. (1994) Power, dominance and social interaction. In M.L. Knapp and G.R. Miller (eds), *Handbook of Interpersonal Communications* (pp. 450–507), Thousand Oaks, CA: Sage.

Berger, J., Rosenholtz, S.J. and Zelditch, J. (1980) Status organizing processes. In A. Inkeles, N.J. Smelser and R. Turner (eds), *Annual Review of Sociology*. Palo Alto, CA: Annual Reviews Inc.

Berger, J. and Zelditch, J. (1993) *Theoretical Research Programs*. Stanford, CA: Stanford University Press.

Berkman, L.F. and Syme, S.L. (1979) Social networks, host resistance, and mortality: a nine year follow-up study of Alameda County residents. *American Journal of Epidemiology*, 109, 186–204.

Berkowitz, L. (1962) *Aggression: a social psychological analysis*. New York: McGraw-Hill.

Berkowitz, L. (1964) Aggressive cues in aggressive behavior and hostility catharsis. *Psychological Review*, 71, 104–22.

Berkowitz, L. (1969) The frustration–aggression hypothesis revisited. In L. Berkowitz (ed.), *Roots of Aggression* (pp. 1–28), New York: Atherton Press.

Berkowitz, L. (1974) Some determinants of impulsive aggression: the role of mediated associations with reinforcements of aggression. *Psychological Review*, 81, 165–76.

Berkowitz, L. (1978) Decreased helpfulness with increased group size through lessening the effects of the needy individual's dependency. *Journal of Personality*, 46, 299–310.

Berkowitz, L. (1983) The experience of anger as a parallel process in the display of impulsive, 'angry' aggression. In R.G. Green and E.I. Donnerstein (eds), *Aggression, Theoretical and Empirical Reviews* (vol. 1), New York: Academic Press.

Berkowitz, L. (1989) The frustration–aggression hypothesis: an examination and reformulation. *Psychological Bulletin*, 106, 59–73.

Berkowitz, L. (1990) On the formation and regulation of anger and aggression – a cognitive-neoassociationistic analysis. *American Psychologist*, 45, 494–503.

Berkowitz, L. (1993) *Aggression: its causes, consequences and control* (pp. 103–33). New York: McGraw-Hill.

Berkowitz, L., Cochran, S. and Embree, M. (1981) Physical pain and the goal of aversively stimulated aggression. *Journal of Personality and Social Psychology*, 40, 687–700.

Berkowitz, L. and Heimer, K. (1989) On the construction of the anger experience: aversive events and negative priming in the formation of feelings. In L. Berkowitz (ed.), *Advances in Experimental Social Psychology* (vol. 22, pp. 1–37), San Diego: Academic Press.

Berkowitz, L. and Knurek, D.A. (1969) Label-mediated hostility generalization. *Journal of Personality and Social Psychology*, 13, 200–6.

Berkowitz, L. and LePage, A. (1967) Weapons as aggression-eliciting stimuli. *Journal of Personality and Social Psychology*, 7, 202–7.

Berndt, T.J. and Heller, K.A. (1985) Measuring children's personality attributions. In S.R. Yussen (ed.), *The Growth of Reflection in Children* (pp. 38–60), New York: Academic Press.

Berrill, M. and Arsenault, M. (1982) Mating behavior of the green shore crab *Carcinus maenas*. *Bulletin of Marine Science*, 32, 632–8.

Berscheid, E. (1985) Interpersonal attraction. In G.

Lindzey and E. Aronson (eds), *Handbook of Social Psychology* (3rd edn, vol. 2, pp. 413–84). New York, Random House.

Berscheid, E. (1991) The emotion-in-relationships model: reflections and update. In A. Ortony, W. Kessen, and F.I.M. Craik (eds), *Memories, Thoughts and Emotions: essays in honor of George Mandler* (pp. 323–35), Hillsdale, NJ: Lawrence Erlbaum.

Berscheid, E. (1992) A glance back at a quarter century of social psychology. *Journal of Personality and Social Psychology*, 63, 525–33.

Berscheid, E. and Walster, E. (1969a) *Interpersonal Attraction*. Reading, MA: Addison-Wesley.

Berscheid, E. and Walster, E. (1969b) A little bit about love. In T. Huston (ed.), *Foundations of Interpersonal Attraction* (pp. 356–82), New York: Academic Press.

Berscheid, E. and Walster, E.H. (1978) *Interpersonal Attraction* (2nd edn). Reading, MA: Addison-Wesley.

Berti, A.E. and Bombi, A.S. (1988) *The Child's Construction of Economics*. Cambridge: Cambridge University Press.

Bertram, B.C.R. (1975) Social factors influencing reproduction in wild lions. *Journal of Zoology*, 177, 463–82.

Bettencourt, B.A., Brewer, M.B., Croak, M.R. and Miller, N. (1992) Cooperation and the reduction of intergroup bias: the role of reward structure and social orientation. *Journal of Experimental Social Psychology*, 28, 301–9.

Betzig, L. (1992) Roman polygyny. *Ethology and Sociobiology*, 13, 309–49.

Bickman, L. and Henchy, T. (eds) (1972) *Beyond the Laboratory: field research in social psychology*. New York: McGraw-Hill.

Bierbrauer, G. (1979) Why did he do it? Attribution of obedience and the phenomenon of dispositional bias. *European Journal of Social Psychology*, 9, 67–84.

Bierhoff, H.W. (1983) Wie hilfreich ist der Mensch? *Bild der Wissenschaft*, Dezember, 118–26.

Bierhoff, H.W. (1990) *Psychologie hilfreichen Verhaltens*. Stuttgart: Kolhammer.

Bierhoff, H.W. (1991) Attribution of responsibility and helpfulness. In L. Montada and H.W. Bierhoff (eds), *Altruism in Social Systems* (pp. 105–29), Lewiston, NY: Hogrefe.

Bierhoff, H.W. (1994) On the interface between social support and prosocial behavior: methodological and theoretical implications. In F. Nestmann and K. Hurrelmann (eds), *Social Networks and Social Support in Childhood and Adolescence* (pp. 159–67), Berlin: de Gruyter.

Bierhoff, H.W., Buck, J. and Klein, R. (1986) Social context and perceived justice. In H.W. Bierhoff, R.L. Cohen and J.P. Greenberg (eds), *Justice in Social Relations* (pp. 165–85), New York: Plenum.

Bierhoff, H.W., Klein, R. and Kramp, P. (1990) *Hemmschwellen zur Hilfeleistung*. Aachen: Mainz.

Bierhoff, H.W., Klein, R. and Kramp, P. (1991) Evidence for the altruistic personality from data on accident research. *Journal of Personality*, 59, 263–80.

Bierhoff, H.W., Lensing, L. and Kloft, A. (1988) Hilfreiches Verhalten in Abhängigkeit von Verghen und positiver Verstärkung. In H.W. Bierhoff and L. Montada (eds) *Altruismus*, (pp. 154–78), Goettingen: Hogrefe.

Bijstra, J.P., Jackson, S. and Van Geert, P. (1991) Progress to conservation: conflict or correct answer? *European Journal of Psychology of Education*, 6, 291–301.

Billig, M. (1976) *Social Psychology and Intergroup Relations*. London: Academic Press.

Binet, A. and Henri, V. (1894) De la suggestibilité naturelle chez les enfants. *Revue Philosophique*, 38, 337–47.

Birns, B. and Hay, D.F. (eds) (1988) *The Different Faces of Motherhood*. New York: Plenum.

Bjorkqvist, K., Osterman, K. and Lagerspetz, K.M.J. (1994) Sex differences in covert aggression among adults. *Aggressive Behavior*, 20, 27–33.

Black, S.L. and Bevan, S. (1992) At the movies with Buss and Durkee: a natural experiment on film violence. *Aggressive Behavior*, 18, 37–45.

Blackburn, R. (1993) *The Psychology of Criminal Conduct: theory, research and practice*. Chichester: John Wiley.

Blakar, R.M. (1985) Towards a theory of communication in terms of preconditions: a conceptual framework and some empirical explorations. In H. Giles and R.N. St Clair (eds), *Recent Advances in Language, Communication and Social Psychology* (pp. 10–40), London: Erlbaum.

Blass, T. (1992) The social psychology of Stanley Milgram. In M.P. Zanna (ed.), *Advances in Experimental Social Psychology* (vol. 25, pp. 277–329), New York: Academic Press.

Blaye, A., Light, P. and Rubtsov, V. (1992) Collaborative learning at the computer: how social processes 'interface' with human–computer interaction. *European Journal of Psychology of Education*, 7, 257–67.

Blazer, D.G. (1982) Social support and mortality in an elderly community population. *American Journal of Epidemiology*, 115, 684–94.

Bless, H., Bohner, G., Schwarz, N. and Strack, F. (1990) Mood and persuasion: a cognitive response analysis. *Personality and Social Psychology Bulletin*, 16, 331–45.

Blumenthal, M., Kahn, R.L., Andrews, F.M. and Head, K.B. (1972) *Justifying Violence: the attitudes of American men*. Ann Arbor: Institute for Social Research.

Blumer, H. (1946) Collective behavior. In A.M. Lee (ed.), *New Outlines of the Principles of Sociology* (pp. 165-220), New York: Barnes & Noble.

Bohner, G., Bless, H., Schwarz, N. and Strack, F. (1988) What triggers causal attributions? The impact of subjective probability. *European Journal of Social Psychology*, 18, 335-46.

Bohner, G., Moskowitz, G.B. and Chaiken, S. (1995) The interplay of heuristic and systematic processing of social information. In W. Stroebe and M. Hewstone (eds), *European Review of Social Psychology* (vol. 6, pp. 33-68), Chichester: Wiley.

Bond, C.F. and Van Leeuwen, M.D. (1991) Can a part be greater than a whole? On the relationship between primary and meta-analytic evidence. *Basic and Applied Social Psychology*, 12, 33-40.

Bonnes, M. (ed.) (1993) *Perception and Evaluation of Urban Environmental Quality: a pluridisciplinary approach in the European context.* ENEL.

Bordens, K.S. and Horowitz, I.A. (1985) Joinder of criminal offences: a review of the legal and psychological literature. *Law and Human Behavior*, 9, 339-53.

Bourhis, R.Y. and Giles, H. (1977) The language of intergroup distinctiveness. In H. Giles (ed.), *Language, Ethnicity and Intergroup Relations*, London: Academic Press.

Bourhis, R.Y., Giles, H., Leyens, J.-P. and Tajfel, H. (1978) Psycholinguistic distinctiveness: language divergence in Belgium. In H. Giles and R. St Clair (eds), *Language and Social Psychology*, Oxford: Basil Blackwell.

Bower, G.H. (1981) Emotional mood and memory. *American Psychologist*, 36, 129-48.

Bowlby, J. (1969) *Attachment and Loss, vol 1: Attachment.* London: Hogarth.

Bowlby, J. (1988) *A Secure Base. Parent–child attachment and healthy human development.* New York: Basic Books.

Box, S. (1972) *Deviance, Reality and Society.* London: Holt, Rinehart & Winston.

Brackwede, D. (1980) Das Bogus-Pipeline-Paradigma: Eine Übersicht über bisherige experimentelle Ergebnisse. *Zeitschrift für Sozialpsychologie*, 11, 56-9.

Bradac, J.J., Friedman, E. and Giles, H. (1986) A social approach to propositional communication: speakers lie to hearers. In G. McGregor (ed.), *Speaking for Hearers* (pp. 127-51), Oxford: Pergamon.

Bradac, J.J., Tardy, C.H. and Hosman, L.A. (1980) Disclosure styles and a hint at their genesis. *Human Communication Research*, 6, 228-38.

Bradac, J.J., Wiemann, J.M. and Schaefer, K. (1994) The language of control in interpersonal communication. In J.A. Daly and J.M. Wiemann (eds), *Strategic Interpersonal Communication* (pp. 91-108), Hillsdale, NJ: Erlbaum.

Bradbury, T.N. and Fincham, F.D. (1990) Attributions in marriage: review and critique. *Psychological Bulletin*, 107, 3-33.

Bradbury, T.N. and Fincham, F.D. (1992) Attributions and behavior in marital interaction. *Journal of Personality and Social Psychology*, 63, 613-28.

Brandstädter, J. (1990) Development as a personal and cultural construction. In G.R. Semin and K.J. Gergen (eds), *Everyday Understanding: social and scientific implications* (pp. 83-107), Newbury Park, CA: Sage.

Branthwaite, A., Doyle, S. and Lightbown, N. (1979) The balance between fairness and discrimination. *European Journal of Social Psychology*, 9, 149-63.

Brantingham, P.L. and Brantingham, P.J. (1993) Nodes, paths and edges: considerations on the complexity of crime and the physical environment. *Journal of Environmental Psychology*, 13, 3-28.

Breckler, S.J. (1984) Empirical validation of affect, behavior, and cognition as distinct components of attitude. *Journal of Personality and Social Psychology*, 47, 1191-1205.

Breckler, S.J. (1993) Emotion and attitude change. In M. Lewis and J.M. Haviland (eds), *Handbook of Emotions* (pp. 461-74), New York: Guilford Press.

Breckler, S.J. and Wiggins, E.C. (1989) Affect versus evaluation in the structure of attitudes. *Journal of Experimental Social Psychology*, 25, 253-71.

Breckler, S.J. and Wiggins, E.C. (1991) Cognitive responses in persuasion: affective and evaluative determinants. *Journal of Experimental Social Psychology*, 27, 180-220.

Bremner, J.G. (1994) *Infancy*, 2nd edn. Oxford: Blackwell.

Bretherton, I. (1992) The origins of attachment theory: John Bowlby and Mary Ainsworth. *Developmental Psychology*, 28, 759-75.

Brewer, M.B. (1979) Ingroup bias in the minimal intergroup situation: a cognitive motivational analysis. *Psychological Bulletin*, 86, 301-24.

Brewer, M.B. and Miller, N. (1984) Beyond the contact hypothesis: theoretical perspectives on desegregation. In N. Miller and M.B. Brewer (eds), *Groups in Contact: the psychology of desegregation*, New York: Academic Press.

Brickman, P., Rabinowitz, V.C., Karuza, J., Coates, D., Cohn, E. and Kidder, L. (1982) Models of helping and coping. *American Psychologist*, 37, 368-84.

Brouwer, D., Gerritsen, M. and DeHaan, D. (1979) Speech differences between women and men: on the wrong track? *Language in Society*, 8, 33-50.

Brown, G.W. and Harris, T. (1978) *Social Origins of Depressions.* London: Tavistock.

Brown, J.D. and McGill, K.L. (1989) The cost of good fortune: when positive life events produce negative health consequences. *Journal of Personality and Social Psychology*, 57, 1103–10.

Brown, J.R. and Rogers, L.E. (1991) Openness, uncertainty and intimacy: an epistemological reformulation. In N. Coupland, H. Giles and J.M. Wiemann (eds), *'Miscommunication' and Problematic Talk* (pp. 146–65), Thousand Oaks, CA: Sage.

Brown, P. and Fraser, C. (1979) Speech as a marker of situation. In K.R. Scherer and H. Giles (eds), *Social Markers in Speech* (pp. 33–62), Cambridge: Cambridge University Press.

Brown, R. (1965) *Social Psychology*. New York: Macmillan.

Brown, R. (1973) *A First Language*. Cambridge, MA: Harvard University Press.

Brown, R. (1980) The maintenance of conversation. In D.R. Olson (ed.), *The Social Foundations of Language and Thought*, New York: Norton.

Brown, R. and Fish, D. (1983) The psychological causality implicit in language. *Cognition*, 14, 233–74.

Brown, R. and Gilman, A. (1960) The pronouns of power and solidarity. In T. Sebeok (ed.), *Style in Language* (pp. 253–76), Cambridge, MA: MIT Press.

Brown, R.C. and Tedeschi, J.T. (1976) Determinants of perceived aggression. *Journal of Social Psychology*, 100, 77–87.

Brown, R.J. (1978) Divided we fall: an analysis of relations between sections of a factory work-force. In H. Tajfel (ed.), *Differentiation between Social Groups: studies in the social psychology of intergroup relations*, London: Academic Press.

Brown, R.J. (ed.) (1984) Intergroup Processes. *British Journal of Social Psychology*, 23.

Brown, R.J. (1988) *Group Processes: dynamics within and between groups*. Oxford: Blackwell.

Brown, R.J., Condor, S., Matthews, A., Wade, G. and Williams, J.A. (1986) Explaining intergroup differentiation in an individual organization. *Journal of Occupational Psychology*, 59, 273–86.

Brown, R.J. and Deschamps, J.-C. (1980-1) Discrimination entre individus et entre groupes. *Bulletin de Psychologie*, 34, 185–95.

Brown, R.J., Hinkle, S., Ely, P.G., Fox-Cardamore, L., Maras, P. and Taylor, L.A. (1992) Recognising group diversity: individualist–collectivist and autonomous–relational social orientations and their implications for intergroup processes. *British Journal of Social Psychology*, 31, 327–42.

Brown, R.J. and Ross, G.R. (1982) The battle for acceptance: an exploration into the dynamics of intergroup behavior. In H. Tajfel (ed.), *Social Identity and Intergroup Relations* (pp. 155–78), Cambridge: Cambridge University Press.

Brown, R.J. and Smith, A. (1989) Perceptions of and by minority groups: The case of women in academia. *European Journal of Social Psychology*, 19, 61–75.

Brown, R.J., Tajfel, H. and Turner, J.C. (1980) Minimal group situations and inter-group discrimination: comments on the paper by Aschenbrenner and Schaefer. *European Journal of Social Psychology*, 10, 399–414.

Brown, R.J. and Turner, J.C. (1979) The criss-cross categorization effect in intergroup discrimination. *British Journal of Social and Clinical Psychology*, 18, 371–83.

Brown, R.J. and Turner, J.C. (1981) Interpersonal and intergroup behaviour. In J.C. Turner and H. Giles (eds), *Intergroup Behaviour* (pp.33–65), Oxford: Basil Blackwell.

Brown, R.J. and Wade, G.S. (1987) Superordinate goals and intergroup behaviour: the effects of role ambiguity and status on intergroup attitudes and task performance. *European Journal of Social Psychology*, 17, 131–42.

Brown, R.J. and Williams, J.A. (1984) Group identification: the same thing to all people? *Human Relations*, 37, 547–64.

Brown, R.J. and Wootton-Millward, L. (1993) Perceptions of group homogeneity during group formation and change. *Social Cognition*, 11, 126–49.

Bruner, J.S. (1957) On perceptual readiness. *Psychological Review*, 64, 123–52.

Bruner, J.S. (1978) Learning how to do things with words. In J. Bruner and A. Garton (eds), *Human Growth and Development* (pp. 54–66), Oxford: Clarendon.

Bruner, J.S. (1983) The acquisition of pragmatic commitments. In R.M. Golinkoff (ed.), *The Transition from Prelinguistic to Linguistic Communication* (pp. 29–47), Hillsdale, NJ: Erlbaum.

Bruner, J.S. and Goodman, C.D. (1947) Value and need as organizing factors in perception. *Journal of Abnormal and Social Psychology*, 42, 33–44.

Bruner, J.S., Goodnow, J.J. and Austin, G.A. (1956) *A Study of Thinking*. New York: Wiley.

Buchanan G.M. and Seligman, M.E.P. (1995). *Explanatory style*. Hillsdale, New Jersey: Erlbaum.

Buck, R. (1984) *The Communication of Emotion*. New York: Guilford Press.

Buck, R. (1985) Prime theory: an integrated view of motivation and emotion. *Psychological Review*, 92, 389–413.

Buehler, R., Griffin, D. and Ross, M. (1995) It's about time: optimistic predictions in work and love. In W.

Stroebe and M. Hewstone (eds), *European Review of Social Psychology* (vol. 6, pp. 1–32), Chichester: J. Wiley.

Bull, N. (1951) *The Attitude Theory of Emotion*. New York: Neurological and Mental Disease Monographs (no. 81).

Buller, D.B. and Burgoon, J.K. (1994) Deception: strategic and nonstrategic communication. In J.A. Daly and J.M. Wiemann (eds), *Strategic Interpersonal Communication* (pp. 191–224), Hillsdale, NJ: Erlbaum.

Burgoon, J.K. (ed.) (1994) Deceptive communication. Special issue of the *Journal of Language and Social Psychology*.

Burke, P.J. (1967) The development of task and social–emotional role-differentiation. *Sociometry*, 30, 379–92.

Burke, P.J. (1974) Participation and leadership in small groups. *American Sociological Review*, 39, 832–42.

Burnstein, E., Crandall, C. and Kitayama, S. (1994) Some neo-Darwinian decision rules for altruism: weighing cues for inclusive fitness as a function of the biological importance of the decision. *Journal of Personality and Social Psychology*, 67, 773–89.

Burnstein, E. and McCrae, A.V. (1962) Some effects of shared threat and prejudice in racially mixed groups. *Journal of Abnormal and Social Psychology*, 64, 257–63.

Burnstein, E. and Vinokur, A. (1973) Testing two classes of theories about group induced shifts in individual choice. *Journal of Experimental Social Psychology*, 9, 123–37.

Burt, C. (1925) *The Young Delinquent*. London: University of London Press.

Buss, A.H. and Perry, M. (1992) The aggression questionnaire. *Journal of Personality and Social Psychology*, 63, 452–9.

Buss, A.R. (1978) Causes and reasons in attribution theory: a conceptual critique. *Journal of Personality and Social Psychology*, 36, 1311–21.

Buss, A.R. (ed.) (1979) *Psychology in Social Context*. New York: Irvington.

Buss, D.M. (1988) The evolution of human intrasexual competition: tactics of mate attraction. *Journal of Personality and Social Psychology*, 54, 616–28.

Buss, D.M. (1989) Sex differences in human mate preferences: evolutionary hypotheses tested in 37 cultures. *Behavioral and Brain Sciences*, 12, 1–49.

Buss, D.M. (1992) Mate preference mechanisms: consequences for partner choice and intrasexual competition. In J.H. Barkow, L. Cosmides and J. Tooby (eds), *The Adapted Mind: evolutionary psychology and the generation of culture* (pp. 249–66), New York: Oxford University Press.

Buss, D.M. (1994) *The Evolution of Desire*. New York: Basic Books.

Buss, D.M. (1995) Evolutionary psychology: a new paradigm for psychological science. *Psychological Inquiry*, 6, 1–30.

Buss, D.M. and Bedden, L.A. (1990) Derogation of competitors. *Journal of Social and Personal Relationships*, 7, 395–422.

Buss, D.M., Larsen, R.J., Westen, D. and Semmelroth, J. (1992) Sex differences in jealousy: evolution, physiology and psychology. *Psychological Science*, 3, 251–5.

Buss, D.M. and Schmitt, D.P. (1993) Sexual strategies theory: an evolutionary perspective of human mating. *Psychological Review*, 100, 204–32.

Butterfield, H. (1963) *The Whig Interpretation of History*. London: Bell.

Buunk, B.P. (1987) Conditions that promote break-ups as a consequence of extradyadic involvements. *Journal of Social and Clinical Psychology*, 5, 237–50.

Buunk, B.P. (1990) Affiliation and helping interactions within organizations: a critical analysis of the role of social support with regard to occupational stress. In W. Stroebe and M. Hewstone (eds), *European Review of Social Psychology* (vol. 1, pp. 293–322), Chichester: John Wiley.

Buunk, B.P. and Bosman, J. (1985) Attitude similarity and attraction in marital relationships. *Journal of Social Psychology*, 126, 133–4.

Buunk, B.P., Collins, R., VanYperen, N.W., Taylor, S.E. and Dakoff, G. (1990) Upward and downward comparisons: either direction has its ups and downs. *Journal of Personality and Social Psychology*, 59, 1238–49.

Buunk, B.P. and Schaufeli, W.B. (1993) Burnout: a perspective from social comparison theory. In W.B. Schaufeli, C. Maslach and T. Marek (eds), *Professional Burnout: recent developments in theory and research* (pp. 53–69), Washington: Taylor & Francis.

Buunk, B.P. & Van Driel, B. (1989). *Variant lifestyles and relationships*. Newbury Park, CA: Sage Publications.

Buunk, B.P. and VanYperen, N.W. (1991) Referential comparisons, relational comparisons and exchange orientation: their relation to marital satisfaction. *Personality and Social Psychology Bulletin*, 17, 710–18.

Buunk, B.P., VanYperen, N.W., Taylor, S.E. and Collins, R.L. (1991) Social comparison and the drive upward revisited: affiliation as a response to marital stress. *European Journal of Social Psychology*, 21, 529–46.

Byrne, D. (1971) *The Attraction Paradigm*. New York: Academic Press.

Byrne, D., Ervin, C.R. and Lamberth, J. (1970)

Continuity between the experimental study of attraction and real life computer dating. *Journal of Personality and Social Psychology*, 16, 157–65.

Byrne, D., London, O. and Griffit, W. (1968) The effect of topic importance and attitude similarity–dissimilarity on attraction in an intrastranger design. *Psychonomic Science*, 11, 303–13.

Cacioppo, J.T. and Gardner, W.L. (1993) What underlies medical donor attitudes and behavior? *Health Psychology*, 12, 269–71.

Cacioppo, J.T., Klein, D.J., Berntson, G.C. and Hatfield, E. (1993) The psychophysiology of emotion. In M. Lewis and J.M. Haviland (eds), *Handbook of Emotions* (pp. 119–42), New York: Guilford Press.

Cacioppo, J.T. and Petty, R.E. (1979a) Neuromuscular circuits in affect-laden information processing. *Pavlovian Journal of Biological Science*, 14, 177–85.

Cacioppo, J.T. and Petty, R.E. (1979b) Effects of message repetition and position on cognitive responses, recall and persuasion. *Journal of Personality and Social Psychology*, 37, 2181–99.

Cacioppo, J.T. and Petty, R.E. (1982) The need for cognition. *Journal of Personality and Social Psychology*, 42, 116–31.

Cacioppo, J.T. and Petty, R.E. (1985) Central and peripheral routes to persuasion: the role of message repetition. In A. Mitchell and L. Alwitt (eds), *Psychological Processes and Advertising Effects* (pp. 91–111), Hillsdale, NJ: Lawrence Erlbaum Associates.

Cacioppo, J.T., Petty, R.E., Kao, C.F. and Rodriguez, R. (1986) Central and peripheral routes to persuasion: an individual difference perspective. *Journal of Personality and Social Psychology*, 51, 1032–43.

Cacioppo, J.T., Petty, R.E. and Sidera, J. (1982) The effects of a salient self-schema on the evaluation of proattitudinal editorials: top-down vs. bottom-up message processing. *Journal of Experimental Social Psychology*, 18, 324–38.

Cacioppo, J.T., Uchino, B.N., Crites, S.L., Snydersmith, M.A., Smith, G., Berntson, G.C. and Lang, P.J. (1992) Relationship between facial expressiveness and sympathetic activation in emotion: a critical review, with emphasis on modeling underlying mechanisms and individual differences. *Journal of Personality and Social Psychology*, 62, 110–28.

Caddick, B. (1982) Perceived illegitimacy and intergroup relations. In H. Tajfel (ed.), *Social Identity and Intergroup Relations* (pp. 137–54), Cambridge: Cambridge University Press.

Calder, B.J. and Ross, M. (1976) Attitudes: theories and issues. In J.W. Thibaut, J.T. Spence and R.C. Carlson (eds), *Contemporary Topics in Social Psychology* (pp. 3–35), Morristown, NJ: General Learning Press.

Calder, B.J., Ross, M. and Insko, C.A. (1973) Attitude change and attitude attribution: effects of incentive, choice and consequences. *Journal of Personality and Social Psychology*, 25, 84–99.

Camden, C., Motley, M.T. and Wilson, A. (1984) White lies in interpersonal communication: a taxonomy and preliminary investigation of social motivation. *Western Journal of Speech Communication*, 48, 309–25.

Campbell, D.T. (1963) Social attitudes and other acquired behavioral dispositions. In S. Koch (ed.), *Psychology: a study of science* (vol. 6, pp. 94–172), New York: McGraw-Hill.

Campbell, D.T., Kruskal, W. and Wallace, W. (1966) Seating aggregation as an index of attitude. *Sociometry*, 29, 1–15.

Campbell, D.T. and McCandless, B.R. (1951) Ethnocentrism, xenophobia, and personality. *Human Relations*, 4, 185–92.

Camras, L.A., Holland, E.A. and Patterson, M.J. (1993) Facial expression. In M. Lewis and J.M. Haviland (eds), *Handbook of Emotions* (pp. 199–208), New York: Guilford Press.

Cannon, W.B. (1929) *Bodily Changes in Pain, Hunger, Fear and Rage*, 2nd edn. New York: Appleton.

Canter, D. (1982) Psychology and environmental design. In S. Canter and D. Canter (eds), *Psychology in Practice: perspectives on professional psychology*. Chichester: John Wiley.

Canter, D., Jesuino, J.C., Soczka, L. and Stephenson, G.M. (eds) (1987) *Environmental Social Psychology*. London: Kluwer.

Cantor, N. and Mischel, W. (1979) Prototypes in person perception. In L. Berkowitz (ed.), *Advances in Experimental Social Psychology* (vol. 12, pp. 3–52), New York: Academic Press.

Caporeal, L.R., Lukaszewski, M.P. and Culbertson, G.H. (1983) Secondary baby talk: judgements by institutionalized elderly and their caregivers. *Journal of Personality and Social Psychology*, 44, 746–54.

Cappella, J.N. and Palmer, M. (1993) The structure and organization of verbal and non-verbal behavior: data for models of production. In H. Giles and P. Robinson (eds), *Handbook of Language and Social Psychology* (pp. 141–61), Chichester and New York: Wiley.

Carey, M. (1978) Does civil inattention exist in pedestrian passing? *Journal of Personality and Social Psychology*, 36, 1185–93.

Carlson, M., Charlin, V. and Miller, N. (1988) Positive mood and helping behavior: a test of six hypotheses. *Journal of Personality and Social Psychology*, 55, 211–29.

Carlson, M. and Miller, N. (1987) Explanation of the

relation between negative mood and helping. *Psychological Bulletin*, 102, 91–108.

Carlson, M., Marcus-Newhall, A. and Miller, N. (1990) Effects of situational aggression cues: a quantitative review. *Journal of Personality and Social Psychology*, 58, 622–33.

Cartwright, D. (1979) Contemporary social psychology in historical perspective. *Social Psychology Quarterly*, 42, 82–93.

Cartwright, D. and Zander, A. (1968) Pressures to uniformity in groups. In D. Cartwright and A. Zander (eds), *Group Dynamics: research and theory*, 3rd edn, New York: Harper & Row.

Carugati, F. and Gilly, M. (1993) The multiple sides of the same tool: cognitive development as a matter of social constructions and meanings. *European Journal of Psychology of Education*, 8, 345–54.

Carver, C.S. (1975) Physical aggression as a function of objective self-awareness and attitudes towards punishment. *Journal of Experimental Social Psychology*, 11, 510–19.

Cate, R.M., Lloyd, S.A. and Long, E. (1988) The role of rewards and fairness in developing premarital relationships. *Journal of Marriage and the Family*, 50, 443–52.

Central Statistical Office (1994) *Social Trends 24: 1994 Edition*. London: HMSO.

Chafetz, J., Feldman, H.M. and Wareham, N.L. (1992) 'There car': ungrammatical parentese. *Journal of Child Language*, 19, 473–80.

Chaiken, S. (1980) Heuristic versus systematic information processing and the use of source versus message cues in persuasion. *Journal of Personality and Social Psychology*, 39, 752–66.

Chaiken, S. (1987) The heuristic model of persuasion. In M.P. Zanna, J.M. Olson and C.P. Herman (eds), *Social Influence: the Ontario Symposium* (vol. 5, pp. 3–39), Hillsdale, NJ: Erlbaum.

Chaiken, S., Liberman, A. and Eagly, A.H. (1989) Heuristic and systematic processing within and beyond the persuasion context. In J.S. Uleman and J.A. Bargh (eds), *Unintended Thought* (pp. 212–52), New York: Guilford.

Chaiken, S. and Maheswaran, D. (1994) Heuristic processing can be biased systematic processing: effects of source credibility, argument ambiguity, and task importance on attitude judgement. *Journal of Personality and Social Psychology*, 66, 460–73.

Chaiken, S. and Stangor, C. (1987) Attitudes and attitude change. *Annual Review of Psychology*, 38, 575–630.

Check, V.P., Perlman, D. and Malamuth, N.M. (1985) Loneliness and aggressive behavior. *Journal of Social and Personal Relationships*, 2, 243–54.

Chemers, M.M. (1983) Leadership theory and research: a systems–process integration. In P. Paulus (ed.), *Basic Group Processes*, New York: Springer.

Cheng, P.W. and Novick, L.R. (1990) A qualitative model of causal induction. *Journal of Personality and Social Psychology*, 58, 545–57.

Cheng, P.W. and Novick, L.R. (1992) Covariation in natural causal induction. *Psychological Review*, 99, 365–82.

Chevalier-Skolnikoff, S. (1973) Facial expression of emotion in nonhuman primates. In P. Ekman (ed.), *Darwin and Facial Expression* (pp. 11-89) New York: Academic Press.

Chiva, M. (1985) *Le doux et l'amer: sensation gustative, émotion et communication chez le jeune enfant*. Paris: PUF.

Chomsky, N. (1959) Review of Skinner (1957). *Language*, 35, 26–58.

Chomsky, N. (1965) *Aspects of the Theory of Syntax*. Cambridge, MA: MIT Press.

Christie, R. and Jahoda, M. (eds) (1954) *Studies in the Scope and Method of the Authoritarian Personality*. New York: Free Press.

Churchman, A. (1993) A differentiated perspective on urban quality of life: women, children and the elderly. In M. Bonnes (ed.), *Perception and Evaluation of Urban Environmental Quality: a pluridisciplinary approach in the European context*. Italia MAB Project II, UNESCO Programme on Man and Biosphere, Rome, 165–78.

Cialdini, R.B., Borden, R.J., Thorne, A., Walker, M.R., Freeman, S. and Sloan, L.R. (1976) Basking in reflected glory: three (football) field studies. *Journal of Personality and Social Psychology*, 34, 366–74.

Cialdini, R.B. and Insko, C.A. (1969) Attitudinal verbal reinforcement as a function of informational consistency: a further test of the two-factor theory. *Journal of Personality and Social Psychology*, 12, 342–50.

Cialdini, R.B., Schaller, M., Houlihan, D., Arps, K., Fultz, J. and Beaman, A.L. (1987) Empathy-based helping: is it selflessly or selfishly motivated? *Journal of Personality and Social Psychology*, 52, 749–58.

Clark, K.B. and Clark, M.P. (1947). Racial identification and preference in Negro children. In H. Proshansky and B. Seidenberg (eds), *Basic Studies in Social Psychology* (pp. 308–17). New York: Holt, Rinehart and Winston (1955 edn.).

Clark, M.S. (1984) Record keeping in two types of relationships. *Journal of Personality and Social Psychology*, 47, 549–57.

Clark, M.S. and Mills, J. (1979) Interpersonal attraction in exchange and communal relationships. *Journal of Personality and Social Psychology*, 37, 12.

Clark, M.S. and Mills, J. (1993) The difference between

communal and exchange relationships: what it is and is not. *Personality and Social Psychology Bulletin*, 19, 684–91.

Clark, M.S., Mills, J. and Powell, M.C. (1986) Keeping track of needs in communal and exchange relationships. *Journal of Personality and Social Psychology*, 51, 233–8.

Clark, M.S., Oullette, R., Powell, M.C. and Milberg, S. (1987) Recipient's mood, relationship type, and helping. *Journal of Personality and Social Psychology*, 53, 94–103.

Clark, M.S. and Reis, H.T. (1988) Interpersonal processes in close relationships. *Annual Review of Psychology*, 39, 609–72.

Clark, N.K. and Stephenson, G.M. (1995) Social remembering: individual and collaborative memory for social information. In W. Stroebe and M. Hewstone (eds), *European Review of Social Psychology* (vol. 6, pp. 127–160), Chichester: J. Wiley.

Coch, L. and French, J.R.R., Jr (1948) Overcoming resistance to change. *Human Relations*, 1, 512–32.

Codol, J.-P. (1975) On the so-called 'superior conformity of the self' behaviour: twenty experimental investigations. *European Journal of Social Psychology*, 5, 457–501.

Codol, J.-P. (1986) Estimation et expression de la ressemblance et de la différence entre pairs. *Année Psychologique*, 86, 527–50.

Cohen, S. and Hoberman, H.M. (1983) Positive events and social supports as buffers of life change stress. *Journal of Applied Social Psychology*, 13, 99–125.

Cohen, S. and Wills, T.A. (1985) Stress, social support, and the buffering hypothesis. *Psychological Bulletin*, 98, 310–57.

Coleman, A. (1985) *Utopia on Trial: vision and reality in planned housing*. London: Hilary Shipman.

Coleman, L.M. and DePaulo, B.M. (1991) Uncovering the human spirit: moving beyond disability and 'missed' communications. In N. Coupland, H. Giles and J.M. Weimann (eds), *'Miscommunication' and Problematic Talk* (pp. 61–84), Thousand Oaks, CA: Sage.

Collins, B.E. and Raven, B.H. (1968) Group structure: attraction, coalitions, communication, and power. In G. Lindzey and E. Aronson (eds), *Handbook of Social Psychology* (2nd edn, vol. 4), Reading, MA: Addison-Wesley.

Collis, G.M. (1985) On the origins of turn-taking: alternation and meaning. In M.D. Barrett (ed.), *Children's Single-Word Speech* (pp. 217–30), Chichester: Wiley.

Combs, B. and Slovic, P. (1979) Newspaper coverage of causes of death. *Public Opinion Quarterly*, 56, 837–43.

Comstock, G. and Paik, H. (1991) *Television and the American Child*. San Diego: Academic Press.

Comte, A. (1853) *The Positive Philosophy*, vol. 1. London: Longmans, Green.

Cook, S.W. (1962) The systematic analysis of socially significant events. *Journal of Social Issues*, 18, 66–84.

Cook, T.D. and Campbell, D.T. (1979) *Quasi-Experimentation: design and analysis issues for field settings*. Chicago, IL: Rand McNally.

Cooper, H. (1990) Meta-analysis and the integrative research review. In C. Hendrick and M.S. Clark (eds), *Research Methods in Personality and Social Psychology*. (Review of Personality and Social Psychology, vol. 11, pp. 42–63), Newbury Park, CA: Sage.

Cooper, J. and Axsom, D. (1982) Effort justification in psychotherapy. In G. Weary and H.K. Mirels (eds), *Integrations of Clinical and Social Psychology*, New York: Oxford University Press.

Cooper, J. and Fazio, R.H. (1984) A new look at dissonance theory. In L. Berkowitz, *Advances in Experimental Social Psychology* (vol. 17, pp. 229–66), Orlando, FL: Academic Press.

Cooper, J. and Worchel, S. (1970) Role of undesired consequences in arousing cognitive dissonance. *Journal of Personality and Social Psychology*, 16, 199–206.

Cooper, J., Zanna, M.P. and Taves, P.A. (1978) Arousal as a necessary condition for attitude change following induced compliance. *Journal of Personality and Social Psychology*, 36, 1101–6.

Corey, S.M. (1937) Professed attitudes and actual behavior. *Journal of Educational Psychology*, 28, 171–280.

Corneille, O. and Leyens, J.-P. (1994) Catégories, catégorisation sociale et essentialisme psychologique. In R. Bourhis and J.-P. Leyens (eds), *Stéréotypes, discrimination, relations intergroupes*, Brussels: Mardaga.

Cosmides, L. (1989) The logic of social exchange: has natural selection shaped how humans reason? Studies with the Wason selection task. *Cognition*, 31, 187–276.

Costanza, R.S., Derlega, V.J. and Winstead, B.A. (1988) Positive and negative forms of social support: effects of conversational topics on coping with stress among same sex friends. *Journal of Experimental Social Psychology*, 24, 182–93.

Cotton, J.L. and Baron, R.S. (1980) Anonymity, persuasive arguments and choice shifts. *Social Psychology Quarterly*, 43, 391–404.

Cottrell, N.B. (1968) Performance in the presence of other human beings: mere presence audience and affiliation effects. In E.C. Simmel, R.A. Hoppe and G.A. Milton (eds), *Social Facilitation and Imitative Behavior* (pp. 245–50), Boston: Allyn & Bacon.

Cottrell, N.B. (1972) Social facilitation. In C.G. McClintock (ed.), *Experimental Social Psychology*, pp. 185–236, New York: Holt, Rinehart & Winston.

Couch, A.S. and Carter, L.F.A. (1952) A factorial study of the rated behavior of group members. Paper presented at the annual meeting of the Eastern Psychological Association.

Coupland, N., Coupland, J. and Giles, H. (1991) *Language, Society and the Elderly: discourse, identity, and aging*. Oxford and New York: Blackwell.

Coupland, N., Coupland, J., Giles, H. and Wiemann, J.M. (1988) My life in your hands: disclosure in intergenerational talk. In N. Coupland (ed.), *Styles of Discourse* (pp. 201–53), London: Routledge and Kegan Paul.

Coupland, N., Wiemann, J.M. and Giles, H. (1991) Talk as 'problem' and communication as 'miscommunication'. An integrative analysis. In N. Coupland, H. Giles and J.M. Wiemann (eds), *'Miscommunication' and Problematic Talk* (pp. 1–17), Thousand Oaks, CA: Sage.

Cousins, S. (1989) Culture and selfhood in Japan and the US. *Journal of Personality and Social Psychology*, 56, 124–31.

Cowles, M. and Davis, C. (1987) The subject matter of psychology: volunteers. *British Journal of Social Psychology*, 26, 289–94.

Cram, F. and Ng, S.H. (1994) Children's understanding of public ownership. *European Journal of Social Psychology*, 24, 469–80.

Critelli, J.W. and Waid, L.R. (1980) Physical attractiveness, romantic love, and equity restoration in dating relationships. *Journal of Personality Assessment*, 44, 624–9.

Cromer, R.F. (1991) *Language and Thought in Normal and Handicapped Children*. Oxford: Blackwell.

Cronin, H. (1991) *The Ant and the Peacock*. Cambridge: Cambridge University Press.

Crook, J.H. (1980) *The Evolution of Human Consciousness*. Oxford: Clarendon Press.

Crosby, F. (1976) A model of egotistical relative deprivation. *Psychological Review*, 83, 85–113.

Croyle, R.T. and Cooper, J. (1983) Dissonance arousal: physiological evidence. *Journal of Personality and Social Psychology*, 45, 782–91.

Crutchfield, R.A. (1955) Conformity and character. *American Psychologist*, 10, 191–8.

Cunningham, J.D. and Kelley, H.H. (1975) Causal attributions for interpersonal events of varying magnitude. *Journal of Personality*, 43, 74–93.

Cunningham, M.R. (1986) Measuring the physical in physical attractiveness: quasi experiments on the sociobiology of female facial beauty. *Journal of Personality and Social Psychology*, 50, 925–35.

Cunningham, M.R., Barbee, A.P. and Pike, C.L.

(1990). What do women want? Facialmetric assessment of multiple motives in the perception of male physical attractiveness. *Journal of Personality and Social Psychology*, 59, 61–72.

Curtiss, S. (1989) The independence and task-specificity of language. In M.H. Bornstein and J.S. Bruner (eds), *Interaction in human development* (pp. 105–38), Hillsdale, NJ: Erlbaum.

Cushman, D. and Cahn, D. (1985) *Communication in Interpersonal Relationships*. Albany: State University of New York Press.

Cutrona, C.C. and Russell, D.W. (1987) The provisions of social relationships and adaptation to stress. In W.H. Jones and D. Perlman (eds), *Advances in Personal Relationships* (vol. 1, pp. 69–108), Greenwich, CT: JAI Press.

Daly, J.A. and Wiemann, J.M. (eds) (1994) *Strategic Interpersonal Communication*. Hillsdale, NJ: Erlbaum.

Daly, M. and Wilson, M. (1982) Whom are newborn babies said to resemble? *Ethology and Sociobiology*, 3, 69–78.

Daly, M. and Wilson, M. (1985) Child abuse and other risks of not living with both parents. *Ethology and Sociobiology*, 6, 197–210.

Daly, M. and Wilson, M. (1988) *Homicide*. New York: Aldine de Gruyter.

Daly, M. and Wilson, M. (1994) Evolutionary psychology of male violence. In J. Archer (ed.), *Male Violence* (pp. 253–88), London: Routledge.

Dance, F.E.X. and Larson, C. (1976) *The Functions of Human Communication*. New York: Holt, Rinehart & Winston.

Dane, F.C. and Wrightsman, L.S. (1982) Effects of defendants' and victims' characteristics on jurors' verdicts. In N.L. Kerr and R.M. Bray (eds), *The Psychology of the other Courtroom*, London: Academic Press.

Danziger, K. (1983) Origins and basic principles of Wundt's Völkerpsychologie. *British Journal of Social Psychology*, 22, 303–13.

Danziger, K. (1990) *Constructing the Subject. Historical origins of psychological research*. Cambridge: Cambridge University Press.

Dardenne, B. and Leyens, J.-P. (1995) Confirmation bias as a social skill. *Personality and Social Psychology Bulletin*, 21, 1229–39.

Darley, J.M. (1992) Social categorization for the production of evil. *Psychological Inquiry*, 3, 199–218.

Darley, J.M. and Batson, C.D. (1973) From Jerusalem to Jericho: a study of situational and dispositional variables in helping behavior. *Journal of Personality and Social Psychology*, 27, 100–8.

Darley, J.M. and Gross, P.H. (1983) A hypothesis-confirming bias in labeling effects. *Journal of Personality and Social Psychology*, 44, 20–33.

Darwin, C. (1859) *On the Origin of Species*. London: John Murray.

Darwin, C. (1871) *The Descent of Man, and Selection in Relation to Sex*. London: John Murray.

Darwin, C. (1872) *The Expression of the Emotions in Man and Animals*. London: Murray (reprinted Chicago: University of Chicago Press, 1965).

Darwin, C. and Wallace, A.R.W. (1858) On the tendency of species to form varieties; and on the perpetuation of varieties and species by natural means of selection. *Journal of the Linnean Society of London (Zoology)*, 3, 45–62.

Davidson, A.R. and Jaccard, J.J. (1979) Variables that moderate the attitude–behavior relation: results of a longitudinal survey. *Journal of Personality and Social Psychology*, 37, 1364–76.

Davidson, A.R. and Morrison, J.M. (1983) Predicting contraceptive behavior from attitudes: a comparison of within-versus-across subjects procedures. *Journal of Personality and Social Psychology*, 45, 997–1009.

Davies, J.C. (1969) The J-curve of rising and declining satisfactions as a cause of some great revolutions and a contained rebellion. In H.D. Graham and T.R. Gurr (eds), *The History of Violence in America: Historical and Comparative Perspectives*, New York: Praeger.

Davis, J.H. (1973) Group decision and social interaction: a theory of social decision schemes. *Psychological Review*, 80, 97–125.

Davis, J.H. (1982) Social interaction as a combinatorial process in group decision. In H. Brandstätter, J.H. Davis and G. Stocker-Kreichgauer (eds), *Group Decision Making* (pp. 27–58), London: Academic Press.

Davis, J.H. (1984) Order in the courtroom. In D.J. Muller, D.E. Blackman and A.J. Chapman (eds), *Psychology and Law* (pp. 251–65), Chichester: Wiley.

Davis, J.H., Kerr, N.L., Atkins, R.S., Holt, R. and Meek, D. (1975) The decision processes of 6- and 12-person juries assigned unanimous and two-thirds majority rules. *Journal of Personality and Social Psychology*, 32, 1–14.

Davitz, J.R. (1964) *The Communication of Emotional Meaning*. New York: McGraw-Hill.

Dawes, R.M. (1980) Social dilemmas. *Annual Review of Psychology*, 31, 169–93.

Dawkins, R. (1976) *The Selfish Gene*. Oxford: Oxford University Press.

De Gilder, D. and Wilke, H.A.M. (1994) Expectation states theory and the motivational determinants of social influence. In W. Stroebe and M. Hewstone (eds), *European Review of Social Psychology* (vol. 5, pp. 243–69), London: Wiley.

de Montmollin, G. (1977) *L'influence sociale. Phénomènes, facteurs et théories*. Paris: Presses Universitaires de France.

de Ridder, R. and Tripathi, R. (eds) (1992) *Norm Violation and Intergroup Relations*. Oxford: Oxford University Press.

Deci, E.L. (1971) Effects of externally mediated rewards on intrinsic motivation. *Journal of Personality and Social Psychology*, 18, 105–15.

Deci, E.L. (1972) Intrinsic motivation, extrinsic reinforcement, and inequity. *Journal of Personality and Social Psychology*, 22, 113–20.

Deci, E.L. (1975) *Intrinsic Motivation*. New York: Plenum.

Decker, S.H. and Wagner, A.E. (1982) The impact of patrol staffing on police–citizen injuries and dispositions. *Journal of Criminal Justice*, 10, 375–82.

Deconchy, J.-P. (1984) Rationality and social control in orthodox systems. In Tajfel, H. (ed.), *The Social Dimension* (vol. 2, pp. 425–45). Cambridge: Cambridge University Press.

DeJong-Gierveld, J. and Van Tilburg, T. (1987) The partner as a source of support in problem and non-problem situations. *Journal of Social Behavior and Personality*, 2, 191–201.

Dennis, G. (1993) *Key Data 1993/4 edition*. Central Statistical Office, London: HMSO.

Dent, H.R. and Flin, R. (1992) *Children as Witnesses*. Chichester: Wiley.

DePaulo, B.M., Brown, P.L. Ishii, S. and Fisher, J.D. (1981) Help that works: the effects of aid on subsequent task performance. *Journal of Personality and Social Psychology*, 41, 478–87.

DePaulo, B.M., Stone, J.I. and Lassiter, G.D. (1985) Telling ingratiation lies: effects of target sex and target attractiveness on verbal and nonverbal deceptive success. *Journal of Personality and Social Psychology*, 15, 247–52.

Derlega, V.J., Metts, S., Petronio, S. and Margulis, S.T. (1993) *Self-disclosure*. Thousand Oaks, CA: Sage.

Deschamps, J.-C. (1977) Effect of crossing category memberships on quantitative judgements. *European Journal of Social Psychology*, 7, 517–21.

Deschamps, J.-C. and Brown, R.J. (1983) Superordinate goals and intergroup conflict. *British Journal of Social Psychology*, 22, 189–95.

Deschamps, J.-C. and Doise, W. (1978) Crossed category memberships in intergroup relations. In H. Tajfel (ed.), *Differentiation between Social Groups*, London: Academic Press.

Desforges, D.M., Lord, C.G., Ramsey, S.L., Mason, J.A., van Leeuwen, M.D., West, S.C. and Lepper, M.R. (1991) Effects of structured cooperative contact on changing negative attitudes towards stigmatized groups. *Journal of Personality and Social Psychology*, 60, 531–44.

Desmond, A. and Moore, J.P. (1991) *Darwin*. London: Joseph (Penguin Books, 1992).

Deutsch, M. (1949) An experimental study of the effects of cooperation and competition upon group process. *Human Relations*, 2, 199–231.

Deutsch, M. and Gerard, H.B. (1955) A study of normative and informational influence upon individual judgement. *Journal of Abnormal and Social Psychology*, 51, 629–36.

Devine, P.G. (1989) Stereotypes and prejudice: their automatic and controlled components. *Journal of Personality and Social Psychology*, 56, 5–18.

Devine, P.G., Hamilton, D.L. and Ostrom, T.M. (eds) (1994) *Social Cognition: contributions to classic issues in social psychology*. New York: Springer-Verlag.

Devine, P.G. and Ostrom, T.M. (1988) Dimensional versus information-processing approaches to social knowledge: the case of inconsistency management. In D. Bar-Tal and A. Kruglanski (eds), *The Social Psychology of Knowledge* (pp. 231–61), Cambridge: Cambridge University Press.

de Waal, F. (1983) *Chimpanzee Politics: power and sex among apes*. New York: Harper and Row.

Di Giacomo, J.P. (1980) Intergroup alliances and rejections within a protest movement: analysis of social representations. *European Journal of Social Psychology*, 10, 329–44.

Di Vesta, F.J. (1959) Effects of confidence and motivation on susceptibility to informational social influence. *Journal of Abnormal and Social Psychology*, 59, 204–9.

Diamond, J. (1991) *The Rise and Fall of the Third Chimpanzee*. London: Radius Books.

Diehl, M. (1988) Social identity and minimal groups: the effects of interpersonal and intergroup attitudinal similarity on intergroup discrimination. *British Journal of Social Psychology*, 27, 289–300.

Diehl, M. (1989) Justice and discrimination in minimal groups: the limits of equity. *British Journal of Social Psychology*, 28, 227–38.

Diehl, M. and Stroebe, W. (1987) Productivity loss in brainstorming groups: toward the solution of a riddle. *Journal of Personality and Social Psychology*, 53, 497–509.

Diehl, M. and Stroebe, W. (1991). Productivity loss in idea-generating groups: tracking down the blocking effect. *Journal of Personality and Social Psychology*, 61, 392–403.

Diener, E. (1980) Deindividuation: the absence of self-awareness and self-regulation in group members. In P. Paulus (ed.), *The Psychology of Group Influence* (pp. 209–42), Hillsdale, NJ: Erlbaum.

Dillehay, R.C. and Nietzel, M.T. (1985) Jury experience and jury verdicts. *Law and Human Behavior*, 9, 179–91.

Dillon, W.R. and Kumar, A. (1985) Attitude organization and the attitude–behaviour relation: a critique of Bagozzi and Burnkraut's reanalysis of Fishbein and Ajzen. *Journal of Personality and Social Psychology*, 49, 33–46.

Dindia, K. (1987) The effects of sex of subject and sex of partner in interruptions. *Human Communication Research*, 13, 345–71.

Dittes, J.E. and Kelley, H.H. (1956) Effects of different conditions of acceptance on conformity to group norms. *Journal of Abnormal and Social Psychology*, 53, 100–7.

Dobash, R.E. and Dobash, R.P. (1977–78) Wives: the 'appropriate' victims of marital violence. *Victimology: An International Journal*, 2, 426–42.

D'Odorico, L. and Franco, F. (1985) The determinants of baby talk: relationship to context. *Journal of Child Language*, 12, 567–86.

Dohrenwend, B.S. and Dohrenwend, B.P. (1974) *Stressful Life Events: their nature and effects*. New York: Wiley.

Doise, W. (1976) *L'articulation psychosociologique et les relations entre groups*. Brussels: de Boeck. Translated as *Groups and Individuals: explanations in social psychology* (Cambridge University Press).

Doise, W., Clémence, A. and Lorenzi-Cioldi, F. (1992) *Représentation Sociale et Analyse de Données*. Grenoble: Presses Universitaires de Grenoble.

Doise, W., Dionnet, S. and Mugny, G. (1978) Conflit sociocognitif, marquage social et développement cognitif. *Cahiers de Psychologie*, 21, 231–45.

Doise, W. and Hanselmann, C. (1990) Interaction social et acquisition de la conservation du volume. *European Journal of Psychology of Education*, 5, 21–31.

Doise, W. and Mugny, G. (1984) *The Social Development of the Intellect*. Oxford: Pergamon.

Doise, W., Mugny, G. and Perret-Clermont, A.-N. (1975) Social interaction and the development of cognitive operations. *European Journal of Social Psychology*, 5, 367–83.

Doise, W. and Palmonari, A. (1984) Introduction: the sociopsychological study of individual development. In W. Doise and A. Palmonari (eds), *Social Interaction in Individual Development* (pp. 1–16), Cambridge: Cambridge University Press.

Doise, W., Rijsman, J.B., Van Meel, J., Bressers, I. and Pinxten, L. (1981) Sociale markering cognitieve ontwikkeling. *Pedagogische Studien*, 58, 241–8.

Doll, J. and Ajzen, I. (1992) Accessibility and stability of predictors in the theory of planned behavior. *Journal of Personality and Social Psychology*, 63, 754–65.

Dollard, J., Doob, L.W., Miller, N.E., Mowrer, O.H. and Sears, R.T. (1939) *Frustration and Aggression*. New Haven: Yale University Press.

Dollard, J. and Miller, N.E. (1950) *Personality and Psychotherapy*. New York: McGraw-Hill.

Doms, M. and Van Avermaet, E. (1980) Majority influence, minority influence and conversion behaviour: a replication. *Journal of Experimental Social Psychology*, 16, 283–92.

Doms, M. and Van Avermaet, E. (1982) The conformity effect: a timeless phenomenon. *Bulletin of the British Psychological Society*, 35, 383–5.

Doms, M. and Van Avermaet, E. (1985) Social support and minority influence: the innovation effect reconsidered. In S. Moscovici, G. Mugny and E. Van Avermaet (eds), *Perspectives on Minority Influence* (pp. 53–74), Cambridge: Cambridge University Press.

Donnerstein, E., Donnerstein, M., Simons, S. and Dittrichs, R. (1972) Variables in interracial aggression. *Journal of Personality and Social Psychology*, 22, 236–45.

Donnerstein, E. and Wilson, D.W. (1976) The effects of noise and perceived control upon ongoing and subsequent aggressive behavior. *Journal of Personality and Social Psychology*, 34, 774–81.

Douglas, W. (1987) Affinity-testing in initial interactions. *Journal of Social and Personal Relationships*, 4, 3–16.

Doyle, A.-B., Beaudet, J. and Aboud, F. (1988) Developmental patterns in the flexibility of children's ethnic attitudes. *Journal of Cross-Cultural Psychology*, 19, 3–18.

Dryden, C. and Giles, H. (1987) Language, social identity and health. In H. Beloff and A. Coleman (eds), *Psychology Survey* (vol. 6, pp. 115–39), Leicester: British Psychological Society.

Duck, S. (1992) *Human Relationships*, 2nd edn. London: Sage.

Duffy, E. (1941) An explanation of 'emotional' phenomena without the use of the concept 'emotion'. *Journal of General Psychology*, 25, 283–93.

Duncan, B. (1976) Differential social perception and attribution of intergroup violence: testing the lower limits of stereotyping Blacks. *Journal of Personality and Social Psychology*, 34, 590–8.

Duncan, S. and Fiske, D.W. (1977) *Face-to-Face Interaction*. Hillsdale, NJ: Erlbaum.

Dunkel-Shetter, C., Blasband, D.E., Feinstein, L.G. and Bennett, H.T. (1992) Elements of supportive interactions: when are attempts to help effective? In S. Spacapan and S. Oskamp (eds), *Helping and Being Helped. Naturalistic studies* (pp. 83–114), Newbury Park, CA: Sage.

Dunkel-Shetter, C. and Wortman, C.B. (1982) The interpersonal dynamics of cancer: problems in social relationships and their impact on the patient. In H.S. Friedman and M.R. Dimatteo (eds), *Interpersonal Issues in Health Care* (pp. 60–100), New York: Academic Press.

Dunn, J. (1988) *The Beginnings of Social Understanding*. Oxford: Blackwell.

Dunn, J. (1993) Social interaction, relationships, and the development of causal discourse and conflict management. *European Journal of Social Psychology*, 8, 391–401.

Durkheim, E. (1898) Représentations individuelles et représentations collectives. *Revue de Métaphysique et de Morale*, 6, 273–302 (English trans. in E. Durkheim (1974), *Sociology and Philosophy*, New York: Free Press).

Durkin, K. (1987) Minds and language: social cognition, social interaction and the development of language. *Mind and Language*, 2, 105–40.

Durkin, K. (1995) *Developmental Social Psychology: from infancy to old age*. Oxford: Blackwell.

Dutton, D.G. and Aron, A.P. (1974) Some evidence for heightened sexual attraction under conditions of high anxiety. *Journal of Personality and Social Psychology*, 28, 510–17.

Duval, S. and Wicklund, R.A. (1972) *A Theory of Objective Self-Awareness*. New York: Academic Press.

Dweck, C. (1975). The role of expectations and attributions in the alleviation of learned helplessness. *Journal of Personality and Social Psychology*, 36, 951–62.

Dweck, C.S. and Leggett, E.L. (1988). A social-cognitive approach to motivation and personality. *Psychological Review*, 95, 256–73.

Eagly, A.H. and Chaiken, S. (1993) *The Psychology of Attitudes*. San Diego, CA and Fort Worth, TX: Harcourt Brace Jovanovich.

Eagly, A.H. and Warren, R. (1976) Intelligence, comprehension, and opinion change. *Journal of Personality*, 44, 226–42.

Ebbesen, E.B., Kjos, G.L. and Konečni, V.J. (1976) Spatial ecology: its effects on the choice of friends and enemies. *Journal of Experimental Social Psychology*, 12, 505–18.

Echabe, A.E., Rovira, D.P. and Garate, J.F.V. (1988) Testing Ajzen and Fishbein's attitudes model: the prediction of voting. *European Journal of Social Psychology*, 18, 181–9.

Echebarria, A. and Paez, D. (1989) Social representations and memory: the case of AIDS. *European Journal of Social Psychology*, 19, 543–51.

Eckardt, G. (1971) Problemgeschichtliche Untersuchungen zur Völkerpsychologie der zweiten Hälfte des 19. Jahrhunderts. *Wissenschaftliche Zeitschrift der Friedrich-Schiller-Universität, Gesellschafts-und sprachwissensschaftliche Reihe*, 20, 4, 7–133.

(Editorial). *European Journal of Social Psychology*, 1971, 1, 5–6.

Edwards, J.R. (1989) *Language and disadvantage*, 2nd edn. London: Cole and Whurr.

Edwards, J.R. and Giles, H. (1984) Applications of the social psychology of language: sociolinguistics and education. In P. Trudgill (ed.), *Applied Sociolinguistics* (pp. 119–58), London: Academic Press.

Egeth, H.E. and McCloskey, M. (1984) Expert testimony about eye-witness behaviour: is it safe and effective? In G.L. Wells and E.F. Loftus (eds), *Eyewitness Testimony: psychological perspectives*, Cambridge: Cambridge University Press.

Ehrlich, I. (1982) The market for offences and the public enforcement of laws; an equilibrium analysis. *British Journal of Social Psychology*, 21, 107–20.

Eibl-Eibesfeldt, I. (1972) Similarities and differences between cultures in expressive movements. In R.A. Hinde (ed.), *Nonverbal communication* (pp. 20–33), Cambridge: Cambridge University Press.

Einhorn, H.J. and Hogarth, R.M. (1986) Judging probable cause. *Psychological Bulletin*, 99, 3–19.

Eisenberg, N. and Miller, P.A. (1987) The relation of empathy to prosocial and related behaviors. *Psychological Bulletin*, 101, 91–119.

Eiser, J.R. and Stroebe, W. (1972) *Categorization and Social Judgement*. London: Academic Press.

Ekman, P. (1972) Universals and cultural differences in facial expressions of emotion. In J.R. Cole (ed.), *Nebraska Symposium on Motivation* (pp. 207–83), Lincoln: University of Nebraska Press.

Ekman, P. (1979) About brows: emotional and conversational signals. In M. v. Cranach, K. Foppa, W. Lepenies and D. Ploog (eds), *Human Ethology* (pp. 169–202), Cambridge: Cambridge University Press.

Ekman, P. (ed.) (1982) *Emotion in the Human Face*, 2nd edn. Cambridge: Cambridge University Press.

Ekman, P. (1984) Expression and the nature of emotion. In K.R. Scherer and P. Ekman (eds), *Approaches to Emotion* (pp. 319–44), Hillsdale, NJ: Erlbaum.

Ekman, P. (1989) The argument and evidence about universals in facial expressions of emotion. In H. Wagner and A. Manstead (eds), *Handbook of Social Psychophysiology*, Wiley Handbooks of Psychophysiology (pp. 143–64), Chichester: John Wiley.

Ekman, P. (1992) An argument for basic emotions. *Cognition and Emotion*, 6, 169–200.

Ekman, P. and Friesen, W.V. (1969) The repertoire of nonverbal behavior: categories, origins, usage, and coding. *Semiotica*, 1, 49–98.

Ekman, P. and Friesen, W.V. (1971). Constants across cultures in the face and emotion. *Journal of Personality and Social Psychology*, 17, 124–9.

Ekman, P. and Friesen, W.V. (1986) A new pan-cultural facial expression of emotion. *Motivation and Emotion*, 10, 159–68.

Ekman, P., Levenson, R.W. and Friesen, W. (1983) Autonomic nervous system activity distinguishes among emotions. *Science*, 221, 1208–10.

Ekman, P., Sorenson, E.R. and Friesen, W.V. (1969) Pan-cultural elements in facial displays of emotion. *Science*, 164, 86–8.

Elander, J., West, R. and French, D. (1993) Behavioral correlates of individual differences in road traffic crash risk: an examination of methods and findings. *Psychological Bulletin*, 113, 279–94.

Elias, N. (1977) *The Civilizing Process*. New York: Urizen.

Elig, T.W. and Frieze I.H. (1979) Measuring causal attributions for success and failure. *Journal of Personality and Social Psychology*, 37, 621–34.

Ellemers, N., van Knippenberg, A., de Vries, N. and Wilke, H. (1988). Social identification and permeability of group boundaries. *European Journal of Social Psychology*, 18, 497–513.

Ellemers, N., Wilke, H. and Van Knippenberg, A. (1993) Effects of the legitimacy of low group or individual status as individual and collective status-enhancement strategies. *Journal of Personality and Social Psychology*, 64, 766–78.

Ellis, B.J. (1992) The evolution of sexual attraction: evaluative mechanisms in women. In J.H. Barkow, L. Cosmides and J. Tooby (eds), *The Adapted Mind: evolutionary psychology and the generation of culture* (pp. 267–88), New York: Oxford University Press.

Ellis, H.C. and Ashbrook, P.W. (1988) Resource allocation model of the effects of depressed mood states on memory. In K. Fiedler and J.P. Forgas (eds), *Affect, Cognition, and Social Behavior* (pp. 25–43), Toronto: Hogrefe.

Elwell, C.M., Brown, R.J. and Rutter, D.R. (1984) Effects of accent and visual information on impression formation. *Journal of Language and Social Psychology*, 3, 297–9.

Emler, N. (1984) Differential involvement in delinquency: toward an interpretation in terms of reputation management. In B. Maher (ed.), *Progress in Experimental Personality Research* (vol. 13, pp. 173–239), New York: Academic Press.

Emler, N. (1990) A social psychology of reputation. In W. Stroebe and M. Hewstone (eds), *European Review of Social Psychology* (vol. 1, pp. 171–94), Chichester: Wiley.

Emler, N. and Dickinson, J. (1993) The child as sociologist: the childhood development and implicit theories of role categories and social organization. In M. Bennett (ed.), *The Child as Psychologist. An introduction to the development of social cognition* (pp. 168–90), New York: Harvester Wheatsheaf.

Emler, N., Ohana, J. and Moscovici, S. (1987) Children's beliefs about institutional roles: a cross-national study of representations of the teacher's role. *British Journal of Educational Psychology*, 57, 26–37.

Emler. N., Reicher, S. and Ross, A. (1987) The social

context of delinquent conduct. *Journal of Child Psychology and Psychiatry*, 28, 99–109.

Emler, N. and Valiant, G.L. (1982) Social interaction and cognitive conflict in the development of spatial coordination skills. *British Journal of Social Psychology*, 73, 295–303.

Endler, N.S. (1965) The effects of verbal reinforcement on conformity and deviant behaviour. *Journal of Social Psychology*, 66, 147–54.

Engler, U. and Braun, O. (1988) Hilfesuchen und helferbezogene Gedanken. In H.W. Bierhoff and L. Montada (eds), *Altruismus* (pp. 253–63), Goettingen: Hogrefe.

Epstein, S. (1966) Aggression toward outgroups as a function of authoritarianism and imitation of aggression models. *Journal of Personality and Social Psychology*, 3, 574–9.

Erber, R. and Fiske, S.T. (1984) Outcome dependency and attention to inconsistent information about others. *Journal of Personality and Social Psychology*, 47, 709–26.

Eron, L.D. and Huesmann, L.R. (1980) Adolescent aggression and television. *Annals of the New York Academy of Science*, 347, 319–31.

Eron, L.D., Huesmann, L.R., Lefkowitz, M.M. and Walder, L.O. (1972) Does television violence cause aggression? *American Psychologist*, 27, 253–63.

Erwin, P. (1993) *Friendship and Peer Relations in Children*. Chichester: Wiley.

Esser, J.K. and Lindoerfer, J.S. (1989) Groupthink and the space shuttle Challenger accident: toward a quantitative case analysis. *Journal of Behavioral Decision Making*, 2, 167–77.

Estes, W.K. (1986) Array models for category learning. *Cognitive Psychology*, 18, 500–49.

Farr, R.M. (1980) On reading Darwin and discovering social psychology. In R. Gilmour and R. Duck (eds), *The Development of Social Psychology* (pp. 111–36), London: Academic Press.

Farr, R.M. (1986) The social psychology of William McDougall. In C.F. Graumann and S. Moscovici (eds), *Changing Conceptions of Crowd Mind and Behavior* (pp. 83–95), New York: Springer-Verlag.

Farr, R.M. and Moscovici, S. (eds) (1984) *Social Representations*. Cambridge: Cambridge University Press.

Farrington, D.P., Biron, L. and LeBlanc, M. (1982) Personality and delinquency in London and Montreal. In J. Gunn and D.P. Farrington (eds), *Abnormal Offenders, Delinquency and the Criminal Justice System*, Chichester: Wiley.

Farrington, D.P., Bowen, S., Buckle, A., Burns-Howell, T., Burrows, J. and Speed, M. (1993) An experiment on the prevention of shoplifting. In R.V. Clarke (ed.), *Crime Prevention Studies* (vol. 1, pp. 93–119), New York: Criminal Justice Press.

Farrington, D.P., Gallagher, B., Morley, L., St Ledger, R.J. and West, D.J. (1986) Unemployment, school leaving and crime. *British Journal of Criminology*, 26, 335–56.

Fazio, R.H. (1989) On the power and functionality of attitudes: the role of attitude accessibility. In A.R. Pratkanis, S.J. Breckler and A.G. Greenwald (eds), *Attitude Structure and Function* (pp. 153–79), Hillsdale, NJ: Erlbaum.

Fazio, R.H. (1990) Multiple processes by which attitudes guide behavior: the MODE model as an integrative framework. In M.P. Zanna (ed.), *Advances in Experimental Social Psychology* (vol. 13, pp. 75–109), San Diego, CA: Academic Press.

Fazio, R.H., Chen, J., McDonel, E.C. and Sherman, S.J. (1982) Attitude accessibility, attitude–behavior consistency, and the strength of the object-evaluation association. *Journal of Experimental Social Psychology*, 18, 339–57.

Fazio, R.H. and Williams, C.J. (1986) Attitude accessibility as a moderator of the attitude–perception and attitude–behavior relations: an investigation of the 1984 presidential election. *Journal of Personality and Social Psychology*, 51, 505–14.

Fazio, R.H. and Zanna, M.P. (1981) Direct experience and attitude–behavior consistency. In L. Berkowitz (ed.), *Advances in Experimental Social Psychology* (vol. 14, pp. 161–202), New York: Academic Press.

Fazio, R.H., Zanna, M.P. and Cooper, J. (1977) Dissonance versus self-perception: an integrative view of each theory's proper domain of aplication. *Journal of Experimental Social Psychology*, 13, 464–79.

Feeney, J.A., Noller, P. and Patty, J. (1993) Adolescents' interactions with the opposite sex: influence of attachment style and gender. *Journal of Adolescence*, 16, 169–89.

Feingold, A. (1992a) Gender differences in mate selection preferences: a test of the parental investment model. *Psychological Bulletin*, 111, 125–39.

Feingold, A. (1992b) Good-looking people are not what we think. *Psychological Bulletin*, 111, 304–41.

Feldman, R.S. and Rimé, B. (eds) (1991) *Fundamentals of Nonverbal Behavior*. Cambridge: Cambridge University Press.

Felson, R.B. (1984) Patterns of aggressive interactions. In A. Mummendey (ed.), *Social Psychology of Aggression. From individual behavior to social interaction* (pp. 107–26). New York, Heidelberg: Springer.

Felson, R.B. and Ribner, S.A. (1981) An attributional approach to accounts and sanctions for criminal violence. *Social Psychology Quarterly*, 44, 137–42.

Ferguson, T.J. and Rule, B.G. (1983) An attributional perspective on anger and aggression. In R. Green and

E. Donnerstein (eds), *Aggression: theoretical and empirical reviews* (vol. 1, *Method and Theory*, pp. 41–74), New York: Academic Press.

Fernald, A. (1989) Intonation and communicative intent in mothers' speech to infants: is the melody the message? *Child Development*, 60, 1497–1510.

Feshbach, S. (1991) Attachment processes in adult political ideology: patriotism and nationalism. In J.L. Gewirtz and W.M. Kurtines (eds), *Intersections with Attachment* (pp. 80–104), Hillsdale, NJ: Erlbaum.

Festinger, L. (1954) A theory of social comparison processes. *Human Relations*, 7, 117–40.

Festinger, L. (1957) *A Theory of Cognitive Dissonance.* Stanford, CA: Stanford University Press.

Festinger, L. (1980) Looking backward. In L. Festinger (ed.), *Retrospection on Social Psychology* (pp. 236–54), New York: Oxford University Press.

Festinger, L. and Carlsmith, J.M. (1959) Cognitive consequences of forced compliance. *Journal of Abnormal and Social Psychology*, 58, 203–10.

Festinger, L. and Maccoby, N. (1964) On resistance to persuasive communications. *Journal of Abnormal and Social Psychology*, 68, 359–66.

Festinger, L., Riecken, H.W. and Schachter, S. (1956) *When Prophecy Fails.* Minneapolis, MN: University of Minnesota Press.

Festinger, L., Schachter, S. and Back, K. (1950) *Social Pressures in Informal Groups: a study of a housing community.* New York: Harper.

Feyereisen, P. and de Lannoy, J.D. (1991) *Gestures and Speech: psychological investigations.* Cambridge and New York: Cambridge University Press.

Fhanér, G. and Hane, M. (1979) Seat belts: opinion effects of law-induced use. *Journal of Applied Psychology*, 64, 205–12.

Fiedler, F.E. (1978) The contingency model and the dynamics of the leadership process. In L. Berkowitz (ed.), *Advances in Experimental Social Psychology* (vol. 12, pp. 59–112), New York: Academic Press.

Fiedler, F.E. and Potter, E.H. (1983) Dynamics of leadership effectiveness. In H.H. Blumbers, A.P. Hare, V. Kent and M. Davies (eds), *Small Groups and Social Interaction* (vol. 1, pp. 407–13), Chichester: Wiley.

Fiedler, K. (1982) Causal schemata: review and criticism of research on a popular construct. *Journal of Personality and Social Psychology*, 42, 1001–13.

Fiedler, K. (1986) Person memory and person judgments based on categorically organized information. *Acta Psychologica*, 61, 117–35.

Fiedler, K. (1991) The tricky nature of skewed frequency tables: an information loss account of distinctiveness-based illusory correlations. *Journal of Personality and Social Psychology*, 60, 24–36.

Fiedler, K., Hemmeter, U. and Hofmann, C. (1984) On the origin of illusory correlations. *European Journal of Social Psychology*, 14, 191–201.

Fiedler, K. and Semin, G.R. (1988) On the causal information conveyed by different interpersonal verbs: the role of implicit sentence context. *Social Cognition*, 6, 12–39.

Fiedler, K., Semin, G.R. and Bolten, S. (1989) Language use and reification of social information: top-down and bottom-up processing in person cognition. *European Journal of Social Psychology*, 19, 271–95.

Field, R.H.G. and House, R.J. (1990) A test of the Vroom–Yetton model using manager and subordinate reports. *Journal of Applied Psychology*, 75, 362–6.

Fillenbaum, S. and Rapaport, A. (1971) *Structures in the subjective lexicon.* New York: Academic Press.

Fincham, F. D. (1983) Clinical applications of attribution theory: Problems and prospects. In M. Hewstone (ed.), *Attribution theory: social and functional extensions* (pp. 187–203). Oxford: Blackwell.

Fincham, F.D. (1985) Attributions in close relationships. In J.H. Harvey and G. Weary (eds), *Attribution: basic issues and applications* (pp. 203–34), Orlando, FL: Academic Press.

Fincham, F.D. and Bradbury, T.N. (1987) The impact of attributions in marriage: a longitudinal analysis. *Journal of Personality and Social Psychology*, 53, 481–9.

Fincham, F.D. and Bradbury, T.N. (1988) The impact of attributions in marriage: an experimental analysis. *Journal of Social and Clinical Psychology*, 7, 147–62.

Fincham, F.D. and Bradbury, T.H. (1991) Cognition in marriage: a program of research on attributions. In W.H. Jones and D. Perlman (eds), *Advances in Personal Relationships* (vol. 2, pp. 159–204), London: Jessica Kingsley.

Fincham, F.D. and Bradbury, T.N. (1992) Assessing attributions in marriage: the Relationship Attribution Measure. *Journal of Personality and Social Psychology*, 62, 457–68.

Fincham, F.D. and Bradbury, T.N. (1993) Marital satisfaction, depression, and attributions: a longitudinal analysis. *Journal of Personality and Social Psychology*, 64, 442–52.

Fincham, F.D., Bradbury, T.N., Arias, I., Byrne, C.A. and Karney, B.R. (1995) *Marital violence, marital distress and attributions.* Manuscript submitted for publication.

Fincham, F.D. and Cain, K. (1986). Learned helplessness in humans: a developmental analysis. *Developmental Review*, 6, 301–33.

Fincham, F.D. and Jaspars, J.M.F. (1980) Attribution of responsibility from man the scientist to man as lawyer. In L. Berkowitz (ed.), *Advances in Experimental*

Social Psychology (vol. 13, pp. 82–139), London: Academic Press.

Fincham, F.D. and O'Leary, K.D. (1983) Causal inferences for spouse behavior in maritally distressed and nondistressed couples. *Journal of Social and Clinical Psychology*, 1, 42–57.

Fischer, D.G., Kelm, H. and Rose, A. (1969) Knives as aggression-eliciting stimuli. *Psychological Reports*, 24, 755–60.

Fishbein, M. (1980) A theory of reasoned action: some applications and implications. In H.E. Howe, Jr. and M.M. Page (eds), *Nebraska Symposium on Motivation, 1979* (vol. 27, pp. 65–116), Lincoln: University of Nebraska Press.

Fishbein, M. and Ajzen, I. (1974) Attitudes towards objects as predictors of single and multiple behavioral criteria. *Psychological Review*, 81, 59–74.

Fishbein, M. and Ajzen, I. (1975) *Belief, Attitude, Intention, and Behavior: an introduction to theory and research* . Reading, MA: Addison-Wesley.

Fishbein, M. and Coombs, F.S. (1974) Basis for decision: an attitudinal analysis of voting behavior. *Journal of Applied Social Psychology*, 4, 95–124.

Fisher, J.D., DePaulo, B.M. and Nadler, A. (1981) Extending altruism beyond the altruistic act: the mixed effects of aid on the help-recipient. In J.P. Rushton and R.M. Sorrentino (eds), *Altruism and Helping Behavior* (pp. 367–422), Hillsdale, NJ: Lawrence Erlbaum.

Fisher, S. and Todd, A.D. (eds) (1983) *The social organization of doctor–patient communication*. Washington: Center for Applied Linguistics.

Fishman, J.A. (1972) The relationship between micro- and macro-sociolinguistics in the study of who speaks what language to whom and when. In J.B. Pride and J. Holmes (eds), *Sociolinguistics* (pp. 15–32), Harmondsworth: Penguin.

Fiske, S.T. (1992) Thinking is for doing: portraits of social cognition from daguerreotype to laserphoto. *Journal of Personality and Social Psychology*, 63, 877–89.

Fiske, S.T. (1993) Social cognition and social perception. *Annual Review of Psychology*, 44, 155–94.

Fiske, S.T. and Neuberg, S.L. (1990) A continuum of impression formation from category based to individuating processes: influences of information and motivation on attention and interpretation. In M.P. Zanna (ed.), *Advances in Experimental Social Psychology* (vol. 23, pp. 1–74), New York: Academic Press.

Fiske, S.T. and Taylor, S.E. (1991) *Social Cognition*. New York: McGraw-Hill (2nd edn).

Flament, C. (1982) Du biais d'équilibre structural à la représentation du groupe. In J.P. Codol and J.-P. Leyens (eds), *Cognitive Analysis of Social Behavior*. The Hague: Nijhoff.

Fletcher, B. (1991) *Work, Stress, Disease and Life Expectancy*. Chichester: John Wiley.

Fletcher, G.J.O. and Fincham, F.D. (eds) (1991) *Cognition in Close Relationships*. Hillsdale, NJ: Erlbaum.

Folkman, S. and Lazarus, R.S. (1985) If it changes it must be a process: study of emotion and coping during three stages of a college examination. *Journal of Personality and Social Psychology*, 48, 150–70.

Ford, C.S. and Beach, F.A. (1951) *Patterns of Sexual Behavior*. New York: Harper.

Forgas, J.P. (1978) The effects of behavioural and cultural expectation cues on the perception of social episodes. *European Journal of Social Psychology*, 8, 203–13.

Forgas, J.P. (1991) *Emotion and Social Judgments*. Oxford: Pergamon Press.

Forgas, J.P. (1992) Affect in social judgments and decisions: a multiprocess model. In M.P. Zanna (ed.), *Advances in Experimental Social Psychology* (vol. 25, pp. 227–75), San Diego, CA: Academic Press.

Forgas, J.P. and Bower, G.H. (1987) Mood effects in person perception judgments. *Journal of Personality and Social Psychology*, 53, 53–60.

Försterling, F. (1985) Attributional retraining: a review. *Psychological Bulletin*, 98, 495–512.

Försterling, F. (1988) *Attribution Theory in Clinical Psychology*. Chichester: Wiley.

Försterling, F. (1995) The functional value of realistic attributions. In W. Stroebe and M. Hewstone (eds), *European Journal of Social Psychology* (vol. 5, pp. 151–80), Chichester: Wiley.

Forsyth, D.R. (1983) *An Introduction to Group Dynamics*. Monterey, CA: Brooks/Cole.

Fox, S. (1980) Situational determinants in affiliation. *European Journal of Social Psychology*, 10, 303–7.

Fraczek, A. (1974) Informational role of situation as a determinant of aggressive behavior. In J. DeWit and W.W. Hartup (eds), *Determinants and Origins of Aggressive Behavior* (pp. 225–30). The Hague: Mouton.

Fraser, C. and Scherer, K.R. (1984) Introduction: social psychological contributions to the study of language. In C. Fraser and K.R. Scherer (eds), *Advances in the Social Psychology of Language* (pp. 1–9), Cambridge: Cambridge University Press.

Frazier, P.A. (1991) Self-blame as a mediator of post rape depressive symptoms. *Journal of Social and Clinical Psychology*, 10, 47–57.

Freedman, J.L. (1984) Effect of television violence on aggressiveness. *Psychological Bulletin*, 96, 227–46.

Freedman, J.L. (1988) Television violence and aggression: what the evidence shows. In S. Oskamp (ed.), *Applied Social Psychology Annual: Television as a social issue* (vol. 8, pp. 144–62), Newbury Park: Sage.

Freedman, J.L., Levy, A.S., Buchanan, R.W. and Price,

J. (1972) Crowding and human aggressiveness. *Journal of Experimental Social Psychology*, 8, 528–48.

Freud, S. (1940) *Gesammelte Werke* (18 vols). London: Imago.

Freud, S. (1953) *Group Psychology and the Analysis of the Ego* (1921 orig.). In J. Strachey (ed.), *The Standard Edition of Complete Psychological Works of Sigmund Freud* (vol. 18), London: Hogarth.

Freud, S. (1993) *New Introductory Lectures in Psycho-analysis*. New York: Norton.

Frey, D. (1986) Recent research on selective exposure to information. In L. Berkowitz (ed.), *Advances in Experimental Social Psychology* (vol. 19, pp. 41–80), New York: Academic Press.

Frey, D. and Gaska, A. (1993) Die Theorie der kognitiven Dissonanz. In D. Frey and M. Irle (eds), *Theorien der Sozialpsychologie* (vol. 1, pp. 275–324), Bern: Huber.

Frey, D. and Rogner, O. (1987) The relevance of psychological factors in the convalescence of accident patients. In G.R. Semin and B. Krahé (eds), *Issues in Contemporary German Social Psychology*, London: Sage.

Frey, D., Rogner, O., Schuler, M., Korte, C. and Havemann, D. (1985) Psychological determinants in the convalescence of accident patients. *Basic and Applied Social Psychology*, 6, 317–28.

Frey, D. and Rosch, M. (1984) Information seeking after decisions: the roles of novelty of information and decision reversibility. *Personality and Social Psychology Bulletin*, 10, 91–8.

Frey, D. and Stahlberg, D. (1986) Selection of information after receiving more or less reliable self-threatening information. *Personality and Social Psychology Bulletin*, 12, 434–41.

Frey, D., Stahlberg, D. and Fries, A. (1986) Information seeking of high- and low-anxiety subjects after receiving positive and negative self-relevant feedback. *Journal of Personality*, 54, 178–86.

Frey, D., Stahlberg, D. and Gollwitzer, P.M. (1993) Einstellung und Verhalten: die Theorie des überlegten Handelns und die Theorie des geplanten Verhaltens. In D. Frey and M. Irle *Theorien der Sozialpsychologie* (vol. 1, pp. 361–98), Bern: Huber.

Frick, R.W. (1985) Communicating emotion: the role of prosodic features. *Psychological Bulletin*, 97, 412–29.

Friedman, L. (1981) How affiliation affects stress in fear and anxiety situations. *Journal of Personality and Social Psychology*, 40, 1102–17.

Friedrich-Cofer, L. and Huston, A.C. (1986) Television violence and aggression: the debate continues. *Psychological Bulletin*, 100, 364–71.

Frijda, N.H. (1986) *The Emotions*. Cambridge and New York: Cambridge University Press.

Frijda, N.H. (1987) Emotion, cognitive structure, and action tendency. *Cognition and Emotion*, 1, 115–43.

Frijda, N.H. (1993a) Moods, emotion episodes, and emotions. In M. Lewis and J.M. Haviland (eds), *Handbook of Emotions* (pp. 381–404), New York: Guilford Press.

Frijda, N.H. (1993b) The place of appraisal in emotion. *Cognition and Emotion*, 7, 357–87.

Frijda, N.H., Kuipers, P. and ter Schure, E. (1989) Relations among emotion, appraisal, and emotional action readiness. *Journal of Personality and Social Psychology*, 57, 212–28.

Frye, D. and Moore, C. (eds) (1991) *Children's Theories of Mind: mental states and social understanding*. Hillsdale, NJ: Erlbaum.

Fuhrer, U. (1990) Bridging the ecological–psychological gap. *Environment and Behavior*, 22, 518–37.

Fultz, J., Batson, C.D., Fortenbach, V.A., McCarthy, P.M. and Varney, L.L. (1986) Social evaluation and the empathy–altruism hypothesis. *Journal of Personality and Social Psychology*, 50, 761–9.

Funder, D.C. (1982) On the accuracy of dispositional vs situational attributions. *Social Cognition*, 1, 205–22.

Funder, D.C. (1987) Errors and mistakes: evaluating the accuracy of social judgment. *Psychological Bulletin*, 101, 75–90.

Furnham, A. (1986) Assertiveness through different media. *Journal of Language and Social Psychology*, 5, 1–12.

Furth, H.G. (1980) *The World of Grown-ups: children's conceptions of society*. New York: Elsevier.

Gabler, H., Schultz, H.-J. and Weber, R. (1982) Zuschaueraggressionen – Eine Feldstudie über Fußballfans. In G. Pilz et al. (eds.), *Sport und Gewalt* (pp. 23–59), Schorndorf: Karl Hofmann.

Gaertner, S., Dovidio, J.F., Anastasio, P.A., Bachevan, B.A. and Rust, M.C. (1993) The common ingroup identity model: recategorization and the reduction of intergroup bias. In W. Stroebe and M. Hewstone (eds), *European Review of Social Psychology* (vol. 4, pp. 1–26). Chichester: Wiley.

Gaes, G.G., Kalle, R.J. and Tedeschi, J.T. (1978) Impression management in the forced compliance situation: two studies using the bogus pipeline. *Journal of Experimental Social Psychology*, 14, 493–510.

Gallagher-Thompson, D., Futterman, A. Farberow, N., Thompson, L.W. and Peterson, J. (1993) The impact of spousal bereavement on older widows and widowers. In M.S. Stroebe, W. Stroebe and R.O. Hansson (eds), *Handbook of Bereavement: theory, research and intervention* (pp. 227–39), Cambridge: Cambridge University Press.

Gangestad, S.W. and Buss, D.M. (1993) Pathogen

prevalence and human mate preferences. *Ethology and Sociobiology*, 14, 89–96.

Garland, H., Hardy, A. and Stephenson, L. (1975) Information search as affected by attribution type and response category. *Personality and Social Psychology Bulletin*, 4, 612–15.

Garton, A.F. (1992) *Social Interaction and the Development of Language and Cognition*. Hove: Erlbaum.

Gates, M.F. and Allee, W.C. (1933) Conditioned behavior of isolated and grouped cockroaches on a simple maze. *Journal of Comparative Psychology*, 15, 331–58.

Geen, R.G. (1990) *Human Aggression*. Milton Keynes: Open University Press.

Geen, R.G. (1991) Social motivation. *Annual Review of Psychology*, 42, 377–99.

Geen, R.G. and O'Neal, E.C. (1969) Activation of cue-elicited aggression by general arousal. *Journal of Personality and Social Psychology*, 11, 289–92.

Geen, R.G. and Stonner, D. (1971) Effects of aggressiveness habit strength on behavior in the presence of aggression-related stimuli. *Journal of Personality and Social Psychology*, 17, 149–53.

Gehm, T.L. and Scherer, K.R. (1988) Relating situation evaluation to emotion differentiation: nonmetric analysis of cross-cultural questionnaire data. In K.R. Scherer (ed.), *Facets of Emotion: recent research* (pp. 61–78), Hillsdale, NJ: Erlbaum.

Gerard, H.B. (1963) Emotional uncertainty and social comparison. *Journal of Abnormal and Social Psychology*, 66, 6, 568–73.

Gerard, H.B. and Mathewson, G.C. (1966) The effects of severity of initiation on liking for a group: a replication. *Journal of Experimental Social Psychology*, 2, 278–87.

Gerard, H.B., Wilhelmy, R.A. and Connelly, E.S. (1968) Conformity and group size. *Journal of Personality and Social Psychology*, 8, 79–82.

Gerbner, G., Cross, L., Morgan, M. and Signorelli, N. (1980) The 'mainstreaming' of America: violence profile no. 11. *Journal of Communication*, 32, 100–27.

Gergen, K.J. (1973) Social psychology as history. *Journal of Personality and Social Psychology*, 26, 309–20.

Gergen, K.J. (1978) Experimentation in social psychology: a reappraisal. *European Journal of Social Psychology*, 8, 507–27.

Gergen, K.J. (1985) Social psychology and the phoenix of unreality. In S. Koch and D.E. Leary (eds), *A Century of Psychology as Science* (pp. 528–57), New York: McGraw-Hill.

Gergen, K.J. and Gergen, M.M. (1983) The social construction of helping relationships. In J.D. Fisher, A. Nadler and B.M. DePaulo (eds), *New Directions in Helping* (vol. 1, pp. 143–63), New York: Academic Press.

Gibbons, F.X. (1978) Sexual standards and reactions to pornography: enhancing behavioral consistency through self-focused attention. *Journal of Personality and Social Psychology*, 36, 976–87.

Gibson, J.J. (1979) *The Ecological Approach to Visual Perception*. Boston: Houghton Mifflin.

Giddens, A. (1992) *Profiles and Critiques in Social Theory*. London: Macmillan.

Gigerenzer, G. and Hug, K. (1991) Domain-specific reasoning: social contracts, cheating, and perspective change. *Cognition*, 43, 127–71.

Gilbert, D.T. (1995) Attribution and interpersonal perception. In A. Tesser (ed.), *Advanced Social Psychology* (pp. 99–147), New York: McGraw-Hill.

Gilbert, D.T. and Hixon, J.G. (1991) The trouble of thinking: activation and application of stereotypic beliefs. *Journal of Experimental Social Psychology*, 60, 509–17.

Gilbert, D.T., Pelham, B.W. and Krull, D.S. (1988) On cognitive business: when person perceivers meet persons perceived. *Journal of Personality and Social Psychology*, 54, 733–40.

Gilbert, S.J. and Horenstein, D. (1975) The communication of self-disclosure: level versus valence. *Human Communication Research*, 1, 316, 22.

Giles, H. (ed.) (1977) *Language, Ethnicity and Intergroup Relations*. London: Academic Press.

Giles, H. and Coupland, N. (1991) *Language: contexts and consequences*. Milton Keynes: Open University Press.

Giles, H., Coupland, N. and Coupland, J. (eds) (1991) *The Contexts of Accommodation: dimensions in applied sociolinguistics*. New York: Cambridge University Press.

Giles, H., Coupland, N., Henwood, K., Harriman, J. and Coupland, J. (1990) The social meaning of R.P.: an intergenerational perspective. In S.M. Ramsaran (ed.), *Studies in the Pronunciation of English: commemorative volume in honor of A.C. Gimson* (pp. 191–221), London: Routledge.

Giles, H. and Farrar, K. (1979) Some behavioural consequences of speech and dress styles. *British Journal of Social and Clinical Psychology*, 18, 209–10.

Giles, H. and Fitzpatrick, M.A. (1984) Personal, group and couple identities: towards a relational context for the study of language attitudes and linguistic forms. In D. Schiffrin (ed.), *Meaning, Form and Use in Context: linguistic applications* (pp. 253–7), Washington, DC: Georgetown University Press.

Giles, H. and Johnson, P. (1981) The role of language in ethnic group relations. In J.C. Turner and H. Giles (eds), *Intergroup Behaviour* pp. 199–243, Oxford: Basil Blackwell.

Giles, H. and Johnson, P. (1986) Perceived threat, ethnic commitment and inter-ethnic language behaviour. In Y. Kim (ed.), *Interethnic Communication: recent research* (pp. 91–116), Beverly Hills: Sage.

Giles, H. and Powesland, P. (1975) *Speech Style and Social Evaluation*. London: Academic Press.

Giles, H. and Robinson, W.P. (eds) (1990) *Handbook of Language and Social Psychology*. Chichester: Wiley.

Giles, H. and Street, R.L. (1994) Communicator characteristics and behavior. In M.L. Knapp and G.R. Miller (eds), *Handbook of Interpersonal Communication* (pp. 103–61), Thousand Oaks, CA: Sage.

Giles, H. and Wiemann, J.M. (1987) Language, social comparison and power. In C.R. Berger and S. Chaffee (eds), *Handbook of Communication Science* (pp. 350–84), Newbury Park, CA: Sage.

Gilly, M. (1989) The psycho-social mechanisms of cognitive constructions. Experimental research and teaching perspectives. *International Journal of Educational Research*, 13, 607–21.

Gilmore,D.G. (1990) *Manhood in the Making: cultural concepts of masculinity*. New Haven and London: Yale University Press.

Gilovich, T. (1981) Seeing the past in the present: the effect of associations to familiar events on judgments and decisions. *Journal of Personality and Social Psychology*, 40, 797–808.

Glachan, M. and Light, P. (1982) Peer interaction and learning: can two wrongs make a right? In G. Butterworth and P. Light (eds), *Social Cognition. Studies of the development of understanding* (pp. 87–102). Chicago: The University of Chicago Press.

Glass, D.C., Gordon, A. and Henchy, T. (1970) The effects of social stimuli on psychophysiological reactivity to an aversive film. *Psychonomic Science*, 20, 255–6.

Glasser, W. (1975) *Reality Therapy: a new approach to psychiatry*. London: Harper & Row.

Gleitman, L.R. and Wanner, E. (1982) Language acquisition: the state of the art. In E. Wanner and L.R. Gleitman (eds), *Language Acquisition: the state of the art* (pp. 3–48), Cambridge: Cambridge University Press.

Goffman, E. (1963) *Behavior in Public Places*. New York: Free Press.

Goldfield, B.A. (1990) Pointing, naming, and talk about objects: referential behaviour in children and mothers. *First Language*, 10, 231–42.

Golinkoff, R.M. (ed.) (1983) *The Transition from Prelinguistic to Linguistic Communication*. Hillsdale, NJ: Erlbaum.

Gollwitzer, P.M. (1990) Action phases and mind-sets. In E.T. Higgins and R.M. Sorrentino (eds), *Handbook of Motivation and Cognition: Foundations of Social behavior* (vol. 2, pp. 53–92), New York: Guilford Press.

Gollwitzer, P.M. (1991) *Abwägen und Planen. Bewußtseinslagen in verschiedenen Handlungsphasen*. Göttingen: Hogrefe.

Gollwitzer, P.M. (1993) Goal achievement: The rule of intentions. In M. Hewstone and W. Stroebe (eds), *European Review of Social Psychology* (vol. 4, pp. 141–85), Chichester: Wiley.

Goodluck, H. (1991) *Language Acquisition: a linguistic introduction*. Oxford: Blackwell.

Gordon, K.H. (1924) Group judgments in the field of lifted weights. *Journal of Experimental Psychology*, 7, 398–400.

Gordon, R.M. (1987) *The Structure of Emotions: investigations in cognitive philosophy*. New York: Cambridge University Press.

Gorsuch, R.L. and Ortberg, J. (1983) Moral obligation and attitudes: their relation to behavioral intentions. *Journal of Personality and Social Psychology*, 44, 1025–8.

Gottman, J. (1982) Emotional responsiveness in marital conversations. *Journal of Communication*, 32, 108–20.

Gottman, J. (1993) Studying emotion in social interaction. In M. Lewis and J.M. Haviland (eds), *Handbook of Emotions* (pp. 475–88), New York: Guilford Press.

Gottman, J. and Levenson R. (1983) Marital interaction: physiological linkage and affective exchange. *Journal of Personality and Social Psychology*, 45, 587–97.

Gottman, J. and Levenson, R. (1988) The social psychophysiology of marriage. In P. Noller and M.A. Fitzpatrick (eds), *Perspectives on Marital Interaction* (pp. 182–200), Clevedon: Multilingual Matters.

Gouldner, A.W. (1960) The norm of reciprocity: a preliminary statement. *American Sociological Review*, 25, 161–78.

Grafen, A. (1982) How not to measure inclusive fitness. *Nature*, 298, 425–6.

Granberg, D. and Holmberg, S. (1990) The intention–behaviour relationship among US and Swedish voters. *Social Psychology Quarterly*, 53, 44–54.

Grant, J.D., Grant, J. and Toch, H. (1982) Police–citizen and decisions to arrest. In V. Konečni (eds), *The Criminal Justice System: a social psychological analysis*, San Francisco, CA: Freeman.

Graumann, C.F. (1976) Modification by migration: Vicissitudes of cross-national communication. *Social Research*, 43, 367–85.

Graumann, C.F. (1983) Theorie und Geschichte. In G. Lür (ed.), *Bericht über den 33. Kongreß der Deutschen Gesellschaft für Psychologie* (vol. 1 , pp. 64–75), Göttingen: Hogrefe.

Grauman, C.F. (1986) The individualization of the social and the desocialization of the individual: Floyd H. Allport's contribution to social psychology. In C.F. Graumann and S. Moscovici (eds), *Changing Conceptions of Crowd Mind and Behaviour*, New York: Springer.

Graumann, C.F. (1987) History as multiple reconstruction of mainstreams, tributaries and undercurrents. In G. Semin and B. Krahé (eds), *Issues in Contemporary German Social Psychology* (pp. 1–11), London: Sage.

Graumann, C.F. (1988) From knowledge to cognition. In D. Bar-Tal and A.W. Kruglanski (eds), *Social Psychology of Knowledge* (pp. 15–29), Cambridge: Cambridge University Press.

Graumann, C.F. and Moscovici, S. (eds) (1986) *Changing Conceptions of Crowd Mind and Behavior*. New York: Springer-Verlag.

Gray, J.A. (1990) Brain systems that mediate both emotion and cognition. *Cognition and Emotion*, 4, 269–88.

Greenberg, M.S., Wilson, C.E., Ruback, R.B. and Mills, M.K. (1979) Social and emotional determinants of victim crime reporting. *Social Psychology Quarterly*, 42, 364–72.

Greenstein, T.N. and Knotterus, J.D. (1980) The effects of differential evaluations on status generalization. *Social Psychology Quarterly*, 43, 147–54.

Greenwald, A.G. (1968) Cognitive learning, cognitive response to persuasion, and attitude change. In A.G. Greenwald, T.C. Brock and T.M. Ostrom (eds), *Psychological Foundations of Attitudes* (pp. 147–170), San Diego, CA: Academic Press.

Greenwald, A.G. (1975a) Does the Good Samaritan parable increase helping? A comment on Darley and Batson's no-effect conclusion. *Journal of Personality and Social Psychology*, 32, 578–83.

Greenwald, A.G. (1975b) On the inconclusiveness of 'crucial' tests of dissonance versus self-perception theories. *Journal of Experimental Social Psychology*, 11, 490–9.

Grice, H.P. (1975) Logic and conversation. In P. Cole and J.L. Morgan (eds), *Syntax and Semantics, vol. 3: Speech Acts* (pp. 41–58), New York: Academic Press.

Griffit, W. and Veitch, R. (1974) Preacquaintance attitude in similarity and attraction revisited: ten days in a fall-out shelter. *Sociometry*, 37, 163–73.

Groebel, J. and Krebs, D. (1983) A study of the effects of television on anxiety. In C.D. Spielberger and R. Diaz-Guerrero (eds), *Cross Cultural Anxiety* (vol. 2, pp. 89–98), Washington, DC: Hemisphere.

Gruder, C.L., Romer, D. and Korth, B. (1978) Dependency and fault as determinants of helping. *Journal of Experimental Social Psychology*, 14, 227–35.

Grusec, J.E. and Redler, E. (1980) Attribution, reinforcement, and altruism: a developmental analysis. *Developmental Psychology*, 16, 525–34.

Gudjonsson, G. and Clark, N.K. (1986) Suggestibility in police interrogation: a social psychological model. *Social Behaviour*, 1, 83–104.

Gudykunst, W.B. (ed.) (1986) *Intergroup Communication*. London: Edward Arnold.

Gudykunst, W.B. and Kim, Y. (1984) *Communicating with Strangers: an approach to intercultural communication*. New York: Random House.

Guimelli, C. (1993) Locating the central core of social representations: towards a method. *European Journal of Social Psychology*, 23, 555–9.

Guimond, S. and Dubé-Simard, L. (1983) Relative deprivation theory and the Quebec nationalist movement: the cognition–emotion distinction and the personal–group deprivation issue. *Journal of Personality and Social Psychology*, 44, 526–35.

Gurr, T.R. (1970) *Why Men Rebel*. Princeton, NJ: Princeton University Press.

Gusella, J.L., Muir, D. and Tronick, E.Z. (1988) The effect of manipulating maternal behavior during an interaction on three- and six-month-olds' affect and attention. *Child Development*, 59, 1111–24.

Gustafson, R. (1986) Human physical aggression as a function of frustration: role of aggression cues. *Psychological Reports*, 58, 103–10.

Gustafson, R. (1989) Frustration and successful vs unsuccessful aggression: a test of Berkowitz's hypothesis. *Aggressive Behavior*, 15, 5–12.

Gutheil, I.A. (1992) Considering the physical environment: an essential component of good practice. *Social Work*, 37, 391–6.

Haaland, G.A. and Venkatesan, M. (1968) Resistance to persuasive communication: an examination of the distraction hypotheses. *Journal of Personality and Social Psychology*, 9, 167–70.

Hagendoorn, L. and Henke, R. (1991) The effect of multiple category membership on intergroup evaluations in a North-Indian context: class, caste, and religion. *British Journal of Social Psychology*, 30, 247–60.

Haines, H. and Vaughan, G.M. (1979) Was 1898 a 'great date' in the history of experimental social psychology? *Journal of the History of the Behavioral Sciences*, 15, 323–32.

Haldane, J.B.S. (1955) Population genetics. In M.L. Johnson, M. Abercrombie and G.E. Fogg (eds), *New Biology* (no. 18, pp. 33–51), London: Penguin.

Halle, T. and Shatz, M. (1994) Mothers' social regulatory language to young children in family settings. *First Language*, 14, 83–104.

Halpin, A.W. and Winer, B.J. (1952) *The Leadership*

Behavior of the Airplane Commander. Columbus: Ohio State University Research Foundation.

Hamilton, D.L. (1981) Illusory correlations as a basis for stereotyping. In D.L. Hamilton (ed.), *Cognitive Processes in Stereotyping and Intergroup Behavior*, pp. 115–44. Hillsdale, NJ: Erlbaum.

Hamilton, D.L. (1988) Causal attribution viewed from an information processing perspective. In D. Bar-Tal and A.W. Kruglanski (eds), *The Social Psychology of Knowledge* (pp. 359–85), Cambridge: Cambridge University Press.

Hamilton, D.L. and Gifford, R.K. (1976) Illusory correlation in interpersonal perception: a cognitive basis of stereotypic judgments. *Journal of Experimental Social Psychology*, 12, 392–407.

Hamilton, D.L., Katz, L.B. and Leirer, V.O. (1980) Cognitive representation of personality impressions: organizational processes in first impression formation. *Journal of Personality and Social Psychology*, 39, 1050–63.

Hamilton, D.L. and Rose, R.L. (1980) Illusory correlation and the maintenance of stereotypic beliefs. *Journal of Personality and Social Psychology*, 39, 832–45.

Hamilton, W.D. (1964) The genetical evolution of social behavior, I and II. *Journal of Theoretical Biology*, 7, 1–52.

Hamilton, W.D. (1975) Innate social aptitudes of man: an approach from evolutionary genetics. In R. Fox (ed.), *Biosocial Anthropology* (pp. 133–55), London: Malaby Press.

Hamilton, W.D. and Zuk, M. (1982) Heritable true fitness and bright birds: a role for parasites. *Science*, 218, 384–7.

Hans, V.P. and Vidmar, N. (1982) Jury selection. In N.L. Kerr and R.M. Bray (eds), *The Psychology of the Courtroom*, London: Academic Press.

Hanson, D.J. and Blohm, E.R. (1974) Authoritarianism and attitudes towards mental patients. *International Behavioural Scientist*, 6, 57–60.

Harcourt, A.H. (1991) Help, co-operation and trust in animals. In R.A. Hinde and J. Groebel (eds), *Cooperation and Prosocial Behaviour* (pp. 15–26), Cambridge: Cambridge University Press.

Hargreaves, D.H. (1967) *Social relations in a Secondary School*. London: Routledge & Kegan Paul.

Harkins, S.G. and Jackson, J.M. (1985) The role of evaluation in eliminating social loafing. *Personality and Social Psychology Bulletin*, 11, 457–65.

Harré, R.M. (1986) *The Social Construction of Emotions*. Oxford: Blackwell.

Harris, P.L. (1989) *Children and Emotion. The development of psychological understanding*. Oxford: Blackwell.

Hartup, W.W. (1991) Social development and social

psychology: perspectives on interpersonal relationships. In J.H. Cantor, C.C. Spiker and L. Lipsitt (eds), *Child Behavior and Development: Training for diversity* (pp. 1–33), Norwood, N.J.: Ablex.

Harvey, D.J. (1965) The history of psychology as sociology of thought. *Journal of the History of the Behavioral Sciences*, 1, 196–202.

Harvey, J.H. (1987) Attributions in close relationships: Research and theoretical developments. *Journal of Social and Clinical Psychology*, 5, 420–34.

Harvey, J.H., Town, J.P. and Yarkin, K.L. (1981) How fundamental is 'The fundamental attribution error'? *Journal of Personality and Social Psychology*, 40, 346–9.

Harvey, J.H., Weber, A.L. and Orbuch, T.L. (1990) *Interpersonal Accounts: a social psychological perspective*. Oxford: Blackwell.

Harwood, J., Giles, H. and Bourhis, R.Y. (1994) The genesis of vitality theory: historical patterns and discoursal dimensions. *International Journal of the Sociology of Language*, 108, 168–206.

Hastie, R. (1980) Memory for information that confirms or contradicts a general impression. In R. Hastie, T.M. Ostrom, E.B. Ebbesen, R.S. Wyer, D.L. Hamilton and D.E. Carlston (eds), *Person Memory: the cognitive basis of social perception* (pp. 155–77), Hillsdale, NJ: Erlbaum.

Hastie, R. and Park, B. (1986) The relationship between memory and judgment depends on whether the judgment task is memory-based or on-line. *Psychological Review*, 93, 258–68.

Hastie, R., Penrod, S.D. and Pennington, N. (1983) *Inside the Jury*. Cambridge, MA: Harvard University Press.

Hatfield, E. (1988) Passionate and compassionate love. In R.J. Sternberg and M.L. Barnes (eds), *The Psychology of Love* (pp. 191–217), New Haven: Yale University Press.

Hatfield, E., Cacioppo, J.T. and Rapson, R.L. (1994) *Emotional Contagion*. Cambridge and New York: Cambridge University Press.

Hatfield, E. and Sprecher, S. (1986) *Mirror, mirror . . . The importance of looks in everyday life*. New York: SUNY Press.

Haugtvedt, C.P. and Petty, R.E. (1992) Personality and persuasion: need for cognition moderates the persistence and resistance of attitude changes. *Journal of Personality and Social Psychology*, 63, 308–19.

Hays, R.B. (1988) Friendship. In S. Duck (ed.), *Handbook of Personal Relationships* (pp. 391–408), Chichester: Wiley.

Hazan, C. and Shaver, P. (1987) Romantic love conceptualized as an attachment process. *Journal of Personality and Social Psychology*, 52, 511–24.

Hearnshaw, L.S. (1964) *A Short History of British Psychology, 1840–1940*. London: Methuen.

Hearold, S. (1986) A synthesis of 1043 effects of television on social behavior. In G. Comstock (ed.), *Public Communication and Behavior* (vol. 1, pp. 65–133), New York: Academic Press.

Hebb, D.O. and Thompson, W.R. (1968) The social significance of animal studies. In G. Lindzey and E. Aronson (eds), *Handbook of Social Psychology*, 2nd edn (pp. 729–74), Reading, MA: Addison-Wesley.

Hecht, M., Collier, M.A. and Ribeau, S. (1993) *African American Communication*. Thousand Oaks, CA: Sage.

Heckhausen, H. (1990) *Motivation und Handeln*. Heidelberg: Springer.

Hedges, L.V. and Olkin, I. (1985) *Statistical Methods for Meta-analysis*. New York: Academic Press.

Heider, F. (1944) Social perception and phenomenal causality. *Psychological Review*, 51, 358–78.

Heider, F. (1946) Attitudes and cognitive organization. *Journal of Psychology*, 21, 107–12.

Heider, F. (1958) *The Psychology of Interpersonal Relations*. New York: Wiley.

Heise, D.R. and O'Brien, J. (1993) Emotion expression in groups. In M. Lewis and J.M. Haviland (eds), *Handbook of Emotions* (pp. 489–98), New York: Guildford Press.

Hellpach, W. (1933) *Elementares Lehrbuch der Sozialpsychologie*. Berlin: Springer.

Helson, H. (1964) *Adaptation-Level Theory: an experimental and systematic approach to behavior*. New York: Harper & Row.

Hemphill, J.K. (1961) Why people attempt to lead. In L. Petrullo and B.M. Bass (eds), *Leadership and Interpersonal Behavior*, New York: Holt, Rinehart & Winston.

Henchy, T. and Glass, D.C. (1968) Evaluation apprehension and the social facilitation of dominant and subordinate responses. *Journal of Personality and Social Psychology*, 10, 446–54.

Henderson, M. and Hewstone, M. (1984) Prison inmates' explanation for interpersonal violence: accounts and attributions. *Journal of Consulting and Clinical Psychology*, 52, 789–94.

Hensley, T.R. and Griffin, G.W. (1986) Victims of groupthink: the Kent State University Board of Trustees and the 1977 gymnasium controversy. *Journal of Conflict Resolution*, 30, 497–531.

Hepworth, J.T. and West, S.G. (1988) Lynchings and the economy: a time series analysis of Hovland and Sears (1940) *Journal of Personality and Social Psychology*, 55, 239–47.

Herek, G.M. (1986) The instrumentality of attitudes: toward a neofunctional theory. *Journal of Social Issues*, 42, 99–114.

Herr, P.M., Sherman, S.J. and Fazio, R.H. (1983) On the consequences of priming: assimilation and contrast effects. *Journal of Experimental Social Psychology*, 19, 323–40.

Hewes, D., Graham, M.L., Doelger, J. and Pavitt, C. (1985) Second guessing: message interpretation in social networks. *Human Communication Research*, 11, 299–334.

Hewstone, M. (1989) *Causal Attribution: from cognitive processes to collective beliefs*. Oxford, UK and Cambridge, MA: Blackwell.

Hewstone, M. (1990) The 'ultimate attribution error'. A review of the literature on intergroup causal attribution. *European Journal of Social Psychology*, 20, 311–35.

Hewstone, M. (1994) Revision and change of stereotypic beliefs. In W. Stroebe and M. Hewstone (eds), *European Review of Social Psychology* (vol. 5, pp. 69–110), Chichester: J. Wiley.

Hewstone, M. and Brown, R.J. (1986) Contact is not enough: an intergroup perspective on the contact hypothesis. In M. Hewstone and R. Brown (eds), *Contact and Conflict in Intergroup Encounters* (pp. 1–44), Oxford: Basil Blackwell.

Hewstone, M. and Jaspars, J. (1987) Covariation and causal attribution: a logical model of the intuitive analysis of variance. *Journal of Personality and Social Psychology*, 53, 663–72.

Hewstone, M., Fincham, F. and Jaspars, J. (1981) Social categorization and similarity in intergroup behavior: a replication with penalties. *European Journal of Social Psychology*, 11, 101–7.

Hewstone, M., Islam, M.R. and Judd, C.M. (1993) Models of crossed categorization and intergroup relations. *Journal of Personality and Social Psychology*, 64, 779–93.

Hiebsch, H. and Vorweg, M. (1980) *Sozial psychologie*. Berlin: Deutscher Verlag der Wissenschaften.

Higgins, E.T. (1980) The 'communication game': implications for social cognition and persuasion. In E.T. Higgins, C.P. Herman and M.P. Zanna (eds), *Social Cognition: the Ontario symposium* (vol. 1, pp. 343–92), Hillsdale, NJ: Erlbaum.

Higgins, E.T. and Bryant, S.L. (1982) Consensus information and the fundamental attribution error: the role of development and in-group versus out-group knowledge. *Journal of Personality and Social Psychology*, 43, 889–900.

Higgins, E.T., Rhodewalt, F. and Zanna, M.P. (1979) Dissonance motivation: its nature, persistence and reinstatement. *Journal of Experimental Social Psychology*, 63, 308–19.

Higgins, E.T., Rholes, W.S. and Jones, C.R. (1977) Category accessibility and impression formation. *Journal of Experimental Social Psychology*, 13, 141–54.

Hildum, D.C. and Brown, R.W. (1965) Verbal reinforcement and interviewer bias. *Journal of Abnormal and Social Psychology*, 53, 108–11.

Hill, C.A. (1987) Affiliation motivation: people who need people but in different ways. *Journal of Personality and Social Psychology*, 52, 1008–18.

Hilton, D.J. (1990) Conversational processes and causal explanation. *Psychological Bulletin*, 107, 65–81.

Hilton, D.J. (1991) A conversational model of causal attribution. In W. Stroebe and M. Hewstone (eds), *European Review of Social Psychology* (vol. 2, pp. 51–82), Chichester: Wiley.

Hilton, D.J. and Slugoski, B.R. (1986) Knowledge-based causal attribution: the Abnormal Conditions Focus model. *Psychological Review*, 93, 75–88.

Hilton, J.L. and Darley, J.M. (1991) The effects of interaction goals on person perception. In M.P. Zanna (ed.), *Advances in Experimental Social Psychology* (vol. 24, pp. 235–67), New York: Academic Press.

Hilton, J.L. and Fein, S. (1989) The role of typical diagnosticity in stereotype-based judgments. *Journal of Personality and Social Psychology*, 57, 201–11.

Hinde, R.A. (1960) Energy models of motivation. *Symposia of the Society for Experimental Biology*, 14, 199–213.

Hinde, R.A. (1974) *Biological Bases of Human Social Behavior*. New York: McGraw-Hill.

Hindelang, M.J., Hirschi, T. and Weis, J.G. (1981) *Measuring Delinquency*. Beverly Hills: Sage.

Hinkle, S. and Brown, R. (1990) Intergroup comparisons and social identity: some links and lacunae. In D. Abrams and M. Hogg (eds), *Social Identity Theory: constructive and critical advances* (pp. 48–70), Hemel Hempstead: Harvester Wheatsheaf.

Hintzmann, D.L. (1986) 'Schema abstraction' in a multiple-trace memory model. *Psychological Review*, 93, 411–28.

Hirsh-Pasek, K. and Treiman, R. (1982) Doggerel: motherese in a new context. *Journal of Child Language*, 9, 229–37.

Hobfoll, S.E. and London, P. (1986) The relationship of self-concept and social support to emotional distress among women during war. *Journal of Social and Clinical Psychology*, 4, 189–203.

Hochschild, A.R. (1979) Emotion work, feeling rules, and social structure. *American Journal of Sociology*, 3, 551–75.

Hochschild, A.R. (1983) *The Managed Heart: the commercialization of human feeling*. Berkeley: University of California Press.

Hoekstra, M. and Wilke, H. (1972) Wage recommendations in management groups: a cross-cultural study. *Nederlands Tijdschrift voor de Psychologie*, 27, 266–72.

Hoffman, M.L. (1990) Empathy and justice motivation. *Motivation and Emotion*, 14, 151–72.

Hogg, M. (1985) Male and female speech in dyads and groups: a study of speech style and gender salience. *Journal of Language and Social Psychology*, 4, 99–112.

Hogg, M. and Abrams, D. (1990) Social motivation, self-esteem and social identity. In D. Abrams and M. Hogg, *Social Identity Theory: constructive and critical advances* (pp. 28–47), Hemel Hempstead: Harvester Wheatsheaf.

Hogg, M. and Sunderland, J. (1991) Self esteem and intergroup discrimination in the minimal group paradigm. *British Journal of Social Psychology*, 30, 51–62.

Hogg, M. and Turner, C. (1987) Intergroup behaviour, self stereotyping and the salience of social categories. *British Journal of Social Psychology*, 26, 325–40.

Hogg, M., Turner, J.C. and Davidson, B. (1990) Polarized norms and social frames of reference: a test of the self-categorization theory of group polarization. *Basic and Applied Social Psychology*, 11, 77–100.

Holahan, C.J. (1976a) Seating patterns and patient behaviour in an experimental day room. *Journal of Abnormal Psychology*, 80, 115–24.

Holahan, C.J. (1976b) Environmental change in a psychiatric setting. *Human Relations*, 29, 153–66.

Hollon, S.D., Shelton, R.C. and Loosen, P.T. (1991). Cognitive therapy and pharmacotherapy for depression. *Journal of Consulting and Clinical Psychology*, 58, 88–99.

Holtgraves, T. (1993) The language of self-disclosure. In H. Giles and P. Robinson (eds), *Handbook of Language and Social Psychology* (pp. 192–207), Chichester and New York: Wiley.

Holtzworth-Munroe, A. and Jacobson, N.S. (1988). An attributional approach to marital dysfunction and therapy. In J.E. Maddux, C.D. Stoltenberg and R. Rosenwein (eds), *Social Processes in Clinical and Counselling Psychology* (pp. 153–70). New York: Springer-Verlag.

Hormuth, S.E. (1979) *Sozialpsychologie der Einstellungsänderung*. Königstein/TS: Verlagsgruppe Athenäum.

Horneffer, K.J. and Fincham, F.D. (1955). The construct of attributional style in depression and marital distress. *Journal of Family Psychology*, 9, 186–95.

Horowitz, I.A. (1969) Effects of volunteering, fear, arousal, and number of communications on attitude change. *Journal of Personality and Social Psychology*, 11, 34–7.

Horowitz, M. and Rabbie, J.M. (1982) Individuality and membership in the intergroup system. In H. Tajfel (ed.), *Social Identity and Intergroup Relations* (pp. 241–74), Cambridge: Cambridge University Press.

Hosking, D.M. (1981) A critical evaluation of Fiedler's

contingency hypothesis. In G.M. Stephenson and J.M. Davis (eds), *Progress in Applied Social Psychology* (vol. 1, pp. 103–54), Chichester: Wiley.

Hough, M. and Mayhew, P. (1983) *The British Crime survey: first report*. London: HMSO.

House, J.S. (1981) *Work Stress and Social Support*. Reading, MA: Addison-Wesley.

Houston, D.A. and Fazio, R.H. (1989) Biased processing as a function of attitude accessibility: making objective judgments subjectively. *Social Cognition*, 7, 51–66.

Hovland, C. and Sears, R.R. (1940) Minor studies in aggression: correlation of lynchings with economic indices. *Journal of Psychology*, 9, 301–10.

Hovland, C.I., Janis, I.L. and Kelley, H.H. (1953) *Communication and Persuasion: psychological studies of opinion change*. Princeton, NJ: Princeton University Press.

Hovland, C.I. and Sherif, M. (1952) Judgmental phenomena and scales of attitude measurement: item displacement in Thurstone scales. *Journal of Abnormal and Social Psychology*, 47, 822–32.

Howe, C.J., Rodgers, C. and Tolmie, A. (1990) Physics in the primary school: peer interaction and the understanding of floating and sinking. *European Journal of Psychology of Education*, 5, 459–75.

Howe, C.J., Tolmie, A. and Rodgers, C. (1992) The acquisition of conceptual knowledge in science by primary school children: group interaction and the understanding of motion down an incline. *British Journal of Developmental Psychology*, 10, 113–30.

Hoyt, M.F., Henley, M.D. and Collins, B.E. (1972) Studies in forced compliance: confluence of choice and consequence on attitude change. *Journal of Personality and Social Psychology*, 23, 205–10.

Hraba, J. and Grant, G. (1990) Black is beautiful: a re-examination of racial preference and identification. *Journal of Personality and Social Psychology*, 16, 398–402.

Hrdy, S.B. (1979) Infanticide among animals: a review, classification and examination of the implications for the reproductive strategies of females. *Ethology and Sociobiology*, 1, 3–40.

Huesmann, L.R., Lagerspetz, K. and Eron, L.D. (1984) Intervening variables in the TV violence–aggression relation: evidence from two countries. *Developmental Psychology*, 20, 746–75.

Huesmann, L.R. and Miller, L.S. (1994) Long-term effects of repeated exposure to media violence in childhood. In L.R. Huesmann (ed.), *Aggressive Behavior: current perspectives* (pp. 153–86), New York: Plenum.

Hutt, C. and McGrew, W.C. (1967) Effects of group density upon social behavior in humans. In *Changes in behavior with population density*. Paper presented at the Meeting of the Association for the Study of Animal Behavior, Oxford, 17–20 July.

Hymes, R.W. (1986) Political attitudes as social categories: a new look at selective memory. *Journal of Personality and Social Psychology*, 51, 233–41.

Ilgen, D.R. and Fujji, D.S. (1976) An investigation of the validity of leader behavior descriptions obtained from subordinates, *Journal of Applied Psychology*, 61, 642–51.

Ingham, A.G., Levinger, G., Graves, J. and Peckham, V. (1974) The Ringlemann effect: studies of group size and group performance. *Journal of Personality and Social Psychology*, 10, 371–84.

Insko, C.A. (1965) Verbal reinforcement of attitude. *Journal of Personality and Social Psychology*, 2, 621–3.

Insko, C.A., Drenan, S., Solomon, M.R., Smith, R. and Wade, T.J. (1983) Conformity as a function of the consistency of positive self-evaluation with being liked and being right. *Journal of Experimental Social Psychology*, 19, 341–58.

Insko, C.A. and Oakes, W.F. (1966) Awareness and the 'conditioning' of attitudes. *Journal of Personality and Social Psychology*, 4, 487–96.

Irving, B. (1980) Police interrogation; a case study of present practice. Research study no. 2, Royal Commission on Criminal Procedure, London: HMSO.

Irving, B. and Hilgendorf, L. (1980) Police interrogation: the psychological approach. Research study no. 1, Royal Commission on Criminal Procedure, London: HMSO.

Isen, A.M. (1990) The influence of positive and negative affect on cognitive organization: some implications for development. In B. Leventhal, N.L. Stein and T. Trabasso (eds), *Psychological and Biological Approaches to Emotion* (pp. 75–94), Hillsdale, NJ: Lawrence Erlbaum Associates.

Isen, A.M. (1994) Towards understanding the role of affect in cognition. In R.S. Wyer and T.K. Srull (eds), *Handbook of Social Cognition* (vol. 3, pp. 179–236), Hillsdale, NJ: Erlbaum.

Isen, A.M., Clark, M. and Schwartz, M.F. (1976) Duration of the effect of good mood on helping: 'Footprints on the sands of time'. *Journal of Personality and Social Psychology*, 34, 385–93.

Isen, A.M., Daubman, K.A. and Nowicki, G.P. (1987) Positive affect facilitates creative problem solving. *Journal of Personality and Social Psychology*, 52, 1122–31.

Isen, A.M., Horn, N. and Rosenhan, D.L. (1973) Effects of success and failure on children's generosity. *Journal of Personality and Social Psychology*, 27, 384–8.

Isen, A.M., Johnson, M.M.S., Hertz, E. and Robinson, G.F. (1985) The effects of positive affect on the unusualness of word associations. *Journal of Personality and Social Psychology*, 48, 1413–14.

Isen, A.M., Means, B., Patrick, R. and Nowicki, G.P. (1982) Some factors influencing decision-making and risk taking. In M.S. Clark and S.T. Fiske (eds), *Affect and Cognition* (pp. 243–61), Hillsdale, NJ: Erlbaum.

Isen, A.M., Shalkner, T.W., Clark, M. and Karp, L. (1978) Positive affect, accessibility of material in memory and behavior: a cognitive loop? *Journal of Personality and Social Psychology*, 36, 1–12.

Isenberg, D.J. (1986) Group polarization: a critical review and meta-analysis. *Journal of Personality and Social Psychology*, 50, 1141–51.

Islam, M. and Hewstone, M. (1993) Dimensions of contact as predictors of intergroup anxiety, perceived outgroup variability, and outgroup attitude: an integrative model. *Personality and Social Psychology Bulletin*, 64, 700–710.

Islam, M. and Hewstone, M. (1993) Intergroup attributions and affective consequences in majority and minority groups. *Journal of Personality and Social Psychology*, 65, 936–50.

Israel, J. and Tajfel, H. (eds) (1972) *The Context of Social Psychology. A critical assessment*. London: Academic Press.

Izard, C.E. (1971) *The Face of Emotion*. New York: Appleton-Century-Crofts.

Izard, C.E. (1990) Facial expression and the regulation of emotions. *Journal of Personality and Social Psychology*, 58, 487–98.

Izard, C.E. (1991) *The Psychology of Emotions*. New York: Plenum Press.

Izard, C.E. (1992) Basic emotions, relations among emotions, and emotion–cognition relations. *Psychological Review*, 99, 561–5.

Jackson, B.S. (1990) *Law, Fact and Narrative Coherence*. Merseyside: Deborah Charles.

Jackson, J.M. and Harkins, J.M. (1985) Equity in effort: an explanation of the social loafing effect. *Journal of Personality and Social Psychology*, 49, 1199–1206.

Jacobs, K.C. and Campbell, D.T. (1961) The perpetuation of an arbitrary tradition through several generations of a laboratory microculture. *Journal of Abnormal and Social Psychology*, 62, 649–58.

Jaffe, Y. and Yinon, Y. (1983) Collective Aggression: the group–individual paradigm in the study of collective antisocial behavior. In H.H. Blumberg, A.P. Hare, V. Kent and M. Davies (eds), *Small Groups and Social Interaction* (vol. 1, pp. 267–75), New York: Wiley.

Jahoda, G. (1962) Development of Scottish children's ideas and attitudes about their countries. *Journal of Social Psychology*, 58, 91–108.

Jahoda, G. (1963) The development of children's ideas about country and nationality: the conceptual framework. *British Journal of Educational Psychology*, 33, 47–60.

Jahoda, G. (1983) European 'lag' in the development of an economic concept: a study in Zimbabwe. *British Journal of Developmental Psychology*, 1, 113–20.

Jahoda, G. (1984) The development of thinking about socio-economic systems. In H. Tajfel (ed.), *The Social Dimension* (vol. 1, pp. 69–88), Cambridge: Cambridge University Press.

Jahoda, G. (1988) Critical notes and reflections on 'social representation'. *European Journal of Social Psychology*, 18, 195–209.

James, W. (1884) What is an emotion? *Mind*, 9, 188–205. Reprinted in M.B. Arnold (ed.) (1968) *The Nature of Emotion: selected readings* (pp. 17–36), Harmondsworth: Penguin.

James, W. (1890) *Principles of Psychology* (2 vols). New York: Holt, Rinehart & Winston.

James, W. (1894) The physical basis of emotion. *Psychological Review*, 1, 516–29.

Janis, I.L. (1972) *Victims of Groupthink*. Boston, MA: Houghton Mifflin.

Janis, I. (1982) *Groupthink*, 2nd edn. Boston, MA: Houghton Mifflin.

Jaspars, J. (1980) The coming of age of social psychology in Europe. *European Journal of Social Psychology*, 10, 421–8.

Jaspars, J. (1983) The task of social psychology. *British Journal of Social Psychology*, 22, 277–88.

Jaspars, J. (1986) Forum and focus: a personal view of European social psychology. *European Journal of Social Psychology*, 16, 3–15.

Jaworski, A. (1993) *The Power of Silence*. Thousand Oaks, CA: Sage.

Jellison, J.M. and Davis, D. (1973) Relationships between perceived ability and attitude extremity. *Journal of Personality and Social Psychology*, 27, 430–6.

Jenni, D.A. (1974) Evolution of polyandry in birds. *American Zoologist*, 14, 129–44.

Jodelet, D. (1984) Représentations sociales: phénomènes, concept et théories. In S. Moscovici (ed.), *Psychologie sociale* (pp. 357–78), Paris: Presses Universitaires de France.

Johnson, C.D. and Gormly, A.V. (1975) Personality, attraction, and social ambiguity. *Journal of Social Psychology*, 97, 227–32.

Johnson, D.J. and Rusbult, C.E. (1989) Resisting temptation: devaluation of alternative partners as a means of maintaining commitment. *Journal of Personality and Social Psychology*, 57, 967–80.

Johnson, D.W., Maruyama, G., Johnson, R., Nelson, D.

and Skon, L. (1981) Effects of cooperative, competitive and individualistic goal structures on achievement: a meta-analysis. *Psychological Bulletin*, 89, 47–62.

Johnson, E. and Tversky, A. (1983) Affect, generalization, and the perception of risk. *Journal of Personality and Social Psychology*, 45, 20–31.

Johnson, M.H. and Morton, J. (1991) *Biology and Cognitive Development: the case of face recognition*. Oxford: Blackwell.

Johnson, M.K. and Raye, C.L. (1981) Reality monitoring. *Psychological Review*, 88, 67–85.

Johnson, T.E. and Rule, B.G. (1986) Mitigating circumstances, information, censure, and aggression. *Journal of Personality and Social Psychology*, 50, 537–42.

Johnson, W.G., Ross, J.M. and Mastria, M.A. (1977) Delusional behavior: An attribution analysis of development and modification. *Journal of Abnormal Psychology*, 86, 421–6.

Johnston, L. and Hewstone, M. (1992) Cognitive models of stereotype change (2): typicality and prototype–exemplar relations. *Journal of Experimental Social Psychology*, 28, 360–86.

Jones, E.E. (1985) Major developments in social psychology during the past four decades. In G. Lindzey, and E. Aronson (eds), *The Handbook of Social Psychology*, 3rd edn (vol. 1, pp. 47–107), New York: Random.

Jones, E.E. (1990) *Interpersonal Perception*. New York: Macmillan.

Jones, E.E. and Aneshansel, J. (1956) The learning and utilization of contravaluant material. *Journal of Abnormal and Social Psychology*, 53, 27–33.

Jones, E.E. and Davis, K.E. (1965) From acts to dispositions: the attribution process in person perception. In L. Berkowitz (ed.), *Advances in Experimental Social Psychology* (vol. 2, pp. 219–66), New York: Academic Press.

Jones, E.E., Davis, K.E. and Gergen, K.J. (1961) Role playing variations and their informational value for person perception. *Journal of Abnormal and Social Psychology*, 63, 302–10.

Jones, E.E. and Gerard, H.B. (1967) *Foundations of Social Psychology*. New York: Wiley.

Jones, E.E. and Harris, V.A. (1967) The attribution of attitudes. *Journal of Experimental Social Psychology*, 3, 1–24.

Jones, E.E. and McGillis, D. (1976) Correspondent inferences and the attribution cube: a comparative reappraisal. In J.H. Harvey, W.J. Ickes and R.F. Kidd (eds), *New Directions in Attribution Research* (pp. 389–420), Hillsdale, NJ: Erlbaum.

Jones, E.E. and Nisbett, R.E. (1972) The actor and the observer: divergent perceptions of the causes of behaviour. In E.E. Jones, D.E. Kanouse, H.H. Kelley, R.E. Nisbett, S. Valins and B. Weiner (eds), *Attribution: perceiving the causes of behaviour* (pp. 79–94), Morristown, NJ: General Learning Press.

Jones, E.E. and Sigall, H. (1971) The bogus pipeline: a new paradigm for measuring affect and attitude. *Psychological Bulletin*, 76, 349–64.

Jones, E.E., Wood, G.C. and Quattrone, G.A. (1981) Perceived variability of personal characteristics in ingroups and outgroups: the role of knowledge and evaluation. *Journal of Personality and Social Psychology*, 7, 523–8.

Judd, C.M. and Kenny, D.A. (1981) *Estimating the Effects of Social Interventions*. New York: Cambridge University Press.

Judd, C.M., Kenny, D.A. and Krosnick, J.A. (1983) Judging the positions of political candidates: models of assimilation and contrast. *Journal of Personality and Social Psychology*, 44, 952–63.

Judd, C.M. and Kulik, J.A. (1980) Schematic effects of social attitudes on information processing and recall. *Journal of Personality and Social Psychology*, 38, 569–78.

Kahneman, D. and Tversky, A. (1972) A judgment of representativeness. *Cognitive Psychology*, 3, 430–54.

Kahneman, D., Slovic, P. and Tversky, A. (eds) (1982) *Judgment under Uncertainty: heuristics and biases*. Cambridge: Cambridge University Press.

Kalin, R. (1982) The social significance of speech in medical, legal and occupational settings. In E.B. Ryan and H. Giles (eds), *Attitudes towards Language: social and applied contexts* (pp. 148–63), London: Edward Arnold.

Kalma, A. (1992) Gazing in triads: a powerful signal in floor apportionment. *British Journal of Social Psychology*, 31, 21–40.

Kalven, H., Jr and Zeisel, H. (1966) *The American Jury*. London: Univeristy of Chicago Press.

Kanter, R.M. (1977) Some effects of proportions on group life: skewed sex ratios and responses to token women. *American Journal of Sociology*, 82, 965–90.

Karney, B.R., Bradbury, T.N., Fincham, F.D. and Sullivan, K.T. (1994) The role of negative affectivity in the association between attributions and marital satisfaction. *Journal of Personality and Social Psychology*, 66, 413–24.

Karpf, F.B. (1932) *American Social Psychology – its origins, development, and European background*. New York: Macmillan.

Katz, D. (1960) The functional approach to the study of attitudes. *Public Opinion Quarterly*, 24, 163–204.

Katz, D. (1967) The functional approach to the study of attitude. In M. Fishbein (ed.), *Readings in Attitude Theory and Measurement* (pp. 457–68), New York: Wiley.

Katz, D. (1978) Social psychology in relation to the social sciences. *American Behavioral Scientist*, 5, 779–92.

Katz, D. and Braly, K. (1933) Racial stereotypes in one hundred college students. *Journal of Abnormal and Social Psychology*, 28, 280–90.

Kaye, K. (1982) *The Mental and Social Life of Babies*. Chicago: Chicago University Press.

Kelley, H.H. (1967) Attribution theory in social psychology. In D. Levine (ed.), *Nebraska symposium on motivation* (vol. 15, pp. 192-238), Lincoln: University of Nebraska Press.

Kelley, H.H. (1972) Causal schemata and the attribution process. In E.E. Jones, D.E. Kanouse, H.H. Kelley, R.E. Nisbett, S. Valins and B. Weiner, *Attribution: Perceiving the causes of behaviour* (pp. 151-74). Morristown, N.J.: General Learning Press.

Kelley, H.H. (1973) The processes of causal attribution. *American Psychologist*, 28, 107–28.

Kelley, H.H. and Thibaut, J.W. (1978) *Interpersonal Relations: a theory of interdependence*. New York: Wiley.

Kelly, C. (1989) Political identity and perceived intragroup homogeneity. *British Journal of Social Psychology*, 28, 239–50.

Kelman, H.C. and Hamilton, V.L. (1989) *Crimes of Obedience: towards a social psychology of authority and responsibility*. New Haven, CT: Yale University Press.

Kendon, A. (1983) Gesture and speech: how they interact. In J.M. Weimann and R.P. Harrison (eds), *Nonverbal Interaction* (pp. 13–45), Beverly Hills: Sage.

Kennedy, C.W. and Camden, C.T. (1983) A new look at interruptions. *Western Journal of Speech Communication*, 47, 45–58.

Kenny, D.A. (1991) A general model of consensus and accuracy in interpersonal perception. *Psychological Review*, 98, 155–63.

Kenrick, D.T. and Cialdini, G.A. (1979) Interpersonal attraction in aversive environments: a problem for the classical conditioning paradigm? *Journal of Personality and Social Psychology*, 37, 572–9.

Kenrick, D.T., Groth, G.E., Trost, M.R. and Sadella, E.K. (1993) Integrating evolutionary and social exchange perspectives on relationships: effects of gender, self-appraisal, and involvement level on mate selection criteria. *Journal of Personality and Social Psychology*, 64, 951–69.

Kenrick, D.T. and Trost, M.R. (1989) A reproductive exchange model of heterosexual relationships: putting proximate economics in ultimate perspective. In C. Hendrick (ed.), *Close Relationships*, pp. 92–118, Newbury Park, CA: Sage.

Kerr, N.L. (1982) The jury trial. In V.J. Konečni and E.B. Ebbeson (eds), *The Criminal Justice System: a social-psychological analysis*, San Francisco: Freeman.

Kerr, N.L. (1992) Issue importance and group decision making. In S. Worchel, W. Wood and J.A. Simpson (eds), *Group Process and Productivity* (pp. 68–88), London: Sage.

Kerr, N.L. and Bruun, S.E. (1983) Dispensability of member effort and group motivation losses: free-rider effects. *Journal of Personality and Social Psychology*, 44, 78–94.

Kerr, S. and Jermier, J.M. (1978) Substitutes for leadership: their meaning and measurement. *Organizational Behavior and Human Performance*, 22, 375–403.

Kerstetter, W.A. and B. Van Winkle (1990) Who decides? A study of the complainant's decision to prosecute in rape cases. *Criminal Justice and Behaviour*, 17, 268–83.

Kidder, L.H. and Campbell, D.T. (1970) The indirect testing of social attitudes. In G.F. Summers (ed.), *Attitude Measurement* (pp. 333–85), Chicago: Rand McNally.

Kiesler, C.A. and Pallak, M.S. (1975) Minority influence: the effect of majority reactionaries and defectors, and majority and minority compromisers, upon majority opinion and attraction. *European Journal of Social Psychology*, 5, 237–56.

Kingdon, J.W. (1967) Politicians' beliefs about voters. *American Political Science Review*, 61, 137–45.

Kirkpatrick, L.A. and Shaver, P.R. (1992) An attachment-theoretical approach to romantic love and religious belief. *Personality and Social Psychology Bulletin*, 18, 266–75.

Kissel, S. (1965) Stress-reducing properties of social stimuli. *Journal of Personality and Social Psychology*, 2, 378–84.

Kitson, G.C., Babri, K.B. and Roach, M.J. (1985) Who divorces and why: a review. *Journal of Family Issues*, 6, 255–94.

Kleck, R.E. and Wheaton, J. (1967) Dogmatism and responses to opinion-consistent and opinion-inconsistent information. *Journal of Personality and Social Psychology*, 5, 249–52.

Kleinginna, P.R. and Kleinginna, A.M. (1981) A categorized list of emotion definitions, with suggestions for a consensual definition. *Motivation and Emotion*, 5, 345–79.

Knapp, M.L. (1983) Dyadic relationship development. In J.M. Weimann and R.P. Harrison (eds), *Nonverbal Interaction* (pp. 179–207), Beverly Hills: Sage.

Knapp, M.L., Ellis, D.G. and Williams, B.A. (1980) Perceptions of communication behaviour associated with relationship terms. *Communication Monographs*, 47, 262–78.

Knapp, M.L. and Vangelisti, A. (1992) *Interpersonal*

Communication and Human Relationships, 2nd edn. Boston: Allyn & Bacon.

Knight, H.C. (1921) *A comparison of the reliability of group and individual judgment*. Unpublished master's thesis, Columbia University.

Knight, J.A. and Vallacher, R.R. (1981) Interpersonal engagement in social perception: the consequences of getting into the action. *Journal of Personality and Social Psychology*, 40, 990–99.

Koch, S. (1985) Foreword: Wundt's creature at age zero – and as centenarian. Some aspects of the institutionalization of the new 'psychology'. In S. Koch and D.E. Leary (eds), *A Century of Psychology as a Science* (pp. 7–35), New York: McGraw-Hill.

Kogan, N. and Wallach, M.A. (1964) *Risk Taking: a study in cognition and personality*. New York: Holt, Rinehart & Winston.

Köhler, B. (1977) Prosoziales Verhalten: Forschungsschwerpunkte und Forschungsthemen. *Zeitschrift für Sozialpsychologie*, 8, 23–49.

Komatsu, L.K. (1992) Recent reviews of conceptual structure. *Psychological Bulletin*, 112, 500–26.

Konečni, V.J. (1975) The mediation of aggressive behavior: arousal level versus anger and cognitive labeling. *Journal of Personality and Social Psychology*, 32, 706–12.

Konečni, V.J. and Ebbeson, E.B. (1979) External validity of research in legal psychology. *Law and Human Behavior*, 3, 39–70.

Kothandapani, V. (1971) Validation of feeling, belief, and intention to act as three components of attitude and their contribution to prediction of contraceptive behavior. *Journal of Personality and Social Psychology*, 19, 321–33.

Krantz, S.E. and Rude, S. (1984) Depressive attributions: selection of different causes or assignment of different meanings? *Journal of Personality and Social Psychology*, 47, 193–203.

Kraut, R.E. and Johnson, R. (1979) Social and emotional messages of smiling: an ethological approach. *Journal of Personality and Social Psychology*, 37, 1539–53.

Kravitz, D.A. and Martin, B. (1986) Ringlemann rediscovered: the original article. *Journal of Personality and Social Psychology*, 50, 936–41.

Krebs, D. (1981) Gewaltdarstellungen im Fernsehen und die Einstellungen zu aggressiven Handlungen bei 12–15 jährigen Kindern – Bericht über eine Längsschnittstudie. *Zeitschrift für Sozialpsychologie*, 12, 281–302.

Krebs, D. and Groebel, J. (1979) *Die Wirkungen von Gewaltdarstellungen im Fernsehen auf die Einstellungen zu Gewalt und die Angst bei Kindern und Jugendlichen*. Projektabschlußbericht. Aachen.

Krosnick, J.A., Betz, A.L., Jussim, L.J. and Lynn, A.R. (1992) Subliminal conditioning of attitudes. *Personality and Social Psychology Bulletin*, 18, 152–62.

Krueger, D.L. (1982) Marital decision-making: a language–action analysis. *Quarterly Journal of Speech*, 68, 273–87.

Kruglanski, A.W. (1975) The endogenous–exogenous partition in attribution theory. *Psychological Review*, 82, 387–406.

Kruglanski, A.W. (1990) Motivations for judging and knowing: implications for causal attribution. In E.T. Higgins and R.M. Sorrentino (eds), *Handbook of Motivation and Cognition: foundations of social behavior* (vol. 2, pp. 13–37), New York: Guilford Press.

Kruglanski, A.W. and Ajzen, I. (1983) Bias and error in human judgment. *European Journal of Social Psychology*, 13, 1–44.

Kruglanski, A.W. and Freund, T. (1983) The freezing and unfreezing of lay-inferences: effects of impressional primacy, ethnic stereotyping and numerical anchoring. *Journal of Experimental Social Psychology*, 19, 448–68.

Kruglanski, A.W. and Mackie, D.M. (1990) Majority and minority influence: a judgemental process analysis. In W. Stroebe and M. Hewstone (eds), *European Review of Social Psychology* (vol. 1, pp. 229–61), Chichester: J. Wiley.

Kruglanski, A.W. and Mayseless, O. (1987) Motivational effects in the social comparison of opinions. *Journal of Personality and Social Psychology*, 53, 834–42.

Kruse, L. (1975) Crowding. Dichte und Enge aus sozialpsychologischer Sicht. *Zeitschrift für Sozialpsychologie*, 6, 2–30.

Kuhn, M.H. and McPartland, T.S. (1954) An empirical investigation of self-attitudes. *American Sociological Review*, 19, 68–76.

Kulik, J.A. (1983) Confirmatory attribution and the perpetuation of social beliefs. *Journal of Personality and Social Psychology*, 44, 1171–81.

Kulik, J.A. and Mahler, H.I.M. (1989) Stress and affiliation in a hospital setting: preoperative roommate preferences. *Personality and Social Psychology Bulletin*, 15, 183–93.

Kuykendall, D. and Keating, J.P. (1990) Altering thoughts and judgments through repeated association. *British Journal of Social Psychology*, 29, 79–86.

La Barre, W. (1947) The cultural basis of emotions and gestures. *Journal of Personality*, 16, 49–68.

Labov, W. (1966) *The Social Stratification of English in New York City*. Washington: Center for Applied Linguistics.

Laird, J.D. (1974) Self-attribution of emotion: the effect of expressive behavior on the quality of emotional experience. *Journal of Personality and Social Psychology*, 29, 475–86.

Lakoff, R. (1975) *Language and the Woman's Place*. New York: Harper & Row.

Lalli, M. (1992) Urban-related identity: theory, measurement, and empirical findings. *Journal of Environmental Psychology*, 12, 285–303.

Lalljee, M. (1981) Attribution theory and the analysis of explanations. In C. Antaki (ed.), *The Psychology of Ordinary Explanations of Social Behaviour* (pp. 119–38), London: Academic Press.

Lamm, H. and Myers, D.G. (1978) Group-induced polarization of attitudes and behaviour. In L. Berkowitz (ed.), *Advances in Experimental Social Psychology* (vol. 11, pp. 145–95), New York: Academic Press.

Lange, C. (1885) *Om Sinsbevaegelser: Et psyko-fysiologiske Studie*. Kopenhagen: Rasmussen.

Lange, F. (1971) Frustration–aggression. A reconsideration. *European Journal of Social Psychology*, 1, 59–84.

Lanzetta, J.T., Cartwright-Smith, J. and Kleck, R.E. (1976) Effects of nonverbal dissimulation on emotional experience and autonomic arousal. *Journal of Personality and Social Psychology*, 33, 354–70.

LaPiere, R.T. (1934) Attitude versus actions. *Social Forces*, 13, 230–7.

Larsen, R.J. and Diener, E. (1992) Promises and problems with the circumplex model of emotion. In M.S. Clark (ed.), *Review of Personality and Social Psychology* (pp. 25–59), Newbury Park, CA: Sage.

Latané, B. (1981) The psychology of social impact. *American Psychologist*, 36, 343–56.

Latané, B. and Darley, J.M. (1969) Bystander 'apathy'. *American Scientist*, 57, 244–68.

Latané, B. and Darley, J.M. (1976) *Help in a Crisis: bystander response to an emergency*. Morristown, NJ: General Learning Press.

Latané, B. and Nida, S. (1981) Ten years of research on group size and helping. *Psychological Bulletin*, 89, 308–24.

Latané, B. and Rodin, J. (1969) A lady in distress: inhibiting effects of friends and strangers on bystander intervention. *Journal of Experimental Social Psychology*, 5, 189–202.

Latané, B., Williams, K. and Harkins, S. (1979) Many hands make light work: the causes and consequences of social loafing. *Journal of Personality and Social Psychology*, 37, 822–32.

Latané, B. and Wolf, S. (1981) The social impact of majorities and minorities. *Psychological Review*, 88, 438–53.

Lau, R.R. and Russell, D. (1980) Attributions in the sports pages. *Journal of Personality and Social Psychology*, 39, 29–38.

Laughlin, P.R. (1980) Social combination processes of cooperative problem-solving groups on verbal intellective tasks. In M. Fishbein (ed.), *Progress in Social*

Psychology (vol. 1, pp. 127–55), Hillsdale, NJ: Erlbaum.

Laughlin, P.R. and Ellis, A.L. (1986) Demonstrability and social combination processes on mathematical intellective tasks. *Journal of Experimental Social Psychology*, 22, 177–89.

Laycock, G. (1985) *Property Marking: a deterrent to domestic burglary?* London: Home Office.

Lazarus, J. (1990) The logic of mate desertion. *Animal Behaviour*, 39, 672–84.

Lazarus, R.S. (1966) *Psychological Stress and the Coping Process*. New York: McGraw-Hill.

Lazarus, R.S. (1984) Thoughts on the relations between emotion and cognition. In K.R. Scherer and P. Ekman (eds), *Approaches to Emotion* (pp. 247–58), Hillsdale, NJ: Erlbaum.

Lazarus, R.S. (1991) *Emotion and Adaptation*. New York: Oxford University Press.

Le Bon, G. (1960) *The Crowd* (1st edn, 1895). New York: Viking.

Le Bon, G. (1895) *Psychologie des foules*. Paris: Alcan.

Leary, M.R. (ed.) (1987) *The Status of Social Psychology: issues, themes, and controversies*. Newbury Park, CA: Sage.

Leavitt, H.J. (1951) Some effects of certain communication patterns on group performance. *Journal of Abnormal and Social Psychology*, 46, 38–50.

Leekam, S. (1993) Children's understanding of mind. In M. Bennett (ed.), *The Child as Psychologist. An introduction to the development of social cognition* (pp. 26–61), New York: Harvester Wheatsheaf.

Leet-Pellegrini, H.M. (1980) Conversational dominance as a function of gender and expertise. In H. Giles, W.P. Robinson and P.M. Smith (eds), *Language: social psychological perspectives* (pp. 97–104), Oxford: Pergamon.

Legerstee, M. (1991) Changes in the quality of infant sounds as a function of social and nonsocial stimulation. *First Language*, 11, 327–43.

Lehman, D.R., Ellard, J.H. and Wortman, C.B. (1986) Social support for the bereaved: recipients' and providers' perspectives on what is helpful. *Journal of Consulting and Clinical Psychology*, 54, 438–46.

Lemaine, G. (1966) Inégalité, comparaison et incomparabilité: esquisse d'une théorie de l'originalité sociale. *Bulletin de Psychologie*, 20, 1–9.

Lemyre, L. and Smith, P.M. (1985) Intergroup discrimination and self-esteem in the minimal group paradigm. *Journal of Personality and Social Psychology*, 49, 660–70.

Lepenies, W. (1977) Problems of a historical study of science. In E. Mendelsohn, P. Weingart and R. Whitley (eds), *The Social Product of Scientific Knowledge* (pp. 55–67), Dordrecht: Reidel.

Lepper, M.R. and Greene, D. (eds) (1978) *The Hidden*

Costs of Reward: new perspectives on the psychology of human motivation. Hillsdale, NJ: Erlbaum.

Lepper, M.R., Greene, D. and Nisbett, R.E. (1973) Undermining children's intrinsic interest with extrinsic reward: a test of the 'overjustification' hypothesis. *Journal of Personality and Social Psychology*, 28, 129–37.

Lerner, M.J. (1980) *The Belief in a Just World: a fundamental delusion.* New York: Plenum.

Levenson, R.W., Ekman, P. and Friesen, W.V. (1990) Voluntary facial action generates emotion-specific autonomic nervous system activity. *Psychophysiology*, 27, 363–84.

Levenson, R.W. and Gottman, J. (1985) Physiological and affective predictors of change in relationship satisfaction. *Journal of Personality and Social Psychology*, 49, 85–94.

Levenson, R.W., Ekman, P., Heider, K. and Friesen, W.V. (1992) Emotion and autonomic nervous system activity in the Minangkabau of West Sumatra. *Journal of Personality and Social Psychology*, 62, 972–88.

Leventhal, H. and Scherer, K.R. (1987) The relationship of emotion to cognition: a functional approach to a semantic controversy. *Cognition and Emotion*, 1, 3–28.

Levine, J.M. and Murphy, G. (1943) The learning and forgetting of controversial material. *Journal of Abnormal and Social Psychology*, 38, 507–17.

Levine, R. (1987) Waiting is a power game. *Psychology Today*, April, 24–33.

Levitt, M.J. (1991) Attachment and close relationships: a life-span perspective. In J.L. Gerwitz and W.M. Kurtinees (eds), *Intersections with attachment* (pp. 105–30), Hillsdale, NJ: Erlbaum.

Levy, R.I. (1984) The emotions in comparative perspective. In K.R. Scherer and P. Ekman (eds), *Approaches to Emotion* (pp. 397–410), Hillsdale, NJ: Erlbaum.

Lewin, K. (1948) *Resolving Social Conflicts: selected papers on group dynamics.* New York: Springer-Verlag.

Lewin, K. (1951) *Field Theory in Social Science: selected theoretical papers.* New York: Harper.

Lewin, K. (1965) Group decision and social change. In H. Proshansky and B. Seidenberg (eds), *Basic Studies in Social Psychology* (pp. 423–37), London: Holt, Rinehart & Winston.

Lewitt, E.M. and Coate, D. (1982) The potential for using excise taxes to reduce smoking. *Journal of Health Economics*, 1, 121–45.

Leyens, J.-P. (ed.) (1991) Prolegomena for the concept of implicit theories of personality. *Cahier de Psychologie Cognitive/European Bulletin of Cognitive Psychology*, 11, 131–6.

Leyens, J.-P., Camino, L., Parke, R.D. and Berkowitz, L. (1975) Effects of movie violence on aggression in a field setting as a function of group dominance and cohesion. *Journal of Personality and Social Psychology*, 5, 229–36.

Leyens, J.-P. and Dardenne, B. (1994) La perception et connaissance d'autrui. In M. Richelle, J. Requin and M. Robert (eds), *Traité de psychologie expérimentale.* Paris: Presses Universitaires de France.

Leyens, J.-P. and Fiske, S.T. (1994) Impression formation: from recitals to symphonie fantastique. In P.G. Devine, D.L. Hamilton and T.M. Ostrom (eds), *Social Cognition: impact on social psychology* (pp. 39–75), New York: Springer-Verlag.

Leyens, J-P. and Herman, G. (1979) Cinéma violent et spectateurs aggressifs. *Psychologie Française*, 24, 151–68.

Leyens, J.-P., Herman, G. and Dunand, M.A. (1982) Towards a renewed paradigm in movie violence research. In P. Stringer (ed.), *Confronting Social Issues: applications of social psychology*, European Monographs in Social Psychology, London: Academic Press.

Leyens, J.-P. and Parke, R.D. (1975) Aggressive slides can induce a weapons effect. *European Journal of Social Psychology*, 5, 229–36.

Leyens, J.-P., Yzerbyt, V.Y. and Schadron, G. (1992) The social judgeability approach to stereotypes. In W. Stroebe and M. Hewstone (eds), *European Review of Social Psychology* (vol. 3, pp. 91–120), Chichester, UK: Wiley.

Leyens, J.-P., Yzerbyt, V.Y. and Schadron, G. (1994) *Stereotypes and Social Cognition.* London: Sage.

Liebert, R.N. and Baron, R.A. (1972) Some immediate effects of televised violence on children's behavior. *Developmental Psychology*, 6, 469–78.

Light, P. (1986) Context, conservation and conversation. In M.P.M. Richards and P. Light (eds), *Children of Social Worlds* (pp. 68–81), Oxford: Polity.

Light, P., Littleton, K., Messer, D. and Joiner, R. (1994) Social and communicative processes in computer-based problem solving. *European Journal of Psychology of Education*, 9, 93–109.

Likert, R. (1932) A technique for the measurement of attitudes. *Archives of Psychology*, 140, 5–53.

Likert, R. (1967) *The Human Organization.* New York: McGraw-Hill.

Lind, E.A. and O'Barr, W.M. (1979) The social significance of speech in the courtroom. In H. Giles and R.N. St Clair (eds), *Language and Social Psychology* (pp. 66–87), Oxford: Basil Blackwell.

Linder, D.E., Cooper, J. and Jones, E.E. (1967) Decision freedom as a determinant of the role of incentive magnitude in attitude change. *Journal of Personality and Social Psychology*, 6, 245–54.

Lindner, G.A. (1871) *Ideen zur Psychologie der Gesellschaft als Grundlage der Sozialwissenschaft.* Vienna: Gerold.

Lingle, J.H. and Ostrom, T.M. (1981) Principles of memory and cognition in attitude formation. In R.E. Petty, T.M. Ostrom and T.C. Brook (eds), *Cognitive Responses in Persuasion* (pp. 399–420), Hillsdale, NJ: Erlbaum.

Linneweber, V. (1988a) Post-occupancy evaluation in a master planned community. *Wissenschaftliche Zeitschrift der Friedrich-Schiller-Universität Jena, Gesellschaftswissenschaftliche Reihe*, 37, 733–46.

Linneweber, V. (1988b) Norm violations in Person x Place transactions. In D. Canter, J.C. Jesuino, L. Soczka and G.M. Stephenson (eds), *Environmental Social Psychology* (pp. 116–34), London: Kluwer.

Linville, P.W. and Carlston, D.E. (1994) Social cognition of the self. In P.G. Devine, D.L. Hamilton and T.M. Ostrom (eds), *Social Cognition: impact on social psychology* (pp. 143–93), New York: Springer-Verlag.

Linville, P.W., Fischer, F.W. and Salovey, P. (1989) Perceived distributions of characteristics of ingroup and outgroup members: empirical evidence and a computer simulation. *Journal of Personality and Social Psychology*, 42, 193–211.

Lippmann, W. (1992) *Public Opinion*. New York: Harcourt and Brace.

Liska, J. (1978) Situational and topical variations in credibility criteria. *Communication Monographs*, 45, 85–92.

Liu, J.L. and Steele, C.M. (1986) Attributional analysis as self-affirmation. *Journal of Personality and Social Psychology*, 51, 531–40.

Livesley, W.J. and Bromley, D.B. (1973) *Person Perception in Childhood and Adolescence*. London: Wiley.

Lloyd-Bostock, S.M. (1979) Common-sense morality and accident compensation. In D.P. Farrington, K. Hawkins and S.M. Lloyd-Bostock (eds), *Psychology, Law and Legal Processes*, London: Macmillan.

Lloyd-Bostock, S.M. (1984) Legal literature, dialogue with lawyers, and research on practical legal questions: some gains and pitfalls for psychology. In G.M. Stephenson and J.H. Davis (eds), *Progress in Applied Social Psychology* (vol. 2, pp. 265–92), Chichester: Wiley.

Locke, D. and Pennington, D. (1982) Reasons and other causes: their role in attribution processes. *Journal of Personality and Social Psychology*, 42, 212–23.

Locksley, A., Hepburn, C. and Ortiz, V. (1982) Social stereotypes and judgments of individuals: an instance of the base-rate fallacy. *Journal of Experimental Social Psychology*, 18, 23–42.

Loftus, E.F. (1974) Reconstructing memory: the incredible eyewitness. *Psychology Today*, August, 116–19.

Loftus, E.F. (1979) *Eyewitness testimony*. Cambridge, MA: Harvard University Press.

Loftus, E.F. (1984) Expert testimony on the eyewitness. In G.L. Wells and E.F. Loftus (eds), *Eyewitness Testimony: psychological perspectives* (pp. 273–82), Cambridge: Cambridge University Press.

Lombardi, W.J., Higgins, E.T. and Bargh, J.A. (1987) The role of consciousness in priming effects on categorization: assimilation versus contrast as a function of awareness of the priming task. *Personality and Social Psychology Bulletin*, 13, 411–29.

Lord, R.G, (1977) Functional leadership behavior: measurement and relation to social power and leadership perceptions. *Administrative Science Quarterly*, 22, 114–33.

Lorenz, K. (1963) *Das sogenannte Böse*. Vienna: Borotha-Schoeler.

Lorenz, K. (1965) *Evolution and Modification of Behavior*. Chicago: University of Chicago Press.

Lorenz, K. (1966) *On Aggression*. New York: Harcourt, Brace & World.

Löschper, G., Mummendey, A., Linneweber, V. and Bornewasser, M. (1984) The judgement of behaviour as aggressive and sanctionable. *European Journal of Social Psychology*, 14, 391–404.

Lösel, F. and Bliesner, T. (1990) Resilience in adolescence: a study on the generalizability of protective factors. In K. Hurrelmann and F. Lösel (eds), *Health Hazards in Adolescence* (pp. 299-320), Berlin: De Gruyter.

Lück, H.E. (1987) A historical perspective on social psychological theories. In G. Semin and B. Krahé (eds), *Issues in Contemporary German Social Psychology*. London: Sage.

Lujansky, H. and Mikula, G. (1983) Can equity theory explain the quality and the stability of romantic relationships? *British Journal of Social Psychology*, 22, 101–12.

Lukes, S. (1973a) *Individualism*. Oxford: Blackwell.

Lukes, S. (1973b) *Emile Durkheim. His life and work. A historical and critical study*. London: Allen Lane.

Lutkenhaus, P., Grossmann, K.E. and Grossman, K. (1985) Infant–mother attachment and style of interaction with a stranger at the age of three years. *Child Development*, 56, 1538–42.

Lutz, C. and White, G.M.L. (1986) The anthropology of emotions. *Annual Review of Anthropology*, 15, 405–36.

Maass, A. and Clark, R.D. III (1983) Internationalization versus compliance: differential processes underlying minority influence and conformity. *European Journal of Social Psychology*, 13, 197–215.

Maass, A. and Clark, R.D. III (1984) Hidden impact of minorities: fifteen years of minority influence research. *Psychological Bulletin*, 95, 428–50.

Maass, A., Clark, R.D. III and Haberkorn, G. (1982)

The effects of differential ascribed category membership and norms on minority influence. *European Journal of Social Psychology*, 12, 89–104.

Maass, A., Corvino, G. and Arcuri, L. (1994) Linguistic intergroup bias and the mass media. *Revue Internationale de Psychologie Sociale*, 7, 31-44.

Maass, A., Salvi, D., Arcuri, L. and Semin, G.R. (1989) Language use in intergroup contexts: the linguistic intergroup bias. *Journal of Personality and Social Psychology*, 57, 981–93.

Mackenzie, K.D. (1976) *A Theory of Group Structures* (2 vols), New York: Gordon & Breach.

Mackie, D.M. (1987) Systematic and nonsystematic processing of majority and minority persuasive communication. *Journal of Personality and Social Psychology*, 53, 41–52.

Mackie, D.M. and Ascuncion, A.G. (1990) On-line and memory-based modification of attitudes: determinants of message recall–attitude change correspondence. *Journal of Personality and Social Psychology*, 59, 5–16.

Mackie, D.M. and Worth, L.T. (1989) Processing deficits and the mediation of positive affect in persuasion. *Journal of Personality and Social Psychology*, 57, 27–40.

Macrae, C.N., Milne, A.B. and Bodenhausen, G.V. (1994) Stereotypes as energy-saving devices: a peek inside the cognitive toolbox. *Journal of Personality and Social Psychology*, 66, 37–47.

Macrae, C.N. and Shepherd, J. (1991) Categorical effects on attributional inferences: a response-time analysis. *British Journal of Social Psychology*, 30, 235–45.

Maier, N.R.F. and Solem, A.R. (1952) The contribution of a discussion leader to the quality of group thinking: the effective use of minority opinions. *Human Relations*, 5, 277–88.

Malt, B.C. (1989) An on-line investigation of prototype and exemplar strategies in classification. *Journal of Experimental Social Psychology: Learning, Memory, and Cognition*, 15, 539–55.

Malt, B.C. (1990) Features and beliefs in the mental representation of categories. *Journal of Memory and Language*, 29, 289–315.

Mandler, G. (1980) Recognizing: the judgment of previous occurrence. *Psychological Review*, 87, 252–71.

Mandler, G. (1984) *Mind and Body: the psychology of emotion and stress*. New York: Norton.

Manis, J.G. and Meltzer, B.N. (1980) *Symbolic Interaction*. Boston, MA: Allyn & Bacon.

Mann, L., Newton, J.W. and Innes, J.M. (1982) A test between deindividuation and emergent norm theories of crowd aggression. *Journal of Personality and Social Psychology*, 42, 260–72.

Mannle, S., Barton, M. and Tomasello, M. (1992). Two-year-olds' conversations with their mothers and preschool-aged siblings. *First Language*, 12, 57–71.

Manstead, A.S. (1990) Developments to be expected in European social psychology in the 1990s. In P.J. Drenth, J. Sargeant and R.J. Takens (eds), *European Perspectives in Psychology*, vol. 3: *Work and Organizational, Social and Economic, and Cross-cultural Psychology* (pp. 183–203), Chichester: Wiley.

Manstead, A.S. (1991) Expressiveness as an individual difference. In R.S. Feldman and B. Rimé (eds), *Fundamentals of Nonverbal Behavior* (pp. 285–328), Cambridge: Cambridge University Press.

Manstead, A.S. and Semin, G.R. (1980) Social facilitation effects: mere enhancement of dominant responses? *British Journal of Social and Clinical Psychology*, 19, 119–36.

Mantell, D.M. (1971) The potential for violence in Germany. *Journal of Social Issues*, 27, 101–12.

Marcus-Newhall, A., Miller, N., Holtz, R., and Brewer, M.B. (1993) Cross-cutting category membership with role assignment: a means of reducing intergroup bias. *British Journal of Social Psychology*, 32, 125–46.

Markova, I. (1982) *Paradigms, Thought, and Language*. Chichester: Wiley.

Markova, I. (1983) The origin of the social psychology of language in German expressivism. *British Journal of Social Psychology*, 22, 315–25.

Markus, H. (1977) Self-schemata and processing information about the self. *Journal of Personality and Social Psychology*, 35, 63–78.

Markus, H. and Kitayama, S. (1991) Culture and the self: implications for cognition, emotion and motivation. *Psychological Review*, 98, 224–53.

Markus, H. and Zajonc, R. (1985) The cognitive perspective in social psychology. In G. Lindzey and E. Aronson (eds), *Handbook of Social Psychology* (vol. 1, pp. 137–230), New York: Random House.

Marlatt, G.A. (1988) Matching clients to treatment: treatment models and stages of change. In D.M. Donovan and G.A. Marlatt (eds), *Assessment of Addictive Behaviors*, London: Hutchinson.

Marlowe, D., Frager, R. and Nuttall, R.L. (1965) Commitment to action-taking as a consequence of cognitive dissonance. *Journal of Personality and Social Psychology*, 2, 864–8.

Marrow, A.J. (1968) *The Practical Theorist: the life and work of Kurt Lewin*. New York: Basic Books.

Martin, L.L., Ward, D.W., Achee, J.W. and Wyer, R.S., Jr (1993) Mood as input: people have to interpret the motivational implications of their moods. *Journal of Personality and Social Psychology*, 64, 317–26.

Marx, M.H. and Hillix, W.A. (1979) *Systems and*

Theories in Psychology, 3rd edn. New York: McGraw-Hill.

Maslach, C. (1982) *Burnout: the cost of caring*. Englewood Cliffs, NJ: Prentice-Hall.

Matsumoto, D. (1987) The role of facial response in the experience of emotion: more methodological problems and a meta-analysis. *Journal of Personality and Social Psychology*, 52, 769–74.

Matsumoto, D. (1989) Cultural influences on the perception of emotion. *Journal of Cross-cultural Psychology*, 20, 92–105.

Mauro, R., Sato, K. and Tucker, J. (1992) The role of appraisal in human emotions: a cross-cultural study. *Journal of Personality and Social Psychology*, 62, 301–17.

Mausner, B. (1954) Prestige and social interaction. The effect of one partner's success in a relevant task on the interaction of observer pairs. *Journal of Abnormal and Social Psychology*, 49, 557–60.

Mayer, J.D. and Salovey, P. (1988) Personality moderates the interaction of mood and cognition. In K. Fiedler and J.P. Forgas (eds), *Affect, Cognition and Social Behavior* (pp. 87–99), Toronto: Hogrefe.

Maynard Smith, J. (1972) *On Evolution*. Edinburgh: Edinburgh University Press.

Maynard Smith, J. (1974) The theory of games and the evolution of animal conflicts. *Journal of Theoretical Biology*, 47, 209–21.

Maynard Smith, J. (1977) Parental investment: a prospective analysis. *Animal Behaviour*, 29, 1–9.

McArthur, L.A. (1972) The how and what of why: some determinants and consequences of causal attributions. *Journal of Personality and Social Psychology*, 22, 171–93.

McArthur, L.Z. and Post, D.L. (1977) Figural emphasis and person perception. *Journal of Experimental Social Psychology*, 13, 520–35.

McCann, C.D. and LaLonde, R.N. (1993) Dysfunctional communication and depression. *American Behavioral Scientist*, 36, 271–87.

McCarthy, E.D., Langner, T.S., Gersten, J.C., Eisenberg, J.G. and Orzeck, L. (1975) Violence and behavior disorders. *Journal of Communications*, 25, 71–85.

McDougall, W. (1908) *Introduction to Social Psychology*. London: Methuen.

McDougall, W. (1920) *The Group Mind*. Cambridge: Cambridge University Press.

McFarland, D.J. (1993) *Animal Behaviour*, 2nd edn. London: Pitman.

McGarty, C. and Penney, R.E.C. (1988) Categorization, accentuation and social judgement. *British Journal of Social Psychology*, 27, 147–57.

McGrath, J.E. (1984) *Groups: interaction and performance*. Englewood Cliffs, NJ: Prentice-Hall.

McGuire, W.J. (1968) Personality and attitude change: an information-processing theory. In A.G. Greenwald, T.C. Brock and T.M. Ostrom (eds), *Psychological foundations of attitudes* (pp. 171–96), New York: Academic Press.

McGuire, W.J. (1969) The nature of attitudes and attitude change. In G. Lindzey and E. Aronson (eds), *Handbook of Social Psychology* (vol. 3, pp. 136–314), 2nd edn, Reading, MA: Addison-Wesley.

McGuire, W.J. (1985) Attitudes and attitude change. In G. Lindzey and E. Aronson (eds), *Handbook of Social Psychology*, 3rd edn (vol. 2, pp. 233–346), New York: Random House.

McLaughlin, M.L., Cody, M.J. and Read, S.J. (eds) (1992) *Explaining one's self to others: reason-giving in a social context*, Hillsdale, NJ: Erlbaum.

McNeill, D. (1970) *The Acquisition of Language. The study of developmental psycholinguistics*. New York: Harper & Row.

McTear, M. (1985) *Children's Conversation*. Oxford: Blackwell.

Mead, G.H. (1934a) *Mind, Self and Society from the Standpoint of a Social Behaviorist*. Chicago: University of Chicago Press.

Mead, G.H. (1934b) *On Social Psychology*, edited by A. Strauss. Chicago: University of Chicago Press.

Medin, D.L. (1989) Concepts and conceptual structure. *American Psychologist*, 44, 1469–81.

Medin, D.L. and Schaffer, M.M. (1978) Context theory of classification learning. *Psychological Review*, 85, 207–38.

Medin, D.L., Goldstone, R.L. and Gentner, D. (1993) Respects for similarity. *Psychological Review*, 100, 254–78.

Meeus, W.H.J. and Raaijmakers, Q.A.W. (1986) Administrative obedience: carrying out orders to use psychological-administrative violence. *European Journal of Social Psychology*, 16, 311–24.

Mehrabian, A. (1968) Relationship of attitude to seated posture, orientation, and distance. *Journal of Personality and Social Psychology*, 10, 26–30.

Meloen, J.D., Hagendoorn, L., Raaijmakers, Q. and Visser, L. (1988) Authoritarianism and the revival of political racism: reassessments in the Netherlands of the reliability and validity of the concept of authoritarianism by Adorno. *Political Psychology*, 9, 413–29.

Mesquita, B. and Frijda, N.H. (1992) Cultural variations in emotion. *Psychological Bulletin*, 112, 179–204.

Messer, D.J. (1983) The redundancy between adult speech and nonverbal interaction: a contribution to acquisition? In R.M. Golinkoff (ed.), *The Transition from Prelinguistic to Linguistic Communication* (pp. 147–69), Hillsdale, NJ: Erlbaum.

Messer, D.M. (1981) Non-linguistic information which could assist the young child's interpretation of adults' speech. In W.P. Robinson (ed.), *Communication in Development* (pp. 39–62), London: Academic Press.

Metalsky, G.I., Halberstadt, L.J. and Abramson, L.Y. (1987) Vulnerability to depressive mood reactions: toward a more powerful test of the diathesis-stress and causal mediation components of the reformulated theory of depression, *Journal of Personality and Social Psychology*, 52, 386–93.

Meyer, C.B. and Taylor, S.E. (1986) Adjustment to rape. *Journal of Personality and Social Psychology*, 50, 1226–34.

Meyer, W.U., Schützwohl, A. and Reisenzein, R. (1993) *Einführung in die Emotionspsychologie*. Bern, Switzerland: Huber.

Miceli, M.P. and Near, J.P. (1992) *Blowing the Whistle: the organizational and legal implications for companies and employers*. New York: Lexington Books.

Michotte, A. (1963) *Perception of Causality*. London: Methuen (first published 1946).

Mikula, G. (1994) Perspective-related differences in interpretation of injustice by victims and victimizers: a test with close relationships. In M.J. Lerner and G. Mikula (eds), *Injustice in Close Relationships: entitlement and the affectional bond* (pp. 175–203). New York: Plenum.

Mikulincer, M., Florian, V. and Weller, A. (1993) Attachment styles, coping strategies, and post-traumatic psychological distress: the impact of the Gulf War in Israel. *Journal of Personality and Social Psychology*, 64, 817–26.

Milgram, S. (1963) Behavioral study of obedience. *Journal of Abnormal and Social Psychology*, 67, 371–8.

Milgram, S. (1965) Some conditions of obedience and disobedience to authority. *Human Relations*, 18, 57–76.

Milgram, S. (1974) *Obedience to Authority: an experimental view*. New York: Harper & Row; London: Tavistock.

Milgram, S., Liberty, H.J., Toledo, R. and Wackenhut, J. (1986) Response to intrusion into waiting lines. *Journal of Personality and Social Psychology*, 51, 683–9.

Milgram, S., Mann, L. and Harter, S. (1965) The lost-letter technique: a tool of social science research. *Public Opinion Quarterly*, 29, 437–38.

Milgram, S. and Toch, H. (1969) Collective behavior: crowds and social movements. In G. Lindzey and E. Aronson (eds), *The Handbook of Social Psychology* 2nd edn (vol. 4, pp. 507–610), Reading, MA: Addison-Wesley.

Miller, A.G. (1986) *The Obedience Experiments: a case study of controversy in social science*. New York: Praeger.

Miller, A.G. (1995) Obedience. In A.S.R. Manstead and M. Hewstone (eds), *The Blackwell Encyclopedia of Social Psychology* (pp. 418–23), Oxford: Blackwell.

Millar, A.G. and Tesser, A. (1989) The effects of affective–cognitive consistency and thought on the attitude–behavior relation. *Journal of Experimental Social Psychology*, 25, 189–202.

Miller, D.T. (1977) Altruism and threat to a belief in a just world. *Journal of Experimental Social Psychology*, 13, 113–24.

Miller, D.T. and McFarland, C. (1991) When social comparison goes awry: the case of pluralistic ignorance. In J. Suls and T. Wills (eds), *Social Comparison: contemporary theory and research* (pp. 287–313), Hillsdale, NJ: Lawrence Erlbaum.

Miller, D.T. and Porter, C.A. (1980) Effects of temporal perspective on the attribution process. *Journal of Personality and Social Psychology*, 39, 532–41.

Miller, D.T. and Ross, M. (1975) Self-serving biases in the attribution of causality: fact or fiction? *Psychological Bulletin*, 82, 213–25.

Miller, F.D., Smith, E.R. and Uleman, J. (1981) Measurement and interpretation of situational and dispositional attributions. *Journal of Experimental Social Psychology*, 17, 80–95.

Miller, J.G. (1984) Culture and the development of everyday social explanation. *Journal of Personality and Social Psychology*, 46, 961–78.

Miller, L.C., Berg, J.H. and Archer, R.L. (1983) Openers: individuals who elicit intimate self-disclosure. *Journal of Personality and Social Psychology*, 44, 1234–44.

Miller, N. and Carlson, M. (1990) Valid theory-testing meta-analyses further question the negative state relief model of helping. *Psychological Bulletin*, 107, 215–25.

Miller, N., Brewer, M.B. and Edwards, K. (1985) Cooperative interaction in desegregated settings: a laboratory analogue. *Journal of Social Issues*, 41, 63–79.

Miller, N.E. (1994) Experimental studies in conflict. In J. McV. Hunt (ed.), *Personality and the Behavior Disorders* (vol. 1, pp. 431–65), New York, Ronald.

Miller, N.E. and Bugelski, R. (1948) Minor studies in aggression: the influence of frustrations imposed by the ingroup on attitudes toward outgroups. *Journal of Psychology*, 25, 437–42.

Miller, N.E., Sears, R.R., Mowrer, O.H., Doob, L.W. and Dollard, I. (1941) The frustration–aggression hypothesis. *Psychological Review*, 48, 337–42.

Miller, R.L., Brickman, P. and Bollen, D. (1975) Attribution versus persuasion as a means of modifying behavior. *Journal of Personality and Social Psychology*, 31, 430–41.

Miller, W.R. (1983) Motivational interviewing with problem drinkers. *Behavioural Psychotherapy*, 11, 147–72.

Mills, J. and Clark, M.S. (1982) Communal and exchange relationships. In L. Wheeler (ed.), *Review of Personality and Social Psychology* (vol. 3, pp. 121–44), Beverly Hills, CA: Sage.

Mittal, B. (1988) Achieving higher seat belt usage: the role of habit in bridging the attitude–behavior gap. *Journal of Applied Social Psychology*, 18, 993–1016.

Mock, D.W. and Fujioka, M. (1990) Monogamy and long-term pair bonding in vertebrates. *Trends in Ecology and Evolution*, 5, 39–43.

Moede, W. (1920) *Experimentelle Massenpsychologie*. Leipzig: Hirzel.

Moerk, E.L. (1992) *A First Language Taught and Learned*. Baltimore: Bookes.

Molleman, E., Pruyn, J. and Van Knippenberg, A. (1986) Social comparison processes among cancer patients. *British Journal of Social Psychology*, 25, 1–13.

Montada, L. and Schneider, A. (1991) Justice and prosocial commitments. In L. Montada and H.W. Bierhoff (eds), *Altruism in Social Systems* (pp. 58–81), Lewiston, NY: Hogrefe.

Moore, B.S., Sherrod, D.R., Liu, T.J. and Underwood, B. (1979) The dispositional shift in attribution over time. *Journal of Experimental Social Psychology*, 15, 553–69.

Morgan, D.L. (1990) Combining the strengths of social networks, social support, and personal relationships. In S. Duck and R.C. Silver (eds), *Personal Relationships and Social Support* (pp. 190–215), London: Sage.

Morojele, N. (1994) *Social Psychological Analysis of a Minnesota Model Centre for Addictions: patients' beliefs and attributions and post-treatment outcomes*. University of Kent, Ph.D. thesis.

Morojele, N. and Stephenson, G.M. (1992) The Minnesota Model in the teatment of addictions: a social psychological assessment of changes in beliefs and attributions. *Journal of Community and Applied Social Psychology*, 2, 25–41.

Moscovici, S. (1961) *La Psychanalyse: Son image et son public*. Paris: Presses Universitaires de France.

Moscovici, S. (1972) Society and theory in social psychology. In J. Israel and H. Tajfel (eds), *The Context of Social Psychology: a critical assessment*. London: Academic Press.

Moscovici, S. (ed.) (1973) *Introduction à la psychologie sociale*. Paris: Larousse.

Moscovici, S. (1976) *Social Influence and Social Change*. London: Academic Press.

Moscovici, S. (1976). *La psychanalyse, son image, son public*, 2nd edn. Paris: Presses Universitaires de France.

Moscovici, S. (1980) Towards a theory of conversion behaviour. In L. Berkowitz (ed.), *Advances in Experimental Social Psychology* (vol. 13, pp. 208–39), New York: Academic Press.

Moscovici, S. (1981a) *L'age des foules*. Paris: Fayard.

Moscovici, S. (1981b) On social representations. In J.P. Forgas (ed.), *Social Cognition: perspectives on everyday understanding* (pp. 181–209), London: Academic Press.

Moscovici, S. (1982) The coming era of representations. In J.-P. Codol and J.-P. Leyens (eds), *Cognitive Analysis of Social Behavior* (pp. 115–50). The Hague: Nijhoff.

Moscovici, S. (ed.) (1984) *Psychologie Sociale*. Paris: Presses Universitaires de France.

Moscovici, S. (1985) Social influence and conformity. In G. Lindzey and E. Aronson (eds), *Handbook of Social Psychology*, 3rd edn (vol. 2, pp. 347–412), New York: Random House.

Moscovici, S. and Hewstone, M. (1983) Social representations and social explanations: from the 'naive' to the 'amateur' scientist. In M. Hewstone (ed.), *Attribution Theory: social and functional extensions* (pp. 98–125), Oxford, UK: Basil Blackwell.

Moscovici, S. and Lage, E. (1976) Studies in social influence. III: majority versus minority influence in a group. *European Journal of Social Psychology*, 6, 149–74.

Moscovici, S., Lage, E. and Naffrechoux, M. (1969) Influence of a consistent minority on the responses of a majority in a colour perception task. *Sociometry*, 32, 365–80.

Moscovici, S. and Nemeth, C. (1974) Studies in social influence. II: Minority influence. In C. Nemeth (ed.), *Social Psychology: classic and contemporary integrations* (pp. 217–49), Chicago: Rand McNally.

Moscovici, S. and Personnaz, B. (1980) Studies in social influence. V: minority influence and conversion behaviour in a perceptual task. *Journal of Experimental Social Psychology*, 16, 270–82.

Moscovici, S. and Zavalloni, M. (1969) The group as a polarizer of attitudes. *Journal of Personality and Social Psychology*, 12, 125–35.

Moston, S., Stephenson, G.M. and Williamson, T.M. (1992) The effects of case characteristics on suspect behaviour during police questioning. *British Journal of Criminology*, 32, 23–40.

Mowrer, D.H. (1975) Foreword. In W. Glasser, *Reality Therapy: a new approach to psychiatry*, New York: Harper & Row.

Mucchi-Faina, A., Maass, A. and Volpato, C. (1991) Social influence: the role of originality. *European Journal of Social Psychology*, 21, 183–97.

Mugny, G. (1982) *The Power of Minorities*. New York: Academic Press.

Mugny, G., Levy, M. and Doise, W. (1978) Conflit sociocognitif et développement cognitif. *Revue Suisse de Psychologie Pure et Appliquée*, 37, 22–43.

Mugny, G. and Papastamou, S. (1980) When rigidity does not fail: individualization and psychologization as resistances to the diffusion of minority innovations. *European Journal of Social Psychology*, 10, 43–62.

Mulac, A., Wiemann, J.M., Widenmann, S. and Gibson T. (1988) Male/female language differences and effects in same-sex and mixed-sex dyads: the gender-linked language effect. *Communication Monographs*, 55, 315–35.

Mulder, M. (1960) Communication structure, decision structure and group performance. *Sociometry*, 23, 1–14.

Mullen, B. (1986) Atrocity as a function of lynch mob composition: a self-attention perspective. *Personality and Social Psychology Bulletin*, 12, 187–97.

Mullen, B. and Johnson, C. (1990) Distinctiveness-based illusory correlations and stereotyping: a meta-analytic integration. *British Journal of Social Psychology*, 29, 11–28.

Mullen, B., Johnson, C. and Salas, E. (1991) Productivity loss in brainstorming groups: a meta-analytic integration. *Basic and Applied Social Psychology*, 12, 3–24.

Mummendey, A., Linneweber, V. and Löschper, G. (1984a) Actor or victim of aggression: Divergent perspectives – divergent evaluations. *European Journal of Social Psychology*, 14, 297–311.

Mummendey, A., Linneweber, V. and Löschper, G. (1984b) Aggression: from act to interaction. In A. Mummendey (ed.), *Social Psychology of Aggression: from individual behavior to social interaction* (pp. 69–106). New York: Springer.

Mummendey, A. and Otten, S. (1989) Perspective specific differences in the segmentation and evaluation of aggressive interaction sequences. *European Journal of Social Psychology*, 19, 23–40.

Mummendey, A. and Otten, S. (1993) Aggression: interaction between individuals and social groups. In R.B. Felson and J.T. Tedeschi (eds), *Aggression and Violence. Social interactionist perspectives* (pp. 145-67). Washington, DC: American Psychological Association.

Mummendey, A., Simon, B., Dietze, C., Grünwert, M., Haeger, G., Kessler, S., Lettgen, S. and Schäferhoff, S. (1993) Categorization is not enough: intergroup discrimination in negative outcome allocations. *Journal of Experimental Social Psychology*,

Münsterberg, D.H. (1908) *On the Witness Stand: essays on psychology and crime*. New York: Clark Boardman.

Murphy, G.L. and Medin, D.L. (1985) The role of theories in conceptual coherence. *Psychological Review*, 92, 289–316.

Murray, N., Surjan, H., Hirt, E.R. and Surjan, M. (1990) The influence of mood on categorization: a cognitive flexibility interpretation. *Journal of Personality and Social Psychology*, 59, 411–25.

Myers, D.G. (1978) Polarizing effects of social comparison. *Journal of Experimental Social Psychology*, 14, 554–63.

Myers, D.G. (1982) Polarizing effects of social interaction. In H. Brandstätter, J.H. Davis and G. Stocker-Kreichgauer (eds), *Group Decision Making*, New York: Academic Press.

Myers, D.G., Wojcicki, S.E. and Aardema, B.S. (1977) Attitude comparison: is there ever a bandwagon effect? *Journal of Applied Social Psychology*, 7, 341–7.

Nadler, A. (1987) Determinants of help seeking behaviour: the effects of helper's similarity, task centrality and recipient's self esteem. *European Journal of Social Psychology*, 17, 57–67.

Nadler, A. and Fisher, J.D. (1986) The role of threat to self-esteem and perceived control in recipient reaction to help: theory development and empirical validation. In L. Berkowitz (ed.), *Advances in Experimental Social Psychology* (vol. 19, pp. 81–122), Orlando, FL: Academic Press.

Nadler, A. and Mayseless, O. (1983) Recipient self-esteem and reactions to help. In J.D. Fisher, A. Nadler and B.M. DePaulo (eds), *New Directions in Helping* (vol. 1, pp. 167–88), New York: Academic Press.

Neisser, U. (1976) *Cognition and Reality*. San Francisco, CA: W.H. Freeman.

Nel, E., Helmreich, R. and Aronson, E. (1969) Opinion change in the advocate as a function of the persuasibility of his audience: a clarification of the meaning of dissonance. *Journal of Personality and Social Psychology*, 12, 117–24.

Nelson, K.E., Bonivillian, J.D., Denninger, M.S., Kaplan, B.J. and Baker, N.D. (1984) Maternal input adjustments and non-adjustments as related to children's linguistic advances and to language acquisition theories. In A.D. Pellegrini and T.D. Yawkey (eds), *The Development of Oral and Written Language in Social Contexts* (pp. 31–56), Norwood, NJ: Ablex.

Nemeth, C. (1982) Stability of fact position and influence. In H. Brandstätter, J.H. Davis and G. Stocker-Kreichgauer (eds), *Group Decision Making* (pp. 185–200), New York: Academic Press.

Nemeth, C. (1986) Differential contributions of majority and minority influence. *Psychological Review*, 93, 23–32.

Nemeth, C. and Kwan, J. (1987) Minority influence,

divergent thinking, and the detection of correct solutions. *Journal of Applied Social Psychology*, 17, 788–9.

Nemeth, C., Mayseless, O., Sherman, J. and Brown, Y. (1990) Exposure to dissent and recall of information. *Journal of Personality and Social Psychology*, 58, 429–37.

Nemeth, C., Swedlund, M. and Kanki, G. (1974) Patterning of the minority's responses and their influence on the majority. *European Journal of Social Psychology*, 4, 53–64.

Nemeth, C. and Wachtler, J. (1974) Creating the perceptions of consistency and confidence: a necessary condition for minority influence. *Sociometry*, 37, 529–40.

Nemeth, C. and Wachtler, J. (1983) Creative problem solving as a result of majority versus minority influence. *European Journal of Social Psychology*, 13, 45–55.

Newcomb, T.M. (1953) An approach to the study of communicative acts. *Psychological Review*, 60, 393–404.

Newman, L.S. (1991) Why are traits inferred spontaneously? A developmental approach. *Social Cognition*, 9, 221–53.

Newman, O. (1972) *Defensible Space*. New York: Macmillan.

Newman, O. (1980) *Community of Interest*. New York: Anchor Press/Doubleday.

Newman, O. and Franck, K.A. (1982) The effects of building size on personal crime and fear of crime. *Population and Environment*, 5, 203–20.

Newton, N. and Newton, M. (1950) Relationship of ability to breast feed and maternal attitudes towards breast feeding. *Pediatrics*, 11, 869–79.

Ng, S.H., Bell, D. and Brooke, M. (1993) Gaining turns and achieving high influence in small conversational groups. *British Journal of Social Psychology*, 32, 265–75.

Ng, S.H. and Bradac, J.J. (1993) *Power in Language*. Thousand Oaks, CA: Sage.

Nisbett, R.E., Caputo, C., Legant, P. and Maracek, J. (1973) Behaviour as seen by the actor and as seen by the observer. *Journal of Personality and Social Psychology*, 27, 154–64.

Nisbett, R.E. and Ross, L. (1980) *Human Inference: strategies and shortcomings of social judgment*. Englewood-Cliffs, NJ: Prentice-Hall.

Nisbett, R.E., Zukier, H. and Lemley, R.E. (1981) The dilution effect: non-diagnostic information weakens the implications of diagnostic information. *Cognitive Psychology*, 13, 248–77.

Nolen-Hoeksema, S., Girgus, J.S. and Seligman, M.E.P. (1992) Predictors and consequences of childhood depressive symptoms: five year longitudinal study. *Journal of Abnormal Psychology*, 101, 405–22.

Noller, P. (1982) Channel consistency and inconsistency in the communications of married couples. *Journal of Personality and Social Psychology*, 43, 732–41.

Noller, P. and Fitzpatrick, M.A. (eds) (1988) *Perspectives on Marital Interaction*. Clevedon: Multilingual Matters.

Noller, P. and Fitzpatrick, M.A. (1990) Marital communication in the eighties. *Journal of Marriage and the Family*, 52, 832–43.

Norman, R. (1975) Affective–cognitive consistency, attitudes, conformity, and behavior. *Journal of Personality and Social Psychology*, 32, 83–91.

Nuttin, J. (1986) *Sociale Psychologie: vijftien inleidende lessen*. Leuven, Wouters.

Nye, R. (1975) *The Origins of Crowd Psychology. Gustave LeBon and the crisis of mass democracy in the Third Republic*. London: Sage.

Oakes, P.J., Haslam, S.A. and Turner, J.C. (1994) *Stereotyping and Social Reality*. London: Blackwell.

Oakes, P.J. and Turner, J.C. (1980) Social categorization and intergroup behaviour: does minimal intergroup discrimination make social identity more positive? *European Journal of Social Psychology*, 10, 295–302.

Oatley, K. (1993) Social construction in emotions. In M. Lewis and J.M. Haviland (eds), *Handbook of Emotions* (pp. 341–2), New York: Guilford Press.

Ofshe, R. and Lee, M. (1981) Status deference, influence and convenient rationalization: an application of Two-Process Theory. *Working paper number 3*, Department of Sociology, University of California, Berkeley.

O'Hair, H.D. and Cody, M.J. (1994) Deception. In W.R. Cupach and B.H. Spitzberg (eds), *The Dark Side of Interpersonal Communication* (pp. 181–213), Hillsdale, NJ: Erlbaum.

Ohbuchi, K. and Kambara, T. (1985) Attacker's intent and awareness of outcome, impression management and retaliation. *Journal of Experimental Social Psychology*, 21, 321–30.

Ohbuchi, K., Kameda, M. and Agarie, N. (1989) Apology as aggression control: its role in mediating appraisal of and response to harm. *Journal of Personality and Social Psychology*, 56, 219–27.

Oliner, S.P. and Oliner, P.M. (1988) *The Altruistic Personality. Rescuers of Jews in Nazi Europe*. New York: Free Press.

Olson, J.M. and Zanna, M.P. (1993) Attitudes and attitude change. *Annual Review of Psychology*, 44, 117–54.

Olweus, D. (1993) *Bullying at School. What we know and what we can do*. Oxford: Blackwell.

Oppenheim, A.N. (1992) *Questionnaire Design, Interviewing and Attitude Measurement*. London: Pinter.

Orford, J. (1992) *Community Psychology: theory and practice*. Chichester: Wiley.

Orne, M.T. (1962) On the social psychology of the psychological experiment: with particular reference to demand characteristics and their implications. *American Psychologist*, 17, 776–83.

Orne, M.T. (1969) Demand characteristics and the concept of quasi-controls. In R. Rosenthal and R.L. Rosnow (eds), *Artifact in Behavioral Research* (pp. 143–79), New York: Academic Press.

Osborn, A.F. (1957) *Applied Imagination*. New York: Scribner's.

Osgood, C.E., May, W.H. and Miron, M.S. (1975) *Cross-cultural Universals of Affective Meaning*. Urbana, IL: University of Illinois Press.

Osgood, C.E., Suci, G.J. and Tannenbaum, P.H. (1957) *The Measurement of Meaning*. Urbana, IL: University of Illinois Press.

Osgood, C.E. and Tannenbaum, P.H. (1955) The principle of congruity in the prediction of attitude change. *Psychological Review*, 62, 42–55.

Osherson, D.N. and Smith, E.E. (1981) On the adequacy of prototype theory as a theory of concepts. *Cognition*, 9, 35–58.

Oster, H., Daily, L. and Goldenthal, P. (1989) Processing facial affect. In A.W. Young and H.D. Ellis (eds), *Handbook of Research on Face Processing* (pp. 107–61), North-Holland: Elsevier Science Publishers.

Osterhouse, R.A. and Brock, T.C. (1970) Distraction increases yielding to propaganda by inhibiting counterarguing. *Journal of Personality and Social Psychology*, 15, 344–58.

Ostrom, T.M. (1969) The relationship between the affective, behavioral and cognitive components of attitude. *Journal of Experimental Social Psychology*, 5, 12–30.

Ostrom, T.M. (1977) Between-theory and within-theory conflict in explaining context effects in impression formation. *Journal of Experimental Social Psychology*, 13, 492–503.

Page, M.M. (1969) Social psychology of a classical conditioning of attitudes experiment. *Journal of Personality and Social Psychology*, 11, 177–86.

Page, M. and Scheidt, R. (1971) The elusive weapons effect: demand awareness, evaluation and slightly sophisticated subjects. *Journal of Personality and Social Psychology*, 20, 304–18.

Paicheler, G. (1976) Norms and attitude change: I. Polarization and styles of behaviour. *European Journal of Social Psychology*, 6, 405–27.

Paicheler, G. (1977) Norms and attitude change: II. The phenomenon of bi polarization. *European Journal of Social Psychology*, 7, 5–14.

Paicheler, G. (1985) *Psychologie des influences sociales*. Paris: Delachaux & Niestlé.

Panksepp, J. (1982) Toward a general psychobiological theory of emotions. *Behavioral and Brain Sciences*, 5, 407–22.

Papousek, M. and Papousek, H. (1989) Forms and function of vocal matching in interactions between mothers and their precanonical infants. *First Language*, 9, 137–58.

Park, B., Judd, C.M. and Ryan, C.S. (1991) Social categorization and the representation of variability information. In W. Stroebe and M. Hewstone (eds), *European Review of Social Psychology* (vol. 2, pp. 211–45). Chichester: Wiley.

Park, R.E. (1972) *The Crowd and the Public*. Chicago: University of Chicago Press.

Parke, R.D., Berkowitz, L., Leyens, J.-P., West, S.G. and Sebastian, R.J. (1977) Some effects of violent and nonviolent movies on the behavior of juvenile delinquents. In L. Berkowitz (ed.), *Advances in Experimental Social Psychology* (vol. 10, pp. 135–72), New York: Academic Press.

Parker, G.A. (1974) Courtship persistence and female-guarding as male time investment strategies. *Behaviour*, 48, 157–84.

Parkinson, B. and Manstead, A.S.R. (1992) Appraisal as a cause of emotion. In M.S. Clark (ed.), *Review of Personality and Social Psychology* (pp. 122–49), New York: Sage.

Passer, M.W., Kelley, H.H. and Michela, J.L. (1978). Multidimensional scaling of the causes for negative interpersonal behavior. *Journal of Personality and Social Psychology*, 36, 951–62.

Patnoe, S. (1988) *A Narrative History of Experimental Social Psychology: the Lewin tradition*. New York: Springer-Verlag.

Patterson, G.R., Littman, R.A. and Bricker, W. (1967) Assertive behavior in children: a step toward a theory of aggression. *Monographs of the Society for Research in Child Development*, 32, 5 (serial no. 113).

Patterson, M.L. (ed.), (1984) Nonverbal intimacy and exchange. Special issue of the *Journal of Nonverbal Behavior*, 8, 4.

Paulus, P.B. and Murdoch, P. (1971) Anticipated evaluation and audience presence in the enhancement of dominant response. *Journal of Experimental Social Psychology*, 7, 280–91.

Peevers, B.H. and Secord, P.F. (1973) Developmental changes in attribution of descriptive concepts to persons. *Journal of Personality and Social Psychology*, 27, 120–8.

Pelz, E.B. (1965) Some factors in 'group decision'. In H. Proshansky and B. Seidenberg (eds), *Basic Studies in Social Psychology*, London: Holt, Rinehart & Winston.

Pennebaker, J.W. (1989) Confession, inhibition, and

disease. In L. Berkowitz (ed.), *Advances in Experimental Social Psychology* (vol. 22, pp. 211–44), New York: Academic Press.

Pennington, N. and Hastie, R. (1993) The story model for juror decision making. In R. Hastie (ed.), *Inside the Juror: the psychology of juror decision making*, Cambridge: Cambridge University Press.

Pepitone, A. (1981) Lessons from the history of social psychology. *American Psychologist*, 36, 972–85.

Perkins, D.D., Wanderman, R., Rich, R.C. and Taylor, R.B. (1993) The physical environment of street crime: defensible space, territoriality and incivilities. *Journal of Environmental Psychology*, 13, 29–49.

Perret-Clermont, A.-N. (1980) *Social Interaction and Cognitive Development in Children*. London: Academic Press.

Perrin, S. and Spencer, C. (1980) The Asch effect: a child of its time. *Bulletin of the British Psychological Society*, 33, 405–6.

Personnaz, B. (1981) Study in social influence using the spectrometer method: dynamics of the phenomena of conversion and covertness in perceptual responses. *European Journal of Social Psychology*, 11, 431–8.

Pessin, J. (1933) The comparative effects of social and mechanical stimulation on memorizing. *American Journal of Psychology*, 45, 263–70.

Peterson, C. (1980) Memory and the 'dispositional shift'. *Social Psychology Quarterly*, 43, 372–80.

Peterson, C., Maier, S.F. and Seligman, M.E.P. (1993) *Learned Helplessness: a theory for the age of personal control*. Oxford: Oxford University Press.

Peterson, C., Seligman, M.E.P. and Vaillant, G.E. (1988) Pessimistic explanatory style is a risk factor for physical health: a thirty-five year longitudinal study. *Journal of Personality and Social Psychology*, 55, 23–7.

Petronio, S., Martin, J. and Littlefield, R. (1984) Prerequisite conditions for self-disclosing: a gender issue. *Communication Monographs*, 51, 268–73.

Pettigrew, T.F. (1958) Personality and sociocultural factors in intergroup attitudes: a cross-national comparison. *Journal of Conflict Resolution*, 2, 29–42.

Pettigrew, T.F. (1971) *Racially Separate or Together?* New York: McGraw-Hill.

Pettigrew, T.F. (1986) The intergroup contact hypothesis reconsidered. In M. Hewstone and R. Brown (eds), *Contact and Conflict in Intergroup Encounters* (pp. 169–95), Oxford: Basil Blackwell.

Petty, R.E. and Cacioppo, J.T. (1981) *Attitudes and Persuasion: classic and contemporary approaches*. Dubuque, IA: Wm C. Brown.

Petty, R.E. and Cacioppo, J.T. (1986a) *Communication and Persuasion: central and peripheral routes to attitude change*. New York: Springer-Verlag.

Petty, R.E. and Cacioppo, J.T. (1986b) The elaboration likelihood model of persuasion. In L. Berkowitz (ed.), *Advances in Experimental Social Psychology* (vol. 19, pp. 123–205), New York: Academic Press.

Petty, R.E., Cacioppo, J.T. and Goldman, R. (1981) Personal involvement as a determinant of argument-based persuasion. *Journal of Personality and Social Psychology*, 41, 847–55.

Petty, R.E., Cacioppo, J.T. and Schumann, D.W. (1983) Central and peripheral routes to advertising effectiveness: the moderating role of involvement. *Journal of Consumer Research*, 10, 134–46.

Petty, R.E., Ostrom, T.M. and Brock, T.C. (eds) (1981) *Cognitive Responses in Persuasion*. Hillsdale, NJ: Lawrence Erlbaum.

Petty, R.E., Priester, J.R. and Wegener, D.T. (1994) Cognitive processes in attitude change. In R.S. Wyer Jr and T.K. Srull (1994), *Handbook of Social Cognition* (vol. 2, pp. 69–142), Hillsdale, NJ: Lawrence Erlbaum.

Petty, R.E., Wells, G.L. and Brock, T.C. (1976) Distraction can enhance or reduce yielding to propaganda: thought disruption versus effort justification. *Journal of Personality and Social Psychology*, 34, 874–84.

Piaget, J. (1928) *Judgement and Reasoning in the Child*. London: Routledge and Kegan Paul.

Piaget, J. (1932a) *The Moral Judgment of the Child*. Harmondsworth: Penguin.

Piaget, J. (1932b) *The Origin of Intelligence in Children*. New York: International University Press.

Piaget, J. (1937) *Main Trends in Psychology*. London: George Allen & Unwin.

Piaget, J. and Weil, A. (1951) The development in children of the idea of the homeland and of relations with other countries. *International Social Science Bulletin*, 3, 561–76.

Piatelli-Palmarini, M. (1980) *Language and Learning. The debate between Jean Piaget and Noam Chomsky*. London: Routledge & Kegan Paul.

Pierce, G.R., Sarason, B.R. and Sarason, I.G. (1990) Integrating social support perspectives: working models, personal relationships, and situational factors. In S. Duck and R.C. Silver (eds), *Personal Relationships and Social Support* (pp. 173–89), London: Sage.

Piliavin, J.A. (1989) The development of motives, self-identities, and values tied to blood donation: a Polish–American comparison study. In N. Eisenberg, J. Reykowski and E. Staub (eds), *Social and Moral Values* (pp. 253–76), Hillsdale, NJ: Lawrence Erlbaum.

Piliavin, J.A., Evans, D.E. and Callero, P. (1984) Learning to 'give to unnamed strangers'. The process of commitment to regular blood donation. In E. Staub, D. Bar-Tal, J. Karylowski and J. Reykowski (eds), *Development and Maintenance of Prosocial Behavior* (pp. 471–92), New York: Plenum.

Pinker, S. (1994) *The Language Instinct*. London: Allen Lane.

Pittam, J. and Scherer, K.R. (1993) Vocal expression and communication of emotion. In M. Lewis and J.M. Haviland (eds), *Handbook of Emotions* (pp. 185–98), New York: Guilford Press.

Pittman, T.S. (1975) Attribution of arousal as a mediator in dissonance reduction. *Journal of Experimental Social Psychology*, 11, 53–63.

Plutchik, P. (1980) *Emotion: a psychobioevolutionary synthesis*. New York: Harper & Row.

Porier, G.W. and Lott, A.J. (1967) Galvanic skin responses and prejudice. *Journal of Personality and Social Psychology*, 5, 253–9.

Potter, J., Edwards, D. and Wetherell, M. (1993) A model of discourse in action. *American Behavioral Scientist*, 36, 383–401.

Potter, J. and Wetherell, M. (1987) *Discourse and Social Psychology: beyond attitudes and behaviour*. London: Sage.

Pratkanis, A.R. and Greenwald, A.G. (1989) A socio-cognitive model of attitude structure and function. In M.P. Zanna (ed.), *Advances in Experimental Social Psychology* (vol. 22, pp. 245–85), San Diego, CA: Academic Press.

Pratt, C. (1993) The representation of knowledge and beliefs. In C. Pratt and A.F. Garton (eds), *Systems of Representation in Children: development and use* (pp. 27–48), Chichester: Wiley.

Prentice-Dunn, S. and Rogers, R.W. (1983) Deindividuation in aggression. In R.G. Geen and E.I. Donnerstein (eds), *Aggression, Theoretical and Empirical Reviews* (vol. 2, pp. 155–71), New York: Academic Press.

Prentice-Dunn, S. and Rogers, R.W. (1989) Deindividuation and the self-regulation of behavior. In P.B. Paulus (ed.), *Psychology of Group Influence*, 2nd edn (pp. 87–109), New York: Academic Press.

Price-Bonham, S., Wright, D.W. and Pittman, J.F. (1983) A frequent 'alternative' in the 1970s. In E. Macklin and R.H. Rubin (eds), *Contemporary Families and Alternative Lifestyles* (pp. 125–46), Beverly Hills, CA: Sage.

Prins, K.S., Buunk, A.P. and Van Yperen, N.W. (1992) Equity, normative disapproval and extramarital sex. *Journal of Social and Personal Relationships*, 10, 39–53.

Promnitz, J. (1992) Peer interactions in young children. In P.C.L. Heaven (ed.), *Life Span Development* (pp. 122–49), Sydney and London: Harcourt Brace Jovanovich.

Quattrone, G.A. (1982) Overattribution and unit formation: when behavior engulfs the person. *Journal of Personality and Social Psychology*, 42, 593–607.

Quattrone, G.A. and Jones, E.E. (1980) The perception of variability within ingroups and outgroups. *Journal of Personality and Social Psychology*, 38, 141–52.

Rabbie, J.M. (1963) Differential preference for companionship under threat. *Journal of Abnormal and Social Psychology*, 67, 643–8.

Rabbie, J.M. (1982) *Are Groups more Aggressive than Individuals?* 'Henri Tajfel' lecture presented at the Annual Conference of the Social Psychology Section of the British Psychological Society, 24–26 September.

Rabbie, J.M. and Horowitz, M. (1969) Arousal of ingroup–outgroup bias by a chance win or loss. *Journal of Personality and Social Psychology*, 13, 269–77.

Rabbie, J.M. and Horowitz, M. (1982) Conflict and aggression between individuals and groups. In H. Hiebsch, H. Brandstätter and H.H. Kelley (eds), *Social Psychology*, Revised and edited version of selected papers presented at the XXII International Congress of Psychology, Leipzig, DDR, no. 8.

Rabbie, J.M. and Lodewijkx, H. (1983) *Aggression toward groups and individuals*. Paper presented to the East–West Meeting of the European Association of Experimental Social Psychology, Varna, Bulgaria, 17–20 May.

Rabbie, J.M., Lodewijkx, H. and Broeze, M. (1985) *Individual and Group Aggression under the Cover of Darkness*. Paper presented to the symposium 'Psychology of Peace' at the third European Congress of the International Society for Research on Aggression (ISRA) devoted to Multidisciplinary Approaches to Conflict and Appeasement in Animals and Men, Parma, Italy, 3–7 September.

Rabbie, J.M., Schot, J.C. and Visser, L. (1989) Social identity theory: a conceptual and empirical critique from the perspective of a behavioural interaction model. *European Journal of Social Psychology*, 19, 171–202.

Ragan, S.L. and Hopper, R. (1984) Ways to leave your lover: a conversational analysis of literature. *Communication Quarterly*, 32, 310–17.

Raven, B.H. and Haley, R.W. (1982) Social influence and compliance in hospital nurses with infection control policies. In J.R. Eiser (ed.), *Social Psychology and Behavioral Medicine* (pp. 413–38), Chichester: Wiley.

Redican, W.K. (1982) An evolutionary perspective on human facial displays. In P. Ekman (ed.), *Emotion in the Human Face* (pp. 212–80), 2nd edn, New York: Cambridge University Press.

Reeder, G. and Brewer, M. (1979) A schematic model

of dispositional attribution in interpersonal perception. *Psychological Review*, 86, 61–79.

Regalski, J.M. and Gaulin, S.J.C. (1993) Whom are Mexican infants said to resemble? Monitoring and fostering paternal confidence in the Yucatan. *Ethology and Sociobiology*, 14, 97–113.

Regan, D.T. and Fazio, R.H. (1977) On the consistency between attitudes and behavior: look to the method of attitude formation. *Journal of Experimental Social Psychology*, 13, 28–45.

Regan, D.T., Straus, E. and Fazio, R. (1974). Liking and the attribution process. *Journal of Experimental Social Psychology*, 10, 385–97.

Reicher, S.D. (1982) The determination of collective behavior. In H. Tafjel (ed.), *Social Identity and Intergroup Relations* (pp. 41–83), Cambridge: Cambridge University Press.

Reicher, S.D. and Emler, N. (1985) Delinquent behavior and attitudes to formal authority. *British Journal of Social Psychology*, 24, 161–8.

Reicher, S.D. and Emler, N. (1986) Managing reputations in adolescence: the pursuit of delinquent and non-delinquent identities. In H. Beloff (ed.), *Getting into Life* (pp. 13–42), London: Methuen.

Reis, H.T. (1986) Gender effects in social participation: intimacy, loneliness, and the conduct of social interaction. In R. Gilmour and S. Duck (eds), *The Emerging Field of Personal Relationships*, Hillsdale, NJ: Erlbaum.

Reis, H.T., Senchak, M. and Solomon, B. (1985) Sex differences in the intimacy of social interaction: further examination of potential explanations. *Journal of Personality and Social Psychology*, 48, 1204–17.

Reis, H.T. and Shaver, P. (1988) Intimacy as an interpersonal process. In S. Duck (ed.), *Handbook of Personal Relationships* (pp. 367–90), Chichester: Wiley.

Reisenzein, R. (1983) The Schachter theory of emotion: two decades later. *Psychological Bulletin*, 94, 239–64.

Revans, R. (1964) *Standards for Morale: cause and effect in hospitals*. London: Tavistock.

Reyes, R.M., Thompson, W.C. and Bower, G.H. (1980) Judgmental biases resulting from differing availabilities of arguments. *Journal of Personality and Social Psychology*, 39, 2–12.

Rhodes, N. and Wood, W. (1992) Self-esteem and intelligence affect influenceability: the mediating role of message reception. *Psychological Bulletin*, 11, 156–71.

Rholes, W.S. and Pryor, J.B. (1982) Cognitive accessibility and causal attributions. *Personality and Social Psychology Bulletin*, 8, 719–27.

Ricci-Bitti, P., Brighetti, G., Garotti, P.L. and Boggi

Cavallo, P. (1989) Is contempt expressed by pan-cultural facial movements? In J.P. Forgas and J.M. Innes (eds), *Recent Advances in Social Psychology: an international perspective* (pp. 329–39), Amsterdam: Elsevier.

Ridgeway, C.L. (1978) Conformity, group-oriented motivation, and status attainment in small groups. *Social Psychology*, 41, 175–88.

Ridley, M. (1994) *The Red Queen: sex and the evolution of human nature*. Harmondsworth: Penguin.

Riess, M., Kalle, R.J., and Tedeschi, J.T. (1981) Bogus pipeline attitude assessment, impression management, and misattribution in induced compliance settings. *Journal of Social Psychology*, 115, 247–58.

Rijsman, J.B., Zoetebier, J.H.T., Ginther, A.J.F. and Doise, W. (1980) Sociocognitief conflict en cognitieve ontwikkeling. *Pedagogische Studien*, 57, 125–33.

Rijt-Plooj, H.H.C. van de and Plooj, F.X. (1993) Distinct periods of mother–infant conflict in normal development: sources of progress and germs of pathology. *Journal of Child Psychology and Psychiatry*, 34, 229–45.

Rimé, B., Mesquita, B., Philippot, P. and Boca, S. (1991) Beyond the emotional event: six studies on the social sharing of emotion. *Cognition and Emotion*, 5, 435–65.

Rimé, B. and Schiaratura, L. (1991) Gesture and speech. In R.S. Feldstein and B. Rimé (eds), *Fundamentals of Nonverbal Behavior*, Cambridge and New York: Cambridge University Press.

Riskind, J.H. (1984) The stoop to conquer: guiding and self-regulatory functions of physical posture after success and failure. *Journal of Personality and Social Psychology*, 47, 479–93.

Roberts, J.V. (1985) The attitude–memory relationships after 40 years: a meta analysis of the literature. *Basic and Applied Social Psychology*, 6, 221–41.

Robertson, L.S. (1986) Behavioral and environmental interventions for reducing motor vehicle trauma. *Annual Review of Public Health*, 7, 13–34.

Robinson, E.J. and Whittaker, S.J. (1986) Learning about verbal referential communication in the early school years. In K. Durkin (ed.), *Language Development in the School Years* (pp. 155–71), London: Croom Helm.

Robinson, J.P. and Shaver, P.R. (1969) *Measures of Social Psychological Attitudes*. Ann Arbor, MI: Survey Research Center, University of Michigan.

Robinson, J.P., Shaver, P.R. and Wrightsman, L.S. (eds) (1991) *Measures of Personality and Social Psychological Attitudes*. San Diego, CA: Academic Press.

Robinson, W.P. (1972) *Language and Social Behaviour*. Harmondsworth: Penguin.

Robinson, W.P. (1984) The development of communicative competence with language in young children: a social psychological perspective. In H. Tajfel (ed.), *The Social Dimension* (vol. 1, pp. 28–51), Cambridge: Cambridge University Press.

Robinson, W.P. (1993) Lying in the public domain. *American Behavioral Scientist*, 36, 359–82.

Roethlisberger, F.J. and Dickson, J. (1939) *Management and the Worker*. Cambridge, MA: Harvard University Press.

Rogoff, B. (1990) *Apprenticeship in Thinking: cognitive development in a social context*. New York: University Press.

Rome-Flanders, T. and Richard, M. (1992) Infant timing of vocalizations in two mother–infant games: a longitudinal study. *First Language*, 12, 285–97.

Room, R. (1993) Alcoholics Anonymous as a social movement. In B.S. McCrady and W.R. Miller (eds), *Research on Alcoholics Anonymous: opportunities and alternatives*, New Brunswick, NJ: Alcohol Research Documentation, Inc., Rutgers Center of Alcohol Studies, ch. 10, pp. 167–87.

Rosch, E. (1975) Cognitive representations of semantic categories. *Journal of Experimental Social Psychology: General*, 104, 192–233.

Rosch, E. (1978) Principles of categorization. In E. Rosch and B.B. Lloyd (eds), *Cognition and Categorization* (pp. 27–48), Hillsdale, NJ: Erlbaum.

Roseman, I.J. (1991) Appraisal determinants of discrete emotions. *Cognition and Emotion*, 5, 161–200.

Roseman, I.J., Spindel, M.S. and Jose, P.E. (1990) Appraisals of emotion-eliciting events: testing a theory of discrete emotions. *Journal of Personality and Social Psychology*, 59, 899–915.

Rosenbaum, M.E. (1986) The repulsion hypothesis: on the nondevelopment of relationships. *Journal of Personality and Social Psychology*, 51, 1156–66.

Rosenberg, M.J. (1968) Hedonism, inauthenticity, and other goads towards expansion of a consistency theory. In R.P. Abelson, E. Aronson, W.J. McGuire, T.M. Newcomb, M.J. Rosenberg and P.H. Tannenbaum (eds), *Theories of Cognitive Consistency: a sourcebook* (pp. 73–111), Chicago: Rand McNally.

Rosenberg, M.J. and Hovland, C.I. (1960) Cognitive, affective, and behavioral components of attitudes. In C.I. Hovland and M.J. Rosenberg (eds), *Attitude Organization and Change: an analysis of consistency among attitude components* (pp. 1–14), New Haven, CT: Yale University Press.

Rosenberg, M. and Simmons, R.G. (1972) *Black and White Self-Esteem: the urban school child*. Washington, DC: American Sociological Association.

Rosenberg, S., Nelson, C. and Vivekanathan, P.S. (1968) A multidimensional approach to the structure of personality impressions. *Journal of Personality and Social Psychology*, 9, 283–94.

Rosenhan, D.L., Underwood, B. and Moore, B. (1974) Affect moderates self-gratification and altruism. *Journal of Personality and Social Psychology*, 30, 546–52.

Rosenhan, D.L., Salovey, P., Karylowski, J. and Hargis, K. (1981) Emotion and altruism. In J.P. Rushton and R.M. Sorrentino (eds), *Altruism and Helping Behavior* (pp. 233–48), Hillsdale, NJ: Lawrence Erlbaum.

Rosenthal, R. (1966) *Experimenter Effects in Behavioral Research*. New York: Appleton-Century-Crofts.

Rosenthal, R. and Rosnow, R.L. (1975) *The Volunteer Subject*. New York: Wiley.

Ross, E.A. (1908) *Social Psychology*. New York: Macmillan.

Ross, L. (1977) The intuitive psychologist and his shortcomings: distortions in the attribution process. In L. Berkowitz (ed.), *Advances in Experimental Social Psychology* (vol. 10, pp. 173–220), New York: Academic Press.

Ross, L., Amabile, T.M. and Steinmetz, J.L. (1977) Social roles, social control and biases in social-perception processes. *Journal of Personality and Social Psychology*, 35, 485–94.

Ross, M. (1989) Relation of implicit theories to the construction of personal histories. *Psychological Review*, 96, 341–57.

Ross, M. and Fletcher, G.J.O. (1985) Attribution and social perception. In G. Lindzey and E. Aronson (eds), *Handbook of Social Psychology* 3rd edn (vol. 2, pp. 73–122), New York: Random House.

Ross, M., McFarland, C. and Fletcher, G.J.O. (1981) The effect of attitude on the recall of personal histories. *Journal of Personality and Social Psychology*, 40, 627–34.

Rothbart, M. and Lewis, S. (1988) Inferring category attributes from exemplar attributes: geometric shapes and social categories. *Journal of Personality and Social Psychology*, 55, 861–72.

Rothbart, M. and Park, B. (1986) On the confirmability and disconfirmability of trait concepts. *Journal of Personality and Social Psychology*, 50, 131–42.

Rothbart, M. and Taylor, M. (1992) Category labels and social reality: do we view social categories as natural kinds? In G.M. Semin and K. Fiedler (eds), *Language, Interaction and Social Cognition* (pp. 11–36), London: Sage.

Rule, B.G. and Ferguson, T.J. (1984) The relation among attribution, moral evaluation, anger, and aggression in children and adults. In A. Mummendey (ed.), *Social Psychology of Aggression: from individual behavior to social interaction* (pp. 143–55), New York: Springer.

Rule, B.G. and Nesdale, A.R. (1976) Emotional arousal and aggressive behavior. *Psychological Bulletin*, 83, 851–63.

Rule, B.G., Dyck, R.J. and Nesdale, A.R. (1978) Arbitrariness of frustration: inhibition or instigation effects in aggression. *European Journal of Social Psychology*, 8, 237–44.

Runciman, W.G. (1966) *Relative Deprivation and Social Justice*. London: Routledge & Kegan Paul.

Rusbult, C.E. (1980) Commitment and satisfaction in romantic associations: a test of the investment model. *Journal of Experimental Social Psychology*, 16, 172–86.

Rusbult, C.E. (1983) A longitudinal test of the investment model: the development (and deterioration) of satisfaction and commitment in heterosexual involvements. *Journal of Personality and Social Psychology*, 45, 101–17.

Rusbult, C.E., and Buunk, A.P. (1993) Commitment processes in close relationships: an interdependence analysis. *Journal of Social and Personal Relationships*, 10, 175–204.

Rushton, J.P. (1980) *Altruism, Socialization, and Society*. Englewood Cliffs, NJ: Prentice-Hall.

Russ, R.C., Gold, J.A. and Stone, W.F. (1979) Attraction to a dissimilar stranger as a function of level of effectance arousal. *Journal of Experimental Social Psychology*, 15, 481–91.

Russell, A. (1987) *The Guinness Book of Records*. London: Guinness.

Russell, D., Cutrona, C.E., Rose, J. and Yurko, K. (1984) Social and emotional loneliness: an examination of Weiss's typology of loneliness. *Journal of Personality and Social Psychology*, 46, 1313–21.

Russell, D.W., Altmaier, E. and van Velzen, D. (1987) Job-related stress, social support, and burnout amongst classroom teachers. *Journal of Applied Psychology*, 72, 269–74.

Russell, J.A. (1980) A circumplex model of affect. *Journal of Personality and Social Psychology*, 39, 1161–78.

Russell, J.A. (1983) Pancultural aspects of the human conceptual organization of emotions. *Journal of Personality and Social Psychology*, 45, 1281–8.

Russell, J.A. (1991) Culture and the categorization of emotions. *Psychological Bulletin*, 110, 426–50.

Rutte, C.G. and Wilke, H.A.M. (1984) Social dilemmas and leadership. *European Journal of Social Psychology*, 14, 105–21.

Rutter, D.R. and Durkin, K. (1987) Turn-taking in mother–infant examination of vocalizations and gaze. *Developmental Psychology*, 23, 54–61.

Rutter, M. and Giller, H. (1983) *Juvenile Delinquency: trends and perspectives*. Harmondsworth: Penguin.

Ryan, E.B., Giles, H. and Bradac, J.J. (eds), (1994) Recent advances in the study of language attitudes. Special issue of *Language and Communication*, 14, 4.

Ryan, E.B., Bartolucci, G., Giles, H. and Henwood, K. (1986) Psycholinguistic and social psychological components of communication by and with older adults. *Language and Communication*, 6, 1–22.

Ryen, A.H. and Kahn, A. (1975) Effects of intergroup orientation on group attitudes and proxemic behaviour. *Journal of Personality and Social Psychology*, 31, 302–10.

Sachdev, I. and Bourhis, R. (1985) Social categorization and power differentials in group relations. *European Journal of Social Psychology*, 15, 415–34.

Sachdev, I. and Bourhis, R. (1987) Status differentials and intergroup behaviour. *European Journal of Social Psychology*, 17, 277–93.

Sadalla, E.K., Kenrick, D.T. and Vershure, B. (1987) Dominance and interpersonal attraction. *Journal of Personality and Social Psychology*, 52, 730–8.

Saegert, S., Swap, W. and Zajonc, R. (1973) Exposure, context and interpersonal attraction. *Journal of Personality and Social Psychology*, 25, 234–42.

Sagar, H.A. and Schofield, J.W. (1980) Racial and behavioral cues in black and white children's perceptions of ambiguously aggressive acts. *Journal of Personality and Social Psychology*, 39, 590–8.

Sahakian, W.S. (1982) *History and Systems of Social Psychology*, 2nd edn. Washington: Hemisphere.

Sampson, E.E. (1977) Psychology and the American ideal. *Journal of Personality and Social Psychology*, 35, 767–82.

Sanbonmatsu, D.M. and Fazio, R.H. (1990) The role of attitudes in memory-based decision making. *Journal of Personality and Social Psychology*, 59, 614–22.

Sanders, G.S. (1981) Driven by distraction: an integrative review of social facilitation theory and research. *Journal of Experimental Social Psychology*, 17, 227–51.

Sanders, G.S. and Baron, R.S. (1977) Is social comparison irrelevant for producing choice shifts? *Journal of Experimental Social Psychology*, 13, 303–14.

Sanders, G.S., Baron, R.S. and Moore, D.L. (1978) Distraction and social comparison as mediators of social facilitation effects. *Journal of Experimental Social Psychology*, 14, 291–303.

Sanna, L.J. (1992) Self-efficacy theory: implications for social facilitation and social loafing. *Journal of Personality and Social Psychology*, 62, 774–86.

Sanna, L.J. and Shotland, R.L. (1990) Valence of anticipated evaluation and social facilitation. *Journal of Experimental Social Psychology*, 26, 82–92.

Sarason, I.G. and Sarason, B.R. (1986) Experimentally provided social support. *Journal of Personality and Social Psychology*, 50, 1222–5.

Sarason, I.G., Sarason, B.R., Slichter, S.J., Beatty, P.G.,

Meyer, D.M. and Bolgiano, D.C. (1993) Increasing participation of blood donors in a bone-marrow registry. *Health Psychology*, 12, 272–6.

Sarnoff, I. and Zimbardo, P.G. (1961) Anxiety, fear, and social facilitation. *Journal of Abnormal and Social Psychology*, 62, 597–605.

Schaap, C., Buunk, B. and Kerkstra, A. (1988) Marital conflict resolution. In P. Noller and M.A. Fitzpatrick (eds), *Perspectives on Marital Interaction* (pp. 203–44), Clevedon/Philadelphia: Multilingual Matters.

Schachter, S. (1951) Deviation, rejection and communication. *Journal of Abnormal and Social Psychology*, 46, 190–207.

Schachter, S. (1959) *The Psychology of Affiliation*. Palo Alto, CA: Stanford University Press.

Schachter, S. (1964) The interaction of cognitive and physiological determinants of emotional state. In L. Berkowitz (ed.), *Advances in Experimental Social Psychology* (vol. 1, pp. 49–80), New York: Academic Press.

Schachter, S. (1970) The assumption of identity and peripheralist–centralist controversies in motivation and emotion. In M.B. Arnold (ed.), *Feelings and Emotions: the Loyola Symposium* (pp. 111–21), New York: Academic Press.

Schachter, S., Nuttin, J., de Monchaux, C., Maucorps, P.H., Osmer, D., Duijker, H., Rommetveit, R. and Israel, J. (1954) Cross-cultural experiments on threat and rejection. *Human Relations*, 7, 403–39.

Schachter, S. and Singer, J.E. (1962) Cognitive, social and physiological determinants of emotional states. *Psychological Review*, 65, 379–99.

Schadron, G. and Yzerbyt, V.Y. (1991) Social judgeability: another framework for the study of social inference. *European Bulletin of Cognitive Psychology*, 11, 229–58.

Schaffer, H.R. (1971) *The Growth of Sociability*. Harmondsworth: Penguin.

Schaffer, H.R. (1984a) Parental control techniques in the context of socialization theory. In W. Doise and A. Palmonari (eds), *Social Interaction in Individual Development* (pp. 65–77), Cambridge: Cambridge University Press.

Schaffer, H.R. (1984b) *The Child's Entry into a Social World*. New York: Academic Press.

Schaffer, H.R. (1989) Early social development. In A. Slater and G. Bremner (eds), *Infant Development* (pp. 78–94), Hillsdale, NJ: Erlbaum.

Schaffer, H.R. (1990) *Making Decisions about Children. Psychological questions and answers*. Oxford: Blackwell.

Schaffer, H.R. and Emerson, P.E. (1964) The development of social attachments in infancy. *Monographs of the Society for Research on Child Development* (no. 29).

Schaffer, H.R., Collis, G.M. and Parsons, G. (1977) Vocal interchange and visual regard in verbal and pre-verbal children. In H.R. Schaffer (ed.), *Studies in mother–infant interaction* (pp. 291–324), London: Academic Press.

Schaller, M. (1992) In-group favoritism and statistical reasoning in social inference: implications for formation and maintenance of group stereotypes. *Journal of Personality and Social Psychology*, 63, 61–74.

Schaufeli, W.B., Maslach, C. and Marek, T. (eds) (1933). *Professional Burnout: Recent developments in theory and research*. Washington, DC: Taylor and Francis.

Scheerer, M. (1954) Cognitive theory. In G. Lindzey (ed.), *Handbook of Social Psychology* (pp. 91–142), Cambridge, MA: Addison-Wesley.

Scherer, K.R. (1979) Voice and speech correlates of perceived social influence in simulated injuries. In H. Giles and R. St Clair (eds), *Language and Social Psychology* (pp. 88–120), Oxford: Basil Blackwell.

Scherer, K.R. (1984) On the nature and function of emotion: a component process approach. In K.R. Scherer and P. Ekman (eds), *Approaches to Emotion* (pp. 293–318), Hillsdale, NJ: Erlbaum.

Scherer, K.R. (1985) Vocal affect signalling: a comparative approach. In J. Rosenblatt, C. Beer, M. Busnel and P.J.B. Slater (eds), *Advances in the Study of Behavior* (pp. 189–244), New York: Academic Press.

Scherer, K.R. (1986) Vocal affect expression: a review and model for future research. *Psychological Bulletin*, 99, 143–65.

Scherer, K.R. (1988) Criteria for emotion-antecedent appraisal: a review. In V. Hamilton, G.H. Bower and N.H. Frijda (eds), *Cognitive Perspectives on Emotion and Motivation* (pp. 89–126), Dordrecht: Nijhoff.

Scherer, K.R. (1992) Social psychology evolving. A progress report. In M. Dierkes and B. Bievert (eds), *European Social Science in Transition. Assessment and outlook* (pp. 178–243), Frankfurt: Campus.

Scherer, K.R. (1993a) Two faces of social psychology: European and North American perspectives. *Social Science Information*, 32, 515–52.

Scherer, K.R. (1993b) Neuroscience projections to current debates in emotion psychology. *Cognition and Emotion*, 7, 1–41.

Scherer, K.R., Abeles, R.P. and Fischer, C.S. (1975) *Human Aggression and Conflict*. Englewood Cliffs, NJ: Prentice-Hall.

Scherer, K.R., Banse, R., Wallbott, H.G. and Goldbeck, T. (1991) Vocal cues in emotion encoding and decoding. *Motivation and Emotion*, 15, 123–48.

Scherer, K.R. and Wallbott, H.G. (1994) Evidence for universality and cultural variation of differential emotion response patterning. *Journal of Personality and Social Psychology*, 66, 310–28.

Scherer, K.R., Wallbott, H.G. and Summerfield, A.B. (eds) (1986) *Experiencing Emotion: a cross-cultural study.* Cambridge/New York: Cambridge University Press.

Schieffelin, B.B. (1990) *The Give and Take of Everyday Life: Language Socialization of Kaluli children,* Cambridge: Cambridge University Press.

Schlegel, R.P. (1975) Multidimensional measurement of attitude towards smoking marijuana. *Canadian Journal of Behavioral Science,* 7, 387–96.

Schlegel, R.P. and DiTecco, D. (1982) Attitudinal structures and the attitude–behavior relation. In M.P. Zanna, E.T. Higgins and C.P. Herman (eds), *Consistency in Social Behavior: the Ontario Symposium* (vol. 2, pp. 17–49), Hillsdale, NJ: Erlbaum.

Schlenker, B.R. (1974) Social psychology and science. *Journal of Personality and Social Psychology,* 29, 1–15.

Schlenker, B.R. (1982) Translating actions into attitudes: an identity-analytic approach. In L. Berkowitz (ed.), *Advances in Experimental Social Psychology* (vol. 15, pp. 59–101), New York: Academic Press.

Schmidt, H.-D. and Schmidt-Mummendey, A. (1974) Waffen als aggressionsanbahnende Hinweisreize: eine kritische Betrachtung experimenteller Ergebnisse. *Zeitschrift für Sozialpsychologie,* 5, 201–18.

Schmitt, B.H., Dubé, L. and Leclerc, F. (1992) Intrusions into waiting lines: does the queue constitute a social system? *Journal of Personality and Social Psychology,* 63, 806–15.

Schneider, D.J. (1973) Implicit theory of personality: a review. *Psychological Bulletin,* 79, 294–309.

Schönbach, P. (1985) *A Taxonomy for Account Phases, revised, explained and applied.* Berichte aus der AE Sozialpsychologie (mimeographed reports). Fakultät für Psychologie der Ruhr-Universität Bochum.

Schriesheim, C.A. and Kerr, S. (1977) Theories and measures of leadership: a critical appraisal of current and future directions. In J.G. Hunt and L.L. Larson (eds), *Leadership: the Cutting Edge* (pp. 51–6), Carbondale, IL: Southern Illinois University Press.

Schroeder, D.H. and Costa, P.T., Jr (1984) Influence of life event stress on physical illness: substantive effects or methodological flaws? *Journal of Personality and Social Psychology,* 46, 853–63.

Schuman, H. and Kalton, G. (1985) Survey methods. In G. Lindzey and E. Aronson (eds), *Handbook of Social Psychology,* 3rd edn (vol. 1, pp. 635–97), New York: Random House.

Schwartz, G.E., Fair, P.L., Salt, P., Mandel, M.R. and Klerman, G.L. (1976) Facial muscle patterning to affective imagery in depressed and nondepressed subjects. *Science,* 192, 489–91.

Schwartz, S.H. (1977) Normative influences on altruism. In L. Berkowitz (ed.), *Advances in Experimental Social Psychology* (vol. 10, pp. 221–79), New York: Academic Press.

Schwartz, S.H. (1992) Universals in the content and structure of values: theoretical advances and empirical tests in 20 countries. In M.P. Zanna (ed.), *Advances in Experimental Social Psychology* (vol. 25, pp. 1–65), San Diego, CA: Academic Press.

Schwartz, S.H. and Bilsky, W. (1987) Toward a universal psychological structure of human values. *Journal of Personality and Social Psychology,* 53, 550–62.

Schwartz, S.H. and Bilsky, W. (1990) Toward a theory of the universal content and structure of values: extensions and cross-cultural replications. *Journal of Personality and Social Psychology,* 58, 878–91.

Schwartz, S.H. and Gottlieb, A. (1976) Bystander reactions to a violent theft: crime in Jerusalem. *Journal of Personality and Social Psychology,* 34, 1188–99.

Schwartz, S.H. and Howard, J.A. (1981) A normative decision-making model of altruism. In J.P. Rushton and R.M. Sorrentino (eds), *Altruism and helping behavior* (pp. 189–211), Hillsdale, NJ: Lawrence Erlbaum.

Schwarz, N. (1985) Theorien konzeptgesteuerter Informationsverarbeitung. In D. Frey and M. Irle (eds), *Theorien der Sozialpsychologie* (vol. III, pp. 269–91), Bern: Huber.

Schwarz, N. (1990a) Assessing frequency reports of mundane behaviors: contributions of cognitive psychology to questionnaire construction. In C. Hendrick and M.S. Clark (eds), *Research Methods in Personality and Social Psychology* (Review of Personality and Social Psychology, vol. 11, pp. 98–119), Newbury Park, CA: Sage.

Schwarz, N. (1990b) Feelings as information. Informational and motivational functions of affective states. In E.T. Higgins and R.M. Sorrentino (eds), *Handbook of Motivation and Cognition* (vol. 2, pp. 527–61), New York: Guilford Press.

Schwarz, N. and Bless, H. (1992) Constructing reality and its alternatives: an inclusion–exclusion model of assimilation and contrast effects in social judgment. In L. Martin and A. Tesser (eds), *The Construction of Social Judgment* (pp. 217–45), Hillsdale, NJ: Erlbaum.

Schwarz, N., Bless, H. and Bohner, G. (1991) Mood and persuasion: affective states influence the processing of persuasive communications. In M.P. Zanna (ed.), *Advances in Experimental Social Psychology* (vol. 24, pp. 161–201), Orlando, FL: Academic Press.

Schwarz, N., Bless, H., Strack, F., Klumpp, G., Rittenauer-Schatka, H. and Simons, A. (1991) Ease of retrieval as information: another look at the availability heuristic. *Journal of Personality and Social Psychology,* 61, 195–202.

Schwarz, N. and Clore, G.L. (1988) How do I feel

about it? The informative function of affective states. In K. Fiedler and J.P. Forgas (eds), *Affect, Cognition, and Social Behavior* (pp. 44–62), Toronto: Hogrefe.

Schwarz, N. and Strack, F. (1991) Context effects in attitude surveys: applying cognitive theory to social research. In W. Stroebe and M. Hewstone (eds), *European Journal of Social Psychology* (vol. 2, pp. 31–50), Chichester: Wiley.

Schwarzer, R. and Leppin, A. (1992) Social support and mental health: a conceptual and empirical overview. In L. Montada, S.H. Filipp and M.J. Lerner (eds), *Life Crises and Experiences of Loss in Adulthood* (pp. 435–58), Hillsdale, NJ: Lawrence Erlbaum.

Scott, M.B. and Lyman, S. (1968) Accounts. *American Sociological Review*, 33, 46–62.

Secord, P.F. (1959) Stereotyping and favorableness in the perception of Negro faces. *Journal of Abnormal and Social Psychology*, 59, 309–15.

Sedikides, C. and Anderson, C.A. (1994) Causal perceptions of intertrait relations: the glue that holds person types together. *Personality and Social Psychology Bulletin*, 20, 294–302.

Sedikides, C. and Ostrom, T.M. (1988) Are person categories used when organizing information about unfamiliar sets of persons? *Social Cognition*, 6, 252–67.

Segal, M.W. (1974) Alphabet and attraction: an obtrusive measure of the effect of propinquity in a field setting. *Journal of Personality and Social Psychology*, 30, 654–7.

Seligman, C. Lambert, W.E. and Tucker, G.R. (1972) The effects of speech style and other attributes on teachers' attitudes toward pupils. *Language in Society*, 1, 131–42.

Selltiz, C., Wrightsman, L.S. and Cook, S.W. (1976) *Research Methods in Social Relations*. New York: Holt, Rinehart & Winston.

Selman, R. (1980) *The Growth of Interpersonal Understanding*. New York: Academic Press.

Semin, G.R. (1986) On the relationship between representations of theories in psychology and ordinary language. In W. Doise and S. Moscovici (eds), *Current Issues in European Social Psychology* (vol. 2, pp. 307–48), Cambridge: Cambridge University Press.

Semin, G.R. and Fiedler, K. (1988) The cognitive functions of linguistic categories in describing persons: social cognition and language. *Journal of Personality and Social Psychology*, 54, 558–67.

Semin, G.R. and Fiedler, K. (1989) Relocating attributional phenomena within a language–cognition interface: the case of actors' and observers' perspectives. *European Journal of Social Psychology*, 19, 491–508.

Semin, G.R. and Fiedler, K. (1991) The Linguistic Category Model, its bases, applications and range. In W. Stroebe and M. Hewstone (eds), *European Journal of Social Psychology* (vol. 2, pp. 1–30), Chichester: Wiley.

Semin, G.R. and Fiedler, K. (eds) (1992) *Language, Interaction and Social Cognition*. Newbury Park, CA: Sage.

Semin, G.R. and Manstead A.S.R. (1979) Social psychology: social or psychological? *British Journal of Social and Clinical Psychology*, 18, 191–202.

Semin, G.R. and Manstead A.S.R. (1983) *The Accountability of Conduct: a social psychological analysis*. London: Academic Press.

Semin, G.R. and Papadopoulou, K. (1990) The acquisition of reflexive social emotions: the transmission and reproduction of social control through joint action. In G. Duveen and B. Lloyd (eds), *Social Representations and the Development of Knowledge* (pp. 107–25), Cambridge: Cambridge University Press.

Semin, G.R. and Strack, F. (1980) The plausibility of the implausible: a critique of Snyder and Swann (1978). *European Journal of Social Psychology*, 10, 379–88.

Senchak, M. and Leonard, K.E. (1993) The role of spouses' depression and anger in the attribution– marital satisfaction relation. *Cognitive Therapy and Research*, 17, 397–409.

Shanab, M.E. and Yahya, K.A. (1978) A cross-cultural study of obedience. *Bulletin of the Psychonomic Society*, 11, 267–9.

Shapland, J.M. (1978) Self-reported delinquency in boys aged 11 to 14. *British Journal of Criminology*, 18, 255–66.

Shaver, K.G. (1981) *Principles of Social Psychology*. Cambridge, MA: Winthrop.

Shaver, K.G. (1985) *The Attribution of Blame: Causality, responsibility, and blameworthiness*. New York: Springer-Verlag.

Shaver, P. and Klinnert, M. (1982) Schachter's theories of affiliation and emotion: implications of developmental research. In L. Wheeler (ed.), *Review of Personality and Social Psychology* (vol. 3, pp. 27–72), Beverly Hills, CA: Sage.

Shaver, P. and Rubinstein, C. (1980) Childhood attachment experience and adult loneliness. *Review of Personality and Social Psychology*, 1, 42–73.

Shaver, P., Hazan, C. and Bradshaw, D. (1988) Love as attachment: the integration of three behavioral systems. In R.J. Sternberg and M.L. Barnes (eds), *The Psychology of Love* (pp. 69–99), New Haven: Yale University Press.

Shavitt, S. (1989) Operationalizing functional theories of attitude. In A.R. Pratkanis, S.J. Breckler and A.G. Greenwald (eds), *Attitude Structure and Function* (pp. 311–38), Hillsdale, NJ: Erlbaum.

Shavitt, S. (1990) The role of attitude objects in

attitude functions. *Journal of Experimental Social Psychology*, 26, 124–48.

Shavitt, S. and Fazio, R.H. (1991) Effects of attribute salience on the consistency between attitudes and behavior predictions. *Personality and Social Psychology Bulletin*, 17, 507–16.

Shaw, M. (1932) A comparison of individuals and small groups in the rational solution of complex problems. *American Journal of Psychology*, 44, 491–504.

Shaw, M.E. (1964) Communication networks. In L. Berkowitz (ed.), *Advances in Experimental Social Psychology* (vol. 1, pp. 111–47), New York: Academic Press.

Shaw, M.E. (1981) *Group Dynamics: the social psychology of small group behavior*, 3rd edn. New York: McGraw-Hill.

Sherif, C.W. and Sherif, M. (1967) Attitude as the individual's own categories: the social judgment–involvement approach to attitude and attitude change. In M. Sherif and C.W. Sherif (eds), *Attitude, Ego-Involvement, and Change* (pp. 105–39), New York: Wiley.

Sherif, M. (1935) A study of some social factors in perception. *Archives of Psychology*, no. 187.

Sherif, M. (1936) *The Psychology of Social Norms*. New York: Harper & Row.

Sherif, M. (1948) *An Outline of Social Psychology*. New York: Harper.

Sherif, M. (1966) *Group Conflict and Co-operation: their social psychology*. London: Routledge & Kegan Paul.

Sherif, M., Harvey, O.J., White, B.J., Hood, W.R. and Sherif, C.W. (1961) *Intergroup Conflict and Cooperation: the robber's cave experiment*. Norman, OK: University of Oklahoma.

Sherif, M. and Hovland, C.I. (1961) *Social Judgment: assimilation and contrast effects in communication and attitude change*. New Haven, CT: Yale University Press.

Sherif, M. and Sherif, C.W. (1953) *Groups in Harmony and Tension: an integration of studies on intergroup relations*. New York: Octagon.

Sherif, M., White, B.J. and Harvey, O.J. (1955) Status in experimentally produced groups. *American Journal of Sociology*, 60, 370–9.

Sherrod, D. (1989) The influence of gender on same-sex friendships. In C. Hendrick (ed.), *Review of Personality and Social Psychology: close relationships* (pp. 164–86), Newbury Park, CA: Sage.

Shiffrin, R.M. and Schneider, W. (1977) Controlled and automatic human information processing. II: perceptual learning, automatic attending, and a general theory. *Psychological Review*, 84, 127–90.

Shultz, T.R. and Schleifer, M. (1983). Towards a refinement of attribution concepts. In J. Jaspars, F.D. Fincham and M. Hewstone (eds), *Attribution Theory and Research: Conceptual, development, and social dimensions* (pp. 37–62). New York: Academic.

Shweder, R.A. (1975) How relevant is an individual difference theory of personality. *Journal of Personality*, 43, 455–84.

Shweder, R.A. (1991) *Thinking through Cultures. Expeditions in cultural psychology*. Cambridge, MA: Harvard University Press.

Shweder, R.A. (1993) The cultural psychology of the emotions. In M. Lewis and J.M. Haviland (eds), *Handbook of Emotions* (pp. 417–34), New York: Guilford Press.

Sighele, S. (1891) *La folla delinquente*. Torino: Fratelli Bocca.

Simmel, G. (1908) *Soziologie – Untersuchungen über die Formen der Vergesellschaftung*. Leipzig: Duncker & Humblot.

Simon, B. (1992a) The perception of ingroup and outgroup homogeneity: re-introducing the intergroup context In W. Stroebe and M. Hewstone (eds), *European Journal of Social Psychology* (vol. 3, pp. 1–30), Chichester: Wiley.

Simon, B. (1992b) Intragroup differentiation in terms of ingroup and outgroup attributes. *European Journal of Social Psychology*, 22, 407–13.

Simon, B. and Brown, R.J. (1987) Perceived intragroup homogeneity in minority–majority contexts. *Journal of Personality and Social Psychology*, 53, 703–11.

Simon, H.A. (1981) *Entscheidungsverhalten in Organisationen. Eine Untersuchung von Entscheidungsprozessen in Management und Verwaltung*. Landsberg am Lech: Verlag Moderne Industrie W. Dummer.

Simons, L.S. and Turner, C.W. (1976) Evaluation apprehension, hypothesis awareness and the weapons effect. *Aggressive Behavior*, 2, 77–87.

Simpson, J.A. (1987) The dissolution of romantic relationships: factors involved in relationship stability and emotional distress. *Journal of Personality and Social Psychology*, 53, 683–92.

Simpson, J.A., Gangestad, S.W. and Lerma, M. (1990) Perception of physical attractiveness: mechanisms involved in the maintenance of romantic relationships. *Journal of Personality and Social Psychology*, 59, 1192–1201.

Sinclair, R.C. and Mark, M.M. (1992) The influence of mood state on judgment and action: effects on persuasion, categorization, social justice, person perception, and judgmental accuracy. In L.L. Martin and A. Tesser (eds), *The Construction of Social Judgments* (pp. 165–93), Hillsdale, NJ: Erlbaum.

Sinclair-de-Zwart, H. (1967) *Acquisition du langage et développement de la pensée*. Paris: Dunod.

Singer, J.L. and Singer, D.G. (1979) Television viewing, family style and aggressive behavior in preschool children. In M. Green (ed.), *Violence and the American Family*, Washington, DC: American Association for the Advancement of Science.

Singh, D. (1993) Adaptive significance of waist-to-hip ratio and female physical attractiveness. *Journal of Personality and Social Psychology*, 65, 293–307.

Sinha, R.R. and Hassan, M.K. (1975) Some personality correlates of social prejudice. *Journal of Social and Economic Studies*, 3, 225–31.

Skrowronski, N.J. and Carlston, D.E. (1989) Negativity and extremity biases in impression formation: a review of explanations. *Psychological Bulletin*, 105, 131–42.

Slavin, R.E. (1983) *Cooperative Learning*. New York: Longman.

Smail, D. (1993) *The Origins of Unhappiness: a new understanding of personal distress*. London: Harper Collins.

Smedslund, J. (1985) Necessarily true culture psychologies. In K.J. Gergen and K.E. Davis (eds), *The Social Construction of the Person* (pp. 73–88), New York: Springer.

Smith, C.A. and Ellsworth, P.C. (1985) Patterns of cognitive appraisal in emotion. *Journal of Personality and Social Psychology*, 48, 813–38.

Smith, C.A. and Ellsworth, P.C. (1987) Patterns of appraisal and emotion related to taking an exam. *Journal of Personality and Social Psychology*, 52, 475–88.

Smith, C.A. and Lazarus, R.S. (1993) Appraisal components, core relational themes, and the emotions. *Cognition and Emotion*, 7, 233–69.

Smith, E.E. (1988) Concepts and thought. In R.J. Sternberg and E.E. Smith (eds), *The Psychology of Human Thought* (pp. 19–49), Cambridge: Cambridge University Press.

Smith, E.E. (1990) Concepts and induction. In M.I. Posner (ed.), *Foundations of Cognitive Science* (pp. 501–26), Cambridge, MA: MIT Press.

Smith, E.E. and Medin, D.L. (1981) *Categories and Concepts*. Cambridge, MA: Harvard University Press.

Smith, E.R. (1991) Illusory correlation in a simulated exemplar-based memory. *Journal of Experimental Social Psychology*, 27, 107–23.

Smith, E.R. (1994) Social cognition contributions to attribution theory and research. In P.G. Devine, D.L. Hamilton and T.M. Ostrom (eds), *Social Cognition: contributions to classic issues in social psychology* (pp. 77–108), New York: Springer-Verlag.

Smith, E.R. and Miller, F.D. (1983) Mediation among attributional inferences and comprehension processes: initial findings and a general method. *Journal of Personality and Social Psychology*, 44, 492–505.

Smith, E.R. and Zárate, M.A. (1992) Exemplar-based model of social judgment. *Psychological Review*, 99, 2–21.

Smith, M.B., Bruner, J.S. and White, R.W. (1956) *Opinions and Personality*. New York: Wiley.

Smith, P.M. (1985) *Language, the Sexes and Society*. Oxford: Basil Blackwell.

Smith, P.M. and Fritz, A.S. (1987) A person-niche theory of depersonalization: implications for leader selection, performance and evaluation. In C. Hendrick (ed.), *Review of Personality and Social Psychology* (vol. 8, pp. 278–94), Beverly Hills: Sage.

Smith, V.L. and Ellsworth, P.C. (1987) The social psychology of eyewitness accuracy: misleading questions and communicator expertise. *Journal of Applied Psychology*, 72, 294–300.

Snow, C.E. (1986) Conversations with children. In P. Fletcher and M. Garman (eds), *Language Acquisition*, 2nd edn (pp. 69–89), Cambridge: Cambridge University Press.

Snyder, C.R. and Forsyth, D. (1991) In C.R. Snyder and D. Forsyth (eds), *Handbook of Social and Clinical Psychology* (pp. 3–17), New York: Pergamon Press.

Snyder, C.R., Lassegard, M.A. and Ford, C.E. (1986) Distancing after group success and failure: basking in reflected glory and cutting off reflected failure. *Journal of Personality and Social Psychology*, 51, 382–8.

Snyder, M. (1974) Self-monitoring of expressive behavior. *Journal of Personality and Social Psychology*, 30, 526–37.

Snyder, M. (1984) When belief creates reality. In L. Berkowitz (ed.), *Advances in Experimental Social Psychology* (vol. 18, pp. 247–305), New York: Academic Press.

Snyder, M. (1992) Motivational foundations of behavioral confirmation. In M.P. Zanna (ed.), *Advances in Experimental Social Psychology* (vol. 25, pp. 67–114), San Diego, CA: Academic Press.

Snyder, M. and DeBono, K.G. (1987) A functional approach to attitudes and persuasion. In M.P. Zanna, J.M. Olson and C.P. Herman (eds), *Social influence: the Ontario Symposium* (vol. 5, pp. 107–25), Hillsdale, NJ: Erlbaum.

Snyder, M. and Kendzierski, D. (1982) Acting on one's attitudes: procedures for linking attitudes and behavior. *Journal of Experimental Social Psychology*, 18, 165–83.

Snyder, M. and Omoto, A.M. (1992) Who helps and why? The psychology of AIDS volunteerism. In S. Spacapan and S. Oskamp (eds), *Helping and Being Helped. Naturalistic studies* (pp. 213–39), Newbury Park, CA: Sage.

Snyder, M. and Swann, W.B., Jr (1976) When actions

reflect attitudes: the politics of impression management. *Journal of Personality and Social Psychology*, 34, 1034–42.

Snyder, M. and Swann, W.B., Jr (1978) Hypothesis-testing processes in social interaction. *Journal of Personality and Social Psychology*, 36, 1202–12.

Snyder, M., Tanke, E.D. and Berscheid, E. (1977) Social perception and interpersonal behavior: on the self-fulfilling nature of the social stereotype. *Journal of Personality and Social Psychology*, 35, 656–66.

Snyder, M. and Uranowitz, S.W. (1978) Reconstructing the past: some cognitive consequences of person perception. *Journal of Personality and Social Psychology*, 36, 941–50.

Softley, P. (1980) *Police Interrogation: an observational study in four police stations*. London: HMSO.

Sokolov, A.N. (1963) *Perception and the Conditioned Reflex*. Oxford: Pergamon.

Solomon, S.D., Regier, D.A. and Burke, J.D. (1989) Role of perceived control in coping with disaster. *Journal of Social and Clinical Psychology*, 8, 376–92.

Sommer, R. (1969) *Personal Space: the behavioural basis of design*. Englewood Cliffs, NJ: Prentice-Hall.

Sommer, R. (1983) Action research is formative: research at the Saskatchewan Hospital, 1957–61. *Journal of Applied Behavioural Science*, 19, 427–38.

Sommer, R. (1987) Crime and vandalism in university residence halls: a confirmation of defensible space theory. *Journal of Environmental Psychology*, 7, 1–12.

Sorrentino, R.M., King, G. and Leo, G. (1980) The influence of the minority on perception: a note on a possible alternative explanation. *Journal of Experimental Social Psychology*, 16, 293–301.

Sparks, R.F., Genn, H.G. and Dodd, D.J. (1977) *Surveying Victims*. Chichester: Wiley.

Spence, K.W. (1956) *Behavior Theory and Conditioning*. New Haven, CT: Yale University Press.

Spivey, E.B. and Prentice-Dunn, S. (1990) Assessing the directionality of deindividuated behavior: effects of deindividuation, modeling, and private self-consciousness on aggressive and prosocial responses. *Basic and Applied Science Psychology*, 11, 387–403.

Sprecher, S. (1986) The relation between inequity and emotions in close relationships. *Social Psychology Quarterly*, 49, 309–21.

Srull, T.K. (1981) Person memory: some tests of associative storage and retrieval models. *Journal of Experimental Psychology: Human Learning and Memory*, 7, 440–63.

Srull, T.K. and Wyer, R.S. (1980) Category accessibility and social perception: some implications for the study of person memory and interpersonal judgments. *Journal of Personality and Social Psychology*, 38, 841–56.

Staats, A.W. (1969) Experimental demand characteristics and the classical conditioning of attitudes. *Journal of Personality and Social Psychology*, 11, 187–92.

Staats, A.W. and Staats, C.K. (1958) Attitudes established by classical conditioning. *Journal of Abnormal and Social Psychology*, 57, 37–40.

Stagner, R. and Congdon, C.S. (1955) Another failure to demonstrate displacement of aggression. *Journal of Abnormal and Social Psychology*, 51, 695–766.

Stahlberg, D. (1987) Assimilation und Kontrast. In D. Frey and S. Greif (eds), *Sozialpsychologie: ein Handbuch in Schlüsselbegriffen* (pp. 111–21), Munich: Urban & Schwarzenberg.

Stahlberg, D. and Frey, D. (1987) Konsistenztheorien. In D. Frey and S. Greif (eds), *Sozialpsychologie: ein Handbuch in Schlüsselbegriffen* (pp. 214–21), Munich: Urban & Schwarzenberg.

Stahlberg, D. and Frey, D. (1993) Das Elaboration-Likelihood-Modell von Petty und Cacioppo. In D. Frey and M. Irle (eds), *Theorien der Sozialpsychologie. Vol I: Kognitive Theorien* (pp. 327–59), Bern: Huber.

Stangor, C. and McMillan, D. (1992) Memory for expectancy-congruent and expectancy-incongruent information: a review of the social and social developmental literatures. *Psychological Bulletin*, 111, 42–61.

Stasser, G., Kerr, N.L. and Davis, J.H. (1989) Influence processes and consensus models in decision-making groups. In P.B. Paulus (ed.), *Psychology of Group Influence* (pp. 279–326), 2nd edn, Hillsdale, NJ: Erlbaum.

Steiner, I.D. (1972) *Group Processes and Productivity*. New York: Academic Press.

Steiner, I.D. (1976) Task-performing groups. In J.W. Thibaut, J.T. Spence and R.C. Carson (eds), *Contemporary Topics in Social Psychology* (pp. 393–422), Morristown, NJ: General Learning Press.

Steiner, J.E. (1979) Human facial expressions in response to taste and smell stimulation. In L.P. Lipsitt and H.W. Reese (eds), *Advances in Child Development and Behavior* (pp. 257–95), New York: Academic Press.

Stephan, W.G. and Stephan, C.W. (1985) Intergroup anxiety. *Journal of Social Issues*, 41, 157–75.

Stephenson, G.M. (1978) Interparty and interpersonal exchange in negotiation groups. In H. Brandstätter, J.H. Davis and H. Schuler (eds), *Dynamics of Group Decisions* (pp. 207–28), London: Sage.

Stephenson, G.M. (1992) *The Psychology of Criminal Justice*. Oxford: Blackwell.

Stephenson, G.M. (1995) Looking to the future: a psychologist's comments on Richard Abel's *Contested Communities*. *Journal of Law and Society*, 22, 1, 133–9.

Stephenson, G.M. and Davis, J.H. (1986) Editorial. *Social Behaviour*, 1, 1.

Stephenson, G.M., Kniveton, B.H. and Wagner, W. (1991) Social influences on remembering: intellectual, interpersonal and intergroup components. *European Journal of Social Psychology*, 21, 463–75.

Stern, D.N. (1985) *The Interpersonal World of the Infant. A view from psychoanalysis and developmental psychology.* New York: Basic Books.

Stern, L.D., Marrs, S., Millar, M.G. and Cole, E. (1984) Processing time and the recall of inconsistent and consistent behaviors of individuals and groups. *Journal of Personality and Social Psychology*, 47, 253–62.

Stern, P.C. (1992) Psychological dimensions of global environmental change. *Annual Review of Psychology*, 43, 269–302.

Stogdill, R.M. (1948) Personal factors associated with leadership. *Journal of Psychology*, 23, 35–71.

Stokols, D. (1972) On the distinction between density and crowding: some implications for future research. *Psychological Review*, 79, 275–8.

Stoner, J.A.F. (1961) *A comparison of individual and group decisions involving risk.* Unpublished master's thesis, Massachusetts Institute of Technology, cited in D.G. Marquis, Individual responsibility and group decisions involving risk, *Industrial Management Review*, 3, 8–23.

Storms, M.D. (1973) Videotape and the attribution process: reversing actors' and observers' points of view. *Journal of Personality and Social Psychology*, 27, 165–75.

Stosberg, M. (1980) Klassische Ansätze in der Einstellungsmessung. In F. Petermann (ed.), *Einstellungsmessung/Einstellungsforschung* (pp. 53–78), Göttingen: Hogrefe.

Stouffer, S.A., Suchmann, E.A., DeVinney, L.C., Star, S.A. and Williams, R.M., Jr (1949) *The American Soldier, vol. 1: Adjustments during army life.* Princeton, NJ: Princeton University Press.

Strack, F., Schwarz, N. and Gschneidinger, E. (1985) Happiness and reminiscing: the role of time perspective, mood and mode of thinking. *Journal of Personality and Social Psychology*, 49, 1460–9.

Strack, F., Schwarz, N., Bless, H., Kübler, A. and Wänke, M. (1993) Awareness of the influence as a determinant of assimilation vs. contrast. *European Journal of Social Psychology*, 23, 53–62.

Strack, F., Stepper, L.L. and Martin, S. (1988) Inhibiting and facilitating conditions of the human smile: a non-obtrusive test of the facial-feedback hypothesis. *Journal of Personality and Social Psychology*, 54, 768–77.

Stratton, P., Heard, D., Hanks, H.G.I., Munton, A.G., Brewin, C.R. and Davidson, C. (1986) Coding causal beliefs in natural discourse. *British Journal of Social Psychology*, 25, 299–31.

Street, R.L., Jr. and Capella, J.N. (eds) (1985) *Sequence and Pattern in Communicative Behaviour.* London: Edward Arnold.

Stroebe, M.S. (1994) The broken heart phenomenon: an examination of the mortality of bereavement. *Journal of Community and Applied Social Psychology*, 4, 47–61.

Stroebe, M.S. and Stroebe, W. (1993) The mortality of bereavement: a review. In M. Stroebe, W. Stroebe and R.O. Hansson (eds), *Handbook of Bereavement: theory, research and intervention* (pp. 175–95), Cambridge: Cambridge University Press.

Stroebe, W. (1977) Self-esteem and interpersonal attraction. In S. Duck (ed.), *Theory and Practice in Interpersonal Attraction* (pp. 79–104), London: Academic Press.

Stroebe, W. (1980) *Grundlagen der Sozialpsychologie.* Stuttgart: Klett-Cotta.

Stroebe, W. and Diehl, M. (1988) When social support fails: supporter characteristics in compliance-induced attitude change. *Personality and Social Psychology Bulletin*, 14, 136–44.

Stroebe, W. and Diehl, M. (1991) You can't beat good experiments with correlational evidence: Mullen, Johnson and Salas's meta-anlaytic misinterpretations. *Basic and Applied Social Psychology*, 12, 25–32.

Stroebe, W. and Diehl, M. (1994) Why groups are less effective than their members. On productivity loss in idea-generating groups. In W. Stroebe and M. Hewstone (eds), *European Review of Social Psychology* (vol. 5, pp. 271–304), London: Wiley.

Stroebe, W., Diehl, M. and Abakoumkin, G. (1992) The illusion of group effectivity. *Personality and Social Psychology Bulletin*, 18, 643–50.

Stroebe, W. and Frey, B.S. (1982) Self-interest and collective action: the economics and psychology of public goods. *British Journal of Social Psychology*, 21, 121–37.

Stroebe, W. and Insko, C.A. (1989) Stereotype, prejudice, and discrimination: changing conceptions in theory and research. In D. Bar-Tal, C.F. Graumann, A.W. Kruglanski and W. Stroebe (eds), *Stereotype and Prejudice: changing conceptions* (pp. 3–34), New York: Springer-Verlag.

Stroebe, W., Insko, C.A., Thompson, V.D. and Layton, B.D. (1971) Effects of physical attractiveness, attitude similarity, and sex on various aspects of interpersonal attraction. *Journal of Personality and Social Psychology*, 18, 79–91.

Stroebe, W. and Stroebe, M.S. (1986) Beyond marriage: the impact of partner loss on health. In R. Gilmour and S. Duck (eds), *The Emerging Field of Personal Relationships* (pp. 203–24), Hillsdale, NJ: Erlbaum.

Stroebe, W. and Stroebe, M.S. (1987a) Bereavement as

a stressful life-event: a paradigm for research on the stress–health relationship. In G.R. Semin and B. Krahé (eds), *Issues in Contemporary German Social Psychology* (pp. 258–72), London: Sage.

Stroebe, W. and Stroebe, M.S. (1987b) *Bereavement and Health*. New York: Cambridge University Press.

Stroebe, W. and Stroebe, M.S (1992) Bereavement and health: processes of adjusting to the loss of a partner. In L. Montada, S.H. Filipp and M.J. Lerner (eds), *Life Crises and Experiences of Loss in Adulthood* (pp. 3–22), Hillsdale, NJ: Lawrence Erlbaum.

Stroebe, W. and Stroebe, M.S. (1995) *Social Psychology and Health*. Buckingham: Open University Press.

Stroebe, W., Stroebe, M.S. and Domittner, G. (1988) Individual and situational differences in recovery from bereavement. A risk group identified. *Journal of Social Issues*, 44, 143–58.

Stroebe, W., Stroebe, M.S., Gergen, K.J. and Gergen, M. (1982) The effects of bereavement on mortality: a social psychological analysis. In J.R. Eiser (ed.), *Social Psychology and Behavioural Medicine* (pp. 527–60), Chichester: Wiley.

Struch, N. and Schwartz, S.H. (1989) Intergroup aggression: its predictors and distinctness from in-group bias. *Journal of Personality and Social Psychology*, 56, 364–73.

Stults, D.M., Messé, L.A. and Kerr, N.L. (1984) Belief-discrepant behavior and the Bogus Pipeline: impression management or arousal attribution. *Journal of Experimental Social Psychology*, 20, 47–54.

Suess, G.J., Grossmann, K.E. and Sroufe, L.A. (1992) Effects of attachment to mother and father on quality of adaptation in preschool: from dyadic to individual organisation of self. *International Journal of Behavioral Development*, 15, 43–65.

Swann, W.B. (1984) Quest for accuracy in person perception: a matter of pragmatics. *Psychological Review*, 91, 457–77.

Swann, W.B., Giuliano, T. and Wegner, D.M. (1982) Where leading questions can lead: the power of conjecture in social interaction. *Journal of Personality and Social Psychology*, 42, 1025–35.

Sweeney, P.D., Anderson, K. and Bailey, S. (1986). Attributional style in depression: A meta-analytic review. *Journal of Personality and Social Psychology*, 50, 974–91.

Symons, D. (1979) *The Evolution of Human Sexuality*. New York: Oxford University Press.

Symons, D. and Ellis, B. (1989) Human male–female differences in sexual desire. In A.S. Rasa, C. Vogel and E. Voland (eds), *The Sociobiology of Sexual and Reproductive Strategies* (pp. 131–46), London: Chapman & Hall.

't Hart, P. (1990) *Groupthink in Government: a study of small groups and policy failure*. Amsterdam: Swets and Zeitlinger.

Tajfel, H. (1969) The cognitive aspect of prejudice. *Journal of Social Issues*, 25, 79–97.

Tajfel, H. (1970) Experiments in intergroup discrimination. *Scientific American*, 223, 96–102.

Tajfel, H. (ed.) (1978) *Differentiation between Social Groups: studies in the social psychology of intergroup relations*. London: Academic Press.

Tajfel, H. (1981) *Human Groups and Social Categories: studies in social psychology*. Cambridge: Cambridge University Press.

Tajfel, H. (1982) Social psychology of intergroup relations. *Annual Review of Psychology*, 33, 1–30.

Tajfel, H. (ed.) (1984) *The Social Dimension: European developments in social psychology* (2 vols). Cambridge: Cambridge University Press.

Tajfel, H., Flament, C., Billig, M.G. and Bundy, R.P. (1971) Social categorization and intergroup behaviour. *European Journal of Social Psychology*, 1, 149–78.

Tajfel, H. and Fraser, C. (eds) (1978) *Introducing Social Psychology*. Harmondsworth: Penguin.

Tajfel, H. and Jahoda, G. (1966) Development in children of concepts and attitudes about their own and other nations: a cross-national study. *Proceedings of the XVIIIth International Congress of Psychology*, 36, 17–33.

Tajfel, H., Nemeth, C., Jahoda, G., Campbell, J.D. and Johnson, N.B. (1970) The development of children's preference for their own country: a cross-national study. *International Journal of Psychology*, 6, 245–53.

Tajfel, H. and Turner, J. (1986a) The Social Identity Theory of intergroup behaviour. In S. Worchel and W.G. Austin (eds), *Psychology of Intergroup Relations* (pp. 7–24), Chicago: Nelson.

Tajfel, H. and Turner, J. (1986b) An integrative theory of intergroup conflict. In W.C. Austin and S. Worchel (eds), *The Social Psychology of Intergroup Relations* (pp. 7–24), 2nd edn, Monterey, CA: Brooks/Cole.

Tajfel, H. and Wilkes, A.L. (1963) Classification and quantitative judgment. *British Journal of Psychology*, 54, 101–14.

Tanford, S. and Penrod, S. (1984) Social influence model: a formal integration of research on majority and minority influence processes. *Psychological Bulletin*, 95, 189–225.

Tannenbaum, P.H. and Zillmann, D. (1975) Emotional arousal in the facilitation of aggression through communication. In L. Berkowitz (ed.), *Advances in Experimental Social Psychology* (vol. 8, pp. 149–92), New York: Academic Press.

Tarde, G. (1895) *Essais et mélanges sociologiques*. Lyon: Storck.

Tarde, G. (1901) *L'opinion et la foule*. Paris: Alcan.

Taylor, B.C. (1992) Elderly identity in conversation: producing frailty. *Comunication Research*, 19, 493–515.

Taylor, D.M. (1981) Stereotypes and intergroup relations. In R.C. Gardner and R. Kalin (eds), *A Canadian Social Psychology of Ethnic Relations* (pp. 151–71), Toronto: Methuen.

Taylor, D.M. and Brown, R.J. (1979) Towards a more social social psychology? *British Journal of Social and Clinical Psychology*, 18, 173–80.

Taylor, R.B. (1987) Toward an environmental psychology of disorder: delinquency, crime, and fear of crime. *Handbook of Environmental Psychology* (vol. 2, pp. 951–86), Chichester: John Wiley.

Taylor, S.E., Crocker, J., Fiske, S.T., Sprinzen, M. and Winkler, J.D. (1979) The generalizability of salience effects. *Journal of Personality and Social Psychology*, 37, 357–68.

Taylor, S.E. and Fiske, S.T. (1978) Salience, attention, and attribution: top of the head phenomena. In L. Berkowitz (ed.), *Advances in Experimental Social Psychology* (vol. 11, pp. 250–89), New York: Academic Press.

Taylor, S.E. and Fiske, S.T. (1981) Getting inside the head: methodologies for process analysis in attribution and social cognition. In J.H. Harvey, W.J. Ickes and R.F. Kidd (eds), *New Directions in Attribution Research* (vol. 3, pp. 459–524), Hillsdale, NJ: Erlbaum.

Taylor, S.E. and Koivumaki, J.H. (1976) The perception of self and others: acquaintanceship, affect and actor–observer differences. *Journal of Personality and Social Psychology*, 33, 403–8.

Tedeschi, J.T. and Felson, R.B. (1994) *Violence, Aggression and Coercive Actions*. Washington, DC: American Psychological Association.

Tedeschi, J.T., Lindskold, A. and Rosenfeld, P. (1985) *Introduction to Social Psychology*. New York: West.

Tedeschi, J.T. and Rosenfeld, P. (1981) Impression management theory and the forced compliance situation. In J.T. Tedeschi (ed.), *Impression Management Theory and Social Psychological Research* (pp. 147–77), New York: Academic Press.

Tedeschi, J.T., Schlenker, B.R. and Bonoma, T.V. (1971) Cognitive dissonance: private ratiocination or public spectacle? *American Psychologist*, 26, 685–95.

Teichman, Y. (1973) Emotional arousal and affiliation. *Journal of Experimental Social Psychology*, 9, 591–605.

Tesser, A. and Shaffer, D.R. (1990) Attitudes and attitude change. *Annual Review of Psychology*, 41, 479–523.

Tetlock, P.E. and Levi, A. (1982) Attribution bias: on the inconclusiveness of the cognition–motivation debate. *Journal of Experimental Social Psychology*, 18, 68–88.

Tetlock, P.E. and Manstead, A.S.R. (1985) Impression management versus intrapsychic explanations in social psychology: a useful dichotomy? *Psychological Review*, 92, 59–77.

Thakerar, J.N. and Giles, H. (1981) They are – so they speak: non-content speech stereotypes. *Language and Communication*, 1, 251–5.

Thibaut, J.W. and Kelley, H.H. (1959) *The Social Psychology of Groups*. New York: Wiley (reprinted by Transaction Books, New Brunswick, 1986).

Thibaut, J.W. and Strickland, L.H. (1956) Psychological set and social conformity. *Journal of Personality*, 25, 115–29.

Thiessen, D. and Ross, M. (1990) The use of a sociobiological questionnaire (SQ) for the assessment of sexual dimorphism. *Behavior Genetics*, 20, 297–305.

Thomas, E.J. and Fink, C.F. (1961) Models of group problem solving. *Journal of Abnormal and Social Psychology*, 63, 53–63.

Thomas, W.I. and Znaniecki, F. (1918) *The Polish Peasant in Europe and America*. Boston: Badger.

Thompson, P.R. (1980) And who is my neighbour? An answer from evolutionary genetics. *Social Science Information*, 19, 341–84.

Thompson, S.C. and Kelley, H.H. (1981) Judgments of responsibility for activities in close relationships. *Journal of Personality and Social Psychology*, 41, 469–77.

Thurstone, L.L. (1928) Attitudes can be measured. *American Journal of Sociology*, 33, 529–54.

Thurstone, L.L. (1931) The measurement of attitudes. *Journal of Abnormal and Social Psychology*, 26, 249–69.

Tinbergen, N. (1951) *The Study of Instinct*. Oxford: Oxford University Press.

Ting-Toomey, S. (1986) Interpersonal ties in intergroup communication. In W.B. Gudykunst (ed.), *Intergroup Communication* (pp. 114–26), London: Edward Arnold.

Toglia, M.P., Hembrooke, H., Ceci, S.J. and Ross, D.F. (1994) Children's resistance to misleading post-event information: when does it occur? *Current Psychology: Developmental, Learning, Personality, Social*, 13, 21–6.

Toi, M. and Batson, C.D. (1982) More evidence that empathy is a source of altruistic motivation. *Journal of Personality and Social Psychology*, 43, 281–93.

Tomkins, S.S. (1984) Affect theory. In K.R. Scherer and P. Ekman (eds), *Approaches to Emotion* (pp. 163–96), Hillsdale, NJ: Erlbaum.

Torestad, B. (1990) What is anger-provoking? A psychophysical study of perceived causes of anger. *Aggressive Behavior*, 16, 9–26.

Torrance, E.P. (1954) The behavior of small groups under the stress of conditions of survival. *American Sociological Review*, 19, 751–5.

Totman, R. (1976) Cognitive dissonance and the placebo response. *European Journal of Social Psychology*, 5, 119–25.

Totman, R. (1979) *Social Causes of Illness*. New York: Pantheon.

Totman, R. (1982a) Psychosomatic theories. In J.R. Eiser (ed.), *Social Psychology and Behavioural Medicine* (pp. 143–75), Chichester: Wiley.

Totman, R. (1982b) Philosophical foundations of attribution theories. In C. Antaki and C. Brewin (eds), *Attribution and Psychological Change*, London: Academic Press.

Totman, R. (1990) *Mind, Stress and Health*. London: Souvenir Press.

Travis, L.E. (1925) The effect of a small audience upon eye–hand coordination. *Journal of Abnormal and Social Psychology*, 20, 142–6.

Trevarthen, C. (1982) The primary motives for cooperative understanding. In G. Butterworth and P. Light (eds), *Social Cognition: studies of the development of understanding* (pp. 201–23), Chicago: University of Chicago Press.

Triandis, H.C. (1994) *Culture and Social Behavior*. New York: McGraw-Hill.

Triandis, K., Bontempo, R., Villareal, M.J., Asai, M. and Lucca, N. (1988) Individualism and collectivism: cross-cultural perspectives on self–ingroup relationships. *Journal of Personality and Social Psychology*, 54, 323–38.

Triplett, N.D. (1898) The dynamogenic factor in pacemaking and competition. *American Journal of Psychology*, 9, 507–33.

Trivers, R.L. (1971) The evolution of reciprocal altruism. *Quarterly Review of Biology*, 46, 35–57.

Trivers, R.L. (1972) Parental investment and sexual selection. In B. Campbell (ed.), *Sexual Selection and the Descent of Man* (pp. 136–79), Chicago: Aldine.

Tulving, E. and Thompson, D.M. (1973) Encoding specificity and retrieval processes in episodic memory. *Psychological Review*, 80, 352–73.

Turnbull, W. and Slugoski, B. (1988) Conversational and linguistic processes in causal attribution. In D. Hilton (ed.), *Contemporary Science and Natural Explanation: commonsense conceptions of causality* (pp. 66–93), Brighton: Harvester Press.

Turner, C.W. and Goldsmith, D. (1976) Effects of toy guns and airplanes on children's free play behavior. *Journal of Experimental Social Psychology*, 21, 303–15.

Turner, C.W. and Simons, L.S. (1974) Effects of subject sophistication and apprehension evaluation on aggressive responses to weapons. *Journal of Personality and Social Psychology*, 30, 341–8.

Turner, J.C. (1980) Fairness or discrimination in intergroup behaviour? A reply to Braithwaite, Doyle and Lightbown. *European Journal of Social Psychology*, 10, 131–47.

Turner, J.C. (1981a) The experimental social psychology of intergroup behaviour. In J.C. Turner and H. Giles (eds), *Intergroup Behaviour* (pp. 66–101), Oxford: Basil Blackwell.

Turner, J.C. (1981b) Some considerations in generalizing experimental social psychology. In G.M. Stephenson and J. Davis (eds), *Progress in Applied Social Psychology* (vol. 1, pp. 3–34), Chichester: Wiley.

Turner, J.C. (1982) Towards a cognitive redefinition of the social group. In H. Tajfel (ed.), *Social Identity and Intergroup Relations* (pp. 15–40), Cambridge: Cambridge University Press.

Turner, J.C. (1987) *Rediscovering the Social Group. A self-categorization theory*. Oxford: Basil Blackwell.

Turner, J.C. (1991) *Social Influence*. Buckingham: Open University Press.

Turner, P.J. (1993) Attachment to mother and behaviour with adults in preschool. *British Journal of Developmental Psychology*, 11, 75–89.

Turner, R.H. and Killian, L.M. (1972) *Collective Behavior*, 2nd edn. Englewood Cliffs, NJ: Prentice-Hall.

Tversky, A. and Kahneman, D. (1973) Availability: a heuristic for judging frequency and probability. *Cognitive Psychology*, 5, 207–32.

Tversky, A. and Kahneman, D. (1974) Judgment under uncertainty: heuristics and biases. *Science*, 185, 1124–31.

Tversky, B. and Tuchin, M. (1989) A reconciliation of the evidence on eyewitness testimony: comments on McCloskey and Zaragoza. *Journal of Experimental Social Psychology: General*, 118, 86–91.

Ulrich, W. (1986) The uses of fiction as a source of information about interpersonal communication: a critical view. *Communication Quarterly*, 34, 143–53.

Underwood, B., Froming, W.J. and Moore, B.S. (1977) Mood, attention, and altruism: a search for mediating variables. *Developmental Psychology*, 13, 541–2.

Upshaw, H.S. (1969) The personal reference scale: an approach to social judgment. In L. Berkowitz (ed.), *Advances in Experimental Social Psychology* (vol. 4, pp. 315–71), San Diego, CA: Academic Press.

US Department of Health, Education and Welfare (1964) *Smoking and Health. Report of the Advisory Committee to the Surgeon General of the Public Health Service*, PHS Publi. no. (HEW) 1103. Washington, DC: USDHEW, Public Health Service., Centers for Disease Control.

Valiant, G., Glachan, M. and Emler, N. (1982) The stimulation of cognitive development through co-operative task performance. *British Journal of Educational Psychology*, 52, 281–8.

Van de Ven, A.H. (1974) *Group Decision-making Effectiveness*. Kent, OH: Center for Business and Economic Research Press.

van Hooff, J.A. (1972) A comparative approach to the phylogeny of laughter and smiling. In R. Hinde (ed.), *Non-verbal Communication* (pp. 209–41), Cambridge: Cambridge University Press.

van IJzendoorn, M.H. (1990) Developments in cross-cultural research on attachment: some methodological notes. *Human Development*, 33, 3–9.

van Koppen, R.J. (1994) From police information to miscarriages of justice. *Issues in Criminological and Legal Psychology*, 21, 11–20.

Vanbeselaere, N. (1991) The different effects of simple and crossed categorizations: a result of the category differentiation process or differential category salience. In W. Stroebe and M. Hewstone (eds), *European Journal of Social Psychology* (vol. 2, pp. 247–78), Chichester: Wiley.

Vanneman, R.D. and Pettigrew, T.F. (1972) Race and relative deprivation in the urban United States. *Race*, 13, 461–86.

VanYperen, N.W. and Buunk, A.P. (1990) A longitudinal study of equity in intimate relationships. *European Journal of Social Psychology*, 20, 287–309.

Vaughan, G.M. (1978) Social change and intergroup preferences in New Zealand. *European Journal of Social Psychology*, 8, 297–314.

Verplanck, W.S. (1955) The control of the content of conversation: reinforcement of statements of opinion. *Journal of Abnormal and Social Psychology*, 51, 668–76.

Vivian, J., Brown, R.J. and Hewstone, M. (1994) Changing attitudes through intergroup contact: the effects of membership salience. Unpublished MS., Universities of Kent and Wales, Cardiff.

Vlaander, G.P.J. and Van Rooijen, L. (1985) Independence and conformity in Holland: Asch's experiment three decades later. *Gedrag*, 13, 49–55.

Voland, E. (1993) *Grundriss der Soziobiologie*. Stuttgart: Fischer.

Vygotsky, L.S. (1962) *Thought and Language*. Cambridge, MA: MIT Press.

Vygotsky, L.S. (1978) *Mind in Society. The development of higher psychological processes*. Cambridge, MA: Harvard University Press.

Wagenaar, W.A., van Koppen, R.J. and Crombag, H.F.M. (1993) *Anchored narratives: the psychology of criminal evidence*. London: Harvester Wheatsheaf.

Wagner, H.L., MacDonald, C.J. and Manstead A.S.R. (1986) Communication of individual emotions by spontaneous facial expressions. *Journal of Personality and Social Psychology*, 50, 637–43.

Walker, I. and Mann, L. (1987) Unemployment, relative deprivation and social protest. *Personality and Social Psychology Bulletin*, 13, 275–83.

Walker, I. and Pettigrew, T.F. (1984) Relative deprivation theory: an overview and conceptual critique. *British Journal of Social Psychology*, 23, 301–10.

Wallbott, H.G. (1985) Movement quality – A neglected aspect of nonverbal behavior in person perception. *Journal of Clinical Psychology*, 41, 345–59.

Wallbott, H.G. and Scherer, K.R. (1995). Cultural determinants of shame and guilt experiences. In J.P. Tangney and K.W. Fischer (eds), *Self-Conscious Emotions: shame, guilt, embarrassment, and pride* (pp. 465–87), New York: Guilford Press.

Walster, E. (1965) The effect of self-esteem on romantic liking. *Journal of Experimental Social Psychology*, 1, 184–97.

Walster, E., Aronson, V., Abrahams, D. and Rottman, L. (1966) The importance of physical attractiveness in dating behavior. *Journal of Personality and Social Psychology*, 4, 508–16.

Walster, E., Walster, G.W. and Berscheid, E. (1978) *Equity: theory and research*. Boston: Allyn and Bacon.

Walters, R.H. and Brown, M. (1963) Studies of reinforcement of aggression. III: Transfer of responses to an interpersonal situation. *Child Development*, 24, 536–71.

Wason, P.C. (1966) Reasoning. In B. Foss (ed.), *New Horizons in Psychology* (pp. 135–51), London: Penguin.

Watson, D. (1982) The actor and the observer: how are their perceptions of causality divergent? *Psychological Bulletin*, 92, 682–700.

Watson, J.B. (1928) *Psychological Care of Infant and Child*. New York: Norton.

Watson, R.I. (1979) The history of psychology conceived as social psychology of the past. *Journal of the History of the Behavioral Sciences*, 15, 103–14.

Wattenmaker, W.D., Nakamura, G.V. and Medin, D.L. (1988) Relationships between similarity-based and explanation-based categorization. In D.J. Hilton (ed.), *Contemporary Science and Natural Explanation: common sense conceptions of causality* (pp. 204–40), Brighton: Harvester Press.

Watzlawick, P., Beavin, J. and Jackson, D.D. (1967) *Pragmatics and Human Communication*, New York: Norton.

Weary, G. (1980) Examination of affect and egotism as mediators of bias in causal attributions. *Journal of Personality and Social Psychology*, 38, 348–57.

Weary, G., Harvey, J.H., Schwieger, P., Olson, C.T., Perloff, R. and Pritchard, S. (1982) Self-presentation and the moderation of self-serving attributional biases. *Social Cognition*, 1, 140–59.

Weaver, F.M. and Carroll, J.S. (1985) Crime perceptions in a natural setting by expert and novice shoplifters. *Social Psychology Quarterly*, 48, 349–59.

Webb, E.J., Campbell, D.T., Schwartz, R.F., Sechrest, L. and Grove, J.B. (1981) *Nonreactive Measures in the Social Sciences*. Boston: Houghton Mifflin.

Weber, R. and Crocker, J. (1983) Cognitive processes in the revision of stereotypic beliefs. *Journal of Personality and Social Psychology*, 45, 961–77.

Webster, D.M. and Kruglanski, A.W. (1994) Individual differences in the need for cognitive closure. *Journal of Personality and Social Psychology*, 67, 1049–62.

Wegener, H., Losel, F. and Haisch, J. (1989) *Criminal Behavior and the Justice System: psychological perspectives*. New York: Springer-Verlag.

Wegner, D.M., Giuliano, T. and Hertel, P. (1985) Cognitive interdependence in close relationships. In W.J. Ickes (ed.), *Compatible and Incompatible Relationships* (pp. 253–76), New York: Springer.

Wegner, D.M., Wenzlaff, R., Kerker, R.M. and Beattie, A.E. (1981) Incrimination through innuendo: can media questions become public answers. *Journal of Personality and Social Psychology*, 40, 822–32.

Weick, K.E. (1985) Systematic observational methods. In G. Lindzey and E. Aronson (eds), *Handbook of Social Psychology*, 3rd edn (vol. 1, pp. 567–634), New York: Random House.

Weigel, R.H. and Newman, L.S. (1976) Increasing attitude–behavior correspondence by broadening the scope of the behavioral measure. *Journal of Personality and Social Psychology*, 33, 793–802.

Weiner, B. (1979) A theory of motivation for some classroom experiences. *Journal of Educational Psychology*, 71, 3–25.

Weiner, B. (1980) May I borrow your class notes? An attributional analysis of judgements of help giving in an achievement-related context. *Journal of Educational Psychology*, 72, 676–81.

Weiner, B. (1985) 'Spontaneous' causal thinking. *Psychological Bulletin*, 97, 74–84.

Weiner, B. (1986) *An Attributional Theory of Motivation and Emotion*. New York: Springer-Verlag.

Weiner, B. (1995) *Judgments of Responsibility*. New York: Guilford.

Weiner, B. and Kukla, A. (1970) An attributional analysis of achievement motivation. *Journal of Personality and Social Psychology*, 15, 1–20.

Weiss, R.S. (1975) *Marital Separation*. New York: Basic Books.

Wells, G.L. (1984) A reanalysis of the expert testimony issue. In G.L. Wells and E.F. Loftus (eds), *Eyewitness Testimony: psychological perspectives* (pp. 304–14), Cambridge: Cambridge University Press.

Wells, G.L. and Loftus, E.F. (1984) Eyewitness research: then and now. In G.L. Wells and E.F. Loftus (eds), *Eyewitness Testimony: psychological perspectives* (pp. 1–11), Cambridge: Cambridge University Press.

Werner, C. and Parmalee, P. (1979) Similarity of activity preferences among friends: those who play together stay together. *Social Psychology Quarterly*, 42, 62–6.

Wertsch, J.V. and Tulviste, P. (1992) L.S. Vygotsky and contemporary developmental psychology. *Development Psychology*, 28, 548–57.

West, C. (1984) *Routine Complications*. Bloomington, IN: Indiana University Press.

Wetherell, M. (1982) Cross-cultural studies of minimal groups: implications for the social identity theory of intergroup relations. In H. Tajfel (ed.), *Social Identity and Intergroup Relations* (pp. 207–40), Cambridge: Cambridge University Press.

Wetherell, M. (1987) Social identity and group polarization. In J.C. Turner, *Rediscovering the Social Group. A self-categorization theory* (pp. 142–70), Oxford: Basil Blackwell.

Wetherell, M., Stiven, H. and Potter, J. (1987) Unequal egalitarianism: a preliminary study of discourses concerning gender and employment opportunities. *British Journal of Social Psychology*, 26, 59–71.

Wexler, K. (1982) A principal theory for language acquisition. In E. Wanner and L.R. Gleitman (eds), *Language Acquisition: the state of the art* (pp. 288–315), Cambridge: Cambridge University Press.

Wheeler, L. and Nezlek, J. (1977) Sex differences in social participation. *Journal of Personality and Social Psychology*, 35, 742–54.

White, G.L., Fishbein, S. and Rutstein, J. (1981) Passionate love and the misattribution of arousal. *Journal of Personality and Social Psychology*, 41, 56–62.

Whitehurst, G.J., Falco, F.L., Lonigan, C., Fischel, J.E., DeBaryshe, B.D., Valdez-Menchaca, M.C. and Caulfield, M. (1988) Accelerating language development through picture book reading. *Developmental Psychology*, 24, 552–8.

Whorf, B. (1956) *Language, Thought and Reality*. Cambridge, MA: MIT Press.

Whyte, W.F. (1948) *Human Relations in the Restaurant Industry*. New York: McGraw-Hill.

Wicker, A.W. (1969) Attitude versus action: the relationship of verbal and overt behavioral responses to attitude objects. *Journal of Social Issues*, 25, 41–78.

Wicklund, R.A. (1975) Objective self-awareness. In L. Berkowitz (ed.), *Advances in Experimental Social Psychology* (vol. 8, pp. 233–75), New York: Academic Press.

Wiemann, J.M. (1977) Explication and test of a model of communicative competence. *Human Communication Research*, 3, 195–213.

Wiemann, J.M. (1985) Interpersonal control and regulation in conversation. In R.L. Street and J.N. Capella (eds), *Sequence and Pattern in Communicative Behaviour* (pp. 85–102), London: Edward Arnold.

Wiemann, J.M. and Bradac, J.J. (1989) Pragmatics of interpersonal competence. In C. Wilder-Mott and J.H. Weakland (eds), *Rigour and Imagination: essays from the legacy of Gregory Bateson* (pp. 283–98), New York: Praeger.

Wiemann, J.M. and Kelly, C.W. (1981) Pragmatics of interpersonal competence. In C. Wilder-Mott and J.H. Weakland (eds), *Rigour and Imagination: essays from the legacy of Gregory Bateson*, New York: Praeger.

Wiemann, J.M. and Knapp, M.L. (1975) Turn-taking in conversations. *Journal of Communication*, 25, 75–92.

Wilder, D.A. (1977) Perceptions of groups, size of opposition, and influence. *Journal of Experimental Social Psychology*, 13, 253–68.

Wilder, D.A. (1984) Intergroup contact: the typical member and the exception to the rule. *Journal of Experimental Social Psychology*, 20, 177–94.

Wiley, N. (1994) *The Semiotic Self.* Cambridge: Polity Press.

Wilke, H.A.M. and Meertens, R.W. (1994) *Group Performance.* London: Routledge.

Wilkinson, S. (ed.) (1986) *Feminist Social Psychology: developing theory and practice.* Milton Keynes: Open University Press.

Williams, J.A. and Watson, G. (1988) Sexual inequality, family life and family therapy. In E. Street and W. Dryden (eds), *Family Therapy in Britain* (pp. 291–311), London: Harper & Row.

Williamson, T.M. (in press) Investigation and interviewing: the changing criminal justice context. In F. Leishman, B. Loveday and S. Savage (eds), *Case Issues in Policing*, London: Longman Higher Education.

Wills, T.A. (1982) Nonspecific factors in helping relationships. In T.A. Wills (ed.), *Basic Processes in Helping Relationships* (pp. 381–404), New York: Academic Press.

Wills, T.A. (1991) Social support and interpersonal relationships. In M.S. Clark (ed.), *Prosocial Behavior* (pp. 265–89), Newbury Park, CA: Sage.

Wills, T.A. (1992) The helping process in the context of personal relationships. In S. Spacapan and S. Oskamp (eds), *Helping and Being Helped. Naturalistic studies* (pp. 17–48), Newbury Park, CA: Sage.

Wilson, D.W. and Schafer, R.B. (1978) Is social psychology interdisciplinary? *Personality and Social Psychology Bulletin*, 4, 548–52.

Wilson, E.O. (1975) *Sociobiology: the new synthesis.* Cambridge, MA: Harvard University Press.

Wilson, M. and Daly, M. (1992) The man who mistook his wife for a chattel. In J.H. Barkow, L. Cosmides and J. Tooby (eds), *The Adapted Mind. Evolutionary psychology and the generation of culture* (pp. 289–321), New York: Oxford University Press.

Wilson, T.D and Dunn, D.S. (1986) Effects of introspection on attitude–behavior consistency: analyzing reasons versus focusing on feelings. *Journal of Experimental Social Psychology*, 22, 249–63.

Wilson, T.D, Dunn, D.S., Kraft, D. and Lisle, D.J. (1989) Introspection, attitude change, and attitude–behavior consistency: the disruptive effects of explaining why we feel the way we do. In L. Berkowitz (ed.), *Advances in Experimental Social Psychology* (vol. 22, pp. 287–343), San Diego, CA: Academic Press.

Wilson, T.D., Laser, P.S. and Stone, J.I. (1982) Judging the predictors of one's own mood: accuracy and the use of shared theories. *Journal of Experimental Social Psychology*, 18, 537–56.

Winnykamen, F. (1990) *Apprendre en imitant?* Paris: Presses Universitaires de France.

Winter, L., Uleman, J.S. and Cunniff, C. (1985) How automatic are social judgments? *Journal of Personality and Social Psychology*, 49, 904–17.

Wishner, J. (1960) Reanalysis of 'impressions of personality'. *Psychological Review*, 67, 96–112.

Witt, L.A. (1989) Authoritarianism, knowledge of AIDS, and affect towards persons with AIDS: implications for health education. *Journal of Applied Psychology*, 19, 599–607.

Wood, W. (1982) Retrieval of attitude-relevant information from memory: effects on susceptibility to persuasion and on intrinsic motivation. *Journal of Personality and Social Psychology*, 42, 798–810.

Wood, W., Lundgren, S., Ouellette, J.A., Busceme, S. and Blackstone, T. (1994) Minority influence: a meta-analytic review of social influence processes. *Psychological Bulletin*, 115, 323–45.

Wood, W., Wong, F.Y. and Cachere, J.G. (1991) Effects of media violence on viewers' aggression in unconstrained social situations: effects of an aggressive model on the behavior of college student and prisoner observers. *Psychonomic Science*, 24, 193–4.

Woodward, W.R. (1980) Toward a critical history of psychology. In J. Brozek and L. Ponfraz (eds), *Historiography of Modern Psychology* (pp. 29–67), Toronto: Hogrefe.

Worchel, S., Andreoli, V.A. and Folger, R. (1977) Intergroup cooperation and intergroup attraction: the effect of previous interaction and outcome of combined effort. *Journal of Experimental Social Psychology*, 13, 131–40.

Word, C.O., Zanna, M.P. and Cooper, J. (1974) The

nonverbal mediation of self-fulfilling prophecies in interracial interaction. *Journal of Experimental Social Psychology*, 10, 109–20.

Wortman, C.B. and Conway, T.L. (1985) The role of social support in adaptation and recovery from physical illness. In S. Cohen and S.L. Syme (eds), *Social Support and Health* (pp. 281–302), Orlando, FL: Academic Press.

Wright, P.H. (1974) The delineation and measurement of some key variables in the study of friendship. *Representative Research in Social Psychology*, 5, 93–6.

Wright, S.C., Taylor, D.M. and Moghaddam, F.M. (1990) Responding to membership in a disadvantaged group: from acceptance to collective protest. *Journal of Personality and Social Psychology*, 58, 994–1003.

Wundt, W. (1874) *Grundzüge der physiologischen Psychologie*. Leipzig: Englemann.

Wundt, W. (1900) *Völkerpsychologie. Eine Untersuchung der Entwicklungsgesetze von Sprache, Mythos und Sitte*. Vol. I. *Die Sprache*. Leipzig: Kröner.

Wundt, W. (1900–1920), *Völkerpsychologie* (10 vols), Leipzig: Englemann.

Wyer, R.S. and Gordon, S.E. (1982) The recall of information about persons and groups. *Journal of Experimental Social Psychology*, 18, 128–64.

Wyer, R.S. and Srull, T.K. (1989) *Memory and Cognition in its Social Context*. Hillsdale, NJ: Erlbaum.

Yang, K.S. and Bond, M.H. (1980) Ethnic affirmation in Chinese bilinguals. *Journal of Cross-cultural Psychology*, 11, 411–25.

Yinin, Y., Goldenberg, J. and Neeman, R. (1977) On the relationship structure of residence and formation of friendship. *Psychological Reports*, 40, 761–2.

Young, L., Giles, H. and Pierson, H. (1986) Sociopolitical change and vitality. *International Journal of Intercultural Relations*, 10, 411–25.

Youngblade, L.M. and Belsky, J. (1992) Parent–child antecedents of 5-year-olds' close friendships: a longitudinal study. *Developmental Psychology*, 28, 700–13.

Youniss, J. (1989) Parent–adolescent relationships. In W. Damon (ed.), *Child Development Today and Tomorrow* (pp. 176–97), San Francisco: Jossey-Bass.

Yuill, N. (1992) Children's production and comprehension of trait terms. *British Journal of Developmental Psychology*, 10, 131–42.

Yuill, N. (1993) Understanding of personality and dispositions. In M. Bennett (ed.), *The Child as Psychologist. An introduction to the development of social cognition* (pp. 87–110), New York: Harvester Wheatsheaf.

Yuille, J.C. and Cutshall, J.L. (1986) A case study of eyewitness memory of a crime. *Journal of Applied Psychology*, 71, 291–301.

Yzerbyt, V.Y. and Schadron, G. (1994) *Stéréotypes et jugement social*. In R.Y. Bourhis and J.-P. Leyens (eds), *Stéréotypes, discrimination et relations intergroupes*. Brussels: Mardaga.

Yzerbyt, V., Schadron, G., Leyens, J.-P. and Rocher, S. (1994) Social judgeability: the impact of meta-informational rules on the use of stereotypes. *Journal of Personality and Social Psychology*, 66, 48–55.

Zahn-Waxler, C. and Radke-Yarrow, M. (1990) The origins of empathic concern. *Motivation and Emotion*, 14, 107–30.

Zajonc, R.B. (1965) Social facilitation. *Science*, 149, 269–74.

Zajonc, R.B. (1968) Cognitive theories in social psychology. In G. Lindzey and E. Aronson (eds), *The Handbook of Social Psychology*, 2nd edn (vol. 1, pp. 320–411), Reading, MA: Addison-Wesley.

Zajonc, R.B. (1980a) Feeling and thinking: preferences need no inferences. *American Psychologist*, 2, 151–76.

Zajonc, R.B. (1980b) Compresence. In P.B. Paulus (ed.), *Psychology of Group Influence* (pp. 35–60), Hillsdale, NJ: Erlbaum.

Zajonc, R.B. (1984) The interaction of affect and cognition. In K.R. Scherer and P. Ekman (eds), *Approaches to Emotion* (pp. 239–46), Hillsdale, NJ: Erlbaum.

Zajonc, R.B. and Nieuwenhuysen, B. (1964) Relationship between word frequency and recognition: perceptual process or response bias? *Journal of Experimental Social Psychology*, 2, 160–8.

Zajonc, R.B., Murphy, S.T. and Inglehart, M. (1989) Feeling and facial efference: implications of the vascular theory of emotion. *Psychological Review*, 96, 395–416.

Zander, A. (1971) *Motives and Goals in Groups*. New York: Academic Press.

Zanna, M.P. and Cooper, J. (1974) Dissonance and the pill: an attribution approach to studying the arousal properties of dissonance. *Journal of Personality and Social Psychology*, 29, 703–9.

Zanna, M.P. and Fazio, R.H. (1982) The attitude–behavior relation: moving toward a third generation of research. In M.P. Zanna, E.T. Higgins and C.P. Herman (eds), *Consistency in Social Behavior: the Ontario Symposium* (vol. 2, pp. 283–301), Hillsdale, NJ: Erlbaum.

Zanna, M.P., Kiesler, C.A. and Pilkonis, P.A. (1970) Positive and negative attitudinal affect established by classical conditioning. *Journal of Personality and Social Psychology*, 14, 321–8.

Zanna, M.P., Olson, J.M. and Fazio, R.H. (1980) Attitude–behavior consistency: an individual difference perspective. *Journal of Personality and Social Psychology*, 38, 432–40.

Zanna, M.P. and Rempel, J.K. (1988) Attitudes: a new

look at an old concept. In D. Bar-Tal and A.W. Kruglanski (eds), *The Social Psychology of Knowledge* (pp. 315–34), Cambridge: Cambridge University Press.

Zebrowitz McArthur, L. and Baron, R.M. (1983) Toward an ecological theory of social perception. *Psychological Review*, 90, 215–38.

Zillmann, D. (1971) Excitation transfer in communication-mediated aggressive behavior. *Journal of Experimental Social Psychology*, 7, 419–34.

Zillmann, D. (1979) *Hostility and Aggression*. Hillsdale, NJ: Erlbaum.

Zillmann, D. (1988) Cognitive-excitation interdependencies in aggressive behavior. *Aggressive Behavior*, 14, 51–64.

Zillmann, D. and Cantor, J.R. (1976) Effect of timing of information about mitigating circumstances on emotional responses to provocation and retaliatory behavior. *Journal of Experimental Social Psychology*, 12, 38–55.

Zillmann, D., Johnson, R.C. and Day, K.D. (1974) Attribution of apparent arousal and proficiency of recovery from sympathetic activation affecting excitation transfer to aggressive behavior. *Journal of Experimental Social Psychology*, 10, 503–15.

Zillmann, D., Katcher, A.H. and Milavsky, B. (1972) Excitation transfer from physical exercise to subsequent aggressive behavior. *Journal of Experimental Social Psychology*, 8, 247–59.

Zimbardo, P.G. (1969) The human choice. Individuation, reason, and order versus deindividuation, impulse, and chaos. In D. Levine (ed.), *Nebraska Symposium on Motivation* (pp. 237–307), Lincoln, NE: University of Nebraska Press.

Zimmerman, D.H. and West, C. (1975) Sex roles, interruptions, and silences in conversation. In B. Thorne and N. Henley (eds), *Language and Sex: differences and dominance* (pp. 105–29), Rowley, MA: Newbury House.

Zuckerman, M. (1979) Attribution of success and failure revisited, or: the motivational bias is alive and well in attribution theory. *Journal of Personality*, 47, 245–87.

Zuckerman, M., Koestner, R., Colella, M.J. and Alton, A.O. (1984) Anchoring in the detection of deception and leakage. *Journal of Personality and Social Psychology*, 47, 301–11.

Zumkley, H. (1981) Der Einfluß unterschiedlicher Absichtsattributionen auf das Aggressionverhalten und die Aktivierung. *Psychologische Beiträge*, 23, 115–28.

Subject Index

Name Index

Criminal Law